The Poetical Works of
CHRISTOPHER SMART

The Poetical Works of

CHRISTOPHER SMART

V

The Works of Horace,
Translated into Verse

EDITED WITH INTRODUCTION
AND COMMENTARY BY

Karina Williamson

CLARENDON PRESS · OXFORD

1996

Oxford University Press, Walton Street, Oxford OX2 6DP

Oxford New York
Athens Auckland Bangkok Bombay
Calcutta Cape Town Dar es Salaam Delhi
Florence Hong Kong Istanbul Karachi
Kuala Lumpur Madras Madrid Melbourne
Mexico City Nairobi Paris Singapore
Taipei Tokyo Toronto
and associated companies in
Berlin Ibadan

Oxford is a trade mark of Oxford University Press

Published in the United States
by Oxford University Press Inc., New York

British Library Cataloguing in Publication Data
Data available

Library of Congress Cataloging in Publication Data
Data available
ISBN 0–19–812772–3

1 3 5 7 9 10 8 6 4 2

Set by Hope Services (Abingdon) Ltd.
Printed in Great Britain
on acid-free paper by
Biddles Ltd.,
Guildford and King's Lynn

TO
NIALL RUDD

Writing thyself or judging others' writ,
I know not which thou'st most, candour or wit.

ACKNOWLEDGEMENTS

PREPARATION of this volume has happily shown me that even in these difficult times the spirit of scholarly communality is still very much alive. As in earlier volumes, I have traded shamelessly on the kindness of friends and colleagues, but in addition I have been fortunate enough to receive generous assistance from scholars I had never met whom I consulted simply on the basis of their reputation. In this way the edition has come to owe an inestimable debt to Professor Niall Rudd, who read the entire text of both the *Phaedrus* and the *Horace* and our commentaries on them; his detailed additions, corrections, and textual emendations have been most gratefully accepted and his critical guidance has been invaluable throughout the work. Any errors or misjudgements that remain are of course entirely my own responsibility.

I owe sincere thanks to Professor Arthur Sherbo, who has done more than anyone else now living to promote Smart's translation of Horace and who went out of his way to pass on timely information and to assist with the collation of texts. I am especially grateful also to Professor Roger Lonsdale: with typical thoughtfulness he not only lent me his two copies of the rare 1767 edition of Smart's *Horace* but also gave me one volume. David Robinson, of the Department of Classics in the University of Edinburgh, was equally generous: he gave me another volume, and provided valuable guidance in the preliminary stages of my editorial work.

It is a pleasure to acknowledge, further, the expert advice and help given by Dr Jonquil Bevan, Professor Kerr Borthwick, Professor Ian Donaldson, Dr Leofranc Holford-Strevens, Dr Alexander Lindsay, and Dr William Zachs; assistance with transcription of the text of Phaedrus given by Alison Bowers; and (again, as often before) the support and hospitality of Professor Betty W. Rizzo. Last in order, but not last in importance, I am deeply grateful to my husband Angus McIntosh. Although his tolerance must have been severely strained at times by having Smart so intrusively about the house, he has been an unfailingly good-humoured and dependable source of wise advice, encouragement, and coffee.

I acknowledge with gratitude the substantial help provided by the award of a Leverhulme Emeritus Fellowship in 1993; it was of critical importance in the final stages of the work, not only financing my travels in Britain and in the United States to examine copies of the editions of Smart's two translations, but also enabling me to enlist the valuable assistance of Anne Becher with the *Phaedrus* volume.

Thanks are also due and gladly expressed to the staffs of: the Bodleian Library; the Library of the Boston Athenaeum; Corpus Christi College Library, Oxford; Edinburgh University Library; the Houghton Reading Room at Harvard University; the National Library of Scotland; the New York Public Library; the New York Society Library; Princeton University Library; and the Beinecke Library at Yale University. In addition, for particular help, I would like to thank John Atterbury of the Burns Library, Boston College; Bernice Bergup of the Davis Library, University of North Carolina at Chapel Hill; Anthony Bliss of the Bancroft Library, University of California, Berkeley; Kenneth D. Craven of the Humanities Research Center, University of Texas at Austin; Thomas V. Lange of the Huntington Library, San Marino; Jean Rainwater of the John Hay Library, Brown University; John Richards of the Hallward Library, University of Nottingham; Carl Spadoni of the Mills Memorial Library, McMaster University; and James Tyler of the Carl A. Kroch Library, Cornell University.

K.W.
Edinburgh

CONTENTS

ABBREVIATIONS AND REFERENCES

For classical references, the abbreviations are those used in the *Oxford Classical Dictionary*. Works cited in the introductions and commentary are published in London unless otherwise indicated.

A. WORKS BY SMART

1756	*The Works of Horace, translated literally into English prose*, 2 vols., 1756.
Hymns	*Hymns and Spiritual Songs*, 1765 (*PW*, vol. ii).
Hymns (1771)	*Hymns for the Amusement of Children*, 1771 (*PW*, vol. ii).
JA	*Jubilate Agno* (*PW*, vol. i).
PW	*The Poetical Works of Christopher Smart* (Oxford: present edition).

B. OTHER REFERENCES

Ainsworth	Robert Ainsworth, *Thesaurus Linguae Latinæ Compendiarius*, 1736.
Borthwick	Prof. E. Kerr Borthwick (personal communication).
Brown	*Horace: Satires I*, ed. P. M. Brown 1993.
Creech	Thomas Creech, *The Odes, Satyrs and Epistles of Horace. Done into English*, 1684.
Francis	Philip Francis, *A Poetical Translation of the Works of Horace*, 4 vols., 6th edn., 1756.
Fraenkel	Eduard Fraenkel, *Horace*, 1957.
Hunter	Christopher Hunter, Life of Smart, in vol. i of *The Poems, of the late Christopher Smart*, 2 vols., 1791.
LS	Lewis and Short, *A Latin Dictionary* (Oxford, 1980).
Mahony and Rizzo	Robert Mahony and Betty W. Rizzo, *Christopher Smart: An Annotated Bibliography 1743–1983*, 1984.
NH	R. G. M. Nisbet and Margaret Hubbard, *A Commentary on Horace, Odes Book I*, 1970; *Odes Book II*, 1978.
OED	*Oxford English Dictionary*.
OLD	*Oxford Latin Dictionary*.
Quinn	*Horace: The Odes*, ed. Kenneth Quinn, 1980.
Rudd	Prof. Niall Rudd (personal communication).
Rudd, 1987	Niall Rudd, *Horace: Satires and Epistles, a verse translation with introduction and notes*, revised edn., 1987.
Rudd, 1989	*Horace Epistles Book II and Epistle to the Pisones*, ed. Niall Rudd, 1989.

INTRODUCTION

Nec verbum verbo curabis reddere, fidus
Interpres—

(Horace, *Ars Poetica*, 133–4)

Nor be so foolishly absurd
As to translate it word for word.

(i) GENERAL

Samuel Johnson, surveying the history of English translation in the *Idler*, 69 (11 Aug. 1759), saw it as a progression from 'servile closeness' in the Renaissance to elegant but often licentious freedom in the reign of Charles II; until at last the happy medium was reached in Dryden's recognition 'that closeness best preserved an author's sense, and that freedom best exhibited his spirit'. Johnson refers here to Dryden's famous discussion of the three modes of translation in the preface to *Ovid's Epistles* (1680). He concludes:

he therefore will deserve the highest praise who can give a representation at once faithful and pleasing, who can convey the same thoughts with the same graces, and who when he translates changes nothing but the language.[1]

By the time Smart embarked on the task of putting the complete works of Horace into English verse he had already tried his hand at both extremes, literal translation (Dryden's 'metaphrase') and free 'Imitation' of this author, and probably also the method halfway between which Dryden labelled 'paraphrase'. The first of his Horatian pieces to be published was *The Pretty Chambermaid* (*PW* iv. 111), an Imitation of *Ne sit ancillae*, *Odes* II. iv, printed in the *Gentleman's Magazine* in October 1746, but already, nearly three years earlier, he had celebrated his graduation with a light-hearted ode written 'in allusion to Horace' (*On taking a Batchelor's Degree*, *PW* iv. 39), based on *Exegi monumentum aere perennius*, *Odes* III. xxx. Other Horatian exercises belonging to his Cambridge years include a free rendering of *Audivere*, *Lyce*, *Odes* IV. xiii (*PW* iv. 166), *The Force of Innocence*, which his friend Charles Burney recognized as 'an elegant

---

[1] *The Idler and the Adventurer*, ed. W. J. Bate, J. M. Bullitt, and L. M. Powell (Yale Edition of the Works of Samuel Johnson: New Haven, Conn., 1963), ii. 217.

application' of *Integer vitae*, *Odes* I. xxii (*PW* iv. 189), and a familiar address in Latin to a university friend, *Christopherus Smart Samueli Saunders* (*PW* iv. 139), in the convivial manner and Sapphic stanza of Horace's invitation to Maecenas, *Odes* I. xx, but with echoes of other Horatian odes also. His most ambitious effort in this period was *The Horatian Canons of Friendship*, an imitation of *Satires* I. iii in the manner of Pope; published in 1750 by John Newbery, it was Smart's first separate publication in London and was perhaps intended to signal his emancipation from academic confines, though he seems to have begun writing it some years earlier while he was still at Cambridge.[2]

These translations fall into Dryden's third category of Imitation, 'where the Translator . . . assumes the liberty not only to vary from the words and sense, but to forsake them both as he sees occasion'. *To Maecenas*, however, a translation of *Odes* I. i, published in the *Midwife* in 1751 and almost certainly by Smart (*PW* iv. 384), is a skilful example of Paraphrase, 'or translation with latitude, where the author is kept in view by the translator, so as never to be lost, but his words are not so strictly followed as his sense, and that too is admitted to be amplified, but not altered'.[3]

Smart's familiarity with the works of Horace from an early age needs no explanation. As Steele mockingly showed in the *Tatler*, 173 (1710), the eighteenth-century schoolboy, whatever his mental capacity or interests, was compelled to construe, memorize, and imitate Horace's poems: '*Horace* and *Virgil* must be thrummed by a boy as well before he goes to an apprenticeship as to the university.'[4] For those with literary aspirations, knowledge of Horace was indispensable; this was perceived by women as well as men, as the number of translations and imitations of Horace's poems by women in the eighteenth century testifies. Those who were deprived of a classical education by gender or class, or both, nevertheless saw that some acquaintance with his poetry was a passport for entry into literary society. Even a domestic servant like Mary Leapor, with no knowledge of Latin but an ardour for learning, an alert under-

---

[2] See *PW* iv. 113 and 423.

[3] Preface to *Ovid's Epistles* in *John Dryden: Of Dramatic Poesy and Other Critical Essays*, ed. G. Watson (1962), i. 268.

[4] *The Tatler*, ed. D. F. Bond (Oxford, 1987), ii. 448. See M. L. Clarke, *Classical Education in Britain 1500–1900* (Cambridge, 1959), pp. 46–73, and R. M. Ogilvie, 'Horace and the Eighteenth Century', in *Latin and Greek: A History of the Influence of the Classics on English Life from 1600 to 1918* (1964), pp. 34–73.

standing, and a shrewd eye for cultural icons could use Horace as
a model, presumably by reading his work in translation.[5]

The status of Horace as 'cultural hero'[6] in a period of increasing
literacy must have contributed to the demand for translations of his
work, though translators and publishers generally address themselves to students of Latin and their tutors rather than to the wider
public. Smart's first full-scale, close translation of Horace was aimed
explicitly at the learners' market. Published by John Newbery in
1756 under the title *The Works of Horace, translated literally into English
prose*, it proclaimed itself for the use of those 'who are desirous of
acquiring or recovering a competent Knowledge of the Latin
Language'. This was a word by word, line by line, faithful translation of the original; when Smart was forced by the exigencies of
English idiom and syntax to interpolate extra words, they were
scrupulously italicized to indicate their alien status. Although it was
not a scholarly edition in the full sense, it was buttressed with a textual apparatus and notes, citing a wide range of editors and commentators. In the preface Smart boasted that

With regard to the Latin text, the best editions have been diligently consulted; and it is presumed the judicious will find in the following sheets
some emendations and improvements, which have escaped former editors.
(a1[b])

All the well-known names in classical scholarship from the
Renaissance onwards appear, such as Joseph Scaliger, Daniel
Heinsius, André Dacier, and Richard Bentley, as well as more
recent Horatians such as the translator Philip Francis, Alexander
Cunningham—one of the many editors of Horace who succeeded
Bentley—and Richard Hurd, whose copiously annotated edition of
the *Ars Poetica* had come out in 1749, only a few years before Smart
started work on his prose translation. The Latin text used in 1756
appears to be eclectic; Smart does not say, and it is impossible to
determine, what edition he used as his basic copy. Textual variants
and emendations noted in the apparatus are quoted more often
from Bentley than from any other single source, but seldom
adopted. The name most conspicuously missing in 1756 from

---

[5] See R. Greene, *Mary Leapor: A Study in Eighteenth-Century Women's Poetry* (Oxford,
1993), p. 170.
[6] See R. A. Brower, 'The Image of Horace', in his *Alexander Pope: The Poetry of Allusion*
(Oxford, 1959), pp. 162–87.

Smart's array of scholarly authorities is that of John Bond, whose edition of Horace was the basis of Smart's translation in 1767 (see below, p. xxxiv).

The tone of Smart's preface in 1756 indicates that even then he found the task of preparing a literal translation for students an uncongenial labour, and later he looked back on the work with shame. In October 1764 John Hawkesworth (writer and literary editor of the *Gentleman's Magazine*) wrote to Smart's sister Margaret Hunter describing a visit he had made to Smart at her request. His letter provides brief but valuable hints of the inception and progress up to that point of Smart's new translation of Horace. Hawkesworth reported that:

he is now busy in translating all Horace into verse, which he sometimes thinks of publishing on his own account, and sometimes of contracting for it with a bookseller; I advised him to the latter, and he then told me he was in treaty about it, and believed it would be a bargain: he told me his principal motive for translating Horace into verse, was to supersede the prose translation which he did for Newbery, which he said would hurt his memory. He intends however to review that translation, and print it at the foot of the page in his poetical version.[7]

It is evident from this account that the verse translation was intended to be of more literary value than a rendering designed simply to meet the needs of young learners of Latin: Smart cannot have meant that the earlier translation would 'hurt his memory' by its failure to fulfil its primary purpose. Its success as a close but readable version was already apparent from the fact that it had gone into a second edition in 1762. Ironically, it remained in print for the best part of two centuries after his verse translation left the press almost stillborn; it kept Smart's memory alive after a fashion, though not in the fashion he wanted, to generations of readers who knew or cared nothing about his poetry. By 1780 it had already reached its fifth edition; it was constantly reprinted throughout the nineteenth century and well into the twentieth, very often as a school 'crib', but also as a popular reading version. It was used for example as the English version of Horace by the Everyman Library from 1911 until recently.

What Smart did not explain to Hawkesworth was the precise way in which his new translation would 'supersede' the prose version.

[7] The letter is printed in Hunter, vol. i, pp. xxiii–xxvi.

Was it to be more 'poetical' or more faithful to the original? (These two principles are not necessarily opposed.) Smart's ideas as set out in his preface in 1767 will be discussed later, but for the present it is worth putting his aims in the context of translations of the classics in the mid-eighteenth century. Thomas Sheridan advanced the interesting notion that verse was the fittest medium for literal translation. In conversation with Boswell in 1762, he said that 'to give the literal meaning of Horace, it should be in verse', but that 'to give an idea of his manner and spirit, it should be imitation and applied to the present time, like Swift's'.[8]

Imitation and translation of Horace's poems in verse was a booming activity throughout the seventeenth and eighteenth centuries but the number of translations of his entire work into verse was small. Smart's chief contemporary rivals were Thomas Creech and Philip Francis. Creech's *Odes, Satyrs and Epistles of Horace*, first published in 1684, was the only complete translation available in the eighteenth century until Philip Francis published *A Poetical Translation of the Works of Horace* in 1747. Reprinted in 1749, 1750, 1753, 1756, 1760, 1765, and after, this immensely popular work dominated the field for the rest of the eighteenth century.[9] In addition to these, there was a composite translation of Horace's *Works in English Verse, by various hands*, edited by William Duncombe and others (1757–9, enlarged edition 1767), and verse translations of parts of Horace's work were also published, such as Thomas Hare's *Translation of the Odes and Epodes of Horace into English Verse* (1737), a work which Smart cited in his 1756 translation.

By mid-century, however, the tide seems to have been turning against verse translations. As Penelope Wilson observes, the most notable development in eighteenth-century translation of the classics was 'the emergence into gradual respectability of literal translation (i.e. of prose translation even for poetry)'.[10] The provision of such versions was associated with the growing demand both for generally educative and for narrowly pedagogical editions of the

---

[8] *Boswell's London Journal 1762–1763*, ed. F. A. Pottle (1950), p. 92.

[9] Previously published in instalments: vols. i–ii, *The Odes, Epodes and Carmen saeculare* in 1743 (Dublin, 1742); vol. iii, *The Satires*, 1746; vol. iv, *The Epistles and Art of Poetry*, 1746.

[10] See 'Classical Poetry and the Eighteenth-Century Reader', in I. Rivers (ed.), *Books and their Readers in Eighteenth-Century England* (Leicester UP, 1982, pp. 69–96), p. 80: this essay and the article by J. W. Draper, 'The Theory of Translation in the Eighteenth Century', *Neophilologus*, 6 (1921), 241–54, are the most detailed sources of information on 18th-c. editions and translations.

major classical authors; Anne Becher draws attention to this development in her introduction to Smart's *Phaedrus* in volume vi. The
potential market was large but divided; on the one hand there was
the increasing number of readers referred to earlier who had no
training in classical languages but wanted to know the major Greek
and Latin poets. On the other hand, there was the new demand
from schools and private tutors for editions of the classics which
could be used as tools of learning in themselves. As John Clarke, a
schoolmaster at Hull grammar school, argued in his *Dissertation upon
the Usefulness of Translations* (1734), the use of dictionaries was laborious, slow, and unhelpful to beginners. Editions with parallel texts
in Latin and English, and explanatory notes (with or without other
aids), were seen as a more useful and agreeable method of induc-
tion into the Latin tongue.

  Both of these audiences, reluctant young scholars and private
readers, seem to have been in the sights of John Watson when he
declared on the title-page of *The Works of Horace, translated into English
Prose* (1743) that the book was 'adapted to the capacities of youth at
school, as well as of private gentlemen'.[11] The growing popularity
of prose translations may in turn account for the defensive tone of
Francis's preface to his verse translation. He begins by saying that
the design of his work was 'to explain, perhaps, the most difficult
author in the Latin tongue', but that 'to preserve his original spirit
in a punctual, regular translation hath been so long considered as
desperate, that it were hardly modest to attempt it'. His solution
was to render his original in such a way that 'the difficult passages
. . . are explained in that sense alone, which seemed most poetical
and most natural', but to supplement the translation where the
meaning was 'really doubtful' with notes giving alternative interpretations drawn from other commentators. By this means, 'a tacit
appeal [is] made to the reader to determine for himself, even
against the present translator'.[12] The rest of the preface is concerned much less with explanation and instruction than with doing
justice to the poetry of Horace itself; the enormous success of his
translation shows that he had hit on a winning formula with his particular combination of *utile* and *dulci*.

  This was the context within which Smart attempted to launch his
own version of Horace in the 1760s. Where Francis seems to know

---

[11] Quoted by Wilson, art. cit., p. 81.
[12] Sixth edn., revised and corrected (1756), pp. vii–viii.

very well the mixed nature of his potential readership, and to be trying to address both classes, Smart appears ambivalent. The title-page is both scholarly and utilitarian, proclaiming the translator's lofty academic credentials, and at the same time advertising 'A Prose Interpretation, for the help of students'. The preface sends out a variety of signals, which need examining more closely. But if we take the edition as a whole, as it appeared in the bookshops in 1767, and put it together with Smart's discussion of the project with Hawkesworth in 1764 and with all we know of Smart's circumstances and writings in the years between 1756 and 1767, a clear enough story emerges. Nothing about Smart in that period suggests that he was now *primarily* interested in or capable of writing hard-headedly for a specific commercial market, as he had so successfully done when he was preparing his prose translation of Horace in 1755. After that had come his breakdown in 1756, the conversion experience described in *Hymn to the Supreme Being* (published in June 1756: *PW* iv. 319–23), and the huge outpouring of religious poetry written during his confinement and afterwards.

Smart emerged from the madhouse in 1763 as much convinced as he was before he entered it that his 'deeds, thoughts, and words' should be devoted to the endless glory of God, as he declared in the *Hymn*. At the same time, he knew very well that he had to write to live. When Horace said that poverty drove him to write verse he was looking back humorously on his early years from the relative comfort of the present, but when Smart quoted Horace's *paupertas impulit audax ut versus facerem* in the dedicatory letter prefixed to his verse translation, he was writing in earnest of his immediate situation. Hawkesworth's letter shows him in the process of negotiating with publishers, but he was in no position to dictate terms by then, still less by the time the translation was completed and he had nothing but a string of critical and commercial failures to add to his record. When he spoke to Hawkesworth of his project, it seems that he was still writing *con amore*, hoping to produce a translation that would both enhance his own reputation and give English honours to the 'Heathen Psalmist' (his title for Horace in the preface), as he had done for the Psalms of David in 1765.

No correspondence of Smart's with the publisher William Flexney survives, but it seems likely that it was Flexney's suggestion that he should add a prose interpretation and adapt his work in other ways to make it attractive to the student market. Provision of a prose version necessitated at least some degree of modification of the 1756 translation both to avoid breach of copyright and to accommodate different readings in the Latin text he was using in the 1760s. In the event, the prose version was so thoroughly revised that it is virtually a new translation.[13]

All this added to Smart's labours without bringing him material benefits, and his circumstances deteriorated in 1765. He was arrested for debt towards the end of the year and only saved from imprisonment by the generosity of friends; the probability that his difficulties stemmed largely from his own improvidence does not make his hardships less real. Throughout 1766 and 1767, while he was presumably struggling to finish his *Horace*, he was constantly in debt or trying to raise money just to survive. From the sour tone at the end of his preface, it appears that an undertaking begun in a spirit of hope, devotion, and self-vindication ended simply as a desperate grind.

That does not mean that his translation necessarily declined in quality as the work progressed. There are certainly unevennesses in it, but these sometimes occur within the course of a single poem, and since we have no knowledge of the order in which he worked it would be a waste of time to search for signs of flagging energy or attention. The frustration Smart expresses at the end of the preface may refer at least as much to dissatisfaction with the printing of the *Horace* as to his own role as translator (see p. xxxv, below).

The preface otherwise is far from self-defensive: Smart presents his account of the qualifications and responsibilities of a translator of Horace with more of a proprietorial than an apologetic air. The epigraph on the title-page of the first volume gives a hint, though a cryptic one, of his conception of the work. It is taken from Horace's *Epistles* I. xix. 21–3, in which the poet says of himself, 'Beholden to no one I blazed a trail over virgin country; nobody had trodden that ground' (Rudd, 1987). Horace was boasting of his originality in the *Odes* and *Epodes*, meaning that he was the first to write lyrics and iambics *in Latin*, in the form and manner of the Greek poets Alcaeus and Archilochus.

It is not obvious what Smart meant by appropriating Horace's claim. To represent his work as the first translation of Horace into verse would have been a totally unjustified boast. If all he meant

[13] See A. Sherbo, 'Christopher Smart's Three Translations of Horace', *Journal of English and Germanic Philology*, 66 (1967), 347–58.

was that his translation was original in style and metre, the quotation is an exaggeration. On the other hand, to refer in this fashion to Horace's originality as a lyrical poet would be merely pedantic. The implication therefore may be that Smart saw himself as the first (in an admittedly not very distinguished line) to give full expression in English verse to the true spirit of the Roman poet. If by the 'three or four applauded persons' whom he acknowledges as predecessors in the dedicatory letter (p. 3) he is thinking of recent translators, as it would seem, the reference must extend to the plodding prose versions of Joseph Davidson (1746), John Stirling (1751–3), and David Watson and Samuel Patrick (1760), and perhaps also to those others who had translated Horace's work only in part.

In the preface, however, Smart distances himself from all rival translators by declaring loftily that his version 'is not written in opposition to others'. This too can only mean that he sees his translation as standing in some special relation to the original. Smart indeed begins his preface by asserting that intelligence and good judgement are insufficient qualifications for a translator of poets such as Phaedrus, Ovid, Virgil, and above all Horace: only a person possessed of 'some rank . . . and affinity in the spirit' could hope to capture their distinctive quality. This idea was a commonplace in Augustan theories of translation: Roscommon's advice in *An Essay upon Translated Verse* (1684) to 'seek a poet who your way does bend, / And choose an author as you choose a friend' was frequently quoted and borrowed.

One problem about founding or judging a translation of Horace on the principle of 'affinity' is that it is singularly difficult to find any general agreement on the character of 'Horace', whether that means the man as revealed in his poetry or the character of the poetry itself. Charles Martindale, who approaches this problem with a modern scepticism about 'the poetics of presence', rightly remarks that 'there are, and always have been, many Horaces, not one Horace'. Because one of these Horaces set his stamp so indelibly on the conception of civilized society in the early eighteenth century, it is often wrongly assumed that the easy philosopher and urbane, witty, moderate, and clubbable man of the *Spectator* circle was the universal image of the poet throughout the century. This was certainly the dominant image, but even in the eighteenth century there were wide divergences of opinion both about the character of the man as revealed in his writings, and, even more, about the distinctive qualities of the poetry itself.[14]

What Smart meant by his implicit claim of affinity with Horace is therefore debatable. Arthur Sherbo points out a number of resemblances between Smart's life and temperament and what Horace represents as his. Both poets were of modest family origins, well educated in the company of young men of wealthy and aristocratic connections; both had lost their paternal estates, and both were indebted to generous patrons.[15] It is easy to see how readily Smart could have personally identified himself with the self-portrait Horace provides at the end of his first book of *Epistles* (I. xx. 19–28):

> When the warmer sun brings you a larger group of listeners,
> You will talk about me: 'He was born in a home of slender means,
> a freedman's son; but his wingspan proved too large for the nest.'
> (In this way what you take from my birth you will add to my merits.)
> 'In war and peace he won the esteem of his country's leaders.
> Of small build, prematurely grey, and fond of the sun,
> he was quick to lose his temper, but not hard to appease.'
> If anyone happens to ask my age, you can let him know
> that I saw the end of my forty-fourth December in the year
> when the consul Lollius was later joined by his colleague Lepidus.
>
> (Rudd, 1987)

In several respects this could be seen as a self-portrait of the translator too: acknowledging his humble background, but taking pride in his achievements and the esteem of people of high station; describing his small stature and his volatile temperament. Horace's *irasci celerem* is heightened in Smart's translation to 'With passion ev'n to phrenzy seiz'd', as if to make it even more closely applicable to himself. Even their ages correspond: in 1766, at the time when he was probably translating these very lines, Smart too was forty-four.

However, it is not this kind of affinity that Smart is concerned with in the preface: his attention is strictly focused on Horace's character as a writer, and particularly with the qualities of his lyri-

---

[14] C. A. Martindale and D. W. Hopkins (eds.), *Horace Made New: Horatian Influences on British Writing from the Renaissance to the Twentieth Century* (Cambridge, 1993), pp. 1 ff. See also Brower, loc. cit., and F. Stack, 'Interpreting Horace', in his *Pope and Horace: Studies in Imitation* (Cambridge, 1985), pp. 3–17.

[15] See *Christopher Smart's Verse Translation of Horace's Odes*, ed. A. Sherbo (ELS Monograph Series, Victoria, 1979), pp. 24–5.

cal poetry. The feature he seizes upon as most distinctive is 'the lucky risk of the Horatian boldness', his 'peculiarity of expression': the gift he takes to be encapsulated in the paradoxical phrase *curiosa felicitas*, used of Horace by Petronius (*Satyricon* 118), which aptly describes the blend of careful artistry and seeming 'good fortune' or even 'inspiration' characteristic of his lyrics. As Niall Rudd points out, Smart's first phrase derives from Quintilian (x. i. 96), *verbis felicissime audax*, 'happily daring in his language'. In this respect, at least, there is a real affinity between the two authors. The creative freedom of Smart's diction has always been noticed; to conventional readers in the eighteenth century it seemed wayward and perturbing, but it is now recognized as the hallmark of a powerful and original imagination.

Examples of Smart's own 'peculiarity of expression' are found everywhere in the odes and epodes: 'Death and the shades anon shall press thee home' (*Odes* I. iv), 'There where the frequent rose-tree blooms' (*Odes* I. v), 'Like Nireus in his form begirl'd' (*Odes* III. xx), 'that dissociable main' (*Odes* I. iii). But they can occur anywhere, as in *Epistles* I. xx, where Horace's *solibus aptum* ('fond of the sun') is transmuted into 'Form'd for th' intensity of day'. Many of Smart's unusual expressions however are not departures from the original but bold literalisms: 'dissociable main', for instance, represents Horace's *Oceano dissociabili*. 'And smooth ambiguous face' (*Odes* II. v) merely adds 'smooth' to *ambiguoque vultu*, but catches the Horatian nuance more effectively than the circumlocutions often resorted to, such as Francis's 'boyish, girlish face'. Similarly, 'And motionless with frost the sharpen'd streams remain' (*Odes* I. ix) is very close to Horace's *geluque flumina constiterint acuto*, but by transferring 'sharpen'd' from the frost to the rivers Smart evades the lurking cliché ('biting frost') to produce an arresting line. Not all of Smart's literalisms are felicitous, it has to be said. They can be clumsy or jarring, as in his singularly maladroit 'putrid eyes' for Horace's admittedly difficult *putres oculos* (*Odes* I. xxxvi). The use of Latinisms like 'inscious' and 'obnoxious' (in the sense of 'vulnerable', as in *Satires* II. vii. 16) makes the verse sound pedantic or inappropriately Miltonic. And Smart's attempts to reproduce Horace's own tropes with exactitude can be sheerly baffling: neither 'flattering farm' for *fundus mendax* (*Odes* III. i. 30), for example, nor 'obliquity' for *obliquum ictum* (*Odes* III. xxii. 7–8) can be understood without knowledge of the original.

Smart's 'peculiar' expressions frequently result from his preference for the concrete and specific to the abstract and generic. In
Odes I. iii, 'a new recruit / Of fevers' reactivates the military force
of Horace's almost buried metaphor, *febrium cohors* (usually translated as 'crowd' or 'throng' of fevers). Where in *Odes* IV. xi (Smart's
IV. x) Horace describes Pegasus as *gravatus*, 'grudging' or 'disdain-
ful' at having to carry a mortal on his back, Smart says he 'scornful neigh'd'. The Phrygian 'wealth' and 'well-stocked homes' of
Arabia in *Odes* II. xii (*Phrygiae . . . opes . . . plenas aut Arabum domos*)
become 'Phrygia's wealthy fleece, / Or all Arabia's ambergreese'.
Smart's method is the more conspicuous when seen in contrast with
Francis, who usually prefers general or conventional literary terms.
Francis translates these last lines as 'the wealth by kings possest, . . .
Or all the treasures of the East'. Again, the boundary between the
unconventional and the bizarre is sometimes overstepped: Smart's
risks are not always lucky. In *Odes* I. vii, for instance, 'the plains /
Of high-manur'd Larissa' has a farmyard pungency quite foreign to
Horace's *Larisae campus opimae* (Francis says merely 'fair Larissa').
But the number of occasions when Smart's bold expression revital-
izes phrases or images worn smooth by familiarity far exceeds the
moments of exasperation. Moreover Smart is usually successful in
varying his diction to match changes of style or tone in the original. One of his best efforts is the translation of *Odes* III. iv, thought
by many to be Horace's greatest ode; Niall Rudd writes, 'it affirms,
in figurative language, the relation between poetic and political
power; Smart rises well to the challenge' (privately communicated).

Affinity in manner of expression may not be the only kind of
'affinity in the spirit' with Horace that Smart meant. Consider
again the motto on the title-page. Smart's translation of these lines
is very free:

> A sheer original from God,
> I stalk'd upon the vacant sod,
> Nor in another's footsteps trod.
>
> (*Epistles* I. xix. 41–3)

Here Smart elevates Horace's portrayal of himself as an innovative
artist, justly proud of his originality as the first to bring Greek lyrical forms and metres into Latin poetry, into that of a *vates*, a poet
owing his originality to divine inspiration. It was in precisely such
terms that Smart described the act of poetic composition in his own

religious verse: the invocation to the 'Muse, through Christ the Word, inventive' (*Hymns* 3, 'Epiphany') is not a mere ·rhetorical trope but a conception of the true source of poetry which is frequently expressed in Smart's later writings. This of course is not at all the way in which Horace's poetry was normally regarded in the eighteenth century or is regarded now. But it appears less unusual if seen in the light of Renaissance interpretations of Horace: in a desire to minimize the gap between pagan and Christian thought, some seventeenth-century scholars took seriously Horace's allusions to the gods and to religious rites and worship, and drew attention to correspondences between his sayings and passages from the Bible and the fathers.[16]

Thus when Smart puts Horace on a par with David by calling him 'the *Heathen Psalmist*' (p. 6), he is presenting Horace as a divine poet, and at the same time signalling his own spiritual affinity. (It is significant that when Hawkesworth visited Smart in 1764 he noticed on the table of his lodgings 'a prayer book and a Horace': see Introduction to *Phaedrus*, vol. vi, p. 16.) There was good reason, however, for underplaying this reading of Horace; Smart knew from experience that his Christian beliefs were liable to be derided as foolish 'enthusiasm' if they were too boldly obtruded. Nevertheless, his translation is tinctured at several points by his religious viewpoint. In *Odes* iii. xxx, for example, *Non omnis moriar multaque pars mei vitabit Libitinam* ('I shall not wholly die, a large part of me will escape the death-goddess') becomes in Smart, 'death shall never have the whole / Of Horace, whose immortal soul / Shall 'scape the pow'rs of human bane'. Horace, however, is talking about his immortal *fame*, not the destination of his soul. In *Odes* iv. vii. 17–24, the phrases 'heav'n . . . daily pray'r . . . keep your soul in tune . . . the pit' give distinct overtones of Christian theology to Horace's Roman rhetoric. In *Satires* i. vi. 114 Horace writes *adsisto divinis*. The standard interpretation of *divinus* here is 'soothsayer', hence 'I loiter by the fortune-tellers' (Rudd, 1987), 'I listen, while diviners tell their tale' (Francis). That was how Smart himself read it in 1756: 'I stand listening among the fortune-tellers.' But *non est qualis erat*; in 1767 he writes (i. vi. 202) 'The temples duly I attend', and his prose version in 1767, 'I assist at the divine services', is even more specific. A subtler instance of Smart's tendency to read or

---

[16] See T. Maresca, *Pope's Horatian Poems* (Columbus, Oh., 1966), pp. 27–8.

infuse spiritual meaning into the text when he can occurs in the epistle to Tibullus, *Epistles* I. iv: Horace writes *Inter spem curamque, timores inter et iras / omnem crede diem tibi diluxisse supremum. / grata superveniet, quae non sperabitur hora.* Smart's version stays close, except for the last line:

> —'Twixt hope and care, 'twixt fear and strife,
> Think every day the last of life.
> Beyond your wish some happy day
> Shall come your grief to over-pay.

The phrase, 'your grief to over-pay' may look like a line-filler, but it is not. It hints at a faith in the compensatory justice of Christian providence which Smart tenaciously held and memorably expressed in 1763 in *On a Bed of Guernsey Lilies* (*PW* iv. 348).

Twice in his footnotes to *Satires* I. v Smart makes references to Christian history: drawing attention to the fact that Appii Forum was the place mentioned in Acts 28: 15 where the Jews met St Paul, and comparing the belief among the Gnatians that incense melts without heating with the 'miracle' of the liquefaction of the blood of St Januarius (presumably a jibe at popish superstition). But the nearest Smart comes to enrolling Horace openly in the select band of divine poets is at the end of *Odes* IV. vi, where *docilis modorum vatis Horati* ('trained in the measures of the poet Horace') becomes 'The numbers of th'Horatian lay, / Skill'd in his mystic verse.' *Mystic* was not a word Smart used lightly: for him, in the hymn for Epiphany quoted above, 'mystic measures' meant poetry inspired by the Christian Muse. Horace is not wholly on the side of the angels, however; in the footnote to *Satires* I. iii. 194–5 Smart takes him to task for not recognizing the divine origins of human language. This is the only occasion in his *Horace* when he gives open expression to the ideas about language and Logos which he worked out in *Jubilate Agno*, and which were so fundamental to his conception of poetry in the 1760s.

Smart's preface is mainly concerned with Horace's lyrical poetry. He has disappointingly little to say about the different set of problems for the translator posed by Horace's hexameter verse. Speaking of the *Satires* and *Epistles*, he mentions only the 'absurdity' of rendering them in heroic verse, and his own choice of 'a more familiar measure, as best agreeing with Conversation pieces, professedly so called'. Smart's early Imitation of *Satires* I. iii had been in heroic couplets, as was his own satire, *The Hilliad*, but he had already shown a talent for composition of conversational verse and familiar epistles in octosyllabic verse. Whether this metre was a wise choice for all of Horace's *sermones* is very doubtful. The shorter line means in practice that a couplet is usually required to translate a single Horatian verse, where a single pentameter would sometimes have been sufficient. Consequently Smart has to resort uncomfortably often to line-fillers, some of them adding colour or explanatory detail, but many of them feeble and inert ('by the bye', 'so fam'd and known', 'on this plan'). At other times, the constriction of his metre leads to over-compression: Smart's style naturally tends towards a close-packed, often unusual syntax, and the extra constraint of a tight metre produces many of the obscurities in his translation.

A further problem with Smart's shorter English line is that it does not leave enough room for manœuvre to give a natural rendering of Horace's conversational style, particularly in the dialogue passages. Pope had brilliantly shown in his *Imitations of Horace* how rhyming pentameters could be used to convey the style and rhythms of colloquial English, and it seems almost a perversity in Smart to forgo a medium so well proven. That is not to say that he has no success with Horace's conversational verse; there are numerous individual lines, sometimes whole passages, in which the cadences of spoken English are effectively caught. In *Satires* II. ii, for example, lines 47–8 (Horace 26–7)—

> Scarce bird! that cost the Lord knows what,
> As if that signified a jot

—and 67–70 (Horace 35–7),

> I see appearance is your guide;
> Why are the pikes so much decried?
> Because they're of a longer sort,
> And mullets naturally short

—strike just the right note of blunt argumentativeness for the rustic Ofellus. But Smart seldom seems able to maintain the familiar style consistently in the *sermones* (his fine rendering of Epistle I. viii is an exception): colloquial lines are often jostled, with jarring effect, by passages of Latinate syntax or mannered diction. Smart's touch in the hexameter poems is thus less sure than it is in the lyrics. Even so his versions are never insipid, servile, or bland. The impression, rarely lost in reading his *Horace*, of an imagination strenuously engaged, ensures that his translations appear as genuine remakings of Horace, not either pallid copies or unlicensed elaborations of the original.

William Clubbe, whose translation of *Six Satires of Horace* was published in 1795, criticized Francis for leaving Horace in too Roman a guise.[17] Most of the time in his translation Smart steers a steady path between the poles of careful historicism and of radical 'imitation' in which Roman names, places, customs, and manners are converted wholesale into English equivalents. From time to time, however, recognizably English details give his versions an engagingly local and immediate flavour. In *Odes* I. i Horace's *otium et oppidi . . . rura sui* (referring to the peace of a country estate), becomes 'his villa's rural ease, / Built amongst bowling-greens and trees'. Similarly in *Satires* II. i, when Scipio and Laelius retire from public life, they go and 'sport upon the green' and play 'at tennis' (ll. 134–6 in Smart's version). In *Odes* I. viii Smart's Horace laments that the love-sick soldier infatuated with Lydia should desert his cavalry friends and no longer ride, 'Dress'd in his regimentals' (*regimentals* is first recorded in *OED* in 1742). In *Satires* II. vii, where Davus says that fear of danger is all that restrains the passionate from sin, Smart translates this grimly into the threat of a London gallows: 'If from Tyburn you'll abate' (*tolle periclum*, l. 73; translation, 116); while the avaricious in *Epistles* I. vi. 36–7 who pursue the goddess Money for the sake of *genus* become very English social climbers in Smart's 'money . . . will heralds buy, / To blaze you of a family' (i.e. 'buy you a pedigree from the College of Arms', ll. 66–9).

One of the hardest challenges for the translator of Horace is to match his metrical virtuosity. Here Smart was on strong ground, as a supple and resourceful metrist in his own original verse. After translating the Psalms he was no stranger to the problem of accommodating a great variety of alien styles and measures to English metre, and as we have seen he was already practised in the art of putting Horace into English verse. With justifiable pride he applies to himself the phrase already quoted from Horace *Odes* IV. vi, *docilis modorum vatis Horati*, 'trained in the metres of the poet Horace'.[18]

---

[17] See Draper, art. cit. (n. 10, above), p. 249.

[18] Smart uses *Odes* IV. vi. 41–4, omitting 42, as a motto for his Latin version (originally published in 1743) of Pope's *Ode on St Cecilia's Day*. It is printed at the end of vol. ii of his

His aim generally seems to be to match the spirit or 'feel' of Horace's metres, not to copy them. Except in his delightful rendering of *Odes* I. xxxviii in English Sapphics, he does not attempt to reproduce Latin quantitative patterns in English verse-forms. Nor does he try to make his metres correspond regularly with Horace's: following the practice of other eighteenth-century translators, Philip Francis and Thomas Hare, Smart sometimes uses the same measure for different originals, sometimes different measures for the same originals. But he does make a point of imitating Horace's rarer metres by producing equivalent versions of his own. In *Odes* II. xviii (one of his happiest efforts) his trochaic metre, rhyming in four-line units, approximates the four-line trochaic strophe used only once by Horace. *Odes* IV. vii, Horace's only ode in alternating hexameters and trimeters, is imitated by Smart's only example of alternating pentameters and trimeters. In *Odes* I. xi and I. xviii, as Smart notes, his rhyming heptameters imitate the long line used by Horace only in these two poems and in *Odes* IV. x (omitted by Smart). For Horace's one-off 'Ionic a Minore' metre in *Odes* III. xii Smart employed a pattern of alternating four- and three-stress dactylics, which he liked enough to use again in *Epodes* iii, vi, and viii (Horace's Epode ix). Altogether he uses twenty-four different metrical patterns in his translation, compared with Horace's nineteen. It is worth noting finally that more than half of his versions of the odes and epodes are in exactly the same number of lines as the originals.

Smart was sensitive to the needs of the general reader with little or no knowledge of Roman history or the Latin language, who might nevertheless prefer a reading version uncluttered with footnotes. He explains in the preface that he tried to be sparing with such notes, aiming instead to make his version 'as much as possible clear and explanatory' (p. 6). As I have already noted, the combination of 'peculiarity of expression' and tight syntax characteristic of Smart's verse works at times against clarity; but he was diligent and ingenious in his efforts to make the text self-explanatory. He avoids using uncommon proper names when he can, sometimes omitting them altogether, otherwise substituting more familiar names or replacing them with descriptive terms or phrases. For example, *Calabrae Pierides* (*Odes* IV. viii) becomes 'Ennius from Calabria

Horace with a note saying it is subjoined 'In order to exercise the student in the Horatian measures'.

sprung'; *Archiacis lectis* (*Epistles* I. v) 'an old-fashion'd seat'; *Cibyratica . . . Bithyna negotia* (*Epistles* I. vi) 'your foreign ware'. At the beginning of Epode i, where editors usually supply notes explaining the contrast between *Liburnis* (light, fast sailing vessels) and *alta navium propugnacula* (the heavy, fortified ships of Antony's fleet), Smart incorporates the contrast into his translation ('In a small ship . . . To face huge vessels tow'ry-stern'd'). Similarly, in Epode vi it has to be explained that *Molossus aut Lacon* refers to two kinds of dog: Smart builds this into his translation with 'a staunch mastiff, or guard of the sheep'.

A particular problem for eighteenth-century editors and translators of the classics was what to do about obscene or even just sexually explicit passages. Smart is by no means unusual in his attitude when he says in the preface that, for the sake of young readers, he has been 'especially careful, concerning all passages of Offence' (p. 6). In 1739 Joseph Spence wondered 'how Horace could say such coarse, obscene things in so polite an age'.[19] It was common practice for eighteenth-century editions, especially school texts, to omit whole poems or large sections, such as *Odes* IV. x, *Epodes* viii and xii, and *Satires* I. ii. 25–134, as Smart does. A reviewer of Smart's edition in 1767 remarked that he was 'not so extremely scrupulous in this point, as some supercilious and unmerciful editors of Horace, who have expunged seventeen of the odes and epodes'.[20] As well as whole poems, shorter 'offensive' passages or single lines were removed, usually silently, by editors especially of school texts. Smart does this with great assiduity though not altogether consistently. Normally both text and translation are expurgated; more rarely the text itself is altered, but Smart is sometimes content with verbal tinkering while leaving the Latin intact. In *Odes* I. iv, for example, he suppresses the erotic wording of Horace's reference to Lycidas, *quo calet iuventus nunc omnis et mox virgines tepebunt* ('for whom all young men now burn and girls will soon grow warm'), substituting the decorous 'doat on Lycidas, as on a son, / Whom for their spouse all little maids design'. In *Odes* III. x, *minstrel* is Smart's euphemism for *Pieria paelice*, 'Pierian concubine'; here his prose interpretation,

[19] *Observations, Anecdotes, and Characters of Books and Men*, ed. J. M. Osborn (Oxford, 1966), no. 539.
[20] *Critical Review*, 24 (Aug. 1767), 104–5. Smart's omissions are noted in the Commentary. On the subject of 18th-c. expurgation generally, see Draper, art. cit., pp. 245–6.

'musical harlot', is less prudish. Francis translates this by 'a song-singing wench'. Again in *Satires* II. vii. 104, Smart's 'raging husband' represents Horace's *domino furenti* (l. 66), meaning 'overmastering lust'.

Smart read out some of his translation to Hawkesworth during the visit mentioned earlier. Hawkesworth comments:

it is very close, and his own poetical fire sparkles in it very frequently; yet, upon the whole, it will scarcely take place of Francis's, and therefore, if it is not adopted as a school book, which perhaps may be the case, it will turn to little account.

History proved Hawkesworth an accurate prophet. A measure of the neglect of Smart's *Horace* is that when his translation of Phaedrus was reprinted in 1831 it was bound up with Francis's translation of Horace, together with an appendix containing 102 translations of individual poems of Horace by other authors: not one of them is by Smart.

Smart's *Horace* attracted little attention from the critics of the time. The *Political Register* (December 1767) summed it up with cruel dismissiveness as 'Unequal' (leaving the reader to deduce whether that meant 'uneven' or 'unequal to the task').[21] The only critical notice of any length it received before the twentieth century came from Smart's old enemy, the *Critical Review*, in August 1767. The tone of the review as a whole is carping. It quotes *Odes* I. v. 1–5 (1–8 in the translation) to show how Smart copes with the *curiosa felicitas* of Horace: 'The word *bedaub'd* gives us an indelicate idea of the lover; *perfumes* and *blooms* do not exactly correspond in sound; the seventh line is at best a deviation from the original; the last is happily expressed.' In Smart's version of *Odes* I. xiii. 17–20 the reviewer finds 'neither delicacy of sentiment, nor elegance of stile'. In *Odes* I. xix. 5–8 Smart 'seems to have preserved the sense, though not the elegance of the original'. Other examples follow of Smart's shortcomings. The criticism is not entirely unfavourable, but the occasional compliments are half-hearted or condescending: *Odes* I. xxxviii 'is prettily translated in the original metre'; the translation of *Odes* I. xxii. 21–4 'is not unpleasing, but may be read without admiration'. The general judgement on Smart's handling of the lyrical poetry is that he 'preserves the sense of his author, and sometimes breathes a true poetic spirit', quoting his version of *Odes* III.

---

[21] Mahony and Rizzo, Item 1258.

xxv in full as an instance. The reviewer dispatches the *Satires* and *Epistles* in a few words, referring contemptuously to Smart's choice of metre and ending with a passage from his translation of the *Art of Poetry* to illustrate the point.[22] Smart had to wait nearly two centuries before the true merits of his *Horace* were first recognized by Robert Brittain in 1950.[23] Brittain's account remains valuable as a critical appraisal but full-scale, detailed study of this remarkable work is still awaited and long overdue.

(ii) THE PRESENT TEXT

Volumes v and vi are the long delayed fulfilment of a hope expressed nearly two hundred years ago by Charles Burney, the son of Smart's old and loyal friend Dr Charles Burney. Writing to the publisher Francis Newbery (Smart's brother-in-law) on 4 April 1800, Burney tentatively suggested that Smart's two major translations from the Latin classics would make a fitting complement to the collection of his original poems already in print, the two-volume *Poems, of the late Christopher Smart*, edited by Francis Newbery with the help of Christopher Hunter, and published in Reading in 1791:

Whether a third Volume might not be made to the Poems, by uniting Smart's poetical translation of *Horace* with his *Phedrus*, it is not for me to determine; but I cannot help regretting, that any writings of so genuine a Poet should be excluded from his Works.—The Originals of the two Roman Bards would of course be left out; as well as the Parsing Index to the Fabulist.

Commercial caution overcame Newbery's family piety, however, and nothing came of the proposal.[24]

Partly as a result, neither of Smart's translations presents any major textual problems, since only one authoritative edition of each

---

[22] *Critical Review*, 24 (Aug. 1767), 94–105.

[23] *Poems by Christopher Smart*, ed. Robert Brittain (Princeton, NJ, 1950), introduction, pp. 67–73. See also Donald Davie, 'Christopher Smart: Some Neglected Poems', *Eighteenth-Century Studies*, 3 (1969–70), 253–61; John P. Beifuss, 'Christopher Smart: Translator of Horace', *Interpretations: Studies in Language and Literature by the Department of English, Memphis State University*, 6 (1974), 24–30; and Sherbo's introduction to the edition cited in n. 15, above. An unpublished study of Smart's *Horace* by Thomas F. Dillingham (*Dissertation Abstracts International*, 34 (1973), 1901–A) is briefly summarized in Mahony and Rizzo, Item 1647.

[24] See *The Annotated Letters of Christopher Smart*, ed. B. Rizzo and R. Mahony (Carbondale, Ill., 1991), pp. 155–8.

has ever been published. Both are now relatively rare, the *Horace* particularly. It was published in 1767 as:

The Works of Horace, Translated into Verse. With a Prose Interpretation, for the Help of Students. And Occasional Notes. By Christopher Smart, A.M. Sometime Fellow of Pembroke Hall, Cambridge, and Scholar of the University. [Epigraph.] In Four Volumes. Vol. I. [II.–IV.] London: Printed for W. Flexney, in Holborn; Mess. Johnson and Co. in Pater-noster-Row; and T. Caslon, near Stationer's-Hall. M DCC LXVII.

> Advertised as forthcoming 'shortly', *Daily Advertiser*, 18 March 1767. Publication advertised, *Daily Advertiser*, 13 July 1767. Royal 8⁰:
> I. A⁸ b⁸ B–T⁸, pp. xxxi, 287.
> *Contents.* A1ᵃ half-title, A1ᵇ blank, A2ᵃ title, A3ᵃ–b8ᵃ dedication, preface, b8ᵇ blank, B1ᵃ half-title, B1ᵇ–T8ᵃ Odes 1.1–3.14 (Latin and English on facing pages), T8ᵇ blank.
> II. π² B–U⁸, pp. 302, [2].
> *Contents.* π1ᵃ half-title, π1ᵇ blank, π2ᵃ title, π2ᵇ blank, B1ᵇ–R2ᵃ Odes 3.15–4.14, Epodes, Secular Ode (Latin and English on facing pages), R2ᵇ note, R3ᵃ title, R3ᵇ blank, R4ᵃ half-title, R4ᵇ–S3ᵃ Carmen cl. Alexandri Pope (Latin and English on facing pages), S3ᵇ blank, S4ᵃ–S6ᵇ De vita Horatii, S7ᵃ–S8ᵇ De Maecenatis, T1ᵃ–T8ᵇ Synopsis chronologica, U1ᵃ–U2ᵇ Specimina carminum Horatii, U3ᵃ–U7ᵇ Syllabus carminum Horatii, U8ᵃ–U8ᵇ Proposals.
> III. π² B–T⁸ U², pp. xiv, 292.
> *Contents.* π1ᵃ half-title, π1ᵇ blank, π2ᵃ title, π2ᵇ blank, a1ᵃ–a7ᵇ Dacerii praefatio, a8ᵃ–a8ᵇ blank, B1ᵃ half-title, B1ᵇ–U2ᵃ Satires (Latin and English on facing pages), U2ᵇ blank.
> IV. π² B–U⁸, pp. 297.
> *Contents.* π1ᵃ half-title, π1ᵇ blank, π2ᵃ title, π2ᵇ blank, B1ᵃ half-title, B1ᵇ–Q5ᵃ Epistles (Latin and English on facing pages), Q5ᵇ blank, Q6ᵇ–U5ᵃ Art of Poetry (Latin and English on facing pages), U5ᵇ blank, U6ᵃ Proposals, U6ᵇ–U8ᵇ blank.
> Flexney's name misprinted 'Fleyney' on title-page.

As may be seen from these collations, a substantial proportion (about a fifth) of the second volume of the *Horace* is made up of other materials: Smart's earlier translation into Latin of Pope's *Ode for Musick on St Cecilia's Day*, given here with a separate title-page as the 'Third Edition'; the life and writings of Horace and a synopsis of Roman history in Latin, both by Rodellius; a genealogy of Maecenas, also in Latin; and a catalogue of the *Odes*, classified by the metres of the original. The third volume is prefaced by André Dacier's preface to Horace's *Satires*, again in Latin. Since this scholarly apparatus is left untranslated, it would not have been very useful to students, whom the edition was professedly designed to help. No doubt it was partly intended to impress, partly useful in filling the pages to bring the volumes to more or less equal length.

As for the edition of *Horace* used, Smart explains in his preface: 'With regard to my original text, I have in general followed *Bond*, who is much admired for his accuracy amongst Scholars abroad.' John Bond's edition of Horace, first published in 1606, was outdated in England by this time. 'Bond's Horace' is jocularly cited as an authority in the *Spectator* in 1711 (no. 286), but the context suggests that it was already old-fashioned by then. The most respected editions in the eighteenth century were those of André Dacier and of course Richard Bentley, whose magisterial work was published in Cambridge in 1711. It is nevertheless true that Bond's *Horace* remained in circulation on the Continent, where editions continued to appear throughout the eighteenth century. Smart had not used Bond's edition for his prose translation of Horace in 1756, and his reason for choosing it for the verse translation can only be guessed. It may have been nothing grander than sheer expediency: Bond's *Horace* was perhaps the only edition he still possessed when he left the madhouse in 1763.

Smart's verse translation of Horace has never been reprinted in full. The only substantial reprint since 1767, even in part, has been Arthur Sherbo's edition of the *Odes*, published in 1979, with an informative introduction, in the ELS Monograph Series (no. 17, University of Victoria). Useful though this edition is, it does not claim to be anything more than a faithful reproduction of the original text of Smart's translation of the *Odes*, with the most obvious misprints or misspellings corrected. Thus there is only a single authorial text, with no surviving manuscripts to help or to complicate editorial judgement. This does not leave the task entirely simple, however. It was necessary first to discover whether there were any differences between surviving copies of the single edition. Of the twenty-five copies of Smart's *Horace* I have been able to trace in libraries or in private hands in Britain, the United States, and Canada, I have personally collated fourteen; the remainder have been checked on my behalf by librarians or kind colleagues. Examination of these copies revealed a small crop of press variants, mostly affecting the running-titles and page numbers, but no variants in the text. The 1767 *Horace* however appears to have been carelessly printed and proof-read. Conspicuous errors have been left untouched, and the press-work itself seems to have been corrected in a perfunctory and unsystematic way. The textual errors mostly involve mistakes in spelling and punctuation, but they are numerous, particularly in the Latin, where they sometimes make nonsense of the original text. In the main they are not of a kind that any competent Latinist would make or that Smart would willingly have tolerated if he had had the chance to correct them. Evidence from editions of his original poems shows that he was vigilant in overseeing his copy through the press when he had the opportunity. With his earlier translation, *The Works of Horace, translated literally into English prose* (1756), he probably had neither the time nor the freedom to be meticulous. The 1756 version was carried out as a pot-boiler for the shrewd and commercial-minded publisher John Newbery (Smart's father-in-law). In a somewhat defensive preface, Smart explained that the translation was designed for cheapness and the convenience of learners, adding disingenuously: 'What errors there may be, either of the press or otherwise, will be found, perhaps, of such a nature, and so seldom to occur, that they may be rather of service, by giving the young student some opportunities of shewing his sagacity in the discovery of them' (a1b–a2).

Smart's verse translation was undertaken in a very different spirit. The comments he made to Hawkesworth in 1764 (see above, p. xvi) imply that he was anxious to repair the damage done to his reputation as a classical scholar and poet by the previous translation, but the signs are that either he was again denied the opportunity to correct his copy during printing, or he was too harassed or unwell to do so. In the convoluted sentence with which his preface concludes, he laments both that a gentleman of his honourable descent should be reduced to the task of translation at all, and that it had not been 'done in a state, he had more reason to be satisfied with'. Smart may have been referring in general to personal and financial difficulties, but his words could also imply dissatisfaction with the conditions under which the work was published. Hawkesworth reported in 1764 that Smart was proposing to publish his verse translation in quarto:[25] even in that he was frustrated and had to make do with the less dignified though still handsome royal octavo.

[25] Hunter, vol. i, p. xxiv.

The careless printing of the 1767 *Horace* has necessitated fairly frequent, though minor, emendation. In particular, the punctuation seems at times to have been distributed almost at random, garbling Smart's syntax where his intention is plain and rendering his more difficult passages almost impenetrable. I have therefore removed, supplied, or changed the punctuation when necessary to restore Smart's sense, as far as it was discernible. In doing so, I have followed wherever possible the pointing in Smart's Latin text and in the 'Prose Interpretation' which accompanies the verse translation throughout; together these provide a useful guide to his intentions in problematic passages.

Quotation marks have been silently supplied where necessary, to differentiate the speakers. Smart often used dashes for this purpose, but inconsistently and confusingly, since dashes are used for other purposes also. Where inverted commas are used but have been manifestly misplaced, they have been corrected without comment. Quotation marks have been standardized according to modern convention: they are given at the beginning and end of the passage only, not at the beginning of each line; single inverted commas used for primary utterances, double for embedded quotations.

The 1767 edition is inconsistent in the use of apostrophes to indicate elision (as in 'threat'ning'): these have been inserted where omitted. Apostrophe *'s*, signifying the possessive singular, has been inserted wherever it was unambiguously needed. Final apostrophe has also been added to proper names (as in *Augustus'*), where required, but not to plural nouns. The possessive suffix *s'* was not in use until about 1780[26] and I have discovered no instance in Smart's translations where its omission causes difficulty. Diacritical marks in quotations from Latin have been omitted. All these minor changes are made without comment in the textual notes.

Spelling posed a further problem, because where unusual forms occurred it was not always clear which were Smart's peculiarities and which were his or the printer's misspellings. In general, my policy has been to alter as little as possible. Known idiosyncrasies of Smart's, such as his use of the form *grutch* for *grudge*, have of course been reproduced, and spellings current in the eighteenth century or even earlier, but since disused, have also been retained as a matter of course (Smart appears to have been somewhat old-fashioned in

---

[26] See H. C. Wyld, *A Short History of English*, 3rd edn. (1927), p. 241.

his orthography). These include many forms which to a modern reader look like misprints, such as *acron (acorn), brethern, cieling, downfal, drought, jobb, recal, steril, stiffled, tauny, tenis, vultur, withold*. Other forms such as *council* (for *counsel*), *die (dye), errant (errand, arrant), muscle (mussel), roast (roost), rout (route), sooth (soothe), straight/ streight (strait), wave (waive)*, which might give rise to confusion, have been glossed in the Commentary where this seemed advisable. Older forms of Latin words and names used by Smart, such as *ediles* (aediles), *Esop* (Aesop), *Rhoecus* (Rhoetus), *Sicambri* (Sygambri), etc., have also been retained. Two departures from the policy of retention are *foul* (when used, misleadingly, for *fowl*) and *discrete* (when used for *discreet*, see Commentary on *Epistles* I. xvii. 1); both forms have been emended. Similarly the name *Lucilius*, which appears sometimes in that form, sometimes as *Lucillius*, has been standardized as *Lucilius*. Smart's quotations from Greek texts have been modernized in style, and errors have been silently corrected.

Otherwise I have not tried systematically to iron out inconsistencies. For example, *Gods* and *Muses* are sometimes initially capitalized, sometimes not. The auxiliaries *would, could, should* are usually but by no means always spelt *wou'd, cou'd*, etc. Other variations include *persue/pursue, plow/plough, tippler/tipler*. These offer no difficulty to the reader, and since it is impossible to know which form Smart preferred (or indeed whether he was consistent himself), it seemed merely officious to interfere. Simple errors, like 'aprobation' and 'Bachus', have been silently corrected, but wherever what looked like a mere misspelling might instead reflect some special usage, the correction has been recorded in the textual notes. In Odes I. vi. 23, for example, I take the original reading *Menerva* to be a misprint for *Minerva* (the form always used elsewhere in the text); but it is just possible that Smart knew *Menerva* as an older Latin form of the name, and chose to use it on this one occasion.

Finally, I have not sought to reproduce the typography and layout of the original editions with complete fidelity. The practice of capitalizing the first word or words of a poem has not been followed, and irregularities in lineation have been silently rectified. Ligatures and ampersands have been expanded both in the text and in quotations in the Commentary. Paragraphing in the longer couplet poems of the *Horace* seems arbitrary at times and can make for confusion; paragraphs have accordingly been realigned in conformity with modern editions of Horace whenever this seemed helpful. Smart's translations of Odes I. xi and I. xviii were intended to be in long lines but were printed in short lines for the printer's convenience (see Commentary on I. xi); they have been restored to their intended format.

The following sigla are used in the textual apparatus:

1767   *The Works of Horace, translated into verse*, 1767
Rudd   Emendations suggested by Niall Rudd

THE
WORKS
OF
HORACE,

Translated into verse

with a

PROSE INTERPRETATION

For the help of students

By

CHRISTOPHER SMART, A.M.

Sometime Fellow of Pembroke Hall, Cambridge,
And Scholar of the University

Libera per vacuum posui vestigia princeps,
Non aliena meo pressi pede, qui sibi fidit
Dux regit examen.—*Hor. de seipso.*

M DCC LXVII

TO THE RIGHT HONOURABLE
SIR FRANCIS BLAKE DELAVAL,
KNIGHT OF THE BATH

SIR,

SHOULD you ask me, what could be my inducement to undertake the following work at my time of day, and after three or four applauded persons, I must fairly answer, that I made my version of Horace for the same reason, as he wrote the original, 5

> —Paupertas impulit audax
> Ut versus facerem—

I had another, however, and far nobler motive, that I cou'd do myself the honour of prefixing the name of such a Gentleman to my performance, distinguished for his taste and 10 encouragement of letters.——The most remarkable Patrons in all ages, have been those, who have put themselves forwards for the Glory of their native Country, assertors of her Dignity, and Champions in her service. Of this class was the gentleman, who thought it no dishonour to be incorporated in the foremost 15 rank of British Grenadiers, who was one of the first to set his foot upon the shore of the common enemy, and who is now adorning peace with experimental improvements of natural Philosophy*.——Of this class also were the Favourers of Horace, and, however unsuccessful I may have been in copy- 20 ing the peculiar felicity of his poetry, yet am I singularly happy in having this opportunity of imitating his example.

I am, Sir,
With the greatest Respect,
Your most obliged,
And most obedient Servant,

CHRISTOPHER SMART.

* And here I cannot omit the acceptable occasion of congratulating you on the merit of your ingenious brother Mr. Edward Delaval, who has been found to deserve a medal from the Royal Society, to the honour of his own family in particular, and the university of Cambridge in general.

---

20 unsuccessful] unsuccessful, *1767*

PREFACE

As the following version was not written in opposition to others, I cou'd wish to be excused from all invidious comparisons; tho' I am so well aware of them, that I hold it necessary to make some apology in order to bespeak the Reader's favour. There are certain interpreters of Horace, which have evidently been misled by the absurd notion, 'That genius is not necessary for a Translator, and that deep learning and sound judgement are the only requisites for such an undertaking.' The works indeed of Euclid, Esop, and that exceeding foolish author, Elian, amongst the Greeks; of Florus, Quintilian, and Columella, amongst the Romans, may be well enough rendered by literary men, who are merely intelligent and judicious: but the redundant elegance of Tully, the concise politeness of Phaedrus, the ingenuous manliness of Livy, the music and painting of Ovid, the easy sweetness of Tibullus, the state and dignity of Virgil, and (above all authors and their excellencies) the lucky risk of the Horatian boldness, cannot be attempted with any success, save by men of some rank with them and affinity in the spirit.

Horace is by no means so much an original in respect to his matter and sentiments (which are rather too frequently * borrowed) as with regard to that unrivalled peculiarity of expression, which has excited the admiration of all succeeding ages.

I beg leave therefore to assure the Reader, that I did not set about my work without the consciousness of a talent, admitted of, and attested to, by the best scholars of the times both at home and abroad. Mr. Pope in particular, with whom I had the honour to correspond, entertained a very high opinion of my abilities as a translator, which one of the brightest men amongst our Nobility will be ready (I trust) to certify, should my veracity in this matter be called in question.

There is a way of staring at an ancient, and being amazed at the magnitude of his spirit, which is owing to littleness of soul and want of penetration together; as a travelling Virtuoso admires the prodigious structure of Stone-Henge, a work that

* From the Greek Lyrics in general, but particularly from Alcaeus and Pindar, as wel such of his Odes as are extant, as his Dithyrambics, which are not.

may easily be conceived as performed by men of gigantic stature, for it is evident that this island or a part of it had formerly such * inhabitants. As for me, I ever look'd upon Horace with extreme approbation, but never supposed him to be so wholly inimitable, that a man might not do him some degree of justice.

In the first place I have especially attended to what the critics call his *curiosa felicitas*, of which many of my predecessors seem not to have entertained the most remote idea. Mr. *Pope* himself, however happy in taking off the spirit and music of *Horace*, has left us no remarkable instance, to the best of my memory, of this kind. In truth this is a beauty, that occurs rather in the Odes, than the other parts of Horace's works; where the aiming at familiarity of style excluded the curiosity of choice diction.

In order to justify my pretensions concerning this point, I beg leave to refer the reader to the † first Ode of the first Book in sundry places, to the fifth, sixth, seventeenth, twenty-second, and (I hope) many others of the same. I have also had the honour to insist upon the like merit before some of the best writers of the age in the following Odes of the second and third Books, viz. the eighth, ninth, tenth, eighteenth and twentieth of the former: and the third, fourth, fifth, eleventh, twenty-fifth, twenty-ninth and thirtieth of the latter. With regard to the fourth Book, which *Horace* wrote with all his might by the united force of judgment and genius, under the patronage and applause of *Augustus* and the whole world; if I have rendered certain of the Odes in such wise, that they may be read after the versions and imitations of *Cowley*, *Pope* and *Atterbury*, I trust it will be thought no mean literary atchievement for a single man, who was very far from having such superlative advantages.

The Epodes of *Horace* are exceedingly beneath his other works, but have always some local or personal propriety

* This has been put beyond all dispute by certain bones dug up at Gog-Magog-hills and other places of the kingdom. I cannot help adding here, that most probably the Giant's Causeway in Ireland, was really, that which it is called.

† This Ode, however amiable for its gratitude, and special for its phrase, is (by the confession of all Commentators as to its spirit) written *Stylo mediocri*. I have endeavoured to raise it all the way, particularly at the conclusion.

PREFACE. 42 attended to] attended to, *1767*

discernible even at this distance; but I have taken particular   60
care and pains with the second, as the images are too pastoral,
and universally pleasing, to escape the approbation of all ranks
and degrees.—The Secular-Ode, that brightest monument of
the *Heathen Psalmist* and *Roman* worship, I have laboured with
all the art and address I am capable of.—As for the Satires and   65
Epistles, I have ever deemed it a great absurdity, that they have
for the most part been done into the Heroic verse; they are
therefore herein submitted to the public in a more familiar
measure, as best agreeing with conversation pieces, professedly
so called.   70

I have likewise given very close attention to the *Art of Poetry*,
(and it is not the first time I have had occasion to consider it)
in which, if I have missed of some niceties, I conceive, I have
made certain new discoveries, and put disputed passages out of
all question. I must not omit to acknowledge, that I have   75
inserted some things, for which I am obliged to the labour of
other men, particularly the Chronological Synopsis of *Rodellius*,
together with his Life of *Horace*, and Essay on the Pedigree of
Maecenas. With regard to my original text, I have in general
followed *Bond*, who is much admired for his accuracy amongst   80
Scholars abroad. As for the notes, the Reader will find I have
been rather sparing of them, hoping that my version in a great
measure precludes the necessity of them, being as much as possible clear and explanatory.—Lastly as I suppose the book will
fall into the hands of young persons, I have been especially   85
careful, concerning all passages of Offence, both in the translation and original.

Besides the *Curiosa Felicitas*, so much of *Horace* by himself,
there is another poetical excellence, which tho' possessed in a
degree by every great genius, is exceeding in our Lyric to sur-   90
pass; I mean the beauty, force and vehemence of *Impression*:
which leads me to a rare and entertaining subject, not (I think)
any where much insisted on by others.

Impression then, is a talent or gift of Almighty God, by which
a Genius is impowered to throw an emphasis upon a word or   95
sentence in such wise, that it cannot escape any reader of sheer
good sense, and true critical sagacity. This power will sometimes keep it up thro' the *medium* of a prose translation; especially in scripture, for in justice to truth and everlasting

preeminence, we must confess this virtue to be far more pow- 100
erful and abundant in the sacred writings.

אשריך וטוב לך

O well is thee, and happy shalt thou be!

דרכיה דרכי נעם
וכל־נתיבתיה שלום 105

Her ways are ways of pleasantness, and all her paths are
peace.—And this charming passage of Zachariah

מה טובו ומה יפיו

How great is his goodness; and how great is his beauty!—
    But to descend from sacred to profane authors, which (tho' 110
a very mean transition) is never the less more home to our present purpose.

  Adsis, O Cytherea, tuus te, Caesar, Olympo,
   Et Surrentini littoris ora vocat!

Behold, *Virgil*, upon the sea-coast with the grateful remem- 115
brance of patronage, and the idea of immortal beauty.

  Come, Venus, come; thee Caesar's vows adore,
  From heav'n, O come——and grutch thy voice no more
 To Echo, pensive-sweet on dear Surrentum's shore!

We must take this along with us, however, that the force of 120
Impression is always liveliest upon the eulogies of patriotism,
gratitude, honour, and the like.

  O nimium dilecte Deo, cui fundit ab antris
  Aeolus armatas hyemes, cui militat aether,
  Et conjurati veniunt ad classica venti. 125

  O fav'rite of thy God, belov'd too dear!
  For whom array'd the host of storms appear;
  At whose command the elements give fire,
  And at whose dread alarm obedient winds conspire!

Genius is certainly that *great witness*, which God never suffered 130
himself to be without even amongst the Heathens: and in general (tho' not in the Augustan age) met with more envy than
encouragement.

τίς τῶν νῦν τοιόσδε; τίς εὖ εἰπόντα φιλήσει;
οὐκ οἶδ'· οὐ γὰρ ἔτ' ἄνδρες ἐπ' ἔργμασιν ὡς πάρος ἐσθλοῖς   135
αἰνεῖσθαι σπεύδοντι, νενίκηνται δ' ὑπὸ κερδέων.
πᾶς δ' ὑπὸ κόλπῳ χεῖρας ἔχων πόθεν οἴσεται ἀθρεῖ
ἄργυρον, οὐδέ κεν ἰὸν ἀποτρίψας τινὶ δοίη,
ἀλλ' εὐθὺς μυθεῖται· "ἀπωτέρω ἢ γόνυ κνάμα·
αὐτῷ μοι τί γένοιτο. θεοὶ τιμῶσιν ἀοιδούς.   140
τίς δέ κεν ἄλλου ἀκούσαι; ἅλις πάντεσσιν Ὅμηρος."

> Is there a worthy breathing nowadays
> That tenders bards, and is in love with praise!
> None such I know—for lucre they adore;
> The spirit of atchievement is no more.   145
> Each folds his sordid arms across his breast,
> Considering for himself—which way is best
> To seize the hoarded talents as his prey
> Alone: nor gives the very rust away:
> And, if besought, he answers your demand,   150
> 'My gauntlet's not yet nearer than my hand,
> Let *me* abundance for *myself* possess,
> And let the Gods their Poets feed and bless.
> Who hears a modern? Homer left behind
> Enough for every age, and all mankind.'   155

It is impossible to keep citing such passages as these without delighting one's self; the reader therefore will the rather indulge me such a refreshment, as my intention is in some measure to form and direct the tastes of young students by this seeming digression.   160

> θύμβρις ἑλισσόμενος πύματον ῥόον εἰς ἅλα βάλλει,
> θύμβρις ἐυρρείτης, ποταμῶν βασιλεύτατος ἄλλων,
> θύμβρις, ὃς ἱμερτὴν διατέμνεται ἄνδιχα Ῥώμην.

> See Tiber big with wave to ocean swell,
> Tiber who looks so fair and flows so well,   165
> Tiber whose royal floods are Roman and excel!

165 flows so well,] flows well, *1767*

I make no doubt but *Sir John Denham* whetted his imagination
by the above lines of *Dionysius*, before he made those famous *
verses upon the *Thames*.

But the finest lines of all heathen antiquity for most glorious   170
Impression (if it is fair to prefer *Homer* to himself) are the following, which are worked up to such a pitch of sublimity, that even
the sour *Scaliger* was compelled to cry out *Divina, inquam, ora-
tio.*——

Ὡς εἰπὼν σύναγεν νεφέλας, ἐτάραξε δὲ πόντον   175
χερσὶ τρίαιναν ἑλών· πάσας δ' ὀρόθυνεν ἀέλλας
παντοίων ἀνέμων, σὺν δὲ νεφέεσσι κάλυψε
γαῖαν ὁμοῦ καὶ πόντον· ὀρώρει δ' οὐρανόθεν νύξ.
σὺν δ' Εὖρός τε Νότος τ' ἔπεσον Ζέφυρός τε δυσαὴς
καὶ Βορέης αἰθρηγενέτης, μέγα κῦμα κυλίνδων.   180

He spoke, and high the forky trident hurl'd,
Rolls clouds on clouds and stirs the wat'ry world;
At once the face of earth and sea deforms,
Swells all the winds, and rouses all the storms:
Down rush'd the night: East, West together roar,   185
And South and North roll mountains to the shore.

By Mr. *Pope*, but not altogether in the sense and spirit of the
original.

Thus speaking, with his lifted trident arm'd,
He troubled Ocean and the clouds alarm'd;   190
Bade all the driving storms at once engage,
Which all the winds are worth in all their rage:
In gloom he shrouded sea and earth and sky,
And night in pow'r descended from on high
East, South fell to, and howling West, and last   195
The Spirit of the Hyperborean blast,
Which swells the boiling wave—and rolls above the mast!

After all, to end this head as we began, there is a littleness in
the noblest poets among the Heathens when compared to the
prodigious grandeur and genuine majesty of a *David* or *Isaiah*.   200

---

* O cou'd I flow like thee, and make thy stream
My great example, as it is my theme;
Tho' deep, yet clear; tho' gentle, yet not dull,
Strong without rage, without o'erflowing, full.——

קוֹל יְהוָה עַל־הַמָּיִם
אֵל־הַכָּדוֹד הִרְעִים
יְהוָה עַל־מַיִם רַבִּים

> The *Word* of infinite command,
> August, adorable and grand,   205
>   The water-flood controuls;
> And in terrific glory breaks
> Upon the billows, and he speaks
>   The thunder, as it rolls.

But (to return to our author) it would be endless to recount all   210
the places that are most beautiful and strong for their impression in Horace; a few however are necessary for our present
purpose: what affectionate tenderness with a cast of melancholy
are *impressed* on this stanza!

> Eheu fugaces, Postume, Postume,   215
> Labuntur anni: nec pietas moram
>   Rugis, et instanti senectae
>   Afferet, indomitaeque morti.

> Ah! Posthumus, the years, the years
> Glide swiftly on, nor can our tears   220
> Or piety the wrinkled age forefend,
> Nor for an hour retard th'inevitable end!

What fire and vivacity on these lines:

> Quo me, Bacche, rapis, tui
> Plenum? quae nemora et quos agor in specus   225
> Velox mente nova?

> Bacchus, with thy spirit fraught,
> Whither, whither am I caught,
> To what groves and grots am driv'n,
> Quick with thought all fresh from heav'n!   230

What strength and grandeur on these:

> Monte decurrens, velut amnis, imbres
> Quem super notas aluere ripas,
> Fervet, immensusque ruit profundo
>   Pindarus ore.   235

Cascading from the mountain's height,
 As falls the river swol'n with show'rs,
Deep, fierce, and out of measure great,
 His verses Pindar pours!

What amazing sweetness on these: 240

 O testudinis aureae
Dulcem quae strepitum, Pieri, temperas!
 O mutis quoque piscibus
Donatura cycni, si libeat, sonum!
 Totum muneris hoc tui est, 245
Quod monstror digito praetereuntium
 Romanae fidicen lyrae:
Quod spiro et placeo, si placeo, tuum est.

O mistress of the golden shell,
 Whose silence you command or break, 250
Thou that canst make the mute excel,
 And ev'n the sea-born reptiles speak,
And like the swan, if you apply
Your touch, in charming accents die!
 This is thy gift, and only thine, 255
  That as I pass along, I hear
  'There goes the bard, whose sweet design
   Made Lyricks for the Roman ear.'
If life or joy I hold or give,
By thee I please, by thee I live. 260

What an air of dignity on these:

 Paulum sepultae distat inertiae
Celata virtus. Non ego te meis
 Chartis inornatum silebo
  Totve tuos patiar labores 265
Impune, Lolli, carpere lividas
Obliviones. Est animus tibi
 Rerumque prudens et secundis
  Temporibus, dubiisque rectus,

Vindex avarae fraudis, et abstinens 270
Ducentis ad se cuncta pecuniae:
 Consulque non unius anni
  Sed quoties bonus atque fidus

Judex honestum praetulit utili et
Rejecit alto dona nocentium   275
   Vultu, et per obstantes catervas
    Explicuit sua victor arma.

   Virtue conceal'd is next, I deem,
To buried sloth—I will not spare
   For ornament, when Lollius is the theme,   280
Nor suffer so much merit, such a world of care
   In black oblivion to be hurl'd.
You, Lollius, have a noble mind,
   Skilful and fraught with knowledge of the world,
Equal to all events or temp'rate, or resign'd.   285
   Of greedy fraud the judge severe,
Forbearing all-attractive gold,
   A Consul, not elected for a year,
But still esteem'd in fact that dignity to hold,
   Whene'er the magistrate prefers   290
Things honest to his private ends,
   And bribing villains with a look deters,
And *draws* against the crowd, and his fair fame defends.

And lastly what elegance and strokes of the master here:

   Quisnam igitur liber? sapiens sibique imperiosus;   295
Quem neque pauperies, neque mors, neque vincula terrent:
Responsare cupidinibus, contemnere honores
Fortis, et in seipso totus teres atque rotundus:
Externi ne quid valeat per laeve morari,
In quem manca ruit semper fortuna—   300

   Who then is free of all mankind?
One wise, and master of his mind,
Whom neither want, nor death, nor bonds
Can terrify—who corresponds
With heav'n and virtue, to defy   305
All lust and fame, beneath the sky:
At once by gift and conduct too
As finely turn'd, as polish'd true,
So that no rub or greater force
Retard him in his level course;   310

Gainst whom dame Fortune is at fault,
* Whene'er she makes her worst assault!

I come now to a piece of classical history, which seems to
have been a secret to all the commentators of *Horace* from the
beginning, and yet I make no doubt, but the fact I am about   315
to insist upon, will shortly be as evident to the Reader as it is
to me. It is the indispensible business of a skilful editor to discover the drift of his author's intention, when there are sufficient materials for that purpose. It is universally allowed, that
Horace his art of poetry is not upon poetry in general, but chiefly   320
the Drama, and certain other particulars. To retard the reader
no longer, the first part of that essay is a manifest ridicule of
the *Metamorphoses* of *Ovid*, who was in high esteem at the *Court
of Augustus* for that work, which, however beautiful for music
and painting, had nothing to recommend it to the judgment   325
and taste of *Horace*, who well knew that the business of poetry
is to express gratitude, reward merit, and promote moral edifi-
cation. The *Metamorphoses* are made up of incredible prodigies,
and impossible transformations, ever shocking common sense,
and seducing imagination into a wilderness of fruitless perplex-   330
ities. Poetry and nature ought never to be set at a distance, but
when a writer is summoned to such a task by real miracles and
divine transcendency. When a new work is made, published,
and is uncommonly successful in its propagation and applause
amongst the people, it is too much the subject of common con-   335
versation, not to suspend the very idea of things, bearing an
older date, unless they be revived by invidious comparisons or
private connections. It was no small mortification to *Horace*,
that this was the case with regard to his poems and those of
Ovid—but to the proofs: 340

Humano capiti cervicem Pictor equinam
Jungere si velit, et varias inducere plumas
Undique collatis membris: ut turpiter atrum
Desinat in piscem mulier formosa superne:
Spectatum admissi risum teneatis, amici?   345

* This subject of *Impression* is altogether a copious one and to use the words of *Mr.
Hurd*, upon another occasion, wou'd require a volume to do it justice; but *Mr. Smart* had
not an opportunity of considering it in its latitude here.

326 knew] know *1767*

> If any painter shou'd design
> A human visage, and subjoin
> A horse's neck with plumage swol'n,
> And limbs from various creatures stol'n,
> Until the figure in th' event,   350
> Which for a beauteous dame was meant,
> At length most scandalously ends
> In a black fish's tail—My friends,
> Admitted to so strange a sight,
> Wou'd not your laughter be outright?   355

These lines are in open contempt of *Ovid*, who has done all these extravagances to a tittle, in his fifth Book of the *Metamorphoses*. As for example:

> Vobis, Acheloides, unde
> *Pluma pedesque avium cum virginis ora geratis?*   360
> An quia cum legeret vernos *Proserpina* flores
> In comitum numero mistae, *Sirenes*, eratis
> Quam postquam toto frustra quaesistis in orbe;
> Protinus ut vestram sentirent aequora curam,
> Posse super fluctus *alarum* insistere remis   365
> Optastis; facilesque Deos habuistis; et *artus*
> Vidistis *vestros subitis* flavescere *pennis*:
> Ne tamen ille canor mulcendas natus ad aures,
> Tantaque dos oris linguae deperderet usum;
> *Virginei vultus* et vox humana remansit.   370

Here you have got the feathers and limbs of birds, the virgin's face and the fish's-tail, which are inevitably implied by the Mermaids, with a pair of horses heads easily suggested to the fancy by an idea of Pluto's chariot, and the rape of Proserpine.

> ——But who cou'd grace   375
> You, charming *Sirens*, with a *Maiden* face
> To your *birds feet and wings*? was it because
> When *Proserpine was lost*, by friendship's laws
> You, then her play-mates, sought her every where?
> And that your marks of love the seas might bear,   380
> You wish'd for *wings to flutter* o'er the main,
> And did your wish from yielding Gods obtain?

Yet lest your voice, contriv'd to charm the ear,
Shou'd lost or useless by the change appear,
Your beauties still, and *virgin looks* remain,   385
And you your old harmonious air retain.
                              Sewell's Ovid.

Inceptis *gravibus* plerumque et *magna professis*
Purpureus late qui splendeat unus et alter
Assuitur pannus—quum lucus et ara Dianae.   390

And a little after:

—Pluvius describitur arcus.

In pompous proems big with threat
The usual pattern that is set,
Is that they place, to make one stare,   395
A piece of patch-work full of glare.

Nothing can be more solemn than the beginning of the
Metamorphoses, where *Ovid* adjures the immortal Gods to
assist his undertaking, for they themselves performed all those
wonders —nam vos mutastis et illas. And as for the splendid   400
patch-work, it means the whole chain of Rhapsodies, from one
end of the book to the other.—But to go on—

As when the *fane* and *sacred wood*
Of *Dian,* or meand'ring flood
In pleasant fields or copious flow   405
Of Rhine, or *many-colour'd bow*
Are all describ'd—

The former part of these verses: As when the fane and sacred
wood of Dian, etc. alludes to the following lines in the VII.
book of the Metamorphoses;   410

Ibat ad antiquas Hecates Persëidos *aras*
Quas *nemus umbrosum* secretaque sylva tegebant.
She now retreats where Hecate's *altar* stood,
All dark and secret in a *shady wood.*
                              Sewell's Ovid.   415

The latter part: Or many-colour'd bow, etc. to this passage in
the XI. book.

Induitur velamina mille colorum
Iris et arquato coelum curvamine signans
Tecta petit jussi sub rupe latentia Regis.   420

Scarce had the Goddess this injunction laid,
Iris in robes of various dies array'd
Her ample bow from heav'n to earth extends,
And to the monarch's dull abode descends.

But the next place I shall cite is so amazingly striking, that it is   425
alone a sufficient key to the close discovery.

  Qui variare cupid rem *prodigialiter* unum
 Delphinum sylvis appingit, *fluctibus aprum*.

And he who works a simple theme
By *monster*, *prodigy* and *dream*,   430
Will paint the *Dolphin in the lawn*,
While *boars* are in the *Ocean* drawn.

If there be any obscurity or obliquity in the other instances,
which I have cited to the argument, here is nothing but open
assault in broad day-light.   435

Mirantur sub aqua lucos, urbesque, domosque
Nereides: *sylvasque* tenent *delphines* et altis
Incursant ramis, agitataque robora pulsant.
Nat lupus inter oves: fulvos vehit unda leones:
Unda vehit tigres, nec vires fulminis *apro*,   440
Crura nec ablato prosunt velocia cervo.

 Beneath the deep the Nereids in surprize
See woods, and groves, and towns, and temples rise:
The *Dolphins now amidst the forests glide*,
Shake the tall oaks, and beat the boughs aside: 445
The wolf now gentle swims among the sheep,
Tygers and lions mingle in the deep:
His swiftness now avails the hart no more,
Nor force of lightning aids *the tusked boar*.
        Sewell's Ovid.   450

In this reprehension however (to use a homely phrase) *Horace*
gives himself a slap of the face; for he does much the same
thing in the second ode of the first book, at the third stanza,
and the truth of the Deluge (which *Ovid* was nearer to knowing

than *Horace*) being admitted, there is no absurdity in these pas- 455
sages at all.——

Over and above all that has been advanced to strengthen my
position, there are yet two remarkable things worth attending
to: first that *Horace* despised elegy in general on *Ovid*'s account,
tho' the epistles are very excellent, and tho' he had a very great 460
affection for *Tibullus*, *Ovid*'s master.

> Quis tamen *exiguos elegos* emiserit author
> Grammatici certant et adhuc sub judice lis est.

> But *him*, who thought it worth his while
> To sing first in so *small* a stile,   465
> Our critics have not yet found out,
> And still the matter is in doubt.

The next is a sneer even to the description of *Ovid*'s person.

> ——Hunc ego me, si quid componere curem,
> Non magis esse velim: quam *pravo* vivere *naso*   470
> Spectandum *nigris oculis, nigroque capillo.*

> If I had anything to write,
> I wou'd no more be such a wight
> Than I wou'd chuse *black hair and eyes*,
> *With nose of most portentous size.*   475

Every school-boy will tell us, why *Ovid*'s parents called him
Naso; and he himself informs us that he had black hair, which
is usually (I suppose) accompanied with black eyes.

> Jam mea cygneas imitantur tempora plumas.
> Inficit et *nigras* alba senecta *comas.*   480

> Now on my temples rests a swan-like down,
> And my *black locks* thro' age are bleach'd upon my crown.

After all we must admit that *Horace* was rather too hard upon
Ovid, who, tho' his inferior with regard to some things, was altogether a better man in others, and his works, with all their 485
defects, have justly intitled him to the *praise*, as his hardships
have in a manner endeared him, to the *affection* of posterity.

Bishop Atterbury, in a little fugitive piece, that I have seen,
takes occasion to make complaint of *Virgil*'s want of gratitude
to Horace (who had celebrated him very frequently) in refusing 490

a place for his panegyric in every part of his works. *Horace* is a
debtor to the pen of *Ovid* in this article.

> Et tenuit nostras numerosus *Horatius* aures,
>   Dum ferit *Ausonia* carmina culta lyra.

> Melodious *Horace* too my ears detain'd   495
> While to his finish'd odes th'*Ausonian* strings he strain'd.

This compliment would have been returned by *Horace,* one of
the most * thankful men that ever lived (if by the bye it was
written in his life-time) had he not, according to our hypothe-
sis, entertained a most extraordinary contempt, both for his   500
writings and himself.—

So much for our conjecture—and now to bring this long
preface to as decent a conclusion as I may; I must confess
myself to the reader, that, tho' I presume upon the whole, he
shall meet with entertainment and information, yet he will find   505
but too many opportunities of exercising his candour and
humanity by the faults, which shall occur. Good-nature is the
grace of God in grain, and so much the characteristic of an
Englishman, that I hope every one deserving such a name will
think it somewhat hard, if a gentleman derived from ancestors,   510
who have abode upon their own Lordship six hundred years in
the County Palatine of *Durham,* should have been reduced in a
manner by necessity to a work of this kind, which if done in a
state he had more reason to be satisfied with, had been more
likely to have given satisfaction.   515

P.S. It is no more than justice to the merit of Mr. *Flexney,* to
acknowledge, that ever since I have been engaged with him in
this work, he has constantly treated me with much friendship
and good-nature, which I hope will serve him amongst such
gentlemen and scholars, as have occasion for a good Bookseller. 520

---

* This is evident not only from the warmth of his language in his Odes and other
works, but from the circumstance of his behaviour to all his friends of all parties, with
whom he always kept himself well to the last.

513–14 a state] a state, *1767*   517 ever] even *1767*

THE ODES

THE
FIRST BOOK
OF THE
ODES OF HORACE

ODE I.
To MAECENAS.

Different men have their several pleasures: Horace affects the name of a poet, especially in the lyric cast.

Maecenas, of a race renown'd,
Whose royal ancestors were crown'd;
O patron of my wealth and praise,
And pride and pleasure of my days!
Some of a vent'rous cast there are,   5
That glory in th'Olympic car,
Whose glowing wheels in dust they roll,
Driv'n to an inch upon the goal,
And rise from mortal to divine,
Ennobled by the wreath they twine.   10
One, if the giddy mob proclaim,
And vying lift to * threefold fame;
One, if within his barn he stores
The wealth of Lybian threshing floors,
Will never from his course be press'd,   15
For all that Attalus possess'd,
To plow, with sailor's anxious pain,
In Cyprian sloop th'Egean main.
The merchant, dreading the south-west,
Whose blasts th'Icarian wave molest,   20
Praises his villa's rural ease,
Built amongst bowling-greens and trees;
But soon the thoughts of growing poor

* To the three greatest honours of Rome; to be either ediles, praetors, or consuls.

Make him his shatter'd barks insure.
There's now and then a social soul   25
That will not scorn the Massic bowl,
Nor shuns to break in a degree
On the grave day's solidity;
Now underneath the shrubby shade,
Now by the sacred fountain laid.   30
Many are for the martial strife,
And love the trumpet and the fife,
That mingle in the din of war,
Which all the pious dames abhor:
The sportsman, heedless of his fair,   35
With patience braves the wintry air,
Whether his blood-hounds, staunch and keen,
The hind have in the covert seen,
Or wild boar of the Marsian breed,
From the round-twisted cords is freed.   40
But as for Horace, I espouse
The glory of the scholar's brows,
The wreath of festive ivy wove,
Which makes one company for Jove.
Me the cool groves by zephyrs fann'd,   45
Where nymphs and satyrs, hand in hand,
Dance nimbly to the rural song,
Distinguish from the vulgar throng.
If nor Euterpe, heavenly gay,
Forbid her pleasant pipes to play,   50
Nor Polyhymnia disdain
A lesson in the Lesbian strain,
That, thro' Maecenas, I may pass
'Mongst writers of the Lyric class,
My muse her laurell'd head shall rear,   55
And top the zenith of her sphere.

ODE II.
To AUGUSTUS CAESAR.

Many storms and tempests are inflicted upon the Roman people, to avenge the death of Julius Caesar. The sole hope of the empire is placed in the safety of Augustus.

Surely at length it may suffice,
These frequent storms of snow and hail,
Which Jove commission'd from the skies,
    So dreadful to prevail!
And hurling from his flaming arm   5
His vengeful bolts, 'midst thunder-show'rs
Has o'er the city spread th'alarm,
    And smote the sacred tow'rs.
Thro' all the world th'alarm is spread,
For fear of those portentous days,   10
When Proteus on the mountain's head
    Made his sea-monsters graze.
On topmost elms the scaly race
Stuck where the ring-doves us'd to be,
And tim'rous deer, expell'd their place,   15
    Swam in the whelming sea.
We saw the sandy Tiber drive
Huge billows from th'Etrurian strand,
And e'en at Vesta's fane arrive
    To mar, what Numa plann'd.   20
Whilst vengeful 'gainst the will supreme
He fondling hears * his wife complain,
And flooding to the left his stream,
    He glories in our bane.
Thinn'd by our crimes our sons shall tell,   25
How Romans whet the sword and spear,
(Against the Persians had been well)
    And all our broils shall hear.

* Ilia, the mother of Romulus, was cast into the Tiber; and hence (as some will have it) poetically called his wife. It is likely she was very fond to walk by that pleasant river, till she was wedded to the place.

ODE ii. 3 Jove] Jove, *1767*

What pow'r to save her sinking name
Shall Rome invoke, what urgent suit   30
Shall Vesta's holy virgins frame
   In hymns that bear no fruit?
What worthy, for the nation's aid,
Our crimes t'atone shall Jove assign,
Come white-rob'd Phoebus, as we've pray'd,   35
   Do thou thyself divine.
Or if thou rather wouldst befriend,
Glad queen of Eryce's perfumes,
Whom love and pleasantry attend
   With their ambrosial plumes—   40
Or, Mars, if thou at length wouldst speed,
O founder of the Roman race,
To visit thy neglected seed,
   Now sunk into disgrace:
Too long indulg'd thy cruel sport,   45
Whom noise, and polish'd helms delight,
And the fierce Moor's determin'd port,
   And aspect in the fight.
Or if the part you can sustain,
By thee the righteous deed be done,   50
You *, which yourself a mortal feign,
   O gentle Maia's son:
Late may'st thou be again receiv'd,
And long in gladness rule our state,
Nor thee at all our vices griev'd,   55
   Th'unwelcome gale translate!
Here rather be the triumph priz'd,
And, father, emp'ror dear to Rome,
Delight thine ear—nor unchastis'd,
   Let scamp'ring Medes presume!   60

---

* The poet here supposes Augustus to be Mercury, in a human shape. There are
many reasons (says Rodellius) wherefore Augustus might be likened to Mercury: for
the courier in ordinary of the Gods was expert in business, quick, and resembling a lively
youth, Octavius, the minister of providence for the repose of mankind, was all this also
at that time being twenty-three. Mercury was the God of genius and address, Octavius
a very great patron of the one, and a most consummate master of the other.

31 virgins] virgin's *1767*   32 fruit?] fruit. *1767*   36 divine.] divine? *176*
37 befriend,] befriend *1767*

ODE III.

He prays that the ship may have a good passage, which was about to carry Virgil to Athens: after which he with great spirit inveighs against the temerity of mankind.

So may the queen of Cyprus' isle
And Helen's brethren in sweet star-light smile,
    And Aeolus the winds arrest,
All but the fav'ring gales of fresh north-west,
    O ship, that ow'st so great a debt,   5
No less than * Virgil, to our fond regret!
    By thee on yon Athenian shore
Let him be safely landed, I implore:
    And o'er the billows, as they roll,
Preserve the larger portion of my soul!   10
    A heart of oak, and breast of brass
Were his, who first presum'd on seas to pass,
    And ever ventur'd to engage,
In a light skiff, with ocean's desperate rage;
    Nor fear'd to hear the cracking masts,   15
When Africus contends with northern blasts;
    Nor Hyads, still foreboding storms,
Nor wrathful south, that all the depth deforms;
    Than whom no greater tyrant reigns
Whether the waves he ruffles or restrains.   20
    How dauntless of all death was he,
Whose tearless eyes could such strange monsters see;
    Cou'd see the swelling ocean low'r,
Or those huge rocks, which in Epirus tow'r!
    Dread Providence the land in vain   25
Has cut from that dissociable main,
    If impious mortals not the less
On this forbidden element transgress:

---

* This ode is to be referr'd to the year of Rome *734*, in which Virgil made a voyage to Athens, intending there to put the last hand to his Eneid at his leisure. He was scarce arrived, when Augustus returning from the East to Italy, brought him back with him; but being taken ill on ship-board, he was put ashore at Brundusium, where, the year following, he died, aged fifty-one.

    Determin'd each extreme to bear,
All desp'rate deeds the race of mortals dare.   30
    Prometheus, with presumptuous fraud,
Stole fire from heav'n, and spread the flame abroad,
    Of which dire sacrilege the fruit,
The lank consumption, and a new recruit
    Of fevers came upon mankind,   35
And for a long delay at first design'd,
    The last extremity advanc'd,
And urg'd the march of death, and all his pangs inhanc'd.
    With wings, not giv'n a man below,
Did Dedalus attempt in air to go.   40
    Th'Herculean toil, exceeding bound,
Broke through the gulf of Acheron profound.
    Nothing too difficult for man,
He'll scale the skies in folly, if he can;
    Nor by his vices every day   45
Will give Jove leave his wrathful bolts to stay.

ODE IV.
To SEXTIUS, a Person of Consular Dignity.*

By describing the delightfulness of spring, and urging the common lot of mortality, he exhorts Sextius, as an Epicurean, to a life of voluptuousness.

    A grateful change! Favonius, and the spring
        To the sharp winter's keener blasts succeed,
    Along the beach, with ropes, the ships they bring,
        And launch again, their watry way to speed.
    No more the plowmen in their cots delight,   5
        Nor cattle are contented in the stall;
    No more the fields with hoary frosts are white,
        But Cytherean Venus leads the ball.

ODE iii. 38 inhanc'd.] inhanc'd, *1767*

---

    * Though this Sextius always had favoured his friend Brutus, and even at this time
respected his memory, insomuch as to preserve busts of him in his house, yet Augustus
in love with such fidelity, not without prodigious applause for his generosity, chose him
his colleague, in the year of Rome *713*, from whence, I conjecture (says Rodellius), that
this Ode was written the year following, there being no reason to call Sextius happy
before his consulate, and the season of the consulate itself not being for indulging the
genius in matter of festivity.

She, while the moon attends upon the scene,
   The Nymphs and decent Graces in the set,   10
Shakes with alternate feet the shaven green,
   While Vulcan's Cyclops at the anvil sweat.
Now we with myrtle shou'd adorn our brows,
   Or any flow'r that decks the loosen'd sod;
In shady groves to Faunus pay our vows,   15
   Whether a lamb or kid delight the God.
Pale death alike knocks at the poor man's door,
   O happy Sextius, and the royal dome,
The whole of life forbids our hope to soar,
   Death and the shades anon shall press thee home.   20
And when into the shallow grave you run,
   You cannot win the monarchy of wine,
Nor doat on Lycidas, as on a son,
   Whom for their spouse all little maids design.

ODE V.
To PYRRHA.

Horace has escaped from the allurements of Pyrrha, as from a ship-wreck. He affirms such as are ensnared by her love to be in a state of wretchedness.

   Say what * slim youth, with moist perfumes
      Bedaub'd, now courts thy fond embrace,
   There, where the frequent rose-tree blooms,
      And makes the grot so sweet a place?
   Pyrrha, for whom with such an air   5
   Do you bind back your golden hair?

   So seeming in your cleanly vest,
      Whose plainness is the pink of taste—
   Alas! how oft shall he protest
      Against his confidence misplac't,   10
   And love's inconstant pow'rs deplore,
   And wondrous winds, which, as they roar,

* Horace, who was a corpulent man, seems to deride a lean rival particularly.

Throw black upon the alter'd scene——
   Who now so well himself deceives,
And thee all sunshine, all serene   1
   For want of better skill believes,
And for his pleasure has presag'd
Thee ever dear and disengag'd.

Wretched are all within thy snares,
   The inexperienc'd and the young!   2
For me the temple witness bears
   Where I my dropping weeds have hung,
And left my votive chart behind
To him that rules both wave and wind.

ODE VI.
To AGRIPPA.

Varius, the tragic and epic poet, will with more address sing the atchievements of Agrippa. Horace is only fit to celebrate revels, and take pictures from middle life.

Brave and victorious in the fight,
Our Varius with Maeonian flight
   Shall thine atchievements blaze,
Whate'er, beneath thy great command,
The troops have done by sea and land,
   In fierce desire of praise.

Agrippa, I cannot attain
The grandeur of the epic strain,
   Tho' rous'd by deeds like thine,
Nor colour up the glowing page
With Peleus' son's immortal rage,
   Nor reach the great design

That artful hero to recount,
Who could by sea such toils surmount;
   Nor sing the barb'rous race
Of Pelops, while the bashful lyre
Thy praise and Caesar's on the wire
   Forbids me to disgrace.

What mortal pen can Mars recite,
In adamantine armour bright,   20
   Or with the life compare
Meriones in dust involv'd,
Or him, Minerva's aid resolv'd
   The Gods themselves to dare?

I sing of sports and am'rous play,   25
(For all these things are in my way)
   And nymphs of sportive veins,
That are so apt to scratch and tear
With nails which to the quick they pare
   Against their fav'rite swains.   30

ODE VII.
To MUNATIUS PLANCUS, a Person of Consular Dignity.*

Some writers praise one city or region, and some another. Horace prefers Tibur to all the world, in which place Plancus was born, whom he exhorts to the washing away of care by wine.

Let others sing the praise of famous Rhodes
   Or Mytilene, or th'Ephesian pride,
Or chant the walls of Corinth in their odes,
   Wash'd by a different sea on either side,
Or Thebes for Bacchus, Delphi justly fam'd   5
   For Phoebus, or Thessalian Tempe's vale;
Some make the feast of Pallas, nymph umblam'd,
   The theme of one uninterrupted tale,
And run all lengths to wear an olive crown—
   Many for Juno, with poetic zeal,   10
Argus so apt for cavalry renown,
   And, rich Mycenae, boast thy public weal.

ODE vi. 23 Minerva's] Menerva's *1767*

---

* Munatius Plancus, upon the death of Caesar, at first sided with Octavius, and was consul with M. Lepidus, in the year of Rome, *712*. After that he went over to Antony, and did not return to Augustus till *722*, who, in consideration of what was past, perhaps not putting any great confidence in him, made no use of him in the war, which that very year was denounced against Antony and Cleopatra. Plancus upon this, being in a state of chagrin, stood in need of that consolation which Horace endeavours to give him in his ode.

With me nor patient Sparta, nor the plains
    Of high-manur'd Larissa e'er cou'd take,
As where Albunea's tinkling fount remains,   15
    Or Anio roaring down into the lake.
And old Tiburnus' grove for ever green,
    Where flow'ring orchards give a strong perfume,
Where marshal'd trees upon the stream are seen,
    And in the waggling waters wave their bloom.   20
As the white south at times serenes the skies,
    Nor are his gath'ring show'rs for ever rife;
So thou, O Plancus, 'gainst thy cares be wise,
    With mellow wine dismiss the toils of life,
Whether the camp, with shining standards gay,   25
    Detain you ready for the hour of fight,
Or in your native Tibur you shall stay,
    And in the dense embow'ring shades delight.
When Teucer by his father was oppress'd,
    And driv'n away from Salamis he fled,   30
He thus his weeping company address'd,
    As, wet with wine, the poplar bound his head.
'Sped on by fortune, kinder than my sire,
    O my co-mates, we'll go where'er she please;
Despair of nothing and to all aspire—   35
    By Teucer's guidance Teucer's auspices.
For Phoebus has of certainty foretold,
    That in a land to us advent'rers new,
Fair Salamis a doubtful name shall hold.
    O brave companions, O my faithful few!   40
Ye that with me have harder things endur'd,
    Than all the evils which ye now sustain,
This day your grief and care with wine be cur'd,
    To-morrow sends us to the depth again.'

ODE vii. 34 please] pleases *1767*   39 hold.] hold, *1767*

ODE VIII.
To LYDIA.

He animadverts upon Sybaris, a youth distractedly in love with Lydia, and wholly dissolved in pleasures.

I charge thee, Lydia, tell me straight,
 Why Sybaris destroy,
Why make love do the deeds of hate,
And to his end precipitate
 The dear enamour'd boy?   5
Why can he not the field abide,
 From sun and dust recede,
Nor with his friends, in gallant pride,
Dress'd in his regimentals, ride,
 And curb the manag'd steed?   10
Why does he now to bathe disdain,
 And fear the sandy flood?
Why from th'athletic oil refrain,
As if its use would be his bane,
 As sure as viper's blood?   15
No more his shoulders black and blue
 By wearing arms appear;
He, who the quoit so dextrous threw,
And from whose hand the jav'lin flew
 Beyond a rival's spear;   20
Why does he skulk, as authors say
 Of Thetis' fav'rite heir,
Lest a man's habit should betray,
And force him to his troops away,
 The work of death to share?   25

ODE IX.
To THALIARCHUS.

The greater the violence of the winter, the more we should indulge in festivity.

See high Soracte, white with snow,
Still more and more a mountain grow,
Nor can the lab'ring woods their weight sustain,
And motionless with frost the sharpen'd streams remain.
Dissolve the cold, a rousing fire   5
Upon the social hearth aspire,
And four years old with bountiful design
Bring in the Sabine jar the long-expected wine.
Leave to th'immortal Gods the rest,
For when they shall have once supprest   10
The winds, that on the boiling surge contend,
Nor cypress shakes a leaf, nor yon old ash-trees bend.
Enquire not of to-morrow's fate,
And whatsoever chance await,
Turn to account, nor fly from sweet amours,   15
Nor let the dance be shunn'd by such address as * yours.
While yet your vig'rous years are green,
Nor peevish age brings on the spleen,
By turns the field, the tenis-court repeat,
And whispers soft at night for assignations meet.   20
Now glad to hear the damsel raise
The laugh, that her retreat betrays,
Steal from her arm the pledge for theft dispos'd,
Or from her finger force, with sham-resistance clos'd.

* The pronoun TU being emphatical in the original, it is likely that Thaliarchus was
an excellent dancer.

ODE X.
To MERCURY.

Whom he praises for his eloquence, his parentage, for the invention of the lyre and * palestra, for his great address in pilfering, and for the offices that he discharges.

> O thou, which, eloquent and chaste,
> From Atlas sprung, rough man to rule,
> And form our sons to toil and taste
>   As in th'Athenian school.
> Thee will I sing, great Jove's courier,   5
> Inventor of the lyre confest;
> Expert to steal and disappear,
>   And turn it to a jest.
> Thee when a boy, with threats injoin'd
> To bring the steers you had withdrawn,   10
> Apollo laugh'd aloud to find
>   His quiver also gone.
> King Priam likewise, thee his guide,
> Deserting Troy with all his wealth,
> Atreus his haughty sons defy'd,   15
>   And hostile camp by stealth.
> The pious souls to realms of love,
> Your golden rod compels to go,
> O grateful to the Gods above
>   And to the pow'rs below.   20

* A school for wrestling, and other manly exercises.

ODE XI.
To LEUCONOE.

He advises Leuconoe to indulge in pleasure, regardless of all care for the mor-
row, by deducing his arguments from the brevity and fleetness of life.

Seek not, what we're forbid to know, the date the Gods decree
To you, my fair Leuconoe, or what they fix for me.
Nor your Chaldean books consult, but chearfully submit,
(How much a better thought it is!) to what the Gods think fit.
Whether more winters on our head they shall command to low'r, 5
Or this the very last of all shall bring our final hour.
E'en this, whose rough tempestuous rage makes yon Tyrrhenian
    roar,
And all his foamy breakers dash upon the rocky shore.
Be wise and broach your mellow wine, which carefully decant,
And your desires proportionate to life's compendious grant.   10
E'en while we speak the moments fly, be greedy of to-day;
Nor trust another for those pranks which we may never play.

ODE XII.
To AUGUSTUS.

Having celebrated the Gods, heroes, and certain famous men, at last he comes
to the divine honours of Augustus.

Clio, to sing on pipe or lyre,
What man, what hero is your choice,
And with what God will you inspire
    Glad echo's mimic voice?
Or in the Heliconian shade,   5
Or Pindus or cool Haemus sped,
Where the vague woods at random stray'd
    With Orpheus at their head?
E'en he who, by his mother's art,
The loud cascade, the rapid wind   10
Cou'd stop—and ears to oaks impart,
    To his soft airs inclin'd?

ODE xi. 4 is!] is? *1767*

First then the usual form of praise
Is his, who men and Gods impow'rs,
The earth, the sea, the world he sways,   15
    The seasons and the hours.
From whom no greater can proceed,
To whom no being's like or near;
Yet Pallas challenges the meed
    Of secondary fear.   20
Nor thee, brave Liber, will I slight,
Nor thee, fair Forrester, the foe
Of beasts, nor thee which aim'st so right,
    Dread Phoebus, with thy bow.
Alcides next, and Leda's twins,   25
In chivalry and cestus too
I praise, whose star, when it begins
    To bless the seaman's view,
Its brightness makes the waves subside,
The winds are still, the clouds disperse,   30
And smooth at their command's the tide,
    That roar'd but now so fierce.
Now shall I Rome's first founder sing,
Or Numa's peaceful reign commend,
Or Priscus great and mighty king,   35
    Or Cato's glorious end?
Great Regulus I will enroll,
The house of Scaurus, Paulus write,
So lavish of his godlike soul,
    And grateful thee recite,   40
Fabricius, with rough Curius join'd;
Him and Camillus too for arms
A hardy poverty design'd
    In their paternal farms.
As imperceptibly the pines,   45
Marcellus, so thy fame aspires:
The Julian star, like Luna, shines
    Amongst the lesser fires.

ᴐᴅE xii. 19 meed] mead *1767*

Sire and preserver of our race,
From Saturn sprung, do thou * convey, 50
That Caesar hold the second place
 In thine eternal sway;
Whether o'er Parthia's threat'ning host
At a just triumph he arrive,
Or, subject to the eastern coast, 55
 Confed'rate Indians drive.
Subordinate to thee alone,
He o'er the happy world shall reign,
While thou shalt thunder from thy throne
 On each polluted fane. 60

ODE XIII.
To LYDIA.

He is very uneasy that his rival Telephus is preferred to him by Lydia.

When Lydia to my rival tells
How Telephus, her Telephus excells;
 And harps upon his manly charms,
His neck so rosy-red, and iv'ry arms;
 Alas! I boil with jealous ire, 5
And all th'internal man is set on fire.
 Then are my pow'rs of reason weak,
My colour comes and goes, and down my cheek
 The trickling tears of anguish steal,
Proof of the ling'ring fever that I feel. 10
 I burn, if in th'immod'rate broils
Of liquor thy white sleeves the tipler soils,
 Or in a raging am'rous fit,
Has left his mark upon the lips he bit.
 Believe me, Lydia, in the end 15
You cannot hope his love will long extend,
 Who to your kisses is so rude
By Venus in nectareous balm imbu'd.

* A word attempted in the peculiarity of Horace—grant by delegation, make over
your right.

O happy thrice, and thrice again!
Who without breach still hug the pleasing chain; 20
    Nor ever any bick'ring strife
Can part them till the last extreme of life.

ODE XIV.

To the Republic of Rome, on the Renewal of the Civil War.

New floods of strife that swell the main,
O ship, shall bring thee out again;
O wherefore venture? 'tis your fort
To keep your station in the port.
Do not you see your sides bereft, 5
Till not a single oar is left,
And, wounded by the rapid blast,
Groan the crack'd sail-yards and the mast?
Nor are there scarcely farther hopes,
That your old keel, despoil'd of ropes, 10
Can longer hold it out to brave
The fury of th'impetuous wave.
Thy canvas is no longer tight,
Nor Gods to sue in evil plight,
Tho' once a Pontic pine you stood, 15
And daughter of a noble wood,
May'st boast a vain descent and form—
The tim'rous seaman in a storm
Trusts not in painted planks—be warn'd,
Lest by the hissing winds you're scorn'd. 20
Late my vexation and my care,
Still my desire and constant pray'r,
Yet may'st thou from those isles be free
That glister in th'Ionian sea.

ODE XV.
The Prediction of NEREUS Concerning the Destruction of Troy

When Paris ship'd in base deceit,
   Against all hospitable laws,
Fair Helen in th'Idean fleet,
   Nereus injoin'd the winds a pause;
And hush'd into the peace they hate
   The rapid murm'rers, while he sung
Each cruel circumstance and date
   Of destiny, that o'er them hung.
'Ill-omen'd her you take to Troy,
   Whom Greece united shall reclaim,
And Priam's ancient reign destroy,
   And your connubials with the dame.
What deaths attend the Dardan realm!
   What toils for man and steed to bear!
See Pallas now her shield, her helm,
   Her car and all her wrath prepare!
In vain, presumptuous in the aid
   Of Venus, you your hair shall tire,
And grateful to each list'ning maid
   Run soft divisions on the lyre.
In vain the spears and Cretan dart,
   So dread to amorous delight,
You shall avoid with timid heart,
   And Ajax swift to urge your flight.
Yet late, too late, adult'rous swain,
   You shall your locks in dust besmear.
See there Ulysses, see the bane
   Of Troy with Pylian Nestor near.
The Salaminian Teucer speeds—
   See warlike Sthenelus arrive,
Who, if there's need of martial steeds,
   Is excellent those steeds to drive.

ODE xv. 5 peace] peace, *1767*   26 besmear.] besmear, *1767*

Thou too Meriones shall know,
  And more heroic than his sire
Hear Diomed, thy deadly foe,   35
  In wrath to find thy post inquire.
Whom you in panting haste shall fly,
  Tho' Helen heard another tale,
As harts the wolf they chance to spy,
  Heedless of pasture in the vale.   40
Long as Achilles' wrath shall last,
  Thy Phrygian dames shall stave their doom,
But Grecia's flames, some winters past,
  Shall Trojan tow'rs consume.'

ODE XVI.
To His MISTRESS.

He is reduced to sing a recantation; for he begs pardon of a young lady whom he had offended with certain Iambics: and he shifts the blame upon his passionate temper, whose uncontroulable violence he describes.

To that lampoon against your fame,
  O fairer than the beauteous dame
    That bore thee, put what shameful end you please,
Whether in flaming fire, or Adriatic seas.
    Cybele, nor the priest possest,   5
    Phoebus himself an inward guest,
  Not Liber can the settl'd temper shake,
Not Corybantian drums with all the noise they make,
    Like baleful ire, which neither blade
    Of Noric temper has dismay'd,   10
  Nor ship-devouring seas, nor fire-flakes red,
Nor Jove himself up-roaring in tremendous dread.
    'Tis said Prometheus when controul'd
    To work into the human mould
  Some portion took from brutes of every kind,   15
And to the stomach's pride the lion's wrath assign'd.
    'Twas wrath that could Thyestes quell,

By such a downfal, great and fell,
That final overthrow of towns, where now
O'er the raz'd walls the foe drive their insulting plough.   20
Take warning and suppress your rage;
Me also, in my blooming age,
Such sallies cou'd seduce too far to dare,
And in the keen Iambic satyrize my fair.
But now I would myself endear,   25
And for the gentle change severe,
Provided she my recantation view,
And be again my sweet, and all my hope renew.

ODE XVII.
To TYNDARIS.

He invites her to Lucretilis, shewing her sundry advantages that she should reap from the place.

Brisk Faunus oft Lyceus flies,
And to Lucretilis applies,
And there defends, in situation sweet,
My goats from showery winds, and from the burning heat.
Secure without another ward,   5
The wives of their unsavoury lord,
At large on thyme and arbute shrubs are fed,
Nor do their kids fierce wolves or lurking adders dread.
But more especial is their peace,
If you the imprison'd notes release,   10
And those sweet strains, O Tyndaris, you play,
Ustica's sloping groupe of marble piles repay.
The Gods protect, the Gods espouse
My lyric muse, and faithful vows,
Here you shall fully taste, a welcome guest,   15
The horn of rural honours heap'd for thee and prest.
Here in a valley's close retreat
You shall avoid the dog-star's heat,
And here shall harp upon the Teian string,
Penelope and Circe vying for the king.   20

ODE xvii. 15 taste,] taste *1767*

Here shaded, innocent and light,
  You shall partake the Lesbian white,
  Nor to your bow'r shall Mars himself betake,
Nor Semele's Thyoneus his disturbance make.
  And, though suspected to be here,   25
    You shall not ruffian Cyrus fear,
  Lest his rude hands should not your sex forbear,
But pull your chaplet off, and the poor night-gown tear.

ODE XVIII.
To QUINTILIUS VARUS.*

Wine moderately taken, makes the heart glad, but drank to excess, creates madness.

† Varus, you shou'd no tree prefer before the sacred vine,
If you to plant the kindly soil of Catilus design.
For to the droughty all things hard has Heav'n and nature made;
Nor can we rankling care escape without the bottle's aid.
Who make a racket in their cups, of want or war's distress,   5
Nor rather Bacchus, sire of joy, and graceful Venus bless?
But lest we shou'd transgress and take more liquor than we
    ought,
The Centaurean battles warn o'er such carousing fought.
Great Bacchus is a warning too as most severely just
Against Sithonians right and wrong confounding in their lust.   10
To thee my candid ‡ Bassareus I will not do despite;
Nor bring from underneath the leaf what best had shunn'd
    the light.
Restrain your Berecynthian horn, and hush your savage drums,
After whose clam'rous din, self-love in partial blindness comes;
Vain glory next, with empty head aloft, is wont to pass;   15
And tattling treachery succeeds seen through as clear as glass.

* Quintilius Varus having enjoyed great posts, and even the consulship itself at Rome, was at last overthrown in Germany with a very great slaughter, called the Varian defeat, and esteemed most deplorable in the judgment of Augustus. This defeat happened shortly after the death of Horace, which (I suppose) makes Rodellius doubt whether this Quintilius Varus, to whom this ode is addressed, be the same.
  † The English metre is the same as in ode the eleventh.
  ‡ A name of Bacchus, from the Hebrew Bassar, which signifies to work in the vineyard.

ODE XIX.
Of GLYCERA.

That he is inflamed with her love.

The mother of the fierce desires
And Semele the Theban's son inspires,
  And wanton wilfulness assures
To render up my heart to fresh amours.
  Bright Glycera my soul inflames,
Whose lustre e'en the Parian polish shames,
  And her sweet archness fans the blaze,
And slipp'ry looks that balk the lover's gaze.
  Her Cyprus now deserting quite,
Venus on me careers with all her might,   10
  Nor lets the Scythian be rehears'd,
Nor Parthian furious with his steed revers'd,
  As things impertinent to sing.
Here, lads, in rolls the living verdure bring,
  And frankincense and vervain place   15
With wine of two years old to crown the vase.
  A victim, welt'ring in his gore,
Her presence will propitiate the more.

ODE XX.
To MAECENAS.

He invites Maecenas to an entertainment by no means sumptuous.

Dear knight, with me you shall partake
In sober cups of Sabine wine,
Poor bev'rage of Horatian make,
  Which with these hands of mine
Was well secur'd that very day,   5
When such applause in thund'ring roar
Was giv'n your merit at the play;
  Till from the sounding shore

ODE xix. 17 victim,] victim *1767*

Of * your own Tiber, back it came,
And at Mount Vatican arriv'd.   10
There echo, pleas'd t'augment your fame,
    The gen'ral peal reviv'd.
You on Calenian juice can dine,
And may rich Caecuban afford;
But Formian or Falernian wine   15
    Appear not at my board.

ODE XXI.
To APOLLO and DIANA.

He exhorts the damsels and boys to sing their praises.

Ye tender virgins, Dian sing,
    Ye lads, the smooth-fac'd Phoebus praise;
And lov'd so much by heav'n's high king,
    Latona likewise grace the lays.
Praise her that loves the streams and groves,   5
    Such as cold Algidus o'ershade,
Or in black Erymanthus roves,
    Or Cragus' ever-verdant glade.
Ye vying youths of Tempe tell,
    And Delos, Phoebus' native place;   10
Him, whom the bow becomes so well,
    And lyre of true Mercurial grace.
He, if tearful war inflicts,
    Or wretched famine, as you pray,
Against the Persians and the Picts   15
    From Caesar shall the plague convey.

---

* Tiber takes its rise from Tuscany, the native country of Maecenas.

ODE XXII.
To ARISTIUS FUSCUS.

Integrity of life is on all sides in security, and that he proves by an instance of himself.

One sound and pure of wicked arts
Leaves to the blacks their spear and bow,
Nor need he deadly tinctur'd darts
   Within his quiver stow.
Whether the suns of southern flame,   5
Or barb'rous Caucasus he braves,
Or goes, where of romantic fame,
   Vast tracts Hydaspes laves.
For careless, out of bounds to rove,
(A song on Lalage my plan)   10
Me swordless in the Sabine grove
   A wolf beheld, and ran.
A monster, such as ne'er was fed
In warlike Daunia's beechen plain,
Nor e'er that nurse of lions bred,   15
   E'en Juba's dry domain.
Me in those lifeless regions place,
Where trees receive no fost'ring gale,
Whence Jove has turn'd away his face,
   And clouds obscure prevail;   20
Or place me, where the sun too near,
No huts can stand the heat above,
Sweet-smiling, sweetly-prattling dear,
   My Lalage I'll love.

ODE XXIII.
To CHLOE.

There is no reason why Chloe should shun the touch of man, whom in the maturity of her bloom she is now fit for.

Me, Chloe, like a fawn you fly,
That seeks in trackless mountains high
   Her tim'rous dam again;
Alarm'd at every thing she hears,
The woods, the winds excite her fears,   5
   Tho' all those fears are vain.
For if a tree the breeze receives,
That plays upon the quiv'ring leaves
   When spring begins to start;
Or if green lizards, where they hide,   10
Turn but the budding bush aside,
   She trembles knees and heart.
But I continue my pursuit,
Not like the fierce Getulian brute,
   Or tyger, to assail,   15
And of thee life and limbs bereave—
Think now at last 'tis time to leave
   Thy mother for a male.

ODE XXIV.
To VIRGIL.

Who lamented inconsolably the death of Quintilius.

What can abash the mournful strains,
Or bounds prescribe to grief, like this,
   For those most precious dear remains,
Of which we have so great a miss?
Melpomene, do thou the dirge inspire,   5
To whom Jove gave the liquid voice and lyre.

Has then eternal sleep possess'd
* Quintilius, mod'rate, just and kind,
  Where shall our grievance be redress'd,
Or where will ye his equal find,   10
O modesty, and faith, the fair allies
Of justice, and the truth without disguise?
    —An object of exceeding grief
To many, virtuous, did he fall—
  But thou, O Virgil, art the chief,   15
More inconsolable than all—
In vain, alas! you to the Gods resent
Him, who was not on such conditions lent.
    What tho' your own majestic lays
  Shou'd, sweeter far than Orpheus' lyre,   20
    Give ears to laurels and to bays,
You cou'd not make his corpse respire,
Or bid the blood in that cold image flow,
Which Mercury, the minister below,
  Has to the gloomy crowd compell'd,   25
In locking up the doors of fate,
  Nor will he be by pray'r withheld,
—However musical and great—
'Tis hard—but manly patience must endure,
And make things lighter, that admit no cure.   30

ODE XXV.
To LYDIA.

He insults her, that now being old, she is deservedly contemned by her gallants.

More sparing the young rakes alarm
  The window-shutters of their toast,
You now may sleep secure of harm;
  The door affects the post,

* This Quintilius is not the same with him to whom the eighteenth ode is addressed, but a native of Cremona, a poet by profession, and a near relation of Virgil; which latter circumstance particularly endeared him to Horace.

Which mov'd so oft its pliant hinge—   5
   —You hear that serenade no more,
'Sleep'st thou, while dying lovers winge,
    O Lydia, at thy door!'
Jilt, thou the scoffing sparks shalt soon
   Lament, neglected in a lane,   10
When, at the changing of the moon,
   The north-west blows amain;
While love and vehement desire,
   Such as the mares for stallions seize,
Shall set your blister'd breast afire,   15
   Join'd to complaints like these,
That gladsome youths on ivy green
   And constant myrtle rather glote;
To Hebrus, winter's comrade keen,
   The wither'd leaves devote.   20

ODE XXVI.
To the MUSE, Concerning * AELIUS LAMIA.

It is not fitting that the votaries of the muses should be liable to solicitude and grief. The poet recommends his friend Lamia to the Pimplean muse.

Friend of the muses, fear and pain
   I throw into the Cretan main,
  To be the sport of ruffian tempests there—
Who the cold north shall sway is far beneath my care.
   I in peculiar unconcern   5
   Profess myself, whatever turn
  The great affairs of Tiridates take,
And all th'alarming dread, that keep his thoughts awake.
   O muse of the Pimplean hill,
   That lov'st to taste the genuine rill,   10
  Weave me those flow'rs that brightest beams receive,
Yea elegance and fragrance for my Lamia weave.

ODE xxv. 19 Hebrus,] Hebrus *1767*

---

* This is the same Lamia with him, ode *xvii.* book *iii.* where we shall have more occasion to take notice of him.

Without that influence of thine,
Vain are the honours I design,
Thou and thy graceful sisters ought to smile,   15
To him devote new strains, and in the Lesbian style.

ODE XXVII.
To his BOTTLE-COMPANIONS.

That they should not quarrel and fight with their cups, as is the manner of barbarians.

With glasses form'd for joy to fight,
Is what the Thracians do in spite;
Let Bacchus know no barb'rous customs here,
But keep the modest God from bloody discord clear.
Can such strange contraries agree,   5
As wine and lights in social glee,
And sabres such as savage Media wears?—
Cease your vile noise, my friends, nor quit your easy chairs.
Me too!—shall I your revels join,
And sour my good Falernian wine?—   10
No, let the brother of the Locrian fair,
Rather his lovesick joys, and darling flame declare.
He will not—On no other plan,
No other terms I take my can—
Whatever damsel e'er thy breast inflam'd,   15
Was of ingenuous birth, nor need you be asham'd.
Whatever be the case speak out
To friendly ears, nor make a doubt.—
'Ah wretch! how thou art hamper'd in a straight,
A lad, whose matchless worth deserv'd a better fate.'   20
What sorceress, what magic art,
What pow'r divine can ease thy smart?—
E'en Pegasus to clear thee will be loth
From one compos'd of * whimsy, wantonness and wrath.

---

* Chimaera. Πρόσθε Λέων ὄπιθεν δὲ Δράκων, μέσση δὲ Χίμαιρα.
                                                        HOM.

ODE xxvii. 7 wears? —] wears — *1767*

ODE XXVIII.

*Archytas a philosopher and geometrician is introduced remonstrating to a certain
sailor, that all must die, and beseeching that he would not suffer his corpse to
lie unburied on the shore.*

Archytas, born to compass land and sea,
  And of the countless sand thy charts to make,
A little boon of dust suffices thee,
  Which on Matinian shores thy relicks take.
Nor is there profit in those airy dreams,   5
  When you the houses of the planets try'd,
And the round world determin'd by your schemes,
  Since in your death all these grand projects dy'd.
The sire of Pelops in like manner fell,
  Tho' with the Gods he feasted in the sky;   10
Tithonus chang'd into a sauterelle,
  And Minos in Jove's secrets wont to pry.
Death too has got * Panthoides again,
  Tho' having taken from the wall his shield,
He cou'd so well the Trojan times explain,   15
  Nor ought to death but skin and nerves cou'd yield.
This was no mean professor in the ways
  Of truth and nature, as you did presume—
But night, a gen'ral night, its wing displays,
  And all at length must travel to the tomb.   20
The furies some expose to martial rage,
  The greedy sailors perish in the wave,
The funerals increase of youth and age,
  None from fell Proserpine themselves can save.
Me, e'en Archytas, the outrageous south,   25
  Upon oblique Orion sure t'attend,
Where that ILLYRIC opes her gulphing mouth,
  Involved at once in an unlook'd-for end.
But thou, O sailor, do not check thy hand,
  Nor grutch on these unburied bones to throw   30
A little portion of the common sand—
  So may the eastern blasts, whate'er you owe,

* Pythagoras asserted that his identical spirit, about seven hundred years before, was
the soul of Euphorbus the son of Panthous, who was slain at the siege of Troy.

Whate'er they threaten to th'Hesperian floods,
 (Thee safe) make Venusinian forrests pay,
And Jove and Neptune, with great store of goods, 35
 Thee to Tarentum's port, in peace convey.
But shou'd you this benevolence neglect,
 A fraud about to hurt your sons unborn,
Perchance, a due reward you may expect,
 Of equal terror, and of equal scorn. 40
If not my prayers, my curses must prevail,
 And no atonement can thy conscience clear,
'Tis not so much (tho' you're in haste to sail)
 To sprinkle thrice the dust in kindness here.

  See this ode finely imitated by Matthew Prior.

ODE XXIX.
To ICCIUS.

*It is a marvel almost up to a prodigy, that Iccius the philosopher, laying aside
his studies, should take a turn to arms, through desire of riches.*

 My friend, you're now invidious grown,
 To make th'Arabian wealth your own,
And 'gainst unconquer'd Saba war declare,
And for the barb'rous Mede his future chains prepare.
 What virgin, when her love is slain, 5
 Shall be a handmaid in thy train?
And, when thou din'st, what youth from out the court,
Shall stand with essenc'd hair, thy splendour to support?
 An archer of paternal craft,
 Skill'd to direct the Indian shaft!— 10
Who now denies but streams their ways may force
Back to the lofty hills, and Tiber change his course,
 When you choice books so dearly bought,
 On doctrines that Panaetius taught,
And your Socratick stock for armour sell, 15
Whose taste for better things at first set out so well?

ODE XXX.
To VENUS.

He requests the goddess to come to the temple, which Glycera had dedicated to
her.

Leave Cyprus, thou that art the queen
  Of Gnidus, and the Paphian isle,
And with my Glycera be seen,
Where, in her temple deck't and clean,
  With frankincense she courts thy smile.   5

With all his ardour bring thy boy,
  The nymphs, the graces loose and free;
Youth's goddess too, that has no joy,
With Mercury, whose mirth wou'd cloy,
  Without thine influence and thee.   10

ODE XXXI.
To APOLLO.

He asks not riches of the God, but only a sound mind in a sound body.

What shall the pious poet pray
  Upon the dedication day;
What vow prefer to this Phoebean shrine,
While from the bowl he pours the first-fruits of his wine?
  Not the rich crop Sardinia yields,   5
  Nor of Calabria's sunny fields
The herds I ask, nor elephants nor gold,
Nor grounds of which still Liris leaves the tale untold.
  Let the Calenian grape be press'd
  By those whom fortune has possess'd;   10
Let the rich merchant in gold cups exhaust
The wine, which to replace his Syrian venture cost:
  Dear to the Gods, since thrice and more
  In one year he can travel o'er

Th' * Atlantic sea undamag'd, while with me   1
Sweet olives, mallows light, and succ'ry best agree.
    Grant, God of song, this humble lot,
    But to enjoy what I have got,
And I beseech thee keep my mind intire
In age without disgust, and with the chearful lyre.   2

ODE XXXII.
To his LYRE.

He addresses his lyre, and requires of it assistance, and that it should not cease
to accompany his song.

If e'er at leisure in the shade
    We've play'd a lesson to remain:
My lyre, the like be now essay'd,
    A true Augustan strain.
Thou whom that † Lesbian touch'd so sweet,
    Tho' with his soldiers arms he bore
Val'rous, or moor'd his shatter'd fleet
    Upon the swampy shore.
Yet Venus and her clinging boy,
    And wine to musick wou'd he set,   1
And on fair maids his skill employ,
    With hair and eyes of jet.
O pride of Phoebus, grateful shell,
    Accepted where the gods regale,
Thou, that canst sooth my toils so well,   1
    'Tis Horace bids thee hail!

---

  * So called from Atlas the highest mountain in Mauritania, which is the extremity of
Africa towards the streight of Gades (now Cadiz) beyond which the Romans at that time
had but little notion of land.
  † Alcaeus.

ODE XXXIII.
To ALBIUS TIBULLUS.

That he should not grieve out of measure, that his rival was unjustly preferred
to him by Glycera.

Tibullus, do not grieve too much,
   Nor in soft elegies complain,
That Glycera's caprice is such,
   And such her insolent disdain,
That she your junior shou'd prefer,   5
Who looks more amiable to her.

For Cyrus fair Lycoria burns,
   So charming with her little face,
But he the fondling damsel spurns
   For squeamish Pholoe's coy embrace;   10
But sooner shall the goats be join'd
To wolves of fierce Appulian kind,

Than Pholoe with a filthy rake
   Commit adult'ry, heinous sin.
Such mischief Venus loves to make,   15
   Who forms and tempers not akin
Pairs with her cruel brazen yoke,
And acts barbarity in joke.

O'er me too in an evil hour
   Had servile Myrtale the sway,   20
A nymph of more tyrannic pow'r
   Than Adria in Calabria's bay,
Tho' at that time a fairer maid
And gentler did my heart invade.

ODE xxxiii. 14 sin.] sin, *1767*

ODE XXXIV.
To HIMSELF.

He repents, that following the Epicureans, he had been wanting in his zeal to the Gods.

A sparing and unfrequent guest
In Jove's high temple at the best,—
While mad philosophy my mind pursu'd,
I now must shift my sail, and have my course renew'd.
For lo! the sempiternal sire   5
(Who us'd to cleave with brandish'd fire
The clouds, as I conceiv'd) of late was seen,
With car and thund'ring horses in the clear SERENE.
Which the still earth and floods that flow,
And horrid Taenarus below,   10
And those Atlantic bounds compels to quake;
'Tis God, and God alone pre-eminent can make
The depths emerge, the mighty poor;
'Tis he, that brings to light th'obscure—
And fortune, at his bidding takes a crown,   15
Here proudly sets it up, there sternly throws it down.

ODE XXXV.
To FORTUNE.

He beseeches her to look to the preservation of Caesar, then on the point of going against the Britons.

O Goddess, whose indulgence sways
Fair Antium sounding with thy praise,
Whose influence can exalt the meanest slave,
Or turn triumphant pomps to sorrow and the grave:
Thee the poor farmer's anxious pray'r   5
Solicits, that his fields may bear;
Thee, mistress of the main, the sailor hails,
As his Bithynian bark o'er Cretan billows sails.

ODE XXXV. 4 grave:] grave. *1767*

Thee the vague Scythians, Dacian rude,
 And cities, nations unsubdu'd,   10
The Latian fierce for battle far and near,
Thee the barbaric queens and purple tyrants fear.
 Let not your hurtful foot displace
 The pillar standing on its base,
Nor let the thronging populace rebel,   15
And roaring out to arms! to arms the state compel.
 * Necessity precedes thy band,
 With nails and wedges in her hand,
Her brazen hand, nor is the hook, nor, hot
With execrable death, the melted lead forgot.   20
 Thee hope, and faith, so scarce, revere,
 And cloath'd in white are ever near,
And still themselves of your own train profess,
Howe'er you bilk the great, and change your seat and dress.
 The faithless mob and courtezan   25
 Behave upon another plan;
And all your friends, when they have drank you dry,
The burthen they should share, in base desertion fly.
 Yet, yet propitiate Caesar's scheme
 On Britain, and the world's extreme,   30
And all our new recruits, that well might brave
The eastern continent, and Erythrean wave.
 O fie upon the barb'rous times,
 Fraternal wounds, and civil crimes,
What has this iron-age refus'd to do!   35
What have we left untouch'd, that honest hearts shou'd rue!
 Our youth, where have they been restrain'd:
 What altars are there left unstain'd—
Yet 'gainst the Scythian and Arabian foe
May all our new-forg'd weapons by thy guidance go! 40

---

* Necessity signifies here the last extremity or death, and things mentioned to belong
to her, were all instruments of torture amongst the Romans.

---

16 arms! to] arms, to *1767*   31 brave] brave, *1767*

ODE XXXVI.
To POMPONIUS NUMIDA.

For whose return from Spain, he rejoices with much exultation.

With the sweet censer and the lyre,
And fatted calf upon the sacred fire,
  The tutelary Gods we bless,
That we our Numida once more caress;
  Who safe and sound from farthest Spain,
Dear to a thousand friends, is come again—
  And yet to none such love he bears,
With none the fond embrace so warmly shares,
  As with lov'd Lamia, mindful still
That they were form'd by one preceptor's skill,
  And both together chang'd their gown—
Set the good day in white memorials down;
  The ready cask by no means spare,
Nor let your feet the morrice-dance forbear.
  Yet Damalis the tippler check,
Lest Bassus she out-drink—the table deck
  With store of parsley, many a rose
And lily, that in transient sweetness blows.
  They all will turn their putrid eyes
On Damalis, who will not quit her prize;
  But her new conquest hugs in hold,
As the ambitious ivies the tall oak infold.

ODE XXXVII.
To his COMPANIONS.

Vhom he invites to indulge their geniuses on occasion of the victory at Actium.
>   To drink and dance with all the glee
>   Of men that find their country free
>   Now, now's the time—now deck the hallow'd shrine,
> Like Mars his active priests, and make the temple fine.
>   Before it was no lawful thing   5
>   The long-kept Caecuban to bring,
>   While for th'imperial capitol the queen
> Ruin and wrath prepar'd, and every deadly scene,
>   With her contaminated train
>   Of eunuchs, arrogant and vain,   10
>   In hopes to compass every point at last,
> Drunk with a long success, and her good fortune past.
>   But now her rage is somewhat tame,
>   Since scarce a ship escap'd the flame,
>   And, tho' at large the Egyptian grape she swill'd,   15
> With real horrors now her frantic soul is fill'd.
>   For as from Italy she flies,
>   His urgent oar Augustus plies,
>   And, as the hawk pursues the dove, he rows,
> Or sportsman hunts the hare trac'd in Aemonian snows,   20
>   That he this monster of her kind
>   Might in coercive fetters bind—
>   But she, while for a nobler death she tried,
> Nor fear'd the hostile sword, nor sought herself to hide.
>   Then to her downcast court she went,   25
>   With look serene, as in content,
>   And to her gen'rous veins the aspicks laid;
> By pre-determin'd death more fierce and desp'rate made.
>   For the Liburnian fleet, she grudg'd
>   The fate to which she was adjudg'd,   30
>   A woman of her pow'r and pomp allow'd,
> In triumph to be dragg'd before the clam'rous crowd.

ODE XXXVIII.
To his SERVANT.

He would have him bring nothing for the gracing of his banquet but myrtle.

In the original metre exactly.

Persian pomps, boy, ever I renounce them:
Scoff o' the plaited coronet's refulgence;
Seek not in fruitless vigilance the rose-tree's
    Tardier offspring.
Mere honest myrtle that alone is order'd,
Me the mere myrtle decorates, as also
Thee the prompt waiter to a jolly toper
    Hous'd in an arbour.

THE
SECOND BOOK
OF THE
ODES OF HORACE

ODE I.
To C. ASINIUS POLLIO.

He advises Pollio to forbear the writing of tragedy for a season, till the state should be settled. And afterwards he praises his compositions.

The war, that rose from civil hate
 In that Metellian consulate,
 Our vices, measures, and the sport of chance,
The famous triple league, the Roman shield and lance,
  With gore unexpiated, smear'd,   5
  A work whose fate is to be fear'd
 You treat, and on those treacherous ashes tread,
Beneath whose seeming surface glow the embers red.
  O spare a little to repeat
  Your tragic verse severely sweet;   10
 Soon, when the public weal you shall replace,
Your grand Athenian works again the stage shall grace.
  Thou who defend'st the poor with zeal,
  To whom the conscript house appeal,
 For whom the fertile laurels, that you wore   15
In that Dalmatian triumph, deathless honour bore.
  E'en now you make my tingling ear
  The din of martial trumpets hear,
 Now clarions bray, and men in armour bright
The routed horse and horsemen with their lightning fright. 20
  Now mighty captains I perceive,
  In clouds of glorious dust atchieve
 Eternal fame, and all the world their own,
Save the ferocious fire of Cato's soul alone.

Juno and every pow'r propense,   2
    Like her, for Africa's defence,
When unreveng'd they left their darling coast,
Offer'd the victor's grandsons to Jugurtha's ghost.
    Say where the blood of Romans slain,
    Has not made fertile every plain   3
Whose monuments record our impious deeds,
And our great downfal heard by the remotest Medes?
    What gulphs, what rivers in their flow
Do not our dire dissensions know?
    What sea is not discolour'd by the gore   3
Of Romans basely slain, what climate, or what shore?
    But leaving mirth, O do not urge
    My Pollio's muse, the Cean dirge—
In some cool grotto sacred to the fair,
With me and sweet * Dione touch a lighter air.   4

ODE II.
To C. SALLUSTIUS CRISPUS.

He applauds Proculeius for his generosity to his brethren. The contempt of mone
makes the wise-man and the monarch.

The hoarded silver is not white,
    Thou foe to metal in the mine,
Unless by circulation bright
    And mod'rate use it shine.
Let † Proculeius live in song,
    A father to his brethren known;
Fame jealous-wing'd, shall bear along
    The bounty, he has shown.
A vaster realm you shall subdue,
    By conq'ring of a greedy mind,   1
Than Lybia and the Gades too
    With either Carthage join'd.

* Dione, a sea nymph, mother of Venus by Jupiter.
† This generous Roman, having several brothers divested of their fortunes, for bear
ing arms against Caesar, divided his substance among them.

—The self-indulging dropsy grows,
   Nor slacks its thirst, until the cause
From out the pallid body flows,   15
   And watry pain withdraws.
The * king restor'd, and repossess'd,
   Not like the crowd fair virtue views,
Nor numbers him amongst the bless'd,
   The language to abuse;   20
The laurel, diadem and reign
   She more to that great man applies,
Who looks upon immod'rate gain
   With unaffected eyes.

ODE III.
To DELLIUS.

Either fortune is to be borne with moderation, since the same condition of mortality equally impends on all.

O Dellius, that art born to die,
   On equanimity rely,
As well in adverse days your spirits buoy,
As keep the hour of wealth from light presumptuous joy.
   Whether you lead a life of woes—   5
   Or in your distant mead repose,
And bless the festal days in rural state,
With right Falernian wine of more interior date,
   Where the tall pine, and poplar white,
   To form a social bow'r delight   10
With blending boughs, and diligent to glide,
The riv'let urges haste against its winding side.
   To wine and unguents here exhort,
   And roses of a bliss too short,
While circumstance and age allow their leave,   15
And those black threads of death the fatal sisters weave.

* Phraates.

ODE iii. 9 poplar] pop'lar *1767*

You must from purchas'd park and seat,
  Which yellow Tiber laves, retreat—
You must retreat, and your appointed heir
Shall soon possess the heaps you pil'd with so much care.   2

  If rich and of Inachian race,
  Or, poor and from a lineage base,
You daily in th'inclement skies remain,
It matters not, you must remorseless death sustain.

  To one point we are all compell'd—   2
  The universal urn is held,
From whence, or soon or late, the lot is cast,
And Charon's boat transports the convicts at the last.

ODE IV.
To XANTHIUS PHOCEUS.

*There is no reason that he should blush for the love he bears to his waiting mai
Phyllis, since the same thing has been the case with sundry great men.*

O Phoceus, think it no disgrace
  To love your maid, since Thetis' heir,
Tho' proud, of old was in your case,
    Briseis was so fair.
—The slave Tecmessa at her feet
  Saw her lord Ajax—Atreus' son
Lov'd his fair captive in the heat
    Of conquest, that he won,
When, beat by that Thessalian boy,
  The Phrygian host was disarray'd,   1
And Hector's death the fall of Troy
    An easy purchase made.
Who knows what wealth thou hast to claim?
  Rich parents may thy Phyllis grace,
Surely the Gods have been to blame   1
    To one of royal race.

ODE iv. 9 When,] When *1767*   11 death ... Troy] death, ... Troy, *1767*   13 claim?
claim, *1767*

You cannot think her meanly born,
　　Nor worthless cou'd her mother be,
Whose heart has such ingenuous scorn
　　　　For wealth, and love for thee.   20
Her face, her limbs so form'd t'engage,
　　I praise with a safe conscience still—
Shun to suspect a man, whose age
　　Is going down the hill.

ODE V.
On LALAGE.

The most beautiful Lalage is a maiden unripe for a husband, wherefore the incli-
nation to possess her ought to be restrained.

As yet her tender neck's unbroke,
Nor to confine her in the yoke
　　Will all your skill avail;
As yet she cannot suit her mate,
Nor stand to bear the mighty weight   5
　　Of an impetuous male.
Your little heifer's fancy feeds
On verdant lawns and flow'ry meads,
　　Whose haunts she has preferr'd;
And by the streams, which willows shade,   10
She loves to have her gambols play'd
　　With younglings of the herd.
Forbear preposterous desire,
Nor at the eager grape aspire,
　　Anon shall autumn speed,   15
And mark each bunch with blooming blue,
And vary into purple hue
　　The clusters ripe to bleed.
She soon shall follow thee of course,
For time goes on without remorse,   20
　　And to her days shall add
The rip'ning years, that make thee old,
And Lalage, maturely bold

ODE v. 15 autumn speed,] autum speed; *1767*

Shall seek a sturdy lad—
Beloved!—coy Pholoe not so well   25
Nor Chloris celebrated belle,
    With chest erect and white,
As Luna shining o'er the sea,
And smiling with celestial glee,
    Or Cnidian Gyges bright;   30
Whom if you place amongst the fair
He'll make sagacious strangers stare,
    As puzzl'd in the case;
Nor can they tell his sex with truth,
By reason of his looks and youth,   35
    And smooth ambiguous face.

ODE VI.
To SEPTIMIUS.

*He wishes to have Tibur and Tarentum for the retreat of his old age, whose
pleasant situation he extols.*

Septimius, who wou'd go with me,
    To Gades, or unconquer'd Spain,
Or Syrtes, where the Moorish sea
    Bids endless tempests reign?
Be Tibur, by a Grecian plann'd,   5
    A seat for Horace in his years,
Weary alike of sea and land,
    And martial hopes and fears.
From whence if driv'n by cruel fate,
    May I Galesus see in peace,   10
Where great Phalanthus rul'd in state,
    And watch'd his cover'd fleece.
With me that little angle takes
    Whose honey's of Hymettian zest,
And with the oil Venafrum makes   15
    Their olives stand the test.

ODE vi. 3 Moorish] moorish *1767*

Where Jove gives winter warmth—and length
   To spring,—and Aulon's heights arise,
Rich with those wines, whose luscious strength
    With true Falernian vies.   20
These scenes to us their site commend—
   Those tow'rs so pleasant to the view:
There the live ashes of thy friend,
    With tears thou shalt bedew.

ODE VII.
To POMPEIUS VARUS.

Whose return to his native country he congratulates.

O Pompey! oft reduc'd with me
   To danger's last extremity,
When Brutus led the van—what pow'r on high
Restores thy native Gods, and an Italian sky?
   Thou principal and dearest friend,   5
   With whom I've made the day suspend
Its course, infringing on the hours of care,
With bays, and precious essence on our shining hair.
   With thee I saw * that fatal field,
   Where shamefully I left my shield   10
In rapid flight, when valour's heart was broke,
And threat'ning heroes fell beneath the hostile stroke.
   But me Mercurius, much dismay'd,
   Quick thro' the midmost foe convey'd
In a thick cloud—Thou wert ingulph'd again   15
In struggling tides of war upon the swelt'ring plain.
   Wherefore to Jove the feast be paid,
   And let your weary limbs be laid,
After long warfare, underneath my bay;
Nor spare the casks I destin'd for this joyful day.   20
   Fill the bright tumblers to the brim,
   And in oblivious Massic swim,
And from large shells the fragrant unguents pour.
—Who runs to parsley beds, or to the myrtle bow'r,

* At Philippi.

For cooling crowns? who throws the most   25
    To take the chair and give the toast?
I will the Bacchanalian priests outdo—
'Tis sweet to lose one's wits at this dear interview.

ODE VIII.
To JULIA BARINE.

There is no reason to give any credit to Barine, when she swears, since she grows
the handsomer for her perjuries.

If any punishment or curse
    Had made thee thy false oath bewail;
Hadst thou but been one tooth the worse,
    Or lost a single nail;
I shou'd have kept my faith,—but thou   5
    Shin'st out more tempting and more fair;
And art, by breaking of thy vow,
    Our youth's peculiar care.
'Tis profit, therefore, to deceive
    Thy mother's ashes in a breath,   10
Stars, moon, and silent heav'n to grieve,
    And Gods, exempt from death.
Yes, Venus laughs, and nymphs, well known
    For mock-simplicity, deride,
And love still whetting on a stone   15
    His darts in crimson dy'd.
But add to this, new dupes abound,
    New slaves, nor will the old relent,
Tho' sworn to quit her impious pound,
    Where their fond hearts are pent.   20
At thee the jealous mothers pine,
    At thee old churls, and maids new wed,
Lest by that winning air of thine
    Their spouses be misled.

ODE IX.
To VALGIUS.

That he would at length desist from bewailing the death of Mystes.

Not show'rs from darkness without end
  Upon the shaggy fields descend,
Nor ruffling whirlwinds o'er the Caspian reign
For ever; nor prolong'd month after month remain,
  Friend Valgius, on Armenia's heights   5
    Of ice and snow, perpetual freights;
Nor to the North do the plantations groan
Of Garganus, nor ash trees their lost leaves bemoan.
    But you, in one continual dirge,
    Th'untimely death of Mystes urge,   10
  Nor with the fondness of your grief have done,
When Vesper comes, or flies the bright-careering sun.
    Yet * he, who for three ages join'd,
    Liv'd an example of mankind,
  Did not, for all the remnant of his years,   15
Antilochus, so loved, lament with ceaseless tears.
    No,—nor did Priam and his wife
    For Troilus, who lost his life
  In ruddy youth, with endless grief deplore,
And ev'n his tender sisters in a whole forbore.   20
    Cease from the softness of your grief,
    And let us rather sing our chief,
  The great Augustus has new trophies won,
And bade the stiff Niphates with submission run.
    Euphrates too must roll his tide   25
    In billows more remote from pride,
  And those Gelonians, added to our reign,
Must in the bounds prescrib'd their cavalry restrain.

---

* Nestor.

ODE X.
To LICINIUS.

A mean is to be observed in either fortune.

A better plan of life you form,
  Not wholly launching out from land,
Nor over-jealous of a storm,
    Too much for shore to stand.
Whoever loves the golden mean,
  From sordid want himself supports,
Nor, safe and sober, is he seen
    In envy-moving courts.
Tall pines are shaken, and the tow'r
  Comes heaviest from the highest wall,   1[0]
And thunderbolts, with greater pow'r,
    On topmost mountains fall.
Hearts, well prepar'd, will see a dawn
  Of hope in woe—in wealth will pray
'Gainst change—heav'n brings the winter on,   1[5]
    And drives the hag away.
If times are evil, by and by
  They shall be better—Phoebus plays
At times upon his minstrelsy,
    Not always shoots his rays.   2[0]
When times are hardest, then a face
  Of constancy and spirit wear;
But wise contract your sails apace,
    When once the wind's too fair.

ODE XI.
To QUINTIUS HIRPINUS.

That waving cares we should live merrily.

Whate'er the warlike Spaniard tries,
Or what the Scythian bands devise,
By Adria's sea disjoin'd, cease to enquire,
Nor bustle for a life, whose term should check desire.
Smooth youth and beauty must give way   5
To wrinkles dry, and ringlets grey,
Which from gallants their wanton loves divorce,
And drive away sweet slumbers from their eyes of course.
Not always does the vernal pride
Of flow'rs remain, nor moon abide   10
In one gay face—Your thoughts why do you teize,
Not made for disquisitions so sublime as these?
Why do we not secure our seat
Beneath this plane-tree from the heat;
Or thrown at random underneath this pine,   15
Drink, while we may presume, and essenc'd roses twine
In wreathes about our hoary hair,
For Bacchus drives off biting care,
Who's there? This same Falernian is too strong,
The passing brook shall quench it, as it purls along.   20
Who shall decoy the gadding lass,
Lyde, to come and take a glass?
Bid her with iv'ry lyre mature her haste,
And hair ty'd up behind in the true Spartan taste.

ODE XII.
To MAECENAS.

Weighty and tragical subjects are not proper for the Lyric stile. Horace will sing
of nothing but the beauty of Lycymnia, and matters pertaining to love.

Numantia's fierce and bloody wars,
And Hannibal, your taste abhors,
    Too dire a subject for a song;
Nor staining the Sicilian sea,
Can Carthaginian blood to me
    And to my warbling lyre belong.
Nor can the Lapithan malign,
Nor over-charg'd with heady wine,
    Hyleus suit the lyric strain,
Nor any giant son of earth,   10
The victim of Herculean worth,
    And dread of Saturn's golden reign.
But, O Maecenas, as for you,
You will for great Augustus do
    Far better in historic prose: 1
With more address you'll tell than sing
The story of full many a king,
    That drag'd in pomp triumphal goes.
Me the harmonious muse allures,
To chant my lady fair, and yours,   20
    And praise Lycymnia's charming voice,
And eyes, that sparkle like the spheres,
With faithful heart, that never veers,
    When she's once settled in her choice.
She's graceful in each bright advance,   2
Whether she lead the seemly dance,
    Or urge the brilliant repartees,
Or with the noble damsels play,
That honour Dian's holiday,
    Uniting dignity and ease.   3
Would you in earnest change one lock
Of sweet Lycymnia, for the stock

ODE xii. 20 yours] your's *1767*

That rich Achemenes possess'd,
Or fertile Phrygia's wealthy fleece,
Or all Arabia's ambergreese,   35
    And houses with all plenty bless'd?
While she declines her blooming cheek,
Where you the burning kisses seek,
    With such benevolent disdain,
And what she'd rather have, than thee,   40
Refuses, till she makes so free
    As to devour them all again.

ODE XIII.

Upon the TREE by whose Sudden Fall He Had Like to
have been Crushed.

*It is never sufficiently evident what a man ought to beware of—the praises of
Sappho and Alceus.*

'Twas on a luckless day, O tree,
   Whatever hand transplanted thee,
  And impious bade thee prosper to disgrace
The village of his birth, and crush his future race.
    He could, no doubt, to death devote   5
    His sire, or cut his mother's throat,
  Or sprinkle his unhospitable ground
At night with stranger's blood, or Colchian drugs compound.
    Or whatsoe'er we may conceive
    Of desp'rate feats he could atchieve,   10
  O log, the man that plac'd thee in my farm,
Hurl'd on thy master's head, that did not dream of harm.
    We never are enough aware
    What we should seek, or what forbear—
From Bosphorus the sailor dreads his fate,   15
Nor heeds what doom at Carthage may his days await.
    The soldiers fear the pointed reed,
    And Parthian shooting in full speed,
  The Parthian fears the Roman strength and chain,
One common lot for all remains, and will remain.   20

36 bless'd?] bless'd. *1767*

How near but now the lot was mine,
  To see the gloomy Proserpine,
 And Eäcus his dread judicial seat,
And those Elysian fields, where melancholy sweet
   Sappho the sland'rous maids of Greece   25
   Arraigns, and in a fuller piece
  Alceus, sings, upon his golden lyre
The conquest or the flight by sea and land how dire!
   Each of these hands th'admiring ghost
   In holy silence hears, but most   30
  Th'attention and the thicking throng augment,
To hear of patriot fights, and kings in exile sent.
   What wonder! since such strains as these
   The many-headed beast can please,
  Who hangs his hellish ears, and furies list,   35
While from their wreathed locks delighted snakes untwist.
   Nay more, Prometheus, and the sire
   Of Pelops to the sound respire,
  Nor 'gainst the ounce or lions of the chace,
Will now Orion urge his visionary race.   40

ODE XIV.
To POSTHUMUS.

Life is short, and death inevitable.

Ah! Posthumus, the years, the years
  Glide swiftly on, nor can our tears
 Or piety the wrinkl'd age forefend,
Or for one hour retard th'inevitable end.
   'Twoud be in vain, tho' you should slay,   5
   My friend, three hundred beeves a day
  To cruel Pluto, whose dire waters roll,
Geryon's threefold bulk, and Tityus to controul.
   This is a voyage we all must make,
   Who'er the fruits of earth partake,   10
  Whether we sit upon a royal throne,
Or live, like cottage hinds, unwealthy and unknown.

ODE xiii. 22 To] So *1767*

The wounds of war we scape in vain,
And the hoarse breakers of the main;
In vain with so much caution we provide 15
Against the southern winds upon th'autumnal tide.
The black Cocytus, that delays
His waters in a languid maze,
We must behold, and all those Danaids fell,
And Sisyphus condemn'd to fruitless toil in hell. 20
Lands, house, and pleasing wife, by thee
Must be relinquish'd; nor a tree
Of all your nurseries shall in the end,
Except the baleful cypress, their brief lord attend.
Thy worthier heir the wine shall seize 25
You hoarded with a hundred keys,
And with libations the proud pavement dye,
And feasts of priests themselves shall equal and outvie.

ODE XV.
Upon the LUXURY of the Age He Lived in.

So great our palaces are now,
They'll leave few acres for the plough.
Wide as the Lucrine lake canals extend,
And steril planes in sum the wedded elms transcend.
Then violet beds, and myrtle bow'rs, 5
And all the nosegay-blending flow'rs,
Shall far and wide their spicy breath renew,
Where for their former lords the fertile olives grew.
There the thick laurel's green array
Shall ward the fervid beams of day. 10
Not so our founder's will, or Cato's lore,
And all our bearded sires commanded things of yore.
Their private fortunes were but small,
But great the common fund of all.
No grand piazzas did there then remain 15
To catch the summer breezes of the northern wane.
Nor did they, by their edicts wise,
The providential turf despise,
Those laws, which bade each public pile be grand,
And with new stone repair'd, the holy temples stand. 20

ODE XVI.
To GROSPHUS.

All men covet peace of mind, which cannot be acquired either by riches or hon
ours, but only by restraining the appetites.

When o'er the Aegean vast he sails
    The seaman sues the gods for ease,
Soon as the moon the tempest veils,
      Nor sparkling guide he sees.
Ease by fierce Thracians in the end;
    Ease by the quiver'd Mede is sought;
By gems, nor purple bales, my friend,
      Nor bullion to be bought.
Not wealth or state, a consul's share,
    Can give the troubled mind its rest,   10
Or fray the winged fiends of care,
      That pompous roofs infest.
Well lives he, on whose little board
    Th'old silver salt-cellar appears,
Left by his sires—no sordid hoard   15
      Disturb his sleep with fears.
Why with such strength of thought devise,
    And aim at sublunary pelf,
Seek foreign realms? Can he, who flies
      His country, 'scape himself?   20
Ill-natur'd care will board the fleet,
    Nor leave the squadron'd troops behind,
Swifter than harts, or irksome sleet
      Driv'n by the eastern wind.
If good, the present hour be mirth;   25
    If bitter, let your smiles be sweet,
Look not too forward—nought on earth
      Is in all points complete.
A sudden death Achilles seiz'd,
    A tedious age Tithonus wore—   30
If you're amerc'd, fate may be pleas'd
      To give to me the more.

A hundred flocks around thee stray,
   About thee low Sicilian kine,
And mares apt for thy carriage neigh,   35
   And purple robes are thine.
Me, born for verse and rural peace,
   A faithful prophetess foretold,
And groundlings, spirited from Greece,
   In high contempt I hold.   40

ODE XVII.
To MAECENAS, when Sick.

If he was to die, Horace has no inclination to survive him.

Why do you send to break my heart
With your complaints? We must not part;
Nor can th'immortal gods consent, nor I,
My glory and my guard, that thou the first shouldst die.
   Ah! if a more untimely fate   5
   On thee, my soul's ally, should wait,
Why should I keep the wretched remnant here,
Imperfect without thee, and never half so dear?
   One day shall be the last of both;
   I have not made a traitor's oath—   10
Yes, we will go, together will we go,
If you precede, I follow to the shades below.
   Me nor Chimera breathing fire,
   Nor Gyas, if he could respire,
With all his hundred hands, should force from thee;   15
So justice, heav'nly pow'r, and so the fates decree.
   If Libra rul'd my natal hour,
   Or Scorpio's more unlucky pow'r,
Ey'd with the menace of an early grave,
Or Capricorn, the tyrant of the western wave.   20
   Our horoscope, at all events,
   Ev'n to a miracle consents—
Thee, lucid Jove sav'd from Saturnian spite,
And clipt the wings of fate, and stopt its rapid flight,

ODE xvii. 23 Jove] Jove, *1767*

Upon the day the crouded town   25
　　Thrice hail'd in claps thy just renown—
Me near that time a falling trunk had brain'd,
If Faunus, shield of bards, had not the stroke refrain'd.
　　These mercies therefore bear in mind,
　　And bring the victims you design'd,   30
And build the fane you vow'd upon the spot;
A slaughter'd lamb from me will suit by humbler lot.

ODE XVIII.

He asserts himself to be contented with a little fortune, where others labour for
wealth, and the gratification of their desires, as if they were to live for ever.

Gold or iv'ry's not intended
　　For this little house of mine,
Nor Hymettian arches, bended
　　On rich Afric pillars, shine.
For a court I've no ambition,   5
　　As not Attalus his heir,
Nor make damsels of condition
　　Spin me purple for my wear.
But for truth and wit respected,
　　I possess a copious vein,   10
So that rich men have affected
　　To be number'd of my train.
With my Sabine field contented,
　　Fortune shall be dunn'd no more;
Nor my gen'rous friend tormented   15
　　To augment my little store.
One day by the next's abolish'd,
　　Moons increase but to decay;
You place marbles to be polish'd
　　Ev'n upon your dying day.   20
Death unheeding, though infirmer,
　　On the sea your buildings rise,
While the Baian billows murmur,
　　That the land will not suffice.

What tho' more and more incroaching,   25
   On new boundaries you press,
And in avarice approaching,
   Your poor neighbours dispossess;
The griev'd hind his gods displaces,
   In his bosom to convey,   30
And with dirty ruddy faces
   Boys and wife are driven away.
Yet no palace grand and spacious
   Does more sure its lord receive,
Than the seat of death rapacious,   35
   Whence the rich have no reprieve.
Earth alike to all is equal,
   Whither would your views extend?
Kings and peasants in the sequel
   To the destin'd grave descend.   40
There, tho' brib'd, the guard infernal
   Would not shrewd Prometheus free;
There are held in chains eternal
   Tantalus, and such as he.
There the poor have consolation   45
   For their hard laborious lot;
Death attends each rank and station,
   Whether he is call'd or not.

ODE XIX.
On BACCHUS.

Filled with the deity, the poet sings his praises.

Bacchus I saw the other day
   (Posterity believe my lay)
Teaching the science of poetic feet,
While nymphs and satyrs listen'd in the rocks secrete.
   Ha! ha! this lab'ring breast of mine   5
   Is shock'd anew—and fraught with wine;
My heart is joy—ha! ha! my Bacchus spare,
Nor rear thine ivy wand too terrible to bear.

Now the mad Thyads I can sing,
Which struck out wine's perennial spring;   10
And rivers that with milky current glide,
And honey trickling down from hollow rocks beside.
Now can I sing the brilliant dame
Of heav'n, thy celebrated flame;
The tow'rs of Pentheus levell'd with the ground,   15
And downfal of Lycurgus to thy praise resound.
You turn the rivers to the main,
You those barbarian seas restrain,
You in the sacred mountains debonaire
Bind in serpentine knot unhurt your handmaids hair.   20
You, when the bands of giants rose
Th'almighty father to depose,
The lion's fangs and horrid jaws assum'd,
Drove Rhoecus back to earth, and to destruction doom'd.
Tho' dance, and lively jests, and sport   25
For thee were fitter by report,
Nor did your military talents strike,
Yet facts have shewn thee proof for peace and war alike.
Thee with your golden horn bedight,
Saw Cerberus devoid of spite,   30
And when from hell you made your last retreat,
His tail he kindly wagg'd, and gently lick'd your feet.

ODE XX.
To MAECENAS.

Horace supposing himself changed into a swan, will fly all the world over; from
which adventure he infers, that his poetry will be immortal.

Above the vulgar and the trite
Transform'd, the poet takes his flight
Thro' heav'n, and will be held on earth no more;
But o'er th'abodes of man, of envious man, shall soar.
Not I, the poor man's offspring scorn'd;   5
Not I thus honour'd and adorn'd,

ODE xix. 14 flame;] flame, *1767*   20 handmaids] handmaid's *1767*

  As by Maecenas to be call'd his friend,
Shall know the Stygian stream, or share a common end.
    Now, ev'n but now, my skin began
    To roughen, and my upper man   10
  Of a white bird the radiant form assumes,
And on my hands and neck spring forth the glossy plumes.
    Now a melodious swan indeed,
    Th'Icarian flight I shall exceed;
  And Bosphorus his roaring rocks will know,   15
And Syrtes, and the plains of Hyperborean snow:
    The Dacians who so poorly feign
    To hold the Romans in disdain;
  The Colchan and Gelonians far remote,
And skilful Spain and Gaul shall learn my works by rote.   20
    No dirges, squalid grief, or moan,
    At mine unreal death be shown;
  Your loud lamentings at my grave restrain,
Nor care to build the tomb this verse has render'd vain.

THE
THIRD BOOK
OF THE
ODES OF HORACE

ODE I.

A happy life is effected not by wealth and honours, but by peace of mind.

I hate the mob, and drive them hence,
Lost to all sanctity and sense;
Hist to the Muse's priest! hist I implore—
I sing for maids and youths the strains unheard before.
 Dread sovereigns their own people sway,   5
 But Jove the kings themselves obey;
He which in triumph hurl'd the giants down,
And rules the universe by his commanding frown.
 One man, perhaps, out-plants his friend,
 In rows that regular extend;   10
Another comes more noble to the poll,
Another pleads his fame, and uncorrupted soul;
 Another will th'ascendant claim
 For clients—but 'tis all the same;
Necessity demands us, dross and scum,   15
And shakes the labell'd lots, and out they all must come.
 He, o'er whose head the naked steel
 Impends, will make no hearty meal
From rich Sicilian fare—his sleep no more
The chirping of the birds or harpers will restore—   20
 Sweet sleep's the lusty lab'rer's lot:
 Sleep does not scorn the lowly cot,
Nor trees that o'er the riv'let interweave,
Nor, Tempe, where the zephyrs play their pranks at eve.
 He who desires but neighbour's fare,   25
 Will for no storm or tempest care;

Him setting bear nor rising goat offends,
Nor all the wizzard wit of diarist portends.
    Not vineyards beaten by the hail;
    Not flattering farm, whose symptoms fail,   30
The trees now laying blame upon the showers,
Now winter's pinching hand, or hot sidereal pow'rs.
    The fishes feel the waters shrink,
    Such loads into the depths they sink;
Here many a proud surveyor with his slaves,   35
And owner of the land, incroach upon the waves.
    But fear and conscience with her cries
    Aboard with the possessor flies;
Nor care will from the top-mast head recede,
And, when he lands, she mounts behind him on his steed. 40
    What if nor stone in Phrygia hewn
    Can keep the troubl'd mind in tune,
Nor purple brighter than the painted sky,
Nor rich Falernian grape, nor Persian luxury;
    Why should I set about a pile,   45
    High-pillar'd in the modern stile—
A bait for envy?—Why should I exchange
For cumbersome expence my little Sabine grange?

ODE II.
To his FRIENDS.

Lads must be habituated from their tender years to poverty, warfare, and a laborious life.

    Train'd up, my friends, in toil severe,
    Let the young lad no hardship fear;
But learn against fierce Parthians to advance,
And on the gallant steed shake his tremendous lance.
    And let him lead a life of care   5
    In bustle and the open air—
Him from the wall the tyrant's consort spies,
And marriagable virgin sends her broken sighs:

ODE ii. 8 sighs:] sighs. *1767*

'Ah me! for fear my royal spouse
    Should this ungovern'd lion rouze,   10
  And with inferior skill provoke his rage,
Which breaks thro' thickest ranks the midmost war to wage.'
    'Tis sweet, 'tis seemly ev'n to die
    For one's dear country—should'st thou fly,
  Death will pursue the youth afraid to fight,   15
Nor spares his timid knees, and back, when turn'd to flight.
    Virtue which in the spirit tow'rs,
    And cannot, like this clay of ours,
  Sustain repulse, her fame unsully'd sees,
Nor takes, nor quits her office, as light voters please.   20
    Virtue, to those that may not die,
    Opes the strait doors of heav'n on high,
  And with her wings in stretch for that sublime,
Scorns the unletter'd mob, and sordid earth, and time.
    There's likewise an undoubted meed   25
    For silence, that its faith can plead;
  Him that mysterious rites has blaz'd—with me,
Nor tent, nor tilt shall cover, or by land or sea.
    Oft the great regent of the day,
    If thoughtless man neglect to pray,   30
  In the same lot have vice and virtue cast.
Justice, tho' lame and blind, will take her due at last.

ODE III.

*A man of virtue is in dread of nothing. The speech of Juno concerning the
destruction of Troy, of the end of the Trojan war, and of the Roman empire
which was to take its rise from the remnant of the Trojans.*

    A man of truth and honour prov'd,
    And in his great resolves unmov'd,
  No clam'rous mob his principles can stir,
Nor ev'n a tyrant's threat his manly heart deter.
    No—nor the south, whose dread command   5
    Fierce Adria's waves cannot withstand,

25 meed] mead *1767*   31 cast.] cast, *1767*

Nor thund'ring Jove—the universe might fall,
And not disturb his thoughts, or make him shrink at all.
    It was upon no other plan
    That Pollux was so great a man,
  And wand'ring Hercules atchiev'd the skies—   10
Augustus too with them to rites divine shall rise.
    'Twas by no other art than this,
    O Bacchus, sire of social bliss,
  Thine unbroke tygers drew thee to the stars,   15
And Romulus 'scap'd death upon the steeds of Mars.
    For to the gods in council join'd
    Juno thus spake her gracious mind—
  'A foreign whore, and that dire * umpire's lust,
Has Troy, ev'n Troy reduc'd to downfal and the dust.   20
    By me and chaste Minerva doom'd,
    E'er since Laomedon presum'd
  The gods to rob of their most due reward,
And subjects shar'd the fate of their deceitful lord.
    No more that ignominious guest   25
    Is of the Spartan dame possest,
  Nor Priam's perjur'd house prevails to break,
By Hector's strength alone, the forces of the Greek.
    War by our diff'rent int'rests drawn
    To such a length, is past and gone—   30
  Henceforward I my wrath to Mars give o'er,
And hatred for the son the Trojan priestess bore.
    Him will I gather and befriend
    Heav'n's lucid mansions to ascend,
  To take his fill from our nectareous bowl,   35
And in the rank of gods his titles to enroll—
    On this condition, that there be
    'Twixt Troy and Rome a raging sea
  For many a league—and let their exiles reign
And prosper where they will—so that there still remain   40
    O'er Paris and o'er Priam's clay
    The trampling herd, the beast of prey,
  And cubs secure—The Capitol shall tow'r,
And vanquish'd Medes confess proud Rome's imperial pow'r.

---

* Alluding to the judgment of Paris.

Let her extend her fame and fear
To every region far and near,
Where the mid-sea from Europe Afric rives,
And where o'erflowing Nile the fertile land revives.
 Deriving from contempt of gold
 A spirit great and uncontroul'd—
Gold best unsought, and cover'd in the sand,
Rather than coin'd for use with sacrilegious hand.
 Whatever pole or place be found
 To give the world his utmost bound,
There let them pride their armies to engage,
Both where cold mists descend, or torrid sunbeams rage.
 But this their fate my word confirms
 For Romans on these only terms—
That they should not an ill-judg'd zeal embrace,
Nor think their mother-town they prosper to replace.
 If Troy's estate should grow again,
 Again their thousands must be slain,
Whilst I, Jove's sister and his wife, command
Against their rising works a new victorious band.
 If thrice their walls of brass should rise,
 By Phoebus helping from the skies,
Thrice should my Grecian champions lay it low;
Thrice leave their dames and sons to widowhood and woe.'
 But whither, Muse, do you aspire?
 These subjects are not for the lyre—
Too grand and grave—cease, wanton, to rehearse
The converse of the gods in light degrading verse.

ODE IV.

The poet mentions his being delivered by the assistance of the Muses from sundry perils, and that it has turned out bad for all that have attempted to act against the gods.

 Descend from yonder bright serene,
 And sing, Calliope, my queen,
 A longer strain—or with your warbling tongue,
Or, if you choose, the lute, or lyre by Phoebus strung.

      Hear ye not plain? Or is my thought   5
      By a transporting frenzy wrought?
   I seem to hear sweet sounds, and seem to rove
Where pleasant airs and streams pass thro' th'Elysian grove.
      Me tir'd to sleep, and yet a child,
      From kind Apulia's bounds beguil'd,   10
   Up in mount Vultur, now so fam'd and known,
The woodland doves conceal'd with foliage newly blown;
      Which was a miracle to tell
      By all th'inhabitants that dwell
   High-nested on the Acherontian brow,   15
Or Bantine chace possess, or fat Ferentum plow,
      That I should there securely sleep,
      Nor bears should rush, nor vipers creep;
   That sacred bays and myrtle should combine
To hide the dauntless boy by providence divine.   20
      Yours, O ye Muses! yours intire,
      I to the Sabine heights aspire—
   Me, whether cool Preneste shall invite,
Or Tibur sweetly slop'd, or Baian baths delight.
      Me, fond of all your sylvan scene   25
      Your founts and gambols on the green;
   Not all our hopes Philippi render'd void,
Nor rough Sicilian wave, nor cursed tree destroy'd.
      Whenever you shall be with me,
      Chearful I'll sail upon the sea   30
   Or raging Bosphorus, or go by land
Through all the length and drougth of that Assyrian sand.
      Th'unhospitable Picts, the race
      Of quiver'd Scythia, will I face;
   And Concanum, with blood of horses fed,   35
And Tanais, secure from detriment and dread.
      You Caesar, of such high renown,
      Soon as he quarters in each town
   His wearied legions, bid his labours cease,
And in Pierian grottoes multiply his peace.   40
      You kindly mod'rate measures urge,
      Rejoicing to refrain the scourge—

ᴼDE iv. 16 plow,] plow. *1767*

We know him who alone the Titans quell'd,
And hurl'd in thunder down the monsters that rebell'd—
    Ev'n he that rules the stormy main,   4
    The sluggish earth, and Pluto's reign,
  And all above, and all beneath the sun,
Both gods and men commands, omnipotent and one.
    Depending upon strength of arm,
    Those desp'rate youths with dire alarm   5
  Insulted Jove, while all the brethren vie
With Pelion on Olympus to ascend the sky.
    But Rhoecus and strong Mimas too,
    Or what could huge Porphyrion do,
  Or what Typhoeus, or with trees up-torn   5
Enceladus assaulting heav'n in impious scorn,
    Rushing against the sounding targe
    Of Pallas?—Here a furious charge
  Was made by Vulcan—there heav'n's royal dame,
And he, who never quits his royal quiver, came,   6
    Who in the pure Castalian spring
    Laves his loose locks, who is the king
  Of Lycian wilds, Apollo is his name,
Who Patara and Delos holds by natal claim.
    Force void of counsel rushes down   6
    By its own weight—but there's a crown
  Of blest event for courage mixt with care;
But rashness heav'n detests, as working for despair.
    That Gyas with his hundred hands,
    Whose story upon record stands,   7
  And he * th'attempter of the spotless maid,
Slain by Diana's dart, confirm what we have said.
    The earth her groaning bosom heaves,
    And for each bury'd monster grieves,
  To dismal hell by thund'ring vengeance doom'd.   7
Nor by the eager flames is Aetna yet consum'd.
    The bird that on the liver preys
    Of Tityus, ever-vengeful stays—
  Three hundred chains Perithous confine,
And gall his am'rous flames, which burn'd for Proserpine.   8

* Orion.

ODE V.

The applause of Augustus, the dispraise of Crassus, the constancy of Regulus,
and his return to the Carthaginians.

The thund'rer, as in heav'n supreme,
We from his dreadful bolts esteem;
And Caesar, like a god, directs our helm,
Picts and vexatious Persians added to our realm.
Have they, who under Crassus fought,   5
With base barbarian wives been caught,
And (O inverted manners, alter'd times!)
With step-fathers grown old in foreign slavish climes?
The Marsian and Appulian band,
Beneath an haughty Mede's command,   10
Forgetting * Numa's shields, and name, and gown,
Jove's Capitol, and Rome subsisting in renown!
The soul of Regulus the great
Precluded such a shameful fate,
Scorning all base conditions ev'n in thought,   15
As exemplary bad, with future mischief fraught:
If not unpity'd and unspar'd,
Their doom the captive youth had shar'd—
'I've seen our standard hung up for a show,
And troops by Punic foes disarm'd without a blow.   20
I've seen our citizens confin'd,
Ty'd with their free-born arms behind;
The hostile gates op'd in defiance wide,
And fields, we ravag'd, till'd in ostentatious pride.
What! shall the soldier bought and sold   25
Be braver when exchang'd for gold?
You add but loss unto an impious stain,
The poison'd wool its whiteness never can regain.
Nor valour, wrought to a reverse,
Can be repair'd by worse and worse—   30

---

* Numa's shields—oval bucklers, used by the priests in processions, one of which being sent down from heaven, was esteemed a token of the establishment of the empire; which, that it might not be known or stolen away, Numa commanded eleven more to be made exactly like it, and to be kept in the temple of Mars.

If rescu'd from the toils, the tim'rous deer
Will turn and fight the hounds—then he shall cease to fear,
    Who once has trusted to deceit;
    And shall the Punic host defeat
  Another time—who felt a ruffian tie
His coward hands with thongs, and was asham'd to die.
    Such, helpless where to fix a ground
    For hope, could peace and war confound—
  O shame! O Carthage! infamously great
By our confirm'd disgrace, and Rome's subverted state!'
    'Tis said, from his chaste wife's embrace
    And little boys, he turn'd his face,
  And look'd as one amerc'd upon the dust,
With aspect manly stern, determin'd to be just,
    Until the conscript fathers all,
    With council most original,
  He did confirm—and 'midst his friends dismay
And tears, the godlike exile forc'd himself away.
    And yet full clearly did he know
    The torments he should undergo—
  But waving all his kin with unconcern,
And crowds of Roman people grutching his return,
    He cooly took his leave, as one,
    The business of the forum done,
  Goes for vacation to Venefran lands,
Or where Tarentum, built by * that fam'd Spartan, stands.

ODE VI.
To the ROMANS, on the Corrupt Manners of his Age.

    Ye Romans, tho' not done by you,
    Ye must your fathers vices rue,
  Unless the holy temples ye repair,
And images defil'd with filth and blackness there.
    You justly claim imperial sway,
    As ye th'immortal gods obey;

* Phalantus.

Thence your beginning, there refer th'event;
Oft heav'n, for our neglect, has doleful vengeance sent.
  Now twice Moneses and the band
   Of Pacorus has made a stand   10
Against our luckless troops, and glad in scorn
Equestrian collars seiz'd, their trinkets to adorn.
  While discord is our business grown,
   Almost we have been overthrown
By Moors and Dacians, those by sea so dread, 15
And these expert for jav'lins whirling at our head.
  Fraught with offence, at first the times
   Defil'd us with domestic crimes,
Our marriage-beds, and families, and race,
Whence all these murders sprang, and national disgrace. 20
  Our virgins, now no longer shy,
   Are proud th'Ionic step to try,
And move by leud prescription in their bloom,
And meditate on incest from the mother's womb.
  Soon, when her husband's at his wine, 25
   To younger sinners she'll incline,
Nor care with whom the lawless bliss she prove,
In hasty stealth, when once the candles they remove.
  But, not without her consort's leave,
   She boldly rises to receive   30
Some broker, that will buy her to his arms,
Or Spanish dupe, that pays full dearly for her charms.
  'Twas not a race from sires like these
   That stain'd with Punic blood the seas,
Slew Pyrrhus and Antiochus the Great, 35
And beat Hamilcar's son at such a glorious rate;
  But a rough set of manly blades,
   And skilful with the Sabine spades
To turn the glebe, and carry clubs of oak,
Such as their rigid mothers from the wood bespoke; 40
  What hour the sun the shades enlarg'd,
   And from the yoke the steers discharg'd,
Fatigu'd with toil, and urg'd with rapid flight
The time for friendly sleep, or neighbourly delight.

DE vi. 40 bespoke;] bespoke. *1767*

What does not mould'ring time impair!   4
Worse than their sires our fathers were,
And we far worse than them, about to fill
The world with baser men, and more degen'rate still.

ODE VII.
To ASTERIE.

*He consoles her in her sorrow for her absent husband, and admonishes her to
preserve the faith she had plighted to him.*

Asterie, why do you bewail
    Him, whom the zephyrs shall restore,
Which fill with vernal breath the sail,
    Wafting Bythinian wealth on shore,
The happy Gyges, whose fair truth is known,   5
And constancy has made so much your own?
    He, driv'n by that autumnal * goat
        And southern winds, is forc'd away,
    His meditations to devote
        On fair Asterie night and day,   10
And joyless, sleepless, spends the year,
With many a melancholy tear.
    And yet the busy footman speeds
        And many a subtle art he tries,
    To urge how Chloe burns and bleeds,   15
        And how she pines, and how she dies:
And, anxious to receive him to her bed,
Has many such like stories in her head,
    'How a false woman could persuade
        King Proetus, credulous too much,   20
    With false pretences that she made
        To murder him, who shunn'd the touch
Of all impurity and shame,
The chaste Bellerophon by name.
    How Peleus was condemn'd almost   2
        To hell, in that he had abstain'd,

* When the constellation of the goat sets at the close of autumn, it generally stirs up
showers and storms.

ODE vii. 25 Peleus] Paleas *1767*

And wary 'scap'd the am'rous post
Where fair Hippolyte remain'd.'
And mentions many a novel tale,
That teaches mortals to be frail.   30
      In vain—for deafer than the rocks
          Of Icarus he hears the lure,
      And as temptation's voice he mocks,
          Asterie, thou art still secure—
And yet—Enipeus—give me leave—   35
Do not with so much joy receive.
      Tho' (to be fair) no man can ride
          Upon the Martian plain so well:
      A goodly sight, of gallant pride,
          And skill equestrian to excel;   40
Nor any active man alike
Can through the yielding Tiber strike.
      Soon as the day begins to close,
          Shut up the doors, shut up the gate,
      Nor in the street yourself expose,   45
          Nor for the scurvy minstrels wait—
The more they call you hard and hard,
The more your doors and ears be barr'd.

ODE VIII.
To MAECENAS.

*Maecenas is not to wonder why Horace celebrates the calends of March,
notwithstanding he has no wife.*

      Why, on the * first of March, so clean,
          Free from the matrimonial god,
      Why flow'rs and frankincense are seen,
      And what these heaps of fewel mean
              Upon the living sod,   5
      Friend, is from your discernment hid,
          Tho' Greek and Latin are your own.

---

* The calends of March were sacred to Juno, and particularly celebrated by married
men and their wives.

Know then I vow'd a feast and kid
To * him, who did my death forbid,
    When down the tree was blown.
This day, the chief of all by far,
  A special festival denotes,
And shall remove from out the jar
The cork smok'd down with pitch and tar,
    When Tullus had the votes.
Take, for the safety of thy friend,
  An hundred bumpers at the least;
On high the wakeful lamps suspend,
Let wrath and clamour have an end,
    Nor interrupt our feasts.
Cease each political conceit,
  Nor Rome let all your cares engage;
The Dacian Cotison is beat,
The hostile Medes, in self-defeat,
    Domestic warfare wage:
The Spanish foe now pays the tax,
  Though by slow steps this wreath was won;
The Scythian troops their bows relax,
And, fearful of the Roman ax,
    The field of battle shun.
The state, not as a man in pow'r,
  But as a private friend, repute;
Leave things that are severe and sour
For pleasures of the present hour,
    Wine, converse, harp, and lute.

ODE IX.
To LYDIA.

It is a Dialogue concerning their former loves, with a proposal for renewing them

HO.   Whilst my growing flame you nourish'd,
      Spotless of a rival's touch,
    Clasp'd within your arms I flourish'd,
      Not the Persian king so much.

* Bacchus.

LY.   Ere you languish'd for another,   5
        And with Chloe was inflam'd,
    Lydia, greater than the mother
        Of the Roman race was nam'd.

HO.   Me indeed that Thracian beauty,
        Sweet musician, holds her slave;   10
    For whose life I deem it duty
        Death, ev'n death itself to brave.

LY.   Me my Calais with such ardour
        Courts and kisses—him to spare—
    Death, or was there aught still harder,   15
        I ten thousand times would bear.

HO.   What if our old flame recover,
        And our hearts again subdue,
    While the portal of your lover,
        Shut to Chloe, opes to you?   20

LY.   Tho' he be as bright as brightness,
        Thou with cork, or with the sea,
    Well compar'd for wrath and lightness,
        I could live and die with thee.

ODE X.
Upon LYCE.

He advises Lyce to lay aside hardheartedness, and to be mild to him in his state of submission.

    Far away, where Tanais flows,
        Had you been a Scythian's wife—
    Yet to see a man expose,
        At your cruel doors, his life,
    To the northern blasts a prey,   5
    Might have fill'd you with dismay.

    Hear you not the creaking door,
        How the winds, in ruffian haste,
    Make the grove-trees howl and roar
        Round the piles of Attic taste;   10
    And how Jove, with purer air,
    Glazes snow that settles there!

To the queen of softer mould
  Cast away ungrateful pride,
Lest you chance to lose your hold,
  When the knot of love's unty'd.
You're not of the Tuscan breed,
Right Penelope indeed.—

Tho' nor bribes nor pray'rs prevail
  On that harden'd breast of thine,
Nor complexion, violet-pale,
  Nor your spouse, who, 'midst his wine,
Wounded by the vocal art
Of a minstrel, yields his heart;

Spare, yet spare your suppliant swains,
  Rougher than th'obdurate oak,—
Or the snakes, which Moorish plains
  To severer spite provoke—
Constitution cannot last,
Thus to bear the stormy blast.

ODE XI.
To MERCURY.

He requests Mercury to suggest to him such strains as may work upon the affec
tions of Lyde, chusing for his subject the tale of the Danaids.

O Mercury! for thou instill'd
  The notes of old Amphion sung,
Who with his voice could cities build,
And thou, O shell! compleatly fill'd,
    When sev'n-times sweetly strung;
Nor vocal, nor in vogue of yore,
  Now known in palaces and fanes,
In such inviting accents soar,
As may tempt Lyde to her door,
    Attentive to thy strains.

ODE x. 24 heart;] heart. *1767*

The tygers, with their woodlands wild,
　　You to your train in pow'r compel;
You make the rapid torrents mild,
Th'enormous hell-hound heard, and smil'd,
　　　You play'd your lute so well.　　　　15
He smil'd—tho' on his Stygian head
　　A hundred twisted snakes are hung,
And steams of pestilential dread,
And matter still with poison fed,
　　　Flow from his triple tongue.　　　　20
Ixion too, and Tityos, shew'd
　　An irksome glimpse of ghastly joy,
While to your melody renew'd,
No more the Danaids pursu'd
　　　Their task of vain employ.　　　　25
Let Lyde hear the rueful tale,
　　And punishment at last injoin'd,
How they still ply the sieve-like pail,
Which ever must be fill'd to fail,
　　　The monsters of their kind.　　　　30
The destiny that must remain
　　For crimes beyond the grave to feel—
Impious! what could be more a stain?
Impious! their bridegrooms all were slain
　　　By their remorseless steel.　　　　35
But * one of many was a bride,
　　Whose merit grac'd the nuptial flame,
To her false father nobly ly'd,
And left her memory the pride
　　　Of everlasting fame.　　　　40
Who bade her youthful spouse 'Arise—
　　Arise (she said) with my reprieve—
Lest a long sleep should seal your eyes
Whence you least fear—my father's spies
　　　And sisters too deceive—　　　　45
Which, like so many beasts of prey,
　　With younglings in their rav'nous claws,
Ev'n now, alas! thy brethren slay—
But I will neither strike nor stay

* Hypermnestra.

Whom gentlest nature awes.   5
With chains let me my father load,
   Because I chose my spouse to spare,
And pity on distress bestow'd—
Or make me settle my abode
    In sharp Numidian air.   5
Convey'd by swiftness and the wind,
   Begone, my love, in peace begone,
While Venus and the night are kind—
But when my monument's design'd,
    Engrave my tale thereon.'   6

ODE XII.
To NEOBULE.

Neobule, smitten with the love of young Hebrus, leads a life of indolence an
sloth.

'Tis wretched in earnest to live like a mope,
   Nor wash down chagrin with sweet wine;
To yield to an uncle all spirit and hope,
   Who rails at your pleasures and mine.
The charms of young Hebrus, and love's flying boy,
   Have stol'n your work-basket away,
And all that fine tap'stry that us'd to employ,
   And give to Minerva the day.
This gay Liparean's a notable knight,
   Bellerophon's self he may seem,
Not beat in the battle, or match'd in the flight,
   When fresh from the cruse and the stream.
The same in each motion's as clean as a cat,
   To hurl at the deer in the park,
Thro' bushes and shrubs the wild-boar can come at,
    And his quickness ne'er misses the mark.

ODE XIII.
To the Fountain BLANDUSIA.

He promises a sacrifice to the fountain, whose pleasantness he highly commends.

Hail, clear as crystal to the eyes,
    Blandusia's fav'rite spring;
O worthy to receive the prize
    Of wine and flow'rs we bring;
To-morrow we shall give thy flood   5
A kid, whose horns begin to bud,
    And fight and wantonness portend:
In vain—his pranks must be no more—
For shortly with his sacred gore
    He thy cool stream shall blend.   10
Thee scorching Sirius cannot touch—
    You yield a pleasing shade,
Which for the steers, when work'd too much,
    And wand'ring flock's display'd.
Thou shalt be register'd by fame,   15
A fountain of illustrious name,
    Whilst I thy useful beauties book;
The oak so happy on the spot,
To overhang thine hollow grot,
    Whence spouts thy prattling brook.   20

ODE XIV.
To the ROMAN PEOPLE.

This ode contains the praises of Augustus, on his return from Spain, after hav-ing defeated the Cantabrians.

Caesar (of whom but now 'twas said,
    That, like Amphytrion's son,
He went, at hazard of his head,
    To buy a wreath from Spain) is sped,
      And has the battle won.   5

ODE xiii. 20 prattling] pratling *1767*

Let * her come forth, whose faithful heart
   Is center'd in her spouse,
So great in military art,
Having to heav'n perform'd her part,
   In rend'ring of her vows.   1⸱

And let Octavia too be there,
   And, with neat fillets bound,
The mothers of the Roman fair,
And youths the gods have deign'd to spare,
   In triumph to be crown'd.   1⸱

O lads and lasses newly bless'd,
   That have your bridegrooms known,
Let not a word be now express'd,
But in such decency is dress'd,
   As modesty may own.   2⸱

This day my festival indeed
   Shall banish care and pain,
Nor will I fear by force to bleed,
But from all trouble shall be freed,
   In Caesar's peaceful reign.   2⸱

Perfumes and garlands bring today,
   And for a measure call,
Whose date preserves the Marsian fray,
If † Spartacus, in quest of prey,
   Has not secur'd them all.   3⸱

Quick, with her hair set off with myrrh,
   Let me Neaera see,
And bring her lute along with her;
If that cross porter should demur,
   Come back again to me.   3⸱

A hoary head dispute abates,
   Though tempted to be sour,
Nor appetite for wrath creates—
I had not borne it, by the fates!
   When Plancus was in pow'r.   4⸱

---

* Livia, the wife of Augustus.
† Spartacus, the famous gladiator, who stirred up the servile war.

ODE XV.
On CHLORIS.

That now being old, she would set some bounds to her impudence and lascivi-
ousness.

    Poor Ibycus his wife,
      At length, methinks, 'tis time
    To quit your wicked life,
      And each flagitious crime:
You should the better, sure, behave,   5
Now you are verging on the grave.
    Sure now you should desist,
      Amidst the brilliant stars,
    To spread a gloomy mist:
      For decency debars   10
That 'mongst the maidens you should play,
Like Pholoe the young and gay.
    Your daughter, with less shame,
      May rouse up our young rakes,
    While Bacchanalian dame   15
      Her timbrel she awakes;
The love of Nothus makes her brisk,
Like goat upon the hill to frisk.
    The fair Lucerian fleece
      Not rosy wreathes to twine,   20
    Nor harps are of a piece
      With such an age as thine;
Nor should an antiquated hag
E'er boast of an exhausted cag.

ODE XVI.
To MAECENAS.

All things are open to gold; but Horace is content with his lot, by which he remains in a state of happiness.

A tow'r of brass, whose doors were barr'd
With oak, while howling, upon guard,
   Stood dogs, prepar'd to bite,
Had been sufficient, to be sure,
Imprison'd Danae to secure
   From rakes that prowl by night;
If Jove, and she of ocean born,
Had not Acrisius laugh'd to scorn,
   With all his anxious tribe;
A way they found was fair and free,   10
When once the god should make his plea,
   Transform'd into a bribe.
Gold through the centinels can pass,
And break through rocks and tow'rs of brass,
   Than thunder-bolts more strong: 1
That * Argive prophet lost his life,
And was undone, because his wife
   Was bought to do him wrong.
The Macedon of such renown,
With gifts the city-gates broke down,   2
   And foil'd his rival kings:
Gifts ev'n can naval chiefs ensnare,
Though rough and honest, they would care
   For more superior things.
Anxiety pursues increase,   2
And craving never like to cease—
   I have myself deny'd
With cause to lift my crest on high,
And with such men as thee to vie,
   O knighthood's peerless pride.   3

---

* Amphiaraus, a Grecian prophet, foreseeing he should die at the siege of Troy, kep
himself concealed; but was betrayed by his wife, for the sake of a golden necklace.

The more a man himself refrains,
The more from heav'n his virtue gains:
    I pitch my tent with those
Who their desires, like me, divest,
And, as an enemy profest,   35
    The slaves of wealth oppose.
More noble in my lowly lot,
Than if together I had got
    Whate'er th'Appulian ploughs;
And poor amongst great riches still,   40
The fruit of no mean toil and skill,
    Could in my garners house.
A wood of moderate extent,
And stream of purest element,
    And harvest-home secure,   45
Make me more happy than the weight
Of Africa's precarious state
    Of empire could ensure.
What tho' nor sweet Calabrian bee
Makes his nectarious comb for me,   50
    Nor Formian wine grows old
Within my cellars many a year,
Though from rich Gallic meads I shear
    No fleeces of the fold:
Yet want's remote, that wretched fate,   55
That makes a man importunate—
    If more I should require,
I should not be refus'd by you—
But I must raise my revenue
    By curbing my desire.   60
And better so, than should I add
The Lydian realm to what I had,
    And all the Phrygian land;
They that crave most, possess the least—
'Tis well where'er enough's the feast;   65
    Heav'n gives with frugal hand.

ODE XVII.
To * AELIUS LAMIA.

He extols the nobility of Lamia—He then advises him to spend the morrow
with merriment.

O sprung from Lamus! fam'd of old,
  Since by our fathers we were told,
That you from him your family derive,
And diaries that feast each rising year revive.
  From him, your fountain-head, you spring,   5
    Who was a most extensive king,
And first the Formian walls was said to found
On Liris for Marica in his current bound.
    To-morrow's eastern blast shall speed
    To strew with leaves and useless weed   10
The groves, unless th'old raven's voice be vain,
That witch of rising winds, and of descending rain.
    On your glad hearth dry billets raise,
    And (while 'tis lawful) let 'em blaze;
Indulge to-morrow on fat pig and wine,   15
And servants call'd from work, with their gay lord to dine.

ODE XVIII.
To FAUNUS.

He beseeches the sylvan god, that in traversing his fields, he would be propitious
to Horace and his stock.

O Faunus! ardent to pursue
  The nymphs that from thee bound,
Propitious all my fields review,
My sunny haunts—and favour shew
  To all my younglings round;   5

* The Aelian family was very illustrious in Rome, and very numerous—it comprehended likewise the house of Lamia, which did to it distinguished honour on account of
its antiquity, insomuch that, if a man was better born that ordinary, he was proverbially
called a Lamia.

ODE xviii. 5 round;] round. *1767*

If yearly with a tender kid
    Thy presence we invoke,
And if to love and feasting bid,
You daily see th'old altar hid
    In wreathes of fragrant smoke.   10
The cattle on the grassy plain,
    Disport in active play;
Both men and flocks at ease remain,
December's nones to entertain,
    Which, Faunus, is thy day.   15
The wolf amongst the lambs is seen,
    And by the sheep's defy'd;
Down falls the foliage ever-green,
The delvers dance with joyous mien,
    And throw their spades aside.   20

ODE XIX.
To TELEPHUS.

He raillies him in a jocose manner, that, describing ancient histories, he neglects things pertaining to a merry life.

How distant from th'Inachian root
Was patriot * Codrus, who so bravely fell,
    You in your histories compute,
Of Peleus' race, and Trojan wars you tell,
    But what a cask of Chian costs,   5
And who the bath shall temper and prepare,
    When I shall 'scape these chilling frosts,
And at whose house, to mention you forbear.
    Fill up, my boy, for this new moon,
For midnight, and Muraena's num'rous † poll,   10
    Mix liquor handily and soon,
Three or nine bumpers in each toper's bowl.

* The last king of Athens, who gave his life for the good of his country. The Lacedemonians being engaged in war with the Athenians, were told by the oracle, that those should get the victory whose general should happen to be slain. Codrus, hearing of this, disguised himself, and went amongst the Lacedemonians, whom he provoked by abuse to put him to death, upon which the Athenians came off victorious.
    † At which Muraena was chosen augur.

    The bard that loves th'odd-number'd train
Of Muses, takes nine bumpers in his glee.
    The Grace, with naked sisters twain,   15
Fearful of wrangling, will admit but three.
    It is my pleasure to be mad,
Why cease to blow the Berecynthian horn?
    Why hang the pipe and harp so sad?
All niggard hearts and sparing hands I scorn.   20
    Bring roses, bring abundance in,
Let neighbour Lycus, and his blooming girl,
    Unfit for Lycus, hear our din,
To mortify that old invidious churl.
    At thee, with bushy hair so spruce,   25
And bright as Vesper, buxom Chloe aims;
    Me slow-consuming cares reduce,
As Glycera now checks, now fans the flames.

ODE XX.
To PYRRHUS.

That he should not force away the beautiful Nearchus from his mistress.

    O Pyrrhus! what art thou about,
      The lioness's cubs to move,
And take her very fav'rite out?
Full soon the plund'rer, none-so-stout,
      Th'attack will disapprove.   5
When she shall pass along the train
      Of rakes, that for their mistress stir,
Who shall have best of the campaign,
Shalt thou thy friend to good regain,
      Or leave to vice and her?   10
Mean time, while you the darts acute
      Present—she wets her dreadful tooth,
Lo! he degrades beneath his foot
That palm, the price of this dispute,
      The long-contested youth,   15

ODE xix. 15 Grace] grace *1767*
ODE xx. 6 she] he *1767*

With his loose locks perfum'd and curl'd,
   For sportive zephyrs there to play,
Like Nireus in his form begirl'd,
Or * who, from Ida and the world,
   To heav'n was snatch'd away.   20

ODE XXI.
To his WINE-JAR.

He pleasantly admonishes it to pour out old wine for the sake of Corvinus, from whence he takes occasion to commemorate the praises of wine in general.

O cask! that bears, like me, thy date
   From Manlius his consulate,
Whether with murmurs, jests, or brawlings fraught,
Or mad amours, or sleep, the kind relief of thought!
   Whatever be your long intent,   5
   Choice Massic, worthy to have vent
On a good day, come forth at the behest
Of my Corvinus, come with mellowness and zest.
   Not he, tho' forward to imbibe
   The lore of the Socratic tribe,   10
Will brutish scorn thee—Cato, as they say,
Would often warm with wine his virtue and his clay.
   To lend to sluggish minds a lift—
   And brighten harshness is thy gift—
You take the cares from out a wiseman's breast,   15
And make our politicians with their secrets jest.
   You doubtful minds by hope ensure,
   The horns exalting of the poor,
Who, after he has fairly drank thee down,
Nor heeds the soldiers arms, nor dreads the tyrant's frown. 20
   Bacchus and Venus on the spot,
   And Graces ever in a knot,
And living lamps shall eke thee out to-night,
Till Phoebus drive the stars with his superior light.

* Ganymede.

ODE xxi. 22 Graces] graces *1767*

ODE XXII.
To DIANA.

He consecrates the pine, which hangs over his villa, to Diana, whose offices he celebrates.

Queen of the mountains far and near,
    And of the woodlands wide,
Who, thrice invok'd, art swift to hear,
    And save the maids with child;
This pine, that o'er my villa tow'rs,   5
And from its eminence embow'rs,
    I dedicate alone to thee;
Where ev'ry year a pig shall bleed,
Lest his obliquity succeed
    Against thy fav'rite tree.   10

ODE XXIII.
To PHIDILE.

The gods are to be worshipped with clean hands, and conscience of a well-spent life.

If, heav'n address'd, your hands and knees
    At each new moon the gods appease,
And if a pig you slay, my rustic dame,
And offer your first-fruits with incense in the flame;
    Your fruitful vineyard then shall scorn   5
    The Afric blast, nor shall your corn
Be scarce or blighted—nor the fatal stroke,
Amidst th'autumnal plenty reach your little folk.
    For the vow'd victim, that is fed
    Where Algidum his snowy head   10
'Midst holms and oaks uprears, or in the mead
Of Alba, must beneath the pontiff's hatchet bleed.
    If you the Lares crown and clean,
    With myrtle and with froth marine,

ODE xxiii. 13 Lares] lares *1767*

'Tis not requir'd that such as you and I   15
Should on our altar cause whole hecatombs to die,
    If there a spotless hand you place,
    A sumptuous victim, in that case,
Will not with heav'n more sure acceptance make,
Than mix'd with good intent the little salted cake.   20

ODE XXIV.
Upon the RICH and COVETOUS.

Though richer than the hoarded gain
Of Araby and Ind unplunder'd yet,
    You of th'Appulian and Tyrrhenian main,
Should with casoons and piers possession get;
    If deepest on the highest head   5
Dire fate his adamantine hooks will drive,
    You cannot rid your fearful soul from dread,
Nor from the snares of death escape contrive.
    The Scythians have a better lot,
Who dwell in plains, and carry in a cart   10
    From place to place their customary cot,
And those rough Getans, negligent of art,
    Whose common acres, unsurvey'd,
Yield corn and fruit, that's bread for all the race;
    Nor do they drive the plough, or ply the spade,   15
Above a year in one continu'd place.
    And when their annual toil is o'er,
Another set the vacant lands receive,
    Who on the self-same terms with those before,
As they succeed, the prior hands relieve.   20
    There her step-children's orphan life
The woman in her innocence will spare;
    Nor does the man obey a portion'd wife,
Nor does she make a well-dress'd rake her care.
    Their parents great and virtuous fame,   25
And, cautious, constant chastity's their dow'r.
    Thus runs the law: 'Keep clear of sin and shame,
Or death's the wages from offended pow'r.'

O that some sage would rise to quell
Our impious slaughter, and our civil rage,   3
   Fond as his country's father to excel—
So call'd beneath his bust—let him engage
   Our monstrous licence to revise—
Fam'd to the latest times—since we, O shame!
   Hate virtue, when she's seen before our eyes,   3
But envious, when she's gone, her worth proclaim.
   For what are all these woful cries,
If sin by punishment is not cut off?—
   Laws without morals!—can mere forms suffice
For any thing but vanity and scoff?   4
   If such presumption still subsists,
That neither torrid zone, nor northern pole,
   Nor solid snow, that mountain-high exists,
Can terrify the merchant's sordid soul?
   The mariners expertly dare   4
The horrid seas; for in their rough account
   Want is disgrace—they rather do or bear
All ills, than virtue's arduous way surmount.
   Let us our gold and gems refund,
Source of our woe, into the neighb'ring main,   5
   Or Capitol, where all our ears are stunn'd
With party clamours, and the servile train.
   If we are penitent in truth,
The very seeds of vice should be eras'd,
   And the too tender spirits of our youth,   5
And nerves with exercise severer brac'd.
   Our noble youth have got no seat
Upon their horse, and fear to urge the chace,
   As far more learned in the idle feat
Of Grecian tops, or law-forbidden ACE.   6
   Mean time the father's perjur'd heart
Imposes on his partner and his guest,
   And hastes to try each method, and each mart,
To make a worthless heir of wealth possest.
   For why? Ill-gotten goods increase—   6
Yet after all their toil and time mis-spent,
   They have acquir'd by far too much for peace,
And far too little to insure content.

ODE XXV.
To BACCHUS.

Roused by an inward goad from Bacchus, he proposes to speak certain new lyrics concerning Augustus.

Bacchus, with thy spirit fraught,
Whither, whither am I caught?
To what groves and dens am driv'n,
Quick with thought, all fresh from heav'n?
In what grot shall I be found,   5
While I endless praise resound,
Caesar to the milky way,
And Jove's synod to convey?
Great and new, as yet unsung
By another's lyre or tongue,   10
Will I speak—and so behave,
As thy sleepless dames, that rave
With enthusiastic face,
Seeing Hebrus, seeing Thrace,
And, where feet barbarian go,   15
Rhodope so white with snow.
How I love to lose my way,
And the vastness to survey
Of the rocks and desarts rude,
With astonishment review'd!   20
O of nymphs, that haunt the stream,
And thy priestesses supreme!
Who, when strengthen'd at thy call,
Can up-tear the ash-trees tall,
Nothing little, nothing low,   25
Nothing mortal will I show.
'Tis adventure—but 'tis sweet
Still to follow at thy feet.
Wheresoe'er you fix your shrine,
Crown'd with foliage of the vine.   30

ODE XXVI.
To VENUS.

Worn out at length with old age, he takes leave of the lyric and his love affairs.

Of late an able am'rous swain,
I made full many a great campaign;
But now my harp and arms, of edge bereft,
Shall hang upon this wall, which rising on the left
In sea-born Venus' temple stands—   5
Here bring the torches and the brands;
Here bring the wrenching-irons and the bows
Against obstructing doors, so big with threats and blows.
Yet, goddess, of rich Cyprus queen,
And Memphis, where no snow is seen,   10
Once gently, with thy long-extended whip,
Touch my coquettish Chloe, till you make her skip.

ODE XXVII.
To GALATEA, on Point to Go Abroad.

He dissuades her especially from the example of Europa.

The screamings of th'ill-omen'd jay,
Or pregnant bitch, or fox attend,
Or tauny wolf in quest of prey,
All wicked wretches on their way,
And to their journey's end: 5
Or let a serpent drive them back,
The road swift crossing like a dart,
And terrify the stumbling hack—
For thee I dread no such attack;
But with an augur's art,   10
In early pray'r I will apply,
That some good-natur'd crow may speed,
And leave the east before the cry
Of birds that bode a stormy sky,
And to their lakes proceed.   15

ODE xxvii. 14 birds] brids *1767*

O Galatea! be thou blest,
   Where'er you choose to take your rout,
And keep my mem'ry in your breast;
Nor raven nor the pye molest
     Your course, as you set out.   20
But look, as he's in haste to set,
   How prone Orion moves the seas,
I well know Adria's gloomy threat,
And how much mischief's to be met
     From yonder whit'ning breeze.   25
May wives and children of our foes
   The rising goat's alarm partake;
To the black surge themselves expose,
Which, roaring to the blast that blows,
     Makes all the land to quake.   30
Thus did Europa trust, of yore,
   To that false bull her snowy limbs,
And, trembling at her boldness, bore
Her midmost course, where, far from shore,
     Full many a monster swims.   35
She, who of late the meadows knew,
   Fair student of the flow'ry bloom,
Wove chaplets to the wood-nymphs due—
Nought now but stars and waves could view,
     All in the glimm'ring gloom.   40
And when she was arriv'd at Crete,
   So famous for its hundred towns,
'O father! lost and indiscreet,
The daughter's duty to defeat,'
     She cry'd, in wrath, and frowns.   45
'Whence? Whither am I come?—Too light
   A punishment one death would be—
Am I awake, and wail of right?
Or is't a vision of the night,
     And I from baseness free?   50
A vision from the iv'ry gate,
   Which brings false fancies to the head—
Say, was it then a better fate
Through the long seas to sail—or wait
     Where new-blown flow'rs are spread?   55

23 Adria's] Adrian's *1767*   43 indiscreet] indiscrete *1767*

O if I had th'audacious steer
   My indignation hates and scorns,
I'd kill him with a falchion here,
And, though he was of late so dear,
      Would strive to break his horns.   60
Shameless I left my father's place,
   Shameless I wait the doom of hell—
Ye gods! if any hear my case—
O that I naked, in disgrace,
      Might roam 'mongst lions fell!   65
Before a virulent decay
   Shall feed upon my blooming cheek,
While yet there's moisture in my clay,
To be the tyger's tender prey,
      With all my charms, I seek.   70
Ah base! thy father to offend,
   Whose passion urges thee to die;
Well did thy girdle thee attend—
Thyself upon this ash suspend,
      And with his will comply.   75
Of if, upon the rocks to split,
   Acute with death, you are inclin'd;
To the fierce storm yourself submit—
Unless, perhaps, you should think fit
      To ply a task injoin'd,   80
And live a tyrant's harlot vile,
   And bear his queen's imperious tongue—'
Thus, as she urg'd her plaintive stile,
Came Venus with perfidious smile,
      And boy with bow unstrung—   85
Anon, when she had jeer'd enough,
   She said, 'forbear your wrath and heat,
Since with his horns, though ne'er so tough,
This bull shall meet a full rebuff,
      When you with him shall treat.   90
Do you not know your fame and fort,
   As matchless Jove's distinguish'd dame—
Learn your high dignity at court—
And let the quarter'd world support
      Your story and your name.'   95

ODE XXVIII.
To LYDE.

He exhorts Lyde to pass the day sacred to Neptune merrily, in drinking and singing.

Neptune, on his festal day,
    How can we so well exalt?
Lyde, bring without delay
    Wine from out our inmost vault;
Thus you, with a fresh resource,   5
Wisdom's fort shall reinforce.

Don't you see the day decline?
    Yet, as if the sun would wait,
You neglect to bring the wine,
    Which is of most pleasant date;   10
For when * Bibulus was chose,
It was laid to its repose.

We will sing alternate lays—
    Neptune and the Nereids green,
I with lively verse will praise—   15
    You, Latona, pow'rful queen,
And swift-darting Dian's laud,
With your twisted lyre applaud.

And the end of all to crown,
    We will chant the queen of smiles,   20
Who with harness'd swans comes down
    Unto all her fav'rite isles;
And as goddess of delight,
We will deify the night.

* Bibulus signifies a toper.

ODE xxviii. 12 its] his *1767*

ODE XXIX.
To MAECENAS.

He invites him to a chearful supper, omitting public concerns.

O from Tyrrhenian monarchs sprung!
    This many a season I forbear
A cask of mellow'd wine, untouch'd by tongue,
With roses for thy breast, and essence for thy hair.
    Dispatch—nor Tibur's marshy meads,
    Nor always Esula admire,
  Whose sloping soil the eye with verdure feeds,
Nor buildings rais'd aloft by * him who slew his sire.
    Leave squeamish plenty, and the pile,
    Whose structures to the skies presume,
  And cease to praise in such a pompous style
The smoke, and wealth, and clamour of your prosp'rous Rome.
    'Tis joy, at times, to shift the scene,
    As men of wealth and pow'r allow,
  And without purple carpets neat and clean,
The poor man's cottage-treat has smooth'd an anxious brow.
    Now Cepheus drives his flaming car,
    Now Procyon's wrath begins to burn;
  Now the mad lion shews his rampant star,
As fiery Phoebus makes the drinking-days return.
    Now weary to the stream and shade
    Go shepherds with their languid sheep,
  Or where Sylvanus spreads his thickest glade,
And on the silent bank vague winds are lull'd asleep.
    What regulations best may suit
    The state, and for the world you care,
  What points the Seres, Bactrians would dispute,
And what discordant Tanais rises to prepare.
    Wisely do heav'nly pow'rs th'event
    Of future times in night suppress,
  And smile when mortal men are too intent
Beyond their reach—Take thought, that moment you possess

---

* Telegonus.

To husband—As for other cares,
    As with the streaming river's course
Now gliding to the Tuscan sea it fares,   35
Now wave-worn rocks, and trunks up-torn with rapid force,
    And flocks and houses in its flood
      Involving, not without the roar
Of Echo—mountains and th'adjoining wood,
When deluge boils the streams above the peaceful shore.   40
    He, master of himself, shall dwell,
      And in a state of joy subsist,
Who every day his heart can fairly tell—
'Why this is life.'—To-morrow with a gloomy mist,
    Or brightness Jove may deck the pole,   45
      Yet shall he never take away
The past, or with his utmost pow'r controul
That bliss, the fleeting hours have ravish'd as their prey.
    Delighted with her cruel pow'r,
      Still trifling insolently blind,   50
Fortune shifts short-liv'd honours ev'ry hour,
Now good, perhaps, to me, now to another kind.
    I praise her while I call her mine;
      But if she spreads her wings for flight,
Wrapt in my virtue, I her gifts resign,   55
And court ingenuous want, whose portion is her mite.
    'Tis not my business, though the mast
      Should with the southern whirlwinds groan,
With wretched pray'rs to deprecate the blast,
Lest in the greedy main my bales be overthrown.   60
    In such a case, my little boat,
      For which two oars alone are made,
Should bear me through th'Egean dread afloat,
Fann'd by the gentle breeze, and safe in Castor's aid.

ODE XXX.
To the MUSE MELPOMENE.

Horace has gained eternal glory by his lyric compositions.

I've made a monument to pass
The permanence of solid brass,
And rais'd to a sublimer height
Than pyramids of royal state,
Which washing rains, or winds that blow   5
With vehemence, cannot o'erthrow:
Nor will th'innumerable tale
Of years, or flight of time avail.
For death shall never have the whole
Of Horace, whose immortal soul   10
Shall 'scape the pow'rs of human bane,
And for new praise his works remain,
As long as priest and silent maid
Shall to the Capitol parade;
Where Aufidus in rapture goes,   15
And where poor Daunus scarcely flows,
Once rural king—I shall be thought
The prince of Roman bards, that brought
To Italy th'Aeolian airs,
Advanc'd from want to great affairs.   20
Assume, Melpomene, that pride,
Which is to real worth ally'd;
And in good-will descending down,
With Delphic bays my temples crown.

THE
FOURTH BOOK
OF THE
ODES OF HORACE

ODE I.
To VENUS.

Horace is now arrived to that time of day, when he ought to alienate himself
from love affairs, and ludicrous verses.

Left alone so long a season,
    What! again new warfare rage?
Spare me, Venus, treason! treason!
    This is not a lover's age.
Now no more my youthful vigour   5
    Good queen Cynara inspires—
Cease to use thy gentle rigour,
    Parent fierce of sweet desires.
Staid, and void of inclination—
    Almost fifty—hence depart   10
To the softer invocation
    Of full many a youthful heart.
On more equable condition
    Drive your purple swans away,
And put Paulus in commission   15
    At a better time of day.
For he's nobly born, and decent,
    Would you fire a worthy breast?
And great instances are recent,
    How he pleads for the distrest.   20
Youth of most accomplish'd merit,
    Of an hundred arts and charms—
He shall bear with strength and spirit
    Far and wide thy conqu'ring arms.

If he smile at times prevailing   25
   O'er a bribing dupe's disgrace,
With sweet wood thy bust empaling,
   He near Alba's lake shall place.
Thine indulgent presence thither
   Shall much frankincense invite,   30
Lyre, and flute, and pipe together
   Shall thy ravish'd ears delight.
Twice a day the lads and lasses
   There thy praises shall resound,
And with foot that snow surpasses,   35
   Salian like, shall shake the ground.

ODE II.

To ANTONIUS JULUS, the Son of Mark Antony, of the Triumvirate.

It is hazardous to imitate the ancient poets.

Whoever vies with Pindar's strain,
   With waxen wings, my friend, would fly,
Like him who nam'd the glassy main,
   But could not reach the sky.
Cascading from the mountain's height,   5
   As falls the river swoln with show'rs,
Deep, fierce, and out of measure great
   His verses Pindar pours.
Worthy to claim Apollo's bays,
   Whether his dithyrambics roll,   10
Daring their new-invented phrase
   And words, that scorn controul;
Or gods he chants, or kings, the seed
   Of gods, who rose to virtuous fame,
And justly Centaurs doom'd to bleed,   15
   Or quench'd Chimera's flame.
Or champions of th'Elean justs,
   The wrestler, charioteer records,
And, better than a hundred busts,
   He gives divine rewards.   20

ODE ii. 12 controul;] controul. *1767*

Snatch'd from his weeping bride, the youth
  His verse deplores, and will display
Strength, courage, and his golden truth,
    And grudges death his prey.
The Theban swan ascends with haste,   25
  Of heav'n's superior regions free;
But I, exactly in the taste
    Of some Matinian bee,
That hardly gets the thymy spoil
  About moist Tibur's flow'ry ways,   30
Of small account, with tedious toil,
    Compose my labour'd lays.
You, bard indeed! with more applause
  Shall Caesar sing, so justly crown'd,
As up the sacred hill he draws   35
    The fierce Sicambrians bound.
A greater and a better gift
  Than him, from heav'n we do not hold,
Nor shall—although the times should shift
    Into their pristine gold.   40
The festal days and public sports
  For our brave chief's returning here,
You shall recite, and all the courts
    Of law contentions clear.
Then would I speak to ears like thine,   45
  With no small portion of my voice,
O glorious day! O most divine!
    Which Caesar bids rejoice.
And while you in procession hie,
  Hail triumph! triumph! will we shout   50
All Rome—and our good gods supply
    With frankincense devout!
Thee bulls and heifers ten suffice—
  Me a calf weaned from the cow,
At large who many a gambol tries,   55
    Though doom'd to pay my vow.
Like the new moon, upon his crest
  He wears a semicircle bright,
His body yellow all the rest,
    Except this spot of white.   60

ODE III.
To MELPOMENE.

Horace was born for poetry, to which his immortality is intirely owing.

He, on whose natal hour you glance
   A single smile with partial eyes,
Melpomene, shall not advance
   A champion for th'Olympic prize,
Nor drawn by steeds of manag'd pride,
In Grecian car victorious ride.

Nor honour'd with the Delphic leaf,
   A wreath for high atchievements wove,
Shall he be shewn triumphant chief,
   Where stands the Capitol of Jove,   10
As justly rais'd to such renown
For bringing boastful tyrants down.

But pleasing streams, that flow before
   Fair Tibur's flow'ry-fertile land,
And bow'ring trees upon the shore,   15
   Which in such seemly order stand,
Shall form on that Eolic plan
The bard, and magnify the man.

The world's metropolis has deign'd
   To place me with her darling care,   20
Rome has my dignity maintain'd
   Amongst her bards my bays to wear;
And hence it is against my verse
The tooth of envy's not so fierce.

O mistress of the golden shell!   25
   Whose silence you command, or break;
Thou that canst make the mute excel,
   And ev'n the sea-born reptiles speak;
And, like the swan, if you apply
Your touch, in charming accents die.   30

This is thy gift, and only thine,
    That, as I pass along, I hear—
'There goes the bard, whose sweet design
    Made lyricks for the Roman ear.'
If life or joy I hold or give,   35
By thee I please, by thee I live.

ODE IV.

To the CITY of ROME, Concerning the Genius of Drusus, and
his Education under Augustus.

As him, by mighty Jove preferr'd
    On high his thunder-bolts to bear,
Deem'd o'er the winged race the sovereign bird,
E'er since he made sweet youth, and innocence his care;
    Of old, green years, but strength innate,   5
        Drove him, unskill'd, upon his prey,
And vernal winds, the winter out of date,
Taught him unwonted flights, but not without dismay.
    Anon, by vivid impulse sped,
        He wages war against the folds,   10
And by his lust of fight and plunder led,
The curv'd-reluctant snakes within his claws he holds.
    Or as a goat in pastures green
        Intent, a lion's tawny whelp
(Whom his fierce mother did but lately wean)   15
Eyes rushing with new fangs, and has no hope of help.
    Such warrior Drusus in his bloom
        The Rhoetian and North-Alpine band
Beheld (which latter whence they did assume
With Amazonian ax long since to arm their hand,   20
    I have omitted to declare,
        Nor can we every matter know);
But far and wide victorious as they were,
The young man's wondrous conduct taught them at a blow,

)DE iv. 8 dismay.] dismay, *1767*   22 know);] know) *1767*

How a well-bent ingenuous mind,   2

   And genius disciplin'd can awe,

Whose plan was in a happy school design'd

By Caesar, more than father to his sons-in-law.

   The brave are gender'd by the brave,

     This truth ev'n genuine steers attest,   3

   The manag'd steeds by progeny behave,

Nor are tame turtles hatch'd in yon fierce eagle's nest.

   Yet learning inward strength assists,

     And education mans the heart;

   Refinement by morality exists,   3

Or else good-nature fails for want of wholesome art.

   What to the Neroes Rome should pay,

     The loud Metaurus witness bears,

   And vanquish'd Asdrubal—and that fair day

Which clear'd the low'ring gloom from our distress'd affairs.

   That day, which many a prize renowns,   4

     First mention'd victory to gain,

   When Hannibal fled thro' th'Italian towns,

Like wind that sweeps the sea, or fire that takes the train.

   From this desirable event   4

     The Roman enterprizes throve,

   And ravag'd, where the Punic plund'rers went,

The temples stood repair'd in every sacred grove;

   Until the traitor said at last,

     'Like stags, of rav'nous wolves the prey,   5

   We follow those heroic bands too fast,

Of whom by craft and flight we solely win the day.

   The nation, which from Troy on fire,

     Held sacred from their numerous woes,

   Brought through the Tuscan seas the son and sire,   5

In fair Ausonia's towns from shipwreck to repose,

   As from the ax the hardy oak,

     Which in dark Algidus abounds,

   Tho' hurt and damag'd by the frequent stroke,

Thrives, and exalts his head, aspiring by its wounds: 6

   Not more increase did Hydra, maim'd,

     Against griev'd Hercules assume,

   Nor was or Thebes, nor was ev'n Colchis, fam'd

For prodigies, more great, more wonderful than Rome.

Sunk to the center, they will rise   65
    More fair, and woe to him that strives;
  From vet'ran victors they will win the prize,
And send the gallant tale to entertain their wives.
    No more my proud couriers I send
        To Carthage fall'n, ah fall'n! and fled   70
    Is all our hope; nor fortune is our friend
(Though once she lov'd our name) now Asdrubal is dead.'
        Nothing so glorious in the field,
            But Claudius will with ease atchieve;
    Whom Jove defends, with prudence for his shield,   75
Thro' intricate distress and war his way to cleave.

ODE V.
To AUGUSTUS.

That he would at length return to Rome.

From gods propitious sprung, O guard
Of Roman greatness! you retard
    Now far too long your stay:
That promise of a quick return
You made the HOUSE, no more adjourn,   5
    But keep a shorter day.
Restore to this thy native place
The light, good chief, for when thy face,
    Like spring, its lustre throws,
The day goes off with more content,   10
And in a better firmament
    A brighter sunshine glows.
As for her son a mother's pain'd,
Above the destin'd year detain'd,
    By southern blasts malign,   15
Beyond Carpathian waves profound,
Where he continues weather-bound,
    For his sweet home to pine,
With calculations, tears, and sighs,
And vows, she calls, nor turns her eyes   20

DE v. 18 pine,] pine. *1767*

From off the winding shore;
Ev'n with that fondness these desires
Caesar his native land requires,
 Still wanted more and more.
For where you are, the grazing steer   25
Roams o'er the meadows, free from fear,
 Ceres yields ampler fruit;
The sailors plow the peaceful main,
And honour, cautious of a stain,
 Keeps accusation mute.   30
Each house is clear of guilt impure,
Example and the laws secure
 The heart from filthy sin;
For penalty sticks close to blame;
Our ladies are of peerless fame   35
 For children like their kin.
The Parthian, or with ice congeal'd
Who fears the Scythian in the field,
 Or who the monstrous host
That Germany brings forth and sends, 40
Or who the threats from Spain attends,
 While Caesar keeps his post?
Each Roman sends the sun to bed
On his own hill, and loves to wed
 To widow'd elms the vine,   45
Thence home at night he goes alert,
And thee, as god of his desert,
 Invites to grace his wine.
Thee their incessant pray'rs adore,
And large libations on the floor,   50
 Are offer'd to thy state;
Thou with the household-gods art join'd,
As Greece her Castor bore in mind,
 And Hercules the great.
Long may'st thou give, O glorious chief! 55
To Rome this leisure and relief,
 So constant patriots pray;
Thus sober in the morn we cry,
Thus in the night with bumpers high,
 When ocean hides the day.   60

ODE VI.
To APOLLO and DIANA.

God, whose dread power the * Theban queen
   Felt for her boastings proud and vain,
And Tityos ravisher obscene,
And Peleus' son, who might have been
     High Ilion's fatal bane;   5
The soldier, braver than them all,
   No match for thee, was taught to fear,
Though him her child did Thetis call,
And though he shook the Dardan wall,
     Arm'd with tremendous spear.   10
As falls to biting steel the pine,
   Or cypress to the eastern gust,
So he was humbled to resign
His life, extended, and recline
     His neck in Trojan dust.   15
He in no woooden horse disguis'd,
   For sacred rites of false report,
The Trojan dupes would have surpris'd,
'Midst feasts and dances ill-advis'd,
     In city and at court.   20
But boldly fierce, with open ire,
   Alas! alas! the dreadful doom
Had gratify'd his vengeance dire,
And infants burnt with Grecian fire,
     Ev'n in their mother's womb.   25
If not by thee wrought to relent,
   And Venus in persuasion skill'd,
The sire of gods had giv'n assent
That for more fortunate event,
     Aeneas walls should build.   30

* Niobe.

DE vi. 7 thee,] thee *1767*   12 cypress] Cypress *1767*

O lyrist, with a master's air,
  By whom the sweet Thalia plays,
Which in cool Xanthus lav'st thy hair,
Make thou the Daunian muse thy care,
    Enlight'ner of our ways.
Phoebus, my spirit, taste, and flame,
  Gives all the gifts that verse adorn;
From him I have the poet's name—
'Ye virgins of unspotted fame,
    And youths most nobly born,
Wards of the Delian maid, so fleet
  'Gainst stags and ounces with her bow,
Take notice of the Lesbian feet,
And, as the time you see me beat,
    Attend to fast and slow,
Extolling with the ritual praise
  Latona's darling in your song,
And her that nightly mends her blaze,
As shedding her fructiferous rays,
    She rolls the months along.
Soon when you're marry'd each shall say,
  "I too was present to rehearse,
Upon that memorable day,
The numbers of th'Horatian lay,
    Skill'd in his mystic verse." '

ODE VII.
To L. MANLIUS TORQUATUS.

All things are changed by time; one ought therefore to live chearfully.

The melted snow the verdure now restores,
  And leaves adorn the trees;
The season shifts—subsiding to their shores
  The rivers flow with ease.
The Grace, with nymphs and with her sisters twain,
  Tho' naked dares the dance—
That here's no permanence the years explain,
  And days, as they advance.

The air grows mild with zephyrs, as the spring
   To summer cedes the sway,   10
Which flies when autumn hastes his fruits to bring,
   Then winter comes in play.
The moons their heav'nly damages supply—
   Not so the mortal star—
Where good Eneas, Tullus, Ancus lie,   15
   Ashes and dust we are.
Who knows if heav'n will give to-morrow's boon
   To this our daily pray'r?
The goods you take to keep your soul in tune,
   Shall scape your greedy heir.   20
When you shall die, tho' Minos must acquit
   A part so nobly play'd;
* Race, eloquence, and goodness, from the pit
   Cannot restore your shade.
For nor Diana's heav'nly pow'r or love,   25
   Hippolytus revives;
Nor Theseus can Perithous remove
   From his Lethean gives.

ODE VIII.
To MARTIUS CENSORINUS.

There is nothing that can immortalize rather than the works of poets.

   Goblets to every friend of gold,
   And statues of Corinthian mould,
   In gratitude I had bestow'd,
   Attending to the present mode;
   And tripods too, which were the meed,   5
   That Greece her valiant sons decreed;
   Nor shou'd you have the meanest prize,
   Were I enrich'd with such supplies,

---

* One of the most illustrious in Rome, he being a descendant of Titus Manlius
'orquatus, so great in history.

DE viii. 5 meed] mead *1767*

As Scopas or Parrhasius send,
The one his colours skill'd to blend;   10
The one, whose excellence is known
To cut a god or man in stone:
But I keep no toy-treasures hid,
Nor do you want them if I did:
Your taste is of a nobler flight,   15
And poetry is your delight;
Which I can furnish, and assign
The merit of the gift divine.

   Not marbles, that the public place
With long inscriptions on the base,   20
By which returns beyond the grave
New life and spirit to the brave;
Not Hannibal what time he fled,
With threats retorted on his head;
Not impious Carthage, all a-flame,   25
To greater brightness raise his name,
(Who, when from conquest he return'd,
The title AFRICANUS earn'd)
Than he, who those achievements sung,
Ev'n Ennius from Calabria sprung;   30
Nor, if our writings shou'd be mute,
Wou'd benefit receive its fruit.
What wou'd the acts of him the son
Of Mars, and what had Ilia done;
If silence, envious of renown,   35
Had borne their matchless merits down?
The virtue, votes, and pow'rful word
Of bards, have Eäcus transferr'd
From Stygian darkness, to the isles
Where happiness eternal smiles.   40
The muse excepts against the doom
Of meritorious men in Rome.
The muse can bless you to the skies—
'Twas thus brave Hercules cou'd rise
To taste with Jove, a welcome guest,   45
Celestial fare amongst the rest.

'Tis thus the fam'd twin-stars obtain,
    To save ships shatter'd on the main;
Thus, ivy-crown'd, the god of wine
Gives furth'rance to each fair design.   50

ODE IX.
To LOLLIUS.

The writings of Horace will never be lost: virtue, without verse, is liable to obliv-
on. He will sing the praises of Lollius, whose particular excellencies he like-
wise commemorates.

Lest you should think the strains will die,
    Which I in skill but newly found
With voice to correspondent strings ally,
Borne where from far the rocks of Aufidus resound:
    Know, that if Homer take the lead,   5
        Yet is not Pindar out of date;
    Nor Cean nor Alcean fire recede,
Nor that * Sicilian bard's authority and weight.
        Nor if of old Anacreon sung,
        Has time his sportive lays suppress'd;   10
    Alive are all the notes of Sappho's tongue,
Which to her lyre she play'd, of genuine warmth possess'd.
        Helen was not the only fair,
            That was enamour'd to admire
    Th'adult'rer's golden garb, and flowing hair,   15
And royal equipage, with all their grand attire.
        Nor Teucer, from Cydonian string,
            Was first that with his darts engag'd;
    Nor Troy but once besieged, nor Cretan king,
Nor Sthenelus alone the well-sung contest wag'd.   20
        Not Hector, val'rous as he was,
            Nor fierce Deiphobus begun
    To bleed and suffer in their country's cause,
Or for a virtuous wife, or for a darling son.

* Stesichorus.

DE ix. 4 resound:] resound. *1767*   12 to] too *1767*

Before great Agamemnon shone,   2
   Heroes there were—but all in night,
Long night, are buried, piteous and unknown,
For want of sacred bards their glories to recite.
   Virtue conceal'd is next, I deem,
     To bury'd sloth—I will not spare   3
For ornament, when Lollius is the theme;
Nor suffer so much merit, such a life of care
   In black oblivion to be hurl'd—
     You, Lollius, have a noble mind;
Skilful and fraught with knowledge of the world,   3
Equal for all events, or temp'rate or resign'd.
   Of greedy fraud the judge severe,
     Forbearing all-attractive gold;
A consul not elected for a year,
But still esteem'd, in fact, that dignity to hold,   4
   Where'er the magistrate prefers
     Things honest to his private ends,
And bribing villains with a look deters,
And draws against the crowd, and his fair fame defends.
   He is not happy, rightly nam'd,   4
     Whom large possessions still increase—
By him more truly is that title claim'd,
Who holds the gift divine in prudence and in peace;
   Who's able hardship to sustain,
     And dreads vile actions worse than death;   5
He for his friends counts any loss a gain,
And for his country's cause will give his dying breath.

ODE X [XI].
To PHYLLIS.

He invites her to a banquet, upon the birth-day of Maecenas.

   Full nine years old my cellar stows
     A cask of good Albanian wine,
   And parsley in my garden grows;
   For Phyllis chaplets to compose,
     Much ivy too is mine:

40 hold,] hold. *1767*

With whose green gloss you shall be crown'd;
   With burnish'd plate the house looks gay,
The altar, with chaste vervains bound,
Craves to be * sprinkled from the wound,
    As we the lambkin slay.   10

All hands are busied—here and there
   Mixt with the lads the lasses fly,
The bustling flames, to dress the fare,
Roll up thick smoke, which clouds the air
    Above the roof on high.   15

But would you know what joy resides
   With me, to tempt you at this time—
You are to celebrate the ides,
The day which April's month divides,
    And Venus calls her prime: 20

A feast observable of right,
   Which I more heartily revere,
Than that which brought myself to light,
From whence my patron to requite,
    Flow many a happy year!   25

Young Telephus, at whom you aim,
   Is not for such as thee at all;
A rich and a lascivious dame
Upon his love has fixt her claim,
    And holds him in sweet thrall.   30

Let blasted Phaeton dissuade
   Presumptuous hope too high to soar;
And † he a dread example made
By Pegasus, who scornful neigh'd
    That he a mortal bore.   35

Things worthy of yourself pursue,
   Nor go where vain desire allures;
'Tis lawless to extend your view
To one that's not a match for you—
    Hail! crown of my amours!   40

* Horace's was a very old altar, so that *avet* and the obsolete *spargier*, are peculiarly
happy.
  † Bellerophon.

For, after this, I will be free
      From every other flame and fair—
Come, learn the song I made for thee,
And join, with charming voice and me,
          To banish gloomy care.

ODE XI [XII].
To VIRGIL.

He describes the approach of spring, and invites Virgil to an entertainment upo
a certain condition.

Now the breezes fresh from Thrace,
      Those attendants on the spring,
Still the sea, yet urge the race
      Of the ships upon the wing:
No more the meadow lands are froze,
Nor roar the streams o'ercharg'd with snows.

Now the bird with mournful scream,
      Aye for Itys wont to pine,
Builds her nest, disgrace extreme
      Of the great Cecropian line
E'er since that most horrid treat
She forc'd the lustful king to eat.

Swains the thriving sheep that tend,
      Thrown upon the mossy sod;
With the pipe their verses blend,
      To divert the rural god:
Whom that sweet scene of flocks and hills,
In Arcady, with rapture fills.

'Tis the time of drinking hard,
      But Calenean would you take,
You must bring a box of nard,
      For your entertainment's sake:
No less can wealthy Virgil frank,
As tutor to our youths of rank.

ODE xi. 5 meadow] meadows *1767*   11 since] since, *1767*

E'en an ounce of that perfume,   25
　　Shall a special cask intice;
Which in the Sulpician room
　　Now sleeps clear of noise and vice:
Fraught with new hopes of cleansing pow'r,
Against the bitter and the sour.   30

To these pleasures if you haste,
　　You must enter with your fee;
You shall not my goblets taste,
　　By my inclination, free:
As in the rich man's house you fare,   35
Without contributing your share.

But, my Virgil, lay aside
　　All delay and thirst of gain;
While 'tis lawful to provide,
　　'Gainst the seats of death and pain: 40
Let mirth relieve each grave concern,
For folly's pleasant in its turn.

ODE XII [XIII].
Upon LYCE, an Antiquated Courtezan.

He insults her with extreme bitterness, that now being old, and yet retaining her lustful appetite, she is contemned by the young gallants.

Lyce, the gods my vows have heard,
　　At length they've heard my vows;
You wou'd be beauteous with a beard,
　　You romp and you carouse:
And drunk, with trembling voice, you court   5
　　Slow Cupid, prone to seek
For better music, bloom, and sport,
　　In buxom Chia's cheek.
For he, a sauce-box, scorns dry chips,
　　And teeth decay'd and green;   10
Where wrinkled forehead, and chapt lips,
　　And snowy hairs are seen.

Nor Coan elegance, nor gems,
   Your past years will restore;
Which time to his records condemns,   1
   With fleeting wings of yore.
Ah! where's that form, complexion, grace,
   That air—where is she, say,
That cou'd my sick'ning soul solace,
   And stole my heart away?   2
Blest! who cou'd Cynara succeed,
   As artful and as fair—
But fate, to Cynara, decreed
   Few summers for her share,
That crow-like Lyce might survive,   2
   'Till lads shou'd laugh and shout,
To see the torch, but just alive,
   So slowly stinking out.

ODE XIII [XIV].
To AUGUSTUS.

Honours, adequate to the merits of Augustus, cannot be attributed by the Roman senate and people.

What can the conscript fathers do,
   Or Romans join'd, with all their souls;
To give th'Augustan worth the honours due,
Grav'd on eternal brass, or written in the rolls.
   O thou, the most illustrious prince,
     Where'er the sun the world illumes;
  'Twas thine the rough north Alpines to convince,
What dignity of rank your martial fame assumes.
   For by your troops did Drusus rout
     The fierce Genaunians, Brennians keen,   1
  And more than once, raz'd many a strong redoubt
They pil'd upon the Alps tremendous to be seen.
   Anon, the elder Nero fought
     A dreadful fight with your success;
  And drove th'enormous Rhetians, quick as thought,   1
From ev'ry post of war they ventur'd to possess.

ODE xii. 24 share,] share. *1767*

Nero, a glorious sight to see,
How he bore down the mighty bane
Of souls, resolv'd to die or to be free,
Ev'n as the south attacks the ocean's proud disdain,   20
While Pleiad, and her sisters, cleave
The clouds, the furious victor sped
Thro' midmost fire, the murm'ring troops to grieve,
And with his warrior horse ev'n there the troops to head.
As Aufidus, that rolls before   25
Appulian Daunus, is in scorn;
And, like the meadow's lord, augments his roar,
And meditates vastation to the fields of corn:
Thus Claudius, thro' each iron rank
Of these barbarians, forc'd renown;   30
And, charging first and hindmost, front and flank,
Victorious, without loss, he mow'd their armies down.
With thine advice, and prosp'rous fates—
For, on that memorable day,
When suppliant Alexandria ope'd her gates,   35
With nought within her courts but terror and dismay;
Before the fifteen years ran out,
Fortune successful in the end
The glory, so long wish'd for, brought about,
And made th'imperial arms their final pow'r extend.   40
Cantabrians, unsubdu'd till now,
Medes, Indians, with submissive mien;
Thee the vague Scythian honour and allow,
Guard of the Latian name, and Rome the world's great queen.
Thee Nilus, that conceals his fount,   45
Thee Danube, rapid Tigris fear;
Thee the swoln waves, on which such monsters mount,
'Till British cliffs, remote, the horrid bellowing hear.
The region of th'intrepid Gaul,
And all Iberia's harden'd race;   50
And thee, their lord, the tam'd Sicambrians call,
And, bloody as they were, thy terms of peace embrace.

ODE xiii. 36 dismay;] dismay. *1767*

ODE XIV [XV].
The Praises of AUGUSTUS.

Willing to sing upon my lyre,
    The fights we dare, the tow'rs we scale;
Apollo bade me check my fond desire,
Nor on the vast Tyrrhenian spread my little sail.
    Caesar, in this thy better age,   5
        Again the fertile fields have throve;
And from proud Parthia's fanes thy godlike rage
Our standards has retook, and giv'n to Roman Jove.
    And Janus' temple too is clos'd,
        Good order from the peace deriv'd;   10
And curbs upon licentiousness impos'd,
Have banish'd vice afar, and ancient arts reviv'd.
    From which the Latin name and strength
        Of Italy are so increast,
And our imperial glory, breadth and length,   15
From the sun's western bed have reach'd remotest east.
    While Caesar the dominion claims,
        Nor civil rage nor active spite,
Can take us from our peace; nor wrath, whose flames
Forge hostile swords, and states in friendship disunite. 20
    Not those that in deep Danube lave,
        Shall now the Julian edicts scorn;
Nor Getans, Seres, or the treach'rous slave
Of Persia, nor the folk upon the Tanais born.
    And we on work and festal days,   25
        Amidst our cups of jovial wine;
With wives and children (first with pray'r and praise,
Having made application to the pow'rs divine)
    Will, like our sires, in songs of joy,
        With many a Lydian air between,   30
Sing our accepted chiefs Anchises, Troy,
And those descendant heirs of love's indulgent queen.

ODE xiv. 7 rage] rage, *1767*   20 swords *Rudd*] sounds *1767*

THE BOOK
OF THE
EPODES OF HORACE

EPODE I.
To MAECENAS.

Horace will accompany Maecenas, going to the Actium expedition against Antony.

In a small ship, my friend,
You soon your course shall bend,
   To face huge vessels tow'ry-stern'd;
Prepar'd to undergo
All perils of the foe,   5
   For Caesar, as thyself concern'd.
And what will come of me,
For life is sweet with thee,
   But on the contrary severe:
What, must I peace pursue,   10
As so enjoin'd by you?
   Peace is not peace if you're not here!
Or shall I danger dare,
Altho' forbid my share
   Of bold adventure in the van: 15
With that degree of heart,
As best beseems the part,
   Of him that acts up to the man?
Yes, yes I will sustain
Each ill of land or main,   20
   Fell Caucasus, or Alpine snows;
Far as remotest west,
With thee my manly breast
   I will to ev'ry foe oppose.

EPODE i. 10 What,] What *1767*   11 you?] you, *1767*   23 breast] breast, *1767*

Perhaps you are to seek,   25
How timorous and weak,
   I with my aid could help you out;
I answer, 'less the fear,
To persons that are near—
   Absence and distance heighten doubt.'   30
As when she leaves her young,
The serpent's forked tongue,
   The bird will fear with more of dread;
Not that her presence there,
Could save her callow care,   35
   Or stave destruction from their head.
With pleasure for your sake,
This voyage would Horace make,
   Or any journey or campaign;
Without a view to bow   40
More steers to pull my plough,
   Upon a more extensive plain;
Or from Calabria's mead,
To turn my flock to feed
   Lucania's marsh when summer reigns;   45
Or spread my marble cot,
To that ambitious spot,
   Which Circe's title still retains.
Your bounty is my store,
Enough for me, and more—   50
   I will not for myself provide
What, like a rake in taste,
I might profusely waste,
   Or like penurious Chremes hide.

30 doubt.] doubt? *1767*   40 bow] bow, *1767*   42 plain;] plain. *1767*
44 feed] feed, *1767*   51 provide] provide; *1767*

EPODE II.
The PRAISES of a Country Life.

A happy man is he,
From business far and free,
Like mortals in the golden days;
With steers at his command,
To till his father's land,   5
Whom int'rest neither plagues nor sways.
Him no dread trump alarms,
To take the soldiers arms,
Nor need he fear the stormy main;
The noisy bar he shuns,   10
Nor to the levy runs
Of men, whose station makes them vain.
Wherefore he rather joins
The marriageable vines
To poplars tall in many a row;   15
Or prunes each fruitless shoot,
That springs to bear no fruit,
And bids the happier tendrils grow.
Or takes a distant gaze
Of lowing herds, that graze   20
As in the valley's mead they roam;
Or steers his tender flock,
Or in the cleanly crock,
Lays up press'd honey from the comb.
But when Autumnus comes,   25
With apples mild and plumbs,
That his delightful aspect crown;
What joy to pluck the pear,
He grafted with such care,
And grape of more than purple down.   30
With gifts select as these,
Priapus to appease,

Or Sylvan, that his bounds defends;
   Now thrown beneath a bough
   Of aged oak, and now   35
On matted grass his limbs extends.
   Mean while the streams beside,
   In their deep channel glide,
And birds within the leafy glade
   Upon the branches sing,   40
   With bubbling fountains spring,
The gentlest slumbers to persuade.
   But when the troubled air
   Is alter'd to prepare
The seasons of the snow and wet;   45
   With hounds on ev'ry hand,
   The wild boar is trepann'd,
Into the interrupting net.
   Or with smooth-shaven stakes,
   A slender toil he makes,   50
Where greedy thrushes are his prey;
   Or tim'rous hare is ginn'd,
   Or stranger cranes are thinn'd
The pleasant prizes of the day.
   'Mongst joys so sweet to thought,   55
   Who does not set at nought,
All love's anxieties and cares;
   But chiefly if a wife,
   Of chaste and virtuous life,
Help in the family affairs.   60
   Such as the Sabine dames,
   Or tann'd by solar flames,
Such as the swift Apulian's spouse;
   Soon as her lord returns,
   Fatigu'd with what he earns,   65
On sacred hearth the fire to rouse.
   And when the kine she's got,
   Within the hurdled spot,

66 hearth] dearth *1767*

She milks their swelling udders dry;
   And bringing this year's wine,   70
   From hogshead sweet and fine,
A gratis feast she can supply.
   Not oysters fetch'd from far,
   Or turbot or the scar,
If a bad wind so well should blow;   75
   To send them from the East,
   To deck a Roman feast,
And on our shores their shoals bestow;
   Not bustards, or the game
   Of Asia would I claim,   80
In preference my taste to please,
   As olives, nicely chose
   From out the special rows
Of fittest and most healthy trees:
   Or sorrel, goodly weed,   85
   That loves the verdant mead,
Or mallow sov'reign cure esteem'd;
   Or lamb, which on the day
   Of Terminus we slay,
Or kid just from the wolf redeem'd.   90
   How sweet, amidst this cheer,
   To see the sheep appear,
Return'd and sated to the full;
   Th'inverted plough to see,
   Which oxen o'er the lea,   95
With languid neck at leisure pull.
   To see the servants swarm,
   As into ranks they form,
To keep the merry house alive;
   The smiling gods to bless   100
   For all this good success,
By which they and their master thrive.
   This speech when Alphius made,
   That, broker of such trade,

8 bestow;] bestow. *1767*   81 please,] please; *1767*

Commencing rustic without doubt;   105
    For all his cash he drew
    Then the first wind that blew,
He chang'd his mind and put it out.

EPODE III.
To MAECENAS.

He expresses his aversion to garlic, which he eat at Maecenas's house, and with
which he was tortured in the bowels.

Has any young profligate been so perverse,
    To slay his old grandsire in wrath;
Why let him eat garlick (not hemlock is worse)
    What stomachs have clowns to their broth!
O what is this poison that's burning within?   5
    Has venom of vipers infus'd
Deceiv'd me! or, as the reward of my sin,
    Canidia the viands abus'd!
Medea, beyond all the Argonaut wights,
    When she captain Jason bespoke;   10
She made him take this as an unction of nights,
    Before the wild bulls cou'd be broke.
With this she prepar'd certain presents she made,
    A desp'rate revenge in her view;
And having Creusa to take them betray'd,   15
    Away on her dragon she flew.
Sure ne'er on the thirsty Apulia before,
    Arose such a muggy offence;
Nor did the gift-shirt that poor Hercules wore,
    Stock closer or burn more intense.   20
If ever such stuff you again shou'd affect,
    With a trick and a jest in your head;
May your wife, hand to mouth, your fond kisses reject,
    Or lie on the post of the bed.

EPODE iii. 4 broth!] broth? *1767*

EPODE IV.
To VOLTEIUS MENA.

A freed man of Pompey the Great.

Not wolves and lambs, by stronger fate
Than thou and I each other hate;
O hamper'd with th'Iberian cord!
And galling fetters of thy lord!
What tho' you strut puff'd up with pelf,   5
That cannot change thy servile self.
As on the sacred way you sweep,
With flowing robes full six ells deep;
Ingenuous scorn do you not trace,
In crowds that turn away their face!   10
'That wretch, corrected to the quick,
Until the officer was sick;
E'en he retains, in his own hand,—
A thousand rood,—Falernian land;—
And on the Appian road proceeds,   15
Which he wears out with gallant steeds;
And sits the first at any fight,
In spite of * Otho, as a knight.
Wherefore so many beaks of brass,
And heavy hulks do we amass,   20
'Gainst pyrates, and the servile band,
With such a fellow in command!'

EPODE V.
Upon CANIDIA the Sorceress.

'But oh, ye pow'rs on high,
Whichever from the sky,
Rul'st human nature, land and sea;
What can this horrid scene,
These screams and aspects mean,   5
All, all so sourly fix'd on me!

* Otho made a law, by which the seats of knights at shows were adjusted.

EPODE iv. 20 amass,] amass; *1767*

         Thee therefore I implore,
         If ever child you bore,
Lucina present to your pray'r;
         By this vain * purple vest,   10
         By Jove, who must detest,
And cannot such proceedings spare!
         Why does your forehead low'r
         On me, with looks as sour
As step-dames on their sons-in-law;   15
         Or like wild beasts, that feel
         The torment of the steel,
Which from their sides they cannot draw?'
         When thus, in trembling mood,
         The boy had spoke,—he stood,   20
Of all his noble robes undrest;
         A tender form and smooth
         And sight enough to sooth
The fierceness of a Thracian breast.
         Canidia, with her hair   25
         Unkempt, as twisted there,
The little snakes infold her head;
         Commands the bastard-fig,
         That from the graves they dig,
And cypress sacred to the dead: 30
         And eggs bedaub around,
         From black toad's filthy wound,
And plumes from owl of nightly scream;
         With drugs Iolchos sends,
         And which Iberia vends,   35
Whose lands with plenteous poison teem:
         And bone, that's snatch'd in spite
         From bitch of greedy bite,
When hungry and about to dine;
         For all these things, the dame   40
         Prepares a Colchian flame,
The magic powder to combine.

   * The praetexta, which young noblemen wore, was ornamented with purple; for the
lad here introduced is supposed to be of rank, in order to aggravate Canidia's barbarity.
———————
EPODE v. 41 Colchian] Colchan 1767

But Sagana, with gown
　　Adjusted, up and down
Is sprinkling the Avernal dew;　　　　　　　　45
　　With hair that stands again,
　　Like urchins of the main,
Or running boar that hounds pursue.
　　Veia, without controul
　　Of conscience, digs a hole,　　　　　　　50
And groans at the severe employ
　　Of sharp laborious spade,
　　That, when the pit was made,
Therein confin'd the buried boy
　　Might famish at the look　　　　　　　　55
　　Of dainties that they cook,
And vary thrice a day the board;—
　　His body hid as far
　　In earth, as swimmers are
In streams, when to their chins they ford.　　60
　　That his exhausted pitch,
　　And liver dry therewith,
For a love-potion might suffice;
　　When settled on the food,
　　They baffle and elude,　　　　　　　　65
The wasting pupils of his eyes.
　　That Folia too did come,
　　E'en from Ariminum,
With lust or masculine excess,
　　In towns both small and great,　　　　　70
　　As well as in the prate
Of idle Naples was the guess:
　　A witch, whose magic art,
　　Can make the stars to start,
At sounds Thessalian, from their spheres;　　75
　　And lunar orb can force,
　　To quit her heav'nly course,
When her inchanting voice she hears.
　　Canidia then in dumps,

45 Avernal] avernal *1767*　　　55 look] look, *1767*　　　69 excess,] excess; *1767*
72 guess:] guess. *1767*

Biting, with her green stumps,   8|

Her thumb, whose nail was never par'd;

What said she, or what not?

'O, conscious on the spot,

Of all these deeds that we have dar'd,

Dian and Night serene,   8|

That rule the silent scene,

What time our mystic blazes burn;—

Now, now present your face,

And on each hostile place,

Your pow'r and your resentment turn.   9|

In gloomy glades of dread,

While now wild beasts are sped,

Indulging as they sweetly doze;

Set all the dogs to bark,

At yon old lech'rous spark,   9|

And to the general laugh expose.

With nard, bedaub'd as rich

As essences, the which

These toiling hands of mine distill;—

Hah! what does magic ail!   10

Why do these charms avail

Less than the fell Medea's skill!

With which empower'd to sate

Her vengeance, wrath, and hate,

Great Creon flying she defy'd;   10|

And with her poison'd cloak,

Consum'd in fire and smoak,

Creusa, Jason's other bride.

Yet neither herb nor root,

Of magical repute,   11|

Have scap'd me by their craggy site;—

He sleeps in beds perfum'd,

By harlots thither doom'd,

Thoughtless of me to pass the night.

Ah! ah! he walks at large,   11

And has his free discharge,

84 dar'd,] dar'd. *1767*   85 Night] night *1767*   101 avail] avail! *1767*

Fresh from a greater wheedler's arms;
  Varus, I will pursue,
  O wretch about to rue,
Pursue thee with unheard of charms.   120
  Again, for me inclin'd,
  You shall return, nor find
Your poor lost wits by Marsian spells;
  A greater, greater bane,
  Of philters will I strain,   125
The more your nice disgust rebels.
  And sooner heav'n shall go,
  To place itself below
The sea, with earth upon the stars,
  Than you shall not desire   130
  My love with such a fire,
As burns this pitch within the bars.'
  At this the boy no more
  Intreated, as before,
The impious hags with gentle tone;—   135
  But doubtful, where to make
  His preface, thus he spake
The curse Thyestes well might own.
  'Your poys'nous drugs are strong,
  Confounding right and wrong,   140
Yet nature cannot be destroy'd;
  Such curses I will urge,
  No sacrifice can purge,
And no atonement render void.
  And when I shall expire,   145
  So destin'd by your ire,
I'll be a fury in the dark;
  And with my crooked claws,
  I'll come to maim your jaws,
(Such pow'r have ghosts) with many a mark.   150
  And lying on your breast,
  I will deprive of rest
Your eyes, by filling them with fear;

129 stars,] stars; *1767*   130 Than … desire] Then … desire, *1767*

And crowds, from town to town,
  Shall join to knock you down,   15
Obscene old witches, far and near.
    Your bodies after all,
    Depriv'd of funeral,
Wolves and Esquilian birds shall share;
    Your horrors and your cries,   16
    My parents ears and eyes
Shall glut, surviving me their heir.'

EPODE VI.
Against CASSIUS SEVERUS.

An abusive and petulant Poet.

Why innocent visitors do you molest,
  'Gainst wolves, a base mongrel, thou cur?
Come here, if you chuse it, and snarl out your best,
  For the kick and the bite I confer.
For like a staunch mastiff, or guard of the sheep,
  A Spartan in colour and breed;
Thro' the snows, ears erect, be they never so deep,
  I will urge all wild beasts that precede.
You, when with fierce barking you fill'd all the field,
  Kept smelling at bones on your plate;—
Have a care, have a care, of the weapon I wield,
  For villains exasp'rate my hate.
Like him false Lycambes despis'd for a son,
  Or he that made Bupalus die;
Shall I, when such mischief's by virulence done,
  Do nought but be boyish and cry?

EPODE VII.
To the ROMAN PEOPLE.

His detestation of the civil war carried on the one side by Brutus and Cassius,
and on the other by Octavius, Antony, and Lepidus.

Where are you rushing on with impious guilt,
　　And hands upon the sheathed swords again;
Is there too little blood profusely spilt,
　　Of Romans on the land and in the main?
And this—not that our army to the ground,　　　　　5
　　With flames invidious Carthage should deface;
Or that unconquer'd Britons, tied and bound,
　　Shou'd up the sacred hill the triumph grace:
But that our Rome, to please the Parthian foe,
　　By her own prowess shou'd be undermin'd;　　　10
A folly neither wolves nor lions know,
　　Save against beasts of a discordant kind.
Madness or mettle, or does vice prevail!
　　Give instant answer—what can be the cause!
They're silent, and their cheeks are deadly pale,　　15
　　As with intense stupidity they pause.
Know then fatality severe, and dread
　　With conscious guilt of fratricide's our own;
E'er since the blood of harmless Rhemus shed,
　　Was left for his descendants to atone.　　　　　20

EPODE VIII [IX].
To MAECENAS.

He has a foretaste of that pleasure, which he shall perceive from Augustus his
victory over Antony and Cleopatra.

What day, my blest knight, in your lofty saloon,
　　This Caecuban hoarded for thee;
(At Caesar's great conquest my spirits in tune)
　　Shall Jove for our banquet decree?

PODE vii. 8 grace:] grace. *1767*　　　19 E'er] E're *1767*

While Doric and Phrygian concertos are play'd,
   Upon the shrill pipes and the lyre;
As lately when Neptune's * sham-son was dismay'd,
   And fled with his ships all a-fire.
But first he had threaten'd all Rome to subdue,
   Till to the same yoke they shou'd bend   10
He took from the slaves to their masters untrue,
   Professing himself for their friend.
Yet still cou'd a Roman, whom frail beauty charms,
   (The fact may our children gainsay)
Most slavishly bear palisadoes and arms,   15
   And e'en haggard eunuchs obey!
Amidst all the standards (O shame to be told)
   That in gallant order arose,
The sun a rich canopy blush'd to behold,
   With squabs for luxurious repose.   20
The Gaul upon this, with two thousand fine horse,
   For Caesar with shoutings decreed;
And their navy's left wing, struck with dread and remorse,
   To port made the best of their speed.
O triumph! you loiter the heifer to bring,   25
   You loiter to bring the gilt car;
O triumph! you brought us Jugurtha the king,
   But Caesar's inferior by far.
Nor, from that long African war, did you crown
   A chief of more excellent name;   30
Tho' Scipio has got him eternal renown,
   By Carthage the tomb of his fame.
Our enemies, vanquish'd by land and by sea,
   Have strip'd their red coats from their back;
And with the most dismal event to agree,   35
   Have cloath'd all their soldiers in black.
And Antony now is a-making for Crete,
   (An hundred fair cities she boasts)
Or is on the Syrtes wind-bound with his fleet,
   Or on some strange region he coasts.   40

* Young Pompey, upon the strength of his father's naval atchievements, called him self the son of Neptune.

EPODE viii. 16 haggard] haggar'd *1767*   37 a-making] a making *1767*

Bring, boy, larger glasses, with Chian replete,
  Or fill'd with right Lesbian wine;
Or Caecuban, which may this sickness defeat,
  Give always good measure for mine!
For anxious concern for great Caesar's affairs,   45
  Which each honest citizen racks;
'Tis better with wine (as your Horace declares)
  With the very best wine to relax.

EPODE IX [X].
Against MAEVIUS the Poet.

Horace wishes he may be ship-wrecked.

The ship ill-omen'd puts to sea,
  With foetid Maevius 'mongst the crew;
Good blust'ring south remember me,
  And with rough waves her course pursue.
And fore and aft her sides assail,   5
  Let east, the wind of black despair,
With floods turn'd upside down prevail,
  And oars and ropes in pieces tear.
Let north too rage, from mountains high,
  As when the trembling oaks are rent;   10
Nor friendly star a ray supply,
  Upon Orion's dread descent.
No gentler breeze their fleet convoy,
  Than what the conq'ring Grecians knew,
When Pallas turn'd her rage from Troy   15
  On Ajax, as the ruffian's due.
O how your sailors toil and curse,
  What woeful paleness in your cheeks;
What pray'rs to Jupiter averse,
  And what extreme unmanly shrieks.   20
When roaring to the dark south-west,
  The shallows of th'Ionian bay
Shall leave your mastless deck distress'd, .
  And break your very keel away.

PODE ix. 6 despair,] despair *1767*   14 knew,] knew; *1767*

But if, upon the winding shore,   2
    Your foulness shall the gulls delight;
With kid and lamb I will adore
    The tempests, as denouncing right.

EPODE X [XI].
To PETTIUS, a Boon-Companion of his.

O Pettius, I delight no more
To scribble verses, as of yore,
    With am'rous pains enslav'd;
This third December now has stole
The leaves from Sylvan, since my soul
    For fair Inachia rav'd.
Ah me! for I'm asham'd of that,
How much I've fill'd the common chat,
    And for their feasts I grieve;
Where listlessness and silence spoke   1
The lover, and such sighs I broke,
    As I cou'd hardly heave.
And oft to you I wou'd complain,
How the poor man's ingenious vein,
    With fortune had no share;   1
Soon as the frontless God of wine,
Had wrought upon this breast of mine,
    To lay its secrets bare.
But if a manly form prevail,
To give these love-tricks to the gale,   2
    Which fan, not sooth the flame;
Then that false shame shall be a jest,
Of coming off the second best,
    With men of greater name.
When thus pot-valiant and austere,   2
This speech I cited in your ear—
    Advis'd to clear the coast,
I stagger'd homewards, to attack
My fair-one's door, and broke my back
    And ribs against the post.   3

EPODE x. 27 coast,] coast; *1767*

EPODE XI [XIII].
To his HUMOUROUS FRIENDS, that they would Pass the Winter Merrily.

The skies with horrid tempests frown,
And even in snow and rain come down,
   The woods and rough profound
Roar with the north wind, fresh from Thrace,
My friends let us the hint embrace,   5
   And while our knees are sound
Let us in seemly sort preclude
The thought of sour solicitude,—
   Bring wine of Manlian date;—
All other matters we forbear,   10
For heav'n, perhaps, these hours of care,
   With joy shall reinstate.
Now is the pleasure and the time,
With odours of the Persian clime,
   Our bodies to perfume;   15
And with the Cyllenean lyre,
To ease our breasts of horrors dire,
   Lest they our frames consume.
Thus the great Centaur to his ward,
Sung lectures, 'O unconquer'd lord,   20
   Whose birth from Thetis rose;
The land of Phrygia thee expects,
Where cool Scamander's stream directs
   Its course, and Simois flows.
From whence (the fates have spun it so)   25
You shall not be allow'd to go
   Home with your blue-ey'd queen;
There thou the ills of every day,
With musick and with wine, allay
   Th'alloquial charms of spleen.'   30

EPODE XII [XIV].
To MAECENAS.

Taken up with his love for Phryne, he cannot finish the promised Iambics.

Why these lethargic fits,
   Have wrought upon my wits,
And in oblivion sunk each sense;
   As I had drank too deep
   Of Lethe, bringing sleep
With greediness of thirst intense.
   Maecenas, candid knight,
   Your questions kill me quite;—
The God of love has un-bespoke
   The strains I promis'd you,   I
   Nor may I them review,
Nor give the master's final stroke.
   You too are all aflame,
   And by as bright a dame
As fir'd the tow'rs of Troy—rejoice—   I
   Me Phryne, just made free,
   Wounds; tho' for more than me,
She gives her person and her voice.

EPODE XIII [XV].
To his MISTRESS NEAERA,

Of whose perjury he makes complaint.

It was a midnight scene,
   When Luna shone serene,
Midst stars in lesser order trib'd;
   When you, about to break
   The league of Gods, didst speak
The form of words that I prescrib'd.
   And round my neck you flung
   Your pliant arms, and clung
With more tenacious fond embrace

EPODE xiii. 9 embrace] embrace; *1767*

Than to the lofty oak   10
   The ivy—while you spoke,
And vow'd your vow upon the place.
   'While wolf the lamb devours,
   And while Orion low'rs
On sailors in the wintry sea;   15
   And while Apollo's hair,
   Flows to the sportive air,
This love of ours shou'd mutual be!'
   O nymph about to pine,
   For these resolves of mine;   20
For if my manhood yet remain,
   I will no rival bear,
   Neaera's bed to share,
But love shall seek for love again.
   Nor will I re-commence   25
   With her, who gave offence,
My flame with any new desire;
   When once the rankling smart,
   Has setled in my heart,
And fix'd me in determin'd ire.   30
   But you, whoe'er you are,
   Of more propitious star,
That strut'st triumphant o'er my woe;
   Tho' rich in land and stock,
   And by your feeding flock   35
For thee in gold Pactolus flow;
   Tho' thou canst con each page,
   Of that transmuted sage,
Than Nireus handsomer appear;
   Yet thou shalt soon lament,   40
   A similar event,
And I in turn shall laugh and sneer.

EPODE XIV [XVI].
To the PEOPLE of ROME.

His commiseration with the Republic on account of the civil wars.

Another age our civil wars compleat,
    And Rome is ruin'd by her own strong hand;
Whom nor the neighb'ring Marsians cou'd defeat,
    Nor threat'ning Porsena's Etruscan band.
Nor Spartacus, nor Capua's rival boasts,
    Nor innovating Allobrox cou'd worst;
Nor rough Germania, with her blue-ey'd hosts,
    Nor Hannibal by Roman parents curst.
But we destroy her, the vile race she bred,
    And beasts again shall seize upon the ground;
Barbarian chiefs shall on her ashes tread,
    And with their horses hoofs her streets shall sound.
And Romulus his bones (dread sight to see!)
    They shall disperse now kept from wind and sun;
Perhaps you all, or a majority,
    Wou'd learn which way this dire distress to shun.
No better scheme than those Phoceans chose,
    And execrating did their place forsake;
And left fields, houses, temples for their foes,
    And for the boars or rav'nous wolves to take.
To go where'er our feet, where'er the wind
    Of south or rude south-west shall us convey;
Can any a more apt expedient find,
    The voyage looks fair, why do we yet delay?
But let us first to these conditions swear,
    That stones shall swim emerging from the deep;
Or Po, ere any to return shall dare,
    Matinian summits in his streams shall steep,
And to the main high Apennine remove,
    And join new monsters in the lustful fit;
Until the kite adulterate the dove,
    And to the stags the tigresses submit;

EPODE xiv. 20 boars] bears *1767*   28 steep,] steep. *1767*   32 submit;] subm
1767

Nor tawny lion the weak flocks elude,
    And shaven goats in the salt wave delight;
This, and whate'er assertion may preclude   35
    Our sweet return, let us, all Rome recite.
All go,—at least the more ingenuous part,
    The soft and hopeless on their couches lie;—
But cease effeminate grief each noble heart,
    And fly the Tuscan shores, set sail and fly.   40
Circumfluent ocean waits us,—steer the fleet
    To plains, the happy plains and blessed isle;
Where each untill'd each year supplies the wheat,
    And undrest vine-trees wear a lasting smile.
Her bud the never-failing olive fills,   45
    And the black figs their native branches grace;—
From hollow oaks flows honey,—and the rills
    Down lofty mountains leap with tinkling pace.
She-goats, unbidden, seek the milk-pail there,
    And kindly flocks, full-udder'd, homeward speed;   50
Nor round the sheep-cote growls the ev'ning bear,
    Nor adders lurk beneath th'unshaven mead!
And still on stronger beauties shall we gaze,
    How the dank east nor lays the bearded ears;
Nor the fat glebe is burnt by torrid rays,   55
    Earth temper'd by the sov'reign of the spheres.
This place the vessel Argo ne'er found out,
    Nor impudent Medea ever knew;
Nor here Sidonian sailors tack'd about,
    Nor here Laertes' son's laborious crew.   60
No murrain hurts the cattle, nor by heat
    Of starry influence are the flocks destroy'd;
Jove did these shores for pious souls secrete,
    When he the golden age with brass alloy'd.
The golden age he first alloy'd with brass,   65
    With iron next he made the times more hard;
Whence, for good Romans, there shall come to pass
    A sure escape, if Horace be a bard.

---

preclude] preclude, *1767*   36 return,] return *1767*   51 sheep-cote] sheep-
at *1767*   63 shores] stores *1767*

EPODE XV [XVII].
To CANIDIA.

He begs of her that she would forgive him, and feigns himself to be over-pow
ered by her magic.

At length to scientific charms
I yield, whose force my heart alarms,
And suppliant pray thee by the reign
Of Proserpine and Dian's fane,
Whose pow'r's inexorably fierce,
And by the books of magic verse,
That make the very stars descend
From heav'n, and cite them to attend.—
No more in cursed mumblings deal,
But backward turn th'electric wheel;
The son of Thetis, when implor'd
By Telephus, the man restor'd;
Tho' he with darts oppos'd his way,
And set his Mysians in array.
The corse of Hector, meant a feast
For dogs and ev'ry bird and beast,
The Trojan matrons cou'd acquire,
For unction and the fun'ral pyre;
When Priam went, and (hard to tell!)
Before the stern Achilles fell;
The crew of * that laborious sage,
Cou'd from their bodies disengage
The bristles of the filthy swine,
Soon as sooth'd Circe gave the sign;
At which their voice and mind, and hue
She did recover and renew:
O lov'd by tars and factors, sure
Enough thou'st giv'n me to endure;
My youthful strength and colour's flown,
With ghastly skin on ev'ry bone;

* Ulysses.

EPODE xv. 15 Hector, ... feast] Hector ... feast, *1767*   16 beast,] beast; *1767*

My hair is with your unguents hoar,
My ceaseless toils are more and more;
Day urges night and night the day,
Nor can my gasping vitals play;
Wherefore I wretched have comply'd,   35
To own what I before deny'd;
That Sabine charms the breast can pain,
And Marsian dirges split the brain.
What wou'd you more, O earth and sea,
I burn to a more fierce degree   40
Than Hercules, what time he wore
The shift besmear'd with Nessus' gore;
More fierce than those Sicilian fires,
Whose wrath from Etna still aspires:
For you your Colchian flames prepare,   45
Till, burnt to ash, I float in air.
What costs? What issue have you plann'd?
Speak out, I'll answer your demand,
Ready to give whate'er you chuse—
An hundred oxen, or my muse,   50
If on the lying lyre you please
To hear such compliments as these.
'You, chaste and good, shall set and rise,
With golden stars that range the skies:'
Castor and he, the other twin,   55
Tho' wroth about their sister's sin;
O'ercome by pray'r, restor'd the light
To * him they had depriv'd of sight:
And thou (for you can do the feat)
Loose me from this delirious heat.   60
O thou ne'er stain'd by parents mean,
And clear of the sepulchral scene;
A prudent woman, that will spare
The nine-days-buried ashes there;

* Stesichorus, who had defamed Helen with scandalous verses, was deprived of sight;
it afterwards restored, by the divine power of Castor and Pollux.

brain.] brain; *1767*   51 please] please, *1767*

You have an hospitable heart,
Pure hands—can do a mother's part;
And tho' you shou'd be brought to bed,
Preserve your strength, your *white* and *red.*

EPODE XVI [XVII].
CANIDIA'S Answer,

In which she shews that she cannot be pacified by any intreaties, because t
poet has made her magical proceedings public.

Why sue your pray'rs to her that mocks,
With listless ears; not beaten rocks,
Where waves the wint'ry Neptune throws,
More deaf attend the sailor's woes.
What, unreveng'd, Cotyttian rites,
Which, sacred to luxurious nights,
Do all free intercourse indulge,
Shall you deride and you divulge;
And with my name the city fill,
As priest of our Esquilian STILL?
What profit, that Pelignian dames
Are richer from my chymic flames;
And that quick poison I contrive,
If thou'rt against my wish alive?
An irksome life thou shalt retain,
For fresh and for perpetual pain.
Still pining at the dainty meats,
For ease false Tantalus intreats;
Prometheus, whom the vultur gnaws,
Wou'd also have his torments pause;
His stone too Sisyphus wou'd prize
Up the high hill; but Jove denies;
To leap from tow'rs on earth beneath,
Or in your breast the sword to sheathe,
Now will you wish, and now will try
The rope about your neck to tye;—

EPODE xvi. 2 ears; . . . rocks,] ears . . . rocks; *1767*   15 shalt] shall *1767*
21 prize] prize, *1767*   24 sheathe,] sheathe. *1767*   25 try] try, *1767*

All this thou shalt attempt in vain,
Thro' tedious grief and sour disdain;—
Mean time I'll on your shoulder ride,
'Till earth shall scarce support my pride: 30
Shall I (as you who pry'd can prove)
Who make the waxen statues move;
The moon can draw from out her course,
By words of sympathetic force;
Can raise burnt bodies out of Styx,   35
And in the cup love-potions mix;
Shall I my fruitless art bemoan,
Without effect on Thee alone?

THE SECULAR ODE.

For the safety of the Roman empire.

Phoebus and Dian, queen of bow'rs,
  Bright grace of heav'n, the things we pray,
O most adorable of pow'rs,
And still by adoration ours,
    Grant us this sacred day,

At which the Sybils in their song,
  Ingenuous youths and virgins warn,
Selected from the vulgar throng,
The gods, to whom sev'n hills belong,
    With verses to adorn.

O fost'ring god, whose fall or flame,
  Can hide the day or re-illume;
Which com'st another and the same,
May'st thou see nothing like the fame,
    And magnitude of Rome!

And thou, to whom the pray'r's preferr'd,
  The matrons in their throes to ease;
O let our vows in time be heard,
Whether Lucina be the word,
    Or 'genial goddess' please.

Make fruitful ev'ry nuptial bed,
  And bless the conscript fathers scheme,
Enjoining bloomy maids to wed,
And let the marriage-bill be sped,
    With a new race to teem.

That years elev'n times ten come round,
  These sports and songs of grave delight
Thrice by bright day-light may resound,
And where the thickest crouds abound,
    Thrice in the welcome night.

SECULAR ODE. 2 pray,] pray; *1767*   5 day,] day. *1767*   7 warn,] warn; *17*
22 fathers] father's *1767*   27 delight] delight; *1767*

And you, ye destinies, sincere
   To sing what good our realm awaits;
Let peace establish'd persevere,
And add to them, which now appear,
     Still hope of better fates.   35

Let fertile earth, for flocks and fruit,
   Greet Ceres with a wheaten crown;
And ev'ry youngling, sprout, and shoot,
Let Jove with air attemper'd suit,
     While wholesome rains come down.   40

Serene, as when your darts you sheathe,
   Phoebus, the suppliant youths befriend;
And all the vows the virgins breathe,
Up to thy crescent from beneath,
     Thou, queen of stars, attend.   45

If Rome be yours, and if a band
   Of Trojans safely came by sea
To coast upon th'Etrurian strand,
And change their city and their land,
     By your supreme decree: 50

For whom, unhurt, thro' burning Troy
   The chaste Aeneas way cou'd find;
He whom the foes could not destroy,
But liv'd to make his friends enjoy,
     More than they left behind: 55

—Ye gods, our youth in morals train,
   With sweet repose old age solace;
On Rome, in general, O rain
All circumstance, increase, and gain,
     Each glory and each grace.   60

And he whose beeves were milky white,
   When to your shrine his pray'rs appeal'd,
Of Venus and Anchises hight,
O let him reign supreme in fight,
     But mild to them that yield.   65

47 sea] sea; *1767*   50 decree:] decree. *1767*   55 behind:] behind. *1767*
62 appeal'd,] appeal'd; *1767*

By sea and land, the Parthians now
  Our arms and ax with dread review;
For terms of peace the Scythians bow,
And, lately arrogant of brow,
    To us the Indians sue.   7●

Now public faith and honour dare,
  With ancient modesty and peace,
To shew their heads, and virtue rare,
And she that's wont her horn to bear,
    With plentiful increase.   7●

The archer with his shining bow,
  The seer that wins each muse's heart;
Phoebus, who respite can bestow,
To limbs in weakness and in woe,
    By his salubrious art: 8●

If, built on Palatine, the height
  Of his own tow'rs his eyes engage;
The Roman and the Latian state,
Extend he to a later date,
    And still a better age!   8●

And may Diana, who controuls
  Mount Algidus and Aventine,
To those great men that keep the rolls,
And to the youths that lift their souls,
    A gracious ear incline!   9●

That Jove, and all the gods, will bless
  Our pray'rs, good hope my thoughts forebode;
THE CHORUS, who such skill possess,
Phoebus and Dian to address,
    In this thanksgiving ode.   9●

---

72 peace,] peace; *1767*   80 art:] art. *1767*   87 Aventine,] Aventine; *1767*

THE SATIRES

Male nominatis,
    Parcite verbis.— — *Hor.*

THE
FIRST BOOK
OF THE
SATIRES OF HORACE

SATIRE I.

He inveighs in the first place against the depraved practice of men, by which it happens that they are never contented in their own station, nor can please themselves by their own determinations, but always prize those of other men. He then takes occasion to be particularly severe upon avarice.

Maecenas, whence is this caprice,
That mortals cannot live in peace?
But their own lot of life disclaim,
Whether by choice, or chance it came,
And give the rest invidious praise!—   5
O happy merchants! (full of days
And worn with toil the soldier cries)
To which the merchant-man replies,
His ship by the south wind distrest,
The military life is best;   10
The troops engage, and in a breath
Glad triumph comes, or instant death.
The lawyer, when his clients knock,
At the first crowing of the cock,
Cries up the country squire, who raves   15
That all but citizens are slaves,
When from his home he's forc'd to dance
Attendance on recognizance:
So many cases of this kind
Are found, that they wou'd break the wind   20
Of talking Fabius to recite;
But lest I tire your patience quite—
Observe—suppose some pow'r divine

Shou'd say, I will to each assign
The part, he chuses—I decree   25
The soldier shall a merchant be,
And he a counsellor of late
Shall have the country squire's estate—
Do you come here to shift the scene,
And you go there—why what do you mean!   30
They hesitate with all their hearts
Tho' in their pow'r to change their parts.
What cause now therefore can they show,
But Jupiter shou'd puff and blow
In wrath, and for the future swear   35
He'll not consent to hear their pray'r.
But to go on and not to smile,
Like some who use a waggish stile,
(Tho' what forbids a man, forsooth,
At once to laugh and speak the truth?)   40
As fondling masters treat their boys
By giving sugar-plumbs and toys,
That they the better may go on,
Their grammar-rudiments to con.

However, raillery apart,   45
Let us the serious matters start.
He that with ploughshare cleaves the clod,
The treach'rous lawyer doom'd to plod,
The soldier and the tars at sea,
Who boldly sail through each *degree*,   50
Assert th'intention of their deed,
Is that in age they may recede
To peace, and to a plenteous board,
When once they've treasur'd up their hoard.
Ev'n as the ant (whose toiling might   55
As most exemplary we cite)
Drags with her mouth all she can reap,
And adds to her constructed heap,
Not unappriz'd, nor unprepar'd
How future matters must be squar'd.   60
However, she will not appear,

38 stile,] stile. *1767*   40 truth?)] truth) *1767*

When once Aquarius damps the year,
And uses in her cell immur'd
The goods her patient toil procur'd.
Whilst then no summer-heat can tire,   65
Nor winter, ocean, sword, nor fire
Divert you from the quest of gain;
And you all obstacles disdain,
So you can make your point in view,
That none shall have more wealth than you.   70
What fruit (inform me) can it bear,
That with that tim'rous over-care
Gold, silver, in immod'rate wealth
You hide up in a hole by stealth?
You answer that a lib'ral use   75
Will sure to nothing all reduce—
But without use what is the rank,
Or what the beauty of the bank?
Suppose your threshing-floor supply
An hundred thousand bowls of rye,   80
Your belly will demand no more
Than mine, of all this mighty store;
As if, 'mongst slaves, you shou'd be sped,
Like Esop, with a load of bread,
Not one crumb more to you wou'd fall,   85
Than him, who carried none at all.
    What does it boot to him that lives
Within the prescript nature gives,
Whether he till an hundred rood,
Or thousand acres for his food?   90
But 'tis a pretty thing you say
With a great capital to play—
If we from little funds can take
Such things, as for our purpose make,
Our garrets why shou'd you despise   95
Compar'd with your great granaries?
As if desirous, when a-dry,
Of but a jug or glass, you cry;

66 fire] fire, _1767_   74 stealth?] stealth. _1767_   90 food?] food. _1767_
92 capital] capitol _1767_   96 granaries?] granaries! _1767_   97 a-dry] a dry _1767_

I'd rather on the river's brink
Than from this little fountain drink.   100
Hence they, that Aufidus approach,
Too large a quantity to broach,
Are hurried down the rapid fall
By him, that swallows banks and all.
While they that want not unto waste   105
Will free from mud their water taste;
Nor, as a needless draught they crave,
Will lose their lives within the wave.
But most thro' false desires unwise
Urge, no finances will suffice;   110
For wealth is character and name,
And, as your riches, such your fame.
What can one do with such as these?
Let them be wretched, if they please;
According as the tale is told—   11_
A churl of Athens, full of gold,
Was wont to scorn the people thus—
The world may hiss and make a fuss,
But I applaud myself the more,
Whilst I at home my bags explore.   120
    When thirsty Tantalus wou'd quaff,
The stream eludes his lips—you laugh—
And yet, if we but change the name,
The story of your life's the same.
O'er bags, which from all hands you scrape,   12_
You cannot sleep, but stare and gape,
Compell'd the plenty to refuse,
As tho' 'twere sacrilege to use;
Nor can they other joy supply,
Than pictures to amuse the eye.   130
What, know you not the real worth
Of money is its help on earth?—
Buy bread, buy herbs, a flask of wine,
To which you likewise may subjoin
Such other articles beside,   13_
As nature grieves to be denied.

131 What,] What *1767*   132 is ... earth?—] is, ... earth— *1767*

But to keep watching and half-dead,
Both night and day to be in dread,
Of thieves, and fire, and slaves, lest they
Shou'd rob the house, and run away: 140
Such wealth with such a life endure,
O rather keep me ever poor!
    —'But if one's body shou'd be seiz'd
With cold, or any way diseas'd,
So that you cannot stir about,   145
You have a friend to help you out,
To bring you medicines, to call in
The doctor, that your loving kin
And children may again enjoy
Your company'—nor wife, nor boy   150
Desire your life—both small and great,
Male, female, all your neighbours hate
Your very name—and is it strange
That no one should good-will exchange,
With one so worthless as to prize   155
His pelf, above all social ties?
But wou'd you gain and keep your friends,
Whom nature without labour sends,
You'd lose your toil in that respect
By their refractory neglect: 160
As who shou'd take an ass to grace
The field, and enter for the race.
    Put then a period to pursuit,
And how much more abundant fruit,
You from your diligence possess,   165
Dread want and poverty the less;
And cease from all this toil of thought,
That being found, for which you sought:
Nor do with your ill-gotten store
As one Umidius did of yore,   170
Who was (the tale will soon be told)
So rich, as ev'n to measure gold;
And yet for fear that he shou'd fast,
Clad, like a slave, unto his last.

140 away:] away. *1767*   156 ties?] ties. *1767*

But him, the flow'r of * Tyndar's breed,   175
A woman he had lately freed,
With a good cleaver split in twain—
  'What part must then a man sustain!
Wou'd you of me a Maenius make,
Shall I like Nomentanus rake?'—   180
Now you are going on to fight
With things, by nature opposite—
Commanded not to be a sneak,
You're not enjoin'd all bounds to break;
There is a medium to be had,   185
No doubt, 'twixt staring and stark mad.
To all things there's a mean assign'd,
And certain boundaries defin'd,
From which remov'd on either hand,
True rectitude can never stand.   190
  But to return—what, are there none
Dislike their lot, but churls alone?
Nor for another's calling votes,
Nor grutches of his neighbour's goats,
And scruples to compare his state   195
With thousands more unfortunate!
But still is anxious to amass
What one or other may surpass:
When from the goal the coursers clear
The whirling car—the charioteer   200
Rushes on him that foremost speeds,
But scorns when he himself precedes.
And hence it is we rarely find
A man so perfectly resign'd,
As to declare this life he leaves,   205
A guest, that to the full receives:
Now tis enough—and lest you think
I've dipt in blear-eyed Crispin's ink,
And stol'n my work from his 'scrutore,
I will not add a sentence more.   210

  * A woman, who was in the spirit of Clytemnestra, the daughter of Tyndarus, who
killed Agamemnon with an axe.

191 what,] what *1767*

SATIRE II.

By examples he confirms the adage: 'while fools avoid vices, they run into the
opposite extreams.'

Each minstrel, quack, and strolling play'r,
Each mime, and scrub is in despair,
And with their ragged race deplore,
Tigellius now can sing no more.
The truth is, he was very good,   5
And lib'ral to the brotherhood.
Another, lest he comes to shame,
Dreads such a spendthrift's very name;
So close, he will not give a friend
What cold and hunger may defend.   10
Another, if you ask him why
His grandsire's, father's fortunes fly,
While cash he borrows but to waste,
And gratify his dainty taste,
He answers, he wou'd not be deem'd   15
Mean-spirited—which is esteem'd
By some as matter worthy fame,
By some of obloquy and blame.
Fufidius, rich in free-hold land,
And money lent at the best hand,   20
Wou'd not be call'd a thief or rake.—
He from the capital will take
Some five per cent. upon the nail,
And the more desperate and frail
A man in circumstance is found,   25
Or life, the more he will be ground.
He hunts for names, and lies in wait
For youths arriv'd at man's estate,
Who just from rigid guardians came—
At this what man will not exclaim,   30
O sov'reign Jove!—But he, we'll say,
Spends in proportion to his pay:

SATIRE ii. 2 mime] mine *1767*   31 he,] he *1767*   32 Spends ... pay:]
Speeds ... pay, *1767*

While it is out of human creed
How much himself he will not heed;
So that the father, whom we see   3.
Presented in the comedy,
And tortur'd at his booby's flight
Was not in such a wretched plight.
Now if you wou'd inquire, my friends,
To what this dissertation tends—   4
'Why fools by ill-concerted schemes,
Shun vice for opposite extremes!'

SATIRE III.

*First he calls those to account, who while they wink at their own vices, ar
quick-sighted at discovering those of others—He then shews, that, after th
example of lovers and parents, in friendship small failings shou'd be cover'd. T
conclude, he digresses to a refutation of that stoic paradox, in which all default
are said to be equal.*

This is the fault of all the quire,
They will not sing at your desire,
But, if you never beg a song
They'll keep a-quav'ring all day long.
Tigellius, that Sardinian spark,
Was a great proof of this remark.
Had Caesar, whose undoubted sway
Might have compell'd him to obey,
Pleaded, to make him shew his tone,
His father's friendship and his own,   1
He wou'd not yet with all have sped—
But did he take it in his head,
A bacchanalian catch he'd grace,
From highest pitch to lowest bass;
Or every note to every string,   1
From egg to apple wou'd he ring.
This man had not the least degree
Of stedfast uniformity.

SATIRE iii. 4 a-quav'ring] a quav'ring *1767*   6 remark.] remark, *1767*

Now wou'd he run as from a foe,
And now with solemn pace and slow,   20
As Juno's sacrifice he bore—
Now with two hundred slaves or more
He liv'd, and now with hardly ten—
One while of kings and mighty men
Was all his talk—another while   25
Submissive in this humble stile—
'A three-leg'd stool let me procure,
A little salt that's clean and pure,
A gown too, which tho' coarse and old,
May serve to keep me from the cold;'   30
A million had you giv'n outright
To this same philosophic wight,
So full of thrift and of content,
In five days every sesterce went.
Each night he sat up, till 'twas day,   35
And snored the sunshine all the way,
Never was heard of such an elf,
So much at variance with himself.
    But here a friend his voice exalts,
And asks me if I have no faults—   40
'Why yes I have, and if you please,
At least about as bad as these'—
At absent Novius Maenius rail'd,
When thus a chap his ear assail'd,
To your own failings are you blind,   45
Or wou'd you cozen all mankind!
Cries Maenius, I can soon excuse
Myself for all my selfish views—
This is a foolish vicious love,
Whost partial way we should reprove.   50
Since you wou'd wink with both your eyes
On all your own impurities,
Why when your neighbours mis-demean,
As eagle or as dragon keen
Do you inspect.—You may depend   55
That in his turn each injur'd friend

o reprove.] reprove, *1767*

Will like to do the same by you,
As sharp and as censorious too.
   A certain man's too prone to rage,
Not well adapted to engage   60
With the shrewd witlings of the town,
And may be laugh'd at, that his gown
On his rough person loosely flows,
With shoes scarce cleaving to his toes.
But he is good to that degree,   65
There is no better man than he,
Your friend, and under this disguise
A most stupendous genius lies.
Then sift yourself, and make essay,
If nature, or an *evil way*,   70
Have sown no *undiscover'd* seeds
Of vice, for 'mongst the other weeds,
The fern, that shou'd be burnt, will yield
His crop, in each uncultur'd field.
   But to forearm in some respects—   75
E'en as a mistress's defects
Deceive at least, if not delight
The lover—or (a case to cite)
Balbinus doats upon the wen
Of his dear Agna—O that men   80
Wou'd thus in friendship be to blame,
Till Virtue found an honest name
For such a fault—let us be mild
To friends, as parents to a child;
And not for blemishes annoy—   85
The father calls his squinting boy
A leering archer full of fun,
And if a man has got a son,
Like Sisyphus, but two-feet tall,
Why him his bantam will he call.   90
One crooked leg'd, with fondling whine,
He ranks as of the Vari-line;
And if club-footed, then he smiles,
And of the house of Scaurus stiles.
One lives too thrifty, let him be   95
Your fav'rite for frugality:

Another's light and apt to boast,
He of his humour makes the most
To entertain—another's rude
To take large freedom, and intrude,   100
Let him be call'd sincere and brave—
Another's hot and giv'n to rave,
But he's a man of spirit still—
For such ways gain and keep good-will—
But we the virtues ev'n invert,   105
On purest vessels throwing dirt.
A man of probity we find
As guilty of an abject mind;
If one amongst us too is slow,
On him the blockhead we bestow.   110
Another's cautious of a snare,
Nor ever lays his bosom bare
To bad men (as he lives in times
With envy fraught and thriving crimes)
Him stead of prudent and discrete   115
We term a man of dark deceit.
If one is unreserv'd and free
To such familiarity,
As I with you, Maecenas, use,
And interrupt you, when you muse,   120
Or read—with any kind of prate
Intrusive or importunate—
At such a guest they take offence
And swear the man wants common sense.
How injudiciously, alas!   125
A law against ourselves we pass;
For no one without faults is bred,
Who has the fewest, is the head.
When my dear friend (as justice pleads)
Weighs 'gainst my bad my better deeds,   130
Let him, if he wou'd win my heart,
Incline unto the major part,
If such indeed my virtues prove,
Then in requital of his love,
The self-same scale shall be applied,   135
Whene'er he's summon'd to be tried.

He that requires his humpt-back shape
Shou'd his friends ridicule escape,
May certainly himself exhort
To wink upon his neighbour's wart,   14
'Tis equal, who for pardon sues
Shou'd not in turn, that grace refuse.

   In fine, since wrath amongst the rest ⎫
Of crimes, that foolish men infest,   ⎬
Cannot be totally suppress'd;   ⎭   14
Why does not human reason rate
Things by its measure and its weight,
And only punish faults, as far
As guilt or provocation are.
If any one his slave shou'd slay,   15
Who when he's bid to take away,
Sequesters one half-eaten fish,
Or licks warm broth from out the dish,
His madness wou'd give more offence,
Than Labeo, with all men of sense.   15
But greater still 'gainst reason's laws
Are follies play'd without a cause.
Your friend has done some slight affair,
Which if you don't forgive and spare,
You shou'd be call'd severe and sour,   16
And yet you from his presence scow'r,
With equal hatred and dismay
As Druso's debtor *on the day*,
Who when the cruel Calends come,
If neither int'rest nor the sum   16
He can procure, by hook or crook,
Must hear him read his *doom's-day-book*,
His servile throat in posture put,
As if preferring to be cut.

   Suppose my friend has by his ale   17
Been forc'd upon my couch to stale,
Or at my board a dish has broke
Which for * Evander was bespoke.

---

* Of such valuable antiquity that it might be supposed to have belonged to Evander
who entertained Aeneas upon his landing in Italy.

For this—or when the servants bring
A chicken, shou'd devour a wing,   175
Which to my seat was rather near,
Shall he for this be held less dear?
What can I do, if he should steal,
Or things of secrecy reveal,
Or break his word?—They who decry   180
All crimes as of an equal die,
Are gravel'd, when you come to facts—
For other laws good sense enacts,
Sound morals, and convenience too,
Source of all justice, that we do.   185
   When first upon the new-form'd earth
Poor mortals crawl'd out from their birth,
A race but just remov'd from brutes,
For caves and caverns their disputes
They did with nails and fists decide,   190
But by degrees their clubs they plied,
And at the last with arms they fought,
Which long experience forg'd and taught,
Till * words at length, and names they found,
To ascertain their thoughts by sound.   195
Hence they began from war to pause,
To wall in towns, and 'stablish laws,
That theft should not unpunish'd be,
Nor rapine, nor adultery.
For long before fair Helen's charms   200
Had woman set the world in arms;
But all those savages are fled,
And all without memorial dead,
Who, like the tenants of the wild,
With vagrant lust themselves defil'd,   205
As still the strong the weaker slew,
And did as bulls for heifers do.
Now laws were a preventive aid
For fears of man's injustice made,

* The understanding of Horace was so benighted, that he supposed language to be gradual, and of human invention—nevertheless The Lord is the WORD, and all good words proceed from him, as sure as nonsense and cant are derivable from the Adversary.

199 adultery.] adultery, *1767*   201 arms;] arms, *1767*

This all must evidence, who mind   210
Each age, and hist'ry of mankind:
Nor can mere nature sep'rate right
From wrong, by as distinct a light,
As she can sever good from ill,
Or what shou'd check, or tempt the will: 21_
Nor e'er can reason make it plain,
That he's as much a rogue in grain,
Who breaks for sprouts his neighbour's hedge,
As he that does a sacrilege.
Some certain rule then let us state   220
To make chastisement adequate,
Lest him you scourge severe and rash,
Who scarce deserves a single lash,
For I do not the least surmise,
That you will with the rod chastise   225
Him that deserves more dreadful doom,
Since your assertions so presume,
That theft is of as great a die
In guilt, as high-way robbery,
And threaten you wou'd cut off all   230
Defaults alike, both great and small,
If man wou'd give you sov'reign sway—
So much for what the Stoicks say.
    * If he is rich who's wise withall,
Tho' but a cobler in his stall,   235
The beauty of the world alone,
And king upon an endless throne,
Why pray for what is in your hand?
'You do not, surely, understand,
What he, the sire of all our sect,   240
Crysippus says in this respect,
"The wise-man makes himself no sole,
Yet is a cobler on the whole." '
How's this?—'Hermogenes, tho' dumb,
His voice can raise and harp can thrum,   245

* The philosopher of the Stoicks (according to Crysippus) was not only, verily, and indeed a king, but also of all trades and professions.

244 this?] this *1767*

Alfenus thus, in lawyer's gown,
His awl, and implements laid down,
Himself a cobler still affirms—
The stoick on no other terms
Is jack-of-all-trades and a king'—   250
The boys that round you form a ring,
Will pluck your beard, and by the press
You shall be brought to last distress,
And snarl and burst your lungs in vain
Unless your staff the mob restrain,   255
Supreme of monarchs—but to wave
Prolixity—while you shall lave
Your body in the farthing bath,
Crispinus following your path,
And my dear friends shall set aside   260
The things, in which my feet shall slide,
Why in return I shall enlarge
My heart, to give them their discharge:
In private life far more THE THING,
Than your imaginary king.   265

SATIRE IV.

He asserts that Lucilius was particularly tart, by following the ancient comedy amongst the Grecians—However he shews his own writings are not to be read in the same view, since (as they were satirical in the general) the most part of mankind conscious of some vice or other, understand themselves to be hinted at therein. Otherwise he professes himself clear of virulence, and to deter men from vice with pleasantry, and by a fatherly kind of chastisement.

Cratinus, Eupolis, with these
And others Aristophanes,
Who made their comedies of yore,
If any man on any score
Was worthy of a shameful note   5
They branded him, in what they wrote,

255 restrain,] restrain *1767*   259 Crispinus] Crysippus *1767*   263 discharge:]
discharge. *1767*   264 far] for *1767*
SATIRE iv. 3 yore,] yore *1767*   4 score] score, *1767*

With perfect freedom and by name,
As thief, adult'rous son of shame,
Cut-throat, or any otherwise
Disgrac'd—with them Lucilius vies,   10
On them depends upon the whole
But changing feet, and measure droll;
Keen—but still making verses halt,
For this was his peculiar fault,
Two hundred verses in an hour   15
(As a great work to shew his pow'r)
Oft wou'd he dictate to his guest,
Still standing hip-hop for a jest.
Mean-time, while muddy was his lay,
There was, what one wou'd wish away—   20
Verbose—too indolent to bear
The toil of writing and the care,
That is the care of writing *clean*,
For *much* is not the thing I mean.
But here Crispinus' wrath I whet   25
To challenge me at any bet.
'Your tablets take, this instant take,
A trial if you choose to make,
Appoint your umpires, hour and place,
To see who writes the greatest pace'—   30
The gods have done the best of all
To make my spirit poor and small,
Who seldom speak and then but spare,
While you may imitate the air,
That's in the leathern bellows pent,   35
There puffs and blows and is not spent,
Until the iron's soft and red—
    The happy Fannius sure is sped,
Who in the library has thrust
Unbid, both manuscripts and bust.   40
While not a soul will read my verse
Who am too tim'rous to rehearse
My works in publick—now the cause
Why few will give, *this kind* applause

12 But] By *1767*   42 rehearse] rehearse, *1767*

Is that the major part are wrong—   45
Take whom you will from out the throng;
Or avarice perverts his ways,
Or desperate ambition sways.
One's mad upon his neighbours wives,
In other filth some waste their lives.   50
This on his silver side-board glotes,
Albius on brazen statues doats:
One with her merchandize will run,
From eastern to the western sun,
Thro' every ill with sails unfurl'd,   55
Like dust that in the wind is whirl'd,
Rush headlong, lest a want should come
To take a farthing from his sum,
Or to enlarge his stock—all these
The muse alarms, the bards displease.   60
'There's hay upon his horn—fly, fly,
Can he but raise a laugh, they cry,
He'll not his father's failings brook,
And, what's once enter'd in his book,
To young and old he'll publick make   65
Who come from bake house or the lake.'
    But come my refutation hear,
As I in my behalf appear.
First then I will myself reject
From men of the poetic sect;   70
'Tis not sufficient for the name,
That merely metre we can frame.
Now if a fellow writes like me
As near to prose, as verse can be,
You must not think he has the *vein*—   75
But one of a diviner strain,
Who has a genius and a tongue,
By which eternal things are sung;
On him this glorious praise confer—
Hence things of comic character   80
If fairly they can be giv'n out
As poems some have made a doubt:

49 neighbours] neighbour's *1767*

Because both words, and things of course,
Have neither spirit, fire, or force;
Men's talk, or, if from talk disjoin'd,   85
By measure of prosaic kind.
But yet you'll say the sire's in rage
Because his son the whores engage,
Who for their sakes neglects a wife,
And all the wealth and sweets of life,   90
A drunkard and (O shame to say)
With flambeaus in the blaze of day.
What? wou'd the loose Pomponius hear
One word less grand, and less severe,
Granting his father were alive?   95
Hence 'twill not answer to contrive
The verses in a style compleat,
All which, if you displace the feet,
A peasant in his wrath might say,
As well as Demea in the play.   100
If from those lines I now indite,
Or those Lucilius us'd to write,
The measure and the pause you take,
And the last words the former make,
You cou'd not find, but wholly lose   ⎫   105
The members of the mangled muse;   ⎬
Not so if Ennius thus you use.   ⎭
WHAT TIME DIRE DISCORD BURST THE BARS,
AND FORC'D THEIR IRON PORTS OF MARS.
    So far of this—another place   110
Shall be reserv'd by me to trace
If comedy's by scene and plot
A poem fairly term'd or not.
But now I only shall debate,
Whether this kind you justly hate.   115
Sharp Sulcius and Caprius hoarse,
As their indictment they enforce
Both to the gang great terror give,
But if a man discreetly live,

He may contemn them both—Tho' you   120
Like Coelus, and like Birrus too,
Upon the road have made full free,
I am not Caprius—fear not me.
To shop, nor stall my volumes come, ⎫
There for the sweaty mob to thumb, ⎬   125
Nor for Hermogenes to hum. ⎭
I never but to friends repeat,
Nor that, but when they much intreat;
Not any where to any croud—
Many there are, that read aloud   130
Ev'n in the market, or the springs
Where people bathe—when he that sings
May by the closeness of the place
Give to his voice a finer grace.
To coxcombs this a grateful task,   135
Who never have the sense to ask
About the purpose, or the time—
    But here they brand me with the crime
Of hurting with a bad intent—
From whence can this 'gainst me be meant?   140
Is any then your voucher, say,
With whom I've liv'd unto this day?
He, who backbites his absent friend,
Nay more, who does not still defend
His fame, and stand on his behalf;   145
He, who wou'd raise a spiteful laugh,
Who no loquacity forbears,
And what he never saw declares,
And he, whose tongue is not controul'd
By what in confidence is told,   150
That fellow is a black in grain,
From him, O Roman youth, refrain:
You'll often see twelve guests repose
Upon three couches—one of those
Ere he has sup'd must needs asperse   155
All beings of the universe,
Except the man, that rules the roast,
And him, ev'n him he'll lash the most,

145 stand] stands 1767

When Bacchus, who the truth reveals,
From his free heart all secrets steals.   16
This man to you, who hate a black,
Seems witty with a pretty knack.
If I one time upon a prank
Have said too frolicksome and frank
That *while Rufillus clogs the sense,*   16
Gorgonius has the goat's offence;
Is churlish envy, then my vice?
If any mention shou'd arise
Of things Petillus stole away,
Made in your presence—you wou'd say,   17
The man thro' habit to defend,
Petillus always was my friend,
And from a child we were as one,
Much for my asking has he done,
And I rejoice he lives in peace,   17
Because it was a strange release
He from the gallows lately had—
This is rank poyson very bad,
Sheer envy, which shall have no part
Or in my writings, or my heart,   18
If I can promise once for all
Or understand myself at all.
  If ought too freely I have spoke,
Or been, perhaps, too much in joke,
Your kind indulgence you'll allow,   18
For that I shall inform you now.
The best of fathers taught me this,
That I shou'd keep from things amiss,
By certain shrewd remarks, he made—
Me, when he wanted to persuade   19
To thrift, and frugally to live,
Content with what he had to give;
'Do you not see (he wou'd observe)
How Albius' son is like to starve,
And Barrus too reduc'd and low—   19
These are great documents to show

170 say,] say *1767*   171 habit to defend,] habit, to defend *1767*   172 Petillus
Petillus, *1767*

The mis'ry of a substance spent.'
Whenever it was his intent
To fright me from loose girls (he cry'd)
'Let not Sectanus be your guide,'   200
Lest I should seek the wedded dame,
When I might have a lawful flame:
'Trebonius, hamper'd in the fact,
Has not his character compact:
Philosophy (says he) my son,   205
May teach you what to seek and shun,
And render reasons more than I;
Let it suffice me to apply
Old rules, traditionally gain'd,
And keep your life and fame unstain'd,   210
As long as you a tutor need;
The riper age will soon succeed
To strengthen every thought and limb,
And then without your corks you'll swim.'
'Twas thus he form'd my tender mind,   215
And if he any thing enjoin'd,
'For this affair you have (says he)
A laudable authority;'
Then wou'd he cite, the point to clench,
One of the sages of the bench.   220
But did he any thing restrain?—
'Can you (says he) a doubt maintain,
But such a thing, in such a case,
Is vain, and nothing but disgrace,
Since He or they are come to shame   225
For doing of the very same!—
As ev'ry neighbour's funeral frights
Sick men with greedy appetites,
And makes them spare themselves, for fear
Their own interment should be near: 230
So tender minds are often warn'd
While others for their vice are scorn'd.'
    Thus instituted I am free
From vices of the first degree,

That post a mortal to his grave,   23

But small and venial faults I have;

And these, perhaps, maturer years,

Sincere advice of my compeers,

And due reflexions on the past

May totally reduce at last: 24

And in my bed, and when I stir,

I am not wanting to confer

Thus with myself, 'this thing is well—

By doing this I shall excell—

By aiming at some certain end   24

I shall be better with my friend—

Such a transaction was oblique,

Shall I then ever do the like?'

All this unto myself I say—

When idle with my pen I play: 25

This is amongst those faults I class't

But as of an inferiour cast;

Which if you will not freely own

As pardonable, be it known,

That all the vast poetic band,   25

Now, more than ever, is at hand,

And like the Pharisee and Scribe

We'll force you to embrace our tribe.

SATIRE V.

*He describes his journey from Rome to Brundusium, after the pattern of
Lucilius, who had given an account of a party of his to the same place. He likewise gives a narrative what laughable matters had occurred in that expedition;
amongst which the squabble between the two buffoons, Sarmentus and Messius,
obtain the first place.*

Arriv'd from all the pomp and din

Of Rome, Aricia took me in,

A guest but sorrily bestow'd;

But my companion on the road

Was Heliodorus, that fam'd Greek,

Who teaches youth the art to speak.

To * Appii-Forum thence we hied,
Where landlords sour and tars reside.
This journey which is but a day
For those that expedite their way,   10
Finding so many things to do
With idleness we split in two.
For them, that often choose to call,
The Appian way is best of all,
And here the water was so vile   15
I mortified my gut, the while
The company sat down to meat
And not without vexation eat.
    Now night was bringing on the shade,
And all the signs of heav'n display'd;   20
Then with the tars our slaves begun,
A spice of their vociferous fun,
Which soon was answered by the crew—
'Why here, you sorry knaves bring to—
You're cramming in the folks too fast,   25
Three hundred are enough—avast!'
Now while their money they demand,
And mule is fasten'd to a stand,
An hour elaps'd—the plaguy gnats,
And frogs, that crowd the fenny flats,   30
Drive off repose—the muleteer
And waterman combin'd to clear
Their pipes, and on the charms enlarg'd
Of their dear girls, with drink o'ercharg'd,
Till the tir'd muleteer began   35
To sleep—the lazy waterman
Tyed the mule's tackle to a stone,
And sent her out to graze alone!
Then snored upon his back—the day
Now sprung, and we had made no way.   40
Then one more hot-brain'd than the rest
Leapt out, and being first possest
From willows of a sturdy tool,
Bang'd head and back of man and mule;

* This is the place where the Jews, residing at Rome, met St. Paul. *Acts xxviii. v.15.*

Till the fourth * hour was more than past,   45
When we were set ashore at last.
Feronia, in thy marble vase
Each of us wash'd his hands and face,
And having din'd, three miles we creep
Beneath white Anxur's rocky steep.   50
Here both Maecenas, and the great
Cocceius, were to come in state,
As they ambassadors were sent,
On an affair of high event,
Us'd separate friends to reunite.—   55
Here, I disorder'd in my sight,
With my black salve my eyes besmear'd—
Maecenas during this appear'd,
Cocceius too, and Capito,
The most accomplish'd man I know,   60
And Antony's especial friend—
From hence our course we trav'lers bend,
And Fundi pass with much good will,
Where † Luscus was the Praetor still,
Not without laughing at the tribe   65
Attending on this crazy scribe,
His robe, and laticlave withal,
And pan of incense in his hall;
From thence to Formiae we roam,
Murena finding us an home,   70
And gen'rous Capito his cook;
Next day the brightest in the book
Arose, for Plotius, Varius came,
And Virgil of eternal name:
At Sinuessa these we met,   75
Of spirits so select a set,
Than which earth ne'er did bear or see,
More candid, or more dear to me.
Oh! what embraces all around,
What joy was at this meeting found;   8c

* They generally went by night from Forum Appi to Feronia, and arrived before
morning; but on account of the delay here mentioned, they did not get there till the
fourth hour after sun-rising, viz. at that time of the year eight o'Clock.

† A little proud magistrate of a petty place, taking upon him the state of the Praetor
who was Lord Mayor of Rome.

There's nothing I wou'd recommend
In pref'rence to a pleasant friend.
With lodging next, the place that's nigh
Campania's bridge did us supply.
Purveyors brought us wood and salt,   85
* For fear of suff'ring, on default:
From hence the mules their packs dispose
At Capua, ere the damps arose.
Maecenas goes to FIVES (as I
And Virgil on our couches lie)   90
For balls are bad things for the blind,
And those that are to coughs inclin'd.
Thence for Cocceius' seat we bear,
Where all good things abound, and where
The Caudian Inns are likewise built.—   95
     Now, muse, deliver if thou wilt,
In a few words the war, enrag'd
Sarmentus and Cicerrus wag'd,
And from what ancestors in pride
These heroes with each other vied: 100
Cicerrus of grand Oscian † race,
Sarmentus is not out of place,
On such illustrious pretence,
The gallant combat they commence:
Sarmentus first, 'you seem disturb'd,   105
Like a mad horse, that should be curb'd.'
We laugh'd, and Messius, ''Tis well said,'
Replied, and shook his furious head.
'O (says Sarmentus) what, if now
Your horn was extant on your brow,   110
Wou'd you atchieve—since ev'n thus maim'd
You have at such distortions aim'd?'
Now a most lamentable scar
Did Messius' grisled forehead mar;
Then pelting him with jests apace,   115
Upon his rubicund grimace,

* They were obliged to do this for all persons sent upon public business. Horace there-
ore availed himself of Maecenas his embassy.
     † The Osci was esteemed the meanest people in all Italy.

ATIRE v. 81 recommend] recommend, *1767*   88 ere] e'er *1767*

Where many a carbuncle and wart
Grew of the right Campanian sort;
'Pray for a dance, Sir, let me ask,
The Cyclops jig—you need no mask,   120
Nor can for buskins be concern'd.'—
To this Cicerrus much return'd.
Ask'd if his household Gods had got
The chain he vow'd shou'd be their lot,
That, tho' by trade a scribbling knave,   125
He was not less his lady's slave;
He kindly beg'd to know for why
He took it in his head to fly,
Since that for one so lank and spare,
A pound of bread was plenteous fare.   130
In short this humorous event,
Prolong'd our meal in merriment.

   To Beneventum thence next day,
Straight as a line, we made our way,
Where, while the meagre thrushes roast,   135
The flames nigh burnt our bustling host,
For thro' th'old kitchen widely spread,
Th'ascending flakes were making head:
Then trembling slaves you might have view'd,
Eager to have the fire subdued,   140
And guests, each greedy of his claim,
Snatching their supper from the flame.
From hence Apulia 'gan to show
The mountains I was born to know,
Which by * Atabulus are swept,   145
And whence we never shou'd have crept,
Unless Trivicum's little sheds
Had found us where to lay our heads,
But not without such clouds of smoke,
As did the very tears provoke,   150
The hearth within a certain house,
Burning both leaves and wet green boughs.

---

* A wind particularly noxious to Apulia.

123 got] got, *1767*   124 their] there *1767*

Miles twenty-four from hence we ran
Bowl'd in post-chariots, for our plan
Was at a place to make our stay,   155
Whose name in * verse we cannot say;
But 'tis describable when told,
By signs, for here the water's sold,
Water the cheapest thing elsewhere,
And here the worst—their bread is fair,   160
And good, so that upon the road
The trav'lers choose to take a load,
For full of grit Canusium sells
Her loaves, nor has she better wells:
Tho' Diomede of brave renown,   165
Chose this same place to build a town.
Here pensive Varius takes his leave
Of friends, that likewise weep and grieve.
      To Rubi next we were convey'd,
All tir'd to death, as we had made   170
A longer journey thro' bad ways,
More tedious for the rainy days.
The morning was a little fair,
But then the ways more dirty were,
As far as Barium's fishy coast—   175
To Gnatia from this place we post,
Which is a city that arose
With all the water-nymphs its foes:
But here they much diversion made,
When us they wanted to persuade,   180
That incense in their sacred shrine
† Melts without heating—I decline
All credit to the tale, the Jews
May think it genuine, if they choose.
For I then learnt the pow'rs above   185
Dwell in security and love;
Nor if a miracle be told
Of Nature, will it therefore hold

---

* *Equotutium*, which will not stand in an hexameter.
† The miracle of the liquefaction of St. Januarius's blood is such another.

The Gods have sent it from the sky
By their profound anxiety—   190
Brundusium, which at length we gain,
Ends the long journey, and the strain.

SATIRE VI.

He finds fault with the futile opinion of the Romans, in regard to Nobility,
which they estimated by antiquity of family, rather than merit, and did not will-
ingly admit any one to the great offices of state without that qualification. That
no one could envy him the friendship of Maecenas, upon the same principle they
envied the post of Tribune, since that was not a matter of chance, but obtained
by the recommendation of virtue. And finally, he demonstrates that his lot in pri-
vate life, is far happier than it could be in the magistracy.

Tho' of the Lydians, that came o'er
To settle on th'Etrurian shore,
Not one is of more rank than you,
And tho' your sire and grandsire too,
Reckon'd on either parent's side,   5
Did o'er such mighty hosts preside;
Yet, friend, the manners of the great
In this you do not imitate,
At low-born men to toss the nose,
Like me who from a free'd-man rose,   10
Because you will not grant that birth,
Tho' mean, can cancel real worth.
  This is a truth that you maintain,
That long before the servile reign,
And pow'r of Tullius, many a one,   15
That merely from themselves begun,
Have both been held of good repute,
And the first honours gain'd to boot:
Whereas Laevinus, tho' the seed
Of great Poplicola, who freed   20
The Romans from proud Tarquin's sway,
Was not a jot the more in play,

SATIRE vi. 10 rose,] rose. *1767*   22 play,] play. *1767*

Ev'n with that judge, so well you know,
The mob, who oftentimes bestow
Their honours on a worthless name,   25
And are the dupes of vulgar fame,
Amazed at titles and a bust—
But how shall we ourselves adjust,
Rais'd from all vulgar thoughts so high?
For granting that the pop'lar cry,   30
Had rais'd Laevinus to the chair,
Rather than placed new Decius there,
Or granted that the Appian frown,
Had from the senate turn'd me down
As not of parents nobly born: 35
(And well I had deserv'd his scorn,
While not content in my own dress)
Yet, after all, we must confess,
Glory's gilt chariot drags along
The gen'rous, as the vulgar throng.   40
What profit, Tullius, wou'd you have
Shou'd you resume your laticlave;
And be a tribune, in that state
The public envy, public hate
Was greater than they could have been   45
In your reserv'd domestic scene.
For soon as an ambitious sot
Has on his legs black buskins got,
With purple robe upon his back,
Such sounds as these his ear attack—   50
'Who's that, and who's his father, speak?'
As if a fellow shou'd be weak,
Like Barrus, whose desire and plan,
Is to be held a pretty man:
That he may tempt the ladies fair,   ⎫   55
Still to enquire with anxious care,   ⎬
What face, leg, foot, what teeth, and hair? ⎭
So he, that promises and swears
That Rome, and all the world's affairs,
That Italy, the public fanes,   60
Shall be protected by his pains,

; born:] born. *1767*   47 sot] sot, *1767*

Drives all mankind to be concern'd,
'Who's this, the man that is *return'd*!
What is his father? was the dame
That bore him of a virtuous fame?
Shall Syrus, you, or Dama's heir,
Or Dionysius' offspring dare,
From the TARPEIAN, men of Rome
Throw down, or unto Cadmus * doom?'
My colleague Novius tho' must sit
One step behind me, as is fit,
For he was of my father's class—
'But do you therefore think to pass,
As Paulus or Messala may—
But here your colleague will huzza;
As if three funerals in the street,
Should with two hundred waggons meet,
And horns and trumpets too outvie,
His gift our choice to justify.'
    Now I return to my own case,
By all still reckon'd in disgrace;
Born of a free'd-man is their scorn,
And I am of a † free'd-man born—
And this, Maecenas, now they do,
Because I am a guest with you;
This too some years ago they said,
When me the Roman band obey'd.
The first is diff'rent from the last,
Because the honour that is past,
No man can envy in degree,
As that I am so well with thee,
So cautious to select such friends,
As unambitious worth commends.
I cannot think it merely chance,
That did me to this rank advance;

* The public executioner.
† This was very far from being a scandal, strictly speaking, as the slaves did not obtai[n]
their freedom, but by great and frequent instances of honesty and fidelity.

69 doom?] doom *1767*   70 colleague Novius] colleague—Nevius *1767*
71 is] if *1767*

For it was not a lucky throw,
But Virgil, Varius, long ago;
Those flow'rs of friendship were the cause,
By fairly saying what I was.
When first into your presence led,   100
Some interrupted words I said;
For stiffled by an aukward shame,
Few words in broken accents came.
I did not at that time aspire,
To be the son of some great sire,   105
Nor drawn by Satureian steeds,
To traverse thro' my native meads;
But, what indeed I was, report—
You, as your custom is, was short
In what you answered—I retir'd;   110
And ere the year was quite expir'd,
You call'd me to your gates again,
And bade me rank amongst your train.
Tis a great honour I confess,
That I could have so much address,   115
With such a person to find grace,
Who picks the best, and spurns the base,
Preferring moral men, and sage,
To those of glorious parentage.
    But if my nature has a spice,   120
Of here and there a little vice,
And otherwise is quite direct;
(As if a critic should detect,
In some fair body certain flaws)
Yet if the crimes against the laws,   125
Or avarice or dirty ways,
No man can urge to my dispraise;
If with clean hands and conscience clear, ⎫
(That I may for myself appear)   ⎬
I live, and to my friends am dear: ⎭   130
All this was from my father's hand,
Who poor, and with a little land,
Yet cou'd not bear to have me brought
To the low school, that Flavius taught;

Where hulking lads in clumsy gaite,   13

Bearing their satchel and their slate,

Sprung from tall soldiers, to a day

Went duly with their quarter's pay;

But dar'd to trust his boy of parts

At Rome, to learn those lib'ral arts,   14

Which every senator, or knight,

Prescribes his children—at the sight

Of all my slaves, and decent gown,

In such a great and populous town,

They might have thought that all this show,   14

Did from some patrimony flow.

Himself the wariest guard and spy,

Still to my masters had an eye:

In short, he kept me chaste and free,   ⎫

(Which is fair virtue's first degree)   ⎬   15

Both from all guilt, and obloquy.   ⎭

Nor did he for his own part care

About the blame, that he might bear,

Shou'd I be forc'd to get my bread

As auctioneer, or even be sped   15

Like him upon the tax to go,

Nor had I murmur'd, were it so.

For this upon the whole you see,   ⎫

More praise from all to him shou'd be,   ⎬

And far more gratitude from me.   ⎭   16

As long as I've my wits intire,

I can't repent of such a sire.

Wherefore I shall not act like some,

Who did not from good parents come,

And plead the fault was not their own—   16

Far wide of all such useless moan

Are both my language and my heart;

For could we from our years depart,

And reach the past of life, and choose

Our parents by ambitious views,   17

Content with mine, I'd not desire

Those, that to higher posts aspire.

For this, by all the revel rout,

I shou'd be deem'd as mad, no doubt;

But you, perhaps, wou'd hold me *sane*, ⎫   175
That from a burthen I refrain,   ⎬
Which I'm unable to sustain.   ⎭
For in that case, without debate
Things must be had in greater state,
More ceremonies than before,   180
With two or three companions more,
For fear I shou'd at home remain,
Or go abroad without a train.
Men slaves, with coaches and a *stand*
Of horses too, I must command.   185
Now can I go serene and cool,
More pleasant on my bob-tail mule,
E'en to Tarentum, if it suit,
With cloak-bag, and myself to boot.
Yet none alive, in this respect,   190
Will stingyness to me object;
In such as Tullius, is thy due,
When five slaves only follow you,
A mighty praetor, as you are,
With wine, and necessary jar.   195
Sage senator, on this account,
Thee, and ten thousand I surmount.
Where'er I will is in my pow'r
To walk, and cheapen greens and flow'r.
The Circus, where they trick and thieve,   200
And Forum I frequent at eve.
The temples duly I attend,
Then homewards make my journey's end;
And take my supper at my ease,
Of onions, pancakes, or of pease.   205
Three slaves the supper serve—at hand
Two large mugs, and a tumbler stand
Upon a marble slab, with ew'r
And bowl, and cruet mean and poor.
I go to sleep, without dismay,   210
That I must rise betimes next day,
And in my rambles stand the shock
Of Marsya's phiz, who tho' a block,

go alive,] alive *1767*

Still signifies with hideous stare,
That he cannot young Novius bear.   21

To the fourth hour I lay me down,
Then take a walk about the town;
Or my still privacy delight
By reading, or by what I write.
Then I take oil—but better chuse,   220
Then Natta robs the lamps to use.
But when the sun with fiercer beam   ⎫
Warns me to seek the cooling stream,   ⎬
I foil the dog-star's heat, and swim.   ⎭
Next after dining in such wise,   225
As with an appetite to rise;
I lounge at home—such are the days
Of men, whom no ambition sways.
With these few comforts I console
Myself, more happy on the whole,   230
Than if my sire and grandsire both,
Had fairly took the Questor's oath.

SATIRE VII.

*He describes a squabble between Rupilius, sirnamed * King, with one Persius a Grecian of mean account.*

How Persius, ev'n that mongrel thing,
Aveng'd himself against one King,
Who by Octavius was proscrib'd,
He had such spite and gall imbib'd,
I make no doubt but long ago,   5
All Barbers and their patients know.
This Persius was compell'd to be
On business at Clazomenae,
Because his bulk of wealth was there,
With King too a perplex'd affair.   10
This man was harsh, and of such hate,
That even King's was not so great,

* This is one of the meanest productions in all Horace, and seems to have been written for the sake of a sorry pun upon the word REX.

Full of all confidence and vain,
And still in such abusive strain,
That he cou'd distance and out do,   15
The Barri and Sisennae too.
    But now return we to this King,
When they cou'd to no issue bring
Their contest, (for when war breaks out,
It's longer, as the men are stout;   20
Thus to such lengths did Priam's son
And spirited Achilles run,
That their intolerable rage,
Cou'd nought but death itself assuage.
And this too was the very cause,   25
Since each deserv'd so great applause;
And if there should begin a fight
'Twixt heroes of unequal might,
The worst by presents must recede,
As Glaucus did by Diomede)   30
When Brutus was the praetor chose
Of Asia, these intrepid foes
Like * Bacchius with Bithus match'd,
Hasted to have th'affair dispatch'd.
With vehemence they both proceed,   35
And were a curious sight indeed:
Persius the first the case expounds,
Till laughter from all sides rebounds;
He praises Brutus and his band,
'The sun of Asia for command,'   40
And all that follow'd him to fight,
He calls his satellites of light,
Except this King, who all things mars,
Curs'd as the Dog amongst the stars.
Made of precipitance and mud,   45
He rush'd on like a wintry flood;
The King then on his running on,
Wou'd have attack'd him pro and con,

* A pair of gladiators.

ATIRE vii. 20 It's] Its *1767*   34 dispatch'd.] dispatch'd, *1767*

According to the cant express
Of clowns, who're sent the vines to dress,   5
For all the passengers gave out,
When he cried cuckold, thief, or lout—
But this same Grecian, dipt in gall
From Italy, began to bawl—
'By all th'immortal Gods, O Brute,
To thee I make my fervent suit,
Thou that are wont all kings to kill,
Use this King also as you will,
For take my word, it is the task
Of him that bears both *ax* and *mask*.'   6

SATIRE VIII.

He introduces the god Priapus, keeper of the gardens, complaining of the witche
Canidia and Sagana, and describing what was done by them in secret.

Cut from the bastard-fig of yore,
A lumpish useless form I bore,
When the pos'd joiner was in doubt,
What in the end I shou'd turn out,
A god, or chipping-block—at last
My lot was for Priapus cast.
Hence as a pow'r divine, I stand
To scare the thieves and birds—my hand
The former checks, but for the crows
A reed is fix'd above my nose,   1
Which still forbids them to parade
In these fine gardens, newly made.
Here sometime since the fellow-slave,
Brought out dead corpses to the grave,
From all their narrow cells thrown out,   1
And in vile coffins borne about.
This was the common burying place,
For wretches of Plebeian race,
Where *fool* Pantolabus they bore,
And Nomentanus rakes no more.   2

53 Grecian, . . . gall] Grecian . . . gall, *1767*   54 Italy,] Italy *1767*

A pillar here inscrib'd, assign'd
A thousand feet in front—behind
Three hundred tow'rds the fields adjoin'd;
A fixt memorial, to assert
It could not to the heir revert.   25
But now so good th'Esquilian air,
That one may like a lodging there,
And on a sunny terras stalk,
Where grieved spectators us'd to walk,
And view with lamentable groans,   30
The place deform'd with human bones.
Tho' both the thieves and ev'ry brute,
That us'd to haunt this place to boot,
Gave me not half the plague and care,
As these old hags that here repair,   35
And with their magic drugs and charms
Turn people's brains—by no alarms
These can I quell or drive away,
When the vague beauteous moon-beams play.
But that both bones they will collect,   40
And simples of a curs'd effect.
    I saw Canidia in black gown
Succinct, and walking up and down
With naked feet, dishevell'd hair,
And howling to the midnight air;   45
With Sagana that elder scold—
They both were ghastly to behold.
Then they began with nails to scratch
The earth, and with their teeth dispatch
A black ewe-lamb alive and crude,   50
His blood into a ditch they spew'd,
That so they might the ghosts compel,
To give them answers out of hell.
A woollen effigy they bring,
And one of wax—the former thing   55
Was largest, and in act express,
As if 'twas punishing the less.
The waxen was in suppliant mood,
As bound to perish on the rood.

SATIRE viii. 41 effect.] effect, *1767*

This hag did Hecate invoke,   60
That fell Tisiphone bespoke;
While serpents and infernal curs,
And moon behind the sepulchres
You might have seen to blush for shame,
Lest she, forsooth, should bear the blame.   65
Now if one lie defile my tongue,
May all the crows my form bedung!
Why should I mention every fact,
And tell each circumstance exact?
How Sagana to a spectre speaks,   70
The one by grumbling, one by shrieks,
And how in earth, with wolf's grim beard,
They teeth of spotted snake interr'd.
How from the image made of wax,
A rousing fire awakes and cracks.   75
How at these furies I was shock'd,
But not intirely foil'd and mock'd;
For as a bladder sounds, when broke,
I from my fig-posteriors spoke.
They scar'd, into the city hied,   80
With laughter then you might have died.
Canidia's artificial bones
For teeth, came tumbling on the stones:
And what the jest shou'd not abate,
Old Sagana soon lost her tete,   85
With magic herbs upon the ground,
And bracelet from her arm unbound.

SATIRE IX.

He describes the impertinence and persevering garrulity of a certain person whom he happened on by chance.

A saunt'ring on the *sacred way*,
(As is my custom every day)
Upon some trivial thing intent,
With all my thoughts engag'd, I went.

When, lo! a chap, whom by his name   5
I barely knew, abruptly came,
And grasping hard my hand in his,
'How does the dearest man, that is?'
'The times consider'd, I can *do*,
With my best wishes, Sir, for you.'   10
But finding that he still kept on,
I ask'd him, what he was upon?
He answer'd, 'Sir, you must know ME,
A scholar of the first degree.'—
I told him on that very score,   15
He must of me be priz'd the more.
Now in the last distress my pace
I mend, and sometime for a space
Stand still—and whisper to my lad,
Sweating from head to foot, like-mad: 20
O blest Bollanus! in my heart
I said, ev'n blockhead as thou art!
Still he went on my ears to greet,
'A noble town! a glorious street!'
Whatever came into his head;   25
But when he found I nothing said,
Says he, 'I know you are in pain
To get away, 'tis very plain.
But you are ne'er the near, good friend!
I'll still keep up, and still attend—   30
And pray, Sir, which way is your route?'
—'You need not go so much about.
It is upon a man to wait,
You do not know at any rate,
Across the Tiber, and as far   35
Almost, as Caesar's gardens are.'
'Brisk, and quite disengaged, I'll cleave
Unto your honour, by your leave.'
Here brought to such a sorry pass,
I hang my ears, like some poor ass,   40
Whose grudging spirit cannot bear
A heavier burthen, than is fair.
Again his tongue began to run,
'Me, if you knew, you wou'd not shun,

Nor wou'd ev'n * Viscus *close ally*,   45
Or Varius be more dear than I.
For who's a better bard than me,
Or writes so fast, or flows so free?
Who dances with an easier grace?
Then for your treble and your base,   50
I raise with voice so tun'd to please,
The envy of Hermogenes.'—
   Here was a respite, to thrust in
A word or two—'Have *you* no kin,
Are you no mother's darling hope,   55
Who would not wish you to elope?'—
'—No not a soul—I've buried all.'—
Thrice blessed in their funeral.
Alas! now I alone survive,
Dispatch and havock me alive.   60
For now the hour is come, foretold
By Sabine sorceress of old,
When for my fate her urn she shook—
'This child (I read it in his look)
Nor poison, nor the hostile spear,   65
Nor pleurisy, nor cough need fear—
Nor shall the gout affect his brain;
Born by a babbler to be slain;
Such he'll avoid, if he is sage,
Shou'd he but live, and come of age.'—   70
   To Vesta's now (one fourth of day
Quite gone and spent) we made our way.
And he, by a most lucky chance,
Was call'd upon recognizance,
Which if he shou'd neglect to do,   75
An instant non-suit must ensue.
'Step in (says he) my dearest bard,
If you retain the least regard.'—
''Sdeath! Sir, I scarce can stand or go,
And hurry to the place, you know—   80

* There is a very pleasant equivocation in the proper name *Viscus*, which likewise signifies *bird-lime*.

SATIRE ix. 56 elope?] elope! *1767*

Nor am I vers'd in civil law.'
Says he, 'Now whether to withdraw
From you, or to desert my cause,
Is that on which I needs must pause.'—
'Me, Sir, I beg you would forbear'—   85
'I cannot do it, Sir, I swear.'—
Then he began to take the lead;
I (for no parley can succeed
Against the victor) creep behind.
'Maecenas, how is he inclin'd?'   90
Cries he, continuing his prate—
'Few men with him are intimate;
A man of excellent good sense,
No one has greater eminence,
By fairly pushing of success.—   95
—Here is your man, whose clean address
Cou'd much assist you, hand and heart,
And finely play an underpart;
Of all the rest you'd soon dispose.'—
—'We are not on such terms as those;   100
Nor is there any house in Rome
More free from that, which you presume.
My circumstance is not concern'd,
Tho' one's more rich, and one's more learn'd,
All have their special ranks and cares.'—   105
—'You tell me marvellous affairs,
Scarce credible!'—''Tis even so.'—
—'Now you inflame me more to know,
And to be near him;' —'To desire
A thing from him is to acquire;   110
Such is your merit, 'twill be done,
And he is easy to be won;
Wherefore he's apt to keep on guard,
And make his first approaches hard.'—
—'I'll not be wanting to my plan,   115
But bribe his servants, man by man.
And if I am repuls'd to-day—
I'll not desist—I'll mark his way,

I will for all occasions wait,
I'll see his honour home in state.   120
The lot of human life is such,
Nought's done but by endeavouring much.'—
      Thus while he rattled without end,
Aristius Fuscus, my dear friend,
One who full well this fellow knew,   125
Came up and met us—how do you do,
And whither bound, each ask'd and told—
I twitch his sleeve, and strive to hold
His arms reluctant—from this scrape,
Nodding and winking to escape.   130
He laugh'd, and scrupled by the dint
Of ill-tim'd jest to take the hint—
I, with my vitals all inflam'd,
Cry 'sure you lately something nam'd,
That you in secret had for me'—   135
'O! I remember it (says he)
But I a fitter time shall choose,
'Tis a great sabbath with the Jews,
When surely you wou'd not offend'—
'I'm not so scrupulous, dear friend.'   140
'But pardon him of weaker turn,
One of the many—we'll adjourn—
Another day—and I'll advise'—
(O that so black a sun shou'd rise!)
Away the traitor runs for life,   145
And leaves my throat beneath the knife—
      By happiest chance the plaintiff came,
And 'where away, thou son of shame?'
He roar'd aloud—then me addrest—
'Sir, will you witness this arrest.'—   150
I yield—he's hurried to the hall—
Both parties make a grievous bawl—
The concourse on all sides is great—
Thus Phoebus stav'd his poet's fate.

127 whither] whether *1767*   148 shame?] shame; *1767*

SATIRE X.

This satire is an answer to those who had taken offence at the Fourth, in which he finds fault with the verses of Lucilius;—and he renders a reason for such reprehension, and shews it to be just.

Well, I did say Lucilius penn'd
Lame verses—who's so much his friend,
And fawning dupe, to praise amiss,
As not at least to grant me this?
But that he smartly lash'd the age,   5
I praise him in the self-same page.
Yet, tho' I this one truth attest,
I cannot grant you all the rest.
For so I might admire each mime,
Laberius wrote, as true sublime.   10
Wherefore 'tis not enough to win
The hearer's ear, and make him grin,
(Tho' this is merit in degree)
But that the period may run free,
Nor with vain words the ear be tir'd—   15
There is a brevity requir'd.
The stile too sometimes shou'd of right
Be grave, and often arch and light,
As acting now the poet's part,
And now the pleader to the heart;   20
And sometime lower'd, to acquit
The part of a familiar wit,
Who will his strength and skill neglect,
The more to heighten the effect.
By satire in a pleasant vein,   25
A weighty point we oft'ner gain,
Than talking in severer strain.
The writers of the Comic cast,
Who wrote their plays some ages past,
Their works on this foundation rear,   30
And all are imitable here.
But these Hermogenes the beau,
And ape Demetrius did not know,

Which last, not learning better things,
Still Calvus and Catullus sings.—
    But this Lucilius cou'd atchieve
A mighty feat, and interweave
His Latin with a deal of Greek.—
O ye late-learn'd, and still to seek—
To think ought wonderful or hard,   40
Performed ev'n by the Rhodian bard!—
But yet, they cry, the stile combin'd
Of diff'rent tongues is more refin'd;
As Chian wine is always best,
Well mixt with the Falernian zest.   45
    Now let me fairly ask your muse,
If for your subject you shou'd choose
Petillus his intangled case,
Wou'd you forget your native place
And Roman sire, to inter-lard   50
Words taken from a foreign bard?
And ape the Canusinian folk,
Where only broken Latin's spoke,
Tho' Pedius and Corvinus sweat
With zeal, and a great pattern set.   55
    To me one time about to speak,
And write my verses all in Greek
Tho' born upon th'Italian coast,
At midnight Romulus his ghost
Appear'd, the hour that dreams are true,   60
My scheme forbidding to pursue:
'The plan wou'd be as wise and good,
To carry timber to the wood,
As to augment th'enormous throng
Of Grecian books in prose and song.'   65
While puff't Alpinus blows his blast,
And butchers Memnon in bombast,
Or * Rhine with muddy head displays,
I sport with these satiric lays;

* A citation from Alpinus himself.

SATIRE x. 57 Greek] Greek, *1767*   58 coast,] coast *1767*

Which nor in Phoebus' temple dare   70
Be shewn, if Tarpa shou'd be there,
Nor in the play-house give delight,
Nor have a run from night to night.
    You, O Fundanius! far surpass
All moderns of the comic class,   75
While you th'arch dialogue repeat,
How Davus and the doxy cheat
That old huncks Chremes—Pollio sings
In lively verse the deeds of kings;
Varius is masterly and strong,   80
Unrival'd in th'heroic song; *
While all the Muses of the field,
The delicate and pleasant yield
To Virgil—writings of this strain,
Which Varro cou'd attempt in vain,   85
And certain others, I pretend
In some degree to recommend,
But of inferior rank in Rome
To him, th' † original, from whom
I shall not dare to pluck the bays,   90
That crown his head with so much praise.—
    But I objected that his song,
Flow'd oft so muddily along,
That the more part of what he said
Shou'd rather be eras'd, than read.   95
Well! well! do you so great a clerk,
No fault in Homer's self remark?
Does not Lucilius revise
In wagg'ry Accius' comedies?
And laugh at Ennius as too free,   100
With his poetic gravity,
When ev'n his noble self he names
No better, than the men he blames?—
    What in like manner can impede
But I, who this Lucilius read,   105
May make enquiry, as I go,
Which was the real cause, to know,

* Virgil had not then published the Aeneid.
† Lucilius.

His subject's nature, or his own,
That he no better skill has shown,
Nor lets his numbers smoother glide,   1
Than if a man shou'd take a pride
The measure with six feet to close,
And lines by hundreds to compose,
Before he sits him down to eat,
And then as many after meat.   1
Such was the * Tuscan poet's trade,
With genius fierce as a cascade,
Whose works gave fuel for the fire,
Upon his own funereal pyre.
    But grant Lucilius form'd to write,   1
At once the hum'rous and polite,
More learn'd than Ennius every piece,
The sire of verse unknown to Greece,
And more correct in ev'ry page,
Than poets of the earlier age—   1
Yet he (continued to our day)
Much from himself had par'd away,
And prun'd off every useless shoot,
On which was neither song nor fruit;
And in the tuning of his wit,   1
Had often scratch'd his head, and bit   }
His nails, in an extatic fit.
    You that wou'd write a taking strain,
And worthy to be read again,
Oft turn your † style in act to blot,   1
Nor care if crouds admire, or not,
Content with readers more select—
What, wou'd you foolishly affect,
To have your verses taught in schools,
To shew poor boys the grammar-rules?   1
Not I—for whom it will suffice,
If knights allow my works the prize;

* Cassius (not Severus) but another poet of that name.
    † The stylus had one end like a graver's needle, and the other flat like a spatula, wi
the former they wrote upon wax, and blotted out with the latter.

138 What,] What *1767*

As in contempt of all the rest,
The hiss'd * Arbuscula profess'd.
Me shall the gnat Pantilius fret,   145
Or shall I feel a thought's regret,
That by Demetrius I am spurn'd,
As soon as e'er my back is turn'd?
Or that Hermogenes's friend,
Weak Fannius loves to discommend—   150
May Plotius, Varius, and the Knight
Of Tuscany, praise what I write!
And Virgil, Valgius, and that best
Of men Octavius, with the rest;
And Fuscus I cou'd wish indeed,   155
And either Viscus wou'd accede!
And here with no ambitious view,
O Pollio! I cou'd mention you,
Messala, and his brother too;
On Servius, Bibulus insist,   160
And candid Furnius in my list:
With many more, whom learn'd and dear,
I wittingly insert not here.
These only, and the like of these,
I do desire my works shou'd please,   165
Such as they are, and shall be griev'd,
If my fond hope shou'd be deceiv'd.
Avaunt Demetrius, and the fool
Tigellius to the singing-school,
There snivel 'midst your female tribe—   170
Ho! quick, my boy, these lines transcribe.

* An actress.

---

48 turn'd?] turn'd. *1767*   152 write!] write? *1767*

THE
SECOND BOOK
OF THE
SATIRES OF HORACE

SATIRE I.

He sets forth the advice given him by Trebatius, in respect to writing the atchievements of Augustus, rather than Satires, and gives his reasons why he cannot follow it.

'There are to whom my lines appear
Far too satiric and severe,
As driving things too great a length—
Others conceive there is no strength
In any thing I sing or say,
And that a thousand lines a day
May be spun out, if such as mine—
Trebatius, what do you opine?'—
'Be quiet'—'you advise, I see,
That I shou'd leave off poetry'—
'Aye'—'may I make a sorry end,
If you are not my worthiest friend,
But then I cannot rest, but start
A' nights'—'why, if your sleep depart,
Good oiling is the best advice,
* And then to swim cross Tiber thrice,
Or take strong liquor in your head,
Some hours before you go to bed.
But if so great an itch to write
Infect you—stand forth to recite

* There is a passage in Cicero which mentions Trebatius as extravagantly fond of swimming; his advice to Horace is therefore very natural.

SATIRE i. 13 A' nights] A nights *1767*

Augustus an unconquer'd Lord,
Sure to acquire a vast reward'—
'Old boy—tho' fervent be my zeal,
Yet I inferior skill must feel;
Nor can a common pen presume   25
To draw the troops, which horrors plume,
And Gauls from shiver'd darts that bleed,
And Parthian dying off his steed.'
—'Yet you might paint him just and brave,
The character Lucilius gave   30
To Scipio, and was therefore wise'—
'I'll not be hindmost for the prize,
Cou'd I bring things to have a face:
Unless in proper time and place
The words of Horace will not speed,   35
To make a mighty chief give heed,
Who like a horse, when strok'd too hard
Will kick, at all times on his guard.'—
'Yet better this—than to defame   ⎫
Pantolabus of merry name,   ⎬   40
And Nomentanus, son of shame;   ⎭
While all men fear you and detest,
Ev'n those, not yet the public jest.'—
    'What shall I do? the dance is led
By brisk Milonius, when his head   45
Is hot, and all the lights augment;
Castor with horses is content,
But he that sprung from the same shell,
Prefers to box, or wrestle well,
For many men of many minds—   50
My spirit consolation finds
To scribble verses, on the plan
Lucilius chose, a better man
Than you or I can boast to be,
Whether in genius or degree.   55
He, as to faithful friends, he chose,
Did to his books his mind disclose,
And this was his amusement still,
If his affairs went well or ill.

7 darts] darts, *1767*   49 well,] well. *1767*

Whence the whole tenor of his days,
His own descriptive page displays,
As if, enjoy'd or undergone,
His life were in a picture drawn.
Him follow I—no matter whom
You're pleased to call me here in Rome,
Lucanian, or Apulian wight,
For all Venusium has a right
The borders of them both to plough;
A race (as old records allow)
Were sent, and this same country held,
What time the Sabines were expell'd,
To such intent, that station'd here,
They might keep guard on this frontier,
If an Apulian disobey'd,
Or fierce Lucanian shou'd invade.
　　But this same pointed style of mine,
Shall not hurt any by design,
And like a scabbard-loving sword,
Mere personal defence afford;
For why shou'd I my weapon draw,
Secure from knaves against the law!
O sire and sov'reign Jove on high,
Grant this my steel in rust may lie,
Nor any person make a breach,
Upon the peace I love and teach!
But he, who such a deed shall dare,
(I give due warning to forbear)
Shall rue, and be a song and jest
Thro' all the city in request.—
　　If Cervius you to wrath inflame,
He threats to take the law—the dame,
Albucius keeps, with poison fights:
Judge Turius all his foes affrights,
Who can such damages denounce—
Thus how all creatures crack and bounce
Against their foes with all their force,
As nature orders in her course,

65 pleased] please *1767*

Observe with me—The wolf with fangs,
The bull with horns will give you pangs,
Whence but by instinct?—to the care   100
Of rakish Scaeva, who is heir,
Shou'd you his long-liv'd mother lend,
His pious hand will not offend.
Strange! but upon the very plan,   ⎫
That wolves will never kick a man,   ⎬   105
Nor bullock bite you, if he can: ⎭
He'll only take th'old lady off
With honey'd hemlock for her cough.
But to make short with our debate,
Whether a tranquil age await,   110
Or death already be my doom,
Poor, wealthy, shou'd I live in Rome,
Or be expell'd for God knows what,
Whate'er the colour of my lot,
I'll still write on'—'O youth! I fear,   115
You cannot long continue here,
But that some favourite bustling slave
Of state, will send you to your grave.'—
   'What if the bold Lucilius durst,
To make these kind of verses first,   120
And all that borrow'd skin to bare,
Which make th'external man seem fair,
Tho' foul within—Did Laelius blame,
Or who from Afric won his name!
Griev'd they at what Metellus hurt,   125
Or Lupus tumbled in the dirt?
But he cou'd at the great ones gibe,
And lash the people tribe by tribe;
As he profess'd to favour none,
But Virtue and her friends alone.   130
With him when Scipio brave and great,
And Laelius gentle and sedate,
Retir'd into the rural scene,
[They] went to sport upon the green,
And strip'd them of their robes, and toil'd   135
At tennis, till the sallad boil'd.

26 dirt?] dirt. *1767*   134 They] And *1767*

Whate'er I am, tho' something worse
Than him in genius and in purse,
Envy must own, till she be griev'd,
That with the great I am receiv'd,   140
And aiming with the file to deal,
Will break her teeth against the steel,
Unless learn'd Sir, you should dissent'—
   'No, on the whole I am content.
But that you may be upon guard,   145
And lest you push your fun too hard,
Thro' inexperience in the laws,
You must observe there is a clause,
"If any man bad verse devise,
His neighbour's fame to scandalize,   150
He may be cast—an action lies." '—
'Granted—bad verse—but if my pen
Shou'd only write good verse—what then?
Shou'd a man send such lines abroad,
Judicious Caesar will applaud,   155
And shou'd he bring a wretch to shame,
Himself the while exempt from blame?'—
'The cause will drop—the judges scoff—
And you may decently walk off.'

SATIRE II.

Under the person of Ofellus he inveighs against persons given to luxury: and a
he recounts the inconveniencies that attend this high way of living, so he like
wise enumerates the benefits which are in a moderate and frugal diet.

What and how great it is to be
A pattern of oeconomy;
(Nor is this doctrine fairly mine,
But what Ofellus wou'd injoin,
A rustic without learning taught,
And wise by downright strength of thought)
Learn, my good friends, while I debate,
But not amongst a glare of plate,

When the maz'd eye is at a loss,
And mind mis-judges, dup'd by gloss,   10
But here, while fasting, let us weigh—
Why so?—I'll tell you, if I may—
    A judge corrupted with a fee,
Cannot the truth so clearly see;
If after hunting of the hare,   15
Or gall'd by some unruly mare,
Or Roman * *Manual* make you weak,
As you are us'd to † play the Greek,
Or while the rapid ball recoils,
The heat of contest cheat your toils,   20
Or if your pleasure is the quoit,
You smite the air in that exploit;
When exercise has cur'd your squeam,
And drougth and hunger are extream,
Then let me see your scorn plain fare,   25
Nor for the best Falernian care,
Unless there's honey in the wine—
Your butler is gone out to dine,
And the tempestuous ocean saves
The fish, by his black wintry waves,   30
Why then a bit of bread and cheese,
The barking stomach will appease.
From whence do you think this wisdom's gain'd?
Whence this philosophy obtain'd?
Not the rich flavour gives delight,   35
The relish is your appetite;
Seek, and you'll not be at a loss
By downright exercise for sauce;
Nor fowls that fly, nor fish that swim,
Can give the least content to him,   40
Who's bloated with th'effects of vice—
    Yet I might fail, shou'd I intice
Your palate to an humble chick,
A peacock ent'ring in the nick,

---

* The manual exercise of the sword and spear.
† To be effeminate.

ATIRE ii. 37 loss] loss, *1767*

Struck by appearance, you regale   4
Upon th'idea of his tail;
Scarce bird! that cost the lord knows what,
As if that signified a jot.
What, do you eat those gaudy dies,
Which you so much extol and prize?   5
And is the bird as much possess'd
Of beauty, when 'tis pluck'd and dress'd?
Yet as there is no odds betwixt
Their several tastes, the truth is fix'd,
That you're deceiv'd by outward shew—   5
Yet grant in this it were not so—
By what conjecture can you dive,
Whether this pike that gapes alive,
Was in main ocean trepann'd
Or Tiber, and was thrown to land   6
Between the bridges, or the head
From whence the Tuscan river's fed—
You ninny, you are apt to praise
A mullet that full three pound weighs,
Which you must mangle, as a dupe   6
To stupid custom in your soupe.
I see appearance is your guide;
Why are the pikes so much decried?
Because they're of a longer sort,
And mullets naturally short.
An appetite with hunger keen,
Will seldom loath the coarse and clean.—
    O cou'd I see a banging fish,
Extended in a swinging dish,
A rav'nous glutton cries aloud,
Whose maw might make a harpy proud!
But, O ye blasts! that taint the air,
Come blow upon their luscious fare;
Tho' there's no mighty need of you,
Since both the boar and turbot too,
First taken are offence to them,
Whose stomach now o'ercharg'd with phlegm

49 What,] What *1767*   50 prize?] prize, *1767*   52 dress'd?] dress'd. *1767*

Prefer the rising food to curb,
The turnip, and the acid herb.
Yet still at sumptuous boards we see   85
Some traits of old oeconomy;
Ev'n to this day eggs first appear,
And the black olives in the rear—
But now the table of the * Cry'r,
Did most notoriously aspire,   90
Exhibiting a sturgeon whole—
Had sea no turbot, nor a sole?
The turbot late was undistress'd,
And safe the stork within her nest,
Until th'exploded Praetor taught,   95
That they might be devour'd and caught;
Wherefore if any fool shou'd boast,
That cormorants were good to roast,
So fond of lies, the Roman youth
Wou'd all receive it as a truth.   100
    But if Ofellus we retain   ⎫
As judge, there's difference again, ⎬
Betwixt the SORDID and the PLAIN.   ⎭
For pomp and pride in vain you shun,
If you to downright meanness run.   105
Avidienus, whom they call
A cur, in justice after all,
Eats olives, which have fairly stood
Five years, and cornels of the wood,
And even spares his wine to pour   110
Into the cup, till chang'd and sour:
Then for his oil, you cannot bear
The scent (tho' 'tis some great affair
He celebrates in white array,
His birth, perhaps, or wedding-day)   115
By his own hand it is distill'd,
From horn that holds two pounds when fill'd,
Upon the cabbage—but for *tart*   ⎫
He is no niggard, and can part   ⎬
From vinegar with all his heart!   ⎭   120

* Gallonius, an infamous gutler, of whom see *Cic. lib. ii. de finibus.*

What food then shall a wise man use,
And which of these examples choose!
For difficulties press around,
And here's the wolf, and there's the hound.
He shall be neat who does not sin   120
In nastiness, and keeps within
Due bounds, no wretch on either side,
Who will not imitate the pride
Of old Albucius, who raves,
Whene'er he's tasking of his slaves—   130
Nor will he bear for want of thought,
That greasy water shou'd be brought,
As noodle Naevius serves his guest,
Which is as bad as all the rest.

Now hear how many and how great   135
The comforts that spare meals await—
First then there is your health preserv'd,
For various things, when they are serv'd,
You well may think can do no good,
When you reflect upon the food,   140
So well digested when a boy,
Too simple to offend or cloy.
But when you once begin your tricks,
And boil'd and roast together mix,
And fish and fowl—the sweetest juice   145
Will turn to bile by gross abuse,
And the tough phlegm, that forms and stays,
Will tumults in your stomach raise.
Observe how pale the guests arise
From courses of varieties;   150
Besides the body overpower'd
With what you yesternight devour'd,
Afflicts the mind, and brings to shame,
Your portion of th'etherial flame.
Another, who but plainly fed   155
Springs active to his early bed,
Betimes arises fresh and gay,
For all the duties of the day.

But he sometimes may have recourse
To better cheer without remorse,   160
At some great festal revolution,
Or on defect of constitution,
When weakness comes, and years implore
More tender usage than before.
But as for you, if sickness come,   165
Or creeping old-age shou'd benumb,
What kind indulgence can be lent,
Which you in youth and strength prevent!
    A rancid boar our fathers chose,
And yet these Romans had a nose.   170
But I presume this was their view,
That for a visitor or two,
At times they'd take it from their shelves,
Rather than eat it all themselves.
O that I had been born and nurst,   175
Amongst such heroes at the first!
Come, are your ears for fame inclin'd,
The more than music of the mind?
Plate, turbots, e'en such show and cheer
Are scandalous as well as dear: 180
To all these items you may add,
Your uncle, and your neighbours mad,
Desp'rate yourself, and without hope
Of death, or credit for a rope.—
    'That Trasius, (you'll be apt to urge)   185
With these invectives you may scourge,
But I have very great estates,
Enough to keep three potentates.'
Why therefore do you not prepare
A fund of what you have to spare?   190
Why shou'd one good man be distress'd,
While you are of such wealth possess'd?
Why do the holy temples fall,
Ingrate! have you no love at all
For native Rome, but she may reap   195
A little from your monst'rous heap?—

68 prevent!] prevent. *1767*   177 Come,] Come *1767*   178 mind?] mind, *1767*
95 Rome,] Rome? *1767*   196 heap?—] heap— *1767*

Must thou alone be still exempt,
O object of your foes contempt
Hereafter—Which shall best confide
In his own heart, when he is tried,   200
He who has us'd to more than due
His pamper'd mind and body too,
Or who with meaner things content,
Prepar'd and cautious of event,
In wisdom knows what peace is for,   205
And hoards supplies against a war?
    But that my doctrine may appear
More acceptable, you shall hear—
I knew Ofellus, when a boy,
Who did not formerly enjoy   210
With more expence his lands intire,
Than now oblig'd those lands to hire.
There may you see him walk about
In fields with elegance laid out,
Stout farmer, tho' his rent be large,   215
With wife and children, all his charge,
Having such things as these to say:
'I never on a common day,
Ought more than herbs and bacon eat,
But when compell'd a friend to treat,   220
After long interval receiv'd,
Or when from all our toils reliev'd,
A neighbour, whom the tempest drives,
Most acceptable guest arrives—
Then we liv'd well, but not so high,   225
As fishes ev'n from Rome to buy:
But pullets, or a kid was caught;
And for the second course they brought
Some grapes, for raisins, hung and dried,
With nuts, and a few figs beside.   230
After this fare we had a * play,
To take our glass in turn, or pay.

* A game like snip, snap, snorum.

---

199 Which] which *1767*   201 due] due, *1767*   206 war?] war. *1767*

Then Ceres by our vows ador'd,
A plenteous harvest to afford,
Smil'd on our jovial cup, to chace   235
The wrinkles of each serious face.
Let fortune rage, new broils foment,
What more 'gainst me can she invent?
Have I, my boys, more sparing been,
Or have we gone less tight and clean,   240
Since the new lord has here been seen?
For nature has appointed none,
To call an earthly thing his own,
Nor him, nor me, nor any third—
He drove us out by war preferr'd;   245
To him his conduct past all shame,
Or quirks in law shall do the same,
Or heir surviving after all—
This field Umbrenus's they call,
Which lately did to me pertain,   250
For none long while shall it remain—
But still be ceded to the plea
Of any person, you or me—
Wherefore act bravely, and oppose
A manly heart to worldly woes.'   255

SATIRE III.

He introduces Damasippus accusing him, that he wrote nothing; and then under the same person he handles that paradox of the Stoics, viz. that all fools are mad.

'Your works so seldom now appear,
You scarcely wrote four times last year;
Employ'd your poems to retouch,
And wroth you have indulg'd so much
In wine and sleep, till all your lays   5
Are far beneath the public praise.
What now? you come here with a view,
The feast of Saturn to eschew—

So now you're sober, drive your trade,
And keep the promise that you made.
Begin—there is no let at all,
In vain you blame your pen, and scrawl }
Upon the harmless, helpless wall.
And yet your features were intent,
As pregnant with some huge event,
If once you compass'd your retreat
To leisure, and your country-seat.
What boots it to make such ado
With Plato and Menander too,
To bring down Eupolis to us,
And that great bard Archilochus?
If you shall think to silence spite,
By quitting valour and the fight, }
They'll call you a most wretched wight. }
That siren indolence divorce,
Or you must lose all fame of course,
You gain'd in better days of yore'—
   'O Damasippus! I implore
All male and female pow'rs above,
For your good council and your love,
A shaver for your beard to send;
But whence are you so much my friend,
And see so deep in my affairs?'—
   'To other men I give my cares,
By no concerns of self controul'd,
E'er since my goods were 'prais'd and sold;
For formerly my chief employ,
Was to be curious in a toy,
And at th' identic vase I guess'd,
Corinthian Sisyphus possess'd.
What cut without the master's hand,
And what too roughly cast, I scan'd,
As connoisseur, for such a head
Some thousand sesterces *I bled*.
I was the only man, that knew
To buy fine seats and gardens too,

And that to such advantage, Sir,
That I was call'd the MANAGER,
Both in the streets and at the 'change'—
　'I know it, and to me 'tis strange,   50
So frantic you shou'd e'er get well'—
'Some new disorders came t'expel
The old, which sometimes is the case,
When pain and sickness shift their place,
And from the head and sides depart,   55
To make advances on the heart.
Or as it is when from his bed
The dull lethargic lifts his head,
And beats the doctor for his fee'—
'So that you do not this to me,   60
Be things as you wou'd have them be.'
——'Do not deceive yourself, good sir,
You're mad, and so are all that err
From wisdom mad, or nearly so,
If truth our great Stertinius know,   65
From whom these admirable rules
I have deriv'd, concerning fools,
What time he order'd me to save
A sapient beard, and never shave,
And speed without concern and pain,   70
From that Fabrician bridge again.
For when, as all my wealth was spent,
I there for self-destruction went,
He very happily stood near,
And have a care (says he) for fear   75
You thro' false shame are on a plan,
Which is unworthy of a man,
Since born amongst the mad-brain'd race,
You dread a personal disgrace.
First then I will inquire to see   80
What's madness? if alone in thee,
I will not add a word, not I
But you may bravely plunge and die.
　Crysippus both his school and sect,
Do madness to all men object.   85

For fools of a malicious mind,
While ignorant of truth, and blind, }
Are madmen properly defin'd.
In this we comprehend you all
Both king and people, great and small,   90
Except the stoic great and wise,
Who bade us thus philosophize.
   Now hear how those, that give to you
The name of madman, are so too.
As in the woods when people stray,   95
Driv'n by some blunder from the way,
If right or left their route's oblique,
The error ends to each alike:
In such conceive yourself *insane*,
So that another, who is vain,   100
And laughs at you, is no less mad,
And hangs his hamper'd tail as bad.
One kind of folly is to fear
All peril, when no hurt is near:
So that upon the open lea   105
Fires, rivers, rocks, they seem to see.
Another opposite direct,
Nor wiser in the least respect:
That is thro' floods and flames to fly.
Let mistress, mother, sister cry,   110
With all his kindred, and his wife:
"This ditch is dreadful—save your life—
This precipice is monstrous steep,
From headlong death your footsteps keep."
He wou'd not hear or be controul'd,   115
Better than * Fusius did of old,
When he was drunk to that degree,
He overslept ILIONE,
The while two hundred thousand roar,
"Hear, mother, hear thy Polydore."   120

---

* Catienus performed Polydore, and Fusius Ilione, in a tragedy of that name written
by Pacuvius. Fusius was only to have shammed to be asleep, which being drunk, he was
in earnest.

---

98 alike:] alike. *1767*   101 you,] you *1767*   109 fly.] fly, *1767*

Now I shall shew you, that the case,
Is parallel with all our race.
If Damasippus is unwise,
For ancient bustos, that he buys,
Are they that lend him money SANE?   125
Well be it so—but to explain.
Here, sir, receive, if I shou'd say,
That which you never can repay,
Is't mad to take me at my word,
Or wou'd you not be more absurd,   130
To spare the purse and its contents,
Which lucky Mercury presents?
Grant that to Nerius there are due
Ten thousand pieces—'twill not do.
Add then a million forms and ties,   135
That quaint Cicuta can devise:
Yet Proteus shifting off his shape,
Shall all these chains and bars escape,
And when you drag him into court,
With your misfortunes making sport,   140
At pleasure boar, or bird, or rock,
Or oak he'll be to stand the shock.
Misconduct if his want of sense,
And care to wisdom claims pretence;
Perillius forward to advance   145
The sum, for which he finds no chance,
Is of a head by far more weak
Than thee, if I my mind may speak.
      Whome'er ambitious thoughts assail,
Who are with watching money pale,   150
Who for luxurious viands pants,
Or sour with superstition cants,
Or finds his intellectual man
At all impair'd, come rear and van
To me, your most especial friend;   155
Adjust your garments and attend,
While I demonstrate to your face,
That madness is a common case.

132 presents?] presents. *1767*   144 pretence;] pretence. *1767*

First to the avaritious tribe,
Most hellebore I must prescribe: 160
Perhaps, these wretches with their hoards,
Claim all * Anticyra affords.
   Staberius' heirs were forc'd to write
The sum he left in black and white
Upon his tomb, for on neglect   165
They were injoin'd to this effect:
That they shou'd to the mob bestow
An hundred fencers, for a show,
With a grand banqueting beside,
Ev'n such as Arrius shou'd provide,   170
With as much corn as in a year,
The fields of fertile Afric bear:
"Whether you deem that this my will
Be right or wrong, yet pray fulfill,
Nor on my mem'ry be too hard."   175
The man, I think, was on his guard.
What therefore do you think he dreamt,
When he commanded on contempt,
His heirs upon his tomb shou'd grave
The money he was said to have?   180
Know then, while yet alive, he sneer'd
At want, as vice, which most he fear'd,
So that he all wou'd self deny,
Lest one mite poorer he shou'd die.
For all things, virtue, fame, and grace,   185
Divine and human must give place
To wealth, which if one can acquire,   ⎫
He's just, fam'd, brave, and sov'reign sire, ⎬
With all things else he can desire.   ⎭
These heaps, as if for merits gain   190
He thought wou'd to his laud remain.—
With him, how little of a piece,
Was Aristippus sprung from Greece,
Who made his slaves by his commands,
Disperse his gold on Lybian sands,   195

* An island in the Archipelago, noted for the growth of hellebore in great abundance.

163 write] write, *1767*   166 effect] affect *1767*   180 have?] have. *1767*
191 laud] land *1767*   195 sands,] sand? *1767*

As going slowly on the road,
Encumber'd with so great a load!
Which is the madder of the two?
—An instance here will little do,
Which strives to help a question out,   200
By bringing up another doubt.—
If any man shou'd buy guittars,
And keep them up with locks and bars,
Unskill'd the lyre or lute to use,
And wholly inscious of the muse;   205
Or be worth many a last and awl,
That is no shoemaker at all;
Or sails and ropes a fool shou'd hoard,
Who never dar'd to go *aboard*,
Why sure delirious and unsound,   210
He wou'd by all his peers be found.
And how I wou'd be told is *he*
From such-like imputations free,
Who dreads to use his hoarded plate,
And money, as if *consecrate?*   215
    Shou'd any person stand before
A heap of corn upon his floor,
And arm'd upon the watch remain,
Yet dare not take a single grain,
And tho' his heart with hunger grieves,   220
Had rather fare upon dry leaves—
Or shou'd a thousand casks possess,
From Chian or Falernian PRESS,
Nay more, three hundred thousand say,
And yet drink vinegar all day: 225
Again, shou'd one of sev'nty-nine,
Lie down on straw, tho' on his *line*
The bedding rot, and in his chest
The food of moths and worms at best,
Yet few wou'd hold him as possest,   230
Because the bulk of all mankind,
Are equally absurd and blind.

197 load!] load. *1767*   198 two?] two— *1767*   212 how] now *1767*
215 *consecrate?*] *consecrate. 1767*   216 before] before, *1767*   225 day:] day. *1767*
230 possest,] possest. *1767*

Thou dotard scorn'd in heav'n and here,
Do you still watch your wealth, for fear
Of want yourself, when in the end,   235
Your son and servant all shall spend?
For what a trifle wou'd each day,
Take from your capital away,
Shou'd you once venture to produce,
Some better oil from out your cruise;   240
Both for your cabbage and your hair,
Uncomb'd, and scurf'd for want of care?
If any pittance will suffice,
For what are all your oaths and lies,
Why do your frauds and thefts abound   245
In ev'ry quarter? are you sound?

   If you shou'd be so indiscreet,
To pelt the mob along the streets,
Or use the slaves you bought as bad,
Each boy and girl wou'd call you mad.   250
You hang your wife, and in despight
Your mother poison, are you right?
For why? because you did not do
The fact at the same place, nor drew
The sword to perpetrate your shame,   255
As mad Orestes slew the dame?
Think you his madness did proceed,
Merely from this flagitious deed,
Or that he was not rather wrought
By furies, ere he ev'n in thought   260
Cou'd cut his mother's throat—but stay—
Ev'n from the time that you wou'd say,
A dang'rous fit had seiz'd her son,
Nought reprehensible was done.
He did not dare Electra seize,   265
Nor draw his sword on Pylades,
He only his hot wrath to vend,
Call'd *her* a fury, and his friend
Some other most outrageous name,
Which from his indignation came.   270

Opimius, who amidst his hoard,
Cou'd nothing to himself afford,
Who us'd to drink from potter's clay
* *Veientan*, on a holiday,   275
While dregs, or any kind of stuff,
Were for a work-day well enough,
Was lately seiz'd, and like to die
Of a prodigious lethargy,
In such that his triumphant heir,
With eager joy already there,   280
About his keys and coffers ran—
His doctor, a most active man,
And faithful too, did thus contrive
The means his patient to revive:
He bade them bring the table out,   285
And throw the money bags about,
Then certain came to count the pelf—
Which, rais'd at once, he did himself.
Then thus the doctor spake, "beware,
Or all goes to your greedy heir;"   290
"What, while I am living?"—"if you chuse
To live, you must the methods use,
Watch—bustle," "what wou'd you persuade?"
"Why your poor body's so decay'd,
Unless your stomach is renew'd,   295
Your veins will fail for lack of food—
Why do you hesitate, th'advice
Is good, here take this bowl of rice:"
"What cost it?" "never mind the price;"
"But what, I say?" "three farthings;" "oh!   300
What signifies which way I go,
Whether I die of my disease,
Or rapine, theft, and doctor's fees."—
    Who therefore is quite *sane* and cool?
Why ev'ry man, that's not a fool.   305
What is the churl? give him his due,
He is both fool and madman too.

* An exceeding bad wine.

But say a person is not *near*,
Are therefore his conceptions clear?
By no means in the world——why so,   310
Good master Stoic?—you shall know;
Suppose that * Craterus shou'd tell
This patient, that his heart is well.
Is he then right, and shall he rise?
The doctor certainly denies,   315
If in his reins, or either side,
The poignant symptoms still abide.
   This person is quite clear of both,
The miser's crime, and breach of oath.
Let him then sacrifice a swine,   320
In honour to the pow'rs divine—
But he is vain and bold—away
Conduct him to † Anticyra.
For what's the difference in th'abuse,
Whether you waste your wealth profuse,   325
Or let it have no end or use?
   Opidius Servius, rich and great,
In an old family estate
Divided (as the story runs)
Two of his farms betwixt his sons,   330
And when upon his dying bed
He call'd his sons, and thus he said—
"Aulus, when thee a little lad,
I saw so free with what you had,
And bear more loosely than the rest   335
Your nuts, and play-things in your breast,
Which you wou'd give or game away—
Thee too, Tiberius, when at play,
I mark'd to count your toys, and hide;
I fear'd lest both there shou'd betide   340
A phrenzy of a diff'rent cast,
Lest he shou'd learn to live too fast

* An eminent physician.
† A place famous for the growth of hellebore.

341 phrenzy] phrenzy, *1767*

Of Nomentanus, and that you
Might, like the scrub Cicuta, do;
Wherefore, by all the Gods adjur'd,   345
Let me have each of you secur'd;
Aulus, lest all by you be spent—
Tiberius, or that you augment
Too much, what in your father's sense
And nature, is a competence.   350
Besides lest glory with its glare
Beguile you, both of you shall swear,
That he who shall be Edile first,
Or Praetor, be cut off and curst.
Wou'd you destroy your wealth and ease,   355
By largesses of * beans and pease,
That in the Circus you may strut
At large, or have your statue cut,
And there in brazen dulness stand,
A dupe depriv'd of cash and land?   360
Yes, you wou'd have Agrippa's praise—
A silly fox that over-plays
His cunning, nor can have the heart
To act the lion's noble part."

   Atrides, whence the royal word,   365
That Ajax shou'd not be interr'd?
"I am a king,"—as you think fit,
Born a plebeian I submit.
"And just was the severe decree,
Which if you do not clearly see,   370
You have my leave to speak your mind."
Great king, may all the gods combin'd,
Grant you from conquer'd Troy to make
A happy voy'ge—so I may take
The liberty of *pro* and *con*,   375
To ask and to reply—"Go on."—
Then why does Ajax so renown'd,⎫
And only to Achilles found⎬
Inferior, rot above the ground?⎭
Oft fam'd for saving yours and you,   380
That Priam, and his people too,

* Distributed by way of bribery to the populace on elections.

May triumph in his fate and shame,
That made their youths endure the same?
"So great the phrenzy of his brain,
By him a thousand sheep were slain,   385
Which at the time he thought *to be*
My brother, and my friends and me."
When thou humanity's disgrace,
At Aulis didst thy daughter place
Before the shrine, and on her head ⎫   390
The consecrated salt you shed,   ⎬
Cou'd you a man of sense be said? ⎭
"Why not?"—why what did Ajax do,
Who without cause the mutton slew?
Why he abstain'd from wife and child,   395
Tho' each Atrides he revil'd:
He hurt not Teucer in his rage,
Nor with Ulysses did engage.
"To loose my fleet from th'hostile shore
Wise I appeas'd the gods with gore."—   400
What, with your own, thou madman?—"yea—
But mad not in the least degree."

　　Who'er false images has built,
Form'd in the hurry of his guilt,
Will be esteem'd disturb'd in mind,   405
Nor does it boot what he's defin'd,
Or fool or furious—Ajax doats,
Who harmless sheep to death devotes:
He who for empty fame commits
An horror, is he in his wits?   410
And is your wicked heart allied,
To purity, when swoln with pride?
If any man shou'd in his *chair*,
Conduct a lamb to take the air,
And for her maids, gold, garments get,   415
And call it *bantling* or *pusette*,
And ev'n design her for the bed
Of some stout youth, to such a head

383 same?] same. *1767*   393 do,] do. *1767*   394 slew?] slew. *1767*
401 What,] What *1767*   418 head] head, *1767*

The Praetor wou'd without delay
All conduct of itself gainsay;   420
And give up to his friends and heirs,
The management of his affairs.
What if a sire his girl depute,   ⎫
A victim for the bleating mute,   ⎬
Are his brains right? no, 'twill not suit. ⎭   425
Wherefore whenever in one mind
Are folly and perverseness join'd,
There's rank insanity, for sin
And raving madness are a-kin.
Fond of frail fame, the warrior's pains,   430
End in the cracking of his brains.

    Come on——let Nomentanus bear
The last, that is the squand'rer's share:
For reason this conclusion makes,
None are more mad than foolish rakes.   435
This fellow, after he was paid
A thousand talents, instant made
An edict, that next morn for state,
The fruit'rer, fishmonger shou'd wait,
The poult'rer and perfumer too,   440
The play'rs, with that indecent crew
That traffic in the * Tuscan street,
With all that dealt in oil or meat.
Well what was the event?——they came.

    The bawd the first began to frame   445
His speech, "whatever I or these
Possess at home, is, if you please
Your own, which you may take away,
Alike to-morrow, or to-day."

    Now hear with what benign concern,   450
The youth bespeaks them in his turn.

    "In boots upon Lucanian snows,
You take a comfortless repose,
That I may sup upon a boar;
You fish upon the wintry shore.   455

---

* Much such another place as Drury-lane.

I pass my time without employ,
This wealth unworthy to enjoy.
Here take ye, every one your due—
A million sesterces for you;
For you as much; for you twice-told,   460
With whose fair spouse I make so bold,
When to my call at midnight sold."
Aesopus' son by folly taught,
To waste a million at a draught,
Dissolv'd in vinegar a pearl,   465
He ravish'd from his fav'rite girl;
Not one jot wiser to be sure,
Than if he'd thrown it in the sew'r.

   The boys of Arrius, curious twins
In trifles as enormous sins,   470
Were wont on nightingales to feed
At any price—say, was their deed
Of sense or fondness, and of right,
To be put down in black or white?

   If once you see a grey-beard take   475
To toys, and baby-houses make,
Yoke mice to go-carts, pebbles hide,
To play at odd and even, ride
About the house upon a cane,
You'd think his phrenzy very plain.   480
If it's as childish as all this
In reason's eye, to love a *miss*,
And that it matters not, if you
Play in the dust, as wont to do
When three years old, or shou'd deplore   485
Your fate in fondness to a whore:
I ask you if you will behave
Like * Polemo reform'd, and wave
The ensigns of your fond disease,
Your mantle, garters below knees,   490

* Polemo, when drunken and crowned with chaplets, went into the school of
Xenocrates, who happened to be upon the topic of temperance, to which the young rake
gave such attention, that he became perfectly reform'd, insomuch, that he lived to succeed the philosopher in his school.

---

469 twins] twins, *1767*   486 whore:] whore. *1767*

And lac'd cravat, as it is said
He did with liquor in his head,
And took by stealth his chaplet off,
Converted by th'abstemious soph.
  If to a boy that's cross in grain   495
You offer apples, he'll refrain—
"Here take them, little rogue."—Not I—
But if they are not giv'n he'll cry.
A whining lover in disgrace,
Barr'd out is in the self-same case.   500
When with himself he argues so,
Whether he shall or shall not go
Unto the place for which he steers,
Altho' unsent for, and adheres
Ev'n to the hated threshold—"What!   505
When dunn'd to see her, shall I not?
Or shall I not myself befriend,
And rather all my sorrows end?
Shut out—recall'd—shall I repeat
My suit—no—shou'd she at my feet   510
Implore me;"—lo! the servant here,
Whose head's a thousand times more clear—
"O Sir, in things that have no mean,
Our conduct cannot be foreseen,
And govern'd by a rule and form: 515
In love these contradictions swarm—
War—peace anon, which as they veer
Like fortune or the atmosphere,
If any one to fix shou'd try,
He'd do no better, by the bye,   520
Than if he rav'd and play'd the fool
By gamut, or by grammar-rule."
  When taking from Picenian fruit,
The seeds you to the cieling shoot,
It gives you joy—are you yourself?   525
Or when you act a fondling elf
In impotence, and lisp, and toy,
Are you then wiser than a boy

Who builds dirt-houses, as he plays?
How think you too of bloody frays,   530
And stirr'd by swords how fire will blaze!
When Marius, who had Hellas smote,
Did death unto himself devote,
Was he then mad, or will you free
The culprit from his lunacy,   535
And so condemn him for the fact
By being in your terms exact?
A wretch in years, a freedman's son,
Was seen about the streets to run
With washen hands, at early day,   540
And "me alone, (for that I pray,
Is no great thing for pow'rs like you,
Ye Gods, which all with ease can do)
Save me alone from death and hell."
This man in eyes and ears was well,   545
But him if e'er his lord should sell,
He must his intellects exclude,
Unless he wanted to be sued.
Such (says Chrysippus) must be clast
'Mongst numbers of * Menenian cast.   550
    "O thou! that giv'st, or canst remove
The worst afflictions, sov'reign Jove!"
(Cries the fond mother of a lad,
Bed-rid five weeks and very bad)
"If this cold quartan shall recede   555
The first day, that a fast's decreed,
In Tiber naked shall he stand."—
Shou'd luck, or some physician's hand,
From dang'rous case restore the boy,
The mother will herself destroy,   560
By stripping him in frantic vein,
And bringing back the fit again.
How driv'n to such a foolish freak?
Why superstition makes her weak.
    These instances, attacks to stave,   565
That *eighth* wise man Stertinius gave

* A crazy person of a numerous family.

In friendship, that some future day
I might the Cavillers repay.
Whoever calls me mad, shall hear
The same re-echoed in his ear,   570
And be compell'd to turn his mind,
Upon the * bag, that hangs behind.'
   'Stoic (so may you re-imburse
Your damages and make a purse)
Of what infatuation, pray,   575
(Since there are many kinds you say)
Am I by thee as guilty found?
For to myself I seem quite sound.'
   'When mad Agave bears the head
Of her unhappy son, that bled   580
By her own hands, does she conceive
Herself a fury?'—'give me leave,
I'll own the truth, I am a fool,
And in my senses not quite cool,
Only speak out, and tell me all   585
That I particularly ail'—'I shall—
First you're a builder, that's to vie
With giants, tho' but two feet high.
Yet you the self same dwarf deride
When little Turbo's strut and pride   590
In armour far too big you see—
Pray are you less a jest than he?
What if Maecenas built in Rome,
Must such a chap as you presume
'Gainst all propriety, so small,   595
And so dissimilar withal?
The young ones of an absent frog,
Crush'd by a bull-calf in the bog,
The mother was inform'd by one
That 'scap'd what an huge beast had done.   600
She asks him of the monster's size,
And puffing up herself she cries,

* Alluding to a fable of Aesop, where Jupiter is feigned to have put bags upon every
man, the one filled with his neighbour's faults before, the other filled with his own
behind, so that he sees the former, but not the latter.

577 found?] found *1767*

"Was he so great?" as great again—
Then after many a grievous strain,
"Was he as big as this?" indeed   60
You would not, shou'd you burst, succeed.
This little piece, that Esop drew,
Bears a strong likeness, sir, to you.
Now introduce your odes and lyre,
That is, add fewel to the fire,   61
The verses, which from men of sense
If e'er they come, you've some pretence.
I do not name your desp'rate wrath—'
'Have done'—'and greater than your cloth
Your coat—' 'my philosophic friend,   61
Pray to your own affairs attend,
And those that nearer reason rave
Thou maddest of all mad-men wave.'

SATIRE IV.

Under the person of one Catius, an Epicurean philosopher, he derides the pre
cepts of that sect, so far as they relate to the culinary art.

'From whence arriv'd, and where away
Good Catius?'—'Sir, I cannot stay—
In haste some maxims to set down,
Form'd to out-rival the renown
And works of Plato's learned ease,
Pythagoras and Socrates'—
'I own myself a little rude,
At such a juncture to intrude
With interruptions indiscreet;
But pardon me, I do intreat.   10
If any thought you lost, you'll find,
So great the presence of your mind,
Whether 'tis nature, or mere skill,
You're great in both, a wit at will.'
—'But I am lab'ring might and main,   1
How I might every thing retain,

As matters to refinement wrought,
Both in the diction and the thought'—
'The name of him you thus applaud,
Is he of Rome, or from abroad?'—   20
'The author's rules shall be reveal'd,
Which I can do; his name conceal'd.
Eggs that are oblong, pray observe,
Are better at a feast to serve,
As being more delicious found,   25
And likewise whiter than the round;
Besides the toughness of the skin,
Premises a male-yolk within.
The greens that grew in drier land,
Are sweeter far than those at hand.   30
In over-water'd gardens shoot
The flashy and insipid root.
If on the even-tide a guest
Comes unawares—why then 'tis best
(Lest the tough hen for want of youth   35
Offend his palate and his tooth)
Live in mix'd wine her body steep—
All this is learning very deep.
The meadow mushrooms are the best:
I cannot warrant all the rest.   40
His summers he in health shall spend,
Who of his dinner makes an end
With mulberries of blacker die,
Gather'd before the sun's too high.
Aufidius with Falernian wine   45
Mix'd honey—wrong—as I opine:
Because on empty veins 'tis fit
Th'emollient only we commit.
With more propriety indeed
You'll wash your stomach with soft mead.   50
If you are costive, in that case
Limpins and cockles shou'd have place,
With sorrel leaves of smaller make,
Which with white *Coan* you shou'd take.

ATIRE iv. 42 end] end, *1767*

The waxing moons, to th'utmost wish,   5
Fill out the lubricating fish.
But every sea is not alike
Productive of the sorts that strike.
The Lucrine muscles far exceed
The burret of the Baian breed.   6
Circean oysters win the prize;
Crabs at Misenum best arise:
But your escallops spreading wide,
Are soft Tarentum's boast and pride.
Let none presumptuously suppose,   6
The table-decking art he knows,
Unless he weigh with previous care
The laws of taste—a nice affair.
Nor is't enough to clear the stall
Of high-pric'd fishes great and small,   7
Unskill'd which sort to stew is right,
And which when roasted will invite
The gutler, that has over-eat
Himself, to re-assume his seat.
The Umbrian boar with acrons fed,   7
Which from the scarlet oak are shed,
The dishes of that person bend,
Whose palate flabby meats offend.
For poorly the Laurentian feeds,
As fatted up with flags and reeds.   8
A connoisseur will be aware,
To chuse the wings of pregnant hare.
Of fowl and fish the sorts and age,
Tho' studied much by many a sage,
Has not as yet been fully known,   8
But by my skill and taste alone.
Some men exhaust their time and taste
In new inventions upon paste.
'Tis not worth labour to discuss
Upon a single point, as thus,   9
Shou'd a man merely rest on this,
That his wine may not drink amiss,

83 fowl] foul *1767*

Careless what oil he shou'd supply,
When he has any fish to fry.
Shou'd you put out the Massic wine,   95
(The weather being very fine)
If it be foul, the air by night
Will make it clear, and banish quite
That smell bad for the nerves—but drawn
And filtred thro' a sieve of lawn,   100
'Twill all its zest intirely lose.
He, who shall skillfully infuse
To wine of Surrentinian kind,
The right Falernian lees, will find
That he can best collect the dregs,   105
By making use of pidgeon's eggs;
Because the yolks, as they descend,
Will make the grosser parts attend.
With roasted shrimps, and cockles live
From Afric's coast you may revive   110
The weary toper—for when sour'd
With too much wine, and over-pow'r'd,
Lettuce will on the stomach rise,
Which seeks the rather for supplies
From sausage, ham, or any thing   115
Which from the slattern-shops they bring.
You'll find 'tis far from any loss
Of time, to learn two kinds of sauce.
The plain is made of oil intire,
Which to improve and render high'r,   120
Add wine and pickles, best by far
When taken from Byzantian jar.
This mixt with shredded greens, and brought
From Corycus, with saffron fraught,
When it has boil'd and stood—then squeeze   125
The olives of Venafran trees.
The apples of Picenum beat
What Tibur bears, as good to eat,
But for their colour these excel.
Venutian grapes for jars are well.   130

3 he] she *1767*   127 beat] beat, *1767*

Yet for preserving in the smoke
Th'Albanian fitter are bespoke.
Th'invention was intirely mine,
This grape with apples to combine,
And vinous lees with herring brine.   135
I was the first who had the knack
White pepper with the salt that's black
Finely to mix, and serve up all
In dishes very neat, tho' small.
'Tis a grand fault to throw away   140
Vast sums upon a market day,
And yet to cramp the spraggling fish
By using of a scanty dish.
'Twill turn your stomach very much,
If waiters take with greasy touch   145
The glass, as they their fingers lick,
Or grime to your old goblet stick.
In saw-dust, napkins, and in brooms,
How small th'expence about your rooms!
Yet if these things you quite neglect,   150
'Tis a most horrible defect

Shou'd you Mosaic pavements sweep
With dirty palm-brooms, as they're cheap,
And tho' he is in purple drest,
Bring out foul cushions for your guest,   155
Forgetting in such things the less
Of care and cost, the greater stress
Is still on the defaulter laid,
Nor are they in the ballance weigh'd
With things of vast expence and state,   160
Pertaining only to the great.'—
—'Learn'd Catius, by the pow'rs divine,
That love with which I call you mine,
Where'er you shall an audience share
With this great man, let me be there,   165
For tho' your mem'ry be so good,
That I have most things understood,

149 rooms!] rooms? *1767*   151 defect] defect. *1767*   152 sweep] sweep, *1767*
167 understood,] understood: *1767*

Yet by mere narrative in brief,
You cannot please me like the chief.
Then add the manner and the dress,   170
And countenance besides, express,
Which strike you not in that degree
As always in your pow'r to see,
But I by vehement desire
Up to the fountain-head aspire,   175
And make myself adept compleat
In precepts of a life so sweet.'

SATIRE V.

*Under the person of Ulysses, consulting the ghost of Tiresias, the poet describes
the wou'd-be-heirs and will-hunters.*

'Besides the things that you have told,
Tiresias, let me be so bold,
As your opinion to demand
How I the loss of house and land
May be enabled to repair   5
By what expedient, art, or care?
Why do you laugh?'—'O fam'd for tricks!
Is't not enough your route to fix,
That you may Ithaca regain,
And in your native country reign?'   10
—'O thou that never spoke a lie, ⎫
You see how stript, how poor am I, ⎬
Returning by your prophecy. ⎭
Where my wife's suitors I shall find,
Nor wealth nor flocks have left behind: 15
But race and virtue without cash,
And property are errant trash'—
'Since poverty so much you dread
There is no further to be said:
Learn how to flourish in a trice.   20
If any thing that's scarce and nice,

171 besides,] besides *1767*

A thrush for your own private snack
Be sent you, presto! in a crack,
The spoil to some old dupe convey,
Who lives in the most splendid way.   2
Whate'er your garden, or your field,
Of fruit, or other dainties yield,
Let him taste first, a guest by far
More venerable than the Lar.
And tho' a wretch of upstart pride, ⎞
A fugitive for laws defied,   ⎬   3
By perjury or fratricide: ⎠
Yet if he chuses at his call
You must attend, and give the wall'—
—'What cheek by jole, shall I be caught   3
With a vile Dama, filthy thought?
Not so still arm'd above my match
At Troy did I myself attach'——
—'The sequel is you must be poor'—
—'This my brave spirit shall endure—   4
And oftentimes I've underwent
Fatigues of greater hardiment,
Yet prithee, prophet, tell me plain,
How I shall cash and substance gain.'—
—'In troth I told you, and repeat   4
The lesson, practise your deceit,
To coax old men to make their will,
And put you in a codicile.
Nor if a cunning knave or two,
Shou'd see the hook and bite it thro',   5
Or from your hope recede dismay'd,
Or for one blank relinquish trade.
If any matter great or small,
Be canvass'd in the judgment-hall,
Whiche'er be rich without a child,   5
Tho' he his betters has revil'd,
Be you the fav'rer of his cause,
And one of honour or applause
Despise, and more so, if he house
A hopeful son, or breeding spouse.   6

"My Lord—your Grace"—(a title suits
And in a drunken ear dilutes)
"Me has your virtue made a friend;
I know the law, can points defend.
And they shall rather have my eyes,   65
Than your great dignity despise,
And with a deaf-nut fob you off:
That you shall have nor loss nor scoff,
Is ever my peculiar care."
Then bid him to his home repair,   70
And cocker up his carcase there.
Persist—hold out—your stumps bestir,
And be yourself sollicitor.
* *Whether the Dog star's* FIERY FEAT
Crack poor dumb statues with his heat,   75
Or fat-gut Furius puff and blow,
And on the Alpine hills below,
Shall disembogue the hoary snow.
"Sir, don't you see (some one will cry
Jogging his elbow by the bye)   80
Your indefatigable friend
So clean the case to comprehend."
With baits like these your plan pursue,
More fish will come to stock the stew.
Again, if any man shou'd rear   85
(Worth you some hundred pounds a year)
An ailing son—lest you shou'd seem
Too open in your courteous scheme,
As batchelor—by slow degrees
Creep in and gradual offices,   90
And for the second heir apply
So haply, if the lad shou'd die,
To all you may yourself advance—
This is an admirable chance.
    Whoever puts into your hand   95
His WILL to read: at first withstand,
And push the parchment rolls aside;
Yet let it be obliquely ey'd

* These lines are citations from one Furius Bibaculus, and another bombastic poet.

So as to catch a glance of that,
The second *item* wou'd be at,   100
Whether with many you're co-heir,
Or come into the whole affair.
Full oft some scriv'ner or old fox
The gaping crow deludes and mocks,
And tho's he's shrewder than the rest   105
Nasica be Coranus' jest'—
—— * 'What, are you mad, or by design
Do you obscurities divine?'—
——'Ulysses all that I foresee
Of surety shall, or shall not be,   110
For from Apollo wise and great,
I have obtain'd this skill in fate.'
—'Then, if you please, pray, sir, unveil
The mystic meaning of your tale.'—
'What time that youth of race divine,   115
Who from Eneas draws his line,
The Parthian's terror shall be crown'd,
And both by sea and land renown'd;
Nasica known for sneaking ways,
Who loves deduction when he pays,   120
† Shall have his stately girl allied
To stout Coranus, as his bride.
The son-in-law shall then proceed
To the old churl to give the deed,
Which, first, he'll frequently refuse,   125
But, being closely press'd, peruse.
And while in silent mood he hums,
He'll find there's neither sum nor sums,
And nothing left for him and his,
But leave to make a rueful phiz.   130
　　To things which we've been led to name,
And also—if a subtle dame

---

* Ulysses speaks again.

† They sometimes had a dowry for their daughters, instead of giving a portion with them; so Nasica expected a handsome legacy at least, from a man most probably advanced in years.

SATIRE V. 101 co-heir] coheir *1767*   107 What,] What *1767*   118 renown'd;]
renown'd. *1767*   122 bride.] bride, *1767*

Or freed-slave manage an old man,
Make one amongst them if you can.
Praise them, that in the self-same strain,   135
You absent may be prais'd again:
This helps—but it is best of all
By far to storm the Capitol.
Does he write verses? sorry stuff?
Be sure to praise them well enough.   140
Is he a wencher? do not wait
For him to be importunate;
But forward of your own accord
Your wife to him you call your lord.'
—'What, wou'd you intimate that she,   145
The chaste and sage Penelope
Can be seduc'd, whom from her course
So many suitors cou'd not force?'—
—'The reason is, that youths of thrift
Were there still grudging of a gift,   150
A race that chose with stomachs keen
The cubbard, rather than the queen.
Thus your Penelope is chaste,
Who if she once had got a taste
Of one old dotard, with a view   155
To share the perquisite with you,
No more wou'd startle from her aim,
Than a staunch hound will quit his game.
     The fact that I'm about to tell,
When I was old, at Thebes befell.   160
Thus by her will an old hag there
Was carried to her grave—the heir
With corpse upon his shoulders went
Naked and oil'd, to this intent,
That she might give the slip at last   165
Tho' dead, to him who stuck so fast.
Wherefore be cautious, nothing spare,
Likewise by no means over-bear.
The splenetic and the morose
Will hate the babler as too gross;   170

Nor keep too silent by the bye;
Be Davus in the comedy,
Stand with your most obsequious head
Aside, as in a state of dread.
Ply him with complaisant grimace;   17
Pray him to veil his precious face,
If once you find the air too brisk,
And from the croud at any risk
Shoulder him out—and if inclin'd
To talk, stick to him ear and mind.   18
If he love praising to excess,
Have at him, keep him up and press,
Till with his hands to heav'n with wrath
He cries, "O 'tis too much in troth."
But keep it up as at the first,   18
Until his tumid bladder burst.
When he at last by his decease,
Shall give your service full release,
And you shall fairly look on this,
In certainty of waking bliss,   19(
"Ulysses is the heir I name,
To the fourth part of all I claim."
What, has my Dama run his race—
O where shall I that man replace?
Likewise appearances to save,   19
Urge now and then how great and brave!
Then cry a little if you will,
'Tis exultation's utmost skill.
Nor be, to your direction left,
His tomb of elegance bereft.   200
The funeral a concourse draws,
With all the neighbourhood's applause.
Mean time if one of your co-heirs
Shou'd think of settling his affairs,
As lab'ring with a dang'rous cough,   20
Tell him you're ready to cut off
Whatever house and farm he likes,
And any sum the bargain strikes.—

193 What,] What *1767*   203 co-heirs] coheirs *1767*   206 you're] your *1767*

But Proserpine, so stern to drive
The Ghosts, recals me—live and thrive.'   210

SATIRE VI.

*He declares himself to be content with such things as he is possessed of, and
that he wishes for no more.*

This was the summit of my views,
A little piece of land to use,
Where was a garden and a well,
Near to the house in which I dwell,
And something of a wood above.   5
The Gods in their paternal love
Have more and better sent than these,
And, Mercury, I rest at ease,
Nor ask I anything beside,
But that these blessings may abide.   10
If I cannot my conscience charge,
That I by fraud my wealth enlarge,
Nor am about by fond excess
To make my little matters less;
If I am not a fool in grain,   15
To make such wishes weak and vain,
'O that I cou'd that nook command
That mars the beauty of my land!
O where there lies a pot of gold,
Might I by some good God be told!   20
Like him who having treasure found,
No longer till'd, but bought the ground!
With Hercules so much his friend!'—
If for what I possess, or spend,
No mean unthankful mind I bear,   25
I supplicate you with this pray'r:
May every thing I have be fat,
My servants, cattle, dog, and cat,
All but my genius—and be still
My guardian, if it is your will!   30

SATIRE vi. 5 above.] above, *1767*

Wherefore, when I from town retreat
To these my mounts, and lofty seat,
How can I of my time dispose
Better than in this measur'd prose?
Here neither worldly pride destroys,   3[5]
Nor pressure of South wind annoys,
Or sickly Autumn, still the gain
Of Libitina's baleful reign.
　　O early sire, or Janus hight,
(If that name more your ears delight)   4[0]
With whom men all their toils commence
In life (for so the Gods dispense)
Do thou thyself begin the song—
At Rome you hurry me along
To give in bail—dispatch me there   4[5]
Lest some one else shou'd do th'affair.
Well—tho' aground the North wind blow, ⎫
Or winter brings the days of snow　　　　⎬
To shorter compass—I must go—　　　　 ⎭
About myself to over-reach—   5[0]
When I in form have made my speech,
At once determinate and loud,
Why I must bustle in the croud,
Sure all slow walkers to offend—
What, are you mad? what mean you, friend?   5[5]
(Some swearing fellow's apt to say)
You jostle all things in your way,
While in post-haste you must be sped,
With great Maecenas in your head—
This *does*, and is too by the bye—   6[0]
A sugar-plumb—I will not lye—
But ere I reach th'Esquilian gloom,
I'm charg'd with all th'affairs of Rome.
'Roscius desires you, as a friend,
The court-house early to attend;   6[5]
The clerks beseech you wou'd return,
Upon a thing of vast concern;
Take care Maecenas seal and sign
To this same instrument of mine.'

55 What,] What *1767*   62 ere] e'er *1767*   68 sign] sign, *1767*

I will *endeavour*, shou'd one say,   70
They'll answer, if you will, you may,
And still keep urging, as before—
    'Tis now the seventh year or more,
Since to Maecenas I was known,
And freely number'd as his own,   75
So far as one he chose to raise
Just to the honour of his chaise,
Conversing as he took his tour,
About such trifles—What's the hour?
Say is * Gallina, who's from Thrace,   80
A match for Syrus face to face?
These morning frosts are very bad
For those who are but thinly clad,
Or any thing, that comes in play,
Which one to leaky ears may say.   85
E'er since this fortunate event,
Th'invidious sons of discontent
Daily increase—'This friend of ours,
On whom her favours fortune show'rs,
A place with great Maecenas claims,   90
With him was present at the games,
Plays in the field with him at ball.'—
Ah, lucky rogue! cries one and all—
Does any bad disheart'ning news,
Its influence thro' the streets diffuse: 95
Whoe'er I meet consults with me.
'Good Sir, (for sure you must be he,
Who all th'affairs of state must know,
As nearer to the gods below)
Ought do you of the Dacians hear?'   100
No—not a syllable—'you jeer:'
May all the gods afflict my heart,
If I know either whole or part.—
'Well—then will Caesar give the lands,
He promis'd to his chosen bands,   105

---

* Gallina and Syrus, two great gladiators.

89 show'rs,] show'rs; *1767*

In Sicily or here, I pray?'
The more I swear, I cannot say—
The more they stare, they cannot sound
A man so close and so profound!—
   Thus do I lose my time and ease,   11
Not without wishes such as these—
O rural scenes! when shall I see
Your beauties, and again be free
Now with those ancient books I chose,
With leisure now, and soft repose,   11
In grateful thoughtlessness to drown
The anxious business of the town?
When shall Pythagoras his beans,
With bacon, and well-larded greens
Be plac'd before me? O ye nights!   12
Of suppers and divine delights,
In which within my proper pale
I and my bosom friends regale;
And make ev'n saucy knaves partake
Of those libations that I make.   12
Each guest according as it suits
May take the glass, no one disputes,
Whether the strong the bumper chuse,
Or weaker chearfully refuse.
A conversation then begins   13
Not on our neighbours wealth or sins,
Or whether Lepos preference claim
For dancing?—but what's more our aim,
And what 'tis evil not to know—
If happiness from riches flow,   13
Or be not rather virtue's prize,
And which it is cement the ties
Of friendship—rectitude or gain, ⎫
And what is real good in grain, ⎬
And how perfection to attain? ⎭   14
   Mean time my neighbour Cervius prates
Old tales, that rise from our debates;

114 books . . . chose,] books, . . . chose *1767*   136 virtue's] virtues *1767*

For if a man who does not know
The world, his eulogy bestow
On great Arellius' cumbrous store,   145
He instantly sets off—'Of yore
A country mouse, as it befel,
Received a cit into his cell,
One chrony to another kind
As intimate time out of mind;   150
This mouse was blunt and giv'n to thrift,
But now and then cou'd make a shift
(However rigid or recluse)
With open heart to give a loose:
In short he wou'd not grudge his guest   155
Or oats or vetches of the best:
And bringing in some berries dried,
With nibbled scrap of ham beside,
Hop'd he variety might plead
To make his daintiness recede,   160
For our grandee wou'd scarcely touch
The things, his squeamishness was such.—
Mean time the master of the treat
Extended on clean straw wou'd eat
Nothing but tares and crusts, to spare   165
For his good friend the nobler fare.
At length the citizen made free
To speak his mind—"my friend, (said he)
How can your mouse-ship hold it good,
To live here on a rugged wood,   170
And how have patience with the place!
Will you not rather turn your face
To view mankind, the town prefer
To these rough scenes that here occur?
Come take my counsel and agree   175
To make a tour along with me.
Since mortal lives must have an end,
And death all earthly things attend,
Nor is there an escape at all
For man or mouse, for great or small;   180

144 eulogy] elogy *1767*   145 Arellius' . . . store,] Arillius . . . store *1767*   150 mind;]
mind, *1767*

Wherefore, good friend, these matters weigh,
And let us for our time be gay,
Let life's contracted period teach
Mice to live jollily"—This speech
Soon as it on the peasant wrought,   185
He nimbly springs from forth his grot,
Then both the destin'd journey take
By midnight gloom their jaunt to make:
And now about that time each mouse
Took refuge in a wealthy house,   190
Where gorgeous carpets crimson-red
Look'd splendid on each ivory bed:
Where many a bit, in many a tray,
Was left from feast of yesterday.
He having then the peasant set   195
Upon a purple coverlet,
Runs like my landlord here and there—
Dish after dish with dainty fare,
And like a handy footman serves,
First tasting every thing he carves.   200
The clown by no means making strange
Begins to chuckle at the change,
And lying on the couch at ease
Lives merrily on all he sees.
But on a sudden, with a roar,   205
Bang open flies the folding door,
And frights our gutlers from their cheer—
Now round the room half-dead with fear,
They scout—new terrors still abound,
With barking dogs the roofs resound.   210
Then (quoth the clown) I have no call
For such a life as this at all;
My cave and wood be still my share, ⎫
There rather let me skulk from care, ⎬
And live upon a single tare.'   ⎭   215

SATIRE VII.

*Horace introduces his slave, rating him soundly for living a different life from
that which he had promised.*

'Long while a list'ner, I wou'd speak,
But somewhat dread my mind to break,
As but a slave'—'What, is it you?
Is't Davus?'—'Davus good and true:
That is so far as to give hope   5
There's no occasion for a rope.'—
'Well, use the right the Roman sire
Allows you by the winter fire,
And since December's come about,
Come let us fairly have it out.'   10
    'There is a portion of mankind
Who're constantly to vice inclin'd,
And let their faults take root and grow.
Many there are that ebb and flow,
One while a sideling to the right,   15
One while to sin obnoxious quite.
Priscus, observ'd at times to wear
Three rings, at times his left-hand bare,
Liv'd so irregular, his way
Was still to shift ten times a day.   20
Sometimes from a most sumptuous scene
He'd seek a place so poor and mean,
From whence a servant just made free
Wou'd scarce appear with decency:
One while a rake at Rome, one while   25
A scholar in th'Athenian style,
Born, when Vertumnus and his airs
Prevail'd the most on man's affairs.
    When Volanerius got the gout
His hands deserv'd his life throughout,   30
The stay'd buffoon hir'd at a price
A substitute to throw the dice:

SATIRE vii. 16 quite.] quite, *1767*

One, who to sin the more in chains
Was much less wretched for his pains,
Than he who plays at fast and loose,   35
All abstinence, or all abuse.'—
'Thou varlet canst thou ever shew
To what this trash pertains?'—'To you'—
'How, scoundrel?'—'You are apt to praise
The peace and forms of ancient days,   40
To which shou'd any God reduce
Your manners, you wou'd beg excuse;
Because you have not that at heart
Which you so clamorously assert,
Or too irresolute and light   45
To stand by what is just and right,
You hesitate with vain desire
To get your foot from out the mire:
In town you for the country sigh,
But Rome's extoll'd up to the sky,   50
When to your villa you're confin'd,
Such is your fickleness of mind.
If uninvited by a friend,

Your peace and sallad you commend,
And hug yourself at home and bless   55
That you shall share no man's excess,
As if by force alone you stirr'd—
But shou'd Maecenas send you word
Late as the lighting of the rooms:
"Ho! quick, who brings me these perfumes?   60
What no one hear a man?"—you cry,
As loud as you can bawl—and fly.
Milvius and play'rs, that hop'd to stay,
In wrath go supperless away,
And leaving many a backward pray'r   65
Too gross for your nice ears to bear.
Some one may say, nor I deny,
That I with appetite comply,
Snuff up my nose at sav'ry food,
Am weak and dull, and to conclude   70

39 How,] How *1767*   46 right,] right *1767*   52 mind.] mind, *1767*
59 rooms:] rooms. *1767*

A sot—but seeing, sir, you are
As bad as I am, and to spare,
Why do you call me to account,
As if your virtues did surmount,
And veil the errors of your ways,   75
In all the art of specious phrase?
But what, and if you shou'd be found
More fool than him, that cost ten pound?
Why then refrain each threatning look,
The hand and wrath I cannot brook,   80
While I into your ears relate
The things I learnt at Crispin's gate.

    You with your robes all thrown aside,
Your ring and your Equestrian pride,
From a grave magistrate evade   85
As Dama in a masquerade,
Still in suspence about your fate,
Art not the thing you personate?
And dreading danger for the nonce,
Are trembling in your honour's bones!   90
What differs it, once bound on oath
For scourge, or broad-sword, or for both,
Or shut within a filthy chest,
Where of the lady's sins possess'd
A maid has cramm'd you neck and heels!   95
Does not the husband hold the seals,
So far as a *just* power to claim
Against both whoring rogue and dame!
A juster with regard to you,
For she nor changes place nor hue: 100
Besides the woman acts in dread,
Nor trusts a word of all you said.
Yet to the yoke you needs must stoop,
The raging husband's destin'd dupe;
Life, body, fortune, soul and all   105
In a most lamentable thrall.
You have escap'd and will beware—
No, no, you'll seek another snare

76 phrase?] phrase. *1767*   78 pound?] pound, *1767*   85 evade] evade, *1767*   88 personate?] personate! *1767*   90 bones!] bones. *1767*   91 on] an *1767*   106 thrall.] thrall, *1767*

Again to fear, again to die,
O wav'rer for servility!   110
What beast so fond as to obtrude
Upon the snares it cou'd elude?
You're no adulterer, you will say,
Nor I a felon by my fay,
When prudent I pass by the plate,   115
But if from Tyburn you'll abate,
Nature, when left unto herself,
Will clear the closet and the shelf.
Inferior then in deed and word
Will you pretend to be my lord,   120
Who punish'd twice and twice again,
Will never from your sins refrain?
    Add we yet more to what we've said
Of equal weight upon this head.
Whether a man, whom slaves obey   125
Be freeman, or a slave, as they,
(For this sometimes is a dispute)
Are you or I of most repute?
For you, o'er me who domineer
To others are in servile fear,   130
And like a poppet wir'd and shown
Have not a motion of your own;
Who then is free of all mankind?
One wise and master of his mind
Whom neither want nor death nor bonds   135
Can terrify—who corresponds
With heav'n and virtue to defy
All lust and fame beneath the sky;
At once by gift and conduct too
As finely turn'd, as polish'd true;   140
So that no rub or outward force
Retard him in his level course;
'Gainst whom dame fortune is at fault,
Whene'er she makes her worst assault!
From all these attributes of fame   145
Have you a single thing to claim?

143 whom *Rudd*] when *1767*

A woman of the town demands
Five talents of your honour's hands,
And after you're turn'd out of bed
Throws down cold water on your head.   150
Anon she calls you—break the chain,
And say, that "I am free again,"
You are not able: for that scourge
And sov'reign of your soul will urge,
And as he calls himself DESIRE   155
Will spur the more, the more you tire.
    When you, in folly so far gone,
Admire a piece by Pausias drawn,
Are you the less to blame than me,
Who, when the prize-fighters I see,   160
Stare at the men or brown'd or black't
In coal or oaker—"'tis the fact,
The very thing, the martial strife,
They strike and parry life and life."
Davus is idle, to be sure,   165
And you a vet'ran connoisseur.
I, if I smell when people bake,
Am call'd to nothing for a cake:
Does your great virtue, godlike soul,
Resist the ven'son and the jole?   170
My fondness for my paunch is wrong:
Why so?—I rue it by the thong.
But are you of all *smarting* clear,
Who buy your things so plaguy dear?
Then those titbits, which you repeat   175
So oft, your palled stomach heat,
And for your body you provide,
Mis-judging feet your steps to guide.
    Shou'd any boy a * strigil take
By night, and pawn it for plumb-cake,   180
Is *he* to blame? And are not *you*,
Who sell your farms for dainties too?

---

* A scraper, or flesh-brush, that they used at the baths.

Besides, you never can command
An hour yourself, nor understand
How you your leisure shou'd amuse,   185
And self to self wou'd fain excuse,
A vagabond from thought, who pine
To banish care by sleep or wine,
In vain—for sticking to your back
He is your constant friend in black.'   190
—'A stone where is there to be had?
A dart?'—'How now, the man is mad,
Or making verse'—'restrain your speech,
Or quick you go to hedge and ditch.'

SATIRE VIII.

Horace interrogates his friend Fundanius, concerning the supper of Nasidienus,
at which he was present.

'How far'd you at the miser's feast?
For there, from yester-noon at least,
You plied the glass, as it was clear
By one I sent to bid you here.'—
—'So well our time we pass'd away,   5
I never had a merrier day.'—
'Say, if 'tis not against the law,
What first appeas'd your rav'nous maw?'—
—'First a Lucanian boar was brought,
Which (as our host affirm'd) was caught,   10
When the South gently blew—the dish
Was garnish'd with both herbs and fish,
Anchovies, lettuce, skirret too,
Such as the appetite renew,
With vinegar from Coan lees,   15
Which all dispos'd of by degrees.
One brisk lad wipes, with purple clout,
The maple table round about;

SATIRE vii. 186 excuse,] excuse *1767*
SATIRE viii. 1 feast?] feast, *1767*   4 here.] here? *1767*   16 degrees.] degrees, *1767*

Another clears off all the rest,
Irksome or useless to the guest.   20
The moor Hydaspes makes parade,
(As with grave rites th'Athenian maid)
Bringing the Caecuban along;
Alcon comes in with Chian strong,
To which no sea had damage done—   25
Here our good host his speech begun:
"Maecenas, if you chuse to dine
With Alban or Falernian wine,
Rather than any thing you see,
Straight you may both command of me." '—   30
'O wretched wealth!—but, prithee show,
Fundanius, for I burst to know,
Who was there with you at this treat,
Where all things were so grand and neat.'

   'Well, I was in the highest place   35
With Viscus, and a little space
Was Varius (as I think) below;
Vibidius too and Balatro,
Which last Maecenas brought to wait
Merely as danglers on his state.   40
Then Nomentanus took his post,
Upon the right hand of our host,
Porcius beneath—despis'd and hiss'd,
For gorging pan-cakes at a twist.

   For this was Nomentanus bid,   45
If ought was unobserv'd or hid,
To point it out—as for the rest,
I, and each undiscerning guest,
We fish and fowl at random took,
Nor saw th'invention of the cook,   50
Which shortly I was giv'n to know,
When he did on my plate bestow
Some turbot-guts, and eels, and plaice,
Such as no other table grace.
Then, willing I shou'd learn, he said,   55
That honey-apples look'd most red,

37 below;] below *1767*

Pluck'd when the moon begins to wane;
Our host himself will best explain
How vast the odds—Vibidius here
Thus whispers in his neighbour's ear—   60
"Unless we tipple to his cost,
All hopes of vengeance will be lost;
Put more capacious tumblers on.'—
On which our host grew wond'rous wan,
As dreading nothing with such hate,   65
As them that drink inordinate;
Whether because they jest too free,
Or swilling to extreme degree,
They blunt the judgment of the taste—
And now whole casks are drank in waste,   70
Both by Vibidius and his friend,
And strangers at the lower end:
Maecenas, and the guests select,
To decency had more respect.

      A lamprey next was usher'd in,   75
With floating prawns in a turrenne.
This (says our host) was caught with spawn,
As tasteless when the row is gone,
For these a sauce of oil was dress'd,
From choice Venafran berries press'd,   80
With pickle from th'Iberian fry,
Wine five years old—but by the bye
Not made beyond sea—all these three,
While it is stewing best agree,
But when once stew'd the Chian wine,   85
No better thing you can divine,
With pepper white, and not without
Such vinegar, as will turn out
By souring Methymnean juice—
"I was the first that brought in use,   90
With these the bitter herb to shred,
And first cut rockets from the bed;
Tho' 'twas Curtillus, I must say,
That to sea-urchins gave the day,
Which in their native salt excel   95
Ought you can get from any shell."

Mean time the tap'stry hung on high
Fell down upon the company,
Bringing black dust, a greater load
Than winds on the Campanian road.   100
We, frighten'd at the first alarm,
Soon as we found was no great harm,
Return each person to his post—
But with his head reclin'd our host
Began to snivel in despair,   105
As if he'd lost his son and heir.
What must have been the end—unless
Sage Nomentanus with address,
Had undertook his friend to cheer.
"O Fortune! which is more severe,   110
Of all th'immortal pow'rs than thee?
With what an everlasting glee,
You love our projects to distress!"
Here Varius, who cou'd not suppress
His laugh, was forc'd the cloth to cram.—   115
Servilius, ever apt to bam,
Cries out with sanctity of face,
"Such are the terms of human race,
Wherefore there's no degree of fame
Can answer your right noble aim,   120
That you shou'd torture and distract
Yourself, so anxiously exact,
That I shou'd be thus well receiv'd!
How, lest the rowls shou'd burn, you griev'd!
Or broth ill-season'd be serv'd up,   125
Or lad in waiting, while we sup,
Neglect the necessary care
Of neat apparel, well-comb'd hair.
Besides, your terror to inhance,
Lo! all these accidents of chance,   130
If hangings shou'd come down, as now,
Or footman, taken from the plough,
Shou'd tumble with a dish upstairs—
But with a noble host it fares,

111 thee?] thee, _1767_   128 hair.] hair, _1767_   132 footman,] footman _1767_

As with great captains in the field;   135
In thriving times their skill's conceal'd,
Which in adversity breaks out,
And brings stupendous things about."
Our Host to this—"pray heav'n may grant,
Both all you wish and all you want;   140
Consid'ring that you are the best
Of men, and most diverting guest"—
And for his sandals he applied
In act to take a turn aside.
Then round the table you might hear   145
A gen'ral buzzing, mouth to ear.
I wou'd not choose a farce, or play,
In preference to such a day.'—
—'But let me have it in a word,
What next to raise the laugh occurr'd?'—   150
'Vibidius with the waiters spoke,
Ask'd if the flaggon too was broke?
Because to his incessant call,
They ministred no wine at all.
And while the laughter is immense,   155
Kept up on many a false pretence,
With Balatro to help us on—
Re-enter host—no longer wan,
As by an happy after-clap
To remedy his dire mishap.   160
Him follow servants, which sustain
The sever'd members of a crane,
In a large charger, sprinkled o'er
With salt and flour, a plenteous store;
A gander's liver next he brings,   165
Fatted with figs, and jointed wings
Of hare, as more the taste to suit
Than if you eat the back to boot.
Then over-roasted mearles appear,
And ring-doves without rumps—fine cheer!   170
Had not their dull loquacious lord
Plac'd all their hist'ries on record,

146 ear.] ear *1767*   164 store;] store, *1767*

And on their natures lectures read,
Whom we in indignation fled,
Nor tasted of his dainty fare,   175
As if Canidia had been there,
And with her fetid breath had blown,
In spite to Afric snakes unknown.'

THE EPISTLES

Ex vitae monstrata via est et gratia regum,
Pieriis tentata modis.   — *Hor.*

THE
FIRST BOOK
OF THE
EPISTLES OF HORACE

EPISTLE I.
To MAECENAS

He affirms that he now throws matter of merriment aside, and adheres only to such things as conduce to virtue.

O subject of my first essays!
Whom as in duty bound to praise,
My muse ev'n to the last persists,
Again you force me to the lists,
With freedom's * rod dismiss'd the stage,   5
As far too much expos'd in age.
No more I have the thirst for fame,
Nor is my time of day the same.
Vejanius having fix'd his arms
Now skreens him in the ground he farms,   10
That from the theatre no more,
He may the mob for life implore.
Something keeps whisp'ring in my ear,
Which purg'd can in the spirit hear,
Loose the old courser, if you're wise,   15
Lest, if he enter for the prize,
He may be scorn'd, as coming last,
And fetch his broken wind too fast.
Wherefore I now will throw away,
All verse and toys of idle play,   20
And all enquiry, thought, and care,

---

* A rod, or wand, given as a token of liberty, by the master of the fencing school, to gladiators, on their dismission.

EPISTLE i. 10 ground] ground, *1767*

But what is true, and what is fair,
And hoard up maxims, and for use
Arrange them, that I may deduce.
And lest, perchance, you shou'd enquire,   25
What school, what master, I admire,
Know I'm addicted to no sect,
Nor swear, as other men direct,
But suit the tenor of my way,
To the complexion of the day;   30
Now active and officious grown,
To state contentions am I prone,
A guard and stedfast partizan
Of virtue, and th'heroic man;
With Aristippus now agree,   35
Not I for things, but things for me.
　　As tedious as the livelong night
To him, whose mistress plays the bite,
As tedious as the livelong day,
To hirelings that must work for pay;   40
As tedious as the livelong year,
To minors under dames severe;
So do all times and seasons go
With me, intolerably slow,
Which in the least retard the thought   45
Of doing all things, as we ought,
And making of that point secure,
Which gain'd is well for rich and poor,
But if neglected will destroy
Alike the hope of man and boy.   50
Add yet, that I myself controul,
And with these dictates sooth my soul.
Like * Lynceus you cannot discern,
Yet do not wholesome eye-salve spurn.
And tho' you are not quite so stout ⎫   55
As matchless Glycon, walk about,   ⎬
By exercise to foil the gout.   ⎭

　　* One of the Argonauts, who had such piercing eyes, that it was said, he could see through a wall.

52 soul.] soul, *1767*

We may begin at least and strive,
Tho' to the goal we cannot drive.
   Does your breast glow inflam'd with vice   60
By lust, or sordid avarice?
Know, there are words and charming sounds,
Whence one may sooth all mental wounds,
May mitigate the pain at least,
If not intirely calm your breast.   65
Are you puff'd up with love of praise,
Philosophers have wrote essays,
Which thrice read o'er your heart will chear,
If your attention be sincere.
The envious, wrathful, slow of will,   70
The wencher, toper, know no ill,
But may be cur'd, if they'll apply
The lectures of philosophy.
   'Tis virtue first from vice to flee,
And the first wisdom to be free   75
From folly—are you not aware,
With how much labour, how much care
Of mind and body, 'tis your aim   ⎞
Want or rejection to disclaim,   ⎬
Things that you rate the greatest shame! ⎠ 80
A merchant to the farthest shore
Of India, to be poor no more,
And with assiduous toil you brave
The rocks, the flames, the wind and wave:
Will you not hear, and learn, and trust   85
Those that are wiser, lest you lust,
And any more those things admire,
Which 'tis a folly to desire?
Is there a fighter for a prize
About the streets, that wou'd despise   90
The honour of th'Olympic crown,
Had he the hopes of such renown,
And, that he takes no pains at all,
Was mention'd as conditional?
   Silver is less of price than gold,   95
And gold than virtue, thousand fold.

Yet, O ye cits! this is the cry,
Let money be the first supply,
And then be honest by and bye.
This is at either Janus taught,   100
And this cant ev'n our youths have got,
This too can each old dotard charm,
With bag and ledger on his arm.
Polite, brave, eloquent, and true,
If certain sesterces be due,   105
Four hundred thousand to fulfil,
You must be a plebeian still.
And yet the very boys at play
Cry, he shall be the king to-day
Whoe'er behaves the best of all.   110
This be thy fort and brazen wall,
To have a conscience clear within,
Nor colour at the charge of sin.

   Say, is the Roscian edict best,
Or does the ballad stand the test,   115
Where the boys offer, as they sing,
The crown to him who lives a king?
Which manly Curius sung of yore,
And brave Camillus long before;
From him does better counsel come,   120
Who bids you scramble up a sum;
Right, if you can; but if your fate
Deny, a sum at any rate,
That you may have the foremost row,
When Puppius plays his tragic woe?   125
Or him who animates your fight,
And wishes you may stand upright,
With lib'ral soul to stem the tide
Of fortune, with her frowns and pride?

   Now shou'd the Romans bid me say,   130
Why I, who walk in the same way,
Have not my sentiments the same,
Nor follow as they praise or blame—
I make my answer in the stile
Of crafty Reynard, all the while,   135

113 charge] change *1767*   121 sum;] sum. *1767*   133 blame—] blame?— *1767*

Who thus unto the lion said,
When he beheld him sick, 'I dread
The footsteps all toward your throne,
But in the home-direction none!'
Thou dost with many heads appear   140
A monster, where must I adhere?
Who's guide? with some it is a charm,
The public revenues to farm,
And some rich widows wou'd intice,
With fruits and sweetmeats, all the price.   145
And others wou'd old dotards get,
Like fish decoy'd into their net.
Many by secret us'ry thrive—
    But grant that all the men alive,
With diff'rent talents are supplied,   150
Can they a single hour abide,
Approving their avow'd persuits?
'No place in all the world disputes
The palm with Baiae, sweet and gay.'
This haply shou'd a rich man say,   155
Anon the lake and sea must feel
The hurry of his lordly zeal.
But if caprice the hint approve—
'To-morrow, masons, all remove
Your chissels and your iron crows,   160
And at Theanum's seat dispose.'
Has he at home a genial bed?
He will advance upon this head,
The happier and the better fate
Is his, who keeps the single state.   165
But if he's single, he'll protest
That married men alone are blest;
What noose for Proteus shall I find,
His many-changing form to bind?
How fares the peasant?—there's the joke—   170
He shifts and turns like other folk;
Changes his loft, and bed of hair,
Bath, barber—when he pays his fare,
In his own barge the rich grandee

Is not more nice and sick than he: 175
Me, if with my hair all cut awry
By some bad barber you espy,
You laugh—and if beneath a coat
That's neat, a ragged shirt you note,
And if my gown but badly fit, 180
Again you laugh to show your wit.
What therefore will you do with me
Whose soul and self cannot agree?
When now I spurn the thing I sought,
Now sigh for what I set at nought, 185
Disorder'd in th'unconstant tide
Of things, that vary far and wide,
Knock down, rebuild, turn square to round?
You judge me but to be unsound
According to the gen'ral trim, 190
And neither ridicule the whim,
Nor think I want a doctor's aid,
Nor keeper by the Praetor paid:
Tho' you're the guard of my affairs,
And liable to real cares, 195
For a cut finger, if your friend's,
Who loves you, and on you depends.
In fine, the Stoics *only* prove,
The wise is less, if less, than Jove,
Whom *free, fam'd, king* 'tis fair to call, 200
And in his senses after all;
Unless a sudden fit of spleen
By some mishap shou'd intervene.

189 unsound] unsound, *1767*   198 Stoics] Stoics, *1767*

EPISTLE II.
To LOLLIUS.

He asserts that Homer, in his poems, shews what is good more fully and better than certain philosophers. He then exhorts to the cultivation of virtue.

O pleader of the highest fame!
Whilst in the Forum you declaim,
I at Praeneste re-peruse,
The battles of th'Homeric muse,
Who what is fair and what is base,⠀⠀⠀⠀⠀5
Of use, or not in any case,
Points fully, on a better plan,
Than Crantor or Crysippus can.
Whence this opinion I will shew,
Unless you've something else to do.⠀⠀⠀⠀10
⠀⠀The argument (in which we read,
For Paris his adulterous deed,
Long war the wasted Grecians wag'd
And with barbarians were engag'd)
The broils of a mad people sings,⠀⠀⠀⠀15
And their infatuated kings;
Antenor's council wou'd propose,
By fair amends, the war to close;
But Paris will not yield to this,
Jealous of safety, as of bliss.⠀⠀⠀⠀20
Nestor wou'd fain make up th'affair
'Twixt Peleus' son and Atreus' heir.
One burns with love, and both with ire:
Mean time how great soe'er the fire
That's kindled by each foolish chief,⠀⠀⠀⠀25
The people feel the loss and grief.
By faction, fraud, by lust, and sin, ⎫
By wrath without the walls, and in, ⎬
Much is the mischief, and the din. ⎭
Again, and in another tale,⠀⠀⠀⠀30
How prudence and a heart avail, .
He has with exemplary art
Explain'd in sage Ulysses' part,

Who politic from Troy's defeat
Made many cities with his fleet,   3.
And got an insight in their ways,
And while on the great sea he strays,
Returning with himself and crew,
Had many hardships to go thro'.
And yet cross fate's severest frown   4c
Could ne'er prevail to sink him down.
The Siren's charms and Circe's cup
You know, which if he'd guzzled up,
As did with glee each foolish mate,
Base in a most disastrous state,   45
The slave of an imperious queen
He must a filthy cur have been,
And had the form and gross desire
Of Swines rejoicing in the mire.

    WE, all mere cyphers from our birth,   5c
Consume the product of the earth;
Ev'n like Penelope's leud knaves,
Or whom Alcinous made slaves;
A youth for their complexion born,
Who us'd to sleep the livelong morn,   55
And so to doze away their cares,
Sooth'd by the harps composing airs.
Robbers get up and kill for pelf—
Will you not rise to save yourself?
Which if you shall not do in health   6c
The dropsy will come on by stealth:
And if you do not call away
For book and light before the day,
And keep not all your thoughts intent
On studies and designs well-meant,   65
With love or envy, when awake,
Your tortur'd heart shall surely ache.
For why do you hasten to remove
Things that your eyes cannot approve,
Yet if ought make the soul impure,   70
You for a year differ the cure?

EPISTLE ii. 71 cure?] cure. *1767*

One half is done if you set out,
Dare to be wise, nor longer doubt.
Whoe'er delays him to be good,
Stands like the clown upon the flood,   75
Expecting till the stream had done,
But that still perseveres to run,
And in eternal motion strong
Shall pass voluminous along.
　　Apt for the purposes of life,   80
And for to bear your heirs, a wife
Is sought—the woodland wild is fell'd,
That there th'improving plough be held.
Yet he that has enough in store
Ought by no means to sigh for more.   85
Nor house, nor farm, nor brass nor gold,
From his sick body can withold
The raging fever of their lord,
Or care's unseen attacks award.
The rich possessor must have health,   90
Or there's no joy in hoarded wealth.
He, on whom lust or terror wait
Enjoys his seat and his estate,
As pictures for the blind are meet,
And poultices for gouty feet,   95
Or all the harping of the spheres,
To those who have obstructed ears.
Unless the vessel is sweet, you pour
The wine therein, to make it sour:
Despise all pleasures light and vain,   100
For pleasure's noxious bought with pain:
The churl a beggar *is* and *seems*,
Then set due limits to your schemes:
A pining takes th'invidious sneak,
Whene'er he sees his neighbour sleek.   105
Sicilian tyrants ne'er cou'd find
A torture like the envious mind.
The man whose passion is not curb'd
Will wish, what in a mind disturb'd
He did, was totally undone,   110
As too great lengths his malice run.

Wrath is short madness, that restrain ⎞
At once, by bridle and by chain,   ⎟
Or what shou'd serve, will always reign. ⎠
The groom is wont the colt to check,   115
While teachable with pliant neck,
To go the road the riders please.
The puppy from the time he sees
The buckskin in the hall, and barks,
Adventures in the woods and parks.   120
Now, child, my words in your pure breast
Imbibe; now offer for the best.
That cask the scent will long retain,
Which it receiv'd, when new, in grain;
But if you loiter in the race,   125
Or urge too much the rapid pace,
I wait not for the slow in speed,
Nor push on them that take the lead.

N.B. All these precepts are drawn from examples in HOMER; a thing (I believe) not
understood by any other editor of Horace. Otherwise, there would not have been such
a complaint of a want of connection, between the former and the latter part of this
Epistle.

EPISTLE III.
To JULIUS FLORUS.

*He interrogates him concerning Claudius Nero, and of the writings of certain of
his friends. He then exhorts Florus himself to the study of wisdom, and to be
reconciled to his brother.*

Fain, Florus, would I understand,
Where Claudius now has got command,
Ev'n Caesar's gallant son-in-law.
Does Thrace, or snows, that never thaw
In Hebrus, now detain your *pow'rs*,
Or seas that run between the tow'rs,
Or in those Asiatic plains
And hills, where such abundance reigns,

127 in] and *1767*

Are you compell'd to take your rout?
What are the courtly wits about?   10
For this I'm anxious too to ask—
Who dares to undertake the task
Great Caesar's history to write,
And eternize each glorious fight,
And happy peace?—Is Titius there?   15
For whom all Rome their praise prepare;
Who fills his cup devoid of dread
At the Pindaric fountain-head,
Lakes, streams, and all the rural scene
Disdaining, as for him too mean.   20
Is he in perfect health, and kind
Enough to bear me in his mind?
Does he the Theban lays aspire
To render on the Roman lyre,
Or rants he with the Muse, his guide,   25
In all the tragic pomp and pride?
On Celsus does my council gain?
So often urg'd, and urg'd in vain,
To strike out matter of his own
And by all means to let alone   30
Such books as have arrang'd themselves
On Palatine Apollo's shelves:
Lest if the feather'd flock come there,
And each demand his proper share,
The vain jack-daw shou'd cause a roar,   35
Strip'd of the borrow'd plumes he wore;
What heights do you attempt to climb,
And active on the flowery thyme,
Whence balmy sweetness do you cull?
For far from mean, and far from dull   40
Your cultivated genius tow'rs:
Whether in keen rhetoric pow'rs
You at the bar attention draw,
Or answer in the civil law,
Or in sweet verse you build renown,   45
And conquer for the ivy crown.

EPISTLE iii. 27 gain?] gain, *1767*

Now cou'd you find it in your heart,
From care's cold comforts to depart,
Then you divinely shou'd proceed
Where'er philosophy wou'd lead.   5
This work, this way shou'd be embrac'd
By great and small, with eager haste,
If we wou'd pass our season here
Or to ourselves, or country dear.

   Of this too you must write me word,   5
Whether Munatius is preferr'd
To such degree of your esteem
As I most necessary deem,
Or, if the wound ill set to rights,
For little purpose re-unites,   6
And is at point to gape again—
Now whether madness of the brain,
Or ignorance of things disturb
Your minds, like colts no skill can curb,
Where'er you live, it is most true   6
No brothers ought to love like you.
However by these presents learn, ⎫
I feed with tenderest concern,   ⎬
A votive runt for your return.   ⎭

EPISTLE IV.
To ALBIUS TIBULLUS.

*He addresses Albius Tibullus, to whom he seems to commend the study of
Philosophy, and recount the talents with which he was adorned from heaven.*

Tibullus, whom I love and praise,
Mild judge of my prosaic lays,
Can I account for your odd turn,
Who in Pedanian groves sojourn:
Are you now writing to out-please
The works of Cassius, or at ease,
And silence, range the healthy wood,
Studious of all things wise and good?

Thou'rt not a form without a heart,
For heav'n was gracious to impart   10
A goodly person, fine estate,
Made for fruition, fortunate.
What more for her most fav'rite boy,
Cou'd a nurse image, to enjoy,
Than to be wise, and ably taught,   15
To speak aloud his noble thought,
To whom grace, fame, and body sound,
Might to pre-eminence abound,
With table of ingenious fare,
And purse with money still to spare?   20
—'Twixt hope and care, 'twixt fear and strife,
Think every day the last of life.
Beyond your wish some happy day
Shall come your grief to over-pay.
Me sleek and fat, as fat can be,   25
I hope you'll shortly come to see:
When you've a mind to laugh indeed
At pigs of the Lucretian breed.

EPISTLE V.
To TORQUATUS.

He invites him to a supper, which he assures him shall be a frugal one.

If, as a guest, you think it meet
To sit on an old-fashion'd seat,
And on a mod'rate dish to sup,
Where herbs make all the banquet up,
At home I'll tarry for my friend   5
Just as the ev'ning rays descend.
Wine you shall drink in casks prepar'd
When Taurus was again declar'd;
Betwixt Minturnian fens 'twas press'd,
And where Petrinum's vines are dress'd,   10
But, if you've better, send for me,
Or else with these commands agree:

EPISTLE iv. 23 day] day, *1767*

Bright shines my hearth, and, to be seen
By you, my furniture is clean.
From airy hopes and Moschus' cause,   15
And broils concerning riches pause:
The festal time of Caesar's birth
Shall give to-morrow peace and mirth;
It shall be lawful to prolong
The summer-night in social song.   20
    What's Fortune, if I must forbear
To use it?—he that lives to spare
For his successor, self-severe,
Is raving mad, or very near.
I will begin to booze and straw   25
Sweet flow'rs, by no means kept in awe,
Tho' held a rake-shame for my pains—
How drinking whets th'inventive brains,
Discloses secrets, strengthens hope,
Makes dastards with the valiant cope,   30
The burthen lifts from anxious hearts,
Adapts a man to learn the arts!
Whose eloquence is not sublime,
That takes off bumpers at a time?
And who so poor and who so bare,   35
But in his cups is free from care?
    These 'tis my duty to provide,
Both with propriety and pride,
And willingly I shall attend,
Lest dirty counterpanes offend,   40
That no foul napkin discompose,
To wrinkles, your discerning nose;
And that the cup and dish, we place,
Shall shine until you see your face,
That there be none to hear and spread,   45
What amongst faithful friends is said.
And that hale fellows be well met,
Brutus shall come to join the set,
Septimius and Sabinus too,
Unless h'as better cheer in view,   50

EPISTLE v. 49 too,] too. *1767*

And prettier maids. There is to boot
Room for such danglers, as shall suit.
But guests, you know, too great a throng,
Are apt, like goats, to smell too strong.
Write back what number you wou'd be,   55
And from all other business free,
Tho' clients in your court-yard wait,
Deceive them at the postern gate.

EPISTLE VI.
To NUMICIUS.

To hold nothing in too high admiration, is a thing which he asserts to be almost solely effectual for the happiness of life.

Of nothing to be over-fond,
Numicius, is contentment's bond;
This makes and keeps the bed of rest—
There are, who with unanxious breast,
Can view the sun, and starry pole,   5
And seasons, which by periods roll.
What think you of earth's golden mine,
And wealth, on either side the line,
With which the wafting ocean stores
The Arabs, and the Indian shores?   10
Then as for plays, and shows of state,
The people's favours to the great,
In what light are they to be view'd,
And what from thence must sense conclude?
Who dreads the contrary of these,   15
Not so the wond'ring fondness flees;
Stupidity o'er each prevails,
If fortune lift, or load the scales:
Rejoice, or grieve, desire, or fear,
What matters it?—shou'd things appear   20
Or better far, or worse than hope,
If man and mind become a mope,

53 guests,] guests *1767*
EPISTLE vi. 16 flees;] flees, *1767*

Let Wise-men bear the name of fools,
The jest of those that break all rules,
If Virtue's self they shall pursue   25
Beyond the laws and limits due.
   Look now on plate with wond'ring eye,
For ancient busts and bronzes sigh!
To all politer arts aspire,
And gems and Tyrian dies admire;   30
Rejoice that when you make harrangue,
On thee ten thousand gazers hang;
Seek to the bar by morning light,
And come not home till late at night,
Lest Mucius from his lady's dow'r,   35
Should reap more corn than in your pow'r,
Still holding it in highest scorn,
That he of meaner parents born,
Shou'd rather show himself than you,
More admirable of the two.   40
Whatever up in earth they lay,
Time shall expose to open day,
And things shall bury deep, and hide,
What now shine in the greatest pride.
Tho' in the Appian way you go,   ⎫   45
And still yourself with grandeur show,   ⎬
Beneath Agrippa's Portico;   ⎭
Yet thither must your course be bent,
Where Numa, and where Ancus went.
   If any virulent disease   50
Your reins, or either side shou'd seize,
Seek remedy—wou'd you excel
In life, as who wou'd not do well?
If worth alone can this atchieve;
For virtue then your pleasures leave.   55
Virtue, perhaps, is understood
As made of words, like trees, of wood.
If so, then make the port with speed,
See, no one your own ship precede,

24 those . . . rules,] those, . . . rules; *1767*   25 pursue] pursue, *1767*   26 laws]
laws, *1767*   32 hang;] hang, *1767*   50 disease] disease; *1767*   53 well?]
well; *1767*

Lest you perchance shou'd lose the FAIR,   60
And selling of your foreign ware:
At once a thousand talents sweep,
An equal sum to crown the heap,
A third to widen the amount,
A fourth to square the whole account;   65
For money, monarch of this life,
Gains you a portion with your wife,
Gives credit, friends—will heralds buy,
To blaze you of a family,
Gives beauty and when wealth is great,   70
There Venus and Suadela wait.
The Cappadocian king, they say,
Has slaves, but has no cash to pay;
Not so your own affairs dispose—
* Lucullus, as the story goes,   75
Ask'd by some persons on the stage,
If he could possibly engage
An hundred cloaks at once to lend—
Cried, how can I so many send?
But I will look amongst my ware,   80
And furnish what there is to spare.
Anon, he writes them word, to call
For full five thousand, part, or all.
'Tis a mean house that has not got
Redundant wealth, which profits not   85
The rich possessor, but deceives,
And is the bait and gain of thieves.

Wherefore, if wealth alone increase
Means and duration for our peace,
Be first this business to atchieve,   90
And be the last of all to leave.
Besides, if fortune's minions are
The splendid and the popular,
Then some shrewd servant let us buy,
The names of voters to supply,   95

---

* This fellow, probably, had the cloathing of a legion.

---

77 engage] engage, *1767*   87 bait] bait, *1767*   88 increase] increase, *1767*
91 leave.] leave: *1767*   92 are] are, *1767*

Jog our left-side, and give a tread
Upon our toes, the hands to spread,
In token of our profer'd grace,
Spite of all obstacle and place.
'This man has interest to bribe   100
The Fabian, or the Veline tribe,
That bustler gives the consulate,
Or takes away the chair of state.'
Then with appellatives endear
With *father*, *brother*, in their ear,   105
According to their sev'ral age,
Adopt them to your patronage.
   If he lives happiest, who feeds
The daintiest, where the gullet leads
Let us set out at earliest day   110
To fish, to hunt, as was the way
Gargilius chose not long ago,
Who nets, poles, servants, for a show
Made thro' the thickest croud to pass:
That one boar, thrown a-cross an ass,   115
Might to the populace appear
When taken with the *silver spear*.
   Let us with loaded stomachs swim,
Confounding decency and whim,
As lawless as Ulysses' crew,   120
Who were determin'd to pursue
All vice and pleasures contraband,
Rather than make their native land.
   If with Mimnermus you agree,
That there is no felicity   125
But what is found in love and jest,
Then rake and rally with the best.—
   Health and long life, my friend, await!
Be candid—and communicate,
If better rules of life you've got,   130
But practise these with me, if not.

114 pass:] pass. *1767*   115 boar,] boar *1767*

EPISTLE VII.
To MAECENAS.

*He excuses himself to Maecenas, that he did not stand to his word, and com-
memorates and extols his patron's liberality towards him; but asserts that liberty and peace of mind ought to be preferred to the benefactions of our friends,
and all manner of riches.*

False to the promise that I made,
Here for all August have I stay'd,
Altho' my honour was at stake
In five days my return to make.
But if Maecenas, you regard   5
The health and spirits of your bard,
The kind indulgence, which you show ⎫
To me, when sick, you will bestow ⎬
When I'm in fear of being so.   ⎭
While early figs and sultry heat   10
Make fun'rals blacken all the street,
While parents tremble for their boys,
And all the business and noise
Of canvassing, and law appeals
Bring illness, which the WILL unseals.   15
   But if on Alban fields the snows
Shou'd come, away your poet goes
Down to the sea his brains to spare,
And read in snug composure there.
Him, my dear friend, you shall receive,   20
If you will deign to give him leave,
When the warm sky the Zephyrs clear
With the first swallow of the year.
You've giv'n me opulence to boast,
But not like the Calabrian host,   25
Who presses you his pears to eat,
'I do it, friend—enough's a treat'
—'But fill your pockets, if you chuse'—
'Good sir, your bounty's too profuse'—

EPISTLE vii. 8 sick,] sick; *1767*   24 giv'n] give *1767*

'By doing so you'll bear away   30
Fit presents for your boys at play'—
'The offer has as much bestow'd,
As if I bore away a load'—
'Do as you please, but, by the bye,
You leave them only for the stye.'   35
The fool's blunt bounty on this plan
Procures no thanks, nor ever can.
The wise and good themselves profess
Ready for merit in distress,
But know, not easy to be bit,   40
The medal from the counterfeit.
I also will present a heart
Of worth to act a thankful part,
But if attach'd, as heretofore,
You'd have me, sir, you must restore   45
My constitution strong and hale,
And those black locks that grew to veil
My narrow forehead, and renew
My pleasantry in converse too:
You must revive my easy smiles,   50
And jeopardy for Cynara's wiles,
As maudlin I was wont to cry
That jilts their faithful swains shou'd fly.
    A female fox, exceeding thin,
Seeing a narrow pass crept in,   55
As leading to a tub of meal—
There having eat a wondrous deal,
She strove to make her way in vain
With her big belly, out again:
To whom a weasel not far off,   60
Cried out in most sarcastic scoff,
If you wou'd fairly make escape,
Resume the *fineness of your shape.*
    If in particular with me
This cited image shou'd agree,   65
I give up all, nor do I praise
The pleasure of the rural ways,

38 profess] profess, *1767*   52 wont] want *1767*

From rank repletion of the town,
Nor yet shall eastern wealth go down,
Nam'd with the liberty and ease,   70
OF WHERE I WILL and WHAT I PLEASE.
    You often have commended me
For diffidence and modesty;
And in return have had your due,
'My sov'reign and my father too'.   75
Behind your back my speech affirms
Your merit in the self-same terms;
Judge then, if I without regret
Cou'd give up all again, as yet.
Telemachus, the genuine heir   80
Of all his Father's patient care,
Well answer'd in a certain case—
'Our Ithaca is not a place
For horses, where no plains abound
Of much extent, nor grass is found: 85
Atrides, I those gifts resign
Which suit your country more than mine.'
The little folk shou'd not presume,
But choose small things—imperial Rome
No longer can have pow'r to please   90
Like Tibur's peace, Tarentum's ease.
    Brave, active, of the highest fame
For pleading, as Philippus came
Near the eighth hour from forth the bar;
Complaining SHIP-STREET was too far   95
For him at such a time of day,
Beheld a person, as they say;
Just from the barber shaven clean,
Paring his nails with easy mien,
'Demetrius (speaking to his slave   100
Quite apt, when his commands he gave)
Go make enquiry and bring word,
Where this man lives and how preferr'd,
Whose son, to whom he pays his court?'
The lad returns and makes report—   105

94 eighth] eight *1767*

'He's a poor man, Mena's his name,
By trade a cryer, free from blame,
One that can bustle, or unbend
His mind, and free to get or spend;
For chronies make up his delight,   110
Besides a certain home at night,
At even, when he's done his trade,
Is at the play or the parade.'
  'I wou'd that he himself explain
The things you mention, go again,   115
And bid him come to sup at eve'—
Poor Mena scarcely cou'd believe,
With silent wonder, and in short
Made answer in a civil sort.
'What, does the scrub deny?'—''tis clear   120
He is indifferent or in fear'—
Next day as he was at his job
Of selling trump'ry to the mob,
Philippus takes him unawares
And first salutes him—he prepares   125
For business his excuse to beg,
Tyed, as he sees him, by the leg,
Or he that morning had address'd,
And been before hand with his guest.
'Think that I make the matter up   130
If you to-night will come and sup.'
—'Content'—'then after nine arrive—
Go now and may your business thrive'—
When supper came discourse they had
Of sundry matters good and bad,   135
At length he's suffer'd to withdraw.
This gudgeon when he often saw
Advancing to the cover'd hook,
Untill the bait unseen he took,
A client by the morning's light,   140
A never-failing guest at night,
He is commanded to attend
Unto his seat his noble friend,

120 What, . . . deny?] What . . . deny 1767

Just at the Latin festivals;
Mounted on horse-back he extols   145
The Sabine air and pleasant ways
Thro' fields, nor ceases in his praise—
Philippus laughs, and while he seeks
Fit objects for his fun and freaks,
And while he gives him to possess   150
Sev'n thousand sesterces—no less—
And promises by way of loan
Sev'n thousand more, besides his own,
He urges him a farm to buy—
He buys one—(not to be too dry   155
And tedious with this story) know
He turns a rustic from a beau,
And all his conversation now
Is of the vineyard or the plough,
Fatigues himself to death with care,   160
And like an old man lives to spare.
But when his sheep he lost by theft,
By murrain of his goats bereft,
His acres to no purpose till'd,
His oxen with hard labour kill'd,   165
Vex'd with his loss he takes his steed,
And ev'n at midnight hies with speed,
And in a passion makes his way
To Philip's house before the day;
Whom soon as Philip chanc'd to see,   170
Rough and untrim'd to that degree,
(Says he) 'my Mena, you appear
By much too harsh and too severe'—
'O Patron!' Mena then rejoin'd
'If I in truth must be defin'd,   175
Wretch is my title to be sure—
And by thy genius, I conjure,
By your right hand and Gods, I pray,
Restore me to my former way'—
As soon as any man perceives   180
That he the better option leaves,
Let him return before too late
Unto his abdicated state.

'Tis just each person shou'd be clear,
What is the compass of his sphere.   185

EPISTLE VIII.
To CELSUS ALBINOVANUS.

Writing to Celsus he wou'd have him admonished by the Muse to bear his good
fortune with moderation and decency.

To Celsus, Muse, that I address,
Wish thou all joy and good success,
Who now with Nero has found grace,
And got his secretary's place.
Shou'd he enquire about my state,   5
* Tell him my threats are fair and great;
But for performance on my plan
Am not a good nor happy man—
Not that the hail my vines has marr'd,
Or frosts destroy'd my olive-yard,   10
Nor dies my heifer, or my goat
With murrain out in fields remote,
But that diseas'd with more defect
Of mind, than body, I object
To hear or learn things for my ease,   15
And faithful doctors salves displease;
I'm angry with the friends that strive
To make this drowsy corpse alive;
I seek the hurtful, good things fly,
At Rome I still for Tibur sigh,   20
At Tibur fickle, as the wind,
I for the city am inclin'd.
Next mind to ask him, how he wears,
How goes himself and his affairs:

---

* These, and the subsequent lines, are all ironical, and a dry rub upon Celsus, and
particularly justify those lines of Persius, viz.

> Omne vafer vitium ridenti Flaccus amico
> Tangit, et admissus circum praecordia ludit.

How with the noble youth he stands,   25
And with the cohort he commands:
Give him much joy, if all be well,
Then in his ear this precept tell—
'Bear thou good luck with meekness due;
And so your friends shall bear with you.'   30

EPISTLE IX.
To CLAUDIUS NERO.

*He recommends Septimius to him, and requests that he wou'd receive him into
a place in his friendship.*

Septimius, sure, of all mankind
Best knows what grace with you I find;
For when he prays in such a way,
As to compel me to obey,
That I in such a point of view   5
Wou'd place him as to come to you,
One worthy to be lov'd and hous'd,
By him, who merit has espous'd,
When he supposes that my fate
Is nearer to your intimate   10
Than I can possibly descry,
He knows my secrets more than I.
Much did I urge to be excus'd,
But was in a degree confus'd,
Lest I shou'd seem *to act a part*,   15
And to dissemble in my heart,
Pretending that my pow'r was none,
Quite bent on serving NUMBER ONE.
Thus to avoid a worse offence
I fly to town-bred confidence.   20
But if assurance in the cause
Of friendship merit your applause,
The *bearer* in your list enroll,
A brave good fellow and *a soul*.

EPISTLE viii. 26 cohort] cohort, *1767*
EPISTLE ix. *Headnote. receive him into*] *receive into 1767*   17 none,] none *1767*

EPISTLE X.
To FUSCUS ARISTIUS.

He extols a country life, with which he is captivated, to Fuscus, a lover of the
town.

I, that the country best approve,
To Fuscus recommend my love;
Who places in the town his bliss,
At wond'rous odds, alone in this,
We in all other things agree,   5
As loving-like, as twins can be.
With spirits of fraternal kind,
Each is, or pleas'd, or disinclin'd,
Each nods to each, in constant mood,
Like two old pidgeons of the wood—   10
You keep the nest—but Horace roves
To streams and moss-grown rocks and groves.
Do you ask why?—I live and reign,
E'er since I treated with disdain
Those very scenes, which with such cries,   15
You're all extolling to the skies;
And like the slave, that flies the priest,
As sick of a perpetual feast;
I want the bread the country bakes
Much rather than your honey'd cakes.   20
    Agreeably to nature's call
If we must live, then first of all,
You shou'd select a pleasant spot,
Where you may build your little cot;
And can you know a better place,   25
Than that which rural beauties grace?
Are warmer summers found elsewhere,
Or is there any milder air
To which a man may have recourse,
What time the Dog-star is in force,   30
Or when the Lion, in his turn,
Does by the Sun's intenseness burn?

EPISTLE X. 2 Fuscus] Fuscus, *1767*   14 E'er] Er'e *1767*

Is there a place, where envious spleen,
Breaks less upon your sleep serene?
Say, do the Lybian stones excel   35
The grass in sightliness or smell;
Or does your water, while it strives
To burst the pipes ere it arrives,
Run purer in the street, than those,
Whose rapid current murmuring flows?   40
Nay, wood is rais'd to please the eyes,
Where variegated pillars rise,
And for applause those buildings stand,
Which have a prospect of the land.
Expel dame nature, how you will,   45
She must herself recover still,
Breaking thro' fashion by degrees
And vain caprice with her decrees.
He that has not discerning sense,
To see how far in excellence   50
The tinctures of Aquinum vie
With purple of Sidonian die,
More loss can never undergo   ⎫
Than those, who have not wit to know ⎬
The truth from that which is not so. ⎭   55
Whom wealth and power too joyful make
At a reverse of things will quake;
Of ought if you are over-fond,
On resignation you'll despond:
One in a cot, for bliss indeed,   60
Kings and their fav'rites may exceed:
   The stag, more warlike than the steed,
Expell'd him from the common mead,
Till long time worsted in the end
He call'd on man to stand his friend,   65
And took the bit—but when he came
Stern conq'ror from the field of fame;
He cou'd not of the rider quit
His back, nor mouth from out the bit.
   Thus he that fears he shall be poor,   70
Must loss of liberty endure,

38 ere] e'er *1767*   50 excellence] excellence, *1767*   51 vie] vie, *1767*

More precious far than gold, must bear
A master, and such fetters wear
As shall eternally enthrall,
Because his income is too small.   75
   A man's concerns that will not do,
May be resembled to a shoe,
Which made too large will soon subvert
Your feet, and if too small will hurt.
   If you're contented with good cheer,   80
My Fuscus, then your wisdom's clear,
And me your old ally chastise, ⎫
Appearing busy in your eyes, ⎬
To gather more than shou'd suffice. ⎭
That money, which we scrape and crave,   85
To all's a tyrant, or a slave,
And yet 'tis easy to decide,
It shou'd be guided, and not guide.
   These lines I wrote in idle vein,
Behind Vacuna's mould'ring fane,   90
Happy in every point of view,
Except the joy to be with you.

EPISTLE XI.
To BULLATIUS Returned from Asia.

He asserts that it is of no consequence to the happiness of life, in what place any man dwells, since this depends upon peace of mind.

Bullatius, how does Chios seem,
And Lesbos of such high esteem?
How Samos, that is built so neat,
And Sardis, Croesus' royal seat:
Is Colophon, or Smyrna's fort,   5
Nobler or meaner than report?
Or are they each a paltry scene
To Tiber, and his meadows green?
Wou'd it your utmost wishes crown,
To have some rich Attalic town,   10

EPISTLE xi. 8 Tiber] Tibur *1767*

Or do you Lebedus admire,
While land and sea the trav'ler tire?
Tho' Lebedus be more obscure
Than Gabii, or Fidenae, sure;
Yet cou'd I live in such a spot,   15
Forgetting all, of all forgot,
Rather than not command the sea
To bluster far enough for me—
    But they, that come from Capua here,
Whom rain, and muck, and dirt besmear,   20
Wou'd not keep always in a hold;
Nor when a man contracts a cold,
The stoves and bagnios will he praise,
So as to love them all his days.
Nor tho' the Southern tempests reign, ⎫   25
Wou'd that the merchant-man constrain ⎬
To sell his ship, across the main.   ⎭
With one that's well, and wise to boot,
Rhodes and fair Mitylene will suit,
As a thick cloak, when summer glows,   30
Or linnen draw'rs in piercing snows,
Or Tiber, when the winter roars,
Or in Mid-August grates and blow'rs.
While yet you may, and fortune's smile
Attends you, in th'applauding stile   35
The praise of absent Rhodes resume,
Of Samos, Chios, here at Rome.
Whatever prosp'rous hour below
The hands of providence bestow,
Let gratitude confirm your own,   40
Nor for the livelong year postpone
To use such things as best can please,
That you may say, I've liv'd at ease,
Whatever region you possess:
For if right reason and address,   45
And not a place that over-bears
Wide ocean, can remove our cares,

12 tire?] tire, *1767*   38 below] below, *1767*   41 postpone] postpone, *1767*

They change their climate, not their soul,
Who go in ships from pole to pole.
In strenuous idleness we strive,   50
We launch our ships, and chariots drive
In order for a happy lot;
But that you seek is on the spot,
And ev'n at * Ulubrae might be,
For men of equanimity.   55

EPISTLE XII.
To ICCIUS.

That he is rich alone, who makes good use of his finances. He writes also of the present state of the Roman affairs.

If, as you take Agrippa's dues,
Sicilian wealth you rightly use,
A greater affluence, my friend,
From Jove himself cou'd not descend:
Cease murm'ring, for you cannot plead   5
You're poor, and have the things you need.
If well with belly, and with back,
And for your feet you nothing lack,
I do not see to make you glad
How ev'n imperial wealth wou'd add.   10
If midst such plenty and such sums
You starve on herbs and *miller's thumbs*,
So very near you'll skin the flint,
That you will raise at least a *mint*,
And fortune shortly shall behold,   15
A pow'ring in a flood of gold;
Because mere money, it is plain,
Can ne'er avail to change the grain,
Or that it is your thought and tone,
That all things yield to worth alone.   20

* A paltry forlorn place in Campania.

EPISTLE xii. 6 need.] need, *1767*   9 glad] glad, *1767*   16 gold;] gold, *1767*

What wonder, if his neighbours cows,
Upon his fields and meadows brouze,
If the old sophist's active mind
Be wand'ring from the man disjoin'd;
When you a scrambler, and a sneak,   25
Will after nothing trivial seek,
But still to things exalted strain:
As how the shores the floods contain,
What rules the year, if on the pole
The stars self-mov'd, or guided roll,   30
What cause the Lunar orb benights,
And what again her beauty lights;
What is the pow'r, and what th'intent
Of all this dissonant consent?
Who most with reason disagrees,   35
Stertinius or Empedocles?

    But whether butchering of a *rough*,
Or leeks and chives, your plate you stuff,
Use Grosphus as a friend, and give
With freedom what he will receive: 40
I'll warrant Grosphus, that his pray'r
Shall only be for what is fair.

    One vast benevolence may reap,
When good men want, true friends are cheap.

    Now that you may not be in doubt,   45
How our affairs at Rome turn out,
The Spanish and Armenian bands,
By Nero's and Agrippa's hands,
Are fall'n—Phraates on his knee,
Does to great Caesar's terms agree;   50
And golden plenty all around
Full-horn'd, th'Italian crops has crown'd.

27 strain:] strain, *1767*   32 lights;] lights, *1767*

EPISTLE XIII.
To VINNIUS ASELLA.

He requires of Vinnius that in presenting his books to Augustus he wou'd have
a due respect to the timing and decency of doing it.

Just as the whole direction stands,
By frequent and by full commands,
Upon your setting out reveal'd,
Deliver up these volumes seal'd,
To Caesar—that is—shou'd you find,   5
He's well, in spirits and inclin'd
To ask for trifles of this kind.
Lest zealous for my works and me
You shou'd be thought to make too free,
And bring an odium, if you press   10
With ill-advis'd officiousness.
But if my budget gall your back,
Rather demolish all the pack,
Than on the pavement rudely throw
Before Augustus, when you go,   15
To bring a jest in the event,
Upon your Asinine descent,
And be the talk of all the town—
Use your best efforts up and down,
Through sloughs and rivers, dale and hill,   20
And when your purpose you fulfil,
Thus bear the parcel, lest, perchance,
You with my volume shou'd advance
As country boobies hug a lamb,
Or Pyrrhia, after many a dram,   25
Stol'n yarn, or routed from his nap,
The drunken cit his fudling-cap.
Lest by a blunder you shou'd say,
How much you sweated all the way
In bringing verse, which may succeed   30
To make great Caesar hear and read.
Intreated by the poet's pray'r,
Proceed—good-bye—be well aware,

Lest you shou'd stumble with your load,
And break my orders on the road.   35

EPISTLE XIV.
To his STEWARD in the Country.

*He reprehends his Steward's desire to live in the city, and in the mean time
capriciously despising the country, which aforetime he secretly longed for.*

O Steward! of my small estate,
Whose woods and fields new life create
In me, tho' scorn'd by you thro' pride,
Where five good families reside;
And which in days of old sent down   5
Five Senators to Varia's town:
Let's try, if I the best succeed,
In plucking up each thorn and weed,
That in the inward man is found,
Or you in clearing of the ground;   10
And which the least offence has got,
Or Horace, or his Sabine spot?
　Albeit the piety and woe
Of Lamia, which no bounds will know,
For his lost brother still severe,   15
Detain me for a season here;
Yet all my heart, and all my mind,
Are solely thither-wards inclin'd,
And fondly longs to break abrupt,
On all barriers that interrupt.   20
I say the country-life is best;
You for the citizen contest;
They with their own are in disgust,
Who for another's portion lust,
And each of us all sense disclaims,   25
Who either place unjustly blames;
The mind's in fault, which cannot shape
Its flight from its own self to 'scape.

EPISTLE xiv. 6 Varia's] Baria's *1767*   28 Its ... its] It's ... it's *1767*

When you was DRUDGE, for country air
You sigh'd with many a secret pray'r;   30
But now you're to a steward rais'd,
The town, the stews, and baths, are prais'd:
I have a more consistent heart,
And always pensively depart,
Whenever back to Rome my fate   35
Drags me to business that I hate.
From different bents we disagree,
For what appears to such as thee,
All horrid scenes, and desart waste,
Are pleasant to a man of taste,   40
Who thinks with me, and must despise
Things that are charming in your eyes.
The greasy taverns, and the stews,
I know, make you the city chuse.
Besides, I rear within my fence,   45
The pepper, and the frankincense;
Nor yield my rocks the grape so quick,
Nor have you there a tavern tick,
Nor minstrel harlot, to whose sound
You gambol cumb'rous to the ground.   50
And yet * you plough with might and main
The fallows, that too long have lain,
And FINELY tend the unyok'd beeves,
And fill them with fresh-gather'd leaves;
Besides the brook, in case of wet,   55
Adds to an idle fellow's sweat,
Best taught by embankations there,
The sunny meadow-land to spare.
    Come now attend, and you shall know
The reason why we differ so;   60
He who well-dress'd in essenc'd hair,
Cou'd scot-free please the venal fair,
He who from jovial noon to night,
Cou'd quaff Falernian with delight,
Now loves short meals, and sweet repose,   65
Where springs green grass, and riv'let flows;

* The purport of his letter to his master.

Nor is it at one time of day,
So much a shame to have been gay,
As not to know one's hand to stay.
There's no one with an evil glance,   70
On my possessions looks askance,
Nor poisons there with secret spite,
Or slander's more audacious bite.
The neighbours smile to see me toil,
Clearing the sods and stone the soil—   75
You'd rather munch upon the fare,
Your fellow-slaves each day prepare,
There are your wishes and your joy—
Mean time the cunning errant-boy
Grudges the fewel and the flocks,   80
And what the kitchen-garden stocks.
The ox wants trappings on his back,
The plough wou'd suit the lazy HACK;
But I determine in that case,
That each shall keep his proper place.   85

EPISTLE XV.
To VALA.

Upon an engagement with himself to go to Velia and Salernum, he makes enquiry how it is to winter with them, and into the temperature of the air.

At Velia—how's the winter there,
And what's Salernum for its air?
What set of men are there bestow'd?
Is there a tolerable road?
For * Musa warrants on his fee,   5
That Baiae is no place for me,
Yet makes me odious at the wells,
While his prescription me compels

* Antonius Musa, a physician, celebrated at Rome, and all over Italy, for his curing Augustus, in the year of Rome *731*, of a grievous disease, by making him bath and drink the waters; for which event, he received a large sum of money both from Caesar and the Senate, with the privilege of the gold ring, which he had not before on account of his being only a free'd-man.

To use cold water every day,
Before the ice is gone away.   10
In truth, the village justly sighs,
To see us myrtle groves despise,
And likewise that chalybeate stream,
Held in such eminent esteem,
As men of chronic ills it rids;   15
And grudges at those invalids,
Who dare their breast and head commit
To Clusian waters, and think fit
To go to Gabii, and those parts,
Where with the cold a traveller smarts.   20
The wonted place I now must change,
And Inns *accustom'd* for the *strange*.
The horses must be driven by—
Hollo! quoth BALD-FACE, where do you hie?
Why, not to Cumae, nor to stay   25
At Baiae, will the rider say,
And pull in wrath the left-hand rein;
But angry speeches are in vain,
For horses are not apt to fear
Rough words, but in the bit they hear.   30
   Your letter too must let me know,
At which place rankest harvests grow;
Whether rain-water there they save,
Or in perennial fountains lave:
For how they there are serv'd with wine,   35
At present, is no care of mine.
When at my feast the bowl I crown,
I can make any thing go down;
But when I come upon the coast,
The rich and mellow suit me most,   40
Which may all anxious thoughts subdue, ⎫
And raising up each pleasing view,   ⎬
Flow in my veins and spirit too.   ⎭
Which may a choice of words suggest,
In which my youth may be exprest,   45
And urg'd to the Lucanian Fair.—
Next mention if the country there

EPISTLE xv. 25 Why,] Why *1767*

Abound with hares, or nurture boars,
And write what shallows near the shores
Most fishes and sea-urchins breed,   50
That I with you so well may feed,
As to do credit to the place,
And part with a * Phaeacian face.
To all these queries you, my friend,
Must speak, and Horace shall attend.   55
     Maenius, who manfully had spent
His father's, and his mother's rent,
Begun upon the comic plan,
And vague from post to pillar ran.
He with a citizen wou'd deal   60
As with a foe, denied a meal:
Made up of most inveterate lies,
Who OUGHT on ANY wou'd devise;
The dearth, and hurricane, and draught
Of markets, whatsoe'er he caught   65
He greedily bestow'd within;
And when with winkers at his sin,
And those poor souls he fill'd with dread,
He little, or ev'n nothing sped,
Whole harslets at a time he'd cram,   70
With all th'intestines of a lamb,
Devouring as his proper share,   ⎫
What wou'd have sated many a bear: ⎬
Now being frugal, as it were,   ⎭
So as to urge, that men shou'd brand   75
The guts of Epicurus' band.
Yet this same Maenius, when he turn'd
Some special booty that he earn'd,
All into ashes, and to smoke,
Then wou'd he Hercules invoke,   80
And swear he cou'd not think it strange,
That men shou'd eat both house and grange,

* A rich, luxurious people.

---

50 fishes] fishes, *1767*   66 within;] within, *1767*   73 bear:] bear, *1767*
74 were,] were: *1767*

While they fat thrushes cou'd prepare,
And feast upon a banging bear.
  In fact, ev'n such a one am I,   85
And when I cannot beg, or buy,
Am very stout 'mongst sorry fare,
But midst the viands nice and rare,
I have another thing to say,
That happiest of all men are they,   90
Who by neat villas make it clear,
They're worth some thousand pounds a year.

EPISTLE XVI.
To QUINTIUS.

After he has described the shape and situation of his Sabine farm, and men-
tioned his happiness in living there, he enquires into the life of his friend, and
warns him not to depend upon vulgar report, but that he should prefer the real-
ity, rather than the character of a good man.

  Lest you shou'd with yourself debate,
Best friend, concerning my estate;
Whether it feeds its lord with corn,
Or olive-yards the spot adorn,
Or rich with fruit and meads it shines,   5
Or elms, that are array'd with vines;
To you I will diffusely write
Of its dimensions, shape, and site.
  A chain of mountains wou'd appear,
Did not a valley interfere,   10
Which wou'd be darken'd by the shade,
Did not the morning sun invade,
Where on the right-hand side 'tis cleft,
And beams at eve upon the left:
What if upon my thorny fence   15
Grow cornels, and the dam'sines dense,
If oak and holmes, whose acrons show'r
To feed the beasts, their lord embow'r?

88 rare,] rare: *1767*
EPISTLE xvi. 3 its] it's *1767*

You'd think Tarentum nearer Rome,
In all its verdant pride and bloom.   20
A fountain too, that well might claim
The rank to give a river name,
(Than which cool Hebrus bounding Thrace,
Shows not a more transparent face)
Flows fraught with salutary aid,   25
When head or bowels pains invade.
This sweet retreat which, dale and hill,
Believe me, are enchanting still,
Preserve your Horace hale and stout,
What time September comes about.   30
   You're a good man, if you take care
To earn the character, you bear.
I with all Rome have long agreed,
That you're a happy man indeed;
But fear from symptoms, that I trace, ⎫   35
You any evidence embrace,   ⎬
Rather than conscience in this case; ⎭
And think man's happiness the prize
Of others than the good and wise;
Lest, tho' the people call you sound   40
In mind and body, there be found
A fever, which you wou'd conceal,
In order to resume your meal,
Until a nervous trembling seize
Your hands, which with good cheer you grease.   45
A fool's false shame his sores will hide,
Till med'cines are in vain applied.
If any man shou'd name to thee
Fights you have fought by land and sea,
And strive your ticklish ear to please   50
With compliments as great as these:
'May Jove! and all the powr's divine!
Who guard the common-wealth and thine,
Still make it doubtful on review,   ⎫
Which is most anxious of the two,   ⎬   55
Or you for Rome, or Rome for you!'   ⎭

27 retreat which,] retreat, which *1767*   33 with] will *1767*   39 others . . . wise;]
others, . . . wise. *1767*   48 thee] thee, *1767*   50 please] please, *1767*

What, wou'd you challenge as your own,
That which is Caesar's praise alone?
When you sit still to hear men call
Thee wise, and without blame at all,   60
Pray will you answer to these terms,
And warrant what a fool affirms:
'Tis granted I, as well as you,
Love to be held both wise and true.
But he, who gives this praise to-day,   65
The next can take it all away;
Ev'n as, when they have giv'n their voice
For one unworthy of their choice
As consul, they can turn him out
Soon as the year is come about—   70
'Resign—'tis ours:'—with aching heart
I do resign, and must depart.
    But shou'd the same *tongues* call me rogue,
Or tax me with each vice in vogue,
Or urge, I with a rope had tied   75
My father's neck, until he died:
Shou'd I change colour, or be stung
At such lies of an evil tongue?
Wrong-prais'd who's *pleas'd*, and *wrong-arraign'd*
Who's *griev'd*, except the false and feign'd?   80
    Who then is good?—I'll tell thee who—
He that observes with rev'rence due
The statutes of the Conscript seers,
And law and equity reveres:
Who great and many things right fair   85
Determines, when he takes the chair;
Whose bond will property maintain,
And testimony causes gain.
Yet he is better understood
In his own house, and neighbourhood,   90
To be all filthiness within,
And clad but in a specious skin.
If by a slave it shou'd be said,
I have not robb'd your house, nor fled,
I answer you have your reward,   95

57 What,] What *1767*   62 affirms:] affirms. *1767*   76 died:] died. *1767*

Ungall'd your shoulders with the cord.
I've kill'd no man—you feed no crows
Upon the gallows—I suppose,
Still I am virtuous good and wise,
All which your Sabine friend denies.   100
    The cautious wolf the pit forbears,
As does the hawk suspected snares,
Nor kite the cover'd hook will take—
Wise men love good for goodness sake.
If you from guilt still keep you clear,   105
'Tis on the principle of fear:
But sure to come off safe and sound,
You sacred and prophane confound.
For if of garner'd beans you stole,
From out a thousand but one bowl,   110
The lighter is my loss and grief,
But you by no means less a thief.
    An honest man *upon your scheme*,
Whom every bar and court esteem,
If he appease the pow'rs divine,   115
At any day with beeves or swine,
Upon Apollo loud he calls,
And after father Janus bawls,
Mean time he mutters to himself,
As dreading hearers, 'Charming elf!   120
Laverna! goddess of deceit,
Grant me the happy knack to cheat!
Grant me a seeming honest face,
And full of sanctified grimace:
In night my gross offences shroud,   125
And o'er my knav'ry cast a cloud!'
I cannot see, the niggard dupe,
Who for a farthing deigns to stoop,
Stuck in the road—how can he be
In any circumstance more free   130
Or better than a common slave;
For he that is so prone to crave,
Must ever lead a life of dread,
And one with terrors in his head,

130 free] free, *1767*

Cannot have freedom in my sense——   135
  They lose their weapons of defence,
And all desert fair virtue's post
That hurry, who shall scrape the most.
Yet if this slave a price will fetch,
'Tis better not destroy the wretch: 140
He may turn out a useful hand,
To feed the flock, or plough the land,
Let him to sea, and winter there,
To stock the market and the fair.
  A wise and good man will be bold   145
To say with Bacchus kept in hold:
'O king of Thebans! how much pain
Will you compel me to sustain,
So much unworthy this foul play?'
'Why I will take your goods away'——   150
'My cattle, bedding, and my plate,
I do suppose——then take them straight.'
'Beneath a surly keeper's nod
You shall be pris'ner here', 'A God
Shall save me, whenso'er I choose,   155
And all these bonds and fetters loose.'
As hinting to the last event,
Death here, I think, the poet meant;
For death's the extremity suppos'd,
By which the line of life is clos'd.   160

EPISTLE XVII.
To SCAEVA.

He admonishes Scaeva not to despise the friendship of people in Power, and that in his cast of life, he should rather imitate Aristippus than Diogenes.

Tho' Scaeva, of yourself discrete,
You know how with grandees to treat,
Yet still to these remarks attend,
And take th'opinion of a friend,
Who'll teach you things of great concern,   5
Himself not yet too old to learn,

As tho' the blind shou'd lead the way;
Howev'r, observing what I say,
You'll see some things, that must conduce
To be of most peculiar use.   10
    If self-indulgence make thee gay,
And kindly sleep till break of day,
If dust and rumbling of the wheels,
And noise in which the tavern deals,
Offend thee, then you must repair   15
To Ferentinum, I declare.
For all the joys beneath the skies,
The rich cannot monopolize;
Nor has he done amiss, whose lease
Of life were secrecy and peace.   20
    If you your family wou'd serve,
And for your own content reserve
A cast upon a higher die,
Betimes you must the nobles ply.
    Had Aristippus been content   25
To dine on herbs, he ne'er had went
Unto the tables of the grand—
Diogenes on t'other hand,
Who to our notions will object,
If he had skill'd in that respect,   30
Might so have liv'd in splendid scenes,
And wou'd have scorn'd his roots and greens:
Whose words and actions of the two
You best approve, I prithee shew;
Or, as you're junior, hear the test,   35
Why Aristippus reasons best.
For he was wont (as stories say)
To keep the Cynic thus at bay.
'The jester's province I profess,
To serve myself with some address,   40
But you to give the mob delight:
So what I practise, as more right,
Is a more honourable thing:
To ride and revel with the king.

EPISTLE xvii. 35 Or, ... junior,] Or ... junior *1767*   41 delight:] delight, *1767*
43 thing:] thing *1767*

I am obsequious in my turn—   45
You beg for what the donors spurn,
Yet are inferior in your soul
To him that gives the sorry dole,
Tho' you mean while your boast have made,
You need not any human aid.'   50
Rare Aristippus, genius born
All lot and station to adorn,
Each look of things a grace he lent,
Tho' still aspiring, still content.
But I shou'd think it very strange,   55
If e'er the churl shou'd brook a change,
Whose obstinacy will but wear
Two rags against th'inclement air.
The one if summon'd to the great,
Will not for purple vestments wait: 60
But be his habit as it may,
To the first place will make his way,
And without awkwardness and pain,
Will any character sustain.
The other fellow a fine cloak,   65
Wrought at Miletum, wou'd provoke
Worse than a mastiff, or a snake,
And he with shiv'ring cold will ache,
Unless his rags you give him back—
Give them—and let him live and lack.   70
    Great actions of heroic lives,
To shew to Rome her foe in gyves,
Ev'n at Jove's throne directly aim,
And there celestial honours claim.
And such immortal chiefs as these,   75
'Tis not the meanest praise to please:
But 'tis not ev'ry fawner's fate,
To gain a point so very great.
    One fearing he shou'd not succeed,
Was prudent to sit still—agreed—   80
What then? was it not bravely done
By him, that hit the mark and won?

51 born] born, *1767*   82 won?] won. *1767*

But here, or no where we must end
The matter, which we now contend.
One dreads the weight, too weak and poor ⎞   85
In limbs and spirit to endure;   ⎟
The other makes the bus'ness sure.   ⎠
The man whose resolution tries
Thro' hardship to attain the prize,
Shou'd be rewarded and renown'd,   90
Or virtue is an empty sound.

   He that before his Lord forbears
To hint the dearth of his affairs,
Is likely to take more away,
Than one too apt to beg and pray.   95
It differs much with modest ease
To take, or greedily to seize;
For in the conduct of your part,
Lies all the myst'ry of your art.
If thus a man his Lord address,   100
'I have a sister portionless,
A mother poor with an estate,
Which will not sell at any rate,
Nor yields it, whence we may be fed:'
Such an one plainly begs his bread;   105
A second will keep up the cant,
For you a dividend to grant.
But if the crow had held her prate,   ⎞
She'd had more victuals and less hate, ⎟
When bick'ring at her cruel fate.   ⎠   110

   If when your Lord shou'd take his rout
Far as Brundusium, or set out
For fair Surrentum, and as friend
Invite his client to attend:
He who of rugged roads complains,   115
Or bitter cold, or heavy rains,
Or for his broken trunk laments,
And for the loss of the contents,
Resembles but too stale a bite,
Which harlots practice every night,   120
Oft wailing they've a garter lost,
Or string of pearls of mighty cost:

So that when really made a prey,
No faith is giv'n to what they say.
Nor cares a man, once made a fool,   125
To be again th'impostor's tool,
Who with pretended broken legs,
Thrown in the road for succour begs,
Ev'n tho' the gypsy stream with tears,
And by the great Osiris swears—   130
'This is no fraud, I pray believe,
And on your backs the lame receive.'
Your tricks upon some stranger try,
All the hoarse neighbourhood reply.

EPISTLE XVIII.
To LOLLIUS.

He instructs Lollius what is to be done, and what avoided, in order to render
friendships permanent; and is particular upon a man's conduct in respect to a
friend in power.

Dear Lollius, if right well I ken
The most ingenuous of men,
Professor of a friendly heart,
You scorn to act a flatt'rer's part.
A Roman matron is not more   5
Distinguish'd from a painted whore,
Than a true friend from the disguise
Of him that faithless deals in lies.
There is a vice reverse of this,
And of the two the more amiss,   10
A clownish harshness blunt and base,
Which wou'd commend itself to grace,
With tweazer'd face, and shaven skin,
And teeth all dirty-black within,
Intending that it shou'd appear,   15
As downright honest and sincere.
Virtue between each vice resides,
Alike remote from both the sides.

EPISTLE xviii. 7 friend] friend, *1767*

    The one's submission's far too great,
And jester of the lowest seat,   20
The rich-man's nod he so reveres,
And so respects, whate'er he hears,
And catches up each word that falls,
Like boys, whose rigid master calls
To say their lesson, or a play'r,   25
That must his under-part prepare.
The other's full of gross abuse,
About the milking of a goose,
And fights with trifles arm'd, 'How now?
What? credit not to me allow?   30
What, boldly shall not I give vent,
Unto my heart's true sentiment?
I wou'd not hold another year,
On terms so monstrously severe!'
But what's the theme of all this fray? ⎞   35
If Castor best his weapon play,   ⎟
Or Docilis shall win the day?   ⎠
Or if Brundusium best to make,
A man the Appian road shou'd take?
    Whom deadly lewdness strips, or dice   40
That speediest lead to want by vice,
Whom vanity too grand shall dress,
And dawbs with essence to excess,
Whom thirst and hunger after gold
Possesses, not to be controul'd,   45
Blushing and shunning to be poor,
Him his rich friend cannot endure,
And oft persues with dread and hate,
Himself far more inordinate.
And, if he does not hate, he rules,   50
And as a pious mother schools
Her son, her virtues to out-do,
He thus adds something pretty true.
'My wealth (pray do not you contend)
Admits of all my follies, friend,   55
Your small estate shou'd make you loth
To cut your coat beyond your cloath,

20 seat,] seat *1767*   31 What,] What *1767*   34 severe!] severe? *1767*

And, if your senses you retain,
Cease contest, where the contest's vain.'
Eutrapelus whene'er intent   60
To do a man much detriment,
Wou'd give him gaudy cloaths, 'For so
Blest in the notion of a beau,
He'll take new measures, form new schemes,
Indulge till noon in pleasing dreams: 65
Will for a whore his trade postpone,
Will give huge int'rest for a loan;
Will learn at last the fencer's art,
Or drive for hire a gard'ner's cart.'—
    Into no secrecies inquire;   70
Keep confidence repos'd intire,
Tho' put to torture by the force
Of wine, or passionate discourse.
Nor must you praise your own persuit,
And that of your great friend dispute: 75
Nor with your poetry solace
Your muse, when he prefers the chace.
For by such means Amphion cross'd
His brother, and his kindness lost;
Till he gave up his lyre at last,   80
To him of the severer cast.
Amphion therefore did give way
To Zethus' temper, as they say:
And do you in likewise attend
The mild injunctions of your friend,   85
And when into the field he gets
His dogs, and his Etolian nets,
Arise, and for a while refuse
Th'ill-bred moroseness of your Muse,
That you may sup upon the spoil,   90
Thus purchas'd by your mutual toil.
This exercise for health and bloom,
Habitual to the sons of Rome,
Is useful ev'n to life, and fame,
And keeps the feet from being lame;   95

88 refuse] refuse, *1767*

But chiefly while you're young and sound,
And can in speed out-strip the hound,
And foil the fury of the boar.

Then add to what we've urg'd before,
Not one of those, which arms profess,   100
Can handle them with more address.
You know what vast applause you gain,
In all those feats on Mars's plain:
In fine, as yet of tender age,
You cou'd in cruel fights engage,   105
And those Cantabrian wars endur'd,
Beneath that chief, who has procur'd
Our standards from the Parthian host,
And fix'd them in their wonted post;
And now does all the acts that tend   110
To make the Roman arms transcend.

And lest you from the sports recede,
Without a good excuse to plead,
(Tho' nothing trifling, or uncooth,
You e'er committed from your youth)   115
Yet, where your rural villa lies,
You pleasant pastimes can devise.
The naval troops divide the boats,
And all the Actian battle floats,
Acted by boys, in hostile pride,   120
Which you, as their commander, guide;
Your brother's the fictitious foe,
And Adria's sea the ponds below,
Till victory, with bays, come down,
And one or other champion crown.   125
Great Caesar, when he once shall see
Your taste and his so well agree,
Shall give you, and your little bands
Immense applause, with both his hands.

Now let me (if a man like you   130
Can need advice) advise you true.
Oft take good heed what, and to whom,
You speak of every man in Rome;
A pumper shun, who will not fail
To bear materials of a tale,   135

Nor can the ears that spring a leak,
With faith retain the things you speak,
And when one word to such you pawn,
It is irrevocably gone.

By frequent observations trace,   140
Him you wou'd recommend to grace;
Lest you anon shou'd be asham'd
Of faults, for which another's blam'd.
We sometimes are deceiv'd, and raise
A person who's not worthy praise.   145
Thus chous'd, forbear to vindicate
Him, whose own conduct mars his fate.
So one well prov'd you shall protect,
If false accusers ought object,
And shield him confident in you;   ⎫   150
If slander's tooth his fame persue, ⎬
Perceive you not your danger too? ⎭
For 'tis a very near concern
To you, when neighb'ring houses burn,
And flames by negligence are fed,   155
And still are wont to get a-head.

The cultivation of esteem
With men in pow'r, to those may seem
Desirous, who have never tried,
But by experience is decried.   160
When once your vessel's under sail,
Ply well your business, lest the gale
Shou'd shift upon th'inconstant main,
And drive your vessel back again.

The sad abominate the gay;   165
These scorn the children of dismay;
The volatile the dull sedate;
Idlers, the brisk and active hate.
They that all night will ply the glass,
Despise you, if your turn you pass,   170
Tho' with solemnity you swear,
You dread th'effects of midnight air.
Your forehead of its gloom uncloud,
For 'tis in general allow'd,

165 sad] sad, *1767*

Too modest men appear, as dark,   175
Too silent, curs that cannot bark.
   In all, with which you are concern'd,
You must consult and read the learn'd,
Who on the proper measures treat,
To make your life serene and sweet;   180
Lest greedy av'rice, ever poor,
Still make you anxious thoughts endure,
Lest fear and hope distract your mind,
For things of an indifferent kind:
That you may know if nature teach,   185
Or virtue be what scholars preach,
What lessens care, encreases smiles,
And your own conscience reconciles;
What makes a perfect calm, a name,
Or wealth, which still is pleasure's aim,   190
Or life's whole passage to fulfil,
Thro' flowery bye-paths snug and still.
   As oft as on Digentia's brink,
Whose cool streams all Mandela drink,
A little village chopt with cold,   195
Myself I at my ease behold,
What are my sentiments, my friend,
For what do you think my knees I bend?
That what I have of present store
Be kept, or rather less than more,   200
That if the Gods more life shou'd give,
I may for self-improvement live,
With choice of the best books to read,
And year's provision for my need,
Lest I shou'd be in fortune's pow'r,   205
Dependent on th'uncertain hour.
Thus much is fit of Jove to pray,
Ev'n he that gives and takes away:
Let him long life and wealth bestow, ⎫
I trust from my own heart to know   ⎬   210
All things that make for peace below. ⎭

188 reconciles;] reconciles, *1767*   206 hour.] hour; *1767*   210 know] know, *1767*

EPISTLE XIX.
To MAECENAS.

He reprehends the false zeal certain writers had to imitate the defects, rather
than the perfections of the poets.

Dear Friend, if you the lore embrace
Of old Cratinus, in this case
No verse can last, or charm the age,
Wrote by the water-drinking sage;
And this has been a maxim fix'd,   5
E'er since the brain-sick bards were mix'd,
By Liber's laws injoin'd to rove
With fawns and satyrs of the grove:
Hence all the muses sweetly gay,
Oft smell of wine at early day.   10
When * Homer call'd the grape divine,
He wrote his verses by his wine;
And Ennius, our reverend sire,
Wou'd not to sing of arms aspire,
Till for his subject made a match   15
By drink—'I therefore shall dispatch
The sneaking milk-sops one and all,
For sentence to the judgment-hall,
Nor will I any licence grant,
For those to sing, who whine and cant.'   20
Soon as this edict was promulg'd,
The poets night and day indulg'd
The bumpers they wou'd not abate.—
   What if a man shou'd imitate
The naked feet and surly frown   25
Of Cato, with his scanty gown?
Wou'd he be instantly endued
With Cato's worth and rectitude?
The mimic, who propos'd to please
By taking off Timagenes,   30

* Ἀνδρὶ δὲ κεκμηῶτι μένος μέγα οἶνος ἀέξει, and sundry other places.

EPISTLE xix. 28 rectitude?] rectitude. *1767*

With envy burst, as he in vain
Did after wit and utt'rance strain.
   Mean imitation foils the base,
As faults are all that they can trace,
As tho', when I've a pallid hue,   35
They shou'd take drugs to be so too.
O mimics! scarce above the brutes!
How very frequently the fruits,
Of that in which each bungler prides,
Provok'd my wrath, or split my sides?   40
   A sheer original from God, ⎫
I stalk'd upon the vacant sod,   ⎬
Nor in another's footsteps trod.⎭
He who as leader can perform
His part in justice heads the swarm.   45
I first made Italy repeat,
Iambics of the Parian beat,
Form'd on Archilochus, to tow'r
At once in harmony and pow'r,
But not pursuing of his scheme,   50
To kill my brother with my phlegm;
And lest I shou'd from Rome receive
A crown that sparing critics weave,
Because I fear'd to undertake
The changing measure of his make: 55
There's Sappho, writing like a man,
Corrects and variegates my plan;
Alcaeus too—but all the while
Diverse in numbers and in stile,
Nor does he now unto his shame   60
Seek his step-father to defame,
Nor strangle, in poetic wrath,
The maid to whom he pledge'd his troth:
Him, who was never known before,
I harp'd upon the Latian shore: 65
For 'tis my pleasure to be new,
And read by an ingenuous FEW.
   Now wou'd you know the real cause,
My readers give me such applause,

60 shame] shame, *1767*

Fond of my arch-instructive tomes,   70
When sung within their private homes;
But soon as e'er they quit their place
Degrade me—this is then the case.
To count the suffrage of the mob,
I ever thought too mean a job,   75
By treating them with dainty fare,
And rags and tatters for their wear.
I hear no writings of the great,
Nor in revenge my own repeat;
Nor do I hie me to the schools   80
Of those that teach the grammar rules—
Hence all this grievance—if I say,
'I am asham'd my worthless lay
In crouds theatric to recite;
As tho' I wou'd to things so light   85
A thought of dignity and weight
In rank presumption arrogate,'
'At us (says one) your honour sneers,
Preserving for celestial ears
Your poetry—for you distill   90
Alone, it seems, the honey'd rill,
A person in your own sweet eyes,
Extremely beautiful and wise.'
At taunts like these, I do not dare
To let my nose have too much air,   95
And lest their nails my skin deface,
I cry, 'I do not like this place',
And beg a truce—for gamesome jest
Brings on a trial, who is best,
Then emulation furthers strife,   100
And THAT ill-blood, and loss of life.

EPISTLE XX.
To his BOOK.

You seem to cast, my vent'rous book,
Towards the town a wishful look,
That thee the chapmen may demand,
Where Janus, and Vertumnus stand;
When polish'd by the binder's art.—   5
Both keys and seals, with all your heart,
You hate, and every thing refuse
Which all your modest volumes chuse.
You grudge that you are shewn to few,
Desirous of the public view,   10
On other principles compil'd—
Away then, since you are so wild—
When once set off there's no return—
Soon shall you say with much concern—
'Ah! wretch, what wou'd I,' when your pride   15
Is by some reader mortified,
And in some narrow nook you stick,
When curiosity is sick.
    But if the augur do not dream,
In wrath for this your desp'rate scheme;   20
At Rome you'll be welcome guest,
As long as you are new at least.
But when all dirty you become,
In witness of the vulgar thumb,
Or groveling book-worms you must feed,   25
Or far as Utica shall speed;
Or bundled up in packthread chain,
Be sent a transport into Spain.
The good adviser, all the while,
To whom you gave no heed, will smile: 30
As he who from the mountain threw
The sulky ass, that wou'd not do
His bus'ness—'then go down the hill—
Who'd save an ass against his will?'

EPISTLE xx. 18 sick.] sick, *1767*   26 far as] for us *1767*   34 will?] will. *1767*

This destiny too must remain—   35
Thee faultring dotage shall detain
About the city-skirts to teach
The boys their rudiments of speech.
    And when the fervency of day
Brings you more hearers, you must say,   40
That poor and meanly born at best,
I spread my wings beyond my nest,
And what you from my birth subtract,
You for my virtues must exact;
That peace or war, I still was great   45
With the first pillars of the state,
Short-siz'd, and prematurely grey,
Form'd for th'intensity of day,
With passion ev'n to phrenzy seiz'd,
But very easily appeas'd.   50
If any person by the bye
Shou'd ask how old I am, reply,
That when the fasces were assign'd
To Lepidus and Lollius join'd,
I was full out, and fairly told,   55
Four times eleven Decembers old.

45 great] great, *1767*   53 assign'd] assign'd, *1767*

THE
SECOND BOOK
OF THE
EPISTLES OF HORACE

EPISTLE I.
To AUGUSTUS.

He complains of the depraved taste amongst the Romans of his time, who esti-
mated the merit of poems by their antiquity, and despised modern ones, for no
other reason than that they were modern.

Since you alone sustain the state,
Midst things so various and so great,
And while your arms our coast defend,
To moral pulchritude attend,
Correcting us with wholesome laws,   5
'Twere sin against the common cause
Was I to pen a tedious strain,
Thy time, Augustus, to detain.
    Rome's Founder, Bacchus, and the seed
Of Leda, men of might in deed,   10
And for their works in heav'n receiv'd,
Yet while on earth conjointly griev'd,
That human favour, human fame,
By no means answer'd to their claim,
As cultivators of mankind,   15
That special property assign'd,
And cities built, and lands dispos'd,
And finally dissentions clos'd.
The man that brought the Hydra down,
And beasts of horrible renown   20
Subdu'd by his predestin'd toil,
Found yet there was a foe to foil,

EPISTLE i. 10 in deed] indeed *1767*   22 there] their *1767*

Ev'n Envy, whose infernal blast
Cou'd not be worsted but the last.
HE galls, whose merits overbear   25
The puny wits, with lust'rous glare,
Hated while he retains his breath,
And lov'd for nothing but his * death.
　　To YOU, tho' with us, we bestow
The full-blown honours, as they grow,   30
And to your name those altars rear,
Which men upon their oath revere,
Confessing that a man like thee,
Nor has been, nor again shall be.
But here your people, wise to own   35
The truth in this one point alone,
(That is to place your matchless fame
Above each Greek and Roman name)
Cannot be made, at any rate,
Thus other things to estimate,   40
And still their futile venom spawn,
On all that are not dead and gone:
Such favourers of dusty shelves,
They will assert the NINE themselves
Upon mount Alban did ordain   45
Those † tables that the laws contain;
The leagues our antient monarchs made,
With neighbours for their mutual aid,
The Pontiff's rolls, and each record
The Augurs College keeps in ward.   50
If, as the oldest Greeks are best,
You say the same thing of the rest
And prove our writers by that test;
Your tongue at once all truth disowns,
Nuts have no shells, nor olives stones.   55

---

　* Witness SHAKESPEAR, MILTON, and BUTLER.
　† These twelve tables containing as it were, the whole body of the Roman laws, were
written in the three hundred and second year of Rome, and in the following publicly
proposed by the Decemviri, who these two years administered the public, in the place
of Consuls. LIVY.

---

35 people,] people *1767*　　36 truth] truth, *1767*　　39 made,] made *1767*
44 themselves] themselves, *1767*　　50 Augurs] Angurs *1767*

We've reached the highest pitch in arts,
In painting, music, shew our parts
And wrestle cleaner on the stage
Than active Greeks, in any age.
    If keeping to a certain date,   60
Like wine one's poems meliorate:
I fain wou'd know the very year
That makes this sage decision clear.
Who died an hundred years ago,
Is he an ancient good or no?   65
Or must he rather be referr'd,
And scorn'd amongst the modern herd?
Here something positive will suit,
To put the matter past dispute—
Well he's an ancient true and good,   70
Who for an hundred years has stood:
But what for him do you decide
Who month or year his junior dy'd?
Him will you condescend to place,
Amongst the vet'rans in this case,   75
Or such as are condemn'd to scoff
Both now and many ages off?
Him then you say, we may be bold
In honesty, to rank as old
Who did the junior depart   80
One month, or year—with all my heart—
From your concessions if you please,
I pull the tail off by degrees,
And certainly shall dock the mare
* If once I work it hair by hair,   85
Till like an heap that falls to ground,
I my opponent shall confound,
Who to the almanacs adheres,
And reckons eminence by years;

---

* Alluding to the story of Sertorius in Plutarch, who having an occasion to shew the preference of skill to main strength, set a strong man to one horse's tail, and a weak one to that of another. The former attempted in vain to pull it off all at once, but the weak one succeeded by going to work gradually.

---

67 herd?] herd. *1767*   75 vet'rans] vet'ran's *1767*

And nothing will applaud at all   90
But trophies from a funeral.
    Ennius th'ingenious and the strong,
* A second Homer for his song,
(As critics estimate the bard)
Seems now but lightly to regard   95
His dreams of what shou'd come to pass,
And figments of Pythagoras.
Naevius, altho' he be not read, ⎫
Is fresh in every person's head,   ⎬
All ancient verse is held so dread. ⎭   100
When critic disputants contest,
Which of the poets is the best,
† Pacuvius is for learning praised,
And Accius reckon'd great and *rais'd*;
Afranius all the town admit   105
His gown wou'd on Menander fit.
    Plautus still keeps each sketch in view,
Sicilian Epicharmus drew:
Caecilius did in weight excel,
And Terence in conducting well.   110
    These mighty Rome by heart has got,
With these cram'd theatres are hot.
These are the poets of the stage
From ‡ Livius to the present age.
    Sometimes the populace are right,   115
Sometimes remote from reason quite.
If poets of the former days
At such a rate th'admirers praise,
So that they nothing will prefer
Or ev'n compare with them, they err;   120
If they but fairly wou'd confess,
Some things are in too stale a dress,
Most lines put down too harsh and rough,
And many errant idle stuff,

---

* Ennius et sapiens Euphorbus et alter Homerus. *Lucill. Frag.*
† Ennius his nephew, by his sister, born at Brundusium.
‡ Livius Andronicus.

---

96 dreams] dreams, *1767*   102 best,] best. *1767*   103 praised,] praised. *1767*

Then are they wisemen, and agree   125
With what is very truth—and me.
I do not for * my part devote
To silence, all that Livius wrote,
Who when a boy, that flogging cull
Orbilius hammer'd in my skull,   130
But am astonish'd they appear
To any beautiful and near
To finish'd—for 'mongst many lines
If but one bright expression shines,
And midst the lamentable whole,   135
One verse or two harmonious roll,
In every righteous man's despite
It carries off th'edition quite.

   'Tis wrath—when works they discommend,
Not that they're stupid or ill penn'd,   140
But merely for their modern date:
And for the ancients arrogate
Rewards and reputation too,
When pardon barely is their due.
Shou'd a man question in this age   145
If Atta tread the † essenc'd stage
With grace or not, our sires wou'd roar
That modesty is now no more,
Those parts by me to be disdain'd,
Whence grave Esopus glory gain'd,   }   150
And which learn'd Roscius too sustain'd. ⌡
Because they think there's nothing right
But which is pleasing in their sight,
Or that they hold themselves disgrace't
If once their juniors *set the taste*,   155
And that when young (they must allow)
They learnt, what they shou'd cancel now.
Who Numa's Salian hymn wou'd praise
And such strange stuff, which now a days

* Here Horace differs from Cicero, who tells us that the comedies of this person were
not worth a second reading.
  † The Roman theatre was sprinkled with saffron-water for the refreshment of the
audience.

131 appear] appear, *1767*   142 arrogate] arrogate, *1767*   152 think] think, *1767*

Cannot be understood when read,   160
Does not so much applaud the dead,
As his invidious taunts he show'rs
On us and every thing of ours.
    But if in Greece new things had been
Thus odious, how shou'd we have seen   165
One ancient, how had they remain'd
With which we all are entertain'd?
When first upon a gen'ral peace
They learn'd to play the fool in Greece,
And into luxury to slide   170
By fortune fav'ring wind and tide,
Now wrestlers, now the race alone,
Now works in iv'ry or in stone,
Now busts, now pictures were admir'd
Thro' which the very soul transpired.   175
Now were they fond of pipe, now plays,
Full of those wild infantine ways,
Like little misses when they're nurst
Soon slighting what so pleas'd at first.
Nought sweeten'd and nought made them sour   180
But had mutations every hour.
Such were the things that peace cou'd do,
And all the prosp'rous gales that blew.
    In Rome it was in much repute,
And held a pleasant task to boot,   185
Betimes each morning to be found
And to a client laws expound;
Cash with great caution to put out;
To be attentively devout
To hear the old—the young direct   190
How wealth may grow and lust be check'd.
    Light fashion now has chang'd our mind,
All are to verse alone inclin'd,
Each boy and rigid elder's crown'd
With bays, and as the cup goes round   195
At supper will their lines rehearse—
Ev'n I, who swear I make no verse,

160 understood] understood, *1767*   176 plays,] plays *1767*

Am found a Parthian to outlie,
And ere the Sun's a second high,
Call for my ink with quick demand,   200
My pen, my paper and my stand.
A man that knows not how to steer
A ship, will such an office fear;
No one with drugs the sick will aid
Who was not 'prentice to the trade—   205
They're doctors who the art profess,
Smiths use their hammers with address,
But wits or blockheads, wrong or right,
We one and all must verse indite.
   But yet this error in degree   210
This tincture of insanity
How much the virtues it can serve
Please in this manner to observe.
The poét seldom on the whole
Has got an avaricious soul,   215
Verse is his study and delight—
At detriments of fire and flight
Of servants he securely smiles,
By craft no neighbour he beguiles,
No pupil of his trust, as fed   220
On homely husks and second bread:
Tho' * slow and useless in the war,
Rome's weal is that he's ever for,
And if you'll grant me this withal
That great things are upheld by small,   225
The infant's mouth the poets frame,
And tune their language lisping-lame,
Weans from bad words their ears betimes,
With friendly care their heart sublimes;
Corrects their rudeness, all the seeds   230
Of envy or of passion weeds;
Records good actions with the pen
And in the lives of glorious men

* Horace is by no means fair in this place, to suppose all poets runaway cocks, because
he was one.

---

199 ere] e'er *1767*   227 lisping-lame,] lisping—lame. *1767*   228 betimes,]
betimes *1767*

Instructs hereafter; to the poor
And weakly gives a gentle cure.   235
How shou'd good boys and girls regard
Their pray'rs, had heav'n denied a bard!
The * chorus for heav'n's aid applies
And feels the present deities,
Sweet in mysterious pray'r the rain   240
They from the highest heav'n obtain,
Avert disease, stave dang'rous fears
Bring peace with rich and fruitful years:
The gods above, the pow'rs below
By verse their consolation know.   245
   Our ancient rustics hale and rough,
And with a little bless'd enough,
Soothing upon their garner'd grain
Their limbs and minds, which cou'd sustain, ⎫
In hopes of respite, grievous pain;   ⎬   250
With children and with faithful wife,   ⎭
And fellow-craft in rural life,
The goddess Tellus with a swine,
Sylvanus with the milk and kine,
All worshipp'd, and with wine and flow'rs   255
The genius of the mental pow'rs
Who's mindful still that life is fleet
And thence invites to make it sweet.
   From sports like these driv'n to excess
Came Fescennine licentiousness,   260
Which pour'd out clownish verse profuse
In dialogue and gross abuse,
Which grateful liberty each year
Was rather cheerful than severe.
At length the jest too far inhanc'd   265
To downright open rage advanc'd,
And while impunity remain'd
Upon ingenuous houses gain'd,
The suff'rers from their bloody fangs
Were tortur'd with most cruel pangs,   270

* He alludes here to his own secular ode.
234 hereafter;] hereafter, *1767*

And many, tho' unhurt, were grieved,
That men such injuries receiv'd.
The senate made a law in fine
Which did a penalty injoin,
If any man they shou'd asperse   275
And point out in satiric verse,
They were oblig'd to change their plan
For fear of beating, and began
Their works poetic to dispense
For pleasure and benevolence.   280
    Bow'd to our arms, the captive Greece
Took the fierce victor on the peace
And introduced politer arts
In Italy's more rustic parts;
Thus lines of barbarism and scoff,   285
Prais'd in Saturnian times, flow'd off,
And elegance, which must be neat
Did squalled filthiness defeat.
Yet this (as former times) retains
Some traces of the rough remains.   290
'Twas late ere they their talents tried
And to the Grecian style applied;
And both the Punic wars were o'er
Ere they set by th'Athenian lore,
And made enquiry by degrees,   295
What Aeschylus, and Sophocles,
And Thespis, had of useful vein,
And strove too, if they might attain
Each author's beauties to translate,
Conscious of natures high and great.   300
For spirit we've enough in Rome,
And wear with grace the Tragic plume,
But cannot bear to be correct,
And hate a blot as a defect.
    The comic muse that draws her scene   305
From things of common life and mean,

272 receiv'd.] receiv'd, *1767*   275 asperse] asperse; *1767*   281 arms, . . . Greece]
arms . . . Greece, *1767*   288 defeat.] defeat, *1767*   291 ere] e'er *1767*
294 Ere] E'er *1767*   296 Aeschylus] Aesculus *1767*

Is thought to smell too much of sweat:
But the less favour it can get,
The more of study it shou'd take.
　　Observe how Plautus paints his rake,　　　310
How stupidly th'old huncks is drawn,
And crafty bawds that huff and fawn;
How much Dorsennus' muse delights
In eating and in parasites,
Who treads the stage an errant slouch　　　315
For while there's money in his pouch,
With him is no concern at all
Whether the Drama stand or fall.
　　He, whom vain-glory's chariot draws
Upon the stage for mere applause,　　　320
Faints when the audience languid grows,
But when they're lively puffs and blows.
So light, so trivial are the things
By which a spirit flags or springs,
That's covetous of praise—Farewel　　　325
All thought in writing to excel,
If glory giv'n or ta'en away
Make me look fat or lean a day—
　　This too makes many a bard withold
And well may terrify the bold,　　　330
That those who're of no worth possess'd
Or name, out-number all the rest,
Unlearn'd and dolts and prone to box
When a knight's taste their fancy shocks:
These midst the most inchanting airs　　　335
Demand the wrestlers and the bears,
For in all such the mob delights:
Nay ev'n the pleasure of our knights,
Driv'n from judicious ears, decoys
Th'uncertain eyes to gewgaw toys.　　　340
—Three or four hours the curtain's drawn
And horse and foot at once come on,
March o'er the stage with hapless kings,
Their hands behind them tied in slings,
Then chariots, litters, ships and wains　　　345
And slaves with iv'ry drag'd in chains,

And Corinth, to conclude the whole,
Is carried on a cloth and pole.
Democritus, was he on earth,
Wou'd fairly burst his sides with mirth,   350
To see the people staring hard
Upon some strange camelo-pard,
Or on an elephant all white;
The mob wou'd more attract his sight,
Than all the fun upon the stage.   355
Mean time he'd find the author's rage,
On a deaf ass was spent in vain,
For who can rant in such a strain,
As all that din to over-bear,
With which they drown both house and play'r?   360
You'd think Garganian forests roar,
Or billows on the Tuscan shore:
With so much clamour from their hearts,
The foreign gems, and wealth, and arts,
In which the actor's trick'd, are view'd;   365
For when he comes, in claps renew'd,
The right-hand and the left agree—⎫
Has he said any thing?—Not he— ⎬
Whence therefore all this wond'rous glee? ⎭
From robe of true Tarentian die,   370
Whose tints may with the violet vie.
And lest you think that I degrade
With sparing praise, what I'm affraid
To undertake myself, when done
By others for a general run,   375
Know then, that far above my hopes
That poet treads the highest ropes,
With fictious grief who wounds my breast,
Inflames, serenes, disturbs my rest
With magic terrors, that he makes,   380
And now to Thebes, now Athens takes.
     But Caesar, take a little care
Of writers, that the stage forbear,

353 white;] white, *1767*   355 stage.] stage, *1767*   357 ass] ass, *1767*
360 play'r?] play'r. *1767*   365 view'd;] view'd, *1767*   371 vie.] vie; *1767*

Who for the closet bards commence,
And dread an haughty audience: 385
So shall that library be fill'd
To Phoebus which you rose to build,
And bards have spurs for new essays,
To gain the Heliconian bays.

   We poets oft (to mar the plot   390
Of our own comrades) are, god wot,
Too apt to do ourselves much wrong,
When we present th' * obtrusive song
To thoughtful patrons, when in league
With sleepy dulness, thro' fatigue: 395
When we are pain'd, if any friend
Has dar'd to call one line ill-penn'd;
When tho' unask'd, we read again
The place that did small praise obtain,
Griev'd that our works so very clear,   400
And finely spun did not *appear*;
When we indulge our hopes, in fine,
That when our verses we divine,
You'll cite us of your own accord,
Force us to write for a reward,   405
Nor dream of want, when you're a Lord.
And yet 'tis worth the while to know,
Who shou'd be virtue's priest below,
Who gives to their immortal tome
Your worth in battle and at home,   410
Themes far too sacred for a bard
That is not worthy prime regard.

   Lov'd by the Macedonian youth
Was Choerilus, whose verse uncouth,
And vilely made, cou'd yet purloin   415
An hoard of royal Philip's coin.

---

  * There are more passages in Horace (particular, a caution to Lollius, and his own reason of forbearance to Trebatius) that shews what extreme address it required to approach Augustus with verses, who tho' he loved them, and could make them, yet did not choose they should interfere with certain times and circumstances.

---

385 audience:] audience, *1767*   387 Phoebus] Phoebus, *1767*   390–1 *brackets supplied* god] got *1767*   411 bard] bard, *1767*   414 Choerilus] Chaerilus *1767*

But as the ink not manag'd right
Leaves blots, so scriblers that indite
Bald verses, must their theme debase,
And the most shining acts disgrace.   420
This same king, who cou'd verses buy
So stupid, at a price so high,
Cou'd make an edict of restraint,
That not a hand his face shou'd paint
Except Apelles, nor in brass   425
Shou'd bustos for his likeness pass,
Save form'd in fam'd Lysippus' mould—
Now shou'd a person make so bold,
This monarch's judgment to refer
To books and bards, one might aver,   430
Or even undertake to swear,
His birth was in Boeotian air.

But those, your fav'rite sons of song,
Virgil and Varius, do not wrong
Your judgment, or the gifts that crown   435
Theirs and the donor's just renown.
Nor are the lineaments more just,
When cast into a brazen bust,
Than in th'immortal poet's lays
Appear the spirit and the ways   440
Of heroes—I am none of those
Who wou'd prefer your creeping prose,
To the describing mighty acts,
Earths, rivers, and extensive tracts,
And tow'rs upon the mountains built,   445
And kingdoms of barbarian guilt,
With all the wars constrain'd to cease,
By proclamation of your peace,
And Janus' temple lock'd and barr'd,
To stand for Concord upon guard,   450
And Rome, that now the Parthians dread,
Because Augustus is our head.
All this supposing I cou'd do,
As well as is my wish, is true.

427 Save] Sav'd *1767*   439 lays] lays, *1767*   444 Earths] Earth's *1767*

But nor your grandeur will admit   455
Of grov'lers, nor can I think fit,
In modesty a theme to try,
Which for my size is far too high.
An author's zeal that's too intense,
Will urge his folly to offence;   460
But most so, when he acts his part
In numbers, and poetic art:
For things ridiculously wrong,
Will to the mem'ry stick more strong,
Than passages of better thought,   465
For praise and admiration wrote.
Were I a patron I shou'd feel
Uneasiness for ill-tim'd zeal,
Nor like by any means to spy
My ugly likeness in a die,   470
Nor choose to be a heroe call'd,
In verses miserably bald,
Lest I shou'd blush, when forc'd to take
The gifts fat dulness comes to make,
And in an open trunk repine,   475
To see my author's name and mine;
Or, carried off, those streets behold,
Where all-spice and perfumes are sold,
And fritter'd into many a scrap,
Be doom'd all sorts of trash to wrap.   480

EPISTLE II.
To JULIUS FLORUS.

He makes his apology to Julius Florus, who complained that he neither sent
him any letter, nor those verses, which he had promised.

Florus, great Nero's faithful friend,
Shou'd any man by chance commend
A little stripling, to be bought
From Gabii, or from Tibur brought,

477 Or, . . . off,] Or . . . off *1767*

And thus begin with you to treat,   5
'This boy, Sir, 's of a temper sweet,
And sightly ev'n from head to foot,
And he his Lord's commands will suit;
Pay me but fifty pounds—he goes—
A little Greek the youngster knows;   10
Like clay for models, you with ease
Can make him learn whate'er you please;
His voice, tho' rude, is well to pass,
And entertaining o'er a glass.
Huge promises will credit lose,   15
When any man is too profuse
In praising what he wants to sell:
Necessity does not compel
That he must needs be sold as yet,
Tho' poor I am in no man's debt;   20
There's not a dealer you cou'd find,
So much unto your honour's mind,
And there's not any man but you
That I wou'd thus oblige—'tis true.
This boy (as often is the way)   25
Did once upon an errant stay
Then fled, thro' fear to feel the pangs
Of whip, that on the stair-case hangs,
Wherefore if this, his only vice,
Offend you not, pay down the price.'   30
The man may for his money call,
And be indemnified withal,
According to my skill in trade;
You wittingly a purchase made
Of him, who for a knave was sold,   35
But the conditions were foretold,
And yet you will th'affair dispute,
And forward an unrighteous suit.
    I told you, when you went away,
That I was idle, out of play,   40
Nor cou'd such offices abide—
I told you that you might not chide,

EPISTLE ii. 10 knows;] knows. *1767*   24 true.] true, *1767*

When from my hands no letter came.
But what's all this, if you disclaim
Conditions for myself I made,   45
And furthermore your friend upbraid,
That he's no better than a liar,
Not sending verse, as you require.

  After much hardship in the fight,
As tir'd he snor'd away the night,   50
A soldier of Lucullus' host,
His money to a farthing lost;
From this a rav'nous wolf he grows,
Wroth with himself, as with his foes,
Fierce rushing, with his hungry fangs,   55
From off their post he soundly bangs
A royal guard (as they report)
And took their stores and strongest fort.
By such great gallantry renown'd,
He is with highest honours crown'd: 60
The Chief besides to him decrees
Full fifty thousand sesterces.
It happen'd just upon this feat,
His captain was intent to beat
The foe, and batter their redoubt—   65
Words that wou'd make a coward stout,
He to the self-same man addrest,
'Go thou the bravest and the best,
Go where thy valour calls, and speed
About to share rewards indeed!   70
Why do you stand debating—march!'—
On which my chap extremely arch,
Tho' but a clown, made answer back,
'Let him go foremost to th'attack,
His lance at your command to couch,   75
Who's fall'n asleep, and lost his pouch.'
  It was my lot in tender age
At Rome to con th'Homeric page,
How by the wrath of Peleus' son,
The Grecian councils were undone;   80

61 decrees] decrees, *1767*

Ingenuous Athens added more,
Of what is call'd the useful lore,
The right from its reverse to know,
And in the search of truth to go,
Where solitary wisdom roves,   85
And thinks in academic groves.
But the perverseness of the time
Displac'd me from that pleasant clime,
And, ere I knew whom I was for,
Involv'd in tides of civil war,   90
And arms, in which there was no hope
That they shou'd with Augustus cope;
From whence when we were all dispers'd,
And from Philippi sent amerc'd,
With my wings clipt, and heart unmann'd,   95
And destitute of house and land,
Compell'd by poverty intense,
I boldly did a bard commence.
But now remote from being poor,
What med'cines cou'd my phrenzy cure,   100
If I should write or verse, or prose,
In preference to my repose?
   The fleeting years from spring to fall,
Have fairly rob'd me of my all,
My jests, my gallantry, my play,   105
And revellings are ta'en away.
Now they're exerting of their force, ⎫
The very Muses to divorce: ⎬
Then how shou'd I direct my course? ⎭
In short, all matters do not strike   110
On every personage alike;
The ode is by your choice preferr'd,
He likes iambics, and a third
The satires written on the plan
Of Bion, that invet'rate man;   115
Here are three guests, cannot approve
Of the same *dish*, or same *remove*;
What shall I give, or what refuse?

87 time] time, *1767*   92 cope;] cope, *1767*   108 divorce:] divorce, *1767*
118 refuse?] refuse, *1767*

You spurn the things that others chuse,
And what's acceptable to you   120
Will give offence to t'other two.
    Besides all this, pray how do you think
A man can harmonize his ink,
At Rome, amidst his toils and cares
And all his intricate affairs?   125
One summons me to be his bail,
And one to hear him without fail,
While he, forsooth, his work recites!
To Mount Quirinus one invites,
The other two I must attend,   130
On Aventine the farther end.
Both must be visited, you see
The distance suits one *charmingly*:
'But never mind, the streets are clear,
Fit for the thoughtful and severe;'   135
A builder hurries with his mules,
And porter bearing chips and tools;
The timber-tug now whirls a stone,
And now a log to break a bone;
Now a dispute is likewise made   140
'Twixt waggon, and the sad parade
Of fun'ral pomp—a mad dog now,
Now rushes a most filthy sow:
Go, poet, make your verses neat,
And let their melody be sweet.   145
Thro' all their choir, the gen'ral run
Of bards love groves, and cities shun,
Due votaries of Bacchus made,
Rejoicing in repose and shade.
Must I then sing the tuneful lay   150
Amidst such din both night and day,
And up hill strive the steps to trace
Of poetry's retarded race?
A genius who has made retreat,
In Athens' leisure-loving seat,   155

129 Mount] mount *1767*   134 mind,] mind *1767*   138 tug] tug, *1767*
153 race?] race. *1767*

And there his constitution wears
Sev'n years immers'd in books and cares,
Sometimes comes out into the town,
A mere dumb statue in a gown,
Till all the people shake their sides—   160
But how in all these boistrous tides
And tempests of the city-throng
Can I associate lyre and song!
 At Rome together liv'd of late,
A dab in tropes and advocate;   165
Those men were brothers, and so near
Allied, that they wou'd only hear
Their mutual praise, in mutual speech,
Gracchus and Mucius, each to each.
Why shou'd this wrath of complaisance   170
Be less in them that sing and dance?
I write but odes, another sings
His elegies, amazing things
Trick't up by all the muses train—
Observe you first, with what disdain,   175
And what importance for ourselves,
We view the * temple's vacant shelves.
Next if your leisure is inclin'd,
Yourself may follow us behind,
And hear us quote and judge the cause   180
We crown each other with applause.
 We work in counterfeited fight,
Like Samnite blades, till candle-light.
I am Alceus the divine,
By his decree—who's he by mine?   185
Callim'chus; if I underrate,
Mimnermus more divinely great.
 Much do I bear to keep in grace
With bards, that irritable race,
Whilst I myself, to get the bays,   190
Submissive court the people's praise,

* Of Palatine Apollo.

---

157 cares,] cares. *1767* 165 advocate;] advocate, *1767* 183 Samnite blades,]
samnite blades *1767* 186 Callim'chus; ... underrate,] Callim'chus, ... underate,
1767 190 myself,] myself *1767*

But having now my studies clos'd,
Quite sound, tho' lately indispos'd,
I can, secure of former fears,
Against reciters stop my ears.   195

   The makers of your wretched strains,
By all are laugh'd at for their pains;
But in the writing they rejoice,
And for themselves will give their voice,
And if you let their praise alone,   200
The men are happy in their own.

   But whoso chuses to compile
A work in genuine form and style,
Shou'd with his pen assume the mind
Of critic, honest and refin'd;   205
He boldly will all words displace,
Devoid of cleanness and of grace,
Such as are destitute of weight,
Such as are not sublime and great;
All these your blotting hand require,   ⎫   210
Howe'er unwilling to retire,   ⎬
And deem'd eternal for their fire.   ⎭

Such phrases, as from Rome have long
Been hid, he will revive in song,
And kindly bring to light again   215
Words, which ideas best explain,
The language of the great and just,
Tho' now disus'd thro' age and rust.
New words he likewise will invent,
All founded on experiment: 220
At once strong, musical, and clear,
Like some pure river he'll appear,
And pour out his redundant store
Abroad upon th'Italian shore;
What's too luxuriant he will pare,   225
To what is harsh he'll give an air;
What has no worth he'll take away.
He'll ape the mimic in the play,
With his invention on the rack,
While now he has the Satyr's knack,   230

214 revive *Rudd*] receive *1767*   227 away.] away, *1767*

And now like Cyclops must advance,
Stupendous in the clumsy dance.
   I'd rather be esteem'd a fool,
And object of all ridicule,
Self-entertain'd, or self-deceiv'd,   235
Than with my wisdom be aggriev'd.
   At Argos once it came to pass,
A personage of no mean class,
Set in a theatre at ease
Alone, and clapt himself to please,   240
Supposing that he heard the play'r,
Divinely tragedizing there:
And yet in other points of view,
This man cou'd all his duty do,
Good neighbour, courteous to his guest,   245
And with kind love his wife carest,
Indulgent to forgive a slave,
So as not actually to rave,
If he had dar'd to tap his wine—
Wou'd well, or precipice decline—   250
At length by care, and by expence
Of friends, recovering his sense.
'Good sirs, (says he) be all assur'd,
You've kill'd me, rather than have cur'd,
Who've rob'd my thoughts of sweet employ,   255
And all my visionary joy.'—
   'Tis granted life is best apply'd
To wisdom, throwing toys aside;
Leave then to boys all childish play,
Theirs is the proper time of day,   260
Nor merely think on words to dwell,
Adapted to the Latian shell,
But method and array to scan,
Which tend to harmonize the man:
Wherefore I with myself converse,   265
And only things like these rehearse:
'If, tho' you drank until you burst,
No water yet wou'd quench your thirst,

253 he] she *1767*

To doctors you wou'd tell th'affair;
How is it that you do not dare,   270
By frank confession to explain,
The more you've got, the more you'd gain?
If from a root or herb prescrib'd,
Your wound no healing balm imbib'd,
That herb, or root, you'd surely shun,   275
By which you found no good was done;
You by some conjuror was told,
To whom the Gods give store of gold,
From him depravity of heart,
And folly shall of course depart;   280
But since you are no wiser grown,
With all this plenitude your own,
Why have you therefore any more
The same advisers, as before?
But if wealth made you wise of soul,   285
Your lusts and terrors to controul,
You ought to blush if earth cou'd shew
A man more covetous than you.'
　　If goods your property are found,
Bought by the penny, and the pound;   290
And some things (as the law assures)
Are wholly by possession yours;
The field that feeds you is your own,
And while he harrows it when sown,
The hind of Orbus still imputes   295
The right to him that has the fruits.
You give your cash receiving more,
Grapes, pullets, eggs, and wine galore,
Till by degrees the farm you've made,
For which p'rhaps the owner paid,   300
(To speak upon a mod'rate guess)
Three hundred thousand sesterces.
What boots it if your food you owe
To things bought now or long ago!
He, who that Aricinian spot,   305
Or field of Veiens lately got,
Sups on bought herbs, tho' he thinks not.

269 affair;] affair, *1767*　　　272 gain?] gain. *1767*

Nay more, he boils his very food
Each frosty night with purchas'd wood;
And yet they're all his freehold lands   310
As far as where the poplar stands,
And is the limit to forefend
Disputes at law 'twixt friend and friend;
As if ought was a man's estate,
Which in one moment of his date,   315
Now by petition, now by pay,
By violence another day,
Or by the common lot of all,
May to some other owner fall.
Then since for ever is not here,   320
Heir making heir still disappear,
As wave o'er wave the billows rise,
Then what are towns, or granaries,
Or cou'd you join, your flocks to feed,
Calabrian with Lucanian mead,   325
Since stern inexorable fate,
Unbrib'd by gold mows small and great?
   Gems, marble, iv'ry, busts, and plate,
Fine pictures, and rich robes of state,
There are who never can acquire,   330
There are who no such things desire.
Why of two brethren one consumes
His time in idling, play, perfumes,
Nor heeds rich Herod's palm-estate;
The other, miserably great,   335
From morn to night with fire and steel,
Seeks with his forest fields to deal;
Our guiding genius here on earth
That rules the planet of our birth,
The best can certify, ev'n he,   340
Our nature's true divinity,
That o'er our heads exerts his might
And cheques our lives with black and white.
   I'll freely take with mod'rate hands
As much as exigence demands,   345

312 to forefend] too forefend, *1767*   313 friend;] friend, *1767*   315 date,] date;
1767   344 hands] hands, *1767*

Nor will I waste a single care,
About th'opinion of my heir,
When at his coming he shall find
No augmentation left behind.
Yet I with measures thus advis'd,   350
Am still inclin'd to be appris'd,
How much the chearful and the free,
Is distant from the debauchee,
And what distinction exists
'Twixt misers and oeconomists.   355
For know there is a diff'rence quite,
Shou'd you waste ev'ry thing out-right,
Or only spread a plent'ous board,
Nor seek addition to your hoard:
But rather self and friend enjoy   360
By fits and starts, as when a boy,
Glad of the breaking-up retreat,
As shorter so by far more sweet.
Let dirty poverty, I pray,
Be far, yea very far away;   365
And be my vessel small or strong,
Let me go uniform along,
The wind, perhaps, is not so fair,
Sails swelling with the Northern air,
And yet I have not in my mouth   370
The tempest of the adverse South.
In force, in genius, figure, weight,
In virtue, station, and estate,
The last of them that foremost go,
But captain of the band below.   375
    You are not covetous—go to—
But have you manhood to subdue
And put to flight all vice beside?
Clear is your breast from worldly pride?
Of wrath and dread of dying clear?   380
Do you at dreams and conj'rer sneer?
Mock wonders, witches, nightly elves?
And ev'n Thessalian charms themselves?

377 subdue] subdue, *1767*

When heav'n another birth-day sends
Art grateful? do you spare your friends?   385
At the approach of hoary age,
Art more good-natur'd and more sage?
Why pluck one thorn from out your mind
And leave so many more behind?
If you no more your life pursue   390
With skill, make room for them that do.
You've play'd, and eat, and drank, your share,
'Tis time your journey to prepare;
Lest youth, that has more decent claim
To every kind of wanton game,   395
Shou'd, midst your cups o'ercharg'd, with scoff
Hiss your last scene, and drive you off.

HORACE

HIS

ART OF POETRY

Inscribed to the HOUSE of PISO.

If any painter shou'd design
A human visage, and subjoin
A horse's neck with plumage swoln,
And limbs from various creatures stol'n,
Untill the figure, in th'event,   5
Which for a beauteous dame was meant,
At length most scandalously ends
In a black fish's tail—my friends!
Admitted to so strange a sight,
Wou'd not your laughter be outright?   10
   Believe me, Pisos, that a book
Will just like such a picture look,
Whose matter, like a sick man's dreams,
Is form'd of vanities and whims;
Where such absurdities prevail,   15
You can make out nor head nor tail.
The painters and the bards, 'tis true,
Claim licence as of both their due.
'Tis a concession that I make,
And hence excuse we give and take: 20
But not so largely as to coop
The tame and savage in a groupe,
And snakes with turtle-doves to mate,
And lambs with tigers copulate.
   In pompous proems, big with threat,   25
The usual pattern that is set
Is that they place, to make one stare,

ART OF POETRY 10 outright?] outright. *1767*   16 tail.] tail; *1767*   26 set] set, *1767*
27 place,] place *1767*

A piece of patchwork full of glare.
As when the fane and sacred wood
Of Dian, or meand'ring flood   30
In pleasant fields, or copious flow
Of Rhine, or many-colour'd bow,
Are all describ'd—but in this case
The foppish trump'ry had no place.
Perhaps a cypress you can draw—   35
But does that signify a straw,
If he that buys what you perform,
Was to be made as in a storm?
The potter had a jar begun;
Why nothing but a pipkin done?   40
In short, the subject what it will,
Be simple and consistent still.
　　Most of us—(I the sire address,
And each good son, the sire express)
Are dup'd by things that seem aright:)   45
I wou'd be brief with all my might,   }
And so become as dark as night!   )
He nerves and spirits must neglect,
Who strives to be extreme correct;
He's apt to swell, who wou'd be grand,   50
And he that dreads to leave the strand,
In terror of the fierce profound,
Is sure to run his ship aground:
And he that works a simple theme,
* With monster, prodigy and dream,   55
Will paint the dolphin in the lawn,
While boars are upon ocean drawn;
A scape from error leads to vice,
If your discernment be not nice.
　　A sculptor near † th'Emilian school,   60
Can skill to fashion with his tool

* I cannot help thinking, but in this and sundry passages, at the beginning of this epistle, there are tacit sneers at Ovid's Metamorphoses, that Horace might at once please Augustus, and gratify (not improbably) a small degree of poetical jealousy.

† The Statuaries had their work-shops near the fencing school, that they might be at hand to take the attitudes of the Gladiators.

30 flood] flood, *1767*　　　　32 Rhine] rhine *1767*　　　　38 storm?] storm. *1767*
44 son,] son *1767*

The nails, or flowing of the hair,
But not compleat the whole affair.
If I had anything to write
I wou'd no more be such a wight,   65
Than I wou'd chuse black hair and eyes,
With nose of most portentous size.
    Your plan, whene'er you tune your lay,
Suit to your faculties, and weigh
How much they can or cannot bear;   70
He who selects his theme with care
Will find no want of flowing style,
With clear arrangement all the while.
But, if the thing I rightly trace,
This is the merit and the grace   75
Of disposition, that the bard
To time and place have just regard,
And mention what shou'd first be known,
But other things a while postpone.
The true professor of the muse   80
Shou'd know to take and to refuse;
Yet if new words he intersperse,
He shou'd be cautious in his verse
And choice—It is exceeding well
To give a common word the *spell*,   85
To greet you as intirely new—
It is a point you must persue,
In modern language to confirm
Each strange and philosophic term,
Words you may use to ancient Rome   90
Unknown, yet modestly presume.
    But new-coin'd words will ever be
Of more approv'd authority,
If from the Grecian fount they fall,
And their mutation be but small,   95
For why shou'd Rome Caecilius give
And Plautus a prerogative,
Which they to Virgil still deny,
And Varius?—Why may not ev'n I

73 clear] clean *1767*   83 verse] verse, *1767*   90 use] use, *1767*   96 give]
give, *1767*

Make some improvements if I can,   100
Nor suffer from th'invidious clan,
Since Ennius' and Cato's phrase
Their native tongue enrich and raise,
And terms exotic introduce—
All have, and must allow the use   105
To make a word, that cleanly chimes,
Stampt with th'impression of the times.
As when the leaves each fleeting year
Are chang'd—the earliest dis-appear
The first; our words in likewise fare,   110
The oldest perish, as it were,
And those new-coin'd are now in flow'r,
Like youths, in all their strength and pow'r.
Ev'n both must fail, our works and we;
Whether the * sovereign of the sea,   115
Receiv'd far up into the land,
(A work with royal grandeur plann'd)
Our fleet from the North wind defends,
Or if a fertile tract extends,
Feeds neighbouring cities, feels the plough,   120
A lake and row'd upon but now—
Or tho' the river's made by force
Of Caesar's word to change his course,
And noxious to his former place
Must learn to run a better race—   125
Yet these as human acts must fail;
Then how much less shall we prevail
To keep the elegance and weight
Of language in a settl'd state.
    Words shall revive that now are gone,   130
And some, which most are look'd upon,
Shall perish, if dame fashion will,
Who has in her dominion still

* Three grand works are here mention'd for the honour of Augustus. The Julian port at Baia, the draining of the Pomptinae paludes, and the cleansing of the channel of the Tiber.

---

114 fail,] fail *1767*   115 footnote. Pomptinae paludes] Pomplinas palades *1767*
129 language] language, *1767*

Supreme prescriptive pow'r to teach
All written and colloquial speech.   135
 Homer has taught us in what verse
The deeds of kings we shou'd rehearse;
And heroes and contentions dire,
With what propriety and fire!
In numbers of unequal lines,   140
Were wrote at first the lover's whines,
But in a while were carried high'r
For bliss and fortunate desire.
But he who thought it worth his while
To sing first in so * *small* a style,   145
Our critics have not yet found out,
So still the matter is in doubt.
 Archilochus his wrathful heat
Made him strike out th'iambic feet:
The sock and stately buskin chose   150
This measure as the nearest prose,
Whence dialogue might aptly please,
And clamours of the mob appease,
Expressive or of mirth or rage,
Fit for the bus'ness of the stage.   155
 The muse has giv'n us on the lyre
In praise divinely to aspire
To sing of Gods and sons of Gods,
And champions crown'd against the odds;
The winning steed and lover's care,   160
And gen'rous claret to declare.
If I'm unskilful to combine
The parts and colours I design,
Why am I hail'd, where'er I go,
As poet, since I nothing know: 165
Why falsely bashful be a fool
Rather than go again to school?
A comic subject will not hold
If 'tis in tragic measure told:

---

* Ovid again tacitly ridiculed for his elegies.

---

157 aspire] aspire, *1767*

Besides, it wou'd an audience shock,   170
In verses fitter for the sock,
The Thyestean feast to tell:
Each kind of writing shall do well,
According to its proper place,
Arrang'd in seemliness and grace.—   175
    But sometimes comedy will rage,
And angry Chremes shake the stage;
And sometimes in the tragic scene
You've wailings melancholy-mean.
Peleus and Telephus when poor,   180
And exiles will no more endure
Their rants and ravings ten feet high,
If they wou'd to the heart apply.
    A poem cannot be compleat,
Tho' beautiful, if 'tis not sweet,   185
Till by its pathos it can seize
The soul, and bear her where it please.
    Expressive or of joy or pain,
As human aspects smile again
Upon the smilers, so their eyes   190
Will with the tearful sympathise.
If you wou'd have me really weep,
Your own distresses must be deep;
Then, Telephus, your tragic part,
Or, Peleus, truly wound my heart.   195
But if you miserably *spout*
Your words, I sleep or else laugh out.
Things of a melancholy turn
Shou'd be express'd with much concern;
But if in wrath the person fret,   200
The aspect shou'd be big with threat.
    In jest the looks shou'd pleasant be,
But serious in severity.
But first there is a sense innate
To every colour of our fate,   205
Which causes passion, gives relief,
Or weighs us to the ground with grief,

192 weep,] weep *1767*   193 deep;] deep, *1767*

Till to the tongue the task's assign'd
To blaze the motions of the mind.
If what the characters shall say   210
Be foreign to the part they play,
The Roman knights and all the croud
Will titter and explode aloud.
It is a diff'rent matter quite
Shou'd Davus speak, or errant knight,   215
A grey old man approach the scene,
Or hot young rake, whose years are green,
A matron full of pomp and show,
Or nurse officious to and fro',
A merchant wont thro' seas to roam,   220
Or one who tills his ground at home,
Assyrian, Colchan, Theban bred
Or Argive on the stage shou'd tread.
   If e'er you write or follow fame,
Or at such sort of stories aim,   225
As with themselves do best agree—
Homer's Achilles shall we see?
Courageous, enemy to sloth,
And most inexorably wroth,
Let him, denying human laws,   230
Claim all things by the sword he draws.
If e'er Medea fill the scene,
Fierce and ungovern'd be the queen.
Be Ino cast to make you cry,
Ixion of perfidious die,   235
Io be rambling drawn and mad,
Orestes most severely sad.
   If to the stage you shall approach
With matter you're the first to broach,
—Let the new character you cast,   240
Be fairly kept up to the last.
   'Tis arduous common things to say
In such a clean peculiar way,
Untill they fairly seem your own,
Wherefore more prudence will be shewn   245

212 knights] knights, *1767*   223 tread.] tread? *1767*   232 scene,] scene *1767*

To plan the Iliad out in acts,
Than your inventive pow'r to tax,
The first to speak upon the stage
Things known not to a former age.
   A tale however blown upon   250
Will as your property, come on,
If you shall not on trifles dwell,
How and ABOUT IT all to tell,
Nor be so faithfully absurd
As to translate it word for word,   255
Nor must you squeeze into a streight
While you too closely imitate,
From whence you can't so well recede
For shame, and for the plan agreed,
Nor yet begin in tumid sounds,   260
Like that old songster of the ROUNDS,
'*The fate of Priam*, SING I SHALL
And many A NOBLE BOUT *withal.*'
What will the boaster bring about
With all this MOWTHING and this rout?   265
The mountain shall again be *laid*,
The little mouse again display'd.
How much more to the purpose HE,
The pattern of propriety—
'To me the man, O Muse! relate,   270
Which after Troy's determin'd fate,
By toil and actual review
The nations and their manners knew.'
He does not meditate by trash,
To give you smoke from out a flash,   275
But chooses rather to procure
Illumination from th'obscure.
By striking out such strokes with ease, ⎫
That Scylla and Antiphates   ⎬
And Cyclops and Charybdis please. ⎭   280
Nor will from Meleager's fate
Returning Diomedes date.
Nor dates the Trojan war 'to wit
When Leda first began * TO SIT,'

* Upon the eggs that brought forth Castor and Pollux.

But ever hastens to the goal,   285
And throws the reader's very soul
Into the center of th'affair,
As tho' he'd been an actor there.
But chuses certain things to leave
Unfit his polish to receive,   290
And with so much discretion *lies*,
Blends truth and falshood in such *wise*,
That the beginning, middle, end,
Do cleanly each on each depend.
   Now hear what all the town with me   295
From you that write expect to see,
If you wou'd have th'applauder stay,
Attending till the actors say,
'Kind gentlemen, pray clap your hands:'
Mark how with every man it stands   300
For manners at a certain age;
And the decorum of the stage
Must be kept up with things assign'd
To time of life and turn of mind;
The boy who just can prattle plain,   305
And on the ground his tread sustain,
Loves with his play-fellows to 'bide,
And wrath contracts or lays aside
For nothing, changing every hour—
The youth out of his guardian's pow'r   310
Delights in horses and in hounds,
And o'er the sunny champaign bounds,
Pliant as wax to vicious ways,
And harsh at what th'adviser says;
A slow provider for the best,   315
And spendthrift with a lofty crest,
Hot in pursuit of new amours,
And quick to leave what he procures.
   From this, by shifting of the plan,
The age and spirit of the man   320
Seeks wealth and friendships and a name,
And dreads an action to his shame.

299 hands:] hands, *1767*   319 this, ... plan,] this ... plan *1767*   320 man]
man, *1767*

Sundry infirmities are found
Which man in his old-age surround,
Because he scrapes and yet abstains,   325
A wretch, that dreads to use his gains;
Or else because he acts when old,
All things too cautious and too cold,
Fain wou'd put off the evil day
And greedy in this world to stay;   330
Harsh, querelous, and loud of tongue
In praising things when he was young,
Censor and punisher too free
Of all who're not so old as he.

    Our growing years, when we are strong,   335
Bring great advantages along,
And when we're going down the hill
We're more and more the losers still.
Then lest the parts that are of age,
Shou'd be assign'd to youthful rage,   340
Or those of youth be giv'n to years,
The strict propriety adheres
Upon those qualities to dwell,
Which suit respective ages well.

    A scene we on the stage behold,   345
Or else we hear the story told;
But things which enter at the ear
Will not affect the mind so near
As what before the eyes is shewn,
And each spectator makes his own.   350
But yet you must not things disclose
Which done within we best suppose.
Some things from sight you'll take away,
Which clean description may display;
Nor let Medea's hand destroy   355
Before the gaping crowd, her boy;
Nor wicked Atreus, full in view,
A dish of human entrails stew,
Or Cadmus turn by change absurd
A snake, or Progne be a bird.   360

358 stew,] stew *1767*

When thus your scenes you represent,
Disgust forbids me to assent.——
   Let not a play you'd have us read,
And put upon the stock, exceed
Five acts—nor let a god be there,   365
Unless some intricate affair
Make you divine assistance seek,
Nor a fourth person strain to speak.
   The chorus shou'd support with art
The duty of his manly part,   370
Nor let him sing amidst the acts
Ought forc'd or foreign to the facts.
Let him the men of worth defend,
And give good council to each friend,
Restrain the wroth, to them that hate   375
Offences be affectionate.
Let mod'rate fare have his applause
And wholesome justice and the laws,
And gen'ral peace, that loves to deal
In open ports—let him conceal   380
Things spoke in confidence, and pray
The Gods, that their propitious day
May to th'unfortunate return,
While haughty loftiness they spurn.
   The flute was not at such a pass   385
Of yore, as to be girt with brass,
Till vying with the trump it roars,
But small and simple with few bores,
To help the chorus with its touch,
And fill the rows not throng'd too much: 390
While they cou'd the spectators hold)
In numbers easy to be told,   }
Chaste, frugal, and not over-bold.   )
   But when victorious Rome began
On all sides to extend her plan,   395
And when an ampler wall embrac'd
The city, and the god of taste

361 represent,] represent *1767*   376 Offences] Offences, *1767*   382 day] day,
1767   385 The] To *1767*

Was serv'd with festal wine by day,
With none the practice to gain-say,
New measures and more notes they found   400
Alike for poetry and sound.
For what degree of taste refin'd
Cou'd be in an unletter'd hind,
Loos'd with his oxen from the yoke,
And mix'd with the politer folk,   405
Where low-liv'd miscreants and base,
With men of honour took their place?
   Thus did the master's skill impart,
New movements to the ancient art,
With all the luxury of *air*,   410
And strutting like a pompous play'r,
Drew on the stage amongst the rest
A train deep-flowing from his vest:
Thus likewise did the sober lyre,
Up to new strings and strains aspire,   415
And an unusual flow of rage,
Rush'd all at once upon the stage;
So what they did of old design,
For things both useful and divine,
Is so far wrested from the mark,   420
That 'tis oracularly dark.
   The bard (a filthy goat the prize)
Who first began to tragedize,
Brought on the fawns, a naked race,
Still joking with a serious face;   425
Because spectators full of wine,
And wild and tir'd with things divine,
Requir'd by novelty and show,
Their minds shou'd relaxation know;
But laughing satyrs we commend,   430
Provided they do not offend,
By turning earnest into jest,
So that a god, or king, that's drest
In gold and purple, do not bawl
The language of the cobler's stall,   435

401 sound.] sound, *1767*   405 folk.] folk. *1767*   412 rest] rest, *1767*
430 commend,] commend. *1767*

Nor while they shun the groveling mire,
To mists and emptiness aspire.
   Grave tragedy shou'd still disdain
All verses in a trivial strain,
And, tho' midst wanton satyrs plac'd,   440
Will yet with decency be grac'd,
Like some grave matron whom the priest
Commands to dance upon a feast.
   As satirist I do not praise
The bald, unornamented phrase,   445
And common cant, nor shall I try
To break the rules of tragedy,
So as to make no odds between
A Davus talking in the scene,
Or Pythias putting to the worse   450
Th'old hunks, and making of a purse,
Or Liber's guardian wont to wait
Upon his pupil god, in state.
   So wou'd I make a tale my own,
Tho' taken from a thing well known,   455
That any man might think to do
The same, but when he once set to
Wou'd sweat and vex himself in vain,
And never to the point attain.
So much effect is in the art,   460
Of clean disposing every part,
And so much novelty and grace,
In common topics, may take place.
   The wood-land fawns shou'd have a care,
(If one may judge in this affair)   465
Lest they shou'd speak as born in town,
And ev'n like them that wear the gown;
Or lest too much they be inclin'd
To verses of infantine kind,
Or ev'n to be too grossly free   470
With ignominious ribaldry:
For every man of rank, or sense,
Or family, will take offence;

470 grossly] grosly *1767*

Nor things that with the mob go down,
Will such hands or excuse or crown.   475
　　*When a long syllable is join'd
Unto a short, and plac'd behind,
The quick iambic foot we frame,
Whence trimeter deriv'd its name;
With only six iambic feet,   480
Consisting of itself compleat:
But to the ear not long ago,
That it might come more grave and slow,
The sober spondee was took in,
As to a league and of a kin,   485
But not to quit the second place,
Or fourth, or last, in any case.
However this is very scarce,
In Accius's applauded farce,
And in the verses Ennius wrote——   490
All bungling lines, like theirs, when brought
Upon the stage, with heavy weight,
Convict them as precipitate,
And wanting care——or, what is worse,
Most grossly ignorant of verse.   495
It is not every judge can see
The negligence of harmony,
And Roman bards in this abuse
Have met with far too much excuse:
But shall a man for this discharge   500
All method, and transgress at large?
Or shall I not suppose the more,
The world will all my faults explore?

---

* This verse at first consisted only of itself, viz. pure iambics as *Suis et ipsa Roma viribus ruit*, [*Epodes* xvi. 2] and all the iambics in that ode. The next degree of correctness in writing this measure, is to have the iambic regularly in the second, fourth and sixth places. When a spondee is put in the last place it is called a Scazon, a noble verse for grave subjects. The verses of Phaedrus which he calls Senarii, have the iambic always for the fifth foot, the former part consisting of all feet promiscuously, except the trochee. Such too are most of the verses of Terence, &c.

---

495 grossly] grosly *1767*　　498 abuse] abuse, *1767*　　500 discharge] discharge, *1767*　　503 will ... explore?] with ... explore, *1767*　　508 patterns,] patterns *1767*

Nor shall my spirit be so poor
As merely pardon to procure;   505
For tho' I 'scape all brand and blame,
I cannot therefore merit fame.
    The Grecian patterns, ye that write,
Peruse by day, peruse by night;
But spite of these, our sires thought fit   510
To praise the verses and the wit
Of Plautus (fools I will not say)
But far too patient at his play:
That is, if either you or I
Have comprehension to descry   515
True repartee from coarser jeers,
And have our fingers and our ears.
    Thespis the first (they say) found out
The tragedy, and bore about
His poems in theatric cart,   520
Which all his actors got by heart,
And play'd in faces daub'd with lees:
Then Eschylus too, by degrees,
Invented masque and decent pall,
And made a little stage withal,   525
Learnt them to aggrandise their talk
And in the tragic buskin stalk.
    To these, with no small share of praise,
Th'old comedy in after days
Succeeded, but its free excess   530
Forc'd pow'r such licence to suppress.
Accordingly a law was fram'd,
And when the right, the Chorus claim'd,
Of personal abuse, was o'er,
He wholly to his shame forbore.   535
Our poets have not left a part
Untried, in all their various art,
Nor do *they* least applause deserve,
Who from the Grecian models swerve,
And our domestic facts rehearse,   540
In tragic or in comic verse;

---

515 descry] descry, *1767*   523 Eschylus] Escalus *1767*   531 suppress.] suppress; *1767*

Nor wou'd our Latium more excel
In feats of arms, than writing well,
Did not her poets in their stile
Disgust the toilsome, tedious file.   545
Do you, my noble friends, reject
All poetry for its defect,
Which many a blot, and many days
Have not chastis'd to perfect phrase.

   Because Democritus contends,   550
That Genius sorry art transcends;
And bars from Helicon each wight,
That has his understanding right,
The greater number of our herd,
Nor pare their nails, nor shave their beard,   555
But walk alone in secret paths,
And keep away from public baths,
And he shall get the name and prize
Of all poetic mysteries,
Whose head, beyond all hopes of cure,   560
Will not the barber's touch endure.
O how unfortunate am I,
Which in the spring to drugs apply!
No man shou'd write a finer style,
But since that's scarcely worth one's while,   565
I'll do the duty of an hone,
And give an edge, tho' I have none.
I will (not writing of a line)
The office of a bard define,
Whence his materials he may gain,   570
How form, and how improve his vein,
What graces, and what must offend,
Where excellence and error tend.

   In taste and wisdom to excel
Is the main spring of writing well,   575
And subjects you may best explore,
Deduc'd from the Socratic lore;
And when you once have plan'd the scheme,
The words will come with ease extream.

544 stile] stile, *1767*   558 prize] prize, *1767*   560 head,] head *1767*

The writer, who the duty knows,   580
Which he his friends and country owes,
And how he may endear the best,
A father, brother, or a guest,
By what behaviour he may grace
A senator's or Praetor's place,   585
Or how his character sustain,
When sent to make the great campaign,
Such skill as his compleatly suits
Each person with just attributes.

    The learned copyist shou'd look   590
At life and manners, as a book,
And from the language most in use,
His style and dialogue deduce.

    Sometimes a play, that shines at starts,
With moral matter for good hearts,   595
Tho' without music, weight or ease,
Will more the Roman people please,
And better on their mem'ry dwells,
Than tuneful toys or senseless bells.

    The Muse has Greece with genius crown'd,   600
They turn the rolling periods round,
Nor can such spirit and such fire,
Ought equal to applause desire.

    The Roman youths with pain and pride
A pound divide and subdivide,   605
'If from five ounces you take one,
How much remains, my little son,'
—'One third part of a pound.'—'O rare!
You'll for yourself take special care—
An ounce is added—what's the whole?'   610
'Why half a pound'—this rust of soul
And hankering after wealth ingrim'd,
The verse harmonious and well-tim'd
Can we expect from sordid elves
With cedar ting'd on cypress shelves?   615

    If poets use their talents right,
'Tis to instruct or to delight,

613 well-tim'd] well-tim'd, *1767*

And in the moral page to plan
The pleasures and concerns of man.
Whate'er you teach be brief and plain,   620
That they conceive you and retain.
When masters make too much a rout,
O'ercharg'd instructions will flow out.
Each fancy-piece for pleasure feign'd,
Shou'd near the truth be still sustain'd,   625
Nor let your tale at any hand,
Exaction of belief demand,
Nor from the witch's belly rive
The boy she din'd upon alive.
The tribe of seniors will decry   630
All verse in which no fruit they spy;
And the young noblemen will sneer,
And slight all writings too austere;
He wins most votes and makes most friends,
That use and entertainment blends,   635
At once delighting all that read,
And urging them to take good heed.
This book brings money to the trade,
By this the longest voyage is made,
And its fam'd author must procure   640
A long memorial to endure.
     But there are failings of the muse
We shou'd be ready to excuse;
Nor in the strings we always find,
Sounds answering to the hand and mind;   645
For oftentimes they will not suit,
And sound a *grave* for an *acute*.
The archer's bow, tho' aim'd aright,
Will not for ever hit the *white*.
     But verses shining in the main   650
I'll not for a few faults disdain,
Which either from a want of heed,
Or human frailty may proceed.
What therefore shall we hence deduce?
As a transcriber wants excuse,   655

618 plan] plan, *1767*   628 rive] rive, *1767*

If oft he err, tho' oft forewarn'd,
And as a harper's justly scorn'd,
By whom one note is always marr'd,
So each incorrigible bard
Becomes a Choerilus to me;   660
In whom if three good lines I see
I smile and wonder—but am wroth,
At Homer's slumbers and his sloth;
But 'tis allowable, perhaps,
If in long works the author naps.   665
  With painting poetry agrees,
And some things will the rather please,
If nearly view'd—but you'll be took
With others at a distant look.
That loves the dark, *this* will endure   670
The light, nor dread the connoisseur.
This piece has pleas'd, one time explor'd,
But this ten thousand times encor'd.
  O youth! the elder of the two,
Tho' from your father you persue   675
The right, and of yourself are wise,
Yet hear the thing that I advise:
Respecting life in many a scene,
The tolerable and the mean
We bear; a lawyer in his room,   680
Or pleader, who cannot presume
With great Messala's worth to vie,
Nor can be seen with Aulus by,
Yet still may be in some request—
But with regard to bards profest,   685
Nor Gods nor men nor rubric post
Can bear them when they're middlemost.
  As musick at an handsome treat,
If bad, will all the joy defeat;
And essence thick, where poppies blend   690
With * Sardian honey-comb, offend;

---

* This honey was bitter, from the nature of the herbs in that country.

660 Choerilus] Chaerilus *1767*   677 advise:] advise, *1767*   686 post] post, *1767*

Because these things might have been spar'd,
So verse, to sooth the soul, prepar'd;
If short of true perfection found,
They lose all worth, and sink aground.   695
   He that cannot the weapons play,
Will from the ring keep far away,
And one unskill'd in quoit or troque,
Forbear, lest he the laugh provoke
Of gaping crowds, at his expence—   700
But poets all our fools commence.—
Why not! the gentleman is free,
Of such estate and family,
Is rated at th'equestrian fine,
And has no sinister design.   705
   But * thou shalt nothing say or do,
Save what Minerva prompts you to;
Such is your judgment, such your will:
But if you e'er assume the quill,
Let Metius your production see,   710
Who is a judge—your sire—and me.—
Nine years your verses be suppress'd,
For while you're of your work possess'd,
You still may blot th'unpublish'd strain,
Which gone, you will recal in vain.   715
   Orpheus, the Gods own seer and priest,
Wild mortals from th'inhuman feast
And savage ways deterr'd, from thence
Inferr'd, upon a fair pretence,
Tygers to tame and lions fell.   720
Amphion, by his tuneful shell,
Was said to build the Theban wall
With stones that heard the charmer's call.
   It was the wisdom of their song
Of old, to sever right and wrong,   725
The public weal from private gain,
And things religious from profane;

* The elder Piso.

---

708 will:] will, *1767*   709 e'er] ere *1767*   716 Gods] God's *1767*   717 feast]
feast, *1767*

Promiscuous Venus to abate,
And institute the marriage state;
Towns and communities to plan,   730
And write the laws of God and Man.
'Twas thus an honour and a name
On bards divine and verses came.

    To worthies as sublime as these,
Succeeded great Maeonides: 735
Tyrtaeus too, by pow'r of verse,
To make the combatants more fierce.
In verse the oracles are made,
Th'oeconomy of life display'd;
And by the soft Pierian strain,   740
The royal favour we obtain;
For these were giv'n th'Olympic bay,
And sports to sooth the toilsome day.
Hear this lest you in scorn refuse
Sweet Phoebus, and the tuneful muse.   745

    It is a question they contest,
If nature or if art be best,
To form the bard—I do not see,
What without parts mere industry
Can profit,—nor can I devise   750
How unform'd Genius shou'd suffice.
Thus one requires the other still,
And friendly mingles force and skill.

    Whoe'er attempts with all his soul,
To run so as to reach the goal,   755
Has from a child endur'd much pain,)
From wine and women must abstain,   }
And sweat and freeze, and sweat again.)
The man that hymns the Pythian God,
Was once at school and fear'd the rod: 760
Nor will it hold for one to cry,
'My wondrous verse is very high,
A murrain seize the hindmost bard,
'Tis shame if ought my course retard,
Or that I shou'd be force'd to own,   765

That what's untaught to me's unknown!'
  As auctioneers with voice aloud,
To buy their goods collect a crowd;
Thus bards with money and with land,
Will hire an assentatious band;   770
But if 'tis one that can afford
To deck with elegance his board;
Or any of the poor to bail,
And save from law-suits, and a jail;
I wonder if he yet can know   775
A friend distinguish'd from a foe.
For making, or intent to make,
A gift of ought for friendship's sake,
Do not lead forth the honour'd boy
To read your verse while big with joy: 780
For then he certainly will roar,
O rare, O bravo, and encore!
Pale at some parts, at some he'll weep,
At some he'll jump about and leap:
As those that wail a corpse for pelf   785
Do more than real grief itself,
By word and deed—so friends that jeer,
Out-act the candid and sincere.
  Kings certain men are said to ply,
With frequent cups their strength to try,   790
That they may see into their heart,
If it can act a friendly part.
Thus, when the verse you make and show,
Learn caution from the fox and crow.
Quintilius, if to him you read   795
Your poems, with great frankness said;
'Pray alter this and that review:'
Which if you urg'd you cou'd not do,
Endeav'ring sundry times in vain,
He'd bid you blot it out again,   800
And to the anvil yet restore

774 jail;] jail. *1767*   775 know] know, *1767*   776 foe.] foe; *1767*   777 making,] making *1767*   779 boy] boy, *1767*   793 show,] show; *1767*   801 restore] restore, *1767*

Bald verses to be hammer'd o'er.
If you chose rather to defend
Your fault, than own it and amend,
He wou'd not waste another word   805
On one resolv'd to be absurd,
But rivalless you might admire
Yourself, and your poetic fire.
 A good man judging as he ought,
Will censure numbers void of thought,   810
 Condemn the harsh, nor will be brook
The incorrect, but cross the book:
Ambitious ornaments he'll pare,
And to th'obscure give light and air;
Ambiguous diction he will spurn,   815
Mark what shou'd have another turn:
In short, he will to thine and thee,
Another Aristarchus be—
Nor will he say, 'I'll not offend,
In trivial matters any friend;'   820
Such trifles sometimes cause offence,
And are of serious consequence
To one expos'd and ill-receiv'd,
Thro' folly not to be retriev'd.
  As one thro' phrenzy wild and vague,   825
Whom scurvy and King's evil plague,
Dreading his touch, each man that's wise,
From the mad-headed poet flies;
The boys attack him in the street;
Some fellow, who are less discreet.   830
He, while he roves about to cant
His verses with extatic rant,
If like a fowler while he eyes,
Intent upon the bird that flies,
Into some ditch or well shou'd fall,   835
Tho' for a long time he might bawl,
'Help, O my Countrymen!' not one,
To take him out, an inch wou'd run.
But shou'd some man his help afford,

820 friend;'] friend' *1767*   822 consequence] consequence, *1767*   837 one,] one
1767

And fairly let him down a cord,   840
I wou'd object, 'how can you prove,
This person chuses to remove!'
And then to make the matter clear,
I'd quote the fam'd Sicilian seer,
Empedocles, what time he schem'd,   845
Ev'n as a god to be esteem'd;
And in cold fit too fond of fame,
Leapt into Etna's burning flame.

    Then let these men of great renown,
Have privilege to hang or drown,   850
For such as save them 'gainst their will,
Are next akin to those that kill.
And often has he thus behav'd,
Nor, shou'd he by mere force be sav'd,
Wou'd he (as man) his lot abide,   855
And scorn the shame of suicide.
Nor is the principle yet known,
Why he shou'd try at verse alone;
Whether he did of old presume
To stale upon his father's tomb,   860
Or e'er remov'd with black intent,
The vengeful thunder's monument.
He's mad, howe'er, by all the fates,
And like a bear that's broke the grates,
Learn'd and unlearn'd, as he recites,   865
He chaces bitterly and frights;
But those he overtakes at last,
With tooth and tongue he holds right fast,
And sticks unto them, like a leach,
Till glutted in all parts of speech.   870

FINIS

852 those] those, *1767*   859 presume] presume, *1767*   861 e'er] 'ere *1767*
866 frights;] frights, *1767*

COMMENTARY

For general abbreviations, see p. xi. The following additional abbreviations are used in this Commentary: H. for Horace; S. for Smart; Fables for Smart's translations of Phaedrus. PI stands for Smart's 'Prose interpretation' in *1767*; PT for his prose translation of *1756*. PT has been used sometimes in preference to PI when a smoother or more literal translation was required. Words italicized in PT to indicate Smart's insertions are given here in square brackets. Unattributed translations are editorial. Biblical quotations are from the Authorized Version (King James Version).

Quotations from Horace in the Commentary are given in the punctuation and orthography of H. R. Fairclough's edition, *Horace: Satires, Epistles and Ars Poetica* (Loeb Classical Library, 1978), unless otherwise indicated. Cross-references to Horace are given according to the numbering of poems and lines in Smart's translation, except when they are prefaced by the letter H, indicating the original text.

Dedication. Francis Blake Delaval (1727–71) was the eldest of three brothers whom S. had known since they were undergraduates at Pembroke College, Cambridge, while he was Fellow. He was MP for Andover from 1754; appointed Knight of the Bath in 1761. S.'s *Occasional Prologue and Epilogue to Othello* (1751) was written for a private performance staged by Francis and his brother John: see *PW* iv. 177 and 435.

ll. 2–3   See Introduction, p. xvii, for other translators of Horace.

ll. 6–7   'Reckless poverty drove me to write verses': *Epistles* (H) II. ii. 51–2.

ll. 14–17   In 1758, during the Seven Years War, Francis Delaval joined the Grenadiers and was sent on the expedition which seized Saint-Malo. Ignoring an order forbidding volunteers to join the landing party, he managed to be the first Grenadier to go up the beach: see F. Askham, *The Gay Delavals* (1955), pp. 91–2.

l. 19 n.   Edward Hussey Delaval (1729–1814), youngest of the Delaval brothers, became Fellow of Pembroke College, Cambridge, and a well-known chemist and experimental philosopher. He was made FRS in 1759, and was awarded the Society's gold medal for his experiments based on Newton's theory of optics.

l. 21   *peculiar felicity*: an adaptation of the phrase *curiosa felicitas* ('studied felicity') which was first used of Horace by Petronius Arbiter (*Satyricon*, 118) in the 1st c. AD. See Preface, ll. 45 ff. and Introduction, p. xxiii.

Preface. ll. 6–8   The quotation is untraced.

l. 10   *Elian* (Aelian): Claudius Aelianus (*c.* AD 170–235), the author of two miscellanies in Greek dealing anecdotally and unsystematically with history, human life, and the animal world.

l. 17   *lucky . . . Horatian boldness*: see Introduction, p. xxiii.

ll. 20 ff.   H.'s broad themes (love, wine, death, etc.) are indeed found in Greek poetry but S.'s complaint that these motifs are too frequently borrowed is absurd. As for the phrasing, too little remains of Alcaeus and Sappho to support a general judgement, but what there is indicates that he would evoke their poetry with a vivid expression (e.g. *nunc est bibendum*, *Odes* I. xxxvii. 1) and then develop his own characteristic treatment (Rudd).

ll. 27–9   S. sent a copy of his translation of Pope's *Ode for Musick on St Cecilia's Day* to Pope sometime in 1743, and wrote again on 6 Nov. 1743, at the instigation of William Murray, Lord Chief Justice (created Baron Mansfield in 1756), proposing to translate Pope's *Essay on Man*. Pope replied on 18 Nov. 1743, encouraging him to translate the *Essay on Criticism* instead, and praising S.'s version of the Ode. He is also reputed to have told S. that the translation of the Ode 'exceeded his own original': see *The Annotated Letters of Christopher Smart*, ed. B. Rizzo and R. Mahony (Carbondale, Ill.: Southern University Press, 1991), pp. 1–10.

l. 29   *one of the brightest men* presumably refers to William Murray.

ll. 36–8   This was a much debated issue at this period. In the years 1757–65 the *Gentleman's Magazine* carried frequent reports of gigantic skeletons discovered in various parts of Britain, and several papers on the subject of giants were printed in the *Philosophical Transactions* of the Royal Society. The nature and origin of the Giant's Causeway was also the subject of scientific discussion: this striking geological formation on the north coast of Co. Antrim derives its name from the legend (which S. endorses in his footnote) that it was built by giants as the first part of a road from Ireland to Staffa in the Hebrides. For S.'s interest in giants, cf. *JA*, C88–92.

l. 43   *curiosa felicitas*: see note on Dedication, l. 21, above.

l. 69   H. describes both his satires and his epistles as *sermones*, 'conversations', in *Epistles* (H) I. iv. 1, II. i. 250–1, and elsewhere.

ll. 71–5   S. is presumably referring both to his carefully annotated translation of the *Ars Poetica* in 1756, in which he drew heavily on the copious notes appended to Richard Hurd's edition (1749), and to the 'discovery' he elaborates below (ll. 313 ff.).

ll. 77–9   These appendices are not included in the present edition.

ll. 79 ff.   See Introduction, pp. xxix and xxxiv, for discussion of S.'s text and annotations.

l. 91   *Impression*: cf. *JA*, B404 and note.

l. 102   Ps. 128: 2.

l. 104   Prov. 3: 17.

l. 108   Zech. 9: 17.

ll. 113–14   [Virgil], *Catalepton* xiv. 11–12; not regarded as Virgilian nowadays.

ll. 123–5   Claudian, *Panegyricus de tertio consulatu honorii Augusti*, 96–8.

l. 130   Perhaps alluding to St Paul's comment on righteous Gentiles who 'shew the work of the law written in their hearts, their conscience also bearing witness' (Rom. 2: 15).

ll. 134–41   Theocritus, *Idyll* xvi. 13–20. The poem is concerned with the difficulty poets experience in securing patronage from the great. The text given here is not the carelessly printed version of *1767* but is taken from *Bucolici Graeci*, ed. A. S. F. Gow (Oxford, 1952), save that the quotation-marks have been adjusted to S.'s interpretation. The edition used by S. has ἐπ' ἔργοις for ἐπ' ἔργμασιν in the second line.

ll. 142–55   Presumably S.'s own free rendering: *folds . . . breast* is evidently intended to suggest a defensive posture equivalent to the original 'having his hands within the fold (of his cloak)'. Similarly, *My gauntlets . . . hand* is S.'s equivalent for the Greek proverbial 'the shin is further than the knee' (Borthwick).

ll. 161–3   Dionysius Periegetes, *Orbis Descriptio* (*Description of the Earth*), 352–4. This poem, now seldom read, was well known in the 16th–18th cc.: editions with Latin translations were common in the first half of the 18th c. The most recent edition, in C. Mueller's *Geographici Graeci Minores*, ii. 102 ff. (1861), has two different readings from S.'s version of these lines.

l. 168   *famous verses*: *Cooper's Hill* (1642), ll. 189–92.

l. 173   The comment is from J. C. Scaliger, *Poetices Libri Septem* (1561), v. iii. 217 B2: 'sour Scaliger' because of his habit of comparing Homer unfavourably with Virgil.

ll. 175–80   Homer, *Od.* 5. 291–6. Text here from the edition of W. B. Stanford (1947).

ll. 189–97   From Pope's translation of the *Odyssey* (1725–6).

ll. 201–3   Ps. 29: 3, 'The voice of the Lord is upon the waters: the God of glory thundereth: the Lord is upon many waters', followed by the version from S.'s *Psalms*, 1765 (see *PW* iii. 65).

l. 215   *Odes* (H) II. xiv. 1.

l. 224   *Odes* (H) III. xxv. 1.

l. 232   *Odes* (H) IV. ii. 5.

l. 241   *Odes* (H) IV. iii. 17.

l. 262   *Odes* (H) IV. ix. 29.

l. 295   *Sat.* (H) II. vii. 83.

l. 312 n.   *to use . . . justice*: this now commonplace expression is used by Richard Hurd in the notes to his edition of *Ars Poetica* (1749): commenting on H's distinction between coarseness and wit (l. 273), Hurd writes, 'The subject is curious, and would require a volume to do it justice.'

ll. 313 ff.   S.'s theory is untenable since H. died in 8 BC, some years before Ovid began to write *Metamorphoses*. The *Critical Review*, 24 (Aug. 1767), 104–5, however, regarded the conjecture as 'new and ingenious'.

l. 341   *Ars Poet.* 1.

l. 359   *Met.* v. 552.

l. 387   *Sewell's Ovid*: George Sewell, *Ovid's Metamorphoses . . . Made English by several hands, . . . The second edition, with great improvements by Mr. Sewell*, 2 vols., 1724 (repr. 1727 and 1751).

l. 388   *Ars Poet.* 14.

l. 392   *Ars Poet.* 18.

l. 400   *nam . . . illas*: *Met.* i. 2, 'For you yourselves have brought about changes.'

l. 411   *Met.* vii. 74.

l. 418   *Met.* xi. 589.

l. 427   *Ars Poet.* 29.

l. 436   *Met.* i. 301.

l. 463   *Ars Poet.* 77.

l. 469   *Ars Poet.* 35.

l. 479   *Trist.* IV. viii. 1.

ll. 488 ff.   The source of this alleged comment is a mystery. In *Reflections on the Character of Iapis in Virgil*, a pamphlet published in 1740, Atterbury described Virgil in contrary terms as 'the most grateful of men to his friends and benefactors': see *Epistolary Correspondence, Visitation Charges, Speeches, and Miscellanies* [ed. J. Nichols], vol. i (1783), p. 337.

l. 493   *Trist.* IV. x. 49.

ll. 507–9   A favourite notion of S.'s: see *Hymns* 21. 43–6, *Hymns* (1771) 14. 1–2, and *Song*, 'A Mason is great and respected', 9–13 (*PW* iv. 366).

l. 516   William Flexney is mentioned in *JA*, D62. He was one of the publishers of S.'s *Poems on several Occasions* (1763) and *Psalms* (1765), to which he also subscribed. In 1767 Flexney and others issued proposals in the *Daily Advertiser* and on the final page of *1767*, vol. iv, for 'A Collection of Miscellaneous Poems' by S., but this publication never materialized.

Odes I. The first three books of Horace's *Odes* were published together in about 23 BC. Horace had already issued his *Epodes* and the two books of *Satires*. The earliest datable ode is I. xxxvii, written after Cleopatra's death in 30 BC.

I. i   *Maecenas*: Gaius Maecenas (*c.* 70–8 BC), a knight descended from a distinguished Etruscan family, was the trusted friend and adviser of Augustus and a generous patron of poets, including Virgil, Propertius, and Varius as well as Horace himself. Some time before 31 BC he presented Horace with his cherished Sabine farm, bounty acknowledged in *Epodes* i and *Epistles* I. vii.

I. i. 3–4   S. makes free with a line which is almost impossible to translate into idiomatic English, *o et praesidium et dulce decus meum*, 'O both my protection and my darling honour' (PT).

I. i. 5–10   S. again alters H.'s syntax to deal with an awkward construction: lit. 'there are some whose delight it is to have collected Olympic dust in the chariot race, and [whom] the goal [nicely] avoided by glowing wheels, and the noble palm, exalts to the Gods' (PT). *Driv'n . . . goal*: it was to the charioteer's advantage to round the turning-post (*meta*) as closely as possible. 'Goal' was the standard 18th-c. translation of *meta*.

I. i. 21–2   A very free expansion of *otium et oppidi laudat rura sui*, 'commends tranquillity and the ruralness of his village' (PT), i.e. the village where he has a country estate.

I. i. 24   *insure*: for *reficit*, 'refit'.

I. i. 26   *Massic*: a wine.

I. i. 27–8   *to break . . . solidity*: for *nec partem solido demere de die* ('nor to infringe upon the business of the day', PI). 'Solidity' suggests both entirety and sober perseverance: cf. Prior, 'Loose and undisciplin'd the soldier lay; / Or lost in drink, and game, the solid day', *Solomon* (1708), ii. 729.

I. i. 34   *pious dames*: 'mothers' in the original.

I. i. 52   For *Lesboum tendere barbiton*, 'tune the Lesbian lute' (PI), referring to lyric poetry in the tradition of Sappho and Alcaeus (Quinn).

I. i. 55–6   *sublimi feriam sidera vertice* ('I shall tow'r to the stars with my exalted head', PT): a proverbial expression (NH).

I. ii. 10–16   'An allusion to the deluge of Deucalion and Pyrrha' (PT, note), i.e. the myth of the universal flood sent by Jove in anger against mankind: see Ovid, *Met.* i. 253–312.

I. ii. 19–20   *Vesta's . . . plann'd*: the temple of Vesta was said to have been built on the left bank of the Tiber (see l. 23) by Numa Pompilius, second king of Rome.

I. ii. 37–8   *thou*: i.e. Venus ('Glad queen'). *Eryce* (Eryx), a mountain and city in Sicily, was famous for its temple to Venus; 'perfumes' is S.'s addition.

I. ii. 56   *translate*: for *tollat*, 'carry away'.

I. ii. 59–60   *nor . . . presume*: for *neu sinas Medos equitare inultos*, 'nor suffer the Parthians with impunity to make incursions' (PT).

I. iii. 1   *queen of Cyprus*: Venus, invoked by mariners as a sea-born goddess and because her planet was useful for navigation.

I. iii. 2   *Helen's brethren*: Castor and Pollux, known as protectors of seafarers and as the constellation Gemini (see *Odes* IV. viii. 47–8).

I. iii. 4   *fresh north-west*: for *Iapyga*. A footnote to PI explains: 'A wind blowing from Japygia, that is, Apulia.' It was the wind that blew ships from Brindisi to Greece (NH).

I. iii. 6 n.   *year of Rome 734*: dating from the foundation of Rome (753 BC), i.e. 19 BC in the Christian calendar, the year of Virgil's death. Since these odes were published in 23 BC the voyage to Greece alluded to here cannot have been Virgil's last journey, as S. surmises.

I. iii. 36–8   *semotique prius tarda necessitas leti corripuit gradum*, 'the slow approaching necessity of death, which till now was remote, accelerated its pace' (PT).

I. iv. 11   *Shakes with alternate feet*: S. keeps close to the original, *quatiunt alterno pede*, to capture H.'s evocation of the simple rhythms of a rustic dance (Quinn).

I. iv. 12   *dum graves Cyclopum Vulcanus ardens urit officinas*, 'while ardent Vulcan inflames the laborious forges of the Cyclops' (PT). Modern editions prefer *visit*, on the grounds that the variant *urit* could not mean 'ignite' (NH); but S. probably followed Ainsworth, who gives 'light up' as a possible sense.

I. iv. 17   S. does not attempt to reproduce the onomatopoeia in H.'s memorable line, *pallida Mors aequo pulsat pede pauperum tabernas*.

I. iv. 22   *win the monarchy of wine*: *regna vini sortiere talis*, win by dice command of the wine. 'The Romans used to cast lots who should be toast-master' (PT, note).

I. iv. 23–4   See Introduction, p. xxx.

I. v. 7–8   An elaboration of H.'s oxymoron *simplex munditiis*, 'plain in thy neatness' (Milton); 'drest with careless art' (Francis). *Munditia* means both 'cleanliness' and 'elegance'.

I. v. 22   *dropping weeds (vestimenta uvida)*: 'dripping clothes'; rescued sailors used to dedicate their clothes to the gods (NH).

I. v. 23   *votive chart (tabula votiva)*: escape from danger was often commemorated by a votive tablet fixed to the temple wall (NH).

I. vi. 2–3   *with Maeonian flight*: i.e. in epic style, like Homer (called 'Maeonian' after his supposed birthplace). *blaze*: proclaim, cf. Fables IV. xx. 9.

I. vi. 7–9   M. Vipsanius *Agrippa* (*c.* 64–12 BC), friend and later son-in-law of Augustus, was distinguished as a military and naval commander during and after the Civil War: his naval operations were principally responsible for Antony's defeat in the decisive battle of Actium (31 BC) celebrated in *Odes* I. xxxvii.

I. vi. 11–14   Referring to the subjects of Homeric epic: *Peleus' son*, Achilles; *That artful hero*, Ulysses.

I. vi. 15–18   *while . . . disgrace*: i.e. lyric poetry is an unfitting medium for tragic and epic subjects. The *race of Pelops* refers to the myths concerning the house of Atreus dramatized by Aeschylus. *wire*: string (of the lyre).

I. vi. 22   *Meriones*: a Cretan charioteer at the siege of Troy.

I. vi. 23–4   *him*: Diomede, another Greek warrior on the Trojan expedition, is called 'a match for the gods' (*superis parem*) because with the help of *Minerva* he wounded Venus and Mars.

I. vi. 29   *With nails . . . pare (sectis unguibus)*: H. means they sharpened them to a point.

I. vii   *Tibur*: modern Tivoli, near Rome. It is frequently mentioned by H. as a pleasant retreat; some think he had a house there. Cf. *Odes* II. vi. 5–6, III. iv. 24, IV. iii. 14, and *Epistles* I. viii. 20–1.

I. vii. 11   *apt for cavalry renown*: for *aptum equis*, 'suitable for horses', a traditional epithet (Quinn).

I. vii. 14   *high-manur'd*: for *opimae*, 'fertile'.

I. vii. 21   *albus ut obscuro deterget nubila caelo saepe Notus*, 'As Notus [the south wind] is frequently serene, and sweeps away the clouds from the gloomy sky' (PI). *albus* means both 'white' and 'favouring', hence here 'clearing' (NH).

I. vii. 29 ff.   *Teucer*, son of Telamon, king of *Salamis*, fought at Troy but on his return was banished by his father, who blamed him for the death of his brother Ajax. He went to Cyprus and founded a new city of Salamis.

I. vii. 39   *doubtful (ambiguam)*: i.e. because the new Salamis would rival its parent city in name (NH).

I. viii. 6   *the field*: i.e. the Campus Martius at Rome, where young men exercised and trained.

I. viii. 22   *Thetis' fav'rite heir*: Achilles. S. omits the phrase which follows, *sub lacrimosa Troiae funera*, 'just before the doleful destruction of Troy' (PI).

I. viii. 23–5   *man's habit* reproduces the ambiguity of the original, *virilis cultus*, which primarily means 'manly dress' but has the secondary sense of 'manly behaviour' (Quinn). H. refers to the legend that Thetis dressed Achilles in woman's clothing to prevent him joining the expedition against Troy.

I. ix. 1–2   *Vides ut alta stet nive candidum / Soracte*: H.'s opening is notoriously unmatchable in translation. S.'s literal rendering in PT, 'You see how [the mountain], Soracte, stands whiten'd with deep snow', has a note: 'As if it were an entire heap of snow.' Cf. Dryden, 'Behold yon' mountains hoary height / Made higher with new mounts of snow', *Sylvae* (1685).

I. ix. 4   *sharpen'd streams*: see Introduction, p. xxiii.

I. ix. 6   *aspire*: 'rise up', as in Shakespeare, *Merry Wives* V. v. 101, 'Whose flames aspire'.

I. ix. 10   *shall have … supprest* misrepresents *stravere* (perfect tense): H. is stating a general truth ('when the gods still storms, the trees are no longer shaken') not talking about the weather at the time of writing, which is calm (see l. 4).

I. ix. 19   *repeat (repetantur)*: 'be sought again'. Cf. Dryden, *Annus Mirabilis* (1667), l. 1028, 'With loathing eyes repeat what they would shun': last recorded use in this sense in *OED* is 1697, again from Dryden.

I. x. 4   For *more palaestrae*, alluding to the wrestling-schools of Athens (of which Mercury was patron), where young men came for logical and rhetorical exercise as well as physical training (NH).

I. x. 5   *courier*: requires stress on the second syllable to rhyme with *disappear* (l. 6); there is no evidence in *OED* for such a pronunciation.

I. x. 13–16   Referring to *Priam*'s secret visit to the Greek camp to recover the body of Hector, in defiance of Agamemnon and Menelaus, sons of *Atreus*: see Homer, *Il.* xxiv. 333 ff. *Atreus his*, the old form of genitive (= Atreus').

I. x. 17   *realms of love*: for *laetis sedibus*, 'joyful mansions' (PI), i.e. the Elysian fields (Quinn).

I. xi   S.'s version is printed in half-lines, with a note: 'In order to imitate the metre of the original, the longest measure in the English language (much in use amongst our old poets) is here introduced: but, for convenience of printing, one line is severed into two.' (H.'s original consists of 8 long asclepiads.)

I. xi. 1   *date*: i.e. the time of our death.

I. xi. 10   *compendious grant*, i.e. short allowance (*spatio brevi*).

I. xi. 11–12   *be greedy … play*: for *carpe diem, quam minimum credula postero*, 'seize the present day, counting as little as possible on the next'.

I. xii. 7–8   *unde vocalem … insecutae Orphea sylvae*, 'Whence the woods followed … the vocal Orpheus' (PI); i.e. through the spell-binding power of his music. *vague*: 'wandering', see note on *Odes* I. xxxv. 9. *at random*: for *temere*, 'pell-mell' (NH).

I. xii. 9   *his . . . art*: 'Calliope was the mother of Orpheus' (PT, note); she was one of the Muses.

I. xii. 14   *his*: Jove's.

I. xii. 19–20   *proximos illi tamen occupavit Pallas honores*, i.e. Pallas is second only to Jove in terms of honours paid to her.

I. xii. 21   *Liber*: Bacchus.

I. xii. 22   *Forrester*: for *virgo*, i.e. Diana, the huntress.

I. xii. 25   *Alcides*: Hercules. *Leda's twins*: Castor and Pollux.

I. xii. 26   *hunc equis, illum superare pugnis*, 'one for success with horses, the other for skill at boxing'. The *cestus* was a leather gauntlet weighted with metal, used by Roman boxers (*OED* 2).

I. xii. 33–44   H. lists heroes of Roman history: early rulers Romulus (33), *Numa*, and Tarquinius *Priscus*, and military commanders and statesmen *Cato* the Younger, *Regulus*, the *Scauri*, L. Aemilius *Paulus*, *Fabricius*, *Curius*, and *Camillus*.

I. xii. 41   *rough*: for *incomptis capillis*, 'with his uncombed locks' (PI), a token of sturdy integrity. Some editions read *intonsis*.

I. xii. 45–8   *Marcellus*: M. Claudius Marcellus, a distinguished general of the 3rd c. BC. His name reminded H. of the promising young Marcellus, nephew and adopted son of Augustus, who died in 23 BC, hence the reference to the 'Julian star'.

I. xii. 49 ff.   Addressed to Jove.

I. xii. 50 n.   *convey* in S.'s version corresponds to H.'s *data*, a verb which could also have legal connotations (see *LS*, *do* II.B, 'grant, permit').

I. xiii. 12   *sleeves . . . soils*: an oddly prudish translation of *turparunt umeros*, 'defiles your shoulders'.

I. xiv. 3   *fort*: 'strong position', in the figurative sense (*OED* 1b), but the following line picks up the military metaphor ('keep your station') only hinted at in H.'s *fortiter occupa* ('firmly seize', PI). Francis's translation, 'with caution keep the friendly port', emphasizes the underlying meaning at the expense of both literal and metaphorical fidelity.

I. xiv. 10   *keel . . . ropes (funibus . . . carinae)*. This strange conjunction can be explained in two alternative ways: (1) 'keel' is used metonymically for 'ship' in both Latin and English poetry (as a Durham man S. would also know 'keel' as the name of a flat-bottomed boat used on the east coast from the Tyne to Norfolk), hence 'ropes' may refer to the ship's tackle generally; (2) *funibus* refers to the cables used by the ancients to strengthen ships' hulls (NH). Swift skilfully catches the spirit in his paraphrase: 'Your cable's burst, and you must quickly feel / The waves impetuous entring at your keel' (*Poetical Works*, ed. H. Davis (1967), p. 282).

I. xiv. 23   *those isles*: the Cyclades. S. footnotes *Cycladas* in the Latin text: 'Islands in the Archipelago, which made the navigation very dangerous.'

I. xv. 18   *tire*: dress.

I. xv. 20   *Run ... divisions*: play melodic passages (see *OED* division, 7).

I. xv. 42   *stave*: i.e. stave off, postpone; S. habitually omits the preposition.

I. xvi. 5–8   *Cybele* (H. *Dindymene*): the 'Great Mother', goddess of nature, worshipped with wild dances and music by her priests, the *Corybantes*. *Liber*: Bacchus.

I. xvi. 10   *Noric*: from Noricum, a region between the Danube and the Alps famous for its iron.

I. xvi. 13–16   *Fertur Prometheus ... nostro*: 'It is said that Prometheus, when compelled to add to our original clay some portion cut out of all sorts of animals, inserted the force of the raging lion in our stomachs.' See Plato's *Protagoras* for this fable. *controul'd* (H. *coactus*) is an extension of the sense 'command(ed)' (*OED* control, *v.* 4), but the construction 'control to [do something]' is not recorded: 'was' in *1767* appears to be an error or misprint. PI has 'upon compulsion'.

I. xvi. 17–18   *Thyestes*, enraged that his brother Atreus, king of Mycenae, would not allow him to share the throne, raped Atreus' wife: this act set in train a bloody vendetta (see note on *Epodes* v. 138). *such a downfal*: i.e. one caused by wrath. *fell*: dire.

I. xvi. 19   *That ... towns*: for *altis urbibus ultimae stetere causae*, 'has been the final cause, that towering cities should fall' (PI).

I. xvi. 26   *for ... severe*: i.e. give up severity for gentleness.

I. xvii. 12   *Ustica*: a hill near H.'s Sabine farm; *marble piles*: smooth rocks (*levia saxa*). *repay*: re-echo.

I. xvii. 19   *Teian string*: i.e. the lyre of Anacreon, born on the island of Teos. He was famed as a writer of love-poetry.

I. xvii. 20   *the king*: Ulysses.

I. xvii. 22   *Lesbian white*: for *innocentis Lesbii*, 'innocuous Lesbian' (wine).

I. xvii. 24   *Thyoneus*: Bacchus, son of *Semele*.

I. xviii. 1   *Varus*: traditionally identified as Quintilius Varus of Cremona, the friend mourned in *Odes* I. xxiv and the critic named in *Ars Poet.* (H) 438 (but see NH for the suggested identification with P. Alfenus Varus). S.'s note is unhelpful.

I. xviii. 3   *droughty (siccis)*: 'abstemious' (PI) is clearly the required meaning, but *droughty* normally meant 'dry' in the opposite sense, i.e. 'thirsty', even 'addicted to drink' (*OED* 3).

I. xviii. 5   *make a racket . . . of (crepat)*: in the 18th-c. sense 'make a fuss about' (*OED* racket, *sb. 3*, 1c).

I. xviii. 8   Referring to the drunken fight between the Lapiths and the Centaurs at the wedding of Pirithous and Hippodamia in N. Thessaly: see Ovid, *Met.* xii. 210–530.

I. xviii. 9–10   the story behind this, if there was one, is unknown; but H.'s *Sithoniis* may simply refer to the Thracians, who were notorious for hard drinking (Quinn). S. translates *Sithoniis* as 'Thracians' in both PT and PI.

I. xviii. 11 n.   The standard derivation of *Bassareus* in the 18th c. as now was from Gk. Bassara, fox or fox-skin, as worn by Bacchantes. S.'s explanation is original as far as I know.

I. xviii. 14   *partial*: i.e. prejudiced in its own favour.

I. xviii. 16   The proverbial notion that 'in vino veritas'. *succeeds*: comes next.

I. xix. 1–3   The object of both *inspires* and *assures* ('encourages', *OED* assure, 8) is 'me' (understood). *mother . . . desires*: Venus. *Semele . . . son*: Bacchus.

I. xix. 8   *et vultus nimium lubricus aspici*: 'and her face too slippery to the sight.' *slippery* could mean both 'deceptive' and 'wanton' (*OED* 4–5); either way she is liable to frustrate ('balk') the lover. *lubricus* reinforces H.'s previous image of polished marble 'Glycera's face is as dazzling as a marble floor, and as treacherous' (NH).

I. xix. 11   *rehears'd*: spoken of.

I. xix. 12   The Parthians were dreaded for their practice of riding towards their enemy, then turning round and shooting over their shoulders as they retreated (hence the phrase 'Parthian shot').

I. xix. 13   *impertinent*: irrelevant.

I. xx. 10   i.e. Mount Vatican too echoed the praises of Maecenas (*et iocosa redderet laudes tibi Vaticani montis imago*).

I. xxi. 2   *smooth-fac'd*: for *intonsum*, usually translated 'unshorn', referring to Apollo's hair, but since the stress is on his youth, S.'s inference that it means 'not yet shaved' ('unrazor'd face', PI) is reasonable.

I. xxi. 4–5   *Latona*: mother of Apollo and Diana. *her*: Diana.

I. xxi. 11   *Him*: Apollo.

I. xxi. 12   Mercury, Apollo's half-brother, invented the lyre.

I. xxii. 8   *Hydaspes*: a river in India, tributary of the Indus.

I. xxii. 14   *Daunia*: Apulia. *beechen plain*: for *aesculetis*, oak-forest.

I. xxii. 16   *Juba's dry domain*: Numidia, a region of N. Africa.

I. xxii. 19–20   i.e. vexed with rain.

I. xxiii. 14   *Getulian brute*: African lion.

I. xxiv   *Quintilius*: See note on *Odes* I. xviii. 1. This ode is a fine example of H.'s sensitivity: he begins by arguing 'what limit can there be to our grief' (aligning himself with the mourners), but then acknowledges that there must be a limit, for laments are futile. Life must go on (Rudd).

I. xxiv. 18   i.e. when Virgil entrusted Quintilius to the gods, he did not mean them to take him away.

I. xxiv. 21   For *auditam arboribus fidem*, [be] 'attended to by the trees' (PI).

I. xxv. 4   *amatque ianua limen*, 'the door hugs its doorstep'.

I. xxv. 7   *winge*, i.e. whinge, a northern dialect word in the 18th c.

I. xxv. 18   *glote*, i.e. gloat, for *gaudeat*: used from the late 17th c. to mean 'cast amorous or admiring glances (on)' (*OED* gloat, 2).

I. xxv. 19   *Hebrus*: a Thracian river. Bentley's conjectural reading *Euro*, east wind (noted but not adopted by S. in *1756*), fits the context much better; cf. *Odes* IV. xi [xii]. 1–2, where winds from Thrace are associated with the spring.

I. xxvi. 7   *Tiridates*: king of Armenia.

I. xxvi. 9   *Pimplean hill*: the mountain of Pimpla, in Pieria, sacred to the Muses.

I. xxvi. 16   *Lesbian style*: see note on *Odes* I. i. 52.

I. xxvii. 11–12   *dicat Opuntiae Megyllae, quo beatus vulnere, qua pereat sagitta*, 'Let the brother of Opuntian Megylla rather declare with what wound he is happy, with what dart he is dying' (PI). Opus was a town of *Locris*, in Greece. H. now starts teasing one particular member of the drinking party about his love affairs (Quinn).

I. xxvii. 13–14   *On . . . can*: for *non alia bibam mercede*, 'I will not drink for any other consideration' (PI).

I. xxvii. 16   *ingenuous*: honourable.

I. xxvii. 19   *hamper'd . . . straight* (strait): for *laboras in Charybdi*, caught in a whirlpool.

I. xxvii. 24   Expansion of *triformi Chimaera*, 'this triple chimera' (PI): *Chimaera* was a fire-breathing monster with a lion's head, goat's body, and dragon's tail; it was killed by Bellerophon mounted on *Pegasus*. Footnote: *Iliad* vi. 181.

I. xxviii. 1   *Archytas*: a Pythagorean philosopher and mathematician of the 4th c. BC. The tradition that he drowned at sea may be founded on this ode.

I. xxviii. 9   *sire of Pelops*: Tantalus. He was admitted to the company of the gods but banished to the underworld for revealing their secrets, according to one version of the story. His punishment was to be tormented by hunger and thirst in the midst of water and fruit which perpetually receded from him: cf. *Sat.* I. i. 121–2.

I. xxviii. 11   *Tithonus* was granted eternal life, but not eternal youth, so he shrivelled away. According to one legend he was transformed into a grasshopper. H. says only that he was *remotus in auras*, 'translated to the skies' (PT), i.e. vanished into thin air (Quinn). For *sauterelle* (grasshopper), cf. *JA*, B28 n.

I. xxviii. 12   *Minos*, son of Jove and one of the three judges of the under-world, was admitted to Jove's council; *pry* is therefore misleading.

I. xxviii. 13–16   *Pythagoras*, son of Panthous (hence *Panthoides*), demon-strated his claim to be Euphorbus reincarnate by recognizing a shield at Argos as the one he (as Euphorbus) had used at Troy. On examination, the name Euphorbus was found inscribed on the back (NH).

I. xxviii. 19   *sed omnes una manet nox*, 'but one night awaits all men' (PI). Night was classically conceived as a dark-winged bird: see e.g. Virgil, *Aen.* viii. 369, and Spenser, *FQ* VI. vii. 44.

I. xxviii. 25–6   *outrageous south*: the raging south wind (*rapidus Notus*). *oblique*: for *devexi*, declining. The constellation Orion sets in Nov., a time when southerly storms are common (NH).

I. xxviii. 27   ILLYRIC: the Illyrian or Adriatic sea.

I. xxviii. 30   *grutch* (grudge): an archaic form even in the 18th c. but habit-ually used by S., cf. *Odes* III. v. 52, *Sat.* I. i. 194.

I. xxviii. 37–40   Modern editions usually read *neglegis immeritis nocituram postmodo te natis fraudem committere? fors et debita iura vicesque superbae te maneant ipsum* ('Do you think nothing of doing a wrong which will one day harm your innocent children? Perhaps the retribution of rights withheld and contempt awaits you too in your turn'). S.'s text reads . . . *committere forsan. Debita iura* etc. S. nevertheless treats the two sentences as related clauses in all his versions, at the cost of some obscurity. H.'s *fraudem* means 'injustice' rather than 'fraud'.

I. xxviii. 44 n.   Prior's imitation of this poem, 'An Ode. Inscribed to the Memory of the Honble. Col. George Villiers', was published in his *Poems on Several Occasions* (1709).

I. xxix   *Iccius*: see *Epistles* I. xii.

I. xxix. 1–4   An unsuccessful expedition was made against *Saba* (Arabia Felix) in 24 BC.

I. xxx. 8–10   *et parum comis sine te Iuventas Mercuriusque*, 'and Youth dis-agreeable without you, and Mercury' (PT).

I. xxxi. 7   *elephants*: for *ebur*, ivory.

I. xxxi. 8   S. makes free with the original: *non rura, quae Liris quieta mordet aqua taciturnus amnis*, 'not those countries which the mute river Liris wears away with its quiet stream' (PI).

I. xxxi. 10   i.e. those to whom fortune has given the vine (*quibus dedit Fortuna vitem*).

I. xxxi. 12   *which . . . cost*: a clumsy rendering of *Syra reparata merce*, got in return for Syrian merchandise.

I. xxxi. 16   *succ'ry*: succory (chicory).

I. xxxi. 20   *disgust*: presumably with the 18th-c. meaning of 'dissatisfaction' or 'vexation', but without the sense of 'dishonour' of the original *turpem senectam*.

I. xxxii. 2   *a lesson to remain*: for *lusimus . . . quod et hunc in annum vivat et plures*, 'any thing . . . that may live for the present year and many others' (PI).

I. xxxii. 10   *Liberum et Musas . . . canebat*, 'would sing of Bacchus and the Muses'.

I. xxxii. 13   *shell (testudo)*: the lyre; a tortoise shell formed the sounding-board of the first lyre (Quinn).

I. xxxiii. 10   *squeamish*: for *asperam*, 'ill-natured' (PI).

I. xxxiv   The Epicureans taught that thunder and lightning were purely physical phenomena, without religious significance; being the result of the movement of clouds, they never came from a clear sky. Some event has caused H. temporarily to doubt this. He then goes on to comment on the unpredictability of the world (Rudd).

I. xxxv   Augustus planned an expedition to Britain in 27 BC but it was not carried out.

I. xxxv. 1 ff.   Fortune had a cult at *Antium*, on the coast of Latium, about 30 miles SW of Ostia.

I. xxxv. 9   *vague (profugi)*: i.e. roaming; a northern dialect word still current in this sense (usually as verb) in the 18th c.

I. xxxv. 17–20 and footnote: *te semper anteit saeva Necessitas, clavos trabales et cuneos manu gestans . . . severus uncus . . . liquidumque plumbum*. H.'s figure of Necessity was commonly interpreted as a torturer in S.'s time: cf. Francis, and Gray's borrowing of these lines in his *Ode to Adversity* (ll. 1–8). Modern scholars interpret the lines as an image of implacable fixity, taking *clavos* (nails or bolts), *cuneos* (dowels or wedges), *uncus* (clamp), and *liquidum plumbum* (molten lead) as building materials (see NH). The reading *serva* (servant) for *saeva* (cruel) in l. 17 is often preferred nowadays, the general idea behind the image being that Fortune operates within a rigid framework of fate (Quinn).

I. xxxv. 32   *Erythrean wave*: the Red Sea.

I. xxxvi. 12   *Set ... in white memorials*: for *Cressa ... nota*, i.e. marked with (Cretan) white chalk, a 'red-letter day' (Quinn).

I. xxxvi. 14   *morrice-dance* is clearly intended to translate into English terms the idea of traditional dancing conveyed by *in Salium pedum*: the *Salii* were 'priests of Mars, who made dancing a principal part of their religious worship' (PT, note).

I. xxxvi. 19   *putrid* (also in PI): for *putres*, usually translated 'languishing'. This is an unusual sense, but cf. Persius v. 58, *in Venerem putris*. L. *puter*, like Eng. *putrid*, normally means 'rotten', hence 'soft' in a somewhat derogatory sense, but *OED* records no such use in English. Ainsworth s.v. *putris* gives 'wanton, lascivious', citing H. only.

I. xxxvi. 22   *ambitious* (also in PI): for *ambitiosor*, 'more embracing'. S.'s word is presumably an intentional Latinism, from the root-word *ambio*, 'go round'.

I. xxxvii   The famous naval battle of Actium (31 BC), at which Octavian (later Augustus) defeated the fleets of Antony and Cleopatra, brought to an end the Civil War which had riven the Roman republic for forty years.

I. xxxvii. 1–4   A free rendering of H. *Nunc est bibendum ... sodales*. 'Now, my companions, is the time to carouse, now to beat the ground with a light foot; now is the time that was to deck the couch of the Gods with Salian banquets' (PT). See note on *Odes* I. xxxvi. 14.

I. xxxvii. 6   *Caecuban*: a wine.

I. xxxvii. 7   *the queen*: Cleopatra. H.'s starting-point was a poem by Alcaeus celebrating the overthrow of the tyrant Myrsilus. Lines 7–22 present the Cleopatra of Augustus' propaganda, a drunken, half-crazed, power-hungry Egyptian (though in fact she was a Greek). Then, with a striking turn, she becomes an implacable Roman Stoic who prefers suicide to humiliation (Rudd).

I. xxxvii. 10   *eunuchs ... vain*: for *turpium morbo virorum*, 'diseased perverts' (Quinn). This phrase evidently gave S. some trouble: he renders it in PT as 'creatures noisome thro' distemper', in PI as 'base emasculated fellows', with a note suggesting the reading *orbo virorum*, presumably meaning 'deprived of manhood'. Ainsworth s.v. *morbus* cites H.'s phrase, noting '*sc.* eunochorum'.

I. xxxviii   S.'s fidelity to Sapphic metre necessitates taking some liberty with H.'s words. Cf. S.'s literal version: 'Boy, I hate the pomp of the Persians; chaplets woven with the inner bark of the linden-tree disgust me. Cease to quest about for the place where the latter rose loiters. It is my diligent care that you make no addition to plain myrtle, nor is the myrtle unbecoming for thee a servant, nor for me drinking under this scant vine'

(Pl). For another 18th-c. version in English Sapphics, see *The Poetical Works of William Cowper*, ed. H. S. Milford (1934), p. 530.

I. xxxviii. 1   *Persian* has three syllables.

II. i   C. Asinius Pollio, senator, writer, and patron of Virgil, was a supporter of Antony in the Civil War, but strove to prevent a rift between him and Octavian. He refused to serve against Antony at Actium, but after the battle he accommodated himself to Augustus' regime. As an author, he wrote tragedies, love-poems, and a history of the Civil Wars from the consulate of Metellus (60 BC) to the battle of Philippi (42 BC). For full interpretation of this difficult poem, see Fraenkel, pp. 234–9.

II. i. 4   *triple league*: 'The triumvirate of Octavius, Lepidus, and Antony' (PT, note). H. says only *graves principum amicitias* ('ill-fated friendships of leaders') which is equally applicable to the first triumvirate of Pompey, Caesar, and Crassus.

II. i. 14   *conscript house*: the Senate. The primary meaning of *conscript* is 'enrolled as a Senator' (*OED a.* 1).

II. i. 15–16   Pollio was awarded a triumph in 39 or 38 BC for his victory over an Illyrian tribe living on the borders of Dalmatia.

II. i. 24   Pompey was defeated by Caesar at Thapsus in 46 BC. After the battle M. Porcius *Cato*, and one of the Scipio clan, committed suicide rather than live in submission. These, in addition to other distinguished Romans who were killed in battle, are 'the victor's grandsons' mentioned in l. 28 below (Rudd).

II. i. 25–8   *Juno* was tutelary goddess of the Carthaginians. H. ascribes the catastrophe at Thapsus to vengeance by Juno and other divine guardians of Africa on the descendants of the Roman destroyers of Carthage (146 BC) and slayers of *Jugurtha*, king of Numidia (104 BC). *propense*: favourably disposed.

II. i. 37–8   H. addresses his own Muse, not Pollio's. *Cean* refers to the Greek poet Simonides, born on the island of Ceos, who was regarded as a master of the pathetic style (NH).

II. ii. 12   *either Carthage*: the Carthaginians were settled in southern Spain as well as N. Africa.

II. ii. 17–20   The subject of this compressed sentence is Virtue: unlike the crowd (*dissidens plebi*), she excludes Phraates from the blessed (*numero beatorum eximit*) and teaches the people not to use false terms (*populumque falsis dedocet uti vocibus*), i.e. not to call him 'blessed'. Phraates IV, king of Parthia, was deposed by Tiridates in 26 BC but quickly regained the throne by ejecting the usurper.

II. iii. 4   *non secus in bonis ab insolenti temperatum laetitia*, 'as secured from insolent exultation in prosperity' (PT).

II. iii. 8   *of more interior date*, for *interiore*: i.e. well-matured. The jars with the longest-stored wine stood further inside the cellar than more recent vintages (Quinn).

II. iii. 9   *Where*: S. adopts Bentley's reading *qua* for the usual *quo* ('to what purpose?').

II. iii. 13   Perhaps meaning 'exhort [people] to enjoy wine,' etc.: for *huc vina et unguenta . . . ferre iube*: order wine, etc. to be brought here.

II. iii. 21   *Inachus* was the first king of Argos in Greece.

II. iv   For S.'s 'Imitation' of this ode see *The Pretty Chambermaid* (*PW*, iv. 111).

II. iv. 2–4   *Thetis' heir*, Achilles, loved his captive *Briseis*.

II. iv. 6–10   Agamemnon (*Atreus' son*) fell in love with the Trojan princess Cassandra who was his captive after the *Phrygian* (Trojan) forces were overcome by Achilles ('that Thessalian boy').

II. iv. 23–4   *whose age . . . hill*: H. specifies that he has passed his fortieth year.

II. v. 14   *eager (immitis)*: sharp, sour.

II. v. 24   *sturdy lad*: for *maritum* (*te* understood), 'you for a husband'.

II. v. 25–30   i.e. Lalage will be more beloved than *Pholoe*, *Chloris*, and *Gyges*.

II. vi. 3   *Syrtes*: dangerous shoals off northern Africa.

II. vi. 5   *Tibur*: see headnote to *Odes* I. vii. *by . . . plann'd*: i.e. founded by Greek settlers (*Argeo positum colono*).

II. vi. 10–11   *Galesus*: a river near Tarentum, a Spartan colony in the south of Italy founded by *Phalanthus*.

II. vi. 12   *cover'd fleece*: for *pellitis ovibus*, 'sheep covered with skins' (PI), with footnote, 'With other skins beside their own to preserve the peculiar delicacy of the fleece.'

II. vi. 13–14   *With me . . . takes*, i.e. 'I have a liking for that little corner [*angulus*]'. Mt. Hymettus in Attica was famous for its honey.

II. vii   In 30 BC, twelve years after the battle of Philippi at which the forces of Brutus and Cassius were defeated by those of Antony and Octavian, a general amnesty was granted; H. availed himself of it at once, but his friend continued the fight (ll. 15–16), perhaps joining Sextus Pompeius.

II. vii. 10   To throw away one's shield in flight was a poetic commonplace (e.g. in Archilochus and Alcaeus); with an ironical poet like H. it is uncertain that he actually did it (Rudd).

II. vii. 13   To be spirited away by a deity was the experience of some epic heroes. *Mercury*, as patron of poets, was the appropriate god to perform this service for H. Again, he is retrospectively making light of a disastrous defeat (Rudd).

II. vii. 19   *bay*, i.e. bay-tree (*lauru*).

II. vii. 22   *Massic*: wine.

II. vii. 25   *who ... most*: a throw of the dice decided who should take the chair, see note on *Odes* I. iv. 22.

II. vii. 28   *at ... interview*: for *recepto ... amico*, 'on the reception [i.e. return] of my friend' (PI).

II. viii. 8   The centre of attention amongst our young men.

II. viii. 19   *pound*: a locked enclosure.

II. ix.   *Valgius*: C. Valgius Rufus was a consul in 12 BC and elegiac poet. He is mentioned as a friend in *Sat.* I. x. 153.

II. ix. 16   *Antilochus*, Nestor's son, was killed in the Trojan War.

II. ix. 24   *Niphates*: S. takes this to mean the river in Armenia rather than the mountain. *stiff*: for *rigidus*, icebound.

II. ix. 27   *Gelonians*: a Scythian tribe.

II. x. 6   i.e. raises himself above squalor.

II. x. 20   *shoots his rays*: for *arcum tendit*, stretches his bow. The contrast is between Apollo as god of the lyre and the angry archer-god of the *Iliad*, book i. S. equates Apollo's arrows with the scorching rays of the sun. 'Not' in *1767* is possibly a misprint for the smoother 'Nor' used in PI.

II. xi. 11–12   *Your thoughts ... these*: for *quid aeternis minorem consiliis animum fatigas?*, 'why do you weary your mind, unequal to such endless plans?' H.'s point is that such matters are the concerns of a public man, not of a philosopher.

II. xi. 19–20   H. describes Falernian wine as *ardentis*, 'fiery', hence the call for a slave to 'quench' it (*restinguet*) with water from the brook.

II. xii. 1   After a long and bloody struggle the Romans laid siege to Numantia in Spain, finally conquering it in 133 BC.

II. xii. 4–5   A reference to the naval battles of the First Punic War, in the 3rd c. BC.

II. xii. 7–9   Referring to the fight between Lapiths and Centaurs: see note on *Odes* I. xviii. 8. *Hyleus* was a centaur.

II. xii. 10–11   *Hercules* helped the gods defeat the earth-born giants.

II. xii. 20–1   The question whether H.'s *dominae Lycymnia* stands for Maecenas' wife or a mistress is much debated. S.'s 'my lady fair' does not make the problem any easier (Rudd).

II. xii. 33   *Achemenes*: king of Persia.

II. xii. 38–42   S.'s confused phrasing makes H.'s complicated syntax impenetrable: 'Or by a mild cruelty denies what she rejoices should be ravished from her more than the petitioner—At times she seizes an opportunity of stealing them herself' (PI).

II. xiii. 6   *or cut . . . throat*: S.'s interpolation. H. says only *illum et parentis crediderim sui fregisse cervicem*, 'I cou'd believe that he had broke his own father's neck' (PT).

II. xiii. 8   *Colchian*: like those of the sorceress Medea of Colchis, see note on *Epodes* iii. 19–26.

II. xiii. 26   *in a fuller piece*: for *sonantem plenius*, 'sounding in fuller strains' (PT).

II. xiii. 31   *thicking*: a variant of *thickening* archaic even in the 18th c.

II. xiii. 34   *many-headed beast*: Cerberus.

II. xiii. 37–8   *sire Of Pelops*: Tantalus, see note on *Odes* I. xxviii. 9.

II. xiii. 39–40   *ounce*: leopard. *visionary*: imaginary. 'Orion, who had loved hunting when he lived, is here described pursuing the same sport, when he died' (Francis).

II. xiv. 8   *Tityus*: see note on *Odes* III. iv. 71–9.

II. xiv. 17   *Cocytus*: 'the river of wailing' in the underworld.

II. xiv. 19–20   *Danaids fell*: 'fierce daughters of Danaus', all punished for murdering their husbands: see *Odes* III. xi. 26–60. For *Sisyphus* see note on *Epodes* xvi [xvii]. 21–2.

II. xv. 4   *platanusque caelebs evincet ulmos*, 'and the single plane-tree will supplant the elm'. Unlike the elm, the plane was not used to support (*maritari*, be 'wedded' to) the vine, hence *caelebs*, 'unmarried'. In this sense it is 'sterile' in contrast to the 'fertile olives' (*olivetis fertilibus*) of l. 8 (Quinn).

II. xv. 11–12   Only Cato is called 'bearded' (*intonsi*) by H. but the word, symbolizing old-fashioned austerity (Quinn), is equally applicable to 'our sires' (*veterum*, ancients).

II. xv. 16   *summer . . . wane*, for *opacam Arcton*, 'the shade of northern breezes' (PI), needed as protection against the scorching sun; *wane* is a variant spelling of *wain*, referring to the constellation Arcturus, known as the *Great* and *Lesser Wain*.

II. xv. 18   *providential turf (fortuitum . . . caespitum)*: 'turf that is there for the collecting', and was useful for simple building purposes (NH).

II. xvi. 11   *fray (summovet)*: scare away (*OED v. 2*).

II. xvi. 26   i.e. rejoice in the present, if it is fortunate. H. says only *laetus in praesens animus*, enjoy the present.

II. xvi. 30   *Tithonus*: see note on *Odes* I. xxviii. 11.

II. xvi. 31–2   *mihi forsan, tibi quod negarit, porriget hora*, 'time perhaps may extend to me what it shall deny to you' (PT). *amerc'd*: deprived.

II. xvi. 37–40   S.'s syntax and wording make this impossibly confused. *Me . . . foretold*: is inverted; *spirited from Greece* qualifies *I*. 'On me faithful providence has bestowed a small country farm, and a little portion of the Grecian poetical spirit, and a disposition to contemn the ill-natured vulgar' (PI).

II. xvii. 13   *Chimera*: see note on *Odes* I. xxvii. 24.

II. xvii. 14   *respire* ('breathe again', *OED* I. 3) spoils the point of *resurgat*, 'rise again': the hundred-handed giant *Gyas* was supposed to be imprisoned under a mountain in Hades (Quinn).

II. xvii. 19   S.'s interpolation.

II. xvii. 23–4   In astrological terms, Jupiter was a friendly planet, Saturn a malevolent one.

II. xvii. 25–6   See *Odes* I. xx. 5–11.

II. xvii. 27–8   See *Odes* II. xiii. *refrain'd*: restrained.

II. xviii. 6   i.e. Since I am not Attalus' heir: *Attalus* III, ruler of Pergamum, died in 133 BC leaving his kingdom to the Roman people.

II. xviii. 41–2   The Titan *Prometheus* was punished by Jupiter for stealing fire from heaven to help mankind. He was chained to a rock with a vulture incessantly devouring his liver (cf. *Epodes* xvi. 19). This story of an attempt to free him by bribery is not known apart from H.'s allusion to it.

II. xviii. 44   *Tantalus*: see note on *Odes* I. xxviii. 9.

II. xix. 4   *secrete*: archaic form of *secret*, for H.'s 'remote'.

II. xix. 9 ff.   H. alludes to Greek legends illustrating the powers of Bacchus. *Thyads*: Maenads, intoxicated followers of the god. Ariadne, abandoned by Theseus on Naxos, was rescued by Bacchus, who wedded her and gave her a crown of seven stars (hence called *the brilliant dame*). It became a constellation after her death. The palace of *Pentheus* king of Thebes was destroyed after he had attempted to suppress the cult of Bacchus. *Lycurgus*, a Thracian king, was likewise driven mad and killed for persecuting Bacchus.

II. xix. 19   *debonaire*: for *uvidus*, 'wet with wine' (PI). The usual meaning of 'debonair' was good-humoured, pleasant, gay in manner, but it could have rakish connotations: *OED* cites Collier (1707), 'He has too debonair and free a Deportment with the Women.'

II. xix. 24   *Rhoecus* (Rhoetus): leader of the giants who rebelled against the gods.

II. xix. 29–32   Alluding to Bacchus' journey to the underworld to bring back his mother Semele. *golden horn*: 'as a god of animal vitality, Dionysus was often represented as a bull' (NH).

II. xx. 14   *Icarian flight*: Icarus attempted to fly on wings of feathers and wax made by his father Daedalus, but the sun melted the wax and he was drowned.

II. xx. 21   *squalid grief*: referring to the black clothes, scratched cheeks, and disordered hair, of traditional mourning rites.

III. i. 2   For *profanum*, but H. means 'profane' in the sense that they are unqualified to take part in the rites of the Muses (Rudd). S. typically takes it in the broader sense of 'irreligious' (PI).

III. i. 13–14   *will . . . clients*: i.e. claims to have more clients.

III. i. 17–18   Alluding to Damocles, who called Dionysius, ruler of Syracuse, the happiest of men: to demonstrate the 'happiness' of a monarch, Dionysius invited him to dinner, where he found himself seated under a naked sword hanging by a single hair.

III. i. 24   *Tempe*, a valley in N. Thessaly, was regarded as a rural paradise.

III. i. 25   *but neighbour's fare*: i.e. only a common sufficiency (*quod satis*).

III. i. 27   *bear . . . goat*: the constellations *Arcturus* and *Haedus*, whose rise and setting in Oct. are a signal for autumn gales.

III. i. 28   *Nor . . . portends*: referring to weather forecasts printed in the almanac.

III. i. 30–2   *Not flattering farm*: *fundusque mendax*, i.e. a farm whose crop fails despite promising signs ('symptoms') of a good harvest. *hot sidereal pow'rs*: *torrentia agros sidera*, 'stars parching the fields' (particularly the Dog-star in summer).

III. i. 34–6   *they*: i.e. the surveyor and his slaves (l. 35), referring to the huge villas built out on to the sea at Baiae and other resorts (Quinn).

III. i. 39   *top-mast head*: for *aerata triremi*, 'brazen-beaked galley' (PI).

III. ii. 27–8   *vetabo, qui Cereris sacrum volgarit arcanae, sub isdem sit trabibus, fragilemque mecum solvat phaselum*: 'I will prohibit that man, who shall divulge the sacred rites of mysterious Ceres, from being under the same roof with me, or from setting sail with me in the same precarious vessel' (PT). *blaz'd*: proclaimed, uttered in public.

III. ii. 29–31   *regent . . . day* stands for *Diespiter*, an old name for Jupiter: when neglected he has often involved the innocent with the guilty (*neglectus incesto addidit integrum*).

III. iii. 12   *to rites . . . rise*: for *recumbens purpureo bibet ore nectar*, 'reclining he shall sip nectar with purple-stained mouth'. Like Francis, S. uses a text with the MS reading *bibit* (present tense), but he translates it into the future, as is theologically requisite.

III. iii. 16   *Romulus*, son of *Mars* and legendary founder of Rome, was said to have disappeared in a thunderstorm, transported in a chariot drawn by his father's horses.

III. iii. 19   *foreign whore*: Helen, carried off from Sparta and brought to Troy by Paris.

III. iii. 22–3   *Laomedon*, king of Troy, employed the gods Apollo and Poseidon to build the walls of the city but then refused to pay them.

III. iii. 25–6   Paris was the *ignominious guest* of Menelaus, king of Sparta, whose wife Helen he stole.

III. iii. 27   *Priam's perjur'd house*: Priam was son of Laomedon and father of Paris.

III. iii. 32   *son . . . bore*: Romulus, son of Ilia by Mars.

III. iii. 40   *so that*: provided that.

III. iii. 49–50   *Deriving* agrees with *her* (l. 45), i.e. Rome: she is *uncontroul'd* by any external nations.

III. iii. 55   *pride*: be proud (*OED v.* 2).

III. iii. 60   i.e. they should not, out of excessive piety and over-confidence (*nimium pii rebusque fidentes*), attempt to restore ancestral Troy. *prosper to replace*: i.e. prosper by replacing.

III. iv   See Introduction, p. xxiv.

III. iv. 16   *chace*: 'chase' in the sense of a hunting-ground.

III. iv. 23–4   The town of *Praeneste* (modern Palestrina) is kept cool by its height. For *Tibur*, see headnote to *Odes* I. vii. *Baiae* was a fashionable seaside resort just north of the Bay of Naples.

III. iv. 28   *Sicilian wave*: H. seems to refer to an occasion (unmentioned elsewhere) on which he narrowly escaped drowning. *cursed tree*: see *Odes* II. xiii.

III. iv. 33–6   H.'s place-names are intended to convey the sense of vast wanderings. S.'s *Picts* stand for 'Britons', representative for H. of the barbaric northern tribes; *Concanum* was in Spain; *Tanais* (the river Don) on the north-eastern borders.

III. iv. 37–40   *You*: i.e. the Muses, who are asked to command Caesar to rest from war.

III. iv. 42   *refrain*: restrain.

III. iv. 43   *him*: Jove.

III. iv. 50–80   Referring to exploits of the giants, who rose against the gods but were defeated and imprisoned in the earth.

III. iv. 64   *Patara*: cult centre of Apollo on the coast of Asia Minor.

III. iv. 69   *Gyas*: cf. *Odes* II. xvii. 14.

III. iv. 71–9   The giants *Orion, Tityus,* and *Perithous* [Pirithous] were all killed for assaults on goddesses. The *spotless maid* was Diana. *Tityus* attempted to ravish Latona, and was killed by her children, Apollo and Diana: for punishment he was kept bound in the underworld while two vultures tore his liver.

III. v. 1–2   *Caelo tonantem credidimus Iovem regnare,* 'We believe from his thunder that Jove rules in heaven.'

III. v. 3–4   In H. these events are all in the future. *Picts*: for *Britannos*, see note on *Odes* III. iv. 33.

III. v. 5–12   'The poet paints the defeat of Crassus, and the cowardice of the Romans in these vivid colours, that he may raise the glory of Augustus, who, by subduing the Parthians, had effaced that ignominy, which so many years had covered the Roman name' (Francis). M. Licinius *Crassus* was allied with Caesar and Pompey in the first triumvirate; after his defeat and murder by the Parthians in 53 BC his soldiers settled among their conquerors.

III. v. 7   *inverted manners*: for *curia*, the (corrupted) Senate. S. alludes to the old tag, *o tempora, o mores* (Cicero, *Cat.* i. 1).

III. v. 11   *gown*: the toga.

III. v. 13   *Regulus*, Roman general in the First Punic War, was defeated and captured by the Carthaginians in 255 BC. He was sent back to Rome on parole in 250 BC to negotiate peace terms but advised the Romans to continue fighting, and returned to Carthage where he was tortured and killed.

III. v. 16   *exemplary*: example, precedent (see *OED sb.* 1).

III. v. 28   *poison'd*: i.e. doctored with dye (*medicata fuco*).

III. v. 31–3   Implying sarcastically that a soldier who has trusted himself to treacherous foes (*perfidis se credidit hostibus*) is as likely to be brave as a deer is likely to fight when disentangled from the snare (*extricata . . . cerva plagis*).

III. v. 43   *amerc'd*, 'attainted' (PI): for *capitis minor*, deprived of civil rights.

III. v. 45   *conscript fathers*: the Senate, see note on *Odes* II. i. 14.

III. v. 51–2   *waving*: brushing aside, a concrete application of *wave*, meaning *waive* (see *OED* waive, *v. 1*, 6d). *grutching*: see note on *Odes* I. xxviii. 30.

III. vi. 1–4   During the Civil Wars many temples had become dilapidated. These lines reflect Augustus' policy of renewal.

III. vi. 9–10   *Moneses . . . Pacorus*: Parthian generals. Pacorus defeated a Roman army in 40 BC.

III. vi. 14–16   Referring to the battle of Actium (see *Odes* I. xxvii) at which Dacian archers and Egyptian sailors fought for Antony and Cleopatra against Caesar.

III. vi. 20   *murders*: for *clades*, meaning defeats on the battlefield (Quinn).

III. vi. 22   Ionian dances were regarded as especially voluptuous and sensual (Quinn).

III. vi. 23   *move by leud prescription*: for *fingitur artibus*, 'is fashioned by arts', i.e. learns to behave coquettishly.

III. vi. 24   *incest*: for *incestos amores*, 'unholy loves'. In 18th-c. English, as in L., 'incest' meant forbidden love of any kind.

III. vi. 35–6   *Pyrrhus*, king of Epirus, was renowned for his military prowess and imperial ambitions: he was killed by the Romans in an attack on Argos in 272 BC. The equally redoubtable *Antiochus* III ('the Great') of Syria was finally defeated by the Romans in 190 and died in 187 BC. *Hamilcar's son*: Hannibal.

III. vi. 39   *clubs of oak*: for *recisos fustis*, here meaning logs cut for firewood, though the primary sense of *fustis* is 'cudgel'.

III. vii. 19–24   *Bellerophon* rejected the advances of the wife of *Proetus*, king of Argos; in revenge, she denounced him to Proetus, who plotted to kill him, but failed.

III. vii. 25–8   *Peleus* likewise escaped death when he repelled *Hippolyte*, wife of King Acastus, who also denounced him to her husband.

III. vii. 35–6   *Enipeus* is the object of *receive*.

III. vii. 38–42   *Martian plain*: the Campus Martius (see note on *Odes* I. viii. 6) was situated by the river.

III. vii. 46   *scurvy minstrels*: for *cantum querelae . . . tibiae*, 'music of the plaintive pipe'. It is usually taken to refer still to Enipeus rather than serenaders generally.

III. viii. 1–2   *Martiis caelebs quid agam Kalendis*, 'what am I, a bachelor, doing on the March calends?' S.'s translation is very confused: *so clean* must refer to himself, meaning something like 'well groomed'. It has no equivalent in H.

III. viii. 8–10   See *Odes* II. xiii.

III. viii. 14–15   'The Romans used to ripen or mellow their wine by fumigation' (PT, note). *When . . . votes*: L. Vocatius *Tullus* was elected consul in 66 BC, the year before H.'s birth.

III. viii. 23   *Cotison*: S.'s habitual spelling of Cotiso, king of the Dacians. He was defeated by the Romans in 30 BC.

III. viii. 26–7   *servit Hispanae vetus hostis orae Cantaber, sera domitus catena*, 'the Cantabrian, our old enemy on the Spanish coast, is subject to us, tho' conquer'd by a long-disputed victory' (PT). The Cantabrians were defeated in 29 BC.

III. viii. 29   S.'s addition.

III. viii. 31–5   A free rendering of H.'s *carpe diem* ending: *neglegens, ne qua populus laboret, parce privatus nimium cavere et dona praesentis cape laetus horae ac linque severa*, 'carefree as a private citizen, cease to worry about [*repute*] how the people are suffering and seize the gifts of the present hour, abandoning serious matters'.

III. x. 13–14   H. says, 'Get rid of your proud disdain, which is unwelcome to Venus.' *ungrateful*: i.e. to Venus.

III. x. 15–16   Replaces H.'s metaphor, *ne currente retro funis eat rota*, 'lest the rope should go back with the turning of the wheel' (PI).

III. x. 17–18   i.e. You are not an old-fashioned Roman lady, nor a faithful Penelope.

III. x. 23–4   *by . . . minstrel*, a euphemism for *Pieria paelice* (see Introduction, pp. xxx–xxxi), perhaps implying that she was a singer, since Mt. Pierus in Thessaly was sacred to the Muses.

III. x. 27–8   *nec Mauris animum mitior anguibus*, 'no gentler in heart than Moorish snakes' (referring to Lyce).

III. xi. 4   *shell* (*testudo*): the lyre (see note on *Odes* I. xxxii. 13); but specifically referring here to H.'s verse.

III. xi. 10/11   S.'s text and translation omit H.'s ll. 9–12 (included in PT), in which Lyde is compared to a 3-year-old filly not yet ready for a mate.

III. xi. 14–20   Alluding to the legend of Orpheus' descent into the underworld: the *hell-hound* is Cerberus. H. does not absurdly say that he 'smil'd', merely that he 'yielded' (*cessit*).

III. xi. 18   *steams . . . dread*: for *spiritus taeter*, foul breath.

III. xi. 21   *Ixion* was bound on an ever-turning wheel in the underworld as punishment for the cruel murder of his father-in-law. For *Tityos* (Tityus) see note on *Odes* III. iv. 71–9.

III. xi. 26–60   According to Greek mythology, a marriage was arranged between the fifty daughters of Danaus (the Danaids) and the fifty sons of his brother Aegyptus. Because of a quarrel between the brothers, Danaus ordered his daughters to stab their husbands on the wedding-night. Only Hypermnestra disobeyed. The rest were condemned to the underworld, where their punishment was to try forever to fill a leaking jar with water.

III. xii. 1   *mope*: gloomy person; cf. Pope, *Dunciad* (1742), ii. 37.

III. xii. 3   In Latin, the *uncle* is traditionally a stern figure.

III. xii. 8   Minerva was goddess of arts and crafts (Quinn).

III. xii. 12   *simul unctos Tiberinis umeros lavit in undis*, 'after he has washed his annointed shoulders in the waters of the Tiber' (PI).

III. xii. 13   *clean as a cat*: a semi-pun, typical of S.'s later poetry. It translates *catus*, 'adroit' (PI): in post-classical Latin, however, *catus* could mean a male cat (*LS*).

III. xiii. 2   *Blandusia* occurs in two codices and is the reading adopted by Bond. Most editors, including S. in *1756*, prefer *Bandusia*.

III. xiii. 15–17   *fies nobilium tu quoque fontium, me dicente*: 'you also will become one of the famous fountains, through my singing.'

III. xiv. 2–4   *Amphytrion's son*: Hercules, referring to his triumphant return after defeating the three-headed monster Geryon in Spain. *To buy a wreath (petiisse laurum)*, i.e. earn the laurel crown awarded to victorious generals, even at the price of death. *sped*: i.e. returned; *repetit penates*, 'revisits his domestic deities' (PI). Augustus was seriously ill during the campaign.

III. xiv. 5   See note on *Odes* III. viii. 26–7.

III. xiv. 11   *Octavia*: Augustus' sister.

III. xiv. 17–20   A textual crux. S. accepts the awkward MSS reading *iam virum expertae, male nominatis parcite verbis* (variously emended by Bentley and others): 'who have experienced a man, forbear words that it is bad to name' (PI).

III. xiv. 27   *measure*, i.e. of wine.

III. xiv. 28   *preserves . . . fray*: i.e. commemorates the Marsian war (90–88 BC).

III. xiv. 29 n.   *Spartacus* successfully led a slave rebellion for two years against the Roman armies until his defeat and death in 71 BC.

III. xiv. 33   S.'s invention, based on H.'s epithet for Neaera *argutae* 'clear-voiced'.

III. xiv. 40   i.e. when H. was a young man (*calidus iuventa*, 'warm with youth', PI). *Plancus*, to whom *Odes* I. vii is addressed, was consul in 42 BC when H. was 23.

III. xv   This ode is the first in Smart's second volume. The title-page has the motto:

> O carminum dulces notae,
> Quas ore pulchre melleo
> Fundis Lyraeque succinis!

'O sweet notes of songs which you pour forth beautifully with honeyed voice, accompanied by the lyre.' The lines are unattributed, presumably therefore written by S. himself.

III. xv. 19–22   i.e. spinning wool is suitable for a woman of your age, not arranging flowers or playing the lyre.

III. xv. 23–4   *nec poti vetulam faece tenus cadi,* 'nor wine-jars drained to the lees, old woman as you are'. *cag:* cask.

III. xvi. 1–12   *Danae* was imprisoned in a brazen tower by her father *Acrisius* to keep her away from suitors, but *Jove* reached her by descending in a shower of gold.

III. xvi. 7   *she . . . born:* Venus.

III. xvi. 16 n.   Amphiaraus was killed in the expedition of the Seven against Thebes, not at Troy; the treacherous wife was Eriphyle.

III. xvi. 19   *The Macedon:* Philip II, father of Alexander the Great, who was notorious for his bribery (Quinn).

III. xvi. 23–4   S.'s interpolation: for his admiration of naval commanders, cf. *Hymns* 17. 19–36 and *Ode to Admiral Sir George Pocock* (*PW* iv. 339).

III. xvi. 31   *refrains:* denies (*negaverit*).

III. xvi. 37–42   i.e. 'I am more glorious as owner of a humble farm (*contemptae dominus splendidior rei*) then if I were reputed to hide the whole Apulian harvest in my granaries (*quidquid arat impiger Apulus occultare meis dicerer horreis*).'

III. xvii. 1   *Lamus:* mythical king of the Lestrygonians, mentioned by Homer, *Od.* x. 81.

III. xvii. 4   *diaries . . . year:* i.e. almanacs (*memores fastos*).

III. xvii. 7–8   *Formiae* was a town on the coast of Latium, *Liris* a river. *Marica* was not a place but the name of a nymph who presided over the local marshes.

III. xviii. 14   *December's nones:* 5 Dec., the festival of Faunalia.

III. xix. 1   *th'Inachian root:* Inachus was the first king of Argos, cf. *Odes* II. iii. 21.

III. xix. 18   Berecyntus was a mountain in Phrygia on which Cybele received orgiastic worship.

III. xx. 5   *disapprove:* for *fugies,* flee. Pyrrhus, the cowardly 'plund'rer' (*raptor*), will have to yield to the fierce 'lioness'.

III. xx. 6–10   A confused rendering of *cum per obstantes iuvenum catervas ibit insignem repetens Nearchum: grande certamen, tibi praeda cedat, maior an illi,* 'when she shall go through the opposing troops of youths, seeking her beautiful Nearchus back again; a grand conflict, whether a greater portion of the prey shall fall to thee or her' (PI).

III. xx. 18   *in his form begirl'd:* S.'s addition. Nireus, according to Homer, *Il.* ii. 671, was the handsomest Greek at Troy, except for Achilles: *begirl'd* is S.'s coinage, presumably meaning 'with an effeminate appearance', but also suggesting 'pursued by girls'.

III. xxi. 2   L. Manlius Torquatus was consul in 65 BC, the year of H.'s birth.

III. xxi. 8   *Corvinus*: Messalla Corvinus, a well-known orator, cf. *Sat.* I. x. 54 and 159.

III. xxi. 16   *our politicians*: S.'s addition.

III. xxi. 18   *addis cornua pauperi*: 'add horns to the poor man.' A note in PI explains: 'To give him confidence and an idea of defence—The figure of Bacchus had sometimes horns affixed to it.'

III. xxi, 22   *ever in a knot*: *segnes . . . nodum solvere*, 'loth to dissolve the knot' (PI), i.e. 'inseparably united. They are painted holding each others hands' (PT, note).

III. xxii. 3   *thrice invok'd*: 'Or invoked by three different names' (PT, note), i.e. Luna in heaven, Diana on earth, Hecate in the underworld.

III. xxii. 9–10   The idea is S.'s invention: H. only describes the boar as 'practising its sidelong jabs' (*obliquum meditantis ictum*).

III. xxiii. 8   *little folk*: for *alumni*, lit. nurslings ('nursery', PI), i.e. young lambs and kids (Quinn).

III. xxiii. 14   *froth marine*: *marino rore*, rosemary.

III. xxiii. 16   *whole hecatombs* (for 'much sacrifice of oxen'): cf. Pope, *The Second Satire of Dr. John Donne*, 116.

III. xxiv. 4   *casoons*: caissons, submerged piers (*caementis*), i.e. foundations for luxury villas built out on the sea (Quinn). Cf. *Odes* III. i. 34–6.

III. xxiv. 49   *refund*, pour back (*OED v. I*, 1): for *mittamus*, cast.

III. xxiv. 60   *ACE*: One on dice (*OED* 1), hence used here metonymically for the game (*alea*).

III. xxiv. 62   *his . . . guest*: his business partner and friends.

III. xxv. 12   *dames*: the Bacchantes.

III. xxv. 21–2   *supreme* agrees with Bacchus; 'supreme over nymphs and priestesses'.

III. xxvii. 22   *prone (pronus)*: i.e. declining, setting (*OED a.* 3).

III. xxvii. 24–5   For *quid albus peccet Iapyx*, 'in what manner Japyx, fair at first, is offensive' (PI): see note on *Odes* I. iii. 4.

III. xxvii. 27   *rising goat's alarm*: for *caecos . . . motus orientis Haedi*, 'the dark tumults of the rising south' (PT): see note on *Odes* III. i. 27. Most editions, including Bond, give *Austri* (south wind) for *Haedi*, but the alternative reading is discussed in Bond's notes.

III. xxvii. 31 ff.   *Europa* was seduced by Jove in the form of a bull as she was gathering flowers: mounted on its back she was carried across the sea to Crete, where she was abandoned.

III. xxvii. 37 *Fair student of:* for *studiosa,* 'eager after' (PI).

III. xxvii. 43–82, 87–95 Quotation-marks supplied. Lines 71–82 in H. are the words Europa imagines her father to say.

III. xxvii. 51–2 False dreams were said to rise from the underworld through an ivory gate, true dreams through a gate of horn: cf. Virgil, *Aen.* vi. 893–8.

III. xxvii. 77 *Acute with death:* acuta leto, 'sharp for death'.

III. xxvii. 80 *a task:* to card wool, according to H.

III. xxvii. 91 *fame and fort:* for *magnam fortunam,* great fortune. For *fort* as forte, strong point, see *OED sb. 1,* 3.

III. xxviii. 1 *Neptune . . . festal day:* 23 July.

III. xxviii. 5–6 *munitiaeque adhibe vim sapientiae,* 'make an attack upon wisdom's stronghold'. S. translated it thus in *1756,* but in PI he gives 'add force to wisdom, however strong', with a footnote: 'Interpreters in general render this passage in this manner, viz. Offer violence to wisdom, which is ever upon its guard.—I rejected this sense, as the Latin will bear a better.'

III. xxviii. 9–12 *parcis deripere horreo cessantem Bibuli consulis amphoram:* 'you delay to bring from the cellar an unused jar of wine dating from Bibulus' consulship.' *Bibulus,* chosen for the sake of his name, was consul in 59 BC, making this a fifteen-year-old wine (Quinn). The meaningless *to his repose* in *1767* is presumably a misprint.

III. xxviii. 20–4 *queen of smiles:* Venus. S. correctly conveys (l. 24) H.'s polite anticipation of love-making (Rudd).

III. xxix. 1 *Tyrrhenian monarchs:* Etruscan kings.

III. xxix. 17–19 *Cepheus . . . Procyon . . . lion:* stars which appear in July.

III. xxix. 24 *vague (vagis):* wandering, see note on *Odes* I. xxxv. 9.

III. xxix. 27–8 The place-names are chosen to suggest far-flung and troublesome parts of the empire. *Seres:* 'People of the East Indies, probably the Chinese' (Ainsworth). *Bactrians:* Bactra was a province of Persia. *discordant Tanais (Tanais discors):* Tanais (the river Don) symbolizes the troubled NE frontier (Quinn); 'a noted river, dividing Europe from Asia' (Ainsworth).

III. xxix. 33–40 To understand S.'s construction *other cares* has to be read as the antecedent of *it fares:* 'as for other cares, everything proceeds like a river' etc.

III. xxix. 44 *Why . . . life:* for *vixi,* 'I have lived'; i.e. the past is unalterable (Rudd).

III. xxix. 56 *whose . . . mite:* for *sine dote,* without a dowry.

III. xxix. 59 *deprecate:* pray for an end of.

III. xxix. 64   *Castor's aid*: see note on *Odes* I. iii. 2.

III. xxx. 9–11   See Introduction, p. xxv.

III. xxx. 13   *silent maid (tacita virgine)*: i.e. Vestal virgin.

III. xxx. 15   *qua violens obstrepit Aufidus*, 'where the wild river Aufidus thunders' (i.e. Apulia, H.'s birthplace).

III. xxx. 16–17   *where . . . king*: for *qua pauper aquae Daunus agrestium regnavit populorum*, 'where Daunus scanty of water once ruled over a rural people'. The name *Daunus*, mythical king of Apulia, stands for the region, not a river, but *scarcely flows* suggests that S. was reminded by *Tanais* in Ode xxix of Pope's famous couplet, 'Lo! where Maeotis sleeps, and hardly flows / The frozen Tanais thro' a waste of snows', *Dunciad* (1742), iii. 87–8.

III. xxx. 19   *th'Aeolian airs*: the verse-forms of Sappho and Alcaeus, who came from Lesbos, colonized by Aeolian Greeks: cf. *Odes* IV. iii. 17–18.

III. xxx. 22   *to real worth ally'd*: H. says 'earned by your achievements' (*quaesitam meritis*), thus modestly attributing his glory to the Muse (Rudd).

IV   The fourth book of *Odes* was a late work; it is usually assigned to 13 BC, but may have been written even later: see introduction to Rudd, 1987, p. 25.

IV. i. 1–2   Several years had elapsed since publication of *Odes* I–III; in the interim H. had written *Epistles*, Book I.

IV. i. 3   *treason! treason!*: for *precor, precor*, 'I beg, I beg'.

IV. i. 13–15   i.e. transfer your attentions more appropriately to Paulus (*tempestivius in domo Pauli . . . comissabere*, 'you will revel more suitably at the house of Paulus'): *Paulus* Maximus (b. 46 BC) married Marcia, cousin of Augustus, at the time of this ode, *c.*16 BC. He later became consul.

IV. i. 25–6   i.e. whenever he prevails exultantly over a rival and all his bribes (*quandoque potentior largi muneribus riserit aemuli*): 'Maximus had probably some rival, who endeavoured to weaken his advantages of birth, wit and beauty, by prodigious expences and magnificent presents' (Francis).

IV. i. 27   *empaling*: enclosing within a wooden fence.

IV. i. 36   The *Salii* (see note on *Odes* I. xxxvi. 14) used to celebrate the feast of Mars annually with processions, songs, and dances. H. says the dances were *ter*, 'in triple time'. S. omits the lines addressed to H.'s beloved boy Ligurinus (H. 29–40) with which this ode concludes, whereas Pope in his 'Imitation' treats them as if they still referred to heterosexual love. They were included in *1756*.

IV. ii. 3   *him . . . main*: Icarus (see *Odes* II. xx. 14). The Aegean, S. of Samos, was called the Icarian sea: cf. *Odes* I. i. 20.

IV. ii. 17   *Elean justs* (jousts): the Games held at Olympia, in Elis.

IV. ii. 25 *Theban swan*: Pindar.

IV. ii. 28–30 *Matinian*: Matinus was a mountain in H.'s native Apulia. *hardly*: i.e. laboriously (*per laborem*). *Tibur*: see headnote to *Odes* I. vii.

IV. ii. 33 Antonius was reputedly author of an epic poem.

IV. ii. 36 *Sicambrians* (Sygambri): a warlike German tribe who defeated a Roman army in 16 BC but hastily made peace when they heard Augustus was setting out against them.

IV. ii. 43–4 *all ... clear*: i.e. clear the courts of legal business. The law-courts were closed on days of public rejoicing.

IV. ii. 55 For *largis iuvenescit herbis*, 'is growing fast on the abundant grass' (Quinn).

IV. ii. 57 *crest*: forehead.

IV. iii. 4–6 S. substitutes the more famous *Olympic* for *Isthmius* (referring to the Isthmian games held at Corinth, rather than those held at Olympia). *champion*: at boxing, according to H: chariot-racing (ll. 5–6) was another of the Isthmian games. *of manag'd pride*: for *impiger*, 'mettlesome' (PI).

IV. iii. 7 *Delphic leaf*: for *Deliis ... foliis*, i.e. Apollo's crown of bay leaves ('wreath' etc. is in apposition to 'leaf'). Both Delos and Delphi were associated with Apollo.

IV. iii. 17–18 For *fingent Aeolio carmine nobilem*, 'shall make him notable for Aeolian verse': referring to the lyric poetry of Alcaeus and Sappho, see note on *Odes* III. xxx. 19.

IV. iii. 25 *shell*: lyre, see note on *Odes* I. xxxii. 13.

IV. iii. 27–30 Expanding *mutis quoque piscibus donatura cygni ... sonum*, 'you who would give the notes of the swan to dumb fishes'. Cr. *JA*, B24. Even the fishes would die melodiously like the swan.

IV. iv This ode celebrates the victories of Tiberius (later emperor) and Drusus, sons of Augustus' wife Livia by her former husband T. Claudius Nero, in 15 BC.

IV. iv. 1–23 H.'s ode has a complex quasi-Pindaric structure which S. makes even less accessible. In simplified form, the syntax here is as follows: 'Like that bird which ... green years but innate strength drove upon his prey, and which vernal winds taught to fly (anon he wages war against sheepfolds [*folds*] and holds squirming snakes in his claws); or like a goat which eyes a lion's whelp ... and has no hope, such a warrior was Drusus ... whom the Rhoetean and North Alpine bands beheld ...' (Rudd).

IV. iv. 4 Referring to Ganymede (named in the original), who was carried off by an eagle to be Jove's cup-bearer.

IV. iv. 9 *vivid impulse*: *vividus impetus*, 'lively impetuosity' (PI).

IV. iv. 12   *curv'd-reluctant*: an attempt to convey the image evoked by *reluctantes*, lit. fighting back, resisting.

IV. iv. 28   *sons-in-law*: i.e. stepsons.

IV. iv. 30–1   *est in iuvencus, est in equis patrum virtus*, 'there is in steers, there is in horses the virtue of their sires' (PT): for the use of *progeny* in the sense of 'parentage', see *OED* 5.

IV. iv. 32   *turtles*: doves.

IV. iv. 33–4   *learning*: a noun (*doctrina*). *mans*: makes manly.

IV. iv. 35–6   *utcumque defecere mores, dedecorant bene nata culpae*, 'whenever morals are deficient, vices disgrace what is naturally good' (PT).

IV. iv. 37 ff.   Referring to the exploits of Drusus' ancestor, C. Claudius Nero, who routed Hasdrubal at the battle of the river Metaurus in 207 BC. This was traditionally regarded as the turning-point of the Second Punic War, leading to the defeat of the Carthaginians under Hannibal.

IV. iv. 41–3   The feeble ll. 41–2 are probably in for metrical reasons. *fled* (43) alters the sense of H: '[that day] which was the first to smile with kindly glory since the terrible African [Hannibal] came galloping through the towns of Italy' (Rudd).

IV. iv. 44   *takes the train*: i.e. ignites from a fuse (the metaphor is S.'s addition).

IV. iv. 47   *ravag'd* is a participial adj. qualifying *temples* (l. 48): i.e. the Romans repaired the havoc wrought by the Carthaginian *plund'rers*.

IV. iv. 49   *traitor*: Hannibal.

IV. iv. 51–2   i.e. we pursue in vain those whom it would be a triumph simply to deceive and evade: *sectamur . . . quos opimus fallere et effugere est triumphus*.

IV. iv. 60   *ducit opes animumque ferro*: 'derives strength and spirit from the steel itself.'

IV. iv. 61–2   *Hydra*: the many-headed monster slain by Hercules. As fast as one head was cut off, another appeared in its place. *griev'd* should go with Hydra (*dolentem vinci*, 'loth to be defeated' (Rudd)).

IV. iv. 69   *couriers*: pronounced as a dissyllable, with stress on the second syllable, cf. *Odes* I. x. 5.

IV. iv. 74   *Claudius*: i.e. the Claudian family, which was intertwined with the Julian line to which Augustus belonged.

IV. v   Augustus was in Gaul for three years after defeating the Sygambri in 16 BC.

IV. v. 23   *Caesar* is the object of *requires*.

IV. v. 31–6   For Augustus' laws against adultery, see note on *Sec. Ode* 21–5.

IV. v. 37–8   i.e. 'who fears the Parthian or the icy Scythian . . .'

IV. v. 44–5   *wed . . . wine*: see note on *Odes* II. xv. 4.

IV. v. 47   *desert*, i.e. dessert (*alteris mensis*, second course).

IV. v. 51   *state*: high position.

IV. vi. 1–15   *Niobe*'s children were killed by Apollo and Diana because she boasted that she was superior to their mother Latona. According to post-Homeric legend, Achilles, son of *Peleus* and *Thetis*, was killed just before the fall of Troy by Apollo disguised as Paris. For *Tityos* (Tityus), see note on *Odes* III. iv. 78.

IV. vi. 16–20   Referring to the famous story of the wooden horse built by the Greeks and hauled into Troy by the Trojans amidst dances and revelry: see Virgil. *Aen.* ii. 15–56 and 234–9. *For sacred rites* . . . It was allegedly an offering to Pallas Athene to secure a safe return for the Greeks.

IV. vi. 26–30   *wrought to relent* qualifies *sire of gods* (Jove). Apollo and Venus interceded with Jove to save the Trojan race; Jove promised that Aeneas should rebuild Troy's walls under better auspices (*potiore ductos alite muros*).

IV. vi. 34   *Daunian*: i.e. of Apulia, Horace's birthplace, cf. *Odes* III. xxx. 16.

IV. vi. 35   For *levis Agyieu*: PI translates 'smooth-shaven Agyeus', explaining in a footnote, 'So called after ἄγυια, a street, because there were altars to him in the open streets'; according to scansion, *levis* could mean either 'smooth' or 'light' (in motion, weight, disposition, etc.): hence S.'s pun 'Enlight'ner of our ways'.

IV. vi. 41   *Delian maid*: Diana.

IV. vi. 43   *Lesbian feet*: another pun, referring to Sapphic metre (see note on *Odes* I. i. 52).

IV. vi. 47   *Latona's darling*: Apollo.

IV. vi. 48   *her*: Diana, the moon-goddess.

IV. vii. 17–23   See Introduction, p.xxv.

IV. vii. 26   *Hippolytus*, a worshipper of Diana, rejected the love of Phaedra, who contrived his death in revenge.

IV. vii. 27–8   *Theseus* conspired with *Perithous* to abduct Proserpine (see *Odes* III. iv. 79–80); *gives*, i.e. gyves, chains.

IV. viii. 2   For *aera*: small bronze statues, especially from Corinth (Quinn).

IV. viii. 9   *Scopas*, a sculptor, and *Parrhasius*, a painter, were celebrated artists of ancient Greece.

IV. viii. 19–26   The construction is 'Not marbles . . . not Hannibal . . . not Carthage . . . raise'. *place* (l. 19) is a verb.

IV. viii. 25–8   Referring to P. Cornelius Scipio Africanus Major, who defeated the Carthaginians under Hannibal in 202 BC.

IV. viii. 30   *Ennius*: Quintus Ennius (239–169 BC), one of the greatest of the early Roman poets, see *Epistles* II. i. 92–3.

IV. viii. 33–4   *son Of Mars*: Romulus. *Ilia*: Rhea Silvia, mother of Romulus.

IV. viii. 37–40   H. states that *Eacus* (Aeacus), one of the judges of Hades, has been promoted to the Isles of the Blest as a result of poets writing about him (Quinn).

IV. viii. 41–2   *dignum laude virum Musa vetat mori*, 'the muse forbids a praiseworthy man to die' (PT).

IV. viii. 47   *twin-stars*: Castor and Pollux.

IV. ix. 2–3   Referring to his lyric poetry.

IV. ix. 4   *Borne* may be a misprint for *Born* (*natus ad Aufidum*: 'I, born on the Aufidus', PI), but it could be intended as a pun, qualifying 'voice'. For the river *Aufidus* in H.'s native Apulia, cf. *Odes* III. xxx. 15.

IV. ix. 7   *Cean . . . fire*: the lyrical poetry of Simonides of Ceos (cf. *Fables* IV. xvii. 11) and Alcaeus.

IV. ix. 17–24   A roll-call of famous names from Trojan legend. *Teucer* (see note on *Odes* I. vii. 29) was the greatest archer on the Greek side. *Cretan king*: Idomeneus. *Sthenelus*: Diomede's charioteer. *Deiphobus*: Hector's brother.

IV. ix. 29–30   *Paulum sepultae distat inertiae celata virtus*, 'Worth concealed is but little different from buried sloth' (PI): *inertiae* is commonly but unnecessarily paraphrased as 'cowardice'. H.'s antithesis is between idleness and active *virtus*.

IV. ix. 34–44   *Lollius*: Marcus Lollius, consul in 21 BC, a prominent supporter of Augustus. For all his supposed indifference to private gain (ll. 40–3) he died immensely rich. *draws* (l. 44): draws his sword.

IV. x [xi]   Smart omits H.'s Ode x to Ligurinus, hence the numbering of *Odes* x–xv differs from that of standard editions.

IV. x [xi]. 9 n.   *spargier*: the old form of the passive infinitive.

IV. x [xi]. 20   *Venus . . . prime*: i.e. Venus' special day. 'The grand festival of Venus was celebrated in this month' (PT, note).

IV. x [xi]. 31–5   *Phaeton* (3 syllables) attempted to drive the horses of his father Helios (the sun), but they bolted; to save the earth from destruction, Jove blasted Phaeton with a thunderbolt. *Bellerophon* was thrown and killed when he tried to fly to heaven mounted on the winged horse *Pegasus*.

IV. xi [xii]   Some think the *Virgil* addressed is not the poet, who had died before this book of *Odes* was published. Others, with equal conviction, believe it *is* the poet, and that H. is recalling earlier days. S. clearly belongs with the latter (Rudd).

IV. xi [xii]. 7–12   Footnote to PI explains: 'See the story of Progne, in Ovid's Metamorphoses.' Procne was descended from Cecrops, legendary ancestor of the Athenians. Her husband Tereus, king of Thrace, raped and mutilated her sister Philomela; in revenge, Procne killed her son *Itys* and served up his flesh to Tereus at a banquet. She was afterwards transformed into a swallow. See Ovid, *Met.* vi. 424–674.

IV. xi [xii]. 23   i.e. nothing less will secure Virgil's entry into noble company (see *OED* frank, *v.* 2, 1c).

IV. xi [xii]. 27   *Sulpician room*: a vintner's warehouse.

IV. xii [xiii]. 28   *dilapsam in cineres*, 'wasted away to ashes' (PI). S. succeeds in making this ode even more offensive than it is in the original. His earlier and freer version, published as *Audivere, Lyce* in 1750 (*PW* iv. 166), is more light-hearted.

IV. xiii [xiv]. 1   *conscript fathers*, the Senate: see note on *Odes* II. i. 14.

IV. xiii [xiv]. 9–14   For *Drusus* and *elder Nero* (Tiberius), stepsons of Augustus, see *Odes* IV. iv. *with your success*: i.e. with success like yours.

IV. xiii [xiv]. 23   *murm'ring*: complaining (*OED* murmur, *v.* 4).

IV. xiii [xiv]. 27   *like the meadow's lord*: for *tauriformis*, bull-like.

IV. xiii [xiv]. 34–6   *that memorable day*: of Augustus' final victory over Antony and Cleopatra in 30 BC. S. fails to make H.'s point that it was on that very day, fifteen years later, that Augustus' stepsons won their victory.

IV. xiii [xiv]. 43   *vague (profugus)*: roving, see I. xxxv. 9 and note.

IV. xiv [xv]   Written soon after Augustus' return from the west in 13 BC and looking forward to a time of peace and prosperity at home and abroad after a period of wars and internal disorder.

IV. xiv [xv]. 9   The doors of *Janus' temple* were kept open in times of war and closed in times of peace.

IV. xiv [xv]. 20   *sounds* in *1767* must be a misprint. PI has 'forges swords'.

IV. xiv [xv]. 22   *Julian edicts*: laws enacted by the Julian line to which Augustus belonged.

IV. xiv [xv]. 31–2   Referring to the legendary descent of Augustus from Aeneas, son of Venus ('love's . . . queen') and Anchises: see note on *Sec. Ode* 63, below.

Epodes. H.'s *Epodes* were published about 29 BC, after the first book of *Satires*, but they include some of his earliest poems.

I   For the battle of Actium (31 BC), see note on *Odes* I. xxxvii. Maecenas may not in the event have joined Caesar's fleet as this poem and *Epodes* viii [ix] anticipate.

I. 1   *small ship*: for *Liburnis*, light, fast sailing vessels.

I. 16–18   *decet qua ferre non molles viros*, 'as becomes brave men to bear'.

I. 25   *you . . . seek*: you ask.

I. 31   *she*: the bird.

I. 36   *stave*: ward off, see note on *Odes* I. xv. 42.

I. 42   S.'s addition.

I. 43–5   Wealthy farmers had different pastures for summer and winter.

I. 46–8   *ut superni villa candens Tusculi Circaea tangat moenia*, 'that my neat villa should extend to the Circaean walls of the upland Tusculum' (Pl). Tusculum was said to be founded by Telegonus, son of Ulysses and Circe.

I. 54   *Chremes*: the name of a miser in comedies by Terence.

II. 11   *levy*: levee, reception.

II. 13–14   *joins . . . marriageable vines (adulta vitium propagine altas maritat populos)*: see note on *Odes* II. xv. 4.

II. 47   *trepann'd*: ensnared.

II. 50   *toil*: net or snare.

II. 52   *ginn'd*: trapped.

II. 53   *stranger*, i.e. migrant (*advenam*): cranes too were caught and killed ('thinn'd').

II. 74   *scar (scari)*: a rare fish of the eastern Mediterranean.

II. 79–80   *bustards*, for *Afra avis*, 'the African bird' (Pl): a footnote explains 'Supposed the turky or bustard', nowadays identified as the guinea-fowl. *game Of Asia*: for *attagen Ionicus* 'Ionic wild-fowl' (Pl), footnoted 'Supposed the woodcock'.

II. 82   *As*: rather than.

II. 96   *at leisure*: i.e. because the day's work is over.

II. 103–8   S.'s awkward phrasing mars H.'s ironical ending. The speaker is now revealed as Alphius, a money-lender *(faenerator)*. On the point of turning countryman *(iam iam futurus rusticus)* he collects in all his money in the middle of the month, but having proclaimed this speech he plans to lend it out again two weeks later: l. 6 now takes on a new flavour.

III. 4   *O dura messorum ilia*, 'O the hardy guts of the mowers!' (Pl). Cf. Virgil, *Eclogues* ii. 10, for mowers' liking for garlic. *clowns*: peasants.

III. 8   For the witch *Canidia* see *Epodes* v and xv–xvi.

III. 9–16   Alluding to the adventures of *Jason* and *Medea* at the court of Aeetes, king of Colchis, and at Corinth, where Jason abandoned Medea in favour of *Creusa*, daughter of King Creon. Medea gave Jason garlic as protection against the fire-breathing bulls of Aeetes, when he was set the task of taming them (ll. 9–12). She also used it to poison a robe and garland send to her rival, Creusa (ll. 13–16): see *Epodes* v. 102–8.

III. 18   A poor translation of *tantus siderum insedit vapor*, 'settled such heat from the stars [i.e. Dog-star]'.

III. 19   Deianira, wife of *Hercules*, sent him a shirt dipped in the poisoned blood of the centaur Nessus, in the belief that it would act as an aphrodisiac; it drove Hercules to his death instead (Ovid, *Met.* ix. 128 ff.). The metre catches the spirit well (Rudd).

III. 23–4   S. primly replaces H's *puella* with 'wife'. *on . . . bed*: for *extrema in sponda*, on the furthest edge of the bed-frame.

IV. 3   *hamper'd*: i.e. 'once hampered', alluding to his former slavery. H. describes him as scarred and calloused from his bonds.

IV. 7   *sacred way*: 'the grand street that led to the Capitol' (PT, note).

IV. 9   *Ingenuous*: honest.

IV. 11   *corrected to the quick*: for *sectus flagellis triumviralibus*, 'cut with the whips of the triumvirs' (officers of justice).

IV. 17–18 n.   By the law of L. Roscius Otho, 67 BC, seats in the Roman theatre were arranged according to rank: senators occupied the seats in front of the stage, with the knights in the fourteen rows behind and above them, and the ordinary people above that.

IV. 19   *beaks of brass*: i.e. ships, *ora navium rostrata* (lit. 'beaked faces of ships'); possibly a defective reading. S. may be thinking of Bentley's suggestion of *aera* for *ora* 'brazen [prows]', as in Virgil, *Aen.* i. 35.

IV. 21   *servile band*: the naval commander Sextus Pompeius, son of Pompey the Great, used runaway slaves to man his ships.

V. 9   *Lucina*: goddess of childbirth.

V. 41   *Colchian*: 'such as Medea of Colchos made use of, that is, according to art' (PT, note).

V. 45   *Avernal*: 'Avernus was a lake in Campania, whose waters were held sacred to the Infernal Deities' (PT, note).

V. 47   *urchins . . . main*: sea-urchins.

V. 92   *are sped* is meaningless. H. says *latent*, lie hidden.

V. 102–8   See *Epodes* iii. 9–16 and note.

V. 117   *veneficae scientioris carmine*, 'by the incantation of some mightier sorceress' (PI).

V. 123   *Marsian*: the Marsi, a people of central Italy, were famed as sorcerers.

V. 138   i.e. like the curse Thyestes uttered when Atreus (in revenge for the rape of his wife) served up to Thyestes the flesh of his own murdered children (see note on *Odes* I. xvi. 17).

VI. 5–6   *qualis aut Molossus, aut fulvus Lacon, amica vis pastoribus*, 'like a Molossian [large hound] or tawny Laconian [Spartan dog], sturdy friend of the shepherds'.

VI. 10   H.'s point is elliptical, but not clarified by S.'s rendering: *proiectum odoraris cibum*, 'you smell at the meat that is thrown to you' (PI), presumably meaning by a malefactor who is being pursued and wants to distract the dog.

VI. 11   *weapon*, for *cornua* (horns), glosses over H.'s abrupt change of metaphor.

VI. 13   Referring to the poet Archilochus, whose ferocious attack on *Lycambes*, when he refused to allow his daughter to marry the poet, was said to have driven father and daughter to their death; cf. *Epistles* I. xix. 46–9.

VI. 14   For *aut acer hostis Bupalo*, 'or the bitter enemy of Bupalus', referring to the poet Hipponax who wrote a lampoon on the sculptor Bupalus and his brother. Pliny relates that they had made a statue caricaturing the poet, but were driven to suicide by his satire.

VII. 19   *Rhemus*: 'He was slain by his brother Romulus, for ridiculing his wall by leaping over it' (PT, note).

VIII [IX]   S. omits H.'s Epode viii because of its obscenity: the numbering of *Epodes* viii–xii is therefore changed. Like the first epode, this poem purports to be written on the eve of the critical battle of Actium. It is an idealized rendering of conversation at a banquet, at which victory is anticipated but not wholly assured (see Fraenkel, pp. 74–5). S.'s sprightly metre hardly does justice to the serious side of H.'s poem.

VIII [IX]. 2   *Caecuban*: a choice wine, cf. *Odes* I. xx. 14.

VIII [IX]. 7 n.   *Young Pompey*: Sextus Pompeius, see note on *Epodes* iv. 21.

VIII [IX]. 10–11   *the same . . . untrue (vincla quae detraxerat servis . . . perfidis)*: i.e. the chains which he had taken off slaves who had deserted their masters and joined him.

VIII [IX]. 13   *whom . . . charms*: for *emancipatus feminae*, 'enslaved to a woman' (PI), referring to Cleopatra.

VIII [IX]. 15   *palisadoes*: stakes used for building defensive barricades.

VIII [IX]. 20   *squabs*: cushions. This detail is S.'s addition.

VIII [IX]. 27   *Jugurtha,* king of Numidia, a region SW of Carthage, was killed in 104 BC (cf. *Odes* II. i. 25).

VIII [IX]. 32   *tomb (sepulcrum):* i.e. memorial to the destruction of Carthage (146 BC) by Scipio Africanus Minor.

VIII [IX]. 43   *this sickness (fluentem nauseam):* S. interprets this figuratively as anxiety for the outcome of the battle. Sometimes translated as 'seasickness', it was used by 19th-c. classical scholars as evidence that the epode was written on board ship at Actium, an interpretation subsequently discredited: see Fraenkel, pp. 71–5.

IX [X]. 13–16   *Pallas* killed *Ajax* (son of Oileus, not Teucer's famous brother) and wrecked his fleet on the homeward voyage from *Troy* because he had attacked Cassandra in her temple: cf. Virgil, *Aen.* i. 39–45.

IX [X]. 28   *as denouncing right:* proclaiming that justice has been done (*OED* denounce, 3).

X [XI]   The original is in fourteen couplets; S.'s text consists of the first eleven couplets, arranged in three-line stanzas by dividing the second line of each in two. *1756* prints the poem complete, in the normal layout. The last six lines are cut because of their homosexual content. Samuel Johnson, who translated this epode in his youth, had no such qualms (see *Poems,* ed. D. Nichol Smith and E. L. McAdam (2nd edn. 1974), p. 17).

X [XI]. 5   *Sylvan:* i.e. the woods.

X [XI]. 14–15   *contrane lucrum nil valere candidum pauperis ingenium,* 'that the fairest genius of a poor man hath no weight against filthy lucre' (PT).

X [XI]. 16   *frontless:* barefaced, shameless (*inverecundus*).

X [XI]. 19–24   *quod si meis . . . summotus pudor:* 'but if a generous indignation should burn in my heart so as to scatter to the winds these futile palliatives which give no relief to my grievous wound, then abandoning false shame I will cease to contend with unequal rivals.'

X [XI]. 25   *pot-valiant:* H. says only *severus,* but S.'s addition is in keeping with the context.

X [XI]. 27   i.e. ordered to get out of the house (*iussus abire domum*).

X [xi]. 30   In the final lines, omitted here, H. declares that he is now infatuated with a male lover.

XI [XIII]   S. omits H.'s Epode xii because of its obscenity.

XI [XIII]. 3   *rough profound:* the sea.

XI [XIII]. 9   *of Manlian date:* see *Odes* III. xxi. 1–2 and note.

XI [XIII]. 12   *reinstate:* for *reducet in sedem,* 'restore to [their former] state'. S. evidently means 'replace', a sense of *reinstate* not recorded by *OED* until 1793, but perhaps already current in 1767.

XI [XIII]. 16   *Cyllenean*: i.e. sacred to Mercury, who was born on Mt. Cyllene in Arcadia.

XI [XIII]. 19   *the great Centaur*: Chiron, renowned for his wisdom and learning in music and medicine. *his ward*: Achilles.

XI [XIII]. 27   *blue-ey'd*: for *caerula*, usually translated here 'sea-blue' (as befitting a sea-nymph), but in *Epodes* xiv [xvi]. 7 'blue-ey'd' for *caerulea* must be correct. *queen*: his mother, Thetis.

XI [XIII]. 30   *alloquial charms*: presumably meaning 'consolatory charms' (for *dulcibus alloquiis*, 'sweet consolations'), but *OED* records no example of *alloquial* used in this sense in English.

XII [XIV]. 7   *candid knight* (*candide Maecenas*): in 18th-c. English, as in Latin, 'candid' was a general term of commendation, here perhaps 'honest' or 'dear'.

XII [XIV]. 9   *has un-bespoke*: for *vetat*, forbids.

XII [XIV]. 13/14   S. omits 4 lines referring to Anacreon's love-poems addressed to the Samian boy Bathyllus: Maecenas also knew an actor of that name.

XII [XIV]. 16–18   For *me libertina, neque uno contenta, Phryne macerat*, 'Phryne, a freed-woman, not content with a single lover, reduces me to a skeleton' (PI).

XIII [XV]. 37–8   *that transmuted sage*: *Pythagorae renati*, 'Pythagoras reincarnate' (see *Odes* I. xxviii. 13 n.); i.e. 'even though you are rich, clever, and handsome'. But one recalls that Pythagoras was the philosopher of change (Rudd).

XIV [XVI]. 1–10   H. contrasts the evils besetting contemporary Rome with threats successfully resisted from outside in the past. He gives as examples *Porsena*, leader of the Etruscans against Rome in the 6th c. BC; *Spartacus*, Thracian leader of a slave rebellion in 73 BC; the claim of *Capua*, chief city of Campania, to command over Rome in the 3rd c. BC; *Allobrox*, collective name of a Gallic people who attempted a revolt in 61 BC; the invasions of *Germanic* tribes in the 1st and 2nd cc. BC; and the campaigns of the dreaded Carthaginian general *Hannibal* in the Second Punic War, 218–207 BC.

XIV [XVI]. 6   *innovating*: attempting revolution.

XIV [XVI]. 17–20   When *Phocaea* (a Greek city in Asia Minor) was besieged by the Persians in 540 BC, most of the citizens chose to emigrate rather than submit.

XIV [XVI]. 20   *boars (apris)*: both verse and prose in *1767* read *bears*, but *1756* has *boars* and it is easier to understand *bears* as a misprint than as a deliberate mistranslation.

XIV [XVI]. 29   *main*: the sea.

XIV [XVI]. 30   *new monsters* are the subject of *join*.

XIV [XVI]. 31   *adulterate (adulteretur)*: debauch, i.e. by miscegenation (see *OED v.* 2). The construction now changes: 'until a, b, c, etc. happen, let us repeat our resolution' (Rudd).

XIV [XVI]. 33   i.e. until the flocks do not flee from the lion.

XIV [XVI]. 34   *shaven*: H. has 'smooth with scales'.

XIV [XVI]. 59   *Sidonian sailors*: Phoenician sea-traders.

XIV [XVI]. 60   *Laertes' son*: Ulysses.

XIV [XVI]. 68   *if . . . bard*: for *vate me*, 'if I am a prophet' (PI).

XV-XVI [XVII]   H.'s Epode xvii is printed as two poems in many early editions. For Canidia, see Epode v and *Sat.* i. viii.

XV [XVII]. 4   *Proserpine* and *Diana* (in her guise as Hecate) are invoked as powers of the underworld.

XV [XVII]. 10   *electric wheel*: for *turbinem*, 'conjuring wheel' (PI). A note in *1756* explains it as 'a kind of wheel, by the turning of which certain sorceries were performed'. S. attributes spiritual powers to the recently discovered force of electricity in *JA*, B260-7, 760-2.

XV [XVII]. 11-26   Examples from Greek mythology of injuries remedied as a result of appeals: *Telephus*, 'king of *Mysia*, opposed the march of the *Greeks* thro' his kingdom in their way to *Troy*. He was wounded by the spear of *Achilles* ["son of Thetis"], and afterwards cured by some filings from the same weapon, for which he was directed to apply by the oracle' (footnote in *1756*). The Trojan women were allowed to administer funeral rites to the body of *Hector* after *Priam* begged Achilles to yield it to them. *Circe* transformed Ulysses' sailors into swine, but restored them to human shape to please him.

XV [XVII]. 15   *meant*: which had been intended as.

XV [XVII]. 21   *laborious (laboriosi)*: 'hard-pressed', in 18th-c. English, as in Latin.

XV [XVII]. 27   *tars and factors (nautis et institoribus)*: sailors and pedlars. *sure*: surely (qualifying *thou'st giv'n me*).

XV [XVII]. 34   *neque est levare tenta spiritu praecordia*, 'nor can I relieve my bursting heart by sighing'.

XV [XVII]. 41-2   See note on *Epodes* iii. 19.

XV [XVII]. 45   *Colchian*: like Medea, see note on *Epodes* iii. 9-16.

XV [XVII]. 62   i.e. she does not haunt graveyards.

XV [XVII]. 64   The last funeral rites were held nine days after death.

XV [XVII]. 67–8   For *et tuo cruore rubros obstetrix pannos lavit, utcunque fortis exsilis puerpera*: 'and yours is the blood that reddened the sheets washed by the midwife, however vigorously you spring forth from the childbed.' S. is squeamish about these details, preferring to veil them in both PT and PI ('and whenever you are brought to bed, you rise up with strength unimpaired by child-bearing'). Francis is even more euphemistic: 'And with a blooming race of boys, / Lucina crowns thy mother-joys.'

XVI [XVII]. 5   *Cotyttian*: referring to the festival held secretly in Athens in honour of Cotytto, goddess of lewdness.

XVI [XVII]. 10   Cf. *Satires* I. viii. 26–45.

XVI [XVII]. 11   *Pelignian dames*: sorceresses.

XVI [XVII]. 18   *Tantalus*: see note on *Odes* I. xxviii. 9.

XVI [XVII]. 19   *Prometheus*: see note on *Odes* II. xviii. 41.

XVI [XVII]. 21–2   *prize* (prise) . . . *hill*: for *collocare in monte*, set on the mountain-top. *Sisyphus* was punished for offending the gods by being forced to roll uphill a huge stone which perpetually rolled down again (cf. *Odes* II. xiv. 20).

XVI [XVII]. 28   i.e. the weariness of life.

XVI [XVII]. 32   Cf. *Sat.* I. viii. 54–9.

Secular Ode. The Ode was commissioned for the Secular Games held by Augustus in 17 BC to celebrate the preservation of the Roman state. It was to be sung by a choir of boys and girls in the temple of Apollo.

7   *warn*: command.

9   *sev'n hills*: i.e. of Rome.

11   *fost'ring god (alme Sol)*: i.e. Apollo the sun-god.

16–20   *thou*: H. identifies Diana with Ilithya, goddess of birth, separating her functions under two names, *Lucina* (for childbirth) and Genitalis (for procreation). S.'s *genial goddess* (quotation marks supplied) signifies this generative power (see *OED a.* 1). *preferr'd*: offered.

21–5   Alluding to the marriage law of 18 BC, *lex Iula de maritandis ordinibus*, imposing penalties on celibacy and rewards for parents with large numbers of children. For *conscript fathers*, i.e. the Senate, see note on *Odes* II. i. 14.

26   The Secular Games were so-called because they were supposed to be held at intervals of 110 years (*saeculum*).

45   *queen of stars*: the moon, i.e. Diana.

59   *circumstance*: material welfare.

63   *clarus Anchisae Venerisque sanguis*: Augustus, born C. Iulius Caesar Octavianus, was supposedly descended from Aeneas, son of Venus and Anchises, through his son Iulus: hence named ('hight') Iulius.

74 The goddess of plenty (*Copia*).

81–2 Referring to the temple of Apollo on the Palatine.

88 *those . . . rolls*: for *quindecim virorum*, the Fifteen Men who were custodians of the Sibylline Books, a collection of oracular sayings kept in a vault under the Temple of the Capitoline Jupiter and consulted at times of national peril. They also had charge of the Secular Games.

93 *Sc.* 'and that he will also bless' the Chorus, etc.

Satires I. Book I of the *Satires* was the first work published by Horace, probably in 35 BC when he was 30 years old.

Motto (from the title-page of S.'s vol. iii). Horace, *Odes* III. xiv. 11–12, 'Refrain from words that it is bad to name.'

I. i For Maecenas, see note on *Odes* I. i.

I. i. 17–18 i.e. when dragged into town from the country to fulfil some legal bond he has entered into (*datis vadibus qui rure extractus in urbem est*).

I. i. 20–1 *wou'd . . . recite*: *loquacem delassare valent Fabium*, 'would fatigue the talkative Fabius to recount them' (PI).

I. i. 27 *counsellor*: i.e. the lawyer of ll. 13–15.

I. i. 41 *fondling*: affectionate.

I. i. 48 S.'s invention: H. has only a crooked innkeeper.

I. i. 55–6 See *Fables* IV. xix, *The Ant and the Fly*.

I. i. 62 January.

I. i. 83–4 *Like Esop* (Aesop) is S.'s addition; I have not traced any fable telling this story. H. posits a gang of slaves, one of whom carries the bag of provisions for them all.

I. i. 101–4 For the turbulent river *Aufidus*, see note on *Odes* III. xxx. 15.

I. i. 105 *want . . . waste*: i.e. want no more than they can use.

I. i. 121–2 *Tantalus*: see note on *Odes* I. xxviii. 9.

I. i. 125 *bags*: i.e. money-bags.

I. i. 143–50 The miser replies (quotation marks supplied).

I. i. 157–62 (H. ll. 88–91) This passage is difficult in the original. The general sense appears to be that it is a waste of effort to try to buy the love of kinsfolk, whom nature gives you freely ('without labour'). S. accepts the reading *at si* (some editors prefer *an si*), hence H. means: 'but if you want to keep the affection of your kith and kin . . . you'll waste your time [i.e. by hoarding money], as if you were to trying to train a donkey for the racecourse.'

I. i. 172 *to measure gold*: i.e. weigh it instead of counting it; a proverbial expression in Latin.

I. i. 173   *fast*: die of starvation (*ne se penuria victus opprimeret*).

I. i. 179–80   *Maenius* and *Nomentanus*: 'two infamous prodigals' (PT, note). For Maenius, see *Epistles* I. xv. 56 ff. Nomentanus reappears in *Satires* I. viii, II. i, and II. iii. 432–3. *rake*: 'live a dissolute life' (*OED v.* 4).

I. i. 181–2   H. seems to mean 'you're trying to bring together as alternatives things which are utterly opposed to each other'.

I. i. 183   *sneak* (for *avarum*): 'A sneaking, mean-spirited, paltry, or despicable person' (*OED sb.*), cf. *Fables* II. prol. 23.

I. i. 185–6   For *est inter Tanain quiddam socerumque Viselli* ('there is some difference between Tanais and the father-in-law of Visellius'). Nothing pertinent is known about either figure, but whoever they were H. intended them as polar opposites (see Rudd, 1987, p. 236). S.'s distinction in l. 186 (his own addition), however, is more one of degree: between looking wild, as if mad (*OED* stare, *v.* 3a), and outright insanity.

I. i. 194–5   *grutches* (grudges): see note on *Odes* I. xxviii. 30. *scruples*: is unwilling.

I. i. 199   *goal*: turning-post (see *Odes* I. i. 8 and note).

I. i. 208   For the character of *Crispinus*, 'a voluminous scribler' (PT, note), see *Sat.* I. iv. 19–26.

I. i. 209   *'scrutore*: 17th–18th-c. form of *escritoire*, writing-desk.

I. ii.   S. prints and translates only the first twenty-four lines of the original, presumably because of the bawdiness of the rest. The *1756* text is unexpurgated.

I. ii. 1   *Each minstrel*: for H.'s jocular *Ambubaiarum collegia*, 'guild of flute-girls'. *Ambubaiae* were Syrian girls in Rome who earned their living as street-musicians and prostitutes; *minstrel* in mid-18th-c. English simply meant a strolling musician, without the romantic connotations it later acquired.

I. ii. 2   *scrub*: beggar, 'person of little account or poor appearance' (*OED sub. 1,* 5).

I. ii. 4   *Tigellius*: see *Sat.* I. iii. 5 ff. and note.

I. ii. 20   *at . . . hand*: to the best advantage.

I. ii. 32   *Spends*: the *1767* reading is surely a misprint; *Speeds*, meaning 'thrives', makes sense but is a feeble and inexact rendering of the original, *in se pro quaestu sumptum facit*, 'expends upon himself in proportion to his gain' (PT).

I. ii. 35–7   Alluding to Menedemus in Terence's comedy *Heautontimorumenos*, 'The man who punished himself' (Rudd, 1987).

I. ii. 42   i.e. they shun one vice only to fall into the opposite.

I. iii   For S.'s 'Imitation' of this satire, see *The Horatian Canons of Friendship* (*PW* iv. 113–26).

I. iii. 5   *Tigellius*: a musician well known in Roman society and on familiar terms with Julius Caesar and Octavian.

I. iii. 16   *egg to apple (ab ovo usque ad mala)*: i.e. throughout dinner, from the first course to the last. H.'s word-order makes the phrase refer unambiguously to Tigellius' persistence in singing, but S.'s positioning suggests a possible second reference, with 'egg to apple' standing for the musical notes E to A.

I. iii. 42   H. says *fortasse minora*, 'perhaps lesser ones'.

I. iii. 87   For *paetum*, lit. 'leering [person]', but applied to Venus it could be a semi-endearment (*LS*). *Paetus* was also the name of an eminent Roman family: throughout these lines (86–94) H. puns on well-known proper names. S.'s *archer* is presumably an allusion to Venus' son Cupid, playing also on the epithet 'arch'.

I. iii. 89   *Sisyphus*: not the mythological character, but a dwarf in the service of Mark Antony.

I. iii. 92–4   *Vari ... Scaurus*: 'The Vari and Scauri were very noble families, and had their names originally from these defects' (PT, note). Varus means 'knock-kneed', Scaurus 'with swollen ankles'.

I. iii. 107–10   These lines (H. 56–8) are usually punctuated *probus quis nobiscum vivit, demissus homo: illi tardo, cognomen pingui damus*, and taken as referring to a single example; i.e. a man of honour and modesty who is called 'slow' and 'stupid'. S. followed that interpretation in *1756*, but in *1767* he emended the text to read *probus ... vivit? multum est homo, illi tardo ... damus*.

I. iii. 115   *discrete*: the sense 'separate, aloof' seems appropriate here. *discreet* in the modern sense would be tautological after *prudent*.

I. iii. 124   *common sense*: a literal translation, but *communis sensus* means 'sense of propriety' rather than 'common sense' in English.

I. iii. 161   *scow'r*: 'run away', in colloquial English (*OED v. 1*, c).

I. iii. 163   *Druso*: S. has *Drusonem* in both *1756* and *1767*, but most editions read *Rusonem*.

I. iii. 167   *doom's-day-book*: for *amaras historias*, dismal histories. The debtor, in Druso's power because he is late with his repayments, has to listen while the money-lender reads out his boring studies in history.

I. iii. 181   *die*: dye. The idea that all sins are on a par was Stoic doctrine.

I. iii. 194 n.   Cf. *JA*, B85 and B237.

I. iii. 194–5 and note   H. says *donec verba, quibus voces sensusque notarent, nominaque invenere*: 'until they found words and names, with which they might give meaning to their cries and feelings.' S.'s eccentric rendering is clearly influenced by his conviction (referred to in his footnote) that language was of divine invention and *preceded* human evolution. For the idea that good words were from God, 'cant' from the devil, cf. *JA*, B85 and 237.

I. iii. 200–1   A bowdlerized version of H.'s *nam fuit ante Helenam cunnus teterrima belli causa*, 'For Helen wasn't the first bitch to cause a war by her foul behaviour' (Rudd, 1987). In *1767* S.'s Latin text substitutes *mulier* for *cunnus*, as does Francis, but *1756* keeps *cunnus*.

I. iii. 217   *in grain*: by nature, genuine, thorough (see *OED* grain, *sb. 1*, 10c); a favourite phrase in S.'s familiar verse, cf. *Sat.* I iv. 151, *Epistles* I. ii. 124, *Fables* III. x. 9, etc.

I. iii. 218   i.e. who steals sprouts from his neighbour's garden: lit. 'who breaks off young cabbage-stalks in a neighbour's garden' (*qui teneros caules alieni fregerit horti*).

I. iii. 233   S.'s addition.

I. iii. 238–41   i.e. if you are already a king in essence, why ask for 'sovereign' power? (see l. 232). 'The doctrine of the Stoics, as explained by Crysippus, was that a wise man was not only *ipso facto* a king, but likewise of all trades and professions whatsoever' (PT, note). *Chrysippus* (*c.*280–207 BC) developed and elaborated the Stoic system of philosophy founded by Zeno.

I. iii. 246–8   *cobler (sutor)*: some MSS have *tonsor* (barber). The problem is to make Alfenus a parallel to Hermogenes. S. gets over it by rendering the epithet qualifying Alfenus, *vafer* ('cunning'), by 'in lawyer's gown', presumably identifying him with Alfenus Varus, the famous jurist (Rudd, 1987). In *1756* S. preferred *tonsor*. *Hermogenes* is unknown: he was formerly identified with Tigellius of the early part of this poem and *Sat.* I. ii. 4, but that identification is no longer accepted (see N. Rudd, *The Satires of Horace* (1966), pp. 292–3).

I. iii. 249   i.e. the philosopher is king by virtue of (*sic rex*) his supremacy in all trades and professions.

I. iii. 257–65   i.e. 'while you enjoy the kingly luxury of a penny bath, accompanied by one silly attendant, I shall live happily as a commoner among my friends; if they forgive me for my follies I will gladly overlook theirs in return.' S. blunts the point by leaving out the epithet, *ineptum*, 'crazy', applied to Crispinus. For *Crispinus*, see *Sat.* I. iv. 19–26.

I. iii. 264   *far . . . THING*: for *magis beatus*, more fortunate.

I. iv.   Gaius *Lucilius* (d. 102 BC) was recognized by H. and his contemporaries as the founder of the tradition of verse satire: see *Sat.* I. x. 123 and II. i. 52 ff. For a comparison of Horace and Lucilius as satirists, see N. Rudd, *The Satires of Horace* (1966), pp. 86–131.

I. iv. 1–2   *Cratinus*, *Eupolis*, and *Aristophanes*: Athenian comic playwrights of the 5th c. BC.

I. iv. 5   i.e. deserved exposure as a villain. H. specifies *malus . . . fur . . . moechus . . . sicarius aut alioqui famosus* (rogue, thief, adulterer, murderer, 'or otherwise infamous').

I. iv. 12   *By* in *1767* must be a misprint. H.'s phrase is correctly translated in PI as 'their feet and numbers only being changed'.

I. iv. 13   *making . . . halt*: for *durus componere versus*, 'harsh in the structure of his verses' (PI).

I. iv. 18   *standing hip-hop*: *OED* records no such phrase, but cites *hip-hop* in the sense 'with a hopping movement'. H.'s *stans pede in uno* (lit. 'standing on one foot') was a proverbial expression for doing something effortlessly ('standing on one's head' is the English proverbial equivalent).

I. iv. 19 ff.   This is the fullest account of *Crispinus*, an otherwise unidentified Stoic philosopher previously mentioned in *Sat.* I. i and I. iii; he reappears briefly in *Sat.* II. vii.

I. iv. 23–4   i.e. not the quantity but the correctness of writing (*scribendi recte*) is H.'s concern.

I. iv. 38   *Fannius*: an unidentified poet, cf. *Satires* I. x. 150. His vanity inspired Pope's portrayal of Lord Hervey as 'Lord Fanny'.

I. iv. 43–5   *now . . . wrong*: the reason why people dislike satire (*genus hoc*, 'this kind') is that the majority are themselves blameworthy (*plures culpare dignos*).

I. iv. 50   *other filth*: H. specifies a passion for boys.

I. iv. 61   *hay . . . horn*: hay was tied as a warning-sign on the horns of dangerous oxen.

I. iv. 66   *bake house . . . lake*: public amenities, where poorer citizens gathered to bake their loaves or draw water.

I. iv. 85–6   *Men's*: emendation suggested by Rudd, i.e. (according to S.) '[Comedy] is men's talk, or, if it differs from talk it does so by virtue of a conversational kind of metre'. H. says, 'except that it [comedy] differs from prose speech by having a fixed metre, it is pure prose' (*nisi quod pede certo differt sermoni, sermo merus*).

I. iv. 87–92   H. uses a stock situation in Roman comedy to outline a hypothetical objection: the angry father, it may be said, speaks with a vehemence *above* normal conversation. The answer given in ll. 93–5 is that the son (Pomponius) would hear the same kind of language if this were a situation in real life.

I. iv. 100   S.'s addition. *Demea* is a character in Terence's comedy *Adelphi*.

I. iv. 108–9   A quotation from Ennius, in which the words themselves are poetic.

I. iv. 114–23   H. likens writers of satire ('this kind') to the paid accusers, *Sulcius and Caprius*, who loudly denounce robbers (*latronibus*, translated 'the gang' by S.); 'but if a man lives decently and keeps his hands clean he may scorn them both', i.e. an innocent citizen need not fear exposure. Even robbers like the unidentified *Coelus* (Caelius) and *Birrus* are safe as far as H. is concerned. S. turns them into highwaymen (l. 122). S. uses the spelling *Coelus* in both PI and PT.

I. iv. 126   *Hermogenes*: H.'s Hermogenes Tigellius. S. imagines him again as the singer Tigellius (see note on *Sat.* I. iii. 246–8), 'humming' H.'s songs. Cf. Francis, 'Or whose soft strains Tigellius can repeat'.

I. iv. 165–6   H. quotes verbatim from *Sat.* (H) I. ii. 27 (from the section omitted by S.): *pastillos Rufillos olet, Gorgonius hircum*, 'Rufillus smells of breath-sweeteners, Gorgonius like a billy-goat'.

I. iv. 169–77   Alluding to a famous lawsuit in which Petillius (usually spelt *Petillus* by S.) was narrowly acquitted on a charge of embezzlement. The phrase *thro' habit to defend* should probably be in parenthesis, qualifying *you* (l. 170).

I. iv. 203–4   *deprensi non bella est fama Treboni*: 'after being caught in the act, Trebonius has a bad name.'

I. iv. 214   *corks*: i.e. for buoyancy.

I. iv. 220   *sages of the bench*: 'select judges' (PI).

I. iv. 231–2   i.e. young minds are deterred from vice by seeing the opprobrium which others incur (*sic teneros animos aliena opprobria saepe absterrent vitiis*).

I. iv. 233   *instituted*: instructed (*OED v.* 3).

I. iv. 247   *Such . . . oblique*: for *hoc quidam non belle*, 'that was not a handsome thing to do'.

I. iv. 257   *Pharisee and Scribe*: for *Judaei*, Jews.

I. v. 2   *Aricia*: a town sixteen miles south-east of Rome.

I. v. 3   For *hospitio modico*, 'in a mean inn' (PI).

I. v. 5   *Heliodorus*: probably Apollodorus, a well-known scholar and teacher in H.'s time, Helios being Greek for 'sun' (Rudd, 1987).

I. v. 13   *them . . . call*: i.e. those who like to make many stops in their journey. H. says merely *minus est gravis Appia tardis*, 'the Appian way is less irksome to the slow'.

I. v. 16   *mortified my gut*: for *ventri indico bellum*, 'declare war on my belly' (PI).

I. v. 32–4   *clear Their pipes . . . girls*: for *absentem cantat amicam*, 'sing their absent mistress' (PI).

I. v. 47   *Feronia*: an Italian goddess, identified with Juno.

I. v. 50   *Anxur*: a hill-town on the coast.

I. v. 51–5   For *Maecenas*, see note on *Odes* I. i. *Cocceius*: L. Cocceius Nerva, consul in 39 BC. Their diplomatic mission (37 BC) was in connection with the strife between Octavian (later Augustus) and Antony. *separate*: estranged.

I. v. 59   *Capito*: Fonteius Capito, consul in 33 BC, the third member of the ambassadorial party.

I. v. 67   *laticlave*: a broad purple stripe on the tunic worn by Roman senators, to which this petty official was not entitled.

I. v. 70–1   *Murena*: Varro Murena, Maecenas' brother-in-law, gave them accommodation, Capito supplied the food.

I. v. 73   *Plotius, Varius*: Plotius Tucca and L. Varius were friends and literary executors of Virgil. Varius was himself a poet: see *Sat.* I. x. 80–1.

I. v. 74   *of eternal name*: S.'s interpolation. S. writes with hindsight: Virgil had written only the *Eclogues*; cf. *Sat.* I. x. 81 n.

I. v. 88   *ere ... arose*: by nightfall (not in H).

I. v. 89   FIVES: for *lusum*, sport.

I. v. 91   *blind (lippus)*: another reference to H.'s eye trouble (cf. l. 56).

I. v. 92   For *crudis*, usually construed 'suffering from indigestion'. There is no evidence to associate *crudus* with the chest or lungs.

I. v. 96–102   S.'s footnote calls attention to the mock-heroic character of this passage. *Sarmentus* was a slave freed by Maecenas who had a job in the Treasury but was accompanying Maecenas as a kind of jester. *Cicerrus* (Messius Ciccirus) was presumably travelling with the diplomats on a similar footing.

I. v. 102–3   H. says only *Sarmenti domina exstat*: 'Sarmentus' mistress is still living.' In other words, there is nothing at all to be said about his ancestry.

I. v. 112   For *sic minitaris*, 'you threaten like this'.

I. v. 118   i.e. the Campanian disease (*Campanum morbum*), an unidentified affliction.

I. v. 120   *Cyclops jig*: i.e. a dance in the manner of the one-eyed giant Cyclops.

I. v. 121   Presumably a taunt about Cicerrus' height: *buskins* were thick-soled boots worn by tragic actors.

I. v. 152/3   S. omits four lines (H. 82–5) relating how H. waited until midnight for a girl who never came, and was assailed with sexual dreams when he finally got to sleep.

I. v. 165   *Diomede*: see note on *Odes* I. vi. 23–4.

I. v. 167   *pensive*: sorrowful (Johnson's Dictionary, 1755).

I. v. 177–8   Implying that Gnatia too lacked water supplies.

I. v. 182 n.   *St. Januarius*, bishop of Benevento, was an early Christian martyr whose relics were deposited in the cathedral at Naples in the 5th c. His blood is said to liquefy every year on his feast-days.

I. v. 183–4   The Romans regarded the Jews as particularly superstitious.

I. v. 185–90   Alluding to Lucretius' *De Rerum Naturae*, in which he expounds the Epicurean doctrine that the gods are free from anxiety and do not intervene in human affairs or the course of nature (Brown). H. says 'I have learned', not 'then learnt'.

I. v. 192   *strain*: S.'s pun, referring both to the strain of the journey and to his narrative 'strain' (*OED sb. 2*, 12b). H.'s *chartae* refers simply to his narrative.

I. vi. 15   *Tullius*: Servius Tullius, sixth king of Rome, was said to have been the son of a maidservant.

I. vi. 19–22   *Laevinus* was a descendant of P. Valerius *Poplicola* (Publicola) who was consul with Brutus in 509 BC and helped in the expulsion of the Tarquins; despite his high birth Laevinus was reputed to have failed to rise in public life because of his dissolute character (Brown). *not a jot . . . play*: for *unius assis non unquam pretio pluris lucuisse*, 'was never thought worth a penny'.

I. vi. 32   *new Decius*: Decius Mus was the first of his family to become consul (340 BC).

I. vi. 33–5   *Appian frown*: i.e. the disfavour of Appius Claudius, who as censor in 50 BC purged the Senate, expelling all sons of freedmen (Brown). H. was himself the son of a freed slave.

I. vi. 37   *my own dress*: i.e. my proper station.

I. vi. 40   *gen'rous*: high-born.

I. vi. 41–2   *Tullius* (*Tillius* in most editions): not the Tullius of l. 15 but an otherwise unidentified praetor. For *laticlave*, see note on *Sat.* I. v. 67.

I. vi. 48   *buskins* (see note on *Sat.* I. v. 121): H. however names a special shoe worn by senators, not buskins.

I. vi. 52–7   H.'s *Barrus* was a homosexual whose glamorous appearance aroused anxious concern among the women (see Rudd, 1987, p. 243): S.'s misleading translation is probably deliberate, to avoid giving 'offence', see Introduction, p. xxv.

I. vi. 63   *return'd*: i.e. elected to the Senate.

I. vi. 66–7   *Syrus, Dama, Dionysius*: 'names of slaves' (PT, note); so when they were emancipated their sons would be sons of freedmen, like H. himself.

I. vi. 68–9   Criminals were sometimes executed by being thrown from the *Tarpeian* rock on the Capitol in Rome.

I. vi. 69–72   The punctuation in *1767* is highly misleading: contrary to both S.'s Latin text and PI, ll. 63–72 are all assigned to one speaker, there is no break after the verb in l. 69, but a break is nonsensically made between *colleague* and *Novius*. The passage has been repunctuated accordingly.

I. vi. 70–2   Seats in the Roman theatre were arranged according to rank, with senators in the front (lowest) rows, then knights, then ordinary people behind and above (see note on *Epodes* iv. 17–18). *Novius* ('new man', upstart: an imaginary character) is identified in l. 72 as a freedman.

I. vi. 74   *Paulus or Messala*: the names of aristocratic families. For Messala, see note on Corvinus in *Sat.* I. x. 54.

I. vi. 75–9   *your colleague*, i.e. Novius: he can shout loudly (sufficient to drown the most deafening traffic noises); that at least finds favour with us (the electorate).

I. vi. 82–7   i.e. they scorn me for being the son of a freedman, as indeed I am, and now for consorting with you, Maecenas; earlier they sneered at me similarly because I was a tribune (l. 87). H. refers to his service as one of the officers commanding a legion in Brutus' army during the Civil War.

I. vi. 89–91   S. makes this needlessly obscure: H. says 'a person might have reason to grudge me that rank, but he shouldn't grudge me your friendship too' (Rudd, 1987).

I. vi. 106   *Satureian*: from a wealthy area near Tarentum.

I. vi. 123   *As if*: 'Or if' in *1767* is clearly a mistake (S.'s text has *velut si*). The printer's eye doubtless picked up 'Or' three lines later.

I. vi. 126   *dirty ways*: for *mala lustra*, evil brothels.

I. vi. 129   i.e. 'if I may praise myself' (*ut me collaudem*).

I. vi. 137   *to a day*: i.e. on the Ides, the customary date for settlement of fees.

I. vi. 155–6   *be sped … go*: i.e. become a tax-collector; but H.'s *coactor* means the man who collects money from the successful bidders.

I. vi. 173   *the revel rout*: the common crowd (*vulgi*).

I. vi. 192   i.e. this objection is made to Tullius. For *Tullius* see note on ll. 41–2 above.

I. vi. 195   *necessary jar*: chamber-pot (*lasanum*).

I. vi. 199   *flow'r*: flour.

I. vi. 202   See Introduction, p. xxv.

I. vi. 213   *Marsya* is the Latin form of the Greek name of Marsyas, a satyr. *phiz*: face (18th-c. slang). 'The statue of Marsyas … was erected in the

Forum, opposite the seat of the magistrates; and the poet pleasantly goes on to say, it stood in such an attitude, as shewed its indignation to behold a man, who had been a slave, now sitting among the magistrates of Rome' (PT, note).

I. vi. 221   *Then*: an acceptable spelling of *than* in the 18th c.

I. vi. 224   For *fugio rabiosi tempora signi*: other editions prefer the reading (given in a 9th-c. MS, now lost) *fugio Campum lusumque trigonem*, 'I escape from the Campus and the ball-game'.

I. vi. 232   i.e. had been members of the Senate.

I. vii. 8   *Clazomenae*: a town on the bay of Smyrna in Asia Minor.

I. vii. 10   *affair*: i.e. lawsuit.

I. vii. 21   *Priam's son*: Hector.

I. vii. 29-30   Referring to the incident in *Iliad* vi. 119-236 when a quarrel between the Greek hero *Diomede* and the Trojan ally *Glaucus* was settled by exchange of gifts instead of fighting.

I. vii. 44   *invisum agricolis sidus*, 'a star hated by farmers' (because it heralded the season of fevers and drought).

I. vii. 48-52 (H. 28-31)   S. makes nonsense of these admittedly difficult lines. The general idea is that King is now reduced to crude abuse of the kind with which vine-dressers silence people who taunt them. Passers-by would shout 'Cuckoo' at the workmen to imply that they were late, since it was thought that vines should be pruned before the coming of the cuckoo (Rudd, 1987).

I. vii. 60   S.'s invention: the *ax* and *mask* were equipment of the public executioner. H. says only *operum hoc tuorum est*, 'the job is made for you': i.e. as you got rid of an earlier *rex* (Julius Caesar) and as your ancestor expelled King Tarquin.

I. viii. 3   *pos'd*: puzzled.

I. viii. 8/9   S. omits H.'s l. 5, alluding to the red phallus which adorned the statue of Priapus.

I. viii. 12-31   These lines describe the conversion of a former paupers' graveyard into a pleasure garden.

I. viii. 19-20   *Pantolabus* ... *Nomentanus*: imaginary characters. The name *Pantolabus* means 'grab-all' in Greek. For Nomentanus, see *Sat.* I. i. 180, II. i. 41, and ii. iii. 432-3.

I. viii. 42-6   *Canidia* ... *Sagana*: see *Epodes* xv-xvi. *Succinct*: tucked up.

I. viii. 59   For *servilibus ut quae iam peritura modis*, 'as one about to perish by the torture appointed to slaves' (PI); 'on the rood' (cross) suggests that this was by crucifixion.

I. viii. 60–1 *Hecate*: goddess of sorcery; *Tisiphone*: one of the avenging Furies.

I. viii. 67/8 S. omits two obscene lines (H. 38–9).

I. viii. 85 *tete*: wig. *OED* cities S.'s use of *tete* in his *1756* translation of *Sat.* I. viii as the first recorded instance.

I. ix. 1 *sacred way*: the street leading from the Capitol to the Forum.

I. ix. 9 For *suaviter, ut nunc est*, 'Pretty hearty, as things are at present' (PI).

I. ix. 19 *my lad*: i.e. his foot-boy.

I. ix. 21–2 *O te Bolane cerebri felicem.* Bolanus is apparently some friend whom H. envies for his imperviousness. 'Hot-tempered' is now the accepted meaning of *cerebri* but S.'s reading is plausible according to earlier scholarship. Francis gives 'impenetrably dull', noting: 'The commentators think he was a choleric who would have made our impertinent feel his resentment. But there seems to be more pleasantry in supposing him a phlegmatic, who could hear with patience; or a stupid, who could be pleased with such a companion.' Cf. 'deaf Bolanus' (Creech).

I. ix. 29 *ne'er the near* (for *nil agis*), 'not a hope': an idiomatic phrase common in the 17th c. and surviving thereafter in dialect use (*OED adv. 1*, 5).

I. ix. 45 *Viscus*: see note on *Sat.* I. x. 156.

I. ix. 46 *Varius*: see *Sat.* I. x. 80–1 and note on *Sat.* I. v. 73.

I. ix. 52 *Hermogenes*: see note on *Sat.* I. iii. 246–8.

I. ix. 56 *elope*: run away.

I. ix. 60 H. says simply *confice*, 'finish me off!' *havock*: destroy, devastate.

I. ix. 71 *Vesta's*: the temple of Vesta in the Forum.

I. ix. 73–6 The bore was involved in a lawsuit and had to appear in court, or lose his case by default.

I. ix. 94 The line as printed in *1767* is hypermetric. The printer probably picked up 'man' from the previous line.

I. ix. 94–5 The bore sees Maecenas as a thrusting opportunist: *nemo dexterius fortuna est usus*, no one has seized the main chance more astutely.

I. ix. 103 i.e. it doesn't worry me (*nil me officit*).

I. ix. 124 *Aristius Fuscus*: unknown except through H.'s references to him. See *Odes* I. xxii, *Sat.* I. x. 155, and *Epistles* I. x.

I. ix. 131 *scrupled*: refused, evaded.

I. ix. 141–2 *At mi, sum paulo infirmior, unus multorum, ignosces*: 'But forgive me, I am a bit weaker, one of the multitude.'

I. ix. 154 *Sic me servavit Apollo*: 'thus Apollo [as patron god of poets] saved me', a humorous translation of *Iliad* xx. 443. *stav'd*: averted, see note on *Odes* I. xv. 42.

I. x. 1   *Lucilius*: see first note on *Sat.* I. iv.

I. x. 9–10   *Laberius*: D. Laberius (*c.*115–43) was a writer of coarse farces ('mimes'), now lost.

I. x. 14   *period*: sentence.

I. x. 28–9   See *Sat.* I. iv. 1–2.

I. x. 32–5   *Hermogenes*: see note on *Sat.* I. iii. 246–8. *Demetrius* is unknown outside Horace. The poets *Calvus* and *Catullus* belonged to the generation before Horace; both were dead when this satire was written.

I. x. 36–8   An opponent's imagined objection.

I. x. 41   *Rhodian bard (Rhodio Pitholeonti)*: identified by Bentley as Pitholaus, a writer of abusive epigrams.

I. x. 45   *zest*: piquancy.

I. x. 48   *Petillus*: see note on *Sat.* I. iv. 169–77.

I. x. 52–4   The people of *Canusium* in Apulia spoke Greek and Oscan ('broken Latin'); serious forensic oratory would forgo Greek flourishes. *Pedius* is unidentified; Messalla *Corvinus*, a well-known orator, is mentioned again in l. 159.

I. x. 66–7   *Alpinus*: 'Alpman', a nickname, probably referring to the ranting poet Furius Bibaculus quoted in *Sat.* II. v. 74–8. The story of *Memnon*, who fought at Troy as leader of the Ethiopian forces and was killed by Achilles, was a stock epic theme.

I. x. 71   *Tarpa*: Spurius Maecus Tarpa, a theatre critic.

I. x. 74–8   For H.'s friend *Fundanius*, see *Sat.* II. viii; he is presented here as the contemporary master of New Comedy, in which the courtesan ('doxy'), the scheming slave *Davus*, and the miserly father *Chremes* were stock characters (Brown). For *Chremes*, cf. *Epodes* i. 54. *huncks*: miser.

I. x. 78–9   *Pollio . . . kings*: referring to tragedy (for Pollio, see note on *Odes* II. i).

I. x. 80   *Varius*: see note on *Sat.* I. v. 73.

I. x. 82–4   *While . . . Virgil*: referring to Virgil's *Eclogues*.

I. x. 84–7   *this strain*: i.e. satire. P. Terentius *Varro* was primarily an epic poet. *I pretend . . . recommend* misrepresents *melius quod scribere possem*, 'which I could write better'.

I. x. 89 n.   *Lucilius*: see ll. 123 ff. below, and note on *Sat.* I. iv.

I. x. 99–101   *Accius*: L. Accius, a tragic dramatist (died *c.*85 BC) whom Lucilius parodied, according to H. *comedies* must be an error: PI correctly translates 'the tragic Accius'. *Ennius* (see note on *Odes* IV. viii. 30) was best known for his tragic and epic poetry; cf. *Sat.* II. i. 92–3.

I. x. 102–3   i.e. he says he is no better that the very poets he criticizes.

I. x. 116 n.   This *Cassius* (named in H.'s text) is unidentified.

I. x. 126–7   i.e. he would have pruned his verse himself if he had lived in present times.

I. x. 130–2   *in an extatic fit* is a gratuitous addition. As in the previous lines, H.'s point is that Lucilius would have recognized the need for careful polishing that modern standards demand (Brown).

I. x. 144   H. quotes the saying attributed to the famous actress *Arbuscula* 'I'm happy if the better classes applaud me' (Rudd, 1987).

I. x. 145   *Pantilius*: unknown, but his name means 'backbiter' (Rudd, 1987).

I. x. 150   *Fannius*: see *Sat.* I. iv. 38–40.

I. x. 151–61   For *Plotius* and *Varius* see note on *Sat.* I. v. 73. The *Knight of Tuscany* is H.'s patron, Maecenas. For C. *Valgius* Rufus, an elegiac poet, see *Odes* II. ix. *Octavius* Musa was a poet and historian. For *Fuscus* see note on *Sat.* I. ix. 124. *either Viscus*: the Visci were sons of Vibius Viscus, a friend of Augustus. *Pollio*: see note on *Odes* II. i. *Messala . . . brother*: Messalla Corvinus is mentioned in l. 54 above; his brother, Gellius Publicola, was consul in 36 BC. *Servius* is usually identified as son of the famous lawyer Servius Sulpicius Rufus, a friend of Cicero, but he may also have been the writer of light erotic verse of that name mentioned by Ovid in *Tristia* ii. 441 (Rudd, 1987). *Bibulus*: L. Calpurnius Bibulus, stepson of Brutus. H. probably knew him from his days as a student in Athens (Rudd, 1987). *Furnius*: a well-known orator, consul in 17 BC.

I. x. 169   For *Tigellius* see *Sat.* I. iii. 5 ff.

II   The second book of Horace's *Satires* was published in 30 BC.

II. i. 8   *Trebatius*: C. Trebatius Testa, an eminent lawyer and friend of Augustus, considerably older than Horace (Rudd, 1987).

II. i. 26   *which horrors plume*: presumably a poeticism for *horrentia pilis*, 'bristling with spears'.

II. i. 30–1   For *Lucilius* see note on *Sat.* I. iv. He accompanied *Scipio* Africanus Minor, the victor of Carthage, on his Spanish campaign (Rudd, 1987). For Scipio, cf. *Epodes* viii [ix]. 31.

II. i. 33   This vacuous line stands for *cum res ipsa feret*, i.e. when the time is ripe.

II. i. 40–1   Cf. *Sat.* I. viii. 19–20 (H. is quoting himself).

II. i. 45–6   *when . . . hot*: i.e. when he is tipsy.

II. i. 48   i.e. *Castor's* twin-brother Pollux: S. explains in a footnote in *1756* that they 'were born of, or rather hatched by *Leda*, in consequence of her amour with *Jupiter* in the shape of a swan'.

II. i. 49–51   The punctuation of *1767* is misleading: l. 50 is a comment on l. 49, with *For* a conjunction ('because') not a preposition. *of* in l. 50 looks like a misprint for *so*: S. clearly has in mind the well-known tag from Terence, *Quot homines, tot sententiae* ('So many men, so many opinions'), which puts H.'s point more succinctly than he does himself. 'My' (l. 51) is then emphatic, asserting where the poet's preference lies.

II. i. 67   *Venusium*: i.e. the people of Venusia, the town in Apulia near which H. was born.

II. i. 76   *style* i.e. pen (*stilus*): see *Sat.* I. x. 135 n.

II. i. 91–2   *dame . . . keeps*: Canidia, see *Epodes* v and xv–xvi.

II. i. 94   *damages denounce*: i.e. impose a big fine.

II. i. 117–18   *slave Of state*: i.e. someone in high station, 'one of your great friends' (*maiorum amicus*).

II. i. 121–2   *detrahere et pellem, nitidus qua quisque per ora cederet, introrsum turpis*, 'to pull off the borrowed skin by means of which many [a] one strutted with a seemly aspect, tho' corrupt within' (PI).

II. i. 123–4   *Laelius*: C. Laelius, nicknamed Sapiens, an orator and friend of Scipio Africanus Minor (*who . . . name*).

II. i. 125–6   Q. Caecilius *Metellus* Macedonicus and L. Cornelius *Lupus* were consuls and political opponents of Scipio.

II. i. 134   *And* in *1767* leaves the sentence without a main clause. The error was probably caused by the compositor picking up 'And' from the following line.

II. i. 141–2   See *Fables* IV. vii, *The Viper and the File*.

II. i. 149–51   H. quotes from the actual libel laws; *He may . . . lies*: 'judgment may be given against you' (PI).

II. ii. 4   *Ofellus*: H.'s neighbour, as we learn, possibly a real person (see N. Rudd, *The Satires of Horace* (1966), pp. 43–4).

II. ii. 17–18   *si Romana fatigat militia adsuetum graecari*, 'if Roman army sports are too tough for someone with Greek habits' (Rudd, 1987): *graecari* implies a more comfortable or luxurious life, not necessarily effeminacy, as S.'s footnote suggests.

II. ii. 20   *cheat . . . toils (fallente laborem)*: i.e. make the hard effort seem light.

II. ii. 23   *squeam* (for *fastidia*, nausea or delicacy): no use of this rare noun is recorded in *OED* before 1798, but the verb *squeam* is recorded in 1576 (see *Fables* IV. vi. 39).

II. ii. 41   *vice*: i.e. excess.

II. ii. 42–6   i.e. he would turn down a chicken in favour of a peacock if it were on offer, just because of its fine tail and its high cost. *in the nick*: just when he was going to eat the chicken.

II. ii. 57   *dive*: discover, 'enter deeply into a matter' (*OED* 4).

II. ii. 73–4   *banging . . . swinging* (= swingeing): dialect terms used for 'large' (see Wright's *English Dialect Dictionary*).

II. ii. 80–4   i.e. the boar and turbot are rank enough already when the stomach is sickened by over-eating and would prefer radishes and sour pickles (S.'s 'turnip' and 'acid herb').

II. ii. 89   *Cry'r*: Gallonius was an auctioneer and glutton ('gutler', l. 89 n.) satirized by Lucilius.

II. ii. 95–6   Alluding to a certain Rufus who, when candidate for the prae-torship, 'entertained the people with a dish of storks. But the people, according to an ancient epigram, revenged the death of the poor birds, by refusing the praetorship to their murderer' (Francis). *exploded*: rejected, dri-ven out (*OED* 2–4), not recorded in this sense as applicable to candidates for office.

II. ii. 125–6   *He . . . nastiness*: for *mundus erit, qua non offendit, sordidibus*, 'he'll be smart enough not to be considered mean' (Rudd, 1987).

II. ii. 129   *raves*: i.e. is savage (*saevus erit*).

II. ii. 161–2   i.e. whether the revolving year brings a festival round, or he wants to renew his weakened body.

II. ii. 167–8   i.e. if you indulge yourself when young and strong, you will have no treats left for your old age.

II. ii. 184   *credit . . . rope*: for *deerit . . . as, laquei pretium*, without a penny to buy a halter.

II. ii. 194–6   The lines in *1767* make sense, but not exactly H.'s sense: *cur, improbe, carae non aliquid patriae tanto emetiris acervo?*, 'Why, abandoned as you are, do you not measure something for your dear country, out of so vast an hoard?' (PI).

II. ii. 210–12   *integris opibus novi non latius usum quam nunc accisis*: 'he spent no more freely when he had all his riches than now when they are reduced.'

II. ii. 215   *tho' . . . large*: fort *metato in agello*, 'his little estate measured off', i.e. assigned to others (see ll. 249–50, below).

II. ii. 219   *Ought* (Aught): anything. *eat*: common 18th-c. form of the past tense.

II. ii. 231–2   *post hoc ludus erat culpa potare magistra*: S. follows most scholars in accepting this reading, taking it to refer to a game of forfeit to decide who should rule the feast (see note on *Odes* I. iv. 22). PI says, 'After this we had a pastime to drink with the cup only, for the mistress of the cere-monies', with footnote: 'This is a much disputed passage, occasioned by two readings, *cuppa* and *culpa*; I have favoured the latter in the poetical version, and the former in the prose interpretation, for the reader to take his choice.' *snip-snap-snorum* was a card-game.

II. ii. 245   *by war preferr'd*: Smart's addition, alluding to H.'s own experience. After serving with Brutus in the Civil War he returned to find his father's farm had been confiscated (see *Epistles* II. ii. 87–95). Such properties were assigned to Octavian's own soldiers.

II. iii.   *Damasippus*: Junius Damasippus, an art dealer mentioned in Cicero's letters.

II. iii. 8   *feast of Saturn*: the Saturnalia, festivities celebrated in Dec.

II. iii. 12   *scrawl*: H. says 'hammer'.

II. iii. 18–21   Damasippus is imagined to have brought with him on his visit to H. books by famous Greek writers: *Plato*, either the great philosopher or Plato the 5th-c. writer of comedies; *Eupolis*, a writer of Old Comedy (cf. *Sat.* I. iv. 1); and *Archilochus*, the iambic poet (see *Epistles* I. xix. 46–51 and note).

II. iii. 31   *your beard*: the trademark of a philosopher, see ll. 68–9 below.

II. iii. 36–40   *'prais'd*: appraised, valued. Damasippus is bankrupt, having formerly been an expert on *objets d'art* and antiques. *curious in a toy*: 'I loved to search for' rare and interesting objects such as the very bronze jar in which *Sisyphus* washed his feet (*quaerere amabam quo ... ille pedes lavisset Sisyphus aere*). The footbath of Sisyphus, mythical founder of Corinth, is mentioned by Aeschylus (Rudd, 1987).

II. iii. 43   *head*: i.e. sculpture.

II. iii. 44   *bled*: 'extorted', a colloquialism (see *OED* bleed, 10).

II. iii. 48   *the* MANAGER: for *Mercuriale*, 'one of Mercury's kind', i.e. a good businessman. Mercury was the god of gain and good luck.

II. iii. 65   *Stertinius*: a Stoic philosopher.

II. iii. 71   *Fabrician bridge*: the bridge between the Campus Martius in Rome and the island in the Tiber.

II. iii. 84   *Crysippus*: see note on *Sat.* I. iii. 241.

II. iii. 102   *hangs ... tail*: for *caudam trahit* ('drags his tail'), usually understood as a reference to the trick of tying a tail on someone to make a fool of him. Ainsworth s.v. *caudam trahere* cites this one instance, explaining 'To be mocked, to have a tail stuck, or tied behind him in mockage'.

II. iii. 116–20   S.'s note fails to explain that Fusius' cue, 'Hear, mother' etc., was spoken by Catienus acting the ghost of Polydore, Ilione's murdered son.

II. iii. 127 ff.   The madness of 'sane' men is illustrated by the folly of money-lenders, *Nerius*, *Cicuta*, and *Perillius*, who are all defeated by a slippery debtor.

II. iii. 131   *spare*: reject.

II. iii. 137   *Proteus*, the sea-god, evaded his enemies by transforming himself into different shapes.

II. iii. 143 ff.   *Si male rem gerere insani est, contra bene sani,* . . . (H. 74–6, 'if to manage things badly is madness, and conversely to manage well is sanity . . .'): S.'s attempt to imitate H.'s compact syntax renders it virtually impenetrable. He is apparently trying to say, 'If to misconduct one's affairs is folly, and careful management deserves the name of wisdom, then Perillius—who was eager to advance a loan which had no chance of being repaid—is weaker in the head than you are.'

II. iii. 152   *cants*: talks sanctimoniously or hypocritically.

II. iii. 160   *hellebore* was supposed to be a remedy for madness.

II. iii. 170   Cicero mentions one Q. *Arrius* who gave a lavish feast at his father's funeral.

II. iii. 178   *on contempt*: i.e. on pain of being in contempt of the law. H. implies that it was a condition of Staberius' will.

II. iii. 190–1   He hoped his riches would redound to his praise, as if they were gained by merit.

II. iii. 193   *Aristippus*: founder of the Cyrenaic school of philosophy. See note on *Epistles* I. i. 35.

II. iii. 205   *inscious*: ignorant; an archaism by this date.

II. iii. 207   *That*: He.

II. iii. 212   *how (quid)*: the *1767* reading *now* makes sense, but is surely a misprint. PI translates 'how'.

II. iii. 227   *on his line*: presumably meaning his clothes-line (S.'s addition).

II. iii. 240   *cruise*: cruse (bottle, jar, etc.).

II. iii. 249   i.e. Or maltreat your own slaves in the same way.

II. iii. 253–70   *the same place*: Argos, site of the legendary calamities of the house of Atreus dramatized in the *Oresteia* by Aeschylus. *Orestes*, son of Agamemnon, conspired with his sister *Electra* and friend *Pylades* to kill his mother Clytemnestra in revenge for the murder of his father. Thereafter he was pursued by the avenging *furies*, the Eumenides.

II. iii. 287   *certain*: certain people.

II. iii. 288   *he*: i.e. Opimius.

II. iii. 306–8   *churl*: miser. *near*: stingy.

II. iii. 316   *reins*: kidneys.

II. iii. 323   Cf. l. 162, above.

II. iii. 342–3   *learn . . . Nomentanus*: learn by the example of Nomentanus. For the spendthrift *Nomentanus* see ll. 432–3 below, and *Sat.* I. i. 180, I, viii. 20, and II. i. 41.

II. iii. 344   *scrub*: contemptible person.

II. iii. 361   M. Vipsanius *Agrippa* distributed his money liberally, as aedile in 33 BC, to win popularity.

II. iii. 365–87   Agamemnon (*Atrides*) ordered that Ajax's body should lie unburied. Ajax had planned to murder Agamemnon, his brother Menelaus, and Ulysses, after losing a contest for possession of the arms of the dead Achilles. Driven mad by resentment, he slew a flock of sheep which he mistook for his enemies, then committed suicide in shame.

II. iii. 383   *the same*: Ajax likewise left the Trojan youths unburied after killing them.

II. iii. 388–91   Agamemnon sacrificed his daughter Iphigenia at *Aulis* to propitiate the gods before the Greek army set sail for Troy.

II. iii. 396–7   *each Atrides*: the brothers Agamemnon and Menelaus. *Teucer*: Ajax's brother.

II. iii. 407   *doats*: dotes, is mad.

II. iii. 413   *chair*: a light vehicle drawn by one horse (first recorded in this sense in 1753, see *OED sb. 1*, 11).

II. iii. 416   *bantling or pusette*: for *pusam aut pusillam*, a textual crux, with many variant readings. S.'s means literally 'girl or little girl'. *bantling* is a small child, *pusette* is unrecorded but is probably connected with *puselle*, 'girl' (see *OED* s.v. pucelle).

II. iii. 418–20   *to such . . . gainsay*: i.e. the Praetor would decree such a person unfit to look after himself.

II. iii. 438   *for state*: as a mark of ceremony.

II. iii. 463–4   *Aesopus*, a famous actor and friend of Cicero, left a large fortune to his son (Rudd, 1987).

II. iii. 469–70   *Arrius*: see note on l. 170 above. *In . . . sins*: in minor follies as much as in great sins.

II. iii. 473   *fondness*: utter folly. *of right*: deserving.

II. iii. 488   *wave*: waive.

II. iii. 506   *dunn'd*: pestered.

II. iii. 522   *gamut*: the whole range or compass of a thing (*OED* 4).

II. iii. 523–5   Shooting apple-pips at the ceiling was supposed by lovers to be a way of discovering if their love was returned.

II. iii. 536   *fact*: crime.

II. iii. 538–46   S. makes a muddle of H.'s story. It is about a freedman, not his son; when the *original* owner sold him, he must have declared his madness or he would have been sued. Presumably he was freed subsequently: a freedman could not be sold.

II. iii. 554   *five weeks*: H. says five months.

II. iii. 566   *eighth wise man*: i.e. after the so-called Seven Sages of Greece.

II. iii. 572   See *Fables* IV. ix, *The Two Bags*.

II. iii. 579–82   *Agave* 'slew her son Pentheus for despising the Bacchanalian ceremonies' (PT, note). In Euripides' tragedy the *Bacchae* she comes on stage carrying the head of her son.

II. iii. 590   *Turbo*: 'a little strutting gladiator' (PT, note).

II. iii. 597–606   See *Fables* I. xxiv, *The proud Frog*.

II. iii. 611–12   *quae si quis sanus fecit, sanis facis et tu*: i.e. if any sane man ever wrote verses, then you are sane.

II. iii. 617–18   *O maior tandem parcas insane minori*: 'you the greater lunatic, spare the lesser one.' *wave*: waive. S. omits from his text and translation Damasippus' interjection (H. 325) *Mille puellarum, puerorum mille furores* ('Your thousand passions for boys and girls'). It is included in *1756*.

II. iv. 30   *those at hand*: i.e. those from the farms near Rome.

II. iv. 38   S.'s addition.

II. iv. 45   *Aufidius*: perhaps M. Aufidius Lurco, said by Pliny to have fattened peacocks for sale, *c*.67 BC.

II. iv. 54   *Coan*: wine from Cos.

II. iv. 56   *lubricating*: oily.

II. iv. 60   *burret*: shellfish.

II. iv. 73   *gutler*: glutton.

II. iv. 80/1   S.'s verse translation omits H.'s l. 43 (*vinea summittit capreas non semper edules*, 'the vineyard does not always send the most eatable kids'), presumably inadvertently: it is included in his Latin text.

II. iv. 82   *wings*: shoulders (of hares or rabbits).

II. iv. 88   *paste*: pastries.

II. iv. 116   *slattern-shops*: 'slovenly eating-houses' (PI).

II. iv. 130   *jars*: i.e. for preserving.

II. iv. 142   *spraggling*: sprawling (*vagos*), a dialect word. Cf. *JA*, B748.

II. iv. 156–61   i.e. forgetting that the less the care and cost of such trifles, the more the blame for neglecting them—more blameworthy than the lack of expensive things which only the rich can provide.

II. iv. 171   *express*: precise (qualifying *countenance*).

II. v. 26–9   The first-fruits were offered to the household gods, the *Lares*.

II. v. 34   *give the wall*: allow to walk on the inside of the pavement, as a mark of respect.

II. v. 36   *Dama*: a common slave name, hence a social inferior.

II. v. 37–8   *haud ita Troiae me gessi, semper melioribus*: 'I did not behave myself in that manner at Troy, contending always with the best' (**PT**).

II. v. 62   *gaudent molles auriculae*: 'delights susceptible ears.'

II. v. 67   *deaf-nut*: nut with no kernel, hence something worthless.

II. v. 71   *cocker up*: coddle.

II. v. 82   *ut amicus aptus? ut acer?* 'how serviceable to his friends, how acute' (**PT**).

II. v. 85–93   *As batchelor* spoils the sense: H. says if your attentions to a bachelor are too blatant, find a man who has a delicate son. *offices*: acts of dutiful attention.

II. v. 103–4   cf. *Fables* I. xiii, *The Fox and the Crow*.

II. v. 106   *Nasica . . . Coranus* (see ll. 119–30): the identity of these characters, presumably familiar to H.'s readers, is now lost.

II. v. 108   *obscurities divine*: speak obscurities by way of prophecy, for *ludis me obscura canendo*: 'deceive me by speaking in obscurities.'

II. v. 115–19   Referring in typically oracular language to Octavian (later Augustus).

II. v. 120   i.e. who hates paying his bills in full (*metuentis reddere soldum*).

II. v. 124   *old churl* is wrong: as S.'s footnote shows, the story depends on the son-in-law being the old man.

II. v. 129–30   i.e. nothing to do except complain (*nil praeter plorare*).

II. v. 152   *nec tantum Veneris quantum . . . culinae*: 'food rather than love.'

II. v. 172   *Davus*: see note on *Sat.* I. x. 74–8.

II. v. 183   *with wrath*: not in H. and far too strong.

II. v. 186   S.'s addition.

II. v. 190   Quoted from Milton, *A Mask* [Comus], l. 262, 'Such sober certainty of waking bliss'.

II. v. 198   *est gaudia prodentem vultum celare*: 'it is well to disguise a countenance betraying too much gladness' (PI).

II. v. 209–10   *Proserpine . . . Ghosts*: for *imperiosa Proserpina*. Proserpine was queen of the underworld.

II. vi. 8   *Mercury*: 'he was supposed to preside over hid treasures, and unexpected gain' (**PT**, note).

II. vi. 23   *Hercules*: guardian of riches.

II. vi. 28   Servants, dog, and cat are S.'s additions.

II. vi. 34   *measur'd prose*: prosaic diction in metrical form.

II. vi. 38–9   *the gain . . . reign*: because it leads to more deaths. The goddess *Libitina* presided over deaths and funerals.

II. vi. 62   *Esquilian gloom*: referring to the cemetery mentioned in *Sat*. I. viii.

II. vi. 100   The *Dacians* fought for Antony against Caesar at the battle of Actium: see *Odes* III. vi. 14–16 and note.

II. vi. 104–6   Italians hoped Caesar would reward his soldiers with grants of land in Sicily (Rudd, 1987).

II. vi. 118   *Pythagoras*: 'alluding to that philosopher's believing the metempsychosis in such an extent, as to imagine souls sometimes transmigrated into beans' (PT, note).

II. vi. 132   *Lepos*: a dancer well known in Rome, supposed to have been favoured by Caesar (Rudd, 1987).

II. vi. 154   *give a loose*: relax restraints; S. may be recalling Dryden's translation of H.'s *Odes* III. xxix, 'Come, give thy Soul a loose, and taste the pleasures of the poor'.

II. vi. 170   *on . . . wood*: the preposition is awkward but not necessarily a misprint. H.'s *praerupti nemoris dorso* is translated in PI 'on the ridge of a rugged wood'.

II. vii   *Heading*. The slave is rating Horace, taking advantage of the freedom allowed during Saturnalia (see ll. 7–10).

II. vii. 6   i.e. that his life is in no danger, referring to the common saying: 'Such a child is too good (*or* too witty) to be long-lived' (PT, note).

II. vii. 7–10   During the Saturnalia (17–19 Dec.) slaves were allowed great liberties in commemoration of the golden age of Saturn, when all people were free and equal.

II. vii. 15   *a sideling*: sidling, inclining.

II. vii. 16   *obnoxious*: guilty (L. *obnoxius*).

II. vii. 20   *shift*: change his clothes.

II. vii. 27   *Vertumnus*: god of the changing seasons.

II. vii. 29–30   *Volanerius* was a parasite whose gout was justly 'deserved' because of his dissipated life. See *Epistles* I. i. 57, where healthy exercise is said to prevent gout.

II. vii. 31   *stay'd*: in the sense of 'hindered', i.e. crippled.

II. vii. 33   *to sin . . . chains*: for *constantior in vitiis*, steadier in his vices.

II. vii. 74   *did surmount*: were superior.

II. vii. 82   In H. Davus has picked up his Stoic doctrine from the philosopher's door-keeper (*Crispini ianitor*). In S. Davus himself is the eavesdropper. For Crispinus, see *Sat.* I. iv. 19–26.

II. vii. 82/3   S. omits from text and translation H.'s ll. 46–52 in which Davus imagines his master having an adulterous affair.

II. vii. 84   Wealthy knights wore a gold ring as badge of their status (Rudd, 1987).

II. vii. 85–6   i.e. the magistrate will turn out to be a slave ('Dama') dressed up. For *evade* meaning 'turn out to be' (L. *evado*), see *OED* 1b.

II. vii. 91 ff.   *bound on oath*: i.e. sworn in as a gladiator. Davus suggests that there is little to choose between the lot of the gladiator, liable for scourging or death by sword, and the perils facing the illicit lover. Lines 93–112 follow on from the passage omitted by S. (see note on ll. 82/3 above).

II. vii. 100   *place nor hue*: rank nor clothing. The adulterous man changes both.

II. vii. 104   *husband*: see Introduction, p. xxxi.

II. vii. 114   *fay*: faith.

II. vii. 115   *plate*: silver.

II. vii. 116   i.e. if the threat of the gallows is removed: see Introduction, p. xxviii.

II. vii. 131   *poppet*: puppet.

II. vii. 140–2   H.'s metaphor is of a smooth-rolling ball (*teres et rotundus*, 'polished and round', PI).

II. vii. 143   i.e. Fortune has no success when she attacks him. *When* in *1767* must be a misprint (emended by Rudd).

II. vii. 158   *Pausias*: a Greek painter of the 4th c. BC famed for his fine technique and erotic subjects (Rudd, 1987).

II. vii. 162–4   *coal or oaker*: i.e. charcoal or red ochre, referring to pictures of gladiators painted on city walls, like modern posters. The words in quotation marks represent the viewer's naïve admiration for the wall-painter's crude artistry.

II. vii. 167–8   A confused rendering of H.'s terse *Nil ego, si ducor libo fumante*, 'I'm good for nothing if I'm tempted by a smoking pasty'.

II. vii. 170   *jole* (jowl): a choice cut of fish.

II. vii. 172   *I . . . thong*: i.e. I'm beaten for pilfering.

II. vii. 175–8   'Then those niceties, sought after without ceasing, pall upon the stomach, and your deluded feet will not support the vicious habit of your body' (PI).

II. vii. 186   There are two conflicting selves, the lower trying to justify itself to the higher.

II. vii. 194   *accedes opera agro nona Sabino*: 'you shall go and make a ninth workman in my Sabine field' (PI).

II. viii   *Fundanius* was the writer of comedies referred to in *Sat.* I. x. 174–8.

II. viii. 22   *ut virgo cum sacris Cereris*: like a maiden bearing the sacred emblems of Ceres.

II. viii. 23–5   *Caecuban . . . Chian*: wines. Sea-water was sometimes added as preservative or flavour enhancer.

II. viii. 40   *danglers . . . state*: hangers-on, to show his important position.

II. viii. 41   *Nomentanus*: perhaps the spendthrift of earlier satires, see *Sat.* II. iii. 432–3.

II. viii. 43   *despis'd and hiss'd*: H. simply calls him *ridiculus*.

II. viii. 44   *at a twist*, 'at a mouthful' (PI).

II. viii. 55   *he*: Nomentanus.

II. viii. 59   *How . . . odds*: how great the difference (cf. *Fables* I. xv. 4).

II. viii. 73–4   A gentlemanly addition by S. Horace says all joined in except the guests on the lowest couch, i.e. Porcius and Nomentanus, who were on either side of the host (Rudd).

II. viii. 78   *row*: roe.

II. viii. 83   *Not . . . sea*: i.e. local.

II. viii. 92   *rockets*: plants used in salads.

II. viii. 116   *bam* was a slang term meaning to deceive, or impose upon, but it translates *suspendens naso*, 'turning up his nose' (PI). S. presumably meant to convey the speaker's mock-consolation.

II. viii. 124   *rowls*: rolls.

II. viii. 132   *footman . . . plough*: for *agaso*, usually translated as 'lackey' here, but the primary sense is one who drives or looks after horses.

II. viii. 144   i.e. to leave the dining-room.

II. viii. 155–6   They invented jokes as an excuse for their laughter (*ridetur fictis rerum*).

II. viii. 159   *after-clap*: 'an unexpected event happening after an event is supposed to be at an end' (Johnson's Dictionary).

II. viii. 166   *wings*: see note on *Sat.* II. iv. 82.

II. viii. 169   *mearles*: blackbirds.

II. viii. 176   *Canidia*: see *Epodes* v and xv–xvi.

II. viii. 178   i.e. more poisonous than African snakes.

Epistles I   H.'s first book of *Epistles* was published some years after the first three books of *Odes*, in 19 BC.

Motto (from the title-page of S.'s vol. iv). Horace, *Ars Poet.* 404–5, 'Song showed the way through life. By means of Pierian tunes a king's favour was sought' (Rudd, 1987).

I. i. 8   *time of day*: time of life; also (colloquially) 'state of affairs' (*OED* time, *sb.* 28c).

I. i. 9   *Vejanius* is evidently a retired gladiator.

I. i. 24   *deduce*: draw from [them] (*depromere*).

I. i. 35   *Aristippus*: founder of the Cyrenaic school of philosophy, whose doctrine was that men should control circumstances rather than be subject to them.

I. i. 38   *plays the bite*: for *mentitur*, i.e. cheats, using 'bite' in the slang sense of a deception (*OED sb.* 9).

I. i. 62–73   Throughout this passage H. applies to philosophy the language of magic and ancient medicine. Perhaps thinking this too obscure for his readers, S. reduces the ambiguities: *Philosophers . . . essays* stands for *sunt certa piacula*, 'there are certain spells'; *lectures of philosophy* for *culturae*, 'treatment'.

I. i. 79   *Want or rejection*: i.e. poverty or losing an election.

I. i. 93–4   i.e. providing he could achieve it without effort.

I. i. 100   *at either Janus*: i.e. from end to end of the arcade of Janus, the centre of the banking world of Rome.

I. i. 106   A fortune of 400,000 sesterces was required for enrolment in the knights (*equites*).

I. i. 113   *colour . . . sin*: for *pallescere culpa* ('turn pale with guilt'); 'change' in 1767 appears to be a misprint.

I. i. 114   *Roscian edict*: the law by which certain seats in the theatre were reserved for knights and senators. See note on *Epodes* iv. 17–18.

I. i. 118–19   *Curius . . . Camillus*: military heroes of Roman history.

I. i. 121   *scramble up a sum*: i.e. make money (*rem facias*).

I. i. 144–5   *rich widows* are the object of *some* (people).

I. i. 162   *genial bed*: the marriage bed (*lectus genialis*).

I. i. 173–5   *when he . . . than he*: i.e. he gets just as seasick when he hires a boat as the rich man who owns his own.

I. i. 192–7   As a friend should, he worries even about a cut finger, while the more important matter of his friend's mental health leaves him unconcerned. A *keeper* was appointed by the Praetor to look after a lunatic (Rudd,

1987), cf. *Sat.* II. iii. 418–22. H. says that Maecenas is irritated at the sight of his client's badly kept finger-nails.

I. i. 199   i.e. the wise man is less than Jove alone.

I. i. 202   *fit of spleen*: for H.'s 'cold in the head' (*pituita*).

I. ii   *Lollius*: Lollius Maximus appears from *Epistles* I. xviii to have served under Augustus as a soldier in Spain. He is now a student of rhetoric in Rome (Rudd, 1987).

I. ii. 8   *Crantor . . . Crysippus*: 'Two eminent philosophers and writers on moral subjects' (PT, note). For Crysippus, see note on *Sat.* I. iii. 241.

I. ii. 11 ff.   Referring to the plot ('argument') of Homer's *Iliad*.

I. ii. 17–18   *Antenor* proposed that Helen should be returned to the Greeks (*Iliad* vii. 347 ff.). *council*: counsel, advice. The spellings *council* and *counsel* were interchangeable in the 18th c.

I. ii. 21–2   *Nestor* tried to reconcile Achilles, son of *Peleus*, and Agamemnon, son of *Atreus*, who had quarrelled over possession of the captive girl Briseis (*Iliad* i. 247 ff.).

I. ii. 34–5   After the defeat of Troy, Ulysses, a prudent ('politic') man, visited many cities.

I. ii. 42   For the *Sirens*, see *Odyssey* xii. 29 ff. *Circe's cup*: see *Odyssey* x. 135 ff.

I. ii. 52   *Penelope's leud knaves*: i.e. her worthless suitors.

I. ii. 53   *Alcinous made slaves*, i.e. by indulging them: see *Odyssey*, books vii and viii.

I. ii. 71   *differ*: older spelling of *defer*.

I. ii. 79   *voluminous* (for *volubilis*): full of windings (*OED* 1). Milton uses it of a serpent in *PL* ii. 652.

I. ii. 89   *award*: ward off (*OED* v. 2).

I. ii. 122   *offer for the best*: this seems to mean 'aim at the best'. H. says simply *te melioribus offer*, 'entrust yourself to your betters'. PI translates 'present yourself to masters of the better sort'.

I. iii. 1–2   Julius *Florus*: a follower of T. *Claudius* Nero (see *Epistles* II. ii. 1), and a writer of satires.

I. iii. 6   *tow'rs*: the towers of Sestus and Abydos, which stand on either side of the straits of Hellespont.

I. iii. 19   H.'s *lacus et rivos apertos* means the tanks and channels from which ordinary people could draw water, as opposed to the natural springs of more remote and difficult access.

I. iii. 27   *Celsus*: Celsus Albinovanus, secretary to Claudius (see *Epistles* I. viii. 4). *council*: counsel.

I. iii. 32   i.e. in the library of the temple of Apollo, on the Palatine in Rome, founded by Augustus in 28 BC.

I. iii. 33–6   See *Fables* I. iii, *The vain Jackdaw*.

I. iii. 69   *runt*: dialect term for heifer (*iuvenca*).

I. iv. 1   Albius *Tibullus* (*c*.50–19 BC) was primarily an elegiac poet.

I. iv. 2   *prosaic lays*: referring to his *Satires* (*sermones*).

I. iv. 6   *Cassius*: another poet, perhaps the Cassius referred to in *Sat.* I. x. 116.

I. iv. 28   *of . . . breed*: i.e. like Epicurus, alluding both to his philosophy and to his reputation as a voluptuary (Rudd, 1987).

I. v   Torquatus is the aristocrat addressed in *Odes* IV. vii.

I. v. 8   T. Statilius *Taurus* was made consul (*declar'd*) for the second time in 26 BC.

I. v. 15   *Moschus' cause*: Torquatus defended Moschus from a charge of poisoning.

I. v. 17   23 Sept.

I. v. 27   *rake-shame* (for *inconsultus*, ill-advised): a common 17th-c. term for drunk and disorderly characters.

I. v. 28   *quid non ebrietas designat?*, 'what cannot wine perform?' (Francis). Modern editions prefer the form *dissignat*, 'unseal'.

I. v. 47   *ut coeat par iungaturque pari*, 'that equals may meet and be associated with equals' (PI).

I. v. 52   *danglers*: hangers-on (cf. *Sat.* II. viii. 40).

I. v. 58   *Deceive them*: i.e. give them the slip.

I. vi. 1   *Nil admirari*, 'Never be dazzled' (Rudd, 1987).

I. vi. 8   *the line*: the equator.

I. vi. 16   *the wond'ring fondness*: i.e. the folly of excessive admiration (see l. 1).

I. vi. 24   *jest* is probably a misprint for *just*. H. says *insani nomen ferat, aequus iniqui*, 'Let the wise man bear the name of fool, the just of iniquitous' (PI). But S. might have intended to make the point that excessive observation of moral laws by wise men earns the derision of those who break them.

I. vi. 40   *admirable*: i.e. to be marvelled at (*mirabilis*).

I. vi. 45–7 *Appian way . . . Agrippa's Portico*: haunts of fashionable Romans.

I. vi. 49   *Numa . . . Ancus*: powerful and popular kings of early Rome.

I. vi. 60   *lose the FAIR*: miss the market (for *portus occupet alter*, 'another should reach port before you').

I. vi. 68–9   *will … family*: will enable you to pay for a coat of arms and claim noble ancestry.

I. vi. 71   *Suadela*: personification of Persuasion.

I. vi. 72   *Cappadocian king*: probably Ariobazarnes III (d. 42 BC), described in Cicero's letters as very poor.

I. vi. 75   L. Licinius *Lucullus*, who commanded the Roman army in the Pontic war (74–67 BC), was renowned for his opulence.

I. vi. 96–9   *Jog … side*: the slave would be walking on the outside of the pavement (cf. *Sat.* II. v. 34), and nudging his master when likely voters appeared. The meaning of the rest, *et cogat trans pondera dextram porrigere*, is debatable. S.'s literal translation, 'make us extend our hand against all impediments' (PI), highlights the difficulty without solving it. His verse translation appears to be an expansion of Francis, 'through the crouded street / To stretch the civil hand to all we meet'. Modern translators usually take *pondera* to refer to the stepping-stones across city streets: 'make us offer a handshake across the stepping stones' (Rudd, 1987).

I. vi. 100–1   *Fabian … Veline*: two of the thirty-five tribes into which Roman citizens were divided (Rudd, 1987). S.'s *bribe* nicely sharpens the original.

I. vi. 102–3   For *cuilibet hic fasces dabit, eripietque curule cui volet importunus ebur*: lit. 'this [man] will procure the fasces for any one; and, by his importunate bustling, will snatch the curule ivory from whom he chooses' (PI). The *curule ebur* ('chair of state') was the official chair, inlaid with ivory, used by higher magistrates.

I. vi. 116–17   *unus ut … populo spectante referret emptum mulus aprum*, 'that in the sight of the mob one mule might return laden with a boar, bought for the purpose'. S. may be using *silver spear* like the proverbial phrase *silver spoon* to imply inherited wealth, underlining the parvenu Gargilius' pretensions, or hinting at a special kind of 'spear', i.e. a purse of silver.

I. vi. 119   i.e. destroying the distinction: 'forgetting what is decent and what not' (PI).

I. vi. 122   *contraband*: forbidden (*OED adj.* 2).

I. vi. 124   *Mimnermus*: an elegiac poet of the 6th c. BC.

I. vii. 11   Cf. Pope, 'While the long fun'rals blacken all the way', *Elegy to the Memory of an Unfortunate Lady*, l. 40.

I. vii. 24   Referring to Maecenas' gift of the Sabine farm (see note on *Odes* I).

I. vii. 36–7   H.'s point is that this is false generosity: *prodigus et stultus donat quae spernit et odit* ('the prodigal fool gives away what he despises and hates').

I. vii. 40   *bit*: deceived.

I. vii. 51–3   'and also the lamentations o'er my liquor at the jilting of the wanton Cynara' (PI). For *Cynara*, cf. *Odes* IV. i and IV. xii [xiii].

I. vii. 69–70   i.e. wealth will not count for me, compared with liberty and ease.

I. vii. 80–7   See *Odyssey* iv. 601 ff.

I. vii. 91   *Tibur*: see headnote to *Odes* I. vii; *Tarentum* (cf. *Odes* III. v. 56) was a wealthy settlement in southern Italy.

I. vii. 93   L. Marcius *Philippus* was a distinguished lawyer.

I. vii. 95   SHIP-STREET: for *Carinae*, a fashionable district only about a quarter of a mile from the Forum (Rudd, 1987).

I. vii. 96   *at . . . day*: for *grandis natu*, 'much advanced in years' (PI).

I. vii. 103   *how preferr'd*: what is his appointment (preferment). H.'s speaker asks about his wealth (*fortunae*).

I. vii. 107   *cryer*: auctioneer.

I. vii. 120   *scrub*: rascal.

I. vii. 125–7   i.e. he excuses himself by saying he is tied down by business.

I. vii. 129–31   *guest*: i.e. host. The two terms were confusable, since French *hôte* could mean either 'host' or 'guest', but the confusion is usually the other way round. In this case, 'host' is the required sense: Mena is apologizing for not having visited Philippus that morning in response to his invitation the previous day. Philippus replies that he will be pacified if Mena comes tonight instead.

I. vii. 144   *Latin festivals*: holidays held in spring, at which time all legal business was suspended.

I. vii. 157   *beau* (for *nitido*): 'smart cockney' (PI) catches the nuance more precisely.

I. vii. 161   *amore senescit habiendi*: 'grows old with his passion for gain.'

I. vii. 184–5   *should . . . sphere*: for *metiri se quemque suo modulo ac pede*, 'ought to measure himself by his own proper foot and standard' (PT).

I. viii. 3   *Nero*: Claudius Nero (cf. *Epistles* I. iii. 2–3 and I. ix).

I. viii. 6–8   *dic multa et pulchra minantem vivere nec recte nec suaviter*: 'tell him I am threatening many and glorious atchievements, but actually live neither laudably, nor agreeably' (PI).

I. viii. 6 n.   Persius, *Sat.* i. 116–17, 'While his friend is laughing, that rascal Horace lays his finger on all his faults; gaining admission, he plays on the conscience' (Rudd, 1987).

I. viii. 20   *Tibur*: see headnote to *Odes* I. vii.

I. ix. 1   *Septimius*: probably the friend addressed in *Odes* II. vi.

I. ix. 9–11   i.e. when he thinks me a closer friend than I am.

I. x. 2   Aristius *Fuscus* was a dramatic writer and scholar, according to the scholiasts.

I. x. 17–18   'The priest's slave, who is tired of living on the delicacies offered to his master's God, runs away from his service, that he may get a little common bread' (Francis).

I. x. 27   H. says 'warmer winters'.

I. x. 30–2   The Dog-star rises on 20 July; the sun enters the constellation of Leo on 23 July.

I. x. 35   *Lybian stones*: referring to the marble chippings (*lapillis*) used for inlaid floors of great Roman villas.

I. x. 41–2   Referring to trees sometimes grown in the colonnaded court-yards of villas.

I. x. 51–2   The expensive *Sidonian* purple was imitated by a dye produced from lichen growing at *Aquinum*.

I. x. 62–9   See *Fables* IV. iii, *The Horse and Boar* for a different version of this fable.

I. x. 78   *subvert*: trip up, overturn, used in a literal sense as in the original (*subvertet*). The last usage in this sense, according to *OED*, is 1697.

I. x. 90   *Vacuna*: 'The goddess of vacations or of idleness' (PT, note); a Sabine goddess with a temple near H.'s farm (Rudd, 1987).

I. xi. 1–5   H. names some of the famous islands and cities of Asia Minor.

I. xi. 10–14   *Attalic*: the cities bequeathed by Attalus III to Rome (see note on *Odes* II. xviii. 6) included Pergamum and Apollonia. *Lebedus*: a town near Colophon, in Asia Minor. *Gabii . . . Fidenae*: small towns in the vicinity of Rome.

I. xi. 16   Cf. Pope, 'The world forgetting, by the world forgot', *Eloisa to Abelard*, l. 208.

I. xi. 17–18   A clumsy expression of H.'s wish to enjoy gazing at the raging sea from a safe distance (*Neptunum procul e terra spectare furentem*).

I. xi. 21   *hold* (for *caupona*, tavern): temporary lodging (*OED sb. 1*, 9).

I. xi. 23   *bagnios*: steam baths.

I. xi. 33   *blow'rs*: a 'blower' was a mechanism for increasing the draught of a fire, but the earliest citation in *OED* is 1795.

I. xi. 46–7   *not . . . ocean: non locus effusi late maris arbiter*. 'Not the bold site, that wide commands the sea' (Francis).

I. xi. 54 n.   *Ulubrae*: situated not in Campania but in the Pomptine marshes in Latium.

I. xii. 1–4   In *Odes* I. xxix H. rallies his friend *Iccius* on deserting philosophy for the pursuit of riches. Now it appears he has become land-agent for the Sicilian estates of M. Vipsanius *Agrippa*, the Roman admiral (see note on *Odes* I. vi. 7–9).

I. xii. 12   *miller's thumbs*: a kind of small fish (cf. *JA*, B148). This is S.'s rendering of *urtica*, usually 'nettles', but used in Pliny's *Historia Naturalis* of a small marine creature, translated in Holland's *Pliny* (1601), ii. 449, as 'The Sea-nettle (a fish so called)'. 'Miller's thumb' was also a proverbial expression for avarice: 'every miller has a thumb of gold' (see Chaucer, *Gen. Prologue*, l. 562).

I. xii. 14   S.'s word-play continues with *mint*, both a herb and a vast sum of money.

I. xii. 16–20   *pow'ring*: pouring. The point of these lines, very obscure in S.'s phrasing, is that a self-denying person would continue to live frugally however wealthy he became. *Because . . . alone* (17–20): *vel quia naturam mutare pecunia nescit, vel quia cuncta putas una virtute minore*: 'either because money cannot change nature, or because you think every consideration inferior to virtue alone' (PI).

I. xii. 21–7   *old sophist*: named by H. as *Democritus*, the Thracian philosopher contemporary with Socrates. H.'s irony is spelt out by Sanadon: 'Democritus was so engaged in his philosophical speculations, that he left his estate a prey to his neighbours. But the severe and frugal life of Iccius rose from very different principles. He denied himself only those pleasures, which his avarice would not allow him to purchase' (quoted by Francis). *scrambler . . . sneak*: colloquial terms for a rapacious person. But H. says that other people, not Iccius, are money-mad.

I. xii. 34   *dissonant consent*: for *concordia discors rerum*, the principle of harmony-from-discord central to western metaphysics from early Greek philosophy onwards.

I. xii. 36   *Stertinius*: a Stoic philosopher of H.'s time, see *Satires* II. iii. 65 ff. *Empedocles*: the 5th-c. Sicilian philosopher.

I. xii. 37   *rough*: the name of a fish.

I. xii. 39   *Grosphus*: see *Odes* II. xvi.

I. xii. 43   i.e. the virtue of benevolence is easily acquired by such modest gestures: S.'s addition, expanding l. 44, H.'s cryptic aphorism, *vilis amicorum est annona, bonis quid deest* ('the price of friends is low, when good men are in need'). S. explains: 'Because they [good men] are always modest and reasonable in their demands' (PT, note).

I. xii. 47–50   Referring to events of 20–19 BC: the victories of *Agrippa* over the Cantabrians, and Tiberius (Claudius *Nero*) over the Armenians, and the restoration by *Phraates*, king of Parthia, of Roman standards captured in 53 BC.

I. xiii. 4 *these volumes*: probably referring to H.'s *Odes*, Books I–III, published in 23 BC.

I. xiii. 12 *budget*: bundle (of papers).

I. xiii. 17 *your Asinine descent*: playing on Vinnius' family name, *Asella* or *Asina* (in some editions), which means 'ass'.

I. xiii. 25–6 *Pyrrhia ... yarn*: 'alluding to a passage in a comedy of Titinius's' (PT, note).

I. xiii. 27 *fudling-cap*: drinking-cap.

I. xiv. 6 *Senators*: for *patres*, meaning merely the heads of households, probably free settlers.

I. xiv. 14 *Lamia*: see *Odes* III. xvii.

I. xiv. 32 *stews*: brothels. H. mentions only *ludos* (games, plays, entertainments, etc.). In l. 43 below, the same word is used correctly for *fornix*.

I. xiv. 48 i.e. there is no local tavern where he can get drinks on credit. The slang use of 'tick' for credit dates from the 17th c.

I. xiv. 50 *ad strepitum salias terrae gravis*: 'you clump up and down on the floor' (Rudd, 1987).

I. xiv. 57–8 i.e. the brook has to be restrained by dykes to prevent it flooding the meadows in rainy weather.

I. xiv. 62 *immunem Cinarae placuisse rapaci*: 'could charm the greedy Cinara without a present.'

I. xiv. 79 *errant-boy*: house-boy.

I. xiv. 82 i.e. the ox longs for the horse's harness.

I. xv. 1–2 *Velia*: a coastal town in southern Italy. *Salernum*: modern Salerno, in Campania.

I. xv. 5–10 *Musa* was famous for prescribing cold-water treatment instead of the usual thermal baths ('the wells'). *Baiae* was a fashionable seaside resort in Campania.

I. xv. 13 *chalybeate*: water infused with minerals (cf. *The Hop-Garden* i. 42, *PW* iv. 43).

I. xv. 18–19 *Clusium* and *Gabii* were more northerly towns.

I. xv. 24 *BALD-FACE*: the driver is not named by H.

I. xv. 30 *in the bit they hear: est auris in ore* ('their ear is in their mouth'): i.e. they are guided by the reins, not by words.

I. xv. 45–6 *Quod me Lucanae iuvenem commendet amicae*, '[words] which may recommend me as a youth to my Lucanian mistress' (PI).

I. xv. 56   *Maenius*: a character from Lucilius mentioned in *Sat.* I. i. 179 as a spendthrift.

I. xv. 58–9   *urbanus coepit haberi, scurra vagus, non qui certum praesepe teneret*: 'gained a reputation as a city wit, a vagabond, with no fixed eating-place.' For *vague*, meaning 'roving', see note on *Odes* I. xxxv. 9.

I. xv. 60–3   When he needed a meal he would slander friends and foes indiscriminately. *of most*: about most of them.

I. xv. 64   *draught*: ruin, by withdrawal of capital investments (see *OED* draught, *sb.* 35).

I. xv. 67–9   *ubi nequitiae fautoribus et timidis nil aut paulum abstulerat*: 'when he got little or nothing from those who laughed at his wit or were afraid of it.'

I. xv. 70   *harslets*: haslets, roast joints or entrails.

I. xv. 74–6   *scilicet ut ventres lamna candente nepotum diceret urendos, correctus*: 'so that he (reformed, as it were) would declare that gluttons ought to have their bellies branded'. Other editions, including *1756*, read *correctus Bestius. idem* for *correctus. Maenius idem*, favoured by Bond and Rodellius.

I. xv. 84   *banging*, huge (cf. *Sat.* II. ii 73 and note); *bear* (*ursa*) in S.'s text and translation appears to be his own emendation for *vulva* (pig's stomach) in all other editions, including *1756*.

I. xv. 86–7   *nam tuta et parvula laudo, cum res deficiunt, satis inter vilia fortis*, 'I praise the safe and humble life when means are lacking, resolute enough where provisions are stingy'.

I. xvi. 16   *dam'sines*: damsons (*damascenes* in PI, *damsons* in PT). A wide variety of spellings were current in the 18th c.

I. xvi. 19   *Tarentum*: see note on *Epistles* I. vii. 91.

I. xvi. 33   *will* in *1767* must be an error (*omnis . . . Roma*, 'All of us at Rome, PI).

I. xvi. 40–5   'Lest' follows 'fear' (l. 35). H. compares people who are concerned with their reputation for virtue to people who force themselves to eat when ill because they are told they are well. *hands . . . grease*: Romans ate with their fingers.

I. xvi. 62   For *tuo nomine*, 'in your own name'.

I. xvi. 80   *false and feign'd: mendosum et mendacem*. Modern editors prefer *medicandum*, 'in need of a doctor', for *mendacem* (itself an emendation of *mendicandum* in the MSS).

I. xvi. 83   *Conscript seers*: for *consulta patrum*, 'decrees of the Fathers' (PI), i.e. the Senate (see note on *Odes* II. i. 14).

I. xvi. 88   *causes gain*: with lawsuits.

I. xvi. 103   *kite*: *milvius* (*miluus*) is translated 'kite' by Francis too: the word primarily denotes a bird of prey, but it is used also of predatory fish by Pliny and usually rendered here as 'pike' by modern translators.

I. xvi. 107   *But sure . . . sound*: for *sit spes fallendi*, 'Let there be but a hope of deceiving the world' (PI).

I. xvi. 146 ff.   A footnote in *1756* explains this as a reference to Euripides' *Bacchae*, 'in which Bacchus, tho' bound in chains by Pentheus, is introduced accosting him in this resolute manner'.

I. xvii. 1   *of yourself discrete*: for *satis per te tibi consulis* 'you're alive to your own interests' (Rudd, 1987). S. may well mean 'discreet' (i.e. prudent), but the spelling *discrete*, often used in this sense earlier, was not so used in the 18th c. (see *OED*). *1767* is inconsistent, printing *(in)discreet* in *Sat.* II. iii. 247, II. iv. 9, and *Art of Poetry* 829, but *(in)discrete(ly)* in *Odes* III. xxvii, *Sat.* I. iii. 115, I. iv. 119, where '(in)discreet(ly)', is clearly meant. The prominence of *discrete* here however suggests that S. may have used it deliberately to mean something like 'self-reliant' rather than prudent.

I. xvii. 16   *Ferentinum*: a lonely town 45 miles SE of Rome (Rudd, 1987).

I. xvii. 23   A higher throw of the dice ('die'), i.e. better fortune: for *paulo que benignius ipsum te tractare*, 'to treat yourself a little more kindly'.

I. xvii. 25 ff.   *Aristippus*: see note on *Epistles* I. i. 35. The adaptability of his philosophy is contrasted with the stubbornness of *Diogenes* the Cynic.

I. xvii. 30   *If . . . skill'd*: if he had had competence. For *skill* meaning to understand, comprehend, see *OED v. 1*, 4.

I. xvii. 39–40   *scurror ego ipse mihi*: 'I play the fool for my own advantage'.

I. xvii. 63   *awkardness*: an acceptable spelling in the 18th c.

I. xvii. 87   *hic subit et perfert*: 'the other undertakes it and carries it out.'

I. xvii. 106–7   i.e. the second chimes in asking for the gift to be divided between them.

I. xvii. 108–10   See *Fables* I. xiii, *The Fox and the Crow*.

I. xvii. 115–24   See *Fables* I. x, *The Wolf and the Fox*, ll. 1–4. *bite*: trick.

I. xvii. 134   *hoarse neighbourhood* (*vicinia rauca*): i.e. the neighbours shout until they are hoarse.

I. xviii. 1   *Lollius*: the friend addressed in *Epistles* I. ii.

I. xviii. 13   S.'s phrases suggest a well-groomed appearance, rather than the skinhead image H. evokes with *tonsa cute*: 'a close-cropped style of hair' (Rudd, 1987).

I. xviii. 28   For *de lana caprina*, about goat's hair: 'A proverbial expression for making much ado about a trifle' (PT, note). S. broadens the satire in *1767* by reducing the topic to nonsense.

I. xviii. 33   i.e. I'd sooner be dead.

I. xviii. 68   *fencer*: gladiator.

I. xviii. 78 ff.   *Amphion*, a musician, and *Zethus*, a herdsman, were twin sons of Zeus and Antiope. Their quarrel over the relative merits of music and hunting was dramatized by Euripides in *Antiope*.

I. xviii. 87   *Etolian nets*: alluding to the mythical boar-hunt organized by Meleager in Calydon, a town in Aetolia.

I. xviii. 103   *Mars's plain*: Campus Martius, the military exercise ground at Rome.

I. xviii. 106–9   Referring to Augustus' campaigns against the Cantabrians in 26 and 23 BC and recovery of the Roman standards from Parthia (see note on *Epistles* I. xii. 47–50).

I. xviii. 114   *uncooth*: an acceptable spelling in the 18th c.

I. xviii. 116–25   At home on their father's estate, Lollius and his brother re-enact in sham fight the famous battle of Actium.

I. xviii. 139/40   S. omits four lines (H. ll. 72–5) advising Lollius not to get over-interested in lovers (boys or girls) when visiting a potential patron.

I. xviii. 146   *chous'd*: deceived.

I. xviii. 175–6   *modestus occupat obscuri speciem, taciturnus acerbi*: 'the shy man gives an impression of being secretive, the silent of being bad-tempered.'

I. xviii. 185–6   i.e. whether virtue is given by nature or acquired by teaching.

I. xviii. 193–4   *Digentia*: a tributary of the Anio, which supplied water for the hillside village of *Mandela*, near H.'s farm.

I. xviii. 195   *chopt*: chapped (for *rugosus*, shrivelled).

I. xix. 2   *Cratinus*: 5th-c. Athenian playwright. In one of his comedies he jokes about his own drunkenness.

I. xix. 11–12   *laudibus arguitur vini vinosus Homerus*: 'Homer is detected as a wine-drinker, by the praises he bestows on wine' (PI). The footnote quotes *Iliad* vi. 261.

I. xix. 15–16   *Till . . . drink*: nisi potus, 'unless well in liquor' (PI).

I. xix. 16–20   *Forum putealque Libonis mandabo siccis, adimam cantare severis*: 'I shall consign the abstemious to the Forum and Libo's Well, and forbid the stern from singing.' The Forum and Libo's Well were the legal and financial areas of the city.

I. xix. 30 *Timagenes*: a rhetorician favoured by Augustus.

I. xix. 33–4 *Decipit exemplar vitiis imitabile*: 'Models deceive: their faults are easy to copy' (Rudd, 1987).

I. xix. 41–3 See Introduction, p. xxiv.

I. xix. 46–51 The iambics of *Archilochus* (a 7th-c. poet from Paros) provided the model for H.'s *Epodes* (Rudd, 1987). *But not . . . phlegm* (50–1): i.e. H. imitates the rhythm and spirit (*numeros animosque*) but not the matter and words which drove Lycambes ('my brother') to destruction: see note on *Epodes* vi. 13.

I. xix. 55 H. says 'to change his measures and his verse-technique'.

I. xix. 56 *Sappho*: 7th-c. lyric poet of Lesbos. H. adopted a form of stanza, used by her, in many of his odes. *writing like a man* is a polite and over-specific interpretation of H.'s *mascula Sappho*.

I. xix. 57 H. says (in defence of his own practice) that Sappho and Alcaeus made only mild alterations to the metrical form of Archilochus.

I. xix. 58 *Alcaeus*: 7th-c. poet also from Lesbos. H. used the Alcaic stanza in his odes more frequently than any other metre.

I. xix. 61–3 Referring again to Archilochus' ferocious satire against Lycambes and his daughter. *step-father*: father-in-law.

I. xix. 64 *Him*: i.e. Alcaeus.

I. xix. 67 *by . . . FEW (ingenuis oculis)*. In both Latin and English 'ingenuous' is used in its primary sense: of good birth or character (cf. *Odes* I. xxvii. 16).

I. xix. 77 Gifts of cast-off clothing; H. does not try to curry favour like a politician by handing out presents.

I. xix. 80–1 A jibe at poets who seek publicity by persuading *grammatici* (school-teachers) to read their poems to the students.

I. xx. 4 The booksellers' quarter of Rome was near the temples of *Janus* and *Vertumnus*.

I. xx. 26 *for us* in *1767* is nonsense. H. says *aut fugies Uticam*, 'or [you] shall fly to Utica' (PI). Utica was a town in north Africa.

I. xx. 45 *was great*: found favour (*placuisse*).

I. xx. 48–9 *Form'd . . . day*: for *solibus aptum*, 'fit for enduring heat' (PI). *passion*: anger.

I. xx. 53–4 i.e. when Lepidus and Lollius were consuls (21 BC): this is the M. *Lollius* of *Odes* IV. ix (see note on *Odes* IV. ix. 34–44).

I. xx. 55 A lame line, to fill out the couplet: H. says 'I completed'.

II. i was written after the *Carmen Saeculare* of 17 BC to which it apparently refers (236–45: H. 132–8), and probably after Drusus' victories in 15 BC.

II. i. 9–10   *Rome's Founder*: Romulus. *seed of Leda*: Castor and Pollux.

II. i. 19   *The man*: Hercules.

II. i. 24   *but the last*: except by death.

II. i. 39–40   i.e. they refuse to judge other matters by the same rule of reason (*cetera nequaquam simili ratione modoque aestimat*).

II. i. 44   *the NINE*: the Muses.

II. i. 46 n.   See Livy, *Ab Urbe Condita*, 331 ff.

II. i. 54   For *non est quod multa loqamur*: 'there is no reason for multiplying words' (PI).

II. i. 76   *to scoff*: to be an object of contempt (*OED sb. 1, 2*).

II. i. 86–7   Referring to *sorites*, the logical puzzle on the pattern of 'How many grains make a heap?': by starting with a heap of objects, then removing them one by one until only a single object remains, it appears that there is no logical point at which the 'heap' ceases to exist (or comes into being).

II. i. 92–7   The poet *Ennius* (cf. *Odes* IV. viii. 30) reports in his *Annals* that the ghost of Homer came to him in a dream and expounded the Pythagorean doctrine of transmigration, telling him that he now possessed Homer's soul. The line in the footnote appears to be a concoction, perhaps by S., relying on memory. According to Jerome, Lucilius simply referred to Ennius as *Homerus alter* (a second Homer): *Remains of Old Latin*, ed. E. H. Warmington (Loeb Classical Library, 1979), iii. 130 (see Rudd, 1989).

II. i. 98   *Naevius* (fl. 240–199 BC) was author of an epic poem and of tragedies and comedies. *be not read*: S.'s text treats H.'s *in manibus non est* as statement, whereas it is a rhetorical question: 'is Naevius not in our hands?' (i.e. still being read).

II. i. 103–10   *Pacuvius* and *Accius* were tragic poets. *Afranius*, *Menander*, *Plautus*, *Epicharmus*, *Caecilius*, and *Terence* were writers of comedy.

II. i. 110   *conducting well*: i.e. artful contrivance, for *Terentius arte*, 'Terence [excelled] in art'.

II. i. 114   *Livius* Andronicus (*c.*284–204 BC): 'the oldest of the Latin poets, and the first of them who composed a play in form' (PT, note). He wrote tragedies, comedies, and a translation of the *Odyssey*.

II. i. 127 n.   See Cicero, *Brutus* 71.

II. i. 129–30   *cull*: 18th-c. slang term for a man. *Orbilius* taught in Rome from 63 BC.

II. i. 139   *'Tis wrath*: for *Indignor*, 'I am enraged'.

II. i. 146   *Atta* (d. 77 BC) was a writer of *togatae*: comedies in Greek form but with Roman characters.

II. i. 149   i.e. to think that those roles should be disdained by me.

II. i. 150–1   *Esopus* (Aesopus) . . . *Roscius*: celebrated actors in the early 1st c. BC.

II. i. 158–60   The priesthood of the *Salii* (see note on *Odes* IV i. 36) was instituted by *Numa*, second king of Rome: their hymns were notoriously unintelligible.

II. i. 194   *rigid*: serious (*severi*).

II. i. 198   Like all long-standing enemies, the Parthians were regarded as untrustworthy.

II. i. 217   *detriments*: damages (*detrimenta*).

II. i. 220–1   It is the poet, not the pupil as S.'s syntax suggests, who is frugally fed ('He lives on husks and brown bread', PI); *second bread*: bread of inferior quality.

II. i. 222 n.   *cock*, used here sarcastically, was a colloquial term for a bold fighter. The story of H.'s flight from the battlefield comes from the poet himself: see *Odes* II. vii. 10–11.

II. i. 245   Weak: H. says the powers were appeased (*placantur*).

II. i. 252   i.e. fellow-labourers (*socios operum*).

II. i. 253–4   *Tellus*: Earth. *Sylvanus*: spirit of the woods and uncultivated places.

II. i. 256   By *genius* H. means the guardian spirit.

II. i. 258   S.'s addition.

II. i. 260–2   Referring to *Fescennine* verses: ribald songs sung at country festivals (Rudd, 1987).

II. i. 268   *ingenuous houses: honestas domos*, decent homes.

II. i. 285–8   *lines . . . times*: H. refers both to the 'Saturnian measure', a metre used by the earliest Latin poets, and to their subject-matter. *squalled*: 17th-c. spelling of *squalid*.

II. i. 289   *this*: i.e. satire.

II. i. 294   *set by*: esteemed (*OED v.* 91c).

II. i. 307–10   *to . . . sweat*: H. says the opposite, *habere sudoris minimum*, 'to involve least sweat'; his point is that comedy is more difficult to write because audiences are more critical.

II. i. 311   *huncks*: miser.

II. i. 312   *huff*: bluster.

II. i. 313–14   *quantus sit Dorsennus edacibus in parasitis*: 'what a buffoon [Dorsennus] is in his ravenous parasites' (Rudd, 1989). Early scholars took *Dorsennus* (Dossennus: 'Hunchback') for the name of a playwright

(Ainsworth, citing this line, glosses *Dossennus* as 'A comic poet'). He is now identified as a character in the old rustic farces; ll. 316–18 are therefore criticizing Plautus.

II. i. 339–40   The visual element, according to Aristotle, was superficial; hence 'uncertain eyes' as opposed to 'judicious ears' (Rudd).

II. i. 347–8   i.e. a picture of Corinth held aloft on a banner: a plausible interpretation of H.'s vague *portata captiva Corinthus*. Corinth was captured in 146 BC.

II. i. 349–50   *Democritus* (see note on *Epistles* I. xii. 21) was called the laughing philosopher, in contrast to Heraclitus, because he ridiculed rather than lamented the follies of humankind.

II. i. 384   i.e. those who aim for a reputation as poets, writing for private reading rather than public performance.

II. i. 386–7   See note on *Epistles* I. iii. 32.

II. i. 390   *(to mar . . . comrades)*: H.'s parenthesis refers mockingly to himself: lit. 'to hack my own vines', a proverbial saying for self-injury. PI: '(that I may kick down my own pail first)', with a footnote giving the literal translation.

II. i. 403–4   *divine* (for *fingere*): either meaning 'devise, conceive' (*OED* 5, archaic even in the 18th c.) or perhaps an error for *design*. *cite*: summon.

II. i. 413–14   *Choerilus*: an epic poet in the train of Alexander the Great ('the Macedonian youth').

II. i. 416   Referring to a famous gold piece coined by Philip II, Alexander's father.

II. i. 425   The works of the famous 4th-c. painter *Apelles* included a portrait of Alexander (Rudd, 1987).

II. i. 427   *Lysippus*: a renowned sculptor of the 4th c. BC.

II. i. 432   The inhabitants of *Boeotia*, a lowland district of Greece, were proverbially dull, supposedly as a result of its damp climate.

II. i. 434   *Varius*: see note on *Sat.* I. v. 73.

II. i. 449   A sign of peace: see note on *Odes* IV. xiv [xv]. 9.

II. i. 451   See note on *Epistles* I. xii. 47–50.

II. i. 456   *grov'lers*: poets writing in a low style.

II. i. 465–6   *wrote* may be a misprint for *wrought*, but in either case S.'s rendering of *quod probat et veneratur* ('that which he [the reader] approves and venerates', PI) is misleading.

II. i. 470   *in a die*: i.e. on an engraved stamp (for impressing on a coin or medal). H. refers to an image in wax.

II. i. 475   For *capsa porrectus aperta* ('stretched out in an open box'). Paper from unsold books was used in the 18th c. to line trunks. Some editions prefer the reading *operta* (closed): Rudd (1989) argues that H. is alluding to a coffin.

II. ii. 1   This epistle was written in 19–18 BC. Julius *Florus*: the friend addressed in *Epistles* I. iii. *Nero*: T. Claudius Nero, stepson of Augustus.

II. ii. 26   *errant* (errand): 'loitered on an errant' (PI).

II. ii. 27–8   *thro' fear . . . hangs*: for *in scalis latuit metuens pendentis habenae*. Many translators prefer to take *in scalis latuit* as referring to the boy (see Rudd, 1989): 'and hid himself under the stairs for fear of the whip hanging [on the wall].'

II. ii. 31–2   H. means that since the seller declared the boy's defect, the buyer will have no come-back (Rudd). S. misses the point.

II. ii. 51   *Lucullus*: see note on *Epistles* I. vi. 75.

II. ii. 56   *bangs*: trounces (*OED* 5).

II. ii. 62   20,000 sesterces, according to H. and PI.

II. ii. 73   *clown*: yokel (*rusticus*).

II. ii. 79–80   Referring to the beginning of the *Iliad*.

II. ii. 90–6   H. served as a tribune in Brutus' army against Octavian; after the defeat of Brutus' forces at *Philippi* (42 BC) he suffered the penalty (was 'amerc'd') of having his land confiscated.

II. ii. 115   *Bion*: an Athenian philosopher (*c*.325–*c*.255 BC), renowned for his biting satire. *invet'rate*: virulent (*OED* 3).

II. ii. 138   *timber-tug* (for *ingens machina*, huge machine): a Kentish term for a special kind of timber-waggon (*OED* timber, *sb. 1*, 10).

II. ii. 152–3   For *contracta sequi vestigia vatum*, 'trace the difficult footsteps of the poets' (PT). This is a textual crux: *contracta* (compressed, restricted) is a reading of the MSS, but in *1756* S. (like Francis) adopted the emendation *cunctata* (delayed). Modern editors read *contracta*, taking it as an allusion to the 'narrow path' recommended to poets by Callimachus (Rudd).

II. ii. 161–2   *in . . . city-throng*: i.e. here in Rome, contrasted with Athens.

II. ii. 165   *A dab in tropes*: a skilled orator (*rhetor*).

II. ii. 169   i.e. one was a Gracchus (the name of a famous orator) to the other, the other a Mucius (famous lawyer) to him.

II. ii. 170   *wrath*: frenzy (*furor*).

II. ii. 177   *vacant shelves*: referring to the library (see note on *Epistles* I. iii. 32). It was divided into separate sections for Greek and Latin books; the Roman shelves still have *vacuam Romanis vatibus*, 'spaces ready for the bards of Rome' (Rudd, 1987).

II. ii. 180–1   i.e. discover how we contrive to win applause.

II. ii. 183   *Samnite blades*: gladiators, whose battles were prolonged because of the heavy armour they wore.

II. ii. 184–7   *Alceus* (Alcaeus): see note on *Epistles* I. xix. 58. *Callim'chus* (Callimachus): famous Alexandrian poet of the 3rd c. BC. *if . . . great*: 'if he seems to have any further demand, he becomes Mimnermus, and thrives by that wished-for name' (PI). For *Mimnermus* see note on *Epistles* I. vi. 124.

II. ii. 193   *indispos'd*: mentally deranged (i.e. writing poetry).

II. ii. 212.   *et versentur adhuc intra penetralia Vestae*: 'and as yet remain in the sanctuary of Vesta' (PI). The general sense appears to be that the rejected words live on, either in the poet's mind or in popular usage, but the allusion to Vesta has never been satisfactorily explained. S. refers here to the flame kept perpetually burning in the temple of Vesta, goddess of the blazing hearth, but in *1756* he had a different interpretation: 'The *Penetralia Vestae* were only to be enter'd by the high priest: in allusion to which Horace humorously makes the poet's closet his *sancta sanctorum*' (PT, note).

II. ii. 214   As Rudd points out, *revive*, which fits the sense exactly, could easily have been misread as *receive* by the printer.

II. ii. 216–17   *which . . . just*: for *quae priscis memorata Catonibus atque Cethegis*, 'which were mentioned by the old Cato's and Cethegus's' (PI). For omission of the proper names, see note on *AP* 86–90.

II. ii. 223   *redundant*: copious, overflowing.

II. ii. 228–32   i.e. like an actor he will make dancing appear fun, in spite of the effort of alternating between the agility of a satyr and the clumsiness of a Cyclops.

II. ii. 236   i.e. rather than be wise and discontented with my work (*quam sapere et ringi*).

II. ii. 246   *carest*: caressed.

II. ii. 252   S. leaves untranslated—presumably by oversight—the line *expulit elleboro morbum bilemque meraco* (H. 137), 'he expelled the disease and spleen with pure hellebore' (PI).

II. ii. 262   *shell*: lyre (see note on *Odes* I. xxxii. 13). *Latian*: of Latium, i.e. Latin.

II. ii. 277   *conjuror*: used ironically in 17th–18th cc. of a claimant to wisdom, a smart alec (see *OED* 3).

II. ii. 289–319 (H. 158–74)   For an interpretation of H.'s passage, with its various legal technicalities, see Rudd, 1989.

II. ii. 295–6   *hind*: bailiff (*vilicus*). Although he does the work, he recognizes as master the person who receives the produce.

II. ii. 312   *forefend*: prevent.

II. ii. 321–2   *heres heredem alterius velut unda supervenit undam*: 'one heir comes upon another, like wave upon wave' (PI).

II. ii. 343   *cheques*: checks, marks out like a chess-board (*OED* check, *v. 2*).

II. ii. 349   'No more than what I have given.'

II. ii. 353   *debauchee*: spendthrift.

II. ii. 355   *oeconomists*: thrifty people.

II. ii. 370   *in my mouth*: i.e. 'in my face'.

II. ii. 374–5   *extremi primorum, extremis usque priores*: 'behind the leaders, but always ahead of the last.'

II. ii. 383   *Thessalian*: cf. *Epodes* v. 75.

Art of Poetry. The title *Ars Poetica* by which this work is generally known was assigned to it by Quintilian in the 1st c. AD but it is in epistolary form and its original title, also commonly used, was probably *Epistula ad Pisones*. In manuscripts it was placed second in order, after the *Odes*, or fourth, after the *Carmen Saeculare*. Its date is controversial, depending on which of the numerous members of the *Piso* family are thought to be addressed, but it is generally assumed to be Horace's last work (see Rudd, 1989).

Smart translates this poem with more than his usual freedom; only the more conspicuous deviations from the literal meaning of the original have been noted.

37–8   *si fractis enatat exspes navibus, aere dato qui pingitur*, 'if what you are paid to paint is a sailor swimming in despair from a shipwreck'.

43–4   (*I . . . express*): *pater et iuvenes patre digni*, 'O father! and youths worthy such a father!' (PI). *express* seems to be used adjectivally, meaning 'exactly like', as in Milton, *PL* vii. 527–8: 'Created thee, in the image of God / Express'.

49   *correct*: for *levia*, smooth.

53   *run . . . aground*: S. gets carried away by the vehicle of the metaphor, at the expense of the tenor. *serpit humi* means 'creeps along the ground' (PI), i.e. writes prosaically.

55 n.   Cf. preface, 313 ff. S.'s theory is untenable because Horace died before Ovid's *Metamorphoses* was written.

66–7   *quam naso vivere pravo, spectandum nigris oculis nigroque capillo*: 'than to live with a crooked nose, though worth looking at for my black hair and eyes.'

73   The *1767* reading *clean* is not impossible but was unlikely to have been S.'s word here. H.'s *lucidus ordo* is translated as 'clear connection' in PI.

85–6   *dixeris egregie, notum si callida verbum reddiderit iunctura novum*: 'You will express yourself admirably well, if a clever connection should impress an air of novelty to a common word' (PI). This appears to be one of the sources of S.'s concept of *Impression* (see preface, 94 ff.). By *spell* S. presumably means some kind of quasi-magic power.

87–91   *It is a point . . . Unknown* paraphrases H. 48–51: *si forte necesse est . . . continget,* 'If novel terms are demanded to introduce obscure material, then you will have the chance to invent words which the apron-wearing Cethegi never heard' (Rudd). As in *Epistles* II. ii. 216–17, S. leaves out the reference to the Cethegi, presumably in accord with his policy of making the text as self-explanatory as possible.

96–104   i.e. why should modern authors like *Virgil* and *Varius*, or H. himself, be denied the licence granted to older writers like *Caecilius, Plautus, Cato,* and *Ennius*? For these writers, cf. *Epistles* II. i. 92 ff. and II. ii. 218.

106   *that cleanly chimes*: Smart's interpolation.

141   *lover's whines*: for *querimonia*, laments ('plaintive ditties', PI), but the reference in H. 75–6 is to sepulchral elegies and dedicatory epigrams.

145   *so . . . style*: for *exiguos elegos*, little elegiacs (probably referring to elegiac metre, rather than the form).

148–50   *Archilochus*: cf. *Epistles* I. xix. 61–3. *sock . . . buskin*: worn by actors on the Roman stage (cf. *Sat.* I. v. 21). The sock was worn for comedy, the buskin for tragedy.

162–3   *to combine . . . design: descriptas servare vices operumque colores*, i.e. to observe the styles and forms appropriate to different genres.

172   *Thyestean feast*: see note on *Epodes* v. 138.

177   *Chremes*: see note on *Epodes* i. 54.

180–3   i.e. to make the sufferings of Peleus and Telephus affect the audience, the writer has to lay aside ranting and bombastic language. *Peleus,* father of Achilles, underwent exile and other ordeals in his youth. For *Telephus*, see note on *Epodes* xv [xvii]. 11–26.

209   *blaze*: proclaim.

215   *Davus*: a slave (*Davus* is an early emendation: modern editions usually prefer *divus*, a god); *errant knight*: for *heros*.

234   *Ino* and her husband Athamas were driven mad by Juno; Athamas killed one of her sons and she leapt into the sea with the other.

235   *Ixion*: see note on *Odes* III. xi. 21.

236   *Io*, transformed into a heifer by her lover Jupiter, was pursued by a gadfly sent by Juno, and forced into long wanderings.

237   *Orestes*: see note on *Sat.* II. iii. 53–70.

261   *old . . . ROUNDS*: for *scriptor cyclicus*, one of the post-Homeric epic poets who treated in order the cycle of myths from the beginning of the world to the end of the heroic age.

266–7   cf. *Fables* IV. xviii, *The Mountain in Labour*. *laid*: brought to bed (*OED* lay *v. 1*, 2).

270–3   The opening of the *Odyssey*, paraphrased.

279–80   All names from the *Odyssey*.

281–4   i.e. Homer does not make his story tedious by starting with all the past history.

308   *contracts*: incurs.

315–16   *utilium tardus provisor, prodigus aeris*, 'a slow provider of things needful, prodigal of money' (PI).

331   *querelous*: a rare but accepted spelling, from late L. *querelosus* (*OED*).

352   *within*: i.e. behind the scenes.

357   *Atreus*: see note on *Epodes* v. 138.

359–60   For the transformation of *Cadmus*, king of Thebes, into a serpent, see Ovid, *Met.* iv. 563 ff. *Progne* (Procne) was changed into a swallow after taking revenge on her husband Tereus for raping and mutilating her sister Philomela.

364–5   *put . . . stock*: i.e. become part of the repertory. *nor . . . there*: H. is referring to the use of a *deus ex machina*.

368   *strain*: for *laboret*, 'be officious' (PI). In Greek tragedy the number of speaking characters on stage at once was restricted to three.

375   *the wroth*: the angry (people).

380   *ports*: gates (already declining in this sense in 18th-c. English usage, but it survived into the 20th c. in Scotland).

397   *god of taste*: for *Genius*, guardian spirit. 'By offering wine and flowers to his Genius, a man indicated that he was enjoying himself' (Rudd, 1989): cf. *Epistles* II. i. 255–6. S. however interprets it as 'the Genius of the place' (PI), equating it with public standards of 'taste'. *Taste* in the 18th c. had a much stronger sense than in modern usage: meaning not only 'relish', but the faculty of critical and aesthetic judgement (*OED sb. 1*, 8).

424–5   *fawns*: i.e. satyrs. l. 424 refers to the 'bard': *incolumi gravitate iocum temptavit*, '[the poet] made an experiment to jest with gravity preserved' (PI).

444   *as satirist*: for *Satyrorum scriptor*, 'writer of satyr-plays'. S. makes the standard 18th-c. mistake of confusing these with *saturae*, satires.

449–51   *Davus, Pythias* (a slave-girl), and the *old hunks* (miser: for H.'s *Simo*) were all stock characters from comedy.

452–3   *Liber's guardian*: Silenus, guardian of Dionysus, a stock figure in satyric drama.

461   H.'s *series iuncturaque*, 'linkage and combination' refers to style, not structural arrangement as S.'s phrase suggests.

481   *primus ad extremum similis sibi*: 'like unto itself from first to last' (PI), i.e. the same throughout.

488–9   *this*: i.e. the iambic foot. S. is being heavily sarcastic, in an attempt to imitate H.'s ironical *in Acci nobilibus trimetris* (in Accius' noble trimeters). *Accius* was renowned for his tragedies.

497   For *immodulata poemata*: unmusical pieces.

500–7   H. rejects both excessive freedom and excessive caution.

517   i.e. are capable of discerning the true rhythm (*legitimumque sonum digitis callemus et aure*).

523   *Eschylus*: the spelling of *Aeschylus* used in PI. *Escalus* is more likely to be a misprint than S.'s mistake.

524   *decent pall*: i.e. lordly robe (*pallaeque honestae*).

526   *Learnt*: taught (still an acceptable usage in the 18th c.).

531   *pow'r*: i.e. the political authorities.

535   *forbore*: i.e refused to speak (*obticuit*). Thus the chorus was no longer a feature of later comedy.

545   *Disgust*: have an aversion to.

550–1   The philosopher *Democritus* (cf. *Epistles* II. i. 349) wrote in his book *On poetry* of the value to the poet of inspiration, but he did not disparage craftsmanship (see Rudd, 1989, on (H) ll. 296–7).

561   *the barber's*: *tonsori Licino*, 'A very wealthy barber, who was afterwards made a senator by Augustus for his hatred to Pompey' (note to PI, copied almost verbatim from Francis).

562–3   *O ego laevus, qui purgo bilem sub verni temporis horam*: 'O unlucky me! who purge my bile at the time of the vernal season' (PI). By curing his melancholy with medicine he deprives himself of the insanity that befits a true poet, according to popular belief.

588–9   Such knowledge enables the playwright to give each character its proper attributes.

590   *learned copyist*: for *doctum imitatorem*, meaning one who is skilled in representing life.

594–5 (H. 319)   *interdum speciosa locis morataque recte*: usually translated 'at times a play marked by attractive passages and properly drawn characters', but *locis* are taken by some as equivalent to *sententiis*, moral reflections

(*Horace: Satires, Epistles and Ars Poetica*, ed. H. R. Fairclough, Loeb Classical Library (1978) p. 476 n.).

599   *quam versus inopes rerum nugaeque canores*, 'than verses void of matter, and harmonious trifles' (Pl).

602–3   i.e. the Greeks (in contrast to the Romans) were interested only in fame.

611–15   Can fine poetry, worthy of being preserved with cedar-oil and kept on cypress shelves, be expected from such mercenary wretches (*elves*)? *this rust . . . ingrim'd* is excessively compressed. Pl spells out S.'s meaning: 'when once the rust and avarice of circumstances has inured their minds to such things as these, can we expect' etc.

626–7   'Nor let the fable require to be believed in everything it chooses' (Pl). *Exaction* seems to mean 'excessive efforts'.

644–7   The metaphor refers to a lyre. *grave . . . acute*: flats and sharps.

649   *the white*: the target (used in the 18th c. for the target itself, not as in later use the circular white band on it). Cf. 'Swift as an arrow to the *White*' in *Ode to Admiral Sir George Pocock*, l. 2 (*PW* iv. 339).

660   *Choerilus*: 'A stupid poet censured by Aristotle' (PT, note); cf. *Epistles* II. i. 413–16.

679   *mean*: average, moderate.

682–3   *Messala . . . Aulus*: distinguished orators in Augustan Rome. *Nor . . . by*: i.e. nor can be compared with Aulus (*nec sit quantum . . . Aulus*, 'does not know as much as Aulus').

686   *rubric post: concessere columnae*, a post with advertisements, a billboard (Rudd, 1989). The Latin phrase is often translated metonymically as 'booksellers' or 'bookshops', but S. prefers to reproduce it literally, with all its bathos.

690–1   *essence* means perfume, whereas poppy-seeds coated with honey were a dessert.

698   *troque: trochi*, a hoop. The only citations in *OED* are from Francis's Horace, including his version of the same line (H. 380): 'The bounding ball, round quoit, or whirling troque.'

701   i.e. all our fools set out to become poets.

704   *census equestrem summam nummorum*: taxed at the fortune of a knight.

710   *Metius* (Maecius): S. Maecius Tarpa, a theatre critic (cf. *Sat.* I. x. 71).

718–20   *from thence . . . fell*: i.e. from Orpheus' influence over human brutality came the fable of his power to tame wild beasts with his music. *lions fell*: 'fierce lions' (Pl).

735–6   *Maeonides*: Homer. *Tyrtaeus*, a 7th-c. Spartan poet, wrote marching songs and elegies.

740–1   Alluding to the poets Simonides, Pindar, and Bacchylides who sought royal patronage in Sicily: *Pieria* in Thessaly was a haunt of the Muses.

759   Referring to the Pythian games held at Delphi in honour of Apollo: they included musical contests.

770   *assentatious band*: crowd of flatterers (*assentatores*). The earliest recorded use of the adjective in *OED* is dated 1860, but the noun *assentation* was in use from the 16th c.

777   *For making*: i.e. if you make.

785–9   As hired mourners make a greater show of sorrow than the genuine grievers, so a scoffer (*derisor*) shows more emotion than the real admirer.

792   i.e. if they will make reliable friends.

794   See *Fables* I. xiii, *The Fox and the Crow*.

795   *Quintilius*: Quintilius Varus, friend of Horace and Virgil (see note on *Odes* I. xxiv).

812   *cross*: draw the pen across.

818   *Aristarchus*: Alexandrian scholar of the 2nd c. BC, proverbial for his severity as a critic.

826   *King's evil*: scrofula.

845   *Empedocles*: Sicilian philosopher-poet of the 5th c. BC.

856   *et ponet famosae mortis amorem*: 'and lay aside his desire for a notable death.' S., unlike most translators, chooses to take *famosae* in its unfavourable sense ('infamous death', PI).

860   *stale*: urinate.

861–2   *an triste bidental moverit incestus*: 'or sacrilegiously disturbed an ill-fated bidental.' The *bidental* was a place struck by lightning and therefore fenced off and consecrated.

864   *grates*: the bars of its cage.

INDEX OF PROPER NAMES

This index includes the more important names mentioned in the text. References to gods and goddesses are omitted, except when used in place-names. Page numbers in square brackets indicate that the subject is referred to but not named. Numbers in parentheses refer to Smart's preface.

HENRY MARTYN
CONFESSOR
OF THE FAITH

By

CONSTANCE E. PADWICK

εἰς τί ἡ ἀπώλεια αὕτη γέγονεν;
Ὁ δὲ Ἰησοῦς εἶπεν,
καλὸν ἔργον εἰργάσατο ἐν ἐμοί.

LONDON
STUDENT CHRISTIAN MOVEMENT
32 RUSSELL SQUARE, W.C.1
1923

First Edition, October 1922
Second Edition, July 1923

*Made and Printed in Great Britain
by Turnbull & Spears, Edinburgh*

EDITORIAL NOTE

THIS volume is the first of a uniform series of new missionary biographies.

The series makes no pretence of adding new facts to those already known. The aim rather is to give to the world of to-day a fresh interpretation and a richer understanding of the life and work of great missionaries.

A group of unusually able writers are collaborating, and three volumes will be issued each year.

The enterprise is being undertaken by the United Council for Missionary Education, for whom the series is published by the Student Christian Movement.

K. M.
A. E. C.

U.C.M.E.
2 EATON GATE,
S.W.1

TO

MY BELOVED

FATHER AND MOTHER

AUTHOR'S PREFACE

WHEN Henry Martyn's journals reached England after his death, Charles Simeon, Mrs Thomason and John Sargent sat closeted together for three mornings of six or seven hours each, reading those travelled pages. In that reading they discovered their friend as sometimes, a monk being dead, his brothers find a hair shirt and a scourge of which they had not guessed. For Martyn's friends knew a man who played with children and with little dogs ; and a friend who bubbled over with welcoming joy ; and a scholar of luminous, beauty-loving mind ; and an adventurer who flung himself unquailing into Paynim camps ; and a saint whose face sometimes abashed them by its shining. But now they were admitted into the confessional, and they saw laid bare before the heavenly Surgeon all the wounds and festering sores of a turbulent soul. They saw the Surgeon's knife and the quivering wince of the penitent spirit ; and they caught the ineffable glance of confidence that passed from time to time between the two. "In every disease of the soul," said their friend, "let me charge myself with the blame and Christ with the cure of it, so shall I be humbled and Christ glorified."

His journal of self-examination before God is the first and greatest source of our knowledge of Martyn, and this book about him, like the rest, is built chiefly on the study of it.

9

But there is danger from the use of such a source, that we know our Martyn chiefly as the great penitent. The first friends, to whom the journal came as a surprise, had in mind the good hours when someone showed Martyn a copy of verses or a new Arabic grammar, when he caught the twinkle in Corrie's eye at Sabat's bombast or the tricks of the Cawnpore school-children, or when the jasmine smelt sweet in the sunset and he drove Mrs Sherwood a devious course in his gig, absorbed in urging upon her the joys of the study of Hebrew. But we who never saw him romp with a child may be misled by meeting him most intimately in hours of penitence. Sargent, his first biographer,[1] " perhaps his dearest friend " and like himself a saint, knew the man so well and all his friends, and their manner of life, that he could not suppose description necessary. Simeon and Wilberforce might yet be met in the street, letters from Corrie and Thomason might come by any mail. It was not for Sargent, with his supreme delicacy, to draw the portraits of the men who might ride to visit him in his rectory under the Downs. Therefore he painted the spiritual story of his friend with the barest earthly background, as in that brief biography which says that " Enoch walked with God."

Yet as the generations pass and the scenes grow dim, we could wish that Sargent had gone down to Cornwall to seek out some old serving-maid of good John Martyn, who could tell us about Laura and Henry and Sally and call to mind the ways of the plain little boy with warts on his fingers. And had he but once described to us how Henry looked up when a friend broke in upon him in his college rooms !

[1] *Henry Martyn*, by John Sargent, 1816, and numerous later editions.

For when the second great biography of Henry Martyn was published in 1892 [1] all who had known the man were gone, and the modest family life in Cornwall had left very little trace on the memory of the neighbourhood. Yet under such disadvantages Dr George Smith, who brought to his book a knowledge of India which Sargent could not claim, put into his task a wealth of research which must make it always the standard reference book on Martyn.

There is nothing new in the present little book. The Church has held most of the records for the greater part of a century : Sargent's "Life" ; the great Journal ; [2] then, as Martyn's generation died, the sidelights from a host of biographies and memoirs of the day ; the Diary of Lydia Grenfell ; [3] stray letters and magazine articles published from time to time ; and at last Dr Smith's great biography in 1892. It is a mass of material, yet with it all there is danger of forgetting a life which is one of the treasures of our spiritual heritage.

For Sargent's book in the religious language of 1816 is almost strange to the children of another century ; and Dr Smith's generous copiousness makes his too costly for those of us who count our pence. We shall always turn gratefully to him in the library ; he cannot be superseded : but for those who are poor and busy he may, nay probably he *must*, be supplemented, as the Church in each generation looks with fresh eyes on the stores of her spiritual

---

[1] *Henry Martyn, Saint and Scholar*, by George Smith, LL.D.

[2] Edited by Bishop Samuel Wilberforce when Rector of Brighstone, Isle of Wight, 1839.

[3] Deposited in the Royal Cornish Institute, Truro. Extracts from it were published by a grand-nephew in 1890.

heritage, and catches the glint of fresh colours in the " variegated " grace of God.

This is not a new book then, but a re-reading of old records, and that not unaided but with the good help of kind people in Cornwall, Cambridge and London too numerous to mention by name, but who have given generous and ready help in regard to anything and everything in which ignorance or carelessness stood in need.   They know that they have my gratitude.

Martyn has never been and never will be the hero of the multitude, but each generation holds some who are his spiritual kindred.   Across the lapse of years and blurred by the clumsy transmission of biographers, these will still catch with understanding ears the response of his spirit to the call of Christ.

C. E. P.

July 1922

CONTENTS

TABLE OF DATES

1803   War declared against Napoleon, May
       Martyn ordained at Ely, October

1805   Wellesley recalled and Cornwallis appointed to India
       Death of Cornwallis
       Sir George Barlow temporary Governor-General
       Martyn sailed for India as Chaplain to the East India Company,
          July 16th
       Battle of Trafalgar, October

1806   *Martyn at the Capture of the Cape of Good Hope, January*
       Death of Pitt, January
       Martyn landed in Calcutta, May
       Martyn proceeded to Dinapore, October

1807   Lord Minto Governor-General of India
       Martyn began the Hindustani New Testament

1809   *Martyn transferred to Cawnpore, April*

1810   The Prince of Wales appointed Regent for George III
       Complete Hindustani New Testament finished for press
       Martyn left Cawnpore with Persian and Arabic versions of the
          New Testament, October

1811   *Martyn reached Shiraz in Persia, June*

1812   *Martyn set out from Shiraz, May, and died at Tokat, Asia*
       Minor, October 16th

1815   *Martyn's Persian New Testament published in St Petersburg*

1816   *Martyn's Persian New Testament, and the Arabic New Testa-*
       ment made by Sabat under his supervision, published in
       Calcutta

CHAPTER I

CALCUTTA OF THE NABOBS

NABOB, noun substantive. [Nobobb, a nobleman, "in the language of the Mogul's Kingdom which hath mixt with it much of the Persian," Sir T. Herbert. Travels, p. 99.] The title of an Indian prince ; sometimes applied to Europeans who have acquired great riches in the East Indies. — *Johnson's English Dictionary* (Ed. 1827).

The style we prefer is the humdrum.—*Traditional answer of Directors of East India Company to an official who asked for guidance in writing despatches.*

WORDS have their day, and the word "nabob" has all but passed out of currency with the passing from English life of the rather pitiable person for whom it stood. But in the last decades of the eighteenth century no better villain could be desired for stage or story than "a rich Nabob" returned from Bengal. Macaulay, who with his sisters burrowed much among the three-volume novels of the eighteenth century, writing in 1840 said,[1] " If any of our readers will take the trouble to search in the dusty recesses of circulating libraries for some novel published sixty years ago, the chance is that the villain or sub-villain of the story will prove to be a savage old Nabob, with an immense fortune, a tawny complexion, a bad liver and a worse heart." All but an alien on his native soil, this villain added

[1] In the *Essay on Clive.*

B
17

to his other crimes, real or imagined, the crime of differing from his caste. "For your Nabobs, they are but a kind of outlandish creatures that won't pass current with us."[1] What more could comedy or melodrama want ?

Yet the nabob-to-be began life much like other small boys of the day, perhaps as one of Squire Roger's younger sons, for whom were neither family acres nor a family living, or maybe as a son of the rectory, where Parson Brown had word one day from an uncle in Leadenhall Street that he had bespoken a writership in the East India Company for " poor Charlotte's boy." At sixteen such a boy spent his last morning rabbiting with his brother and the dogs in the churchyard spinney, while his mother sobbed her heart out over piles of lavender-scented linen. The coach bore away a ruddy English lad with a smattering of the classics and a capacity for honest affection. Forty years later the countryside would know him again as "the rich Nabob " who called for curricles with the airs of a prince, and showed a pitiable disregard for the cost of living and the laws of fox-hunting. "Why wherever any of them settles, it raises the price of provisions for thirty miles round," cries the Mayor in Foote's comedy quoted above ; while Lady Oldham explains to the audience the family embarrassment when " preceded by all the pomp of Asia, Sir Matthew Mite, from the Indies, came thundering amongst us ; and, profusely scattering the spoils of ruined provinces, corrupted the virtue and alienated the feelings of all the old friends of the family."

The process to which the nabob-to-be was sub-

[1] Foote, *The Nabob*, acted at Theatre Royal, Haymarket, 1778.

mitted from the moment when the East Indiaman left Tilbury on her voyage of seven or more months is little enough pictured by us now.

" Such things as I should not want till my arrival in India were made very large, the Captain saying I should grow very much during the passage," one of those young " writers " tells us.[1]

We are forgetful of the completeness of exile in those days of long, slow travel, when often enough it took eighteen months to receive the reply to a letter sent home. We hardly realize the gradual wearing down of standards as home memories grew faint and the physical and moral climate did their enervating work. We are apt to see the India of the Company through the stories of men like Clive, Warren Hastings, or Wellesley the imperious. Such as these could not but be chief actors on any stage. They were men of vivid, restless genius, and of political imagination, in whose actions, good or bad, we find something of " the grand style." For men of such gifts life is not dull, and through their eyes we see romance.

But for the boy of ordinary gifts life in " the East Indies " was often a tedious affair. " The waste of spirits in this cursed country is a disease unconquerable, a misery unutterable," wrote Francis, the archfoe of Warren Hastings. At the age when his brother entered the University our boy was cast upon a Calcutta that had only one carriage road, the dusty " Course," and one small theatre, built by subscription and managed by amateur actors, who in their zeal for the drama were apt to undertake parts beyond their power, with the result that

[1] *Travels in India a Hundred Years Ago*, Thomas Twining, 1893.

" many went to see a tragedy for the express purpose
of enjoying a laugh." [1] He found indeed a little
coterie of English hostesses who received every
evening, and beyond a doubt were kind to striplings
fresh from home. But the balls of Calcutta provided no blushing English maidens for the boy to
adore or play with. Ladies he found there of
strange descent and stranger history, and Hicky's
Bengal Gazette, the first English newspaper in India
(published Calcutta, 1780), shows plainly enough how
the little, bored society looked for the enlivenment
of their hard, hot lives to the relish of betting and
unsavoury scandal. " I don't think the greatest sap
at Eton can lead a duller life than this " Lord
Cornwallis wrote to his schoolboy son, during his
first governor-generalship (1786-1795). And our
nabob-to-be soon learnt to echo the sentiments of
that industrious and high-minded chief, and to seek
distraction in arrack punch and heavy dinners or in
stables for which his salary during his first five years
as an " apprentice " was inadequate. But " a
Company's servant," as a contemporary letter tells
us, " will always find numbers ready to support his
extravagance ; and it is not uncommon to see
writers within a few months after their arrival
dashing away on the Course four-in-hand." [2]

The boy's intercourse with the people of that
eastern world, in which his station was a tiny island
of European life, would seem to have been of the
slightest. Unless he aimed ambitiously at diplomatic tasks—when he studied Persian, the language
of eastern court etiquette—he did not take seriously

---

[1] Mrs Eliza Fay, *Original Letters from India*, p. 279.
[2] *Ibid.*   Letter written on 29th August 1780.

the learning of any oriental language. And when he did take lessons, his teacher was regarded by this young lord of creation as only another servant of a rather superior grade, " permitted by many of the more liberal students to enter the apartments without taking off his shoes ; an omission for which the other servants would be severely punished." [1] Throughout his long years of exile the Company's English servant may never have experienced the intellectual and spiritual adventure of friendship with an eastern gentleman. When even Sir William Jones, who reached European fame as an orientalist, was yet " quite unintelligible in Calcutta to any native in any eastern tongue," it is not surprising that our more ordinary boy never reached converse with the more thoughtful minds of India. " Portuguese was the ordinary medium of communication between the Europeans and their domestics. . . . Even in Calcutta Portuguese was more commonly used by the servants of the Company and the settlers than the language of the country. . . . Down to so late a period as 1828, the governor of Serampore,[2] a Norwegian, received the daily report of his little garrison of thirty sepoys from the native commandant, a native of Oude, in Portuguese." [3]

The ordinary boy's intercourse with the people of India was limited to business relationships in which he depended much on the clumsy aid of the interpreter, and to his dealings, some of them, alas, deplorable, with what seemed to him at first a vast

---

[1] D'Oyley, *The European in India*, 1813.

[2] Serampore was a Danish settlement on the Hooghly sixteen miles above Calcutta.

[3] Marshman, *History of the Serampore Mission*, pp. 21, 22.

and wondrous docile army of servants round his new home—a cringing and salaaming population whose servility tempted him to think them made for his good pleasure. The charge sheet of the Calcutta superintendent of police in 1778 contains the following among similar items :

" 129.   A slave girl of Mr Anderson, Piggy, having run away from her master and being apprehended by the Chowkedar—ordered her five rattans and to be sent to her master."

So late as 1800 Lord Wellesley, his imagination aflame with the vision of his ideal administrator, was pulled up short by what he knew of the down-ward, sensuous pull of a servile population. Of English boys sent to up-country stations he wrote in unvarnished words that "sloth, indolence, low debauchery, and vulgarity are too apt to grow on those young men who have been sent at an early age into the interior part of the country and have laid the foundations of their life and manners among the coarse vices and indulgences of those countries."

John Clark Marshman, who knew his Calcutta as few men knew it, tells the same tale :

The number of English ladies in the country was lamentably small. . . . In the days of Warren Hastings (Governor 1772-85) the arrival of a spinster from England was an event, and it was inaugurated by a succession of balls. The great bulk of the Europeans both in and out of the service, lived un-married with native females, and their leisure was spent in the most debasing associations. The young civilian was told that one of his first duties was to "stock a zenana."

William Macintosh, a political journalist, who

sheltered his possibly libellous attacks on the friends of Warren Hastings under the transparent veil of initials and dashes, published in 1782 an account [1] of " The Manner in which the Day is commonly spent by an Englishman in Bengal." Political opponents criticizing his book said that he made an unfair use, in writing the sketch, of the hospitality of a plump, good-natured soul who gave him the freedom of his Calcutta house. They do not call in question the truthfulness of the picture, though they would have us remember that there were other more energetic households, and that as a general rule " the young gentlemen, as soon after their arrival as they can, muster money to buy a horse, ride a little before daybreak until eight o'clock, then breakfast and go directly to the public offices." [2] Macintosh's description must be read with his own spelling :

About the hour of seven in the morning, his durvan (porter or door-keeper) opens the gate, and the viranda (gallery) is free to his circars, peons (footmen), har-carrahs (messengers or spies), chubdars (a kind of constable), houccabadars and consumas (or steward and butler), writers and solicitors. The head-bearer and jemmadar enter the hall, and his bedroom at eight o'clock. A lady quits his side, and is conducted by a private staircase, either to her own apartment, or out of the yard. The moment the master throws his legs out of bed, the whole possé in waiting rush into his room, each making three salams, by bending the body and head very low, and touching the fore-head with the inside of the fingers, and the floor with the back part. He condescends, perhaps, to nod or cast an eye towards the solicitors of his favour and

[1] In his *Travels in Europe, Asia, and Africa.*
[2] Captain J. Price, *Some Observations on a late Publication entitled "Travels in Asia,"* 1783.

protection. In about half-an-hour, after undoing and taking off his long drawers, a clean shirt, breeches, stockings and slippers, are put upon his body, thighs, legs and feet, without any greater exertion on his part than if he were a statue. The barber enters, shaves him, cuts his nails, and cleans his ears. The chillumjee and ewer are brought by a servant, whose duty it is, who pours water upon his hands to wash his hands and face, and presents a towel.

The superior then walks in state to his breakfasting parlour in his waistcoat; is seated; the consumah makes and pours out his tea, and presents him with a plate of bread or toast. The hair-dresser comes behind, and begins his occupation while the houccabadar softly slips the upper end of the snake or tube of the houcca into his hand. While the hair-dresser is doing his duty, the gentleman is eating, sipping, and smoking by turns. By and by his banian presents himself with humble salams, and advances somewhat more forward than the other attendants. If any of the solicitors are of eminence they are honoured with chairs.

These ceremonies are continued perhaps till ten o'clock; when, attended by his cavalcade, he is conducted to his palanquin, and preceded by eight to twelve chubdars, harcarrahs and peons with the insignia of their professions, and their livery distinguished by the colour of their turbans and cumberbands (a long muslin belt wrapt round the waist) they move off at a quick amble; the set of bearers, consisting of eight generally relieve each other, with alertness, and without incommoding the master. If he has visits to make, his peons lead and direct the bearers; and if business renders his presence only necessary, he shews himself, and pursues his other engagements until two o'clock, when he and his company sit down, perfectly at ease in point of dress and address, to a good dinner,[1] each attended by his

[1] Mrs Eliza Fay gives an account to her sister at home of the daily dinner in her Calcutta home, a household of only moderate means, in the summer of 1780. She and her husband dined on " a soup, a roast fowl, curry and rice, a mutton pie, a forequarter of lamb, a rice

own servant. And the moment the glasses are introduced, regardless of the company of ladies, the houccabadars enter, each with a houcca, and presents the tube to his master, watching behind and blowing the fire the whole time.[1] As it is expected that they shall return to supper, at four o'clock they begin to withdraw without ceremony, and step into their palanquins ; so that in a few minutes, the master is left to go into his bedroom, when he is instantly undressed to his shirt, and his long drawers put on ; and he lies down on his bed, where he sleeps till about seven or eight o'clock : then the former ceremony is repeated, and clean linen of every kind, as in the morning, is administered ; his houccabadar presents the tube to his hand, he is placed at the tea table, and his hair-dresser performs his duty as before. After tea, he puts on a handsome coat, and pays visits of ceremony to the ladies :[2] returns a little before ten o'clock, supper being served at ten. The company keep together till between twelve and one in the morning, preserving great sobriety and decency ; and when they depart, our hero is conducted to his bedroom, where he finds a female companion to amuse him until the hour of seven or eight next morning.

The record gives rise to many reflections, among them one as to the comparative modernness of the habit of the daily tub.[3] It must be remembered

pudding, tarts, very good cheese, fresh churned butter, fine bread, excellent Madeira." This tiffin was eaten without ice. There were giants in those days !

[1] If ladies were present it was considered a delicate compliment for a beau to whip from his pocket a silver mouthpiece, fix it to his hookah and offer it to the lady at his side.

[2] Mrs Eliza Fay again enlightens us as to the ways of that almost forgotten little world. "Formal visits are paid in the evening," she tells her sister. "Gentlemen call to pay their respects and if asked to put down their hats, it is considered as an invitation to supper."

[3] D'Oyley's *European in India*, published thirty years later, tells us that three or four pots of cold water were sometimes thrown over the master's head to brace him before dressing for dinner.

that the Englishmen who suffered themselves to be dressed and carried like luxurious dolls were living in a Bengal where the swing punkah was yet unknown [1] and from which there was no escape to a hill station. Yet even so, one whose daily life is here described has travelled far in spirit, and his mother's seven-or-eight-months-old letters must strike a wistful note when she writes in her Italian hand to tell of little Fanny's first ball and the moss rosebuds in her hair.

No one can read the despatches to the India House without realizing that in the great affairs of the Company many men must have lived more laborious lives than this. Yet it is significant that the lively author of the description quoted above felt impelled to no further comment than the remark that " with no greater exertions than these do the Company's servants amass the most splendid fortunes."

One is forced to the conclusion that, with the great exceptions of high-minded men like Cornwallis, Shore, Wellesley, or Grant, the latter eighteenth century had settled down quite complacently to regard " the East Indies " as a gold mine.

There is more of the spirit of the counter than one likes to confess among " The Honourable the Court of Directors for the affairs of the United Company of Merchants of England trading to the East Indies " *Auspicio Regis et Senatus Angliæ*. They were decorously anxious for dividends. Warren Hastings was appointed to Bengal for his good management of warehouses in Madras, and his first business was to make Bengal pay. The Directors suffered many a financial tremor in the days of the

---

[1] It was still a novelty in 1801.

patrician Wellesley " who endeavoured in redundantly eloquent despatches to reconcile his deeds with the pacific tone of his instructions." [1] They felt that creator of great schemes and enterprises to be an ornament to their administration, but how expensive an ornament ! Small wonder if their servants caught their spirit. Sir Harry Verelst described the English in Bengal as " a colony of merchants, governed by laws and influenced by principles merely commercial." [2]

We looked no further than the provision of the Company's investment. We sought advantages to our trade, with the ingenuity, I may add the selfishness of merchants. . . . All our servants and dependents were trained and educated in the same notions ; the credit of a good bargain was the utmost scope of their ambition.

Little guessed that old, bourgeois Calcutta of the merchants that she was the stage set for a drama of spiritual adventure. Yet so it was. The saints were coming to town. As when a Christian man first trod the forum of some lustful Roman city, and his spirit, fain of the eternal beauty, felt the unclean life around him to be " earthly, sensual, devilish " ; or as when two brothers of St Francis, their hearts singing with the beauty of poverty for Christ, first visited the greedy court of an Italian merchant prince, so when men who had caught the spirit of Christ first touched the sordid life of old Calcutta, there followed struggle and the hardness of moral choice in many lives.

They came in the rather prosaic garb of chaplains

---

[1] A. F. Pollard, *History of England.*
[2] Letter to Council of Fort William, December 1769.

of the East India Company : in matters of taste,
men of their day, with a power of enjoying if not of
producing " poetical effusions " that leave us cold,
and a habit in penitent moments of describing themselves as " contemptible and wretched worms."
But behind the high neck-cloths and the language
of eighteenth-century religious diaries we find the
infallible marks of the friends of Jesus.

The precursor and father of the little group
arrived when Calcutta was sweltering in the hot
weather of 1786, with his wife and a baby born at
sea. The Company had sent for " a clergyman and
a married man " to take charge of their new Military
Orphan Asylum. The Reverend David Brown who
responded to their call was the son of a Yorkshire
farm-house, who brought to his Calcutta home, along
with a solid classical education, a certain wholesome
shrewdness, and the tradition of hearty and generous
hospitality. Through twenty-five years of service
with only one fortnight of furlough he kept the
countryman's fresh colouring. He was no pallid
saint. But Calcutta found in that Yorkshireman a
spirit that was strange to her.

When he discovered that he was to have the
charge of five hundred orphans instead of the forty-
five of whom he had been told, and that the salary
was considerably less than had been represented, he
accepted the situation with the remark in his diary
that " since a larger field of usefulness was thus
opened to my view, I regretted not the diminution
of salary." [1] This Yorkshireman must be reckoned
with. He had a disconcerting habit of continual
reference to a standard that Calcutta had forgotten.

[1] *Memorial of the Rev. David Brown*, 1816, p. 298.

" I now sit down in a house of my own," he wrote,
" but my good Master had not where to lay His head.
. . . He emptied Himself of all and was literally
the poorest of men."

His habit of reference to another standard led
David Brown to do strange things. He found in
the city an ugly and at that time glaring building
known as " The Red Church " (now " The Old
Mission Church," Mission Row), built sixteen years
before his coming at the private expense of a Danish
missionary, and still the only Church in Bengal.[1]
Calcutta society affirmed that " by Gad, the place
is only fit for stable-boys and low Portuguese."
Church-going was not modish, and Sunday was the
day for races. Moreover it was impossible to go
to Church without considerable ceremony. " If you
were a person of fashion yet did not choose to go
to Church in your yellow chariot, you would arrive
in a neat sedan chair, gleaming with black lacquer.
You brought at least seven servants with you,—four
chair-bearers, two running footmen with spears and
one parasol bearer.[2] A lady told David Brown that
" she had been more than twelve years a resident
of Calcutta, and twice married ; but it had been out
of her power in all that time to go to Church, because
she had never had an offer from any beau to escort
her there and hand her to a pew."

The very small group of very mixed parentage
that looked to " the Red Church " for help, was now
without a shepherd, and David Brown " thought of
those with whom his Divine Master associated "

---

[1] But another was then a-building and was consecrated in June
1787 as St John's Church, now generally known as " The old Cathedral."

[2] Hyde, *The Parish of Bengal*, p. 190.

and offered himself as unsalaried chaplain. Calcutta sniffed, but in spite of herself was drawn to the big-hearted man who never took a baptism or a marriage service without a deep human emotion that could not be altogether hidden from the men and women he had come to serve.

Like draws to like, and David Brown had not been many days in Calcutta before he was asked to dine with the " Senior Merchant " of the Company and found a friend.

Charles Grant, later to be celebrated in the Councils of the East India Company " for an understanding large enough to embrace, without confusion, the entire range and the intricate combinations of their whole civil and military policy, and for nerves which set fatigue at defiance," [1] was a Highland Scot whose father had been fighting for the Stuarts at Culloden at the very hour of his birth. He was known in Calcutta as a man long of limb and long of face, his sagacious countenance under massive brows singularly steadfast and immovable, but softening when he glanced at the adorable wife whom he had brought to India as a bride of seventeen, an apt musician and a charming dancer. She made his house a home of rare delight and gave him two baby girls, loved by both parents with the almost desperate affection that surrounds the delicate babes of a household in the tropics. The head of the house for all his home affections followed the ordinary standards of Calcutta society, and the one shadow in the household was cast by the master's gambling debts which piled up far higher than his means of payment.

Then, with dreadful suddenness, the light went out

---

[1] Sir James Stephen, *Essays in Ecclesiastical Biography.*

from their home as, within a few days, first one little daughter and then the other was carried off by smallpox, and the twenty-year-old mother was left distraught with grief, springing up now and then in the belief that she was waking from a nightmare and would find her babies in their nursery, only to suffer her first agony over again when she reached the empty room.

To the father's conscience it seemed " a judgment from heaven " on his selfish and worldly courses. Atonement must be made. In agony of soul he broke through his lifelong reserve and went to Dr Kiernander the old Danish missionary who had built the Red Church. " I found him lying on the couch. My anxious enquiries as to what I could do to be saved appeared to embarrass and confuse him exceedingly ; and when I left him the perspiration was running from his face in consequence, as it appeared to me, of his mental distress." [1] Charles Grant came away from the only religious specialist within his ken, as miserable as he went. It was his young wife who brought him peace. She noticed, even in her own sorrow, his heavy spiritual anxiety and turned to search such good books as she had, for help for both of them. In the New Testament she found the way of peace and wrote her Charles a letter to tell of her discovery :

Now is not this the sinner whom our blessed Saviour invites to come unto Him with promises of lightening his burden and giving him rest ? I think it is.[2]

He thought so too when her faith led the way, and together they remodelled the life of their house-

[1] George Smith, *Twelve Indian Statesmen*, p. 12.
[2] Morris, *Life of Charles Grant*, p. 64.

hold, as those who openly confessed that One was their Master, even Christ. Charles Grant set himself grimly to the task of paying off his gaming debts and cleared them in four years. His work for the Company, in which his calmly sane intellect shone out, became the work of one who cared for India and her peoples with a disinterested love that rose above party politics or dividends. "The views which are entertained by statesmen and others for the welfare of India," he wrote in a letter of 1784, "are so disturbed by party as to be sometimes indistinct. Ambition and party, in a word, have marred all that has been intended for the benefit of this country for ten years past. . . . How few . . . . rise above the mists of present passions to objects having respect to 'Him who is invisible.'"

To one trying to guide his personal and public life by standards so different from those current in Calcutta, the coming of David Brown was a great event. In nothing were these two more unique than in their relationships with the people of India. David Brown at once "dedicated some attention to the languages of the country" and though he made it plain to Calcutta that he was not the man for nautch displays, he proceeded to go "among the Hindoos in a way not usual with the English. He attended, in their domestic circles, their literary and religious entertainments" and behaved there "with urbanity and respect."[1] David Brown, Charles Grant, and two like-minded friends,[2] persisted in seeing in the people of India men and women with

---

[1] *Memorial of the Rev. David Brown*, p. 71.

[2] Mr William Chambers, the East India Company's chief linguist, and Mr George Udny, indigo planter.

spiritual struggles as interesting to God as their own. With all appearances in Church and State against them, they dared to see a vision of spiritual kinship with India, and to believe that her people might come to share in what was for them the supreme experience of life, the touch of the Living Christ on the spirit of a man.

They did not stop at dreaming, but wrote out a proposal which they sent home to clergy and members of Parliament, calling for volunteer missionary schoolmasters to come to Bengal where the Company had not yet raised a finger for the intellectual or moral enlightenment of its eastern subjects. They asked for " fit men, of free minds, disinterested, zealous, and patient of labour, who would accept of an invitation, and aspire to the arduous office of a missionary. . . . His work must be his business, his delight, and reward. . . . Men who are ready to endure hardships and to suffer the loss of all things."

Knowing their England they sent this appeal to ardent souls, clergy whose zeal had earned them the name of " Methodist," and philanthropists like William Wilberforce and Robert Raikes. Raikes in his reply suggested that they had made a false step in asking the " methodist " clergy to forward their adventure, for, said he, the bishops " never like to give the reins into the hands of men of warm imaginations."

Charles Grant and David Brown, for all their spiritual daring, were government officials used to working through official channels ; and while they were under no delusions as to the difficulties ahead, it yet never occurred to either of them that their

c

new scheme should be independent of the official sanction of the leaders of Church and State. They were before the day when great private and voluntary societies within the Church undertook her missionary enterprises. The immense growth of these in the nineteenth century was at once a forward and a backward step ; forward in that the societies revealed a number of the Church's sons and daughters awakening to a forgotten fundamental of that Church's life, but backward in so far as the primary task of the whole Church was thereby relegated to smaller groups within her. But that day had not yet come, and to Charles Grant and David Brown it seemed a natural course to approach the Archbishop of Canterbury and good King George the Third. They were not over-sanguine as to official countenance for they knew the age-long character of Christian teachers as those who " turn the world upside down," and measured the probable opposition. "The truth, as we presume to think," they wrote, " is, that all objections to the extension of Christianity arise rather from Indisposition to the thing itself than any persuasion of its Impracticability. . . . Some may oppose political Considerations, the danger of disturbing the present Order of things, and of introducing a spirit destructive of that subjection and Subordination, which have made the Natives of Bengal so easy to govern."

It was a true forecast. When Charles Grant went home in 1790 to one of the " Chairs " of the East India Company's Directors, he found an England increasingly panic-stricken by the news of revolution in France, and regarding the Church as an institution for the moral policing of the nation and the support of the existing powers. In such an atmosphere he made his main purpose in life the enlisting of that Church in spiritual service for India. He knocked unbidden at the door of Lambeth until he had persuaded the bland and very bourgeois prelate, Dr Moore,[1] to step into his purple-liveried coach and lay before King George himself a copy of the scheme drawn up with such eager hope by the group of friends in Calcutta.

Dr Moore did not like the task; but Charles Grant's pertinacity and his own sense of duty at last drove him to St James's. We are told what the King said, and can picture the interview; the light from the high windows falling on the amiable and full-bodied prelate as he knelt on the carpet (for George III was a stickler for this posture) in his purple coat, full wig and abbreviated cassock; the elderly, stooping king with his good, obstinate face, a born lover of mediocrities, "testy at the idea of all innovations and suspicious of all innovators,"[2] grunting a little at first, then, with the usual oscillations of his body and precipitate, tumbling speech finding words to say that he "hesitated to countenance such ideas" owing to "the alarming progress of the French Revolution and the proneness of the period to movements subversive of the established order of things"; the kneeling Archbishop hastily assuring his "royal patron" that an exactly similar hesitation arose in his own mind, then rising ponderously from the floor, only too thankful to be quit of an ungrateful task.

[1] The only gentleman to appear on the walls of the National Portrait Gallery in a pair of immaculate grey gloves.

[2] Thackeray, *Four Georges.*

Charles Grant had to report to David Brown that the whole of officialdom, whether in Parliament, in Leadenhall Street or in episcopal palaces proved prosaic and timid. The Bishop of Llandaff did send his copy of the scheme to Pitt, but with an apologetic covering letter doubting "whether the present is the fittest time for making the attempt." [1] Leadenhall Street in a panic decided to give no licence to any captain of an East Indiaman for any passenger calling himself a missionary, and the friends now found their hopes of spiritual service for India limited to the possibility of sending out as official chaplains of the Company men with hearts as high as their own and with an equal sense of the spiritual rights of every human soul.

To this end Charles Grant now used his ever-increasing influence in the Councils of Leadenhall Street, with the result that David Brown was joined in the course of years by a group of younger men who dared to share his vision. Among them came Henry Martyn, that youth in years who yet knew the abasement and the rapture of the saint, and who flung at the feet of Christ a scholar's dreams and the heart of a lover.

---

[1] Bishop Watson's Anecdotes of his Life, p. 197.

CHAPTER II

CORNWALL

Not lolling at ease or in the indecent posture of sitting, drawling out one word after another; but all standing before God, and praising Him lustily, and with good courage.—JOHN WESLEY.

There is a fair prospect in Cornwall from Launceston to the Land's End.—WESLEY'S *Journal for August* 27, 1789.

THE curate of Truro in the year 1747 received a surprising letter from the master of the Grammar School. That good man explained that his physician had ordered him French wines, but having failed to obtain any in Cornwall that had not been smuggled into the country he now desired to pay the duty himself on the quantity he had bought. He enclosed a sum of money and requested the clergyman, as a well-known and respectable character above suspicion by the excise men, to hand it in to the authorities as conscience money from an anonymous source. The obliged writer would in that way gain the satisfaction of having tried to keep the precept of Jesus about the things that should be rendered to Cæsar.

The Reverend Samuel Walker was a genial clergyman whose company was often sought by neighbouring squires "to supper on a roasted pig." He was interested in character, and never having met on that smuggling coast with such sensibility on a point of conscience, he forthwith sought the friend-

ship of the ingenious and respectable writer. Their
friendship was momentous in the life of Truro ; for
Samuel Walker, level-headed, and well-known in
his Oxford days for devotion to logic, now saw in
the Grammar School master an aspect of religion
which had hitherto escaped him, and which trans-
cended logic. He witnessed in his friend a personal
relationship with Christ which became central for
the man who experienced it and altered all his
thinking. He went further and sought that vital
experience for himself, and in the power of it he
transformed Truro. There was a new force about
the man which drew all the city to him, so that they
had to shut up the cockpit for want of patrons. Of
a Sunday the people flocked now to their lovely
perpendicular parish Church of St Mary in such
numbers that " you might fire a cannon down every
street in Truro in church time without a chance of
killing a single human being."

Samuel Walker, a careful organizer, drew the
" serious people " of his flock into what would nowadays be called a guild or fellowship for mutual
stimulus and prayer. He was untiring in the preparation of courses of sermons and lectures, and his
people must have been some of the most instructed
Christians in the land.

Among the regular members of his " Society " was
one John Martyn, cashier in a Truro mercantile
office and himself in a modest way a citizen of
substance, with shares of his own in the Wheal
Unity mine.

" Whether at Church or at Prayer-meetings John
Martyn always attended Mr Sam Walker, the
Curate of St Mary's, but at Mr Walker's decease

seemed to prefer the Prayer-meeting to the Church." [1]
Be that as it may, John Martyn together with most
of Samuel Walker's flock remained in connexion
with the mother church throughout those days of
stir. Samuel Walker before his death in 1761 had
considerable correspondence with John Wesley, that
most arresting leader who came more than any other
man of dominant spirit into immediate contact with
the masses of the people.

In Cornwall, as in all England, John Wesley was
facing and taming ill-conditioned mobs, and he
could not but appreciate the changes in Truro that
he found through Samuel Walker's life-work. He
wrote in his journal for August 30, 1755, of his first
contact with Walker's flock : "As I was riding
through Truro one stopped my horse and insisted
on my alighting. Presently two or three more of
Mr Walker's society came in, and we seemed to
have been acquainted with one another many years."

The two men, both priests of the English Church,
akin in spiritual experience and both preachers now
of "the new birth," yet differed in policy. Walker
dreaded the masses. "It has been a great fault all
along," he wrote to Wesley, "to have made the low
people of your council." So he tilled his own plot,
working no stupendous upheaval but a gradual
transformation in the life of the little city.

When Walker died, leaving a sober and a godly

---

[1] So writes Polwhele in his *Biographical Sketches of Cornwall*, i. 91,
adding: "It is much to be lamented that Mr Walker should have
instituted prayer meetings." Mr Polwhele sees so red if the word
methodism be but breathed never so softly that his account of Henry
Martyn is malicious and unreliable. His scorching *Anecdotes of
Methodism* are a breath from the heated atmosphere in which the
spiritual upheaval of the evangelical revival took place in Cornwall.

Truro, John Wesley was only at the beginning of his series of marvellous meteoric visits to a half-pagan Cornwall, whose miners and fisher folk (not without the spur of some local persecution) flocked to hear him in the open fields and made his hymns their folk-songs.

Meanwhile "serious" John Martyn attended his prayer-meetings, took to himself a wife, begat a son named John after himself, and amused his leisure with the study of mathematics. The mail coach for London would carry up to the office of *The Gentleman's Diary or Mathematical Repository* John Martyn's solutions to problems which beginning airily "Suppose a fire engine" required the discovery of "the diameters of the cylinder and pumps, the height of the stroke, the depth of the engine pit shaft, and the quantity of gallons of water this engine will draw in one hour, friction excepted."

Young John's mother died early, and John Martyn the elder brought home a new bride from Ilfracombe to his house in Truro near the Coinage Hall. Her name was Fleming; she gave him a daughter Laura, then on February 18, 1781, when young John was fifteen, a second little son whom they named Henry. Two years later another baby, Sally, had been born and the mother had died, leaving to her children a constitution of singularly weak resistance. None of John Martyn's family outlived early middle life.

The baby Henry opened his eyes upon a discreet and dignified little city which lived its life without much reference to the rest of England. One of the aldermen had never travelled farther than Bodmin, and news trickled in slowly when the journey by stage to Exeter took two days. The gentry of the Cornish countryside instead of careering up to London had their town houses of sober grey stone in Truro, where they might meet one another for routs and dances and the high affairs of matrimony between families of standing.

It was a trim city, but even while the stage rattled over the cobbled street you could hear if you listened the call of the gulls among the shipping, and catch a tang of the salt sea from the estuary below the bridge. Henry Martyn's childhood was spent in a house of two aspects. Its fairer face looked down a garden to the little river just before it emptied itself into the estuary where the curlews whistle; but the back of the house looked out on the very heart of the city's life. Coinage Hall Street was narrow [1] but just opposite the Martyns' house the buildings gave way to leave a little open square before the pillared cloister of the Coinage Hall. Years afterwards in dreams in India Henry would find himself walking down that street, with the discreet dwellings of the citizens (for it was not yet the shopping quarter of the town) and brother John's house on the other side a few doors lower than his own, and the cloisters of the ancient Coinage Hall where his father, tall and erect, would take a daily constitutional.

Under those early English arches Wesley preached on more than one of his fifteen visits to Truro, with the people in the square before him, " enabled to speak exceeding plain on ' Ye are saved through

[1] Coinage Hall Street and Powder Street with the houses between them known as Middle Row were thrown into the present spacious Boscawen Street.

faith.' "[1] The little boy in John Martyn's house
might still sometimes see the erect figure of that
"human gamecock," though he no longer rode up
the street on horseback but stepped out of a chaise.
"His face was remarkably fine; his complexion
fresh to the last week of his life, his eye quick and
keen and active. When you met him in the street
of a crowded city he attracted notice, not only by
his band and cassock and his long hair, white and
bright as silver, but by his pace and manner, both
indicating that all his minutes were numbered and
that not one was to be lost."[2]

One day when Henry was eight years old the street
east of his door was blocked with soldiers, and westward with "numberless tinners, a huge multitude,
nearly starved" assembled to demand a living wage.
Into the heart of the throng stepped John Wesley,
and standing in front of the Coinage Hall, between
the two opposing hosts, he preached his gospel to
them all alike. Whether or no the child Henry
listened to those sermons of the veteran, he was
growing up in a world half-moulded by the Wesleys.
Their hymns were the songs of his home to which
he turned again and again for solace in the remote
places of the earth.

There is no record of a beloved nurse or any
woman who took the place of the lost mother in the
lives of John Martyn's little children. Physically
Henry sounds a neglected and untempting child
with hands covered with warts, and red eyelids
devoid of eyelashes set in a plain little face; but
the father who gave his own leisure to those

[1] John Wesley's *Journal*, August 27, 1776.
[2] Southey's *Life of Wesley*.

problems in the *Gentleman's Diary* saw with delight uncommon promise in his small son.

At the age of seven he entered little Henry at the Truro Grammar School and never ceased to hold before him a career of scholarship. The seven-year-old child trotted across the square and dived down an opposite lane to find himself in a large low room that held the wonderful new world of school.

Opposite the door was a moulded painting where the civic ship rode yellow on very blue waves ; and below the ship stood a throne whereon sat one of Truro's great ones. The Reverend Doctor Cornelius Cardew, a magistrate, a member of the corporation, twice mayor of the city, and its schoolmaster for more than a generation, looked out over a formidable beak with the searching quizzical glance of one who knew what was in boys. He thrashed soundly, he believed his boys to be " good material," and assisted by only one usher he turned out able men, so that in the distant Universities they began to speak with respect of the little western Grammar School.

Down either side of the room as in the choir of a church were yellow benches carved with the names of the more daring scholars ; and here sat the sixty boys, more terrible to the new seven-year-old than the master himself, who thought him a babe of promise. There they sat, while bland plaster angels looked down from the green and white vaulted ceiling with perfect unconcern on despairing faces turned up in search of an answer. It soon became noticeable that little Henry, though no one called him studious, showed a happy faculty for hitting on the right answer without consulting the angels.

The " great boys " were wonderful. There was

Clement Carlyon who was going to be a doctor;
there was John Kempthorne from Helston whose
father was a real live admiral and fought on the
high seas; and most wonderful of all was Humphry
Davy from Penzance, the son of a wood-carver,
round-shouldered and clumsy, a youth who dipped
his finger in the inkpot when he wanted to blot out
a mistake in his exercise, but the inventor of wonderful things to do. He could make lamps of scooped-
out turnips, and tales of chivalry and gory ballads
and Latin verses that pleased Dr Cardew, and
he invented fireworks that really went off, and
" thunder-powder " which exploded on a stone.
You paid in pins to see it.

Only while these great ones were occupied with
their work and their plans for fishing, Henry finding
his level among the " lesser boys " had his temper
sorely tried. He was " a good-humoured plain little
fellow," Carlyon said, and no coward; " he quailed
before no man." But he was considerably under the
average in size and in staying power, and in the hurly-
burly of the small boy world he was always pushed
to the wall, when he broke into the bitter rages of
one who is helpless before his tormentors yet un-
cowed. His puny but intensely violent rages made
him a tempting subject for the bullies of that boy
community and Henry's schooldays would have been
dark for him but for the searching critical eye of
the pedagogue in white bands at the end of the
room.

Dr Cardew saw that Henry's knowledge of the
classics would be small unless he had protection.
He turned the whipper-snapper over to the great,
beneficent Kempthorne, a diligent senior boy who

was later a clergyman and lord of a manor in the Lizard district. Kempthorne " had often the happiness of rescuing him from the grasp of oppressors " and never forgot " the thankful expression of his affectionate countenance when he happened to be helped out of some difficulty."

Seated near the big, safe presence little Martyn blossomed out, into no very great diligence at his book it is true—he seemed in those days rather to absorb the classics than to learn them—but into marked sociability, forgetting his helpless rages and becoming one of the friendliest souls in the school.

So the years passed and Henry Martyn, still small for his years, was no longer one of the babes but played the big boy to his own younger cousin Fortescue Hitchins, learned to shoot, and began to look to the future. Oxford was the University of most of his acquaintance, for the Cornishmen went in numbers to Exeter College, and when Henry was fifteen, they sent him up to compete for a scholarship at Corpus. The fact that in spite of his extreme youth he all but won the prize is a testimony to the classical training of Dr Cardew's boys. Henry now sat among the " great boys " at the annual school sermon in St Mary's and on holidays scoured the country with a gun.

He belonged to a family of mine agents that never intermarried with the great gentry of the land, but had a sprinkling of cousins and relatives by marriage up and down the Cornish countryside in the ranks of solicitors, clergy or mining accountants. It was a hospitable world and what with school-fellows and cousins Henry could ride all over the

county and be sure of a welcome at some town-
place sheltering among sycamores or in the one
street of some country town. There grew in him
a great love of the Cornish land so that later even
Cambridge seemed "a dreary scene" when he
thought of misty headlands crowned with scilla or
sea pink above the slow wash of an opal sea. The
holiday rides that meant the most to him were
those to St Hilary Vicarage where a little church
among its trees stood as a landmark to the sailors
in Mount's Bay. Here lived his father's cousin,
Malachy Hitchins. He was a man of varied interests,
who in youth had helped to make a survey of Devon-
shire, and now divided his energies between his
work as the parson of the villages of Gwinear and
St Hilary (a preacher of formal old-fashioned
sermons) and his other task as assistant to Green-
wich Observatory in compiling the *Nautical Almanac*.
He wrote to the *Gentleman's Magazine* under the
signature "ultimus vatum" ("You know that
Malachi was the last of the prophets") and he
loved his garden. In that house of many interests
Henry Martyn always found a welcome, and with
his cousins Tom and Josepha and Fortescue in
the old vicarage garden his happiest hours were
spent.

So the Cornish land bred him and made him for
ever her own—small, passionate, affectionate, a boy
of parts and of imagination, wholly incapable of
passing easily and light-heartedly through sunny
shallows, a born plunger into the depths whether
of good or of evil.

In the winter of 1796-7, when the West Country
was set buzzing by the daring of three French

frigates that sailed into Ilfracombe harbour, and when eyes were beginning to turn to an officer named Nelson who first hoisted his flag that spring as Admiral of the Blue, John Martyn told his boy that he should leave school at Midsummer and prepare for the larger world of the University.

CHAPTER III

UNDERGRADUATE

The gentleman's Muse wears Methodist shoes ; you may know by her pace, and talk about grace, that she and her bard have little regard for the taste and fashions, and ruling passions, and hoidening play of the modern day.—W. COWPER *to the* REV. JOHN NEWTON, *June* 1781.

Unless God has raised you up for this very thing, you will be worn out by the opposition of men and devils.—JOHN WESLEY *to* CHARLES SIMEON, *February* 1791.

HENRY MARTYN left the Grammar School in the summer of 1797, and after a September spent in "his favourite employment of shooting and . . . reading for the most part travels and Lord Chester-field's *Letters*" he went up to St John's College, Cambridge, following in the steps of his beloved Kempthorne.

In that summer when Henry left the Grammar School, Jane Austen, all unknown in a Hampshire village, was putting the final touches to *Pride and Prejudice* ; Charles Lamb spent his brief, idyllic holiday with Coleridge and Sara at Nether Stowey ; and Coleridge "the rapt one of the godlike fore-head," writing a few weeks later to the excellent Mr Cottle, announced that "Wordsworth and his exquisite sister" were staying with him.

But none of these voices had stirred the Cambridge to which Martyn went. Rather was she still listening to the rolling echoes of the most sonorous of English voices, hushed only that summer with the death of Burke.

Fanny Burney said of Burke that when he spoke of the French Revolution his face immediately assumed " the expression of a man who is going to defend himself against murderers." Just such a look stole into the faces of the authorities at Cambridge when, turning for a moment from the worship of Newton, they heard the strange clash of revolutionary forces in politics or literature. Every year saw its goodly crop of orthodox pamphlets against the writings of Thomas Paine—pamphlets in which the forces seem to be fighting in confusion on the wrong side of the battle. For Tom Paine with his harsh earnestness, his daring if unlettered mind, his championship of common folk, and his life of self-forgetful adventure seems far nearer in spirit to the Christ whom he denied, than the comfortable gentlemen who, with more dignity and learning but with less of love and sacrifice, wrote tracts under such stimulating titles as *A Layman's Protest against the Profane Blasphemy, false Charges, and illiberal Invective of Thomas Paine.*

But Henry Martyn, with four months yet to run before he was seventeen, was still outside the warring world of pamphlets. There was Cambridge, with all her beauty calling to his Cornish soul ; his own college, St John's, of whose " blushing bricks " old Fuller writes, not the least fair, its three courts containing some of the loveliest Tudor brickwork in that city of rare brick. The music at King's College chapel became one of Martyn's dear delights,

D

and another he was to find in St John's walks and
Fellows' Gardens, where yet

> . . . *The elm clumps greatly stand*
> *Still guardians of that holy land,*

and whence in Martyn's day, when patches of heath
crept almost to the gates of the colleges, one looked
out over open champaign country that grew " the
best saffron in Europe."

In the then much smaller city of Cambridge the
eighteenth century was dying hard. Pitt was a
familiar figure there, coming twice a year to visit
his constituency, and walking the college courts
with a cocked hat and almost military step. Men
who might have stepped out of the pages of Fielding
yet walked the Cambridge streets. A certain well-
known Dr Glynn, Fellow of King's and champion
of the old school of physicians, took his walks
abroad in a scarlet cloak, powdered wig and three-
cornered hat, wielding an enormous gold-headed cane,
while he ordered blisters for his patients with the
unvarying and depressing formula " emplasma vesi-
catorium amplum et acre."

Cambridge still thought umbrellas effeminate, and
there was said to be but one in all the city, kept at
a shop in Benet Street and let out by the hour.
But even in Cambridge old ways were passing, and
fathers who brought boys to the University were
shocked to see M.A.s in round hats rather than
cocked ones. Powder too was going out of fashion,
though the graver seniors still wore powdered wigs
which went to a shop on Saturday to be curled and
dressed for Sunday, and Trinity cherished a joyful
story of the bribing of the shopman, and of certain

statues seen at dawn with curled wigs on their heads, while College dignitaries fumed into Sunday morning chapel in their second-best headgear. But very few junior members of the University wore powdered hair. Pitt had done much to change the fashion by his hair-powder tax to pay for the French war, and young poetic democrats like Coleridge, Southey and Savage Landor at Oxford, had done their part by railing against powder " as inconsistent with republican simplicity." It was necessary, however, to wear your hair curled at Cambridge, unless you would be classed among the " very rustic and unfashionable."

Undergraduates were bound to wear white stockings, garterless and reaching to short knee-breeches, and men who cared for appearances donned white waistcoats and silk stockings for dinner in hall at about two o'clock. Dinner was followed by disputations in the mathematical school at three o'clock, but these were much deserted for the sake of exercise, and from three till half-past five men rode or walked. The richer and the gayer sort drove curricles, and kept race-horses and hunters, but as yet the rowing man was not, and the river was left to lonely dreamers.

After five-thirty chapel, for missing which at St John's one was ordered an imposition, men made tea in their rooms, or, in the fireless days of summer, repaired to coffee-houses in the town. Reading men then settled in for a long unbroken evening, and social spirits sat down to hazard and burgundy. Few cared to disturb the evening for the supper served in hall at eight forty-five.

Tutors did not in those days give individual

lessons, but lectures on the set books for the degree examinations, chiefly "treatises by Wood and Vince on optics, mechanics, hydrostatics and astronomy." Rapid bookwork was in great demand, and King's College used to quote an answer to a question in a tutor's lecture: "Sir, I do not know what the centre of percussion is, but I can work the problem upon it."

Martyn's tutor, Mr Catton, was an astronomer who had been Fourth Wrangler, but in Cambridge opinion should have been Senior. He lived for a little observatory on one of the towers at St John's. When he came down from his observations of occultations and contemplated his new pupil, he found a spare boy under the usual height, who had been taught no mathematics, and whose idea of learning it seemed to be the committing of Euclid to memory. The astronomer called in the help of T. H. Shepherd a second-year man, who thus tells the tale:

"Mr Catton sent for me to his rooms, telling me of Martyn, as a quiet youth, with some knowledge of classics, but utterly unable as it seemed to make anything of even the First Proposition of Euclid, and desiring me to have him into my rooms, and see what I could do for him in this matter. Accordingly, we spent some time together, but all my efforts appeared to be in vain; and Martyn, in sheer despair, was about to make his way to the coach office, and take his place the following day back to Truro, his native town. I urged him not to be so precipitate, but to come to me the next day, and have another trial with Euclid. After some time light seemed suddenly to flash upon his mind, with clear comprehension of the hitherto dark problem, and he threw up his cap for joy at his Eureka. The Second Proposition was soon taken, and with perfect success ; but in truth his progress was such and so rapid, that he distanced everyone in his year." [1]

" A quiet youth " Mr Catton had called the slight demure boy, whose faintly ceremonious manners bore to the end of his life a trace of his studies in Lord Chesterfield before coming up to Cambridge. The undergraduate who stopped that despairing rush to the Blue Boar Inn for the next western coach saw that the " quiet youth " was an impetuous one. With friends he was known also as a sociable one, showing a bright delicacy of spirit and a liveliness all too apt to pass into quivering irritation. But few guessed what a storm centre was the inner life of this freshman not yet seventeen. The Henry Martyn of those early Cambridge days had his being in a spiritual whirlwind. He was swept by great devastating emotions, longings, exaltations, rages, ambitions ; raised to an ecstasy by music ; cast to despair by a slip in mechanics. " A life of woe " he called it, looking back on those early storms from the comparative security of twenty-three.[2] In general the outward visible sign of the inward stress was only an " exquisite irritability," but now and again passion would master him. In such a moment he flung a knife at his friend Cotterill, and those who saw it quivering in the wall knew that the inner Martyn was no " quiet youth."

The safeguards of his storm-swept soul lay in his always warm affections. It is true that there was no mother to be impressed with each new Cambridge phase, to be teased, and to be trusted for unfailing

[1] Smith's *Henry Martyn*, p. 19, note.   [2] *Journal*, June 27th, 1804.

love. But at Cambridge there was Kempthorne, and at home there was his father. The big, safe Kempthorne of the Truro Grammar School was still one of the great ones in Martyn's world, having become the Senior Wrangler of 1797. From these heights he was a good friend to "little Henry Martyn" from his old school. He found the boy swept away by the new delights and freedoms of a first term, and told him he must work. Kempthorne believed in work. He had won his own honours by unflagging diligence, covering more reams of paper, it was said, than any man in the University, as he worked out every problem in a fair hand, perhaps a hundred times, till he had first stripped the argument of each unnecessary step, and then reduced the necessary steps to the most lucid economy of word, line and letter. Such diligence he recommended to Martyn.

The beloved Kempthorne had spoken; and work Martyn did, with a greedy ambition only stimulated by his quick success in the college examinations, then conducted twice a year by the Fellows in hall on the lecture subjects for the term. Martyn was never for half-measures. The boy who knew no mathematics when he came up was soon "nettled to the quick" when he took second instead of first place in his college examinations. He now set his heart on following Kempthorne's footsteps as the Senior Wrangler of his year, no small ambition in a student whose natural bent was for literature and above all for language.

The good Kempthorne dreaded so engrossing a concern with examination results and tried "to persuade me that I ought to attend to reading, not for the praise of men, but for the glory of God. This seemed *strange* to me, but *reasonable*." Reasonable, no doubt, but also quite uninteresting to the Martyn of those days.

His love for his father fostered his ambition. The gentle and sympathetic old man, himself a self-trained mathematician, who all along had set before Henry a career of scholarship, was now waiting as eagerly as the boy himself for tidings of each examination. When at Christmas 1799 Henry was first in the college examination it " pleased my father prodigiously."

Only sister Sally, aged sixteen, and a devout Christian girl after the type of piety left in Cornwall by the Wesleys, was full of heavy concern for Henry's passionate soul. Her overtures, nay her exhortations on religion when he went home were " grating " to the ears of a brother two years older than herself, and he was apt to reply to her " in the harshest language." (Oh Henry !) The maiden did extract a promise, one day, that he would read the Bible for himself. " But on being settled at college, Newton engaged all my thoughts." [1] It was in the autumn term of 1799 that Newton so held the ascendancy, and it was at the Christmas examinations of the same term that Henry obtained that first place which so " prodigiously " pleased his father.

It seems that Henry did not that Christmas make

---

[1] Twelve years afterwards on a ship in the Indian Ocean Martyn wrote : " I bless God for Sir I. Newton, who, beginning with the things next to him, and humbly and quietly moving to the things next to them, enlarged the boundaries of human knowledge more than the rest of the sons of men."

the tedious journey to Cornwall. The vacation
lasted four weeks exactly, and the journey would
cut out the best part of two of them. Although
there was daily communication with London there
was but one coach weekly from Cambridge to
Birmingham. This left Cambridge early on Thursday
morning and carried western passengers, at a fare
of £1. 11s. 6d., to Birmingham by Friday evening,
in time for a Cornishman to catch the night coach
to the west. On the western coach there were two
days between Birmingham and Exeter, and Henry
had further yet to go; but even such speed was too
much to hope for through the miry lanes of winter.
Henry did not go home, but letters from Truro
told him that his father was " in great health and
spirits."

What then was my consternation, when in January
I received from my [half] brother an account of my
father's death.

The affectionate boy, too young to remember his
mother's death, found his first great sorrow staring
at him, and he quite alone, in what seemed only
a greater isolation because, with the chimes of
Trinity and St Clement's, there floated in the sound
of eager talk on the staircase, and shouting and
sudden spurts of laughter from the court below.

Alone, Martyn found himself shivering before
realities he would gladly have forgotten.

I began to consider seriously that invisible world
to which he had gone and to which I must one day
go. As I had no taste at this time for my usual
studies, I took up my Bible [how often had the pious
little Sally in Cornwall prayed for that moment !]
thinking that the consideration of religion was rather
suitable to this solemn time.

But tormented as he was by memories of his own "consummate selfishness" at home, as set against his father's unfailing "patience and mildness," Martyn found no peace of forgetfulness through his effort at Bible reading. He was turning for escape to other books when Kempthorne came in. That steady, comfortable friend, the link between Cambridge and the world of home, now advised Martyn "to make this time an occasion for serious reflection."

Once more Kempthorne had spoken, and Martyn obediently turned again to his Bible. "I began with the Acts as being the most amusing, but I found myself insensibly led to enquire more attentively into the doctrines of the apostles." His interest once awakened, he remarked with approval how the notions he had gathered as a little child from the Cornish Christians of the evangelical revival "corresponded nearly enough" with what he now read in the Epistles.

It was not Martyn's habit at that time to pray, but prayer seemed a suitable exercise for one urged by Kempthorne to "serious reflection." He knelt and "began to pray from a precomposed form, in which I thanked God in general for having sent Christ into the world." It was his first stumbling footstep in the way of prayer, wherein his spirit was to know such hard-won and such exquisite delight.

Kempthorne not only advised "reflection" but lent Martyn one of the religious classics of the day to guide him in it. He chose Doddridge's *Rise and Progress of Religion in the Soul,* a book to which young William Wilberforce owed the awakening of his spirit, and a book in which the wonderful confidence of the eighteenth century in the power of reason may be seen extending even to her evangelists, who sought to save men by a logical order of convictions, starting in this case with the proposition of the guilt of all created beings before an offended Creator. " I will labour to fix a deep and awful *Conviction of Guilt* upon his conscience, and to strip him of his vain *Excuses* and his flattering hopes " says Doddridge in the " general plan of the work." And he does labour. Good and sincere man as he is, we feel with Leslie Stephen that he is " lashing a jaded imagination rather than overpowered by an awful vision." " I am sensible I can do it no otherwise," Doddridge tells us, " than by way of deep Humiliation." Henry Martyn, dejected though he was, read and rebelled. " It appeared to make religion consist too much in humiliation " he said. " I was not under great terror of future punishment " he tells his sister ; and moderns feel a sneaking gladness that he would not be terrified into the Kingdom of Heaven.

But in despite of too logical " plans of salvation " the vision of a Living Person was slowly stealing into Martyn's heart. " I am brought to a sense of things gradually " he wrote. He still " read the Bible unenlightened " but having worked through the Acts and the Epistles he now turned to the Gospels. " Soon I began to attend more diligently to the words of our Saviour in the New Testament, and to devour them with delight." Then when the same voice made " offers of mercy and forgiveness " Martyn's heart responded and he found himself, he knew not how, praying " with eagerness and hope." His spirit had discovered not a doctrine but a

Person. None was to know more than he of the humiliation that marks the saint, but he learnt it, not under Doddridge's guidance by the contemplation of his guilty state, but under Other guidance when he came to see "the light of the knowledge of the glory of God, in the Face of Jesus Christ."

This was a conversion. Four years later he could write, "The work is real. I can no more doubt it than I can my own existence. The whole current of my desires is altered, I am walking quite another way, though I am incessantly stumbling in that way."

Henceforth we know the same Martyn, but with a liberating change : a Martyn with emotions still intense, perhaps even intensified ; all his life more quickly moved than most men whether to delight or tears ; his heart raised to rapture by music or by quiet scenery ; while, as the price of ecstasies too intense for his physical frame, he must know a fastidiousness and quivering irritation almost inconceivable to men of firmer build. But no longer was this Martyn to be the slave of his own storms. In finding a Master he was set free. No more pent up in himself, his whole spiritual being found a great escape through contact with the infinite life of his Lord. That vital contact now begun was maintained, as it seemed to himself, precariously enough and with difficulty at first, through what he felt to be a surprising "reluctance to prayer, unwillingness to come to God the fountain of all good." But for all that, the contact was maintained and cultivated, growing daily more sure, until he became at home in the new realm that he now entered, "tasting the powers of the age to come," and growing into gradual harmony with that "undisturbèd song of pure concent" whose notes were for the first time stealing into his ears as he read "the words of our Saviour in the New Testament" in January 1800.

Martyn was far too rapturous a being ever to reach a stoic composure, but he came at last very near to the quite different composure of the charity that "beareth all things, hopeth all things, endureth all things," and those who read his story see that most sensitive and irritable of beings grow to such indomitable patience that a friend, in writing of a maddening character, could say, "There is little hope that any person but Martyn could bear with him." [1]

But the life of inner discipleship, then as ever, had to find expression in outward relationships, and Henry Martyn made new friendships both at Cambridge and at home. The little religious sister in Cornwall, now recognized as a comrade in experience, received, as she also delightedly wrote, long letters on their common experience in Christ. The brother and sister used, naturally enough, the vocabulary of the evangelical revival under the Wesleys, which had created the religious atmosphere that Sally breathed. For them, any "means of grace" from the Holy Communion to personal study of the Scriptures was "a sacred ordinance," a group meeting for Bible study was "a Society" [2] and

[1] D. Corrie to D. Brown, October 4th, 1810.

[2] John Wesley's *Journal* for May 1st, 1738, after his visit to the Moravians, tells of the first meeting of such a "society" in Fetter Lane. It was to meet weekly in groups of not more than ten for confession, spiritual conference and mutual prayer. This was the forerunner of the Wesleyan Class Meeting. Charles Simeon, in order to know his

united prayer was "engaging in a social exercise,"
while private devotions were "secret duties" as
against Church services or "public duties." The evil
which distressed them in their inner life they
commonly referred to as their "corruption," over
which indeed they were in deep concern as they
strove by "a realizing faith" to reach a "happy
frame" of "breathings after God" and a "lively
view of eternal things." The vocabulary may be
studied in the hymns and religious diaries of that
day. Its historical lineage is interesting, many of
the phrases leading one back to sixteenth century
divines and worthies, or to the Moravian brethren
and the German pietists. To-day when it is almost
obsolete as an expression of life it sounds stilted
enough, but for Martyn it was pulsing with the
unconquerable vitality of

> *The children of the Second Birth*
> *Whom the world cannot tame.*

Almost the same phraseology was in use among
the small group of religious men at Cambridge,
with whom Henry Martyn was now to ally himself.
The usual nickname for those in the University
who took Christian discipleship with any seriousness
was still "Methodist," a tribute to the amazing
influence of John Wesley's work. In Martyn's time
a few such "Methodist" undergraduates were found
at Queens' under the Mastership of Isaac Milner,
genial and full-bodied, "a man of boundless good
will to his fellow creatures at every period of life,

---

flock more individually, started something between a cottage meeting
and a Bible class which he also called "a society." He had six
"societies" meeting regularly, each with about 20 members.

provided that they were not Jacobins or sceptics," [1] and the most brilliant talker in the University. "He was equally at home on a steeplechase and on final perseverance ; and explained with the same confidence the economy of an ant-hill and the policy of the Nizam." [2] His lectures on optics, illustrated both by his humour and by "experiments" of the nature of "exhibitions of the magic lanthorn," were among the joys of undergraduate life.

Another group of religious men belonged to Magdalene where the Master wailed that there must be "something in the air of Magdalene that makes men Methodists. We have elected fellows . . . whom we considered to be most anti-Methodistical but they all become Methodists." The central personality here was Professor Farish, a chemist of distinction and a man of charm, later to become well known to Martyn.

But the strongest religious influence in the University, and as some said in all England, was wielded by a Fellow of King's, whose erect soldierly figure might any day be seen riding to the Gogmagog Hills on one of the best-bred horses in the neighbourhood. Undergraduates who a few decades later would be designated by the first syllable of the word "pious" then had the first syllable of the word "Simeon" shouted under their windows at night, in compliment to the Reverend Charles Simeon of King's College, one of the most typically English saints that ever lived, and perhaps the most intrepid and arresting personality of Martyn's Cambridge.

[1] Trevelyan, *Life and Letters of Lord Macaulay*, p. 40.
[2] Stephen, *Essays in Ecclesiastical Biography*.

Twenty years before Martyn, Charles Simeon had come up to King's College from Eton, a most active, vehement and vivid black-eyed boy, given to dominating the circle in which he found himself. He combined an intense interest in clothes, then largely expressed in shoe-buckles and silk waistcoats, with a yet intenser interest in horse-flesh, that abode with him to the day of his death. Under the noise of his vehement talk, Charles Simeon had in him an unguessed depth of reverence, and when he found, three days after his arrival, that undergraduates were, by a now vanished college rule, compelled to take the Sacrament at half-term and again on Easter Day, his soul revolted from a formal and official entrance to the Holy of holies. He set himself to preparation, reading Law's *Whole Duty of Man*, "the only religious book I had ever heard of." For three months his discomfort only grew, until in Passion Week when he was in " distress of soul," light came like a flash to his always vivid mind. "Has God provided an Offering for me, that I may lay my sins on His head ? Then God willing, I will not bear them on my own soul one moment longer." To Simeon as later to Martyn came the revelation of a Person. On Easter Sunday he awoke with the words " Jesus Christ is risen to-day, Hallelujah ! " upon his lips and in his heart, and went to church in a passion of glad conviction. After the service some morsels of the Consecrated Bread remained, and the clergyman handed them to Simeon and some others. Simeon, his heart still at worship, covered his face in prayer while he ate, then looked up to find that, inconceivable as it may now seem, the clergyman was smiling at so rare and so unnecessary a display of "enthusiasm."

From that day the taint of "enthusiasm," so much dreaded in the eighteenth century, made Simeon a marked man in the University and a considerable anxiety to his family, his brother writing plaintively enough "I trust that in the common course of things your zeal will slacken a little." Simeon suffered under his isolation, for he was warm-hearted ; but there was also that in him which leapt to the call of battle.

Henceforth there were two sides to Charles Simeon. On one side he lived, almost unhelped by men, a life of very simple discipleship, of which we learn by stray phrases that reveal the man ; as when he breaks out wistfully, "Oh that Jesus were to be at the wedding, with what joy I should go then" ; or as when a friend, failing to make him hear, burst into his room to find that active, dominating person lost in contemplation and murmuring again and again "Glory, glory, glory to the Son of God." This little-known side of his life he maintained by rising at four, and spending the hours till breakfast in meditation with his "little old quarto Bible."

He had another and a very different side "to face the world with" as he proceeded magnificently to defy the scorn of Cambridge. Shortly after his ordination to a fellowship of King's in 1782 he accepted, against a fury of local opposition, a living of the value of £40 a year, in order that Trinity Church might give him a pulpit from which to speak his message to the city. It is doubtful whether Simeon in all his long life ever knew what it was to speak in an uncertain tone ; and in his pulpit, preaching, as he would have said, to perishing souls of the truths of eternity and the deepest convictions of his own heart, his vehement earnestness of voice and gesture struck Cambridge as " lively " but " grotesque." " Oh, Mamma, what is the gentleman in a passion about ? " cried a little girl who heard such preaching for the first time. Mamma might very properly have replied that Simeon was in a passion, and never out of it, for the neglected honour of his Lord.

It went the round that this Fellow of King's (like the members of the Holy Club at Oxford half a century before) was in the habit of visiting poor felons in the jail and of poking into cottages in insalubrious lanes. But the limit was reached when the respectability of Trinity Church was invaded by the great unwashed. The same treatment was meted out to Simeon as had been given to Romaine when his preaching drew " the unsavoury multitude " into the sacred precincts of St George's, Hanover Square. The respectable pew-holders locked up their square family pews and sat in satisfied propriety at home, leaving Simeon to preach to such of the peasantry of the neighbouring villages (for these tramped miles to hear him) and Cambridge lanes as could stand in the aisles. He placed benches in the aisles, but the churchwardens, with all the joy of battle, threw them out into the churchyard. He started an evening service, a shocking innovation in days when evensong was generally droned through in the sleepiest part of Sunday afternoon, and the cost of candles saved.

Such a " Methodist " with such outrageous practices was fair game for undergraduate wit, and

E

it became a regular Sunday " rag " to bait Simeon. You could stand outside and throw pebbles at the windows while you waited to harry the congregation on their way out ; or you could go inside and stand upon the seats or stroll about the aisles, with suitable cat-calls to a friend in another part of the church, and witty comments on all that Simeon did. " Why, how long the old hypocrite goes on a-praying ! " you felt bound to say, as he bowed his head before the sermon which was to be for you an opportunity of aping his grotesque and passionate gesture. The sermon was the great encounter, and Simeon knew it, and knew too that he could expect no support from University authorities. He had only his own dominating personality and his terrible eye with which to oppose the rowdies. And Sunday after Sunday the miracle happened, and the man with his overwhelming earnestness imposed silence so long as he chose to preach, the hurly-burly breaking out again when he left the pulpit and they were no longer under the domination of that flashing eye. As an old man he used to say that he had never met but two gownsmen who " ever were daring enough to meet my eye."

But Simeon did more than quell men to silence ; week after week he drove the ploughshare of conviction deep into some soul to whom he became ever afterwards a father in God, a robust and fearless leader.

In Martyn's days he was midway in his career, still doubtful whether another Fellow would be seen to walk across the grass of the college court with him ; his disciples still running the gauntlet of University scorn, but forming now a perceptible group, in which "Father Simeon" held his half-tender and half-autocratic sway. When Henry Martyn became a regular attendant at Trinity in 1799, Simeon had already started tea-drinkings, later to become his famous "conversation parties" for gownsmen, at which, after welcoming his guests with the polish and the dignity of a courtier, he sat erect in a high chair, by a scientifically-mended fire (a special crotchet) and dealt out the counsel of a tried and courageous Christian, while two servants handed tea to the slightly embarrassed undergraduates.

This was Martyn's leader in the new path ; a man always vivid, often quaintly humorous, generally domineering, but with touching gentlenesses ; a man of whom the landlady of the "Eagle and Child" was heard to remark confidentially in the London coach, "He looks proud, he walks proud, he talks proud, and he *is* proud," but a man in whom his relationship to Christ worked wonderful flashes of humility : as when he wrote in apology to a groom whom he had rated for putting the wrong bridle on his horse, "I earnestly beg his pardon, and am sorry for what I said to him " : or as when, after snapping at an undergraduate for trampling the yellow gravel of King's College court into the carpet of his bachelor domain, he would return after a few moments to say, "My brother, I was annoyed and spoke too strongly, but [and how human is that but !] I do love a clean carpet."

The literary sense was not strong in Simeon, who was rather a born organizer. He had none of Martyn's love for pure scholarship, but in him common sense was carried almost to the point of genius, and his counsel to the delicately sensitive

Martyn "without one torpid nerve about him," was nearly always robust. A specimen of the guidance Martyn had is found in Simeon's treatment of what was still the favourite subject for theological worry—the Arminian and Calvinistic controversy. A letter written long after Martyn had left Cambridge may yet serve to show us Simeon's habitual and most independent treatment of such questions :

The truth is not in the middle, and not in one extreme but in both extremes. . . . Here are two extremes, Calvinism and Arminianism (for you need not to be told how long Calvin and Arminius lived before St Paul). "How do you move in reference to these, Paul ? In a golden mean ? " "No"—"To one extreme ? " "No." "How then ? " "To both extremes ; to-day I am a strong Calvinist, to-morrow a strong Arminian"—"Well, well, Paul, I see thou art beside thyself ; go to Aristotle and learn the golden mean."

But I am unfortunate ; I formerly read Aristotle, and liked him very much ; I have since read Paul and caught some of his strange notions, oscillating (not vacillating) from pole to pole. Sometimes I am a high Calvinist, at other times a low Arminian, so that if extremes will please you, I am your man ; only remember, it is not one extreme that we are to go to, but *both* extremes.

. . . We shall be ready (in the estimation of the world, and of *moderate* Christians) to go to Bedlam together.[1]

In lesser questions his "young friends" found his advice both fatherly and robust. He would have them work ; but "remember," said he, "your success in the Senate House depends much on the care you take of the three-mile stone out of Cambridge." Most sound counsel for one of Martyn's build who in 1799 and 1800 was all but a recluse,

[1] H. C. G. Moule, *Charles Simeon*, p. 97.

working with the eagerness that gained for him the title of "the man who never lost an hour"; yet working without the old frenzy, since he knew now a deeper interest than his work, and was almost jealous of the necessary absorption in reading. "The labourer as he drives on his plough," he wrote to Sally, "and the weaver as he works at his loom, may have his thoughts entirely disengaged from his work, and may think with advantage upon any religious subject. But the nature of *our* studies requires such a deep abstraction of the mind from all other things, as to render it completely incapable of anything else, and that during many hours of the day."

The examination for degrees took place in January 1801. Henry knew that, having no advantage of family or wealth, his social prospects, and in part those of his sisters also, depended upon the honours that he took. It was true that he was now easily first in his college examinations; but the year was said to be an unusually brilliant one in the University. Among leading names from other colleges were those of Charles and Robert Grant of Trinity, the two sons of Charles Grant of Calcutta, who had learnt their first Latin from the Reverend David Brown.

The examination of those days began before breakfast on a January morning, a moment at which spirits are apt to be at a low ebb. As Martyn passed under the fluted columns of the Senate House portico, there flashed into his agitated mind the text of a sermon heard not long ago—"Seekest thou great things for thyself? Seek them not, saith the Lord." Steadied, as an over-excited child by his father's voice, he went in and wrote with a mind "composed and tranquillized," and retained his calm through the three long mornings of the *viva voce*, when the honours men sat round a table in the ice-cold Senate House with an examiner at their head, who propounded a problem which all worked at topmost speed. When the first man had handed in his solution another problem was read out, with the result that the slower men missed many of the questions. At night in the rooms of one of the moderators more difficult work was set, in which the race for speed was not so great, and men had a choice of problems offered them.

The results were published on the fourth day; and, at not quite twenty years of age, Henry Martyn found that his darling ambition had been realized, and he was Senior Wrangler. His first sensation was keen disappointment. His father was not there to glory in the news. "I obtained my highest wishes," he says, "but was surprised to find that I had grasped a shadow." Be that as it may he did later find much seductive pleasure in the sense of distinction, and in the subtle tone of regard that crept into the voices of University officials when they talked to one at once so young and so distinguished.

Cambridge had given to her young son her highest honours, but at the cost of a diligence that cut him off from many of the richer interests of life. She had given him a formal intellectual training; she had yet in store for him that training in the humanities which only comes of friendship and of fruitful meditation.

CHAPTER IV

FELLOW OF ST JOHN'S

I have seen a great deal of him, have studied his sentiments and heard his opinion on subjects of literature and taste; and upon the whole, I venture to pronounce that his mind is well informed, his enjoyment of books exceedingly great, his imagination lively, his observations just and correct, and his taste delicate and pure. . . . His person can hardly be called handsome, till the expression of his eyes, which are uncommonly good, and the general sweetness of his countenance, is perceived. At present I know him so well that I think him really handsome; or at least almost so.—JANE AUSTEN, *Sense and Sensibility*.

Oh dear Sir, do not think it enough to live at the rate of common Christians. . . . And oh, dear Sir, let me beseech you frequently to attend to the great and precious duties of secret fasting and prayer.—*Letter of* DAVID BRAINERD.

THE ordeal of the degree examination was followed two months later by what was then considered the still more searching test of the examination for the Smith's Prizes, in which less was required of the reproduction of book-work, and more of mathematical thought. Martyn held his own and went home at Easter to receive the congratulations of his old schoolmaster and all the Cornish cousinry, as Senior Wrangler and first Smith's Prizeman of a brilliant year.

Only Sally was dissatisfied and told him so. Cambridge meant little to her, and her brother's religion meant much; in this she was not content with his rate of progress.

He returned to Cambridge to take pupils and prepare for the examination for a fellowship that was an almost certain reward of such distinctions as his.

This second stage of Martyn's Cambridge life was less crowded with relentless tasks and richer in friendship and in growth than his undergraduate days. Martyn was never by nature a mathematician only. A friend writes : [1] "His mathematical acquisitions clearly left him without a rival of his own age : and yet, to have known only the employment of his more free and unfettered moments would have led to the conclusion that poetry and the classics were his predominant passions."

We have no record of what was the poetry on which he slaked his thirst for beauty until a few years later, when we find him steeped in the older traditions. For with all his transcendent abilities, Martyn was no originator in literary thought. The intellectual realm in which he was to come into his own was the then little explored field of the comparative philology of Eastern languages. In regard to English literature he was content to be a finely appreciative follower of the taste of his own day, sometimes too of the day just before his, for Blair's *Grave* gave him " much pleasure." He was at Cambridge in those days just before the " Renascence of Wonder " when men had on them a great industry for compilations, and were busy over encyclopædias,[2] periodicals full of facts, and public lectures packed with information. But they had also a fresh and genuine interest in landscapes of the common

---

[1] Archdeacon C. J. Horne quoted by Sargent, p. 439.
[2] The *Encyclopædia Britannica* was first published in 1771.

countryside, and Marianne Dashwood must possess "every book that tells her how to admire an old, twisted tree."

This taste, so largely due to the loving subtlety with which Cowper drew his bird-haunted shrubberies and placid reaches of the Ouse, was one of the deepest in Martyn's nature ; for he, like the poet of his own religious school, knew the relief of escape from his own too eager emotions to quiet fields and waters.

The recognized versifier of the clan of cousins and cousinly friends in Cornwall was Fortescue Hitchins,[1] a boy three years younger than Martyn, whose home with his grandfather, the Rev. Malachy Hitchins of Marazion, had been one of the favourite haunts of Henry's boyhood. Fortescue Hitchins wrote and published by subscription verses full of local landscapes, Cornish shores and sea-birds.

> *My steps the barren sands*
> *(Though barren not unpleasing) oft invite,*
> *Where not a trace is seen, save the light print*
> *Of sea-bird . . .*
> *. . . So smooth the sea,*
> *It seems a mirror of ethereal blue,*
> *Dappled with varied plumage. O'er its plain*
> *Swift wheels the timid sanderling, gregarious,*
> *Nimble, alert, and mingling on the shore*
> *With dotterell and plover.*

For this type of quiet verse-making Martyn's appetite was keen. "Some of Fortescue's poems," he says, "set me into a pensive meditation on the happy mornings I had passed near Kea." He would

---

[1] Later a solicitor at St Ives and compiler of a *History of Cornwall*.

often rest his own mind by composing verses as he walked into the country round Cambridge.

Always, too, there were the immortals and he tells us that he read now " some choruses of Sophocles," or again, " Euripides till very late," and confesses that just before he left for India he allowed himself an Æschylus and a Pindar, not without scruples as to whether he should afford the price.

There was more space now in Martyn's Cambridge life for friendship, and Charles Simeon drew him into closer intimacy and would often ask him to drink tea when they would sit together, Simeon erect in his high chair under that " beautiful old painting of the Crucifixion " which he hoped they would hang before him on his deathbed, and quietly rubbing his hands together, as was his way in moments of placid enjoyment, while he talked with one so eagerly and so respectfully responsive.

To Simeon Martyn owed many of the friendships of these years, and above all his very beautiful intimacy with John Sargent of King's, who had taken his degree with Martyn but was not personally known to him till Simeon's introduction.

Young Sargent, heir of a Sussex squire, had shown at Eton " a decided superiority in the manly sports of the playground, with high classical attainments." When he came up to Cambridge he was one of the only two gownsmen whom Simeon's eye had been unable to quell, a fact which the latter did not fail to appreciate. And when conviction entered the soul of the young rioter, and Sargent placed himself on the side of the " serious " undergraduates, Charles Simeon welcomed him to a life-long friendship.

Through the pen of his son-in-law [1] we see Sargent
as a man of gracious charm. Both he and Martyn
" belonged to a school of Attic elegance which is
declining amongst us—a school of men who studied
the classics, not as a means by which to obtain
distinction, nor merely to acquire in the knowledge
of another language a key to fresh mental attainments, but for their own sweetness. These were
men whose whole spirit breathed of classical
refinement."

" A friend indeed " Martyn called Sargent, writing
to Sally in September 1801, " and one who has made
much about the same advances in religion as myself."
For one so sensitive as Martyn, this was a wholesome friendship, for though none ever possessed
" a softer touch " than Sargent, he was " frank and
sparkling," with " a perpetual spring of holy, guileless
gaiety." As yet he was a young disciple, but he
was growing towards that freedom and spontaneity
as of a child at home in his father's house, which
his son-in-law shows as one of the dominant notes
in his religious life, a rare note in those days of rather
portentous solemnity.

It might be from mingling in the sports and merri-
ments of childhood ; it might be from the excitement
of intellectual conversation ; that he was called upon to
turn his attention at once to holy things. The transition was effected in a moment. It was natural and
reverend ; free from anything of sternness ; and
impressing upon everyone the evident truth that his
religion was no gloomy system of prohibitions and
restraint.

[1] Bishop Samuel Wilberforce who wrote a short memoir of Sargent
as an introduction to the *Journals* of Henry Martyn. The details
given about him are largely from this sketch.

To these two friends Charles Simeon sounded a call. To them as to all the choice youth whom he gathered into the inner circle of his friendship it was his way to speak again and again of "the transcendent excellence of the Christian ministry." But in Sargent and in Martyn the words of their leader roused very different feelings.

Sargent who "seemed scarcely able to comprehend the pleasure of owning anything unless he could give it to another" was destined to become a substantial Sussex landowner. He carried in the year 1801 the spirit of a son of Francis in the year 1210. "Could I have been assured that it was God's will that I should serve Him as a minister, were it to preach to the wild Indians," he told a friend, "*nothing* should stand in my way." But parental orders were distinct. He was to go to the Temple and "follow the profession of the law" as a valuable training for the future head of a landed family.

With intense pain of spirit, after being "tossed about for a long time" he decided that Simeon's call was not for him, and bent to the parental will as to discipline from his Divine Master. The effect of the self-conquest was manifest to his friends. "Sargent seems to be outstripping us all" wrote Martyn. But Sargent himself was chiefly conscious of the difficulties of his new course. "Do not forget I beseech you," he wrote, "to pray for me, that the love of Jesus may attend me, and His right hand lead me through the perils of the profession I am entering."

In Martyn's mind Charles Simeon's exhortations had struck a very different and a jarring note.

"Few could surpass him," wrote Sargent of his friend, "in an exquisite relish for the various and refined enjoyments of a social and literary life." His University honours placed him in a position to choose his path, and the very profession from which Sargent shrank seemed to Martyn alluring, as a path to money, position and studious leisure. "I could not consent," he says, "to be poor for Christ's sake." He knew the humiliation served out to Simeon's friends in clerical life, and had seen how, if Simeon were absent, his curate was left with a perfectly impossible burden of duty because no cleric in the town or University would demean himself by serving in that notorious parish.

But Martyn's attitude to life was changing, in part through Sargent's friendship, and still more through great draughts of Bible reading and solitary prayer in green places by the Cambridge river during the long vacation of 1801. That summer marks an epoch in his life. "Not until then," he said, "had I ever experienced any real pleasure in religion." The taste which grew in him then for solitude, and especially for solitude out of doors, went with him through life.

In the pages of his Cambridge journal we can trace how the desire grew upon him for the Companionship which he found in that solitude in which he was never alone. In that journal we are allowed to watch with a rare intimacy the growth of a saint. "My object in making this journal," he says, "is to accustom myself to self-examination, and to give my experience a visible form, so as to leave a stronger impression on the memory, and thus to improve my soul in holiness; for the review of such a lasting testimony will serve the double purpose of conviction and consolation." Whatever we may think of the value of such a plan, Martyn's scrupulously transparent journal, written without a shred of self-excuse, as in the sight of God and all His angels, is perhaps the most remarkable human document left by the Church of his day, ranked by Dr George Smith among "the great spiritual autobiographies of Catholic literature."

Entry after entry like those which follow serves to give us a glimpse of the growing taste for solitude, a solitude at first full of conscious effort, but into which there stole the sense of a Presence so sweet that all earthly joys went less to that communion.

I walked in the fields and endeavoured to consider my ways, and to lift up my heart to God.

Walked to the hawthorn hedge. . . . I devoted myself to Him solemnly, and trust that when tempted to sin I shall remember this walk.

Had a sweet, supporting sense of God's presence in the evening, when I walked by moonlight.

I determined to give all the rest of the day to acts of devotion without going into hall to dinner. So I retired to the garden.

During my walk, my mind was too much engaged in the composition of poetry, which I found to leave me far short of that sweetness I seemed in a frame to enjoy. Yet on the spot where I have often found the presence of God, the spirit of prayer returned.

My imagination takes to itself wings and flies to some wilderness where I may hold converse in solitude with God.

Was empty and tired for want of being alone.

Let me but ply heart-work in secret, let me but walk alone in communion with God, and I shall surely be able to offer Him sacrifices more pure.

From the church I walked to our garden, where I was alone an hour, I trust with Christ.

The sudden appearance of evil thoughts made me very unhappy, but I found refuge in God. O may the Lord . . . make me to find in Himself, the source and centre of beauty, a sweet and satisfied delight.

What is this world, what is religious company, what is anything to me without God ? They become a bustle and a crowd when I lose sight of Him. The most dreary wilderness would appear paradise with a little of His presence.

A man cannot yield himself to such Companionship without being moulded by it, and the Martyn who thought that he " could not consent to be poor for Christ's sake " found himself writing to Sally in September 1801 :

The soul that has truly experienced the love of God will not stay meanly inquiring how much he shall do, and thus limit his service ; but will be earnestly seeking more and more to know the will of our heavenly Father that he may be enabled to do it.

He did not reach his final decision as to the choice of a career until the long vacation of 1802. That summer, after a walking tour in Wales, he spent a Cornish holiday in sister Laura's married home, a lovable white house called Woodbury on the winding banks of the Fal Estuary. Here where the curlews called and the steep woods met the lapping water he wandered alone with the Book of the Prophet Isaiah, passing " some of the sweetest moments of his life." When he returned to Cambridge his mind was made up. He would seek ordination and accept an invitation from Charles Simeon to become his curate. The decision was not easy to announce in Cambridge, as his journal shows.

Was ashamed to confess to —— that I was to be Simeon's curate, a despicable fear of man.

Five months before reaching this determination Martyn had obtained his fellowship (April 5th, 1802), and had followed it up by winning the first of the only University prizes open to middle bachelors, the Members' Prize for a Latin essay which he must declaim in public. Sargent says that "men of great classical celebrity" contested it with him. We can only wonder the more at the ease of the stride with which, after three years of close mathematical work, he returned to the classics that he loved.

The new Fellow, in rooms in the corner of the lovely second court of St John's, lived a life at once sociable and solitary. Men found him accessible, for with all his love of pretty manners he was remarkable, an old schoolfellow tells us, for "simplicity and ease." The journal shows a large acquaintance and it shows too that the men who climbed his staircase had a way of staying to talk long, and sometimes longer than he liked.

Interrupted by R. who stayed till nine. Our conversation was on mathematics.

Some of my acquaintance drank wine with me. I was more careful about offending them by overmuch strictness than of offending God by conformity to the world.

From seven to twelve wasted by repeated calls of friends.

Insensibly passed the whole time in talking about music.

I had promised to walk with —— which was perfectly hateful to me at this time, when I had such need of being alone with God.

For he was living now in two worlds and the man who at one moment had all heaven before his eyes, at another was terribly mortified because "fear of man" kept him from saying grace when two visitors from Clare Hall came to breakfast. The *Journal* shows him always accessible to younger men in need of help with mathematics, and his schoolfellow, Dr Carlyon, had memories of running to Martyn's room in trouble over the Eleventh Book of Newton and watching him push aside a massive Bible, pick up an odd sheet of paper and with a few miraculous lines sweep away all his difficulties.

As Fellow, Martyn took his share in conducting the college examinations, then largely oral; at different times he examined in Butler, Locke, Xenophon, Juvenal and Euripides. It cost him a good deal of nervous *malaise* to examine before his brother Fellows. He "doubted of his fitness," but when it came to the point examined "with great ease to myself and clearness," and found the "attention and respect" of the Fellows after his performance in hall "remarkable." Yet here again he was living in two worlds. "There was something of a sacred impression on my mind during the examination in hall; several of the poetical images in Virgil in which they had been examining, especially those taken from nature, together with the sight of the moon rising over the venerable walls, and sending its light through the painted glass, turned away my thoughts from present things and raised them to God." Did any trembling candidate wonder at a sudden and other-worldly illumination in the face of the man who was examining him "with great ease and clearness"?

And did the dining Fellows catch a strange light on his face in hall at times like that when the con-

F

versation at their table was of "stones falling from
the moon," and "my imagination began to ascend
among the shining worlds hung in the midst of
space, and to glance from one to another; and my
heart bounded at the thought that I was going a
much surer way to behold the glories of the Creator
hereafter, than by giving up my time to speculations
about them"?

Those were the years when men expected Bona-
parte to sail across the Channel, and the loyal
University formed its volunteer corps with "a
grave uniform," dark blue jacket, black stock, grey
trousers and short black gaiters. So clad, Martyn
used to drill the Fellows, perhaps as the youngest
and most active member of that learned body.
One would like to know whether Mr Catton came
down from the observatory tower to present arms
at his former pupil's bidding. The drills took place
on Sidney Piece (now the Master's Garden) or on
Parker's Piece, and sometimes there was a field
day at Cherry Hinton chalk-pits. Martyn wrote
to Sargent that he was passing his summer "amid
the din of arms. I give our drilling this lofty title."

With all his share in college life and work, Martyn
yet gave the impression to his colleagues of one
who had his being in another world, and they re-
sented it as men always resent the involuntary
absorption of the artist or the saint.

On preparing to go out B. called upon me, and our
conversation lasted till near dinner time. He thought
that by immoderate seclusion I deadened those fine
feelings that we should cultivate, and neglected the
active duties of life: that a thorough and universal
change of heart and life was not necessary to make us
Christians, of whom there might be all degrees, as of

everything else. His amazing volubility left me unable to say anything.

Martyn on his part found their tastes as mysterious as they found his gauche and bizarre :

It sometimes appeared astonishing that men of like passions with myself, of the same bodies, of the same minds, alike in every other respect, knew and saw nothing of that blessed and adorable Being in whom my soul findeth all its happiness, but were living a sort of life which to me would be worse than annihilation.

Under such circumstances that matchless combination room of St John's with its bossy ceiling and its long row of Tudor windows was not always a place of joy for Martyn. Sometimes, indeed, after an intellectual triumph this very junior Fellow found there " respect and admiration " from which he shrank as " dangerous " ; but there were other days on which the Johnians had great relish from a little mockery of their resident " Methodist." Martyn must have provided plenty of scope for wit ; like Charles Simeon in the early years after his conversion, he found it necessary to cut himself off from much that a maturer disciple could have enjoyed without danger. " I was tinder and did not like to go near sparks," Simeon would explain in later years. To the immature disciple it was a question of entering into life were it blind or halt or maimed ; but to the genial souls in the combination room such young severity must have seemed delicious. " Went into the combination room after dinner, where some of those present kept me constantly employed by asking me questions to make me speak against the usual amusements of men."

So he walked among them uncomprehended and

often uncomprehending, with that involuntary aloofness of the poet or the saint, and yet equally with a new yearning towards every human soul, that would lead him at the end of a long day's work to read aloud to his bedmaker. It is a strange picture of the rapt young scholar by the lamp, reading St Luke to the frowzy old lady who could not read for herself. Did she catch the meaning of his ministrations, or did she twiddle her thumbs and possess her soul in patience under the unaccountableness of her gentleman's new whim?

This new-found care of the once fastidious Martyn for the souls of dull and shabby personages was immensely strengthened when in the autumn of 1802 he read the life of David Brainerd [1] and found his hero. He who would know Martyn must ask what manner of man was that Brainerd who called out his depths of admiration.

Martyn's hero was born at Hartford, Connecticut, in 1718, of a Puritan family that named him David and his brothers Hezekiah, Nehemiah, John and Israel. Surrounded by the influences that commonly went with a choice of names in which the Old Testament held so heavy a predominance, and suffering from a wretched constitution and the loss of both parents before he was fourteen, young David hardly surprises us when he writes: "I was, I think from my youth something sober, and inclined rather to melancholy than the contrary extreme; but do not remember anything of conviction of sin, worthy of remark, till I was, I believe, about seven or eight years of age."

[1] *An Account of the Life of David Brainerd* by Jonathan Edwards, Edinburgh, 1798.

Yet for this boy, bred in so dour a school, there was in store an evangelical experience that might be recorded of one of the mystics of Catholicism. It came to him on a "Sabbath evening" in July of 1739 when he was twenty-one. He was, he tells us,

walking in the solitary place where I was brought to see myself lost and helpless . . . endeavouring to pray (though being as I thought very stupid and senseless) for near half an hour (and by this time the sun was about half an hour high as I remember), then as I was walking in a thick dark grove *unspeakable glory* seemed to open to the view and apprehension of my soul. I do not mean any external brightness, for I saw no such thing ; nor do I intend any imagination of a body of light, somewhere away in the third heavens, or anything of that nature ; but it was a new inward apprehension or view that I had of God, such as I never had before, nor anything which had the least resemblance of it. I stood and wondered and admired. . . . My soul was so captivated with the excellency, loveliness, greatness and other perfections of God, that I was even swallowed up in Him ; at least to that degree that I had no thought (as I remember) at first about my own salvation, and scarce reflected that there was such a creature as myself. . . . At this time the *way of salvation* opened to me with such infinite wisdom, suitableness and excellency, that I wondered I should ever think of any other way of salvation ; was amazed that I had not dropt my own contrivances, and complied with this lovely, blessed and excellent way before.

In turning over the yellow leaves of the life of Martyn's hero, one finds that this son of Calvinistic Independents, this Presbyterian minister of the mid-eighteenth century was a saint spiritually akin to Francis and to Raymond Lull, to all the bearers of the stigmata and all the great spiritual lovers throughout the ages.

In the forenoon, [says Brainerd] while I was looking on the Sacramental elements, and thinking that Jesus Christ would soon be " set forth crucified before me," my soul was filled with light and love, so that I was almost in an ecstasy; . . . and I felt at the same time an exceeding tenderness and most fervent love towards all mankind.

Henceforth this Christo-centric love for men was one of the marks of David Brainerd :

God enabled me so to agonize in prayer, that I was quite wet with sweat, though in the shade, and the wind cool. My soul was drawn out very much for the world ; I grasped for multitudes of souls.

The language of my thoughts and disposition (although I spoke no words) now were, Here I am, Lord, send me to the ends of the earth ; send me to the rough, the savage Pagans of the wilderness ; send me from all that is called comfort in earth . . . send me even to death itself if it be but in Thy service and to Thy kingdom.

To the wilderness he was sent, little strength and little taste as he had for it. A hillside which for Martyn's generation would have been " romantic " was for Brainerd and his fellow-settlers, who thought of it in terms of weary and dangerous travel, " a hideous mountain." Into the " hideous and howling wilderness " Brainerd was sent to be the missionary and shepherd of the Indian tribes pushed backwards by advancing settlers. " My Indians," " my poor Indians," or " my dear little flock " he called them, gave them his heart and lived for them under conditions that to him were hateful. His diet as he told his brother John was " mostly of hasty pudding, boiled corn, and bread baked in the ashes and sometimes a little meat and butter. My lodging is a little heap of straw, laid upon some boards, a little way from the ground, for it is a log room,

without any floor that I lodge in." For his Indians
he made apostolic journeys to camps on the Susquehannah river, himself fast dying of consumption.

Near night, my beast that I rode upon hung one of
her legs in the rocks, and fell down under me. . . .
She broke her leg ; and being in such a hideous place,
and near thirty miles from any house . . . was obliged
to kill her, and to prosecute my way on foot . . . just
at dark we kindled a fire, cut up a few bushes, and made
a shelter over our heads to save us from the frost, which
was very hard that night.

When Brainerd died at the age of thirty-two,
having spent his last night on earth in "very
proper discourse" with brother John concerning
"the interest of religion among the Indians," the
forest round his settlement was full of leafy cells
into which his Indian Christians would steal at
dawn for secret prayer.

This was the life that made an irresistible appeal
to Martyn in the days when, by all accepted canons
of taste around him, he should have been listening
to the dulcet tones of that divine of whom George III
said that he "wished every youth in the kingdom
might possess a copy of the Bible and of Blair."
Blair, whose "fortune was easy," "lived much in
the style of a gentleman" and wrote in a corresponding style. So much did the age enjoy his
ornate and measured periods that he received £600
a volume for his sermons. His address to youth
was conciliatory : and we feel no incongruity at
finding extracts from his sermons bound up with
Chesterfield's *Advice to his Son* and Rochefoucauld's
Maxims as a gift for the young.

"While some by wise and steady conduct," says

this most urbane of mentors, "attain distinction
in the world, and pass their days with comfort and
honour ; others of the same rank, by mean and
vicious behaviour, forfeit the advantages of their
birth, involve themselves in much misery, and end
in being a disgrace to their friends, and a burden on
society. . . . Shall happiness grow up to you of
its own accord, and solicit your acceptance, when,
to the rest of mankind it is the fruit of long cultivation, and the acquisition of labour and care ?
Deceive not yourselves with such arrogant hopes.
Whatever be your rank, Providence will not, for
your sake, reverse its established order. By listening to wise admonitions, and tempering the vivacity
of youth with a proper mixture of serious thought
you may ensure cheerfulness for the rest of your life.
We call you not to renounce pleasure but enjoy
it in safety. Instead of abridging it, we exhort
you to pursue it on an extensive plan. We propose
measures for securing its possession and for pro-
longing its duration." [1]

In an age of Blairdom, Martyn preferred his
Brainerd sleeping on the ground by the Susquehannah river, waking in a cold sweat, spitting blood,
dragging himself on, listening unseen to the pow-
wows of medicine men, teaching Indians to fence
their corn by day and to answer the questions of
his catechism by night, battling against a strain
of morbid melancholy, consumed with a longing
" to be a flame of fire in the divine service."

So Martyn pored alone over the chronicle of " the
fatigues and perils of another journey to Susquehannah," the very river of dreams where, but a

[1] Blair's *Sermons*, Vol. I., Sermon XI.

few years since, young Coleridge of Jesus College, Cambridge, with Robert Southey of Balliol College, Oxford, had planned a "social colony." That "Pantisocracy" where all selfishness was to be proscribed made a glorious theme for the glorious talk of young republican poets. But "Mr C.'s cooler friends could not ascertain that he had received any specific information respecting this notable river. 'It was a grand river'; but there were many other grand and noble rivers in America; and the preference given to the Susquehannah, seemed to arise solely from its imposing name." [1] For Henry Martyn and his hero the Susquehannah was no river of vague ideal beauties. The contemplation of the wayfarer of Christ roused in Martyn, Sargent tells us, "a holy emulation," and pointed the way to the hardest struggle he had yet known. Again and again the name of Brainerd finds its way into the *Journal:*

I thought of David Brainerd, and ardently desired his devotedness to God and holy breathings of soul.

Read David Brainerd to-day and yesterday, and find as usual my spirit greatly benefited by it. I long to be like him; let me forget the world and be swallowed up in a desire to glorify God.

The rest of the evening in conversing and writing letters. My heart was not in visible disorder during all this, but it is not the spiritual life that Brainerd led.

Read Brainerd. I feel my heart knit to this dear man, and really rejoice to think of meeting him in heaven.

It was to Simeon the leader that Martyn owed the suggestion of the path by which he was to follow Brainerd. Charles Simeon had been one of those "Methodist" clergy to whom Grant and

[1] Joseph Cottle, *Reminiscences of Coleridge and Southey*, p. 22.

Brown wrote in 1787 of their proposed mission to Bengal. " We understand that such matters lie very near your heart " they had said. Simeon's ardent mind had caught fire, and from that moment, as he lived his industrious days in Cambridge colleges and lanes, his eyes had been set towards the east. India did lie very near his heart. To Martyn on his return from Cornwall in 1802 with the resolution to be ordained, he said some eager words about the good done " by *one* missionary in India," the immortal cobbler Dr Carey, whose *Periodical Accounts* from Serampore were earnestly followed by Simeon.

Martyn listened to his leader ; then he read Brainerd ; the appeal of Simeon's words and of Brainerd's life lived together in his mind through the autumn of 1802 ; against them were all the inclinations of his nature. When the last leaves were falling from the elms in the Fellows' garden " he was at length fixed in a resolution to imitate Brainerd's example." And he proposed to do it by offering himself as a missionary to the tiny new society formed in London by some of Simeon's acquaintance under the title of " The Society for Missions to Africa and the East." [1]

Martyn's decision startled his world almost as much as if he had proposed a flight to the moon ; and not the least surprised people were the committee of the little missionary society gathered in the study of a London rectory. Since their foundation in 1799 no Englishman had offered to serve them as

---

[1] Known to-day as the Church Missionary Society. The group who formed it were friends of Simeon and invited him to become a " country member."

a foreign missionary, and in the month when Martyn
sent his enquiry (November 1802) they had inter-
viewed two young German pietists, an interview not
without its difficulties, since neither the committee
nor the candidates knew many words of the other
party's language. The Germans had been accepted
as " catechists " for West Africa and sent to
Clapham to learn a little English.[1] The secretary
of the committee now received an astonishing
enquiry about service from a young scholar who,
as far as university preferments were concerned,
had the ball at his feet.

Both in Cambridge and in Cornwall Martyn's
step was regarded as fantastic and absurd.

Walked out in the evening in great tranquillity and
on my return met with Mr C., with whom I was obliged
to walk an hour longer. He thought it a most improper
step for me to leave the University to preach to the
ignorant heathen, which any person could do.

Such was the University opinion of the missionary
vocation.

In Cornwall it was much the same :

Breakfasted with ——, he presently entered into the
highest points of the Calvinistic scheme . . . my heart
was much frozen by the conversation ; he had but a
slight opinion of missionary work, though he has, I know,
great affection for me. . . . Dined at ——'s who used
every argument to dissuade me from going to India.

To Sally he confided, " The thought that I might
be unceasingly employed in the same kind of work,
amongst poor ignorant people, is what my proud
spirit revolts at. To be obliged to submit to a
thousand uncomfortable things that must happen to

[1] See Eugene Stock, *History of the Church Missionary Society*, I. 83.

me whether as a minister or a missionary is what the flesh cannot endure."

Even Sally was not encouraging. Perhaps she was beginning to be absorbed in her own love affair. At all events she does not seem to have realized that Henry was no longer the flighty schoolboy for whom she used to pray. "Received a letter from my sister in which she expressed her opinion of my unfitness for the work." She told him that he was lacking in "that deep and solid experience necessary for a missionary."

Martyn was half inclined to agree with her and the *Journal* shows a picture of steady self-discipline, "to fit me for a long life of warfare and constant self-denial."

How mortally do I hate the thought, yet certainly I will do the will of God, if I be cut piece-meal.

I resolved on my knees to live a life of far more self-denial than I had ever yet done, and to begin with little things. Accordingly I ate my breakfast standing at a distance from the fire, and stood reading at the window during the morning, though the thermometer stood at freezing-point. . . . I rejoiced that God had made this life a time of trial. To climb the steep ascent, to run, to fight, to wrestle was the desire of my heart.

CHAPTER V

A CURACY AMONG THE EVANGELICALS

Read Mr Edward's piece on the affections again and again.—*Letter of* DAVID BRAINERD.

That great man, Jonathan Edwards.—HENRY MARTYN'S *Journal.*

Many spirits are abroad, more are issuing from the pit; the credentials which they display are the precious gifts of mind, beauty, richness, depth, originality. Christian, look hard at them with Martin in silence, and ask them for the print of the nails.—J. H. NEWMAN, *The Church of the Fathers.*

We must speak out. Their *Christianity* is *not* Christianity. It wants the radical principle. It is mainly defective in all the grand constituents.—WILLIAM WILBERFORCE, *A Practical View of Christianity.*

ON an October morning in 1803 Henry Martyn hired a gig and bowled out of Cambridge through the autumn lanes to Ely, to be examined by the Bishop's chaplain, and to be ordained next day in the Cathedral. He went into the Bishop's chapel, and kneeling there before his examination felt "great shame at having come so confidently to offer myself for the ministry of the Lord Jesus Christ with so much ignorance and unholiness." The examination of candidates for ordination in 1803 was an almost casual affair, and Martyn's preparation, mental and spiritual, had been left to his own devices.

Rarely did a candidate present himself with mind more soaked in Holy Scripture, or who took with

a more awful reverence "authority to read the
Gospel in the Church of God and to preach the
same." Three times daily in his college rooms he
bathed his soul in Holy Writ; and on walks to
Lolworth or Shelford, or on solitary rides he learned
whole books by heart. The details in the *Journal*
show that his imagination, jealously watched
and repressed in some directions, had free play
here :

I addressed myself with earnest prayer and a strong
desire to know and learn the Epistle to the Romans in
the Greek.

Read the Psalms with a bright light shining upon
them.

Read the Acts this morning with great delight. I
love to dwell in sacred scenes other than those which
pass before me, and especially those in which the men
of God are concerned.

Read at night the first three chapters of the Revelation,
and found them as usual very searching and awful.

Read the latter end of the Revelation, and so very
lively was the impression on my mind, that I was often
in tears. So awful, so awakening was this book to me.

But the book that was above all the home of his
spirit and to which, perhaps insensibly, he returned
the most, was the prophecy of Isaiah :

Hoped to enjoy some of the peace and joy I used to
feel in reading Isaiah but was interrupted. [Or again]
In great sorrow I read some of Isaiah.

It was his lifelong love, and in the great Bible
that he took with him to India this book more than
any other is interlined, in his free and delicate
penmanship, with readings from the Septuagint or
Hebrew.

Butler and Paley he read as the indispensable

apologists of his day; and on them the examining chaplain set most of his questions.

But Martyn had also browsed in experimental divinity. He had found for himself St Augustine's *Confessions,* then strangely out of fashion, and dismissed a generation later by Macaulay as " an interesting book marred in places by the style of a field preacher," but calling to the deeps in Martyn. William Law: " rather a favourite of mine " . . . " Rose at half after five according to the impulse I received from reading Law." Bishop Hopkin's [1] sermons: " Never did I read such energetic language." But above all other divines the man of Martyn's heart, at whose name examining chaplains would have shuddered, was one Jonathan Edwards, born in Connecticut in the days of good Queen Anne, and educated at " Yale College," bred up a Calvinist and ordained a Presbyterian minister, a man whose books show him " a seer oppressed by his tremendous faith."

There was room in Edwards at one and the same moment for an awful sense of sin, a passion of adoration and a terribly lucid intellectual view of the universe.

My wickedness as I am in myself, has long appeared to me perfectly ineffable, and infinitely swallowing up all thought and imagination, like an infinite deluge, or infinite mountains over my head. I know not how to express better what my sins appear to me to be, than by heaping infinite upon infinite and multiplying infinite by infinite. I go about very often for these many years

---

[1] 1634-1690, Bishop of Derry. He won the appreciation of the early evangelicals. Doddridge remarks of him in his *Lectures on Preaching :* " His motto *aut suaviter aut vi* well answers to his works. Yet he trusts most to the latter. He awakes awfully."

with such expressions in my mind, and in my mouth
" Infinite upon Infinite !   Infinite upon Infinite ! "

Yet this burdened soul bore about with him what
he called " a sort of inward, sheer delight in God."

I often used to sit and view the moon for a long time ;
and so in the day time, spent much time in viewing the
clouds and sky, to behold the sweet glory of God in these
things. . . . And scarce anything, among all the works
of nature, was so sweet to me as thunder and lightning
. . . it rejoiced me.   I felt God at the first appearance
of a thunderstorm.

This vivid, emotional nature so congenial to
Martyn was joined with a lucid, systematizing mind.
Before going to his first cure Edwards recorded
among his resolutions : " Resolved, when I think
of any Theorem in Divinity to be solved, immediately to do what I can towards solving it if Circumstances don't hinder."   And so there came thundering out of the wilderness books to which Martyn
turned again and again as the most satisfying body
of divinity : Jonathan Edwards on *The Great
Christian Doctrine of Original Sin Defended*, virile,
incisive, terrible.   Jonathan Edwards on *The History
of Redemption*, clear-cut and all but debonair.   But
above all Jonathan Edwards, *Concerning Religious
Affections*, as searching in its scrutiny of human
motive as the discipline of any monastic confessor.

Such reading was Martyn's preparation for the
ministry.   The examining chaplain gave him a test in
New Testament Greek, in theological Latin, with some
questions in Christian evidences, and set him free.

After leaving the palace I was in very low spirits.   I
had now nothing to think of but the weight and difficulty
of the work which lay before me.

His depression was not helped by finding the other candidates flippant at dinner ; good enough boys perhaps, sent by their fathers for ordination to a family living, without a thought of the mysteries profaned. Martyn begged one of them in a quiet moment " to read the ordination service," and he " was much affected."

Next morning

At half-past ten we went to the cathedral. During the ordination and Sacramental services I sought in vain for a humble heavenly mind. The outward shew which tended to inspire solemnity affected me more than the faith of Christ's presence, giving me the commission to preach the gospel.

With inward struggle, then, Martyn's ministry began, and with struggle it continued. Without other training than a resident fellowship in the University, he was thrust as Simeon's curate into the care of the little parish of Lolworth four miles out of Cambridge. There, among his country folk, or in the almshouses and lanes of the city where Simeon set him to visit, he felt " a mere schoolboy " with words and manner smacking of college rather than of life, and perhaps hiding from his hearers the very realities he was struggling to express.

H. and my other friends complained of my speaking too low and with too little elocution. These things, with the difficulty I had found in making sermons, and the poorness of them, made me appear exceedingly contemptible to myself. I began to see (and amazing is it to say) for the first time, that I must be content to take my place among men of second-rate abilities.

C. told me I was far above the comprehension of people in general. Nothing pains and grieves me more than this, for I had rather be a preacher of the Gospel among

G

the poor, and to the poor, so as to be understood by them, than be anything else upon earth.

Later, Mr Cecil, of St John's, Bedford Row, added his brisk advice :

Brother Martyn, you are a humble man, and would gain regard in private life ; but to gain public attention you must force yourself into a more marked and expressive manner.

Mr Cecil has been taking a great deal of pains with me.   My insipid inanimate manner in the pulpit, he says, is intolerable.   Sir, said he, it is cupola-painting, not miniature, that must be the aim of a man that harangues a multitude.

Diligent pastoral visiting was the rule for Simeon's curates, and it was no easy rule to Martyn.   " It is my will rather to sit down, to please myself with reading, and let the world perish."

The work of visiting the people of Cambridge and reading to and praying with them appeared hateful to me.

Yet day after day he was driven out from the congenial world of books by a sense of terrible responsibility.   It is clear that he often stayed too long in a sick-room, but he left his people with no possible doubt that someone cared for their souls. The *Journal* is full of vignettes.

He was lying in his clothes and hat, on the bed, dying : his wife was cleaning the room as if nothing was the matter ; and on the threshold was the daughter, about thirty-three years old, who had been deranged thirteen years.   Her mother said that the poor creature sometimes talked of religion : so I asked her, several times, before I could arrest her attention, Who came into the world to save sinners ?   After several wild looks she hastily answered, " Christ," and then talked on as before.

The dying man was almost insensible to anything I could say.

Wished for nothing but to be doing the work of Christ and went in this frame to visit the woman and her son. The room was so exceedingly offensive that I could scarcely endure it for an instant, yet by care I was able to continue for about half an hour.

Went to see a poor young woman, who after a life of sin, appears to be in a dying state, though only seventeen ; she was in too much pain to attend to me much, and so I withdrew, affected almost to tears. My heart was ready to burst when I thought of the man who had seduced her.

After church called at two of the cottages. In one the man, the father of a large family, and in the other the mother . . . told me in the course of conversation that they used the belief as their favourite prayer at night. I was perfectly shocked.

All his life Martyn would be " perfectly shocked " at what another man would meet with a rueful smile. All his friends note in him a certain " simplicity" which always credited others with the spiritual standards of his own life, and left him unshielded against many a rude encounter with things as they were.

There is no denying the fact that these years in Simeon's parish were years of overwork. College life and interests went on as before, and to these were added the cure of Lolworth, with cottage visiting and catechizing in the school (" I seem able to instruct children "), and a share of the work in Trinity parish, sermons, week-day services, visits to hospital, almshouses, workhouse, sick-beds and meetings of " Societies " for Bible study.

The incessant employment of my thoughts about the necessary business of my life, parishes, pupils, sermons, sick, leave far too little time for my private meditations ; so that I know little of God and my soul. Resolved I would gain some hours from my usual sleep if there were no other way.

Martyn's reward and relaxation after work was the grammar of some Eastern language. A grammar was to him what a novel is to the ordinary tired mortal :

Finished the Bengalee [1] grammar which I began yesterday.
Wasted much time in looking over an Arabic grammar.
Finding myself in great stupidity I took up the Hindoostanee grammar, that the time might not pass away without any profit.
Very unwillingly left Bengalee for writing sermon.

Thus greedily and by snatches, as a delightful relaxation, Martyn worked on Persian and Arabic, Gilchrist's Hindustani Dictionary and Reader (a pioneer work) and Halhed's Bengali Grammar for which the first printed type ever made in that script was punched with his own hands by Sir Charles Wilkins, the orientalist who under Warren Hastings first made Britain aware of the treasures hidden in Sanskrit literature.

The friends who allowed, nay encouraged, Martyn at an all but intolerable strain, to forsake scholarship for a busy parochial round were men whose gifts lay along the lines of the more active duties. Charles Simeon, essentially an organizer, had found his ideal senior curate, and perhaps the most

---

[1] Here as elsewhere in quotations from Martyn or others of his day their spelling of oriental words is preserved ; perhaps it may help to place them in their setting as pioneer workers before the days of comparative phonetics.

intimate friend of his life, in Thomas Thomason, a mathematical tutor who learned to dread "the mathematical religion prevalent at Cambridge," and turned for leadership to that intrepid figure in Trinity Church with his forward-pushing chin and his warm urgency of manner. To Simeon Thomason gave as a personal friend an almost filial care, and as a curate all the support of the reliable, unresting diligence of himself and his good wife.

Martyn went often to Thomason's home at Shelford to talk in the riverside garden with Simeon and his host. He would come away full of self-abasement at the sight of Thomason's unfussed diligence, and the piety of his orderly household. For all their love to him the group that he left under the chestnut trees at Shelford did not realize the half of the effort at which he was doing the pastoral duties so delightful to themselves.

So Martyn, Cornish, imaginative, scholarly, took his place among men who for all their solid abilities half agreed with old John Newton (still living in London and laying down the law with homely shrewdness), that æsthetic interests only stimulated the "depraved nature" of man.

"I think it probable," said Newton to a friend who was admiring sculpture in Rome, "I think it probable from many passages in the Apostle Paul's writings, that he likewise had a taste capable of admiring and relishing the beauties of painting, sculpture, and architecture . . . but then he had a higher, a spiritual, a divine taste, which was greatly shocked and grieved by the ignorance, idolatry and wickedness which surrounded him, in so much that he could attend to nothing else."

A minister of the Gospel, he would say, is better
without " a large stock of other people's dreams
and fables."

In the fellowship of such a group, Martyn learned
Christ. If they pointed him to intellectual privation,
what was that ?

The pursuits of science [he wrote] and all the vain
and glittering employments of men seemed a cruel
withholding from their perishing brethren of that time
and exertion which might save their souls.

I was led to think a good while on my deficiency in
human learning. . . . I cannot but think (though it is
not easy to do so) that it must be more acceptable to God
to labour for souls, though the mind remains uninformed.

Such entries in his journal would have been read
with warm approval by old John Newton, and by
Charles Simeon himself. But another side of Henry
Martyn struggled for life. At one moment he
renounced earthly beauty as " ensnaring " and set
off to pray by a bed in the workhouse. At another
he gave her a hesitating welcome as a handmaid
to worship.

The music and the sight of a rural scene of solitude
had the effect of fixing my thoughts on heaven.

I heard the chant at King's with the same emotions
of devotion. [We almost feel John Newton stirring
uneasily in his chair.]

The sanctity of the place and the music, brought
heaven and eternal things and the presence of God very
near to me.

But with what circumspection he admits her,
even as a handmaid, to the sanctuary and with
what jealousy lest his profane love assume more
than the handmaid's place ! Henry Martyn's hymn-
book like John Wesley's would have been prefaced

with the caution that "what is of infinitely more moment than the spirit of poetry is the spirit of piety."

At this moment in his life, like his namesake who slashed at his cloak that the beggar might have half, Martyn was cutting ruthlessly at his own intellectual and æsthetic life, for the sake of the souls of the poor. Like his leader Simeon, he observed days of fasting and abstinence, but his true fast was that which he imposed on his intellectual and artistic appetites. Yet even as he crushed back his desires for beauty he found (with an experience rare among the early evangelicals as his nature of æsthetic hungers was rare amongst them) that his lips were laid at her very source.

My heart adored the Lord as the author and source of all the intellectual beauty that delighted me; as the creator of all the fair scenes that employ the poet's pen; and as the former of the mind that can find pleasure in beauty. . . . My soul seems labouring still with the mysterious glories of religion. What shall appear to this soul when I die? What shall appear of God's glory while I live? Since I have known God . . . painting, poetry and music, have had charms unknown to me before. I have received what I suppose is a taste for them: for religion has . . . made my mind susceptible of impressions from the sublime and beautiful.

With the unfailing paradox of the Gospel, Henry Martyn had lost his life only to find it, heightened and summed up in Christ,

Ubi non praevenit rem desiderium
Nec desiderio minus est praemium.

The *Journal* during the Cambridge curacy shows signs of unwilling preoccupation with legal business. Martyn suddenly learned that the slender fortune left him by his father was totally lost, and his unmarried sister Sally entirely dependent on him. Dr Smith tells us of a tradition in the family of his half-brother John that Henry and his sisters litigated with them at this time.[1] However that may have been, Henry's plans were now thrown into confusion. He could not feel justified in accepting the subsistence allowance of a missionary, and leaving Sally in distress. Bishop Wilberforce says that for nearly three years (1803-5) the family financial questions "often harassed his conscience, engrossing much of his time, and deeply depressing his spirits." "Unless Providence should see fit to restore our property," Martyn told Sargent, "I see no possibility of my going out [to India]." But his friends pointed out another opening.

Charles Grant, from one of the Chairs in Leadenhall Street, was looking anxiously for like-minded chaplains to work with David Brown in Bengal. The Company's salary would enable Martyn to support Sally; and the need for good men was great. "The clergy in Bengal," Sir John Shore had written home in 1795, "are not respectable characters." If they did not die "of drinking punch in the torrid zone," they were apt to retire with large fortunes amassed in a surprisingly short time. The Bishop of Llandaff having refused a chaplaincy when at Cambridge thanked God afterwards for denying him "an opportunity of becoming an Asiatic plunderer."[2]

---

[1] We know however from an appeal published by Charles Simeon after Henry Martyn's death, that on John's coming to financial disaster Henry was the chief support of his brother's family.

[2] Bishop Watson, *Anecdotes of his Life*, p. 21.

Martyn was not sanguine. Professor Farish warned him of the danger of "worldly-mindedness" as a Company's servant. He read Tennant's *India* and decided that the life would be odious to the last degree. Then he turned to the Bengali Grammar or to Brainerd's *Life* and was all aflame to go, no matter how.

The business involved interviews in London and visits to the India House. There were journeys to town on the "Telegraph" coach, which told an incredulous public that it could travel in seven hours from Cambridge to the City. There were visits to Leadenhall Street when Martyn must go past the two gorgeous porters into the very house where sat a clerk with a snuff-coloured coat and an unforgettable smile, by name Charles Lamb.

Martyn was ushered into the stately presence of Charles Grant, whose mastery of Indian commerce was making him "the real ruler of the rulers of the east, the Director of the Court of Directors," but who none the less met with considerable opposition when he proposed to send men of the "Methodist" taint to India. Between the business interviews there was all London for the Cornishman to see. The slight black-clad figure "called at the booksellers"; visited the British Museum; listened to the Gresham Lecture on Music; sat on a bench in St James's Park beside a poor man "of a very passionate and disappointed spirit," into whose hand he slipped a coin; or went to the New London Tavern in Cheapside to hear a farewell charge given to the two young German missionaries starting for West Africa. "I shook hands and almost wished to go with them, but certainly to go to India."

Another day he stood at the gate of St James's to see the nobility go to court. The yellow coaches rolled past with turbans and fans, garters and swords, to the dull court of the dull old king, and Martyn standing on the pavement wondered at "such a glare of finery on poor old shrivelled people." But in the streets where the "first gentleman of Europe" set the fashion, temptation waited for Martyn, for "him even," when arch glances were directed at him and buxom charms displayed. He "made a covenant with his eyes," and kept it, throwing himself at once into prayer for the bold hussy or the fine lady who caught his eye. "After asking of God, that she might be as pure and beautiful in her mind and heart as in body, and be a temple of the Holy Ghost. . . . I dare not harbour a thought of an opposite tendency."

So he saw the streets; but a social circle was waiting too for Simeon's curate, in the rural villas bordering Clapham Common. Charles Grant took him down one afternoon from the India House, giving him upon the road "much information on the state of India" and introducing him, in time for dinner, to William Wilberforce, a wiry bright-eyed figure, with powdered hair, a diamond brooch in his linen, and an eyeglass which he fingered while he talked his unforgettable talk, swift-wheeling as a swallow's flight, described by spell-bound listeners as "vivacious," "radiant," "aerial."

Here Martyn found his welcome in the innermost circle of the men then fighting the slave-trade and slashing indeed at the devil wherever they per-

ceived him. "The first 'friends of the negro,'"
Mr G. K. Chesterton calls them, "whose honest
industry and philanthropy were darkened by a
religion of sombre smugness, which almost makes
one fancy that they loved the negro for his colour,
and would have turned away from red or yellow
men as needlessly gaudy." The enjoyable sentence
tells a half truth which must be faced, for in their
own generation Sydney Smith brought much the
same taunt against Martyn's friends.[1] Looked at
closely the life on Clapham Common, as compared
with other middle-class life of the day, seems in
part a home of smugness and in part a gallant
escape from it.

If to the dwellers in Clapham villas theirs was
the best of all possible Commons that is small
matter for surprise. When the Bishop of London's
coach had orders to set a lady down at the nearest
public-house rather than be seen to stop at Clapham
Rectory, the saints of Clapham were thrown in
upon one another by a mild ostracism from outside.
But nothing of ennui appears in the most intimate
accounts of their life together.

It is true that like the rest of their class they
were deeply in love with " our happy establishment,"
and it is also true that their edifying conversation
was often expressed in language of an almost unbearable smugness (hard as the word is to associate

---

[1] In his article on "Indian Missions" in the *Edinburgh Review*,
April 1808, in which he is very funny on Brother Carey's piety during
sea-sickness, and the "difficulty of the Mission in getting converts
shaved " occur these words : " Ennui, wretchedness, melancholy,
groans and sighs, are the offerings which these unhappy men make to
a Deity who has covered the earth with gay colours, and scattered it
with rich perfumes."

with William Wilberforce, that Ariel among the reformers), but what is sometimes forgotten is that the possibly less edifying conversation of countless other middle class homes was expressed in language of equal heaviness. A wave of smugness had swept over the great middle class in Martyn's England, that middle class which knew how to appreciate the solid unimaginative virtue of George III and told him so in New Year Odes:

> *Still o'er our fields waves Concord's silken wing,*
> *Still the Arts flourish, and the Muses sing ;*
> *While moral truth and Faith's celestial ray,*
> *Adorn, illume and bless, a George's prosp'rous sway.*[1]

From this prevailing atmosphere adventurous spirits sought escape. The Prince of Wales led off the rakes : the poets, untamed sons of light, escaped to shimmering horizons and

> . . . *Aëreal kisses*
> *Of shapes that haunt thought's wildernesses.*

The group among whom Martyn was now numbered, knowing no key to faery realms, and never to find linguistic escape or shake off the intellectual trappings of their day and class, yet made a spiritual escape. For in so far as they reached vital contact with One whom no man ever yet accused of smugness, they became free of a realm where man was face to face with the beauty and the terror of reality. The best known literary work of the circle was Wilberforce's *Practical View of Christianity.* He wrote in prose, and he set out to be " practical " ; but when a few men of the solid middle class heard

---

[1] Ode for the New Year 1803 by Henry James Pye, Esq., Poet-Laureate.

he call to the discipleship taught by the Lake of
Galilee, incalculable spiritual forces were let loose
and incalculable elements of romance broke in upon
the prevailing smugness. " It is probable that
Pietism in Germany and the Evangelical movement
in England did much to prepare the ground for the
reception—perhaps even for the creation—of the
new spirit that was coming into poetry." [1]

For Christianity even at Clapham made room
in life for spiritual adventure. They spoke smugly,
but their souls knew how to worship and to dare.
Granville Sharp the ordnance clerk " sat at his
desk with a soul as distended as that of a Paladin
bestriding his warhorse," [2] and being persuaded that
America was right in her War of Independence
threw away his livelihood rather than copy the
account of a cargo of munitions which had been
used against her. Young Clarkson wrote a Latin
Essay for a university prize, on the set subject
" Is it right to make slaves of other men against
their will ? " No doubt his periods were smug
enough, but he was not the man to shelter under
phrases. " If the contents of my essay are true,"
he cried, " it is time some one should see these
calamities to their end," and forthwith threw himself into a lifelong grapple with vested interests
and semi-sacred institutions. In Parliament the
group were known as " men who looked to the
facts of the case and not to the wishes of the
minister." [3]

Their interests were far-flung. Now it is a

[1] C. E. Vaughan in *The Cambridge Modern History*, Vol. VII. p. 826.
[2] Stephen, *Essays in Ecclesiastical Biography.*
[3] Trevelyan, *Life and Letters of Lord Macaulay*, p. 71.

crusade against bull-baiting, now provision for widows of the fallen in the Napoleonic Wars, now a translation of the Bible into Arabic. Martyn's first evening at Clapham was spent in conversation about India—" They wished me to fill the Church in Calcutta very much,"—and in questioning a Mr Richard Johnson from New South Wales as to what could be done for the convict centre at Botany Bay, left for sixteen years without moral or spiritual care.[1]

So Martyn joined the group and fell like the rest of them under the spell of Wilberforce's voice of rare cadences. That was a red-letter day when he dined alone with Wilberforce at Palace Yard.

It was very agreeable, as there was no one else. Speaking of the slave trade . . . and found my heart so affected that I could with difficulty refrain from tears. . . . Went with Mr W. to the House of Commons, where I was surprised and charmed with Mr Pitt's eloquence.

They introduced him, too, to old John Newton, the friend of Cowper, now the Nestor of the evangelicals, widowed and blind, but with undiminished courage and a pawky humour.

Breakfasted with the venerable Mr Newton. . . . He said he had heard of a clever gardener, who would sow the seeds when the meat was put down to roast, and engage to produce a salad by the time it was ready, but the Lord did not sow oaks in this way. . . . When I spoke of the opposition that I should be likely to meet with, he said he supposed Satan would not love me for what I was about to do.

[1] Through the influence of Wilberforce with Pitt this same Mr Johnson was appointed first chaplain to Botany Bay, and Mr Thornton of Clapham took him to Woolwich and introduced him to a flock of two hundred and fifty convicts on one of the hulks there.

On one of these London visits Martyn, having just reached the age of twenty-four, was ordained priest at the Chapel Royal, St James's. "A solemn ordinance to me . . . yet very little like what it ought to be." He was now ready at any time to obey a summons to India, but it was not till three months later that he wrote in his journal :

April 2, 1805. Went with Mr Grant towards the India House. He said that he was that day about to take the necessary steps for bringing forward the business of the chaplains, and that by to-morrow night I should know whether I could go or not.

Next day :

Going to Mr Grant's I found that the chaplaincies had been agreed to after two hours' debate, and some obloquy thrown upon Mr Grant by the Chairman for his connexion with Mr Wilberforce, and *those people*. Mr Grant said that though my nomination had not taken place, the case was now beyond danger.

Mr Grant little understood with what hidden distaste the chaplaincy was accepted. "I could have been infinitely better pleased to have gone out as a missionary, poor as the Lord and His apostles," Martyn confided to his journal. There is no doubt that it was true. To the man inspired by David Brainerd the acceptance of a handsome salary and the obligations of Government service were no alleviation but an addition to the difficulties of his path.

Martyn decided to leave Cambridge at once and take up his abode in London, serving as temporary curate to Mr Cecil in Bloomsbury and holding himself in readiness for orders to proceed to India with the summer fleet.

On Palm Sunday five days later, he rode out to Lolworth for the last time and preached his farewell sermon to his country folk. There were partings afterwards at the church door.

An old farmer of a neighbouring parish, as he was taking leave of me, turned aside to shed tears ; this affected me more than anything. Rode away with my heart heavy.

At night he must preach his last sermon to Mr Simeon's crowded congregation at Trinity Church. " I prayed over the whole of my sermon for the evening," he writes. When he stood up he read as his text :

Thou, O Lord of Hosts, God of Israel, hast revealed to Thy servant saying, I will build thee an house. . . . Now let it please Thee to bless the house of Thy servant, that it may continue for ever before Thee : for Thou, O Lord God, hast spoken it : and with Thy blessing let the house of Thy servant be blessed for ever.[1]

The listeners felt the poignancy of such words of settled permanence from one passing out from among them after so brief a sojourn, impelled in spirit to some pilgrim course. It was not usual in 1805 for the people to stand as the clergy left the church, but that night, when Martyn went out, the kneeling people rose as one man and turned to watch his figure down the aisle.

---

[1] 1 Chronicles xvii. 25-27.

CHAPTER VI

THE LOVER

I find a pleasing mournfulness of spirit to-night.—LYDIA GRENFELL'S *Diary, November* 19, 1803.

Passed a happy morning reading Edwards on the Affections.— LYDIA GRENFELL'S *Diary, November* 15, 1804.

ON Monday in Holy Week 1805 Martyn left Cambridge. "A great many," he says, "accompanied me to the coach which took me up at the end of the town; it was a thick, misty morning, so the University, with its towers and spires, was out of sight in an instant."

The Cambridge chapter was ended, but there was another farewell which cost him more; for Henry Martyn was in love.

He had discovered it nine months before, during a summer visit to Cornwall, when although he did not know how soon the way to India might be opened, he regarded himself as among his own folk for the last time. It was a crowded visit. He must say good-bye to his sisters and to all the clan of cousins and cousinly friends. He must preach too in the churches which they opened to him, though not in the church of his baptism, since he was deeply tainted with "Methodism," and his old schoolmaster, hitherto proud of his pupil, now led the outcry against his pernicious views.[1]

[1] The heated feelings of the day are hard to picture now. One of the Cornish clergy who speaks of Martyn as "this poor deluded en-

H   113

It was not permitted me to occupy the pulpit of my native town. . . . The clergy seemed to have united to exclude me from their churches, so that I must now be contented with my brother-in-law's two little churches about five miles from Truro.

Kenwyn, which had welcomed John Wesley, had a welcome for Henry Martyn, and when he preached there in the church among the trees through whose branches you peer down over the Truro house-tops, the people of the city came up the hill to hear him. "The church at Kenwyn was quite full, many outside, and many obliged to go away. At first beginning the service I felt very uneasy from the number of people gazing, but my peace soon returned."

Another church was open to Martyn in the ancient town of Marazion that looks sleepily from among its yellow sea poppies to St Michael's Mount, the trysting-place of Cornish legend and Cornish history. Marazion church was then a chapel-of-ease under the care of Martyn's cousin Malachy Hitchins, who lived two miles away on a wooded hill-top beside the church of St Hilary with its whitewashed spire, a landmark to the ships that made for Falmouth or Penzance. Here in the Vicarage garden with

thusiast" wrote a tract on the Methodists, divided under the following headings :

Ignorance with Itching Ears	Vainglory
Prevarications	Uncharitableness
Lying	Profaneness
Hypocrisy	Uncleanness
Knavery	The Spirit of Family Discord
Contempt of the Regular Clergy	Freakishness and Distraction
An Intractable and Revengeful	and
Spirit	Insanity
Political Restlessness	

Cousin Tom Hitchins a few years older than himself " all the happier hours " of Martyn's boyhood had been spent.

Their walks and rides had been shared by a young brood of Grenfells from a square house in Marazion Street, children of the Commissary for the States of Holland in the ancient port of Penzance. When Cousin Tom Hitchins grew up he married one of the Grenfell maidens, and Tom and his Emma at Plymouth Dock were among Martyn's dearest friends. The rest of the Grenfell family were now established in life : the eldest son, the pride of the house, a Member of Parliament in Buckinghamshire ; the girls, with one exception, settled in homes of their own in Cornwall, partly, it was said, through the energies of their stirring and practical mother, Mrs Mary Grenfell. The one exception was the youngest daughter Lydia, whose love story had come to grief, and who now at the ripe age (very ripe for those days) of thirty was still at home, a steady annoyance to her matter-of-fact mother because of her Methodistical leanings and inclination to pious brooding. It rarely occurred to the matron of the day that a daughter of thirty was old enough to make her own decisions, and Lydia, when the maternal fiat went forth, refrained from attending the Methodist meeting-house that was for her the gate of heaven, but did not refrain from confiding her yearnings and sorrows to a religious diary.

Mr Hitchins asked Henry Martyn to Marazion for old times' sake, and on the Sunday which he spent there he made the discovery of his love for Lydia.

At St Hilary Church in the morning, my thoughts wandered from the service and I suffered the keenest

disappointment. Miss Lydia Grenfell did not come. . . .
Called after tea on Miss Lydia Grenfell and walked with
her and ——, conversing on spiritual subjects. All the
rest of the evening and at night I could not keep her out of
my mind. I felt too plainly that I loved her passionately.

The discovery was overwhelming. It was impossible for a Henry Martyn to be a lukewarm lover.
Yet this new love and his vocation seemed to
him in deadly rivalry. To him the missionary call
meant probable hardship and banishment for life.
Supposing she could love him, could he involve his
Lydia in this ?

True, there was the chance of an East Indian
chaplaincy ; but that was yet in the air. He had
lost his patrimony. His family needed his help.
What had he to offer a bride, or a bride's very
practical mother, unless he were to forsake his
missionary vocation, and settle down at Cambridge, or
perhaps in a college living ? A country rectory with
Lydia, and a quiet study, and children in the garden !
But no.

The direct opposition of this to my devotedness to
God in the missionary way, excited no small tumult in
my mind. . . . At night I continued an hour and a
half in prayer, striving against this attachment. . . .
One while I was about to triumph, but in a moment my
heart had wandered to the beloved idol. I went to bed
in great pain, yet still rather superior to the enemy ;
but in dreams her image returned, and I awoke in the
night, with my mind full of her.

His sense of vocation and his love grappled in
deadlock. Next morning the call to sacrifice was
uppermost. "I again devoted myself to the Lord,
and with more of my will than last night." He
took horse and rode away from St Hilary.

But there was yet a month to spend in Cornwall, a month when he was near her, and would hear friends speak of her, when a ride across the hawthorn-dotted uplands brought him to her door. An old friend, knowing nothing of his inner tumult, gave him *Thomas à Kempis* as a parting gift. The book was new to Martyn and daily during that month he read it, sometimes in a cave on the Cornish coast and sometimes late at night, drinking in its spirit of surrender.

At the end of August came his farewell to St Hilary. Lydia Grenfell's diary on August 26th, 1804, tells us that she heard " H. M. preach a precious sermon." Martyn's on the same day omits the sermon but tells of the evening when he " walked with Mr Grenfell and Lydia up the hill, with the most beautiful prospect of the sea, but I was unhappy from feeling the attachment to Lydia, for I was unwilling to leave her."

The next day was the last. There was a ride to a cottage, printed for ever on his memory and referred to again and again. Five miles by wren-haunted lanes or over uplands with the peewits calling and the soft, large sea-winds buffeting, and Lydia at his side.

Rode with Lydia to an old man, five miles off. . . . When we arrived the old man was out, but his sister, a blind woman of seventy, was confined to her bed. . . . Lydia and myself said everything we could to cheer her. . . . When the old man arrived we formed a little circle before the door, under the trees, and he conversed . . . concerning the things of God. I then read Psalm lxxxiv. (How amiable are thy tabernacles, O Lord). Our ride home was delightful.

He spent that afternoon alone with his love.

Reading in the afternoon to Lydia alone, from Dr Watts, there happened to be among other things a prayer on entire preference of God to the creature. Now thought I, here am I in the presence of God, and my idol. So I used the prayer for myself, and addressed it to God, who answered it I think, for my love was kindled to God and to divine things. . . . I continued conversing with her, generally with my heart in heaven, but every now and then resting on her. Parted with Lydia, perhaps for ever in this life, with a sort of uncertain pain, which I knew would increase to greater violence.

So he walked away "dwelling at large on the excellence of Lydia," and for the kingdom of heaven's sake he had not breathed his love. But it was not therefore unknown. A part of that "holy simplicity" which his friends all attribute to Martyn was a transparency which neither could nor would hide from their eyes the adventures of his heart.

And what of the lady ?

Lydia Grenfell, carrying soup to cottages, or transcribing hymns for favoured friends, had a heart that brooded on its own love story. The year 1800 when she was twenty-five had been the momentous year of her life. She then became engaged to the man of her heart, a solicitor of Penzance, Mr Samuel John, "to whom her heart was more closely united than to any earthly object." In the same year too she experienced a conversion, and became a devout believer, drawing her inspiration from the homely warmth of "the people called Methodists." Before the end of the year she had discovered that her betrothed was an impossible scoundrel. She broke off the engagement, but she could not break her love. Her diary shows a mind turned inward upon its own distresses ; unguided self-examination run to seed ; genuine religion mixed with morbid scruple and brooding sentiment. In a home with her active managing mother there were few demands on her powers. She was only too free to yearn and to renounce with a daily glow of pious sentiment, " hoping for pardon " for her " broken vows " to her betrothed, and blaming herself for every bad story that she heard of him whom she yet loved. Those " broken vows " seemed to her to render any other marriage a spiritual adultery. While Samuel John remained unmarried Lydia Grenfell told herself that she was bound to maidenhood. Nothing but his marriage could free her.

Six months before Martyn's appearance Mr John had announced his engagement to a London lady, and Lydia's diary shows that she received her freedom with a pang.

February 25th, 1804. My slumbers last night were distracted on his account, and through the day he has much occupied my thoughts—too much—but now duty will, I trust, compel me to turn from one who will soon be united to another.

March 5th. I now enter into a resolution and engagement from this hour to resist the temptation of employing my thoughts on one whom I must cease to love.

That summer, to a Lydia daily expecting the undesired freedom that would be hers with her first lover's marriage ; solacing herself with abstracts of sermons or with prayers by cottage death-beds ; a Lydia aged thirty and believing that for her romance was over, to such a Lydia came Henry Martyn, transparently and reverentially in love.

July 25th. I was surprised this morning by a visit from H. M.

August 8th. I was surprised again to-day by a visit from my friend.

There is no doubt that her surprise was genuine. He was remembered as a boy cousin, or all but a cousin, six years younger than herself, a vast chasm of years when boys and girls play together. She knew that he too, a year later than herself, had experienced conversion; and she knew of his Cambridge honours. Tom Hitchins, her sister's husband, and old Mr Malachy, himself an astronomer, would not fail to blazon forth their cousin's prowess. Now he returned, with the romance upon him of one dedicated to a lonely pilgrimage. And he preached such a sermon as her soul found " precious," and spoke to her with tremulous eagerness of the joys of the life to come. And there was no mistaking the light in his eyes.

But her first love, the habit of years, could not be suddenly replaced by an equal feeling for one who till lately had seemed merely a boy cousin who did well at books. Yet to a woman still starved of affection while her sisters ruled their homes, such reverent devotion was very sweet. She talked it out with Emma, her good sister, connected by marriage with the Martyn family. The upshot of the consultation was that Martyn, passing through Plymouth on his way from Cornwall, was told by Cousin Emma " that his attachment to her sister was not altogether unreturned."

Such news to a Martyn, who for the kingdom of heaven's sake was leaving Cornwall with his love untold, brought " both pleasure and pain."

Next day he went on by coach to Exeter. "My thoughts were almost wholly occupied with Lydia, though not in a spirit of departure from God, for I considered myself as in His hands."

A young attorney on the coach claimed his attention, one who said that he "knew the necessity of a change, but could not begin." While they changed horses the two went into a garden, and sat by some water on the grass slopes reading the 23rd Psalm.

Martyn's spirit was regaining buoyancy. As they drove out of Bath, early on a harvest morning, "Nothing seemed desirable but to glorify God." So he returned to his last months under Simeon, telling himself that the love story was over. "My dear Lydia and my duty call me different ways, yet God hath not forsaken me but strengthened me. . . . At chapel my soul ascended to God, and the sight of a picture at the altar, of John the Baptist preaching in the wilderness, animated me exceedingly to devotedness to the life of a missionary."

But a great love refused so soon to be deposed. They gave him an East India chaplaincy with a salary that would keep Sally and a bride as well. And they showed him a letter from David Brown saying, "Let him marry and come out at once." And then there was always that word of Cousin Emma's about an attachment "not altogether unreturned."

Was all this further temptation or was it an indication of his path ? Tossed in spirit he wrote through Cousin Emma to beg for the honour of Lydia's correspondence. But no letter came from

Lydia. She on her part was waiting with all her old morbid scruple for a letter to say that her first love was safely married. And Mr John, as if to tantalize her, still deferred his wedding. Martyn was "keenly disappointed at finding no letter from Lydia," yet inclined to agree with Simeon, himself unmarried, who "said he wished me to be properly a missionary dead to the world. . . . I thought of my dear Lydia when he said this."

Between them the saints tore him in pieces with contrary advice. Mr Cecil "said I should be acting like a madman if I went out unmarried. A wife would supply by her comfort and counsel the entire want of society." "Mr Atkinson, whose opinion I revere, was against my marrying." A letter from Mr Simeon "immediately convinced me of the expediency of celibacy." "Mr Pratt coming in argued strongly on the other side." "I could attend to nothing else." What lover could ?

My heart was sometimes ready to break with agony, at being torn from its dearest idol ; and at other times I was visited by a few moments of sublime and enraptured joy. Such is the conflict : why have my friends mentioned this subject ? It has torn open old wounds.

The time came to sail, and the celibates had it. He sent to Emma and to Lydia each a keepsake, "a little *Pilgrim's Progress* enclosed in the tea-caddy," and set off to join the East India fleet at Portsmouth, riding on the way to Sargent's Sussex home to bid his friend good-bye.

July 10*th*, 1805. I went to Portsmouth, where we arrived to breakfast, and found friends from Cambridge.

Sargent, newly married, felt that he must see the

last of that lonely figure and rode down from Midhurst to Martyn's Portsmouth inn, to find him surrounded by " numerous friends " from Cambridge and London, led by Simeon himself, who was deeply stirred, and with his usual energy despatched Bibles for distribution on Martyn's ship, and gave him a keepsake of a massive volume weighing 11 lb. 11 oz. from himself, and a silver compass from his Cambridge hearers who arranged that the day of his sailing should be set apart by them for fast and prayer.

July 16th. The Commodore called at the inn to desire that all persons might be awakened, as the fleet would sail to-day. We went immediately to the quay ; but after waiting five hours Mr Simeon took his last leave of me, [at a long farewell it was Simeon's way to take his friend's hand in both of his and raise it to his lips] and the rest accompanied me on board.

A " triumphal occasion," Sargent called the moment of parting.

But even this was not the end of his farewells. " To my no small surprise I found we were bound to Falmouth." The news brought a torturing bliss. He was to see Cornwall again and to come once again within reach of Lydia. Was it that he might win her ?

In three days' time the fleet dropped anchor in the great harbour which " braggeth that a hundred sail of ships may anchor within his circuit, and no one of them see the other's top." " I seemed to be entirely at home," said Martyn, " the scene about me was so familiar, and my friends so near." The fleet was delayed day after day. Shore visits were possible, and " after much deliberation " he decided to go to Marazion and tell his love and ask his Lydia if she could bring herself to come to him in India.

He went on the early mail, and did ever another lover in such case find leisure to speak to the coachmen about the welfare of their souls ?

I arrived at Marazion in time for breakfast and met my beloved Lydia. In the course of the morning I walked with her . . . with much confusion I declared my affection for her, with the intention of learning whether, if I saw it right in India to be married, she would come out ; but she would not declare her sentiments. She said that the shortness of arrangement was an obstacle, even if all others were removed.

" She would not declare her sentiments : " but she copied a hymn for her lover.

As I was coming on board this morning, and reading Mr Serle's hymn you wrote out for me, a sudden gust of wind blew it into the sea. I made the boatmen immediately heave to, and recovered it.

To Cousin Emma, Lydia's sister, and so far the encouraging confidante of Henry's love, he wrote :

The consequence of my Marazion journey is, that I am enveloped in gloom. May He give me grace to turn cheerfully to my proper work and business. . . . Another consequence of my journey is, that I love Lydia more than ever.

There were yet one or two more meetings, and at the last a hurried parting, when as he sat reading to his lady and her mother a servant came in with news that the fleet had immediate sailing orders and a horse was at the door that he might catch his ship.

" It came upon me like a thunderbolt. Lydia was

evidently painfully affected by it; she came out,
that we might be alone at taking leave." There
at the door he told her that if it seemed right for
him to marry she must not be offended at receiving
a letter from India.

"In the great hurry she discovered more of her
mind than she intended; she made no objection
whatever to coming out." But "you had better
go out free," she stipulated, implying, he thought,
that the freedom need not be for ever. There was
no time to ask her to explain herself. He mounted
and galloped away, reaching Falmouth by the aid
of relays of horses just as his ship was getting under
way.

Next morning being Sunday, he held a service
on the deck. As he read the words, "But now
they desire a better country, that is an heavenly,"
St Michael's Mount and St Hilary spire and trees
were fast fading from sight. His letter to Cousin
Emma still showed a lover's interest in those re-
ceding hills.

Lydia I knew was about that time at St Hilary. If
you have heard from Marazion since Sunday I should be
curious to know whether the fleet was observed passing.
. . . Do not forget to tell me as much as you can about
Lydia.

The fleet was so long held up in the Cove of
Cork that Martyn had Cousin Emma's answer there.
Her letter is not preserved. But it told him more
of Lydia than she herself had let him know, for
it explained that his lady who had said him neither
yea nor nay, was still held back by some insuperable
obstacle. From later letters it would seem that
the obstacle was a double one. Her own obstinate

scruple against a second engagement before her
former lover's marriage (and the exasperating person
delayed his wedding until 1810) was added to the
difficulty of obtaining Mrs Grenfell's consent to her
faring forth to the terribly remote East Indies to
marry a man as "methodistical" as herself and
(who can gainsay the motherly prudence ?) showing
signs already to observant eyes of the consumptive
tendency now making itself seen in both his sisters.

Henry Martyn was ill prepared for the letter.
Lydia's hesitating farewell speech had left him
sanguine. But he was loyal to his lady, though
his reply to Cousin Emma breathed more serenity
than he could always feel.

Whatever others have said, I think that Lydia acts
no more than consistently by persevering in her present
determination.   I confess, therefore, that till this obstacle
is removed my path is perfectly clear, and blessed be God !
I feel very, very happy in all that my God shall order
concerning me. . . . The Lord teaches me to desire Christ
for my all in all . . . surely the soul is happy that thus
breathes in a medium of love ?

CHAPTER VII

THE NINE MONTHS AT SEA

Common parlancy won't do with a common seaman. It is not here as in the Scriptures, "Do this and he doeth it;" (by the bye that chap must have had his soldiers in tight order) but it is, " Do this d——n your eyes " and then it is done directly.

The ship lurched, did it ? . . . and pray Mr Cooper why has heaven granted you two legs with joints at the knees ? . . . There take that, you contaminating, stage-dubbing, gimlet-carrying quintessence of a bung-hole !—

Mr Chucks the boatswain in CAPTAIN MARRYATT'S *Peter Simple.*

I am born for God only. Christ is nearer to me than father or mother or sister—a nearer relative, a more intimate friend ; and I rejoice to follow Him and to love Him.—*Journal* of HENRY MARTYN on board the *Union* Transport.

THAT summer of 1805 the beacons were in train on all the south coast heights, to give warning in case the French fleet sailed out of Brest for the invasion of England. Sir Home Popham, the Commodore who was to convoy the East India fleet, was held up in Cork Harbour in case his ships were needed to do battle against invaders, and every man in the convoy was given his battle station—Martyn's to be " with the surgeons in the cockpit."

It was August 28th before the convoy stood out to sea, a great fleet of one hundred and fifty sail. All the summer sailing of both East and West Indiamen were there with their burden of trade and with the new officials and cadets of the East

India Company ; one vessel was a " Botanyman," the
Pitt, with a load of one hundred and twenty women
convicts for transportation to the dreadful Bay ;
and with the merchant vessels passing " on their
lawful occasions " was a fleet of fifty transports
carrying five thousand troops under Sir John Baird,
to some unknown destination. "We are to join
in some expedition," Martyn told the Plymouth
cousins, "probably the Cape of Good Hope or the
Brazils."

The Commodore had no great naval force to escort
so large a fleet, for the Admiralty in that summer
before Trafalgar was scraping together ships enough
to fit out a fleet for Nelson, and Mr Snodgrass,
surveyor to the East India Company's shipping,
was showing them how to strengthen crazy vessels
with double planking and diagonal bracings that
would hold them together for one more conflict
in that great sea year. Sir Home Popham's whole
naval strength for convoying one hundred and fifty
sail was two men-of-war, the *Diadem* and the
Belliqueuse each of sixty-four guns,[1] and two naval
frigates the *Leda* and *Narcissus*—no great force even
though manned by " hearty souls ready to fight the
devil if so be as he should hoist the tricolour ensign."
Neither the transports nor the merchantmen, however, were quite defenceless. They all carried a
few guns on the chance of a scrap on the high seas
with an enemy privateer.

In spiritual charge of this assemblage of sea-dogs
and fighting men ranging from raw village lads to
blasphemous veterans, was Henry Martyn, aged

[1] Most of the British ships at Trafalgar had 74 guns ; the *Victory*
had 100.

twenty-four, at home in polite literature and in college courts, all delicate ear and sensitive scruple. Never were flock and shepherd more strangely assorted. He sailed on the *Union*, a transport carrying a load of treasure and his Majesty's 59th together with some of the East India Company's cadets and their officers. His cabin was stacked with books — commentaries, oriental grammars, works on India and the life of David Brainerd for himself, together with Simeon's parting gift of an enormous Bible, and for the men a store of Scriptures, hymn-books and tracts.

The Commodore gave Madeira as the first rendezvous of the fleet, and between leaving Cork Harbour on August 28th and reaching Funchal on September 29th Martyn had an epitome of life at sea. Packed with humanity as the little wooden vessel was, she yet meant for Martyn a discipline of loneliness, always one of the marks of his spirit but now first accentuated. For at Cambridge, although in the society of his own college he moved solitary as regards his deepest interests, there was in reserve the delightful intimacy of Sargent and Corrie and Simeon and half a dozen more, to atone for the disdain of the crowd. And at the Fellows' table the men who shrank from his opinions were at least men who shared the same intellectual interests and vocabulary. On the *Union* he felt himself not only friendless in all the deeper sense of friendship but a foreigner, a " raw academic " as he called himself, out of place among men whose dinner talk was all of "regiments and firemen."

It was impossible that a Henry Martyn should not suffer in the first months after leaving England,

I

as he believed, for ever. His delicately strung
nature had payment to exact for the strain of overwork during his Cambridge curacy, as well as for
the strain of loving and leaving his Lydia. He was
as homesick as a child, waking "from disturbed
dreams, to find myself with a long sea rolling between
myself and all that I hold dear in this life."
"England had gone, and with it all my peace . . .
the pains of memory were all I felt." For Lydia had
not given him permission to write. "I cannot write
to her," he told Emma Hitchins, "or I should find the
greatest relief and pleasure even in transmitting
upon paper the assurances of my tenderest love."

Unable to endure the fetid atmosphere below,[1]
Martyn spent the first days of the voyage on deck
"standing in the air in a sort of patient stupidity,
very sick and cold," longing for the relief of being
alone, but surrounded by a crowd, "the soldiers
jeering one another and swearing, the drums and
fifes constantly playing." The common miseries of
sea-sickness were followed by fever and faintness;
but the struggle that was darkening his days was in
its essence spiritual. He was torn by conflicting
desires. "The world in a peculiar form" (he might
have said in a gracious feminine form) "has a hold
upon my soul, and the spiritual conflict is consequently dreadful. . . . I am now in the fire fighting
hard."

Next day he wrote again :

Once more I struggled, determined to rise through
God, above the body, the flesh and the world, to a life
of ardour and devotedness to God.

---

[1] The air below decks became too foul even for those unsqueamish
days, and at intervals one or other of the lower decks was cleared of
humans and fires were lighted to purify the atmosphere.

And the following morning :

Beginning to grow quite outrageous with myself and like a wild bull in a net, I saw plainly this was coming to nothing, and so in utter despair of working any deliverance for myself, I simply cast myself upon Jesus Christ, praying that if it were possible, something of a change might be wrought in my heart.

Relief came to him two days later ; but not the relief of a traveller who regains the sheltered pastures where " love is of the valley." " I gave you up entirely," he told Lydia afterwards. The relief that came to Martyn was rather the relief of the traveller who has climbed through clouds to some upland meadow where gentians drink the sunlight of a peak. As the essential struggle had been on the spiritual plane, so was the victory. This evangelical parson on a troopship in Trafalgar year suddenly carries us into the company of all the mystics when they try to tell us of what came to them as they passed through purging pains to the soul's illumination.

At last the Lord hath appeared for the comfort of His creature [he says]. In prayer launched sweetly into eternity. . . . Thy work may be prosecuted best by my soul's remaining in heaven. The transcendent sweetness of the privilege of being always with God would appear to me too great, were it not for the blessed command " Set your affections on things above."

And again :

I seemed at a long distance from the earth and time, and near the blessed God.

Or again :

Separated from my friends and country for ever, there is nothing to distract me from hearing " the voice of my Beloved," and coming away from the world and walking with Him in love, amid the flowers that perfume the air of Paradise.

Looking back in the light of such experience on the struggle he had just passed through, he felt that God had been also in the cloud, and the words of a sermon preached on the poop of the *Union* convey his confidence. " It may be you will still be kept in darkness, but darkness is not always the frown of God ; it is only Himself—thy shade on thy right hand."

Meanwhile, whether the chaplain's soul were in heavenly places or in the nethermost hell, men went through with the routine of seafaring days. The sailors of the *Union* threatened mutiny because of the miseries of their diet of salt junk. And there was a night of storm when several sails were torn away and the wind in the rigging above and the clatter on deck made sleep impossible. Men lay awake in the creaking wooden ship, very near to the wailings and demon howls of the wind. At 4 A.M. one of the East India Company's officers came and sat shivering in Martyn's cabin " for company." When dawn came, the cabin floor was awash with water, and going up on deck they found that they " were going under bare poles, the sea covered with so thick a mist from the spray and rain that nothing could be seen but the tops of the nearest waves, which seemed to be running even with the windward side of the ship."

The *Union* was the heaviest sailer in the fleet and she dropped out of sight of the rest of the convoy so that she ran considerable risk of capture. Only in port could the other ships share in the chaplain's ministrations, when they sent for him or came in boats with babes to be baptized. At sea the *Union* was his whole parish and earned the title of "a very praying ship."

Martyn's own mess was with the officers of the 59th and East India Company's cadets and writers in the cuddy, "pleasant and orderly," but he sought his flock in every corner of their crowded little world. "I have now free access to the soldiers and sailors," he wrote home. A surprising figure he must have been on a transport of the Napoleonic wars, a figure frail and careful of dress, faintly academic in phrase, wincing at a blasphemy, but no coward on his business. "Went below decks," he says, "there was a quarrel amongst the soldiers and sailors ; one of the former who was stripped for fighting I went up to." And the tumult ceased, perhaps from sheer surprise, for it was far from usual in 1805 to meet a padre on the orlop deck. This chaplain was everywhere. They found him sitting among pig-tailed sailors on the gun-deck, where the hammocks of the crew were slung, "in the boatswain's berth" oblivious to everything in "a long and close conversation with the carpenter." The seamen ear-ringed and tattooed, packed together, miserably fed, and flogged for robbing a sugar basin, swore with every breath, and their language was quite literally pain and grief to their chaplain. "Every oath they swore was a call on me to help them" he told himself.

The most astonishing conquest that he made on the gun-deck was when the chief mate for his sake ceased to swear, and ranged himself beside Martyn as protector and stout friend, telling those who rebelled at the chaplain's ministrations that one

day " their consciences would be overhauled." " He
is the image of a blunt good-natured seaman," wrote
Martyn of this new friend, adding with naïve surprise
that they could not converse " very long on religious
subjects," since the mate was " so soon out of his
depth."

Below the gun-deck were the soldiers; and amid-
ships, just under the main hatchway, their wives,
one of whom had come aboard as a stowaway at
Portsmouth and remained unnoticed in the crowded
confusion sharing a single ration with her husband
until they reached Madeira, when the Captain found
her, forgave her handsomely, and put her on the
ration list. Martyn went below every afternoon
and amid " the noise of the children, of the married
people and the sailors who were all about us, talking
as if nothing were going forward," he read aloud to
a small group from the *Pilgrim's Progress*. Later,
he hit upon the more popular plan of teaching them
to sing. His offer to teach the men to read they
would have none of. The subalterns of the 59th
chose to regard his singing class as " most
dangerous," " unfitting the men to be soldiers."
(It is possible that Martyn had felt called to re-
monstrate with the subalterns on the subject of
foul language.) Some of the men agreed with them
or tried to make the chaplain think so: " B. said
he was determined he would never pray, for if he
did, he should not be able to fight, that he was a
soldier and robbery was his business." The senior
officers, however, saw no harm in Martyn's unusual
course if it gave him any pleasure; his audience
was not so large as to cause any serious fear of the
demoralization of the army. For Martyn had

neither Sargent's humour nor Simeon's arresting vehemence nor any of the gifts of the street preacher.

It was never easy to him to thread his way through a crowd in the dark and stifling lower decks, and win for himself a hearing from the figures lolling round or busy with domestic concerns. With intense pain he would rouse himself to rebuke some blasphemy, knowing well that such a rebuke was no ingratiating opening for his message, and listening to the snigger that followed his effort in full consciousness of his own shortcomings.

I do not know how to push things. I have a delicacy about me which no doubt proves ruinous to souls. . . . I do not, that I know of, shrink from any known method of diffusing the light of truth, but I am not ingenious in methods ; . . . I want the essence of zeal, which if no way be open will make a way.

Against humanity in the raw, humanity familiar with salt pork and curses, grog and cutlasses and bumboat women, he felt himself " a schoolboy, a raw academic."

" I pictured myself strutting about the streets and walks of Cambridge wrapt in content, thinking myself very amiable and admired." He longed to escape from " the academic contagion," never doubting that his gospel was for the seamen and the Company's Cadets and for his Majesty's 59th, but longing to break through the barriers that education had built between his mind and theirs. " I could have willingly forgotten all I had ever read or learnt, to be a man of the ancient primitive simplicity." " The words of Milner have been much upon my mind, ' to believe, to suffer and to love, was the primitive taste.' I do not know that any uninspired sentence ever affected me so much."

Martyn never found, and never would find his way to the warm heart of a mob. But his presence in the ship, with his refusal of all compromise, proved there, as wherever the clear flame of his spirit passed, a touchstone for other souls. Many of doubtful mind "offended at his sayings" "went back and walked no more with him." Yet here and there "with tears" a rough and hearty seaman or corporal changed his allegiance and began to follow Christ on no easy path. The loyal few, for whom Martyn's cabin was open at all hours, were led on to harder loyalties than they had known before. One of the cadets' officers, a Mr Mackenzie, became almost Martyn's shadow, reading with him and sometimes with the surgeon or another "serious" officer, the *Confessions of St Augustine*, Milner's *Church History*, Leighton's *Commentaries*, or the *Letters of David Brainerd*. Mr Mackenzie even went below decks to Martyn's hymn-singing, running the gauntlet of much banter in the cuddy afterwards. On his appearance a cheerful subaltern would sing out, "Come now, let's have a little of the humbug," and the cuddy would be indulged with a choice nasal parody of psalm-singing. The cadets whom Mr Mackenzie commanded were seriously afraid that their officer in turning "Methodist" would try to make them all "melancholy mad." It was Mr Mackenzie's none-too-easy task to try to explain the saint to the ship's company and the ship's company to the saint. He brought to Martyn the current reports about his preaching: "Martyn is a good scholar but not much of an orator" they said, and Mackenzie told him " It was a want of easy flow, arising from a want of confidence in his own abilities."

" If it be not remedied," said the disconsolate Martyn, " I am afraid I shall make but a dull preacher to the Indians."

The one service on Sunday was held on the poop, weather permitting, at any hour that seemed good to the authorities. Sometimes Martyn, expecting a service in the morning, would go up to find " the sailors all at work on the poop and the boatswain swearing at them " and Church would not be rigged till 5 P.M. Sometimes it was put off till too late— " The sun was down before they rigged the Church " —and the men were piped to hammocks.

Between two and three hundred came to the services but the soldiers were " not very attentive " to the chaplain's preaching. The boatswain's mate told him, to his deep humiliation, that the sermons were too difficult for the young lads among the soldiers. On reading them one finds that, direct and simple as he made his thought, and relentlessly as he made each sentence do its perfect work, Martyn's words and especially his sentence-building have a faintly classical tinge that must have given them an almost foreign ring in the ears of boys from the tail of the plough, who could not sign their names when they took King George's shilling.

His preaching was far too direct and unequivocal to be popular among the officers. " Mr Martyn sends us to hell every Sunday " was their comment, which considerably surprised the preacher. " Major Davidson told me that I set the duties of religion in so terrific a light that people were revolted. I felt the force of this remark and determined to make more use of the love of God in the Gospel." But his audience, used to the comfortable flowing periods of a moral essay, threatened to stay away unless he would preach a sermon "like one of Blair's." Martyn continued his hot-gospellings ; his flaming conviction, his all-compelling God-consciousness strangely clad in carefully-turned classical sentences. It was as though an Old Testament prophet stood among them on the poop and delivered his burning message of "righteousness, temperance and judgment to come," clad all the while in the black gown and white bands associated with plump velvet pulpit-cushions and afternoon slumber induced by a gently flowing voice and the buzz of a blue-bottle in a window not made to open.

The officers were annoyed and rude at the chaplain's failure, his deliberate failure too, to accommodate his preaching to their wishes. They arranged themselves behind him, ready to walk out at any statement of which they disapproved, and one of them conspicuously "employed himself in feeding the geese."

Such storms were usual enough when one of the "serious" clergy first made his appearance and preached the tremendous doctrine of sin and justification in days which held it "monstrous" that a high-born lady should be told "she had a heart as sinful as the common wretches." The doctrinal storm on the *Union* gradually died away as such storms do, and two of the ringleaders eventually told the chaplain that "he had persuaded them that a religious character was an amiable one." But Martyn was regarded to the end as too severe a preacher. Charles Simeon himself, sharing to the full Martyn's conviction of the exceeding sinfulness of sin, had yet told him that his condemnations were those of a man who saw black against white and did not distinguish the grey of mingled motives in human action. Dean Church perhaps throws light upon this note in Martyn's preaching when, in a suggestive sentence, he points out a likeness between Henry Martyn and Hurrell Froude who, thirty years later, was to be the youngest and shortest-lived figure in the group that led the Oxford Movement. Both men, he says, "were made by strong and even merciless self-discipline over a strong and for a long time refractory nature." [1] And he goes on to write of Froude words that might have been set down of Martyn, and go far to explain the severity of his relentless earnestness :

He " turned his thoughts on that desolate wilderness, his own conscience, and said what he saw there." A man who has had a good deal to conquer in himself, and has gone a good way to conquer it, is not apt to be indulgent to self-deceit or indolence, or even weakness. . . . It was as unbearable to him to pretend not to see a fallacy as soon as it was detected, as it would have been to him to arrive at the right answer of a sum or a problem by tampering with the processes.

Newman who loved him wrote of Froude, " I should say that his power of entering into the minds of others was not equal to his other gifts." Such words are true of Martyn too, and it follows that both men would rouse opposition where others of less utterly sincere devotion might serve acceptably.

But there are pleasanter pictures of Martyn with

[1] Dean Church, *The Oxford Movement*, p. 37.

his flock, as when he stole unobserved down three ladders to visit the sick in the cockpit, where he had to feel his way to their hammocks, a light being forbidden. "At night," he writes, "got below without being observed, and with some Madeira and water for two of the sick men."

Or as when a corporal stole up to him and pressed into his hand a letter with the confession of spiritual need that he could never make otherwise on the crowded deck, and Martyn sought him out and spent a Sunday evening by his side at the main hatchway "looking out at a raging sea."

Or as in the *Journal* of another day :

On deck I had some conversation with one of the sergeants, who said with some emotion that many of the men were the better for my coming among them, and that for himself he had been brought up in this persuasion, and now things he had almost forgotten were brought to his mind. At his request I supplied him with a Bible.

The first break in the monotony of sea life was at Funchal, Madeira, where the fleet put in for water, upsetting the whole economy of the island by the demands of its great numbers. "Not a bed or a meal to be had at either of the two inns" and the whole town in the greatest bustle and confusion at having to water one hundred and fifty sail in a few hours. Martyn had letters of introduction to the English community and characteristically enough persuaded one of his island acquaintance to come to his lodging to hear him read aloud the whole of a volume of French sermons in order to criticize his pronunciation "with great care and attention."

It was his first glimpse of foreign parts.

I went to the great Catholic Church . . . the splendour of the church was beyond anything I had conceived . . . the few devotees there, while on their knees, would laugh and talk together. A poor negro woman crossed herself at this time with much fervour and apparent contrition. I thought she might be truly an awakened soul, and longed to be able to speak to her.

Before they set sail the Captain of the *Union* took Martyn aboard H.M.S. *Diadem* where the Commodore was giving orders to colonels of regiments and captains of vessels about the mysterious destination of the troops. Martyn, pacing the larboard side of the quarter-deck and observing the eager group, coveted for the business of his own campaign " Sir Home's earnestness of manner in expressing himself." When the fleet had sailed the men learned that San Salvador (now Bahia) Brazil, was the next rendezvous on their tortuous passage to India, but the troops were still in the dark as to where they were to take the field.

The month of October (October 3rd to November 12th) they spent in crossing the Atlantic, all unaware that during their voyage the French fleet had sailed out of Cadiz to meet the English under Cape Trafalgar. During this month Martyn made strides with Hindustani in which he was to do original and originative work. He had with him Gilchrist's *Grammar* and *Dictionary* and was making himself master of all the roots, but his problem was to compare the language of grammars with the language of life, and to produce books, not indeed forgetful of classic elegance—ere a Martyn forgot that his right hand must forget her cunning—but still less forgetful of the language of common speech. In his claim for the value of the spoken tongue and his delicate care for actual spoken sound Martyn was a pioneer among oriental scholars. Men of the type of Sir William Jones built their work upon dictionaries and comparison of written roots; Martyn, as much in love as they with such research, had a message for life, and the living language must be his care. The officers of the *Union* saw their most astonishing chaplain sit down among the Lascars and test on them the sentences from his grammar. He found, as might be expected, that the Hindustani of the grammars was "vastly too fine for these men" and too full of Arabic and Persian words. Slowly he made himself better understood: the *Journal* for Trafalgar Day shows Martyn seated on the gun deck, the centre of a group of Lascars, and reading aloud

the prayer of Parboter which I had been translating into Hindoostanee. They seemed to understand me perfectly; Cade corrected my pronunciation in a few words, and one or two other words they did not understand, but I was surprised at being able to gain their attention at all.

Later he bore one of them off to his cabin to test his work sentence by sentence and word by word. A Company's official who invited "blacks" to his cabin must be demented, and the officers henceforth gave Martyn up as "a mad enthusiast."

They ran at last into San Salvador after a day spent in battle stations owing to the presence of a strange sail on the horizon. The Captain of the *Union*, which had as usual fallen behind the rest of the fleet, told Martyn "in a great ferment" that he "would rather fight till the ship sunk than strike to a privateer." But the stranger showed no signs of fight, and amid much " furious bellowing " from Captain to pilot, the *Union* made the harbour of San Salvador.

Here Martyn went ashore on a new continent and spent one of the sunniest fortnights of his life. " Nothing but negro slaves " was his first impression, " very good-natured cheerful looking people."

A slave was sent to gather three roses for me. . . . A slave in my bedroom washed my feet. I was struck with the degree of abasement expressed in the act ; and as he held the foot in the towel with his head bowed down towards it, I remembered the condescension of our blessed Lord.

Looking for a shady spot where he could be alone under the orange trees, Martyn stumbled on to the estate of a Portuguese gentleman, who, charmed with the manners and the learning of the stranger, gave him great and genial hospitality ; carried him about through the sunny air in a palanquin, and showed him off to his friends as " one who knew everything, Persian, Arabic, Greek." Martyn half amused and wholly interested in his new experiences in the pleasant, lazy land was allowed at intervals the solace of time alone in the garden where trees made a shade near water, the ground covered with oranges, like apples on an English orchard floor. Here, in great peace, he crooned over well-loved hymns, read psalms that carried him to Lydia and Cornwall, and prayed aloud in the security that no Brazilian listener could understand his words.

His home letters tell of the " indescribable slops " of Portuguese feasts, and venture playfully to send kind remembrances to Lydia's mother " if she considers me as now at a sufficient distance."

They beg for news. To Cousin Emma he writes: "The simplest narrative in the world will delight me,—what texts Cousin Tom preached on—what sick he went to see—and a thousand nameless little occurrences will present a living picture of you to my mind. Can you send me by Mr Corrie, or by any other means, your profile and Cousin Tom's and Lydia's?"

In the delights of the tropical garden; in genial hours when Señor Antonio, his wife and a slave played cards, and Martyn "sat at the table learning Hindoostanee roots"; in a rapid devouring of the Portuguese grammar; and in Latin discussions, not unheated, with the Franciscan fathers of the place, the pleasant Brazilian interlude flew by; and Martyn was rowed back to the crowded life on board, by white-robed Lascars singing chants in honour of Mohammed.

The fleet stood out to sea and now at last the object of the military expedition was disclosed.

December 6th. Our Captain going aboard the Commodore by a signal, brought back the information that the Cape was our object, that a stout resistance was expected; and that it would be five weeks before we should arrive thither. The minds of all were set in motion by this account, as few, I believe, expected hard fighting.

The "side show" for which this expedition had been despatched was the wresting from the French (then masters of the "Batavian Republic") of the Dutch settlement of Cape Colony, which, in view of Napoleon's eastward-straining ambition, loomed large as a naval stronghold that was the halfway house to India.

So through strange seas and under other stars than the stars of home, the *Union* carried her load of fighting men to battle. In this, the third stage of her voyage, many of the men went sick. Martyn staggered amongst them, himself down with dysentery. His journal reveals something of the miseries of illness at sea in 1805.

The ship's steward lay convulsed with a gunner standing by him, holding a burning lamp that would scarcely burn; the air was so bad and the place withal so hot, being directly under the copper, that it was altogether most intolerable.

Had no service below as I was taken up in going to and fro to the sick, of whom there is now a great number. . . . The condition of the sick is miserable. I could not stand it till I got some aromatic vinegar.

The Captain himself was stricken down.

About seven this morning I was sent for by the surgeon to the captain; I saw that he was a dying man; his eyes rolled in his head, . . . but he was in general sensible. I began to read the most encouraging passages I could find. . . . He repeated " Lord, evermore give us this bread " . . . I prayed. . . . On my being interrupted by the doctor, he said " Mind him," meaning that he was to attend to me, and shortly died. We bore down to give notice of it to the Commodore. . . . The *Sarah Christiana*, when she saw our signal, fired minute guns so that the whole scene was very affecting.

When 1806 was three days old, the high lands of the Cape were discovered, yet eighty miles off; " a most stately thing, and the finest cape we saw in the circumference of the earth," Sir Francis Drake had called it; seen now with what eager suspense by cadets who for the first time would go into battle. Martyn's journal and a letter to Sargent give us a picture of the deck of the *Union*

K

when she came to anchor in Table Bay on Saturday night, January 4th.

About sunset the fleet came to an anchor between Robbers' Island and the land. The instant our anchor was down, a signal was given for the 59th regiment to prepare to land. Our men were soon ready and received thirty-six rounds of ball cartridge; before the three boats were lowered down and fitted it was two o'clock; I stayed up to see them off. The privates were keeping up their spirits by affecting to joke about the approach of danger, and the ladies sitting in the cold night upon the grating of the after-hatchway overwhelmed with grief.

Martyn, although an official chaplain of the East India Company's troops, was left on deck with the women. Señor Domingo in Brazil had already put him to shame by asking " if the soldiers had a minister to attend them in their dying moments, to instruct and administer consolation "; and Martyn " hardly knew what to say to explain such neglect amongst the Protestants," at which his Portuguese friend was shrugging his shoulders in horror. He was now left to strain his eyes in following his men as they were rallied among the flowering heaths and myrtle bushes near the shore, and as they marched, breasting the Blue Mountains to meet the Dutch resistance, ranged " with twenty-three pieces of cannon " between them and the town. He heard the artillery speak and " it seemed as if the mountain itself were torn by intestine convulsions." He could see his men rush down the hill to meet the Dutch, and then, as the enemy who had stood fire were broken by a bayonet charge, Martyn escaped from the *Union* and got ashore to his men. On the sandy beach he came first upon the cadets of his own ship who had made a shelter of bushes and straw and hailed him in to eat with them. But he did not stay long, for two wounded Highlanders walking into the lines brought news of a number of wounded lying out along the army's line of march. A party with " slings and barrows " went in search and Martyn was off with them six miles through the soft burning sand dotted with heath and geranium.

We were attracted by seeing some English soldiers; wounded men of the 24th; three were mortally wounded. One who was shot through the lungs was spitting blood. The surgeon desired me to spread a greatcoat over him as they left him. As I did this I talked to him a little of the blessed Gospel.

The wounded were being carried into a Boer farmhouse.

All whom we approached cried out instantly for water. One poor Hottentot . . . lay with extraordinary patience under his wound on the burning sand; I did what I could to make his position comfortable, and laid near him some bread which I found on the ground. Another Hottentot lay struggling with his mouth in the dust and the blood flowing out of it, cursing the Dutch in English. . . . While the surgeon went back to get his instrument in hopes of saving the man's life, a Highland soldier came up, and asked me in a rough tone, " Who are you ? " I told him an Englishman, he said, " No, no, you are French," and was going to present his musket. As I saw he was rather intoxicated, and might in mere wantonness fire, I went up to him and told him that if he liked he might take me prisoner to the English Army, but that I was certainly an English clergyman. The man was pacified at last. The surgeon on his return found the thigh of the poor Hottentot broken and therefore left him to die. Oh! that ambitious men at home could see the agonies of dying men left on the field.

Cape Town surrendered on January 10th. About five the Commodore fired a gun which was answered by the other men-of-war. " On looking out for the cause, we saw the British flag flying on the Dutch fort. . . . I prayed that the capture of the Cape might be for the advancement of Christ's kingdom."

The fleet lingered nearly a month at the Cape and Martyn took shore lodgings, rejoiced in " honest English apples and pears, tea and bread and butter for breakfast," and came into personal contact with one of his Cambridge heroes, Dr Vanderkemp, the old Dutch missionary to Kaffraria whose report he had found so " infinitely entertaining " that he " could read nothing else while it lasted."

From the moment of his arrival in South Africa Martyn had been " anxiously enquiring about Dr Vanderkemp. At last, to my no small delight, heard that he was now in Cape Town. But it was long before I could find him. At length I did. He was standing outside of the house, silently looking up at the stars. A great number of black people were sitting around. On my introducing myself he led me in and called for Mr Read."

From the exuberance of Martyn's delight at meeting men who shared the same allegiance, we gather how great had been the repression and loneliness of the months at sea. " I was beyond measure delighted." " I hardly knew what to do." He visited them daily, and with the younger man, Mr Read, he was " so charmed . . . that I fancied myself in company with David Brainerd." Mr Read in a bush station among the Hottentots had often been reduced to penury. At such times, he told Martyn, " it seemed to be suggested to him ' If thou wilt be my servant, be contented to fare in this way : if not, go and fare better.' His mind was thus satisfied to remain God's missionary." " Walking home I asked Dr Vanderkemp if he had ever repented of his undertaking. ' No,' said the old man, smiling, ' and I would not exchange my work for a kingdom.' Dear Dr Vanderkemp gave me a Syriac Testament as a remembrance of him."

So passed a month and the East India fleet was once more ready to sail. Before leaving Africa Martyn went with two or three friends up Table Mountain ; and wandering away from his party he scrambled up the kloof alone. At the end of the last steep pull he came upon a little hollow, green and decked with flame-coloured blossoms waving in the breeze. " It seemed to be an emblem of the beauty and peacefulness of heaven as it shall open upon the soul." He left the kloof and stood alone on the roof of the world, looking from sea to sea, " where there was neither noise nor smaller objects to draw off my attention. One might be said to look round the world from this promontory." Gazing out eastward over the watery road to India, the calmness of wide spaces came into his soul. " I felt commanded to wait in silence and see how God would bring His promises to pass."

None of the travellers found it easy to go back to the close-packed life of their voyagings : " A gloom seemed to hang upon all the passengers, at beginning so long a trip as from hence to India, after the weariness of so long a voyage." They set sail on February 9th, 1806, shortly before Martyn's twenty-fifth birthday, and seven months after leaving England, and they plunged at once into storms and sea-sickness. Martyn propped up in his cabin a water-colour of St Hilary Vicarage, and longed for a picture of Lydia. But there was a quietness dwelling on his spirit :

I pray that this may be my state, neither to be anxious to escape from this stormy sea that was round the Cape, nor to change the tedious scene of the ship for Madras . . . but to glorify God where I am and where He puts me.

A change was coming over his experience. During the first months of his voyage, along with the acceptance of loneliness and rebuff there had come to him moments of illumination and escape, which he could only describe as "walking with my Beloved amid the flowers of Paradise."

Now as he left South Africa his climbing soul made fresh discovery. Such moments of ecstasy, like sunlit peaks, were not the summit he was seeking, but only outlying bulwarks of "those shining tablelands."

"I perceived for the first time the difference between sensible sweetness in religion, and the really valuable attainments." He dwelt first with surprise, but later with consent, on a stern sentence of Leighton. "Mortify all affections towards inward sensible spiritual delight in grace, and the following of devotion with sensible sweetness in the lower faculties or powers of the soul, which are in no wise real sanctity or holiness in themselves, but certain gifts of God to help our infirmity." Strong meat for strong climbers this, and no milk for babes. "For the many that come to Bethlehem there be few that go on to Calvary."

The last stage of the *Union's* voyage was the

weariest. The ship was several times becalmed in the Indian Ocean and people grew fretful in the heat and tedious delay. It is curious to see the moral ascendancy which Martyn had insensibly won over the men he sailed with. There was little peace for his Hindustani grammar, he was " much teased with the accusations of the Captain, the commander of the troops, the sick, etc. all of whom complain of and abuse one another to me," and was constantly in request to mediate quarrels between the cadets and their officers, or between the King's officers and the Company's. As the delays lengthened, the new Captain confided in Martyn his fears that the provisions might not hold out. Sickness continued among the men and there was no diet fit for invalids. Martyn sent down to them his own allowance of Madeira and water. Coffee gave out, then tea. There was no fresh meat to spare and Martyn's own helping went, when he could manage it, to the convalescents, while he ate salt junk himself.

Read Hindoostanee ; the gale of wind continuing and much water flying over the sides, all the hatches were shut down, so that there was perfect darkness below ; however I visited the sick man, being obliged to feel my way to him. I am always surprised at the perfect contentment in which they seem to lie. This man was swinging in his hammock in darkness, and heat, and damp, without a creature to speak to him, and in a burning fever.

B. still delirious and dying fast ; the first thing he said to me when I visited him this afternoon was, " Mr Martyn, what will you choose for a kingdom ? ". . . All I can get from breakfast and at night I thought it right to give to Beasant, who is still on the borders of the grave from . . . want of proper meat after the weakening effect of his disease. . . . Among the sick whom I went to afterwards I found but one sensible.

Word was brought to me this morning that Beasant had just died. He was crawling upon his hands and knees to his breakfast, when he was taken worse and died as they were lifting him into his hammock.

Martyn was himself a sick man with constant headache, dysentery and "a distressing sensation of shortness of breath," contending too against "nervous irritability." And how he did contend, through those torpid days when nerves were raw, forever putting himself to some new fence, soul and body tensely trained for the enterprise in India that was never far from his thoughts.

In general I find that, in beginning to pray, I transport myself in imagination to some solitary spot . . . and there fancy myself praying. The bad consequence of this is that when I open my eyes and am conversant with the things around me, I am distressed and unable to maintain such a sense of God's presence; imagination seems to be a sort of help like music. . . . Yet I feel that I ought to learn to live without it.

Began to pray for the setting up of God's kingdom . . . especially in India. . . . My whole soul wrestled with God. I knew not how to leave off.

After two months at sea Martyn, coming on deck early from his sleepless cabin, "saw the island of Ceylon bearing west three or four leagues. . . . The smell from the land was exceedingly fragrant." All spirits rose and on April 25th at sunlight the *Union* anchored in the Madras roads. Martyn, amid a white-clad chattering crowd, went ashore to the country of his dreams. A round of invitations waited for him, a kindly welcome from the chaplain, Dr Kerr, and pleasant words of approval from the Governor, Lord William Bentinck, before whom he preached. But already his heart was given to the

east. " While the turbaned Asiatics waited upon us
at dinner I could not help feeling as if we had got
into their places ; " he was perhaps the first Englishman in India to think just that thought. He engaged a servant who " could speak Hindustani,"
and escaping from the European settlement walked
out with him by field paths to his native village.
" Here all was Indian ; no vestige of anything
European." Martyn, for the first time alone in
the east, felt now the power of the spiritual force
against which his life was hurled. The man who
stood there in the village street, though frail of
body, was a young athlete in the spiritual realm.
It was no untrained soul that felt there the " power
of the air," and shuddered

as if in the dominions of the prince of darkness. I fancy
the frown of God to be visible . . . the veil of the
covering cast over all nations seems thicker here ; the
fiends of darkness seem to sit in sullen repose in this land.

The battle was set.

CHAPTER VIII

CALCUTTA, 1806

The mornings are so pleasant in the garden. Very early, at about three in the morning, the Bheem-raj, a little bird, begins his song; half an hour afterwards, all the bushes and trees burst into melody . . . and the gay little humming-birds, with their brilliant colours, dive into the flowers for honey, with busy twitters. Oh, it is so cool and pleasant in the morning till ten o'clock, when the warmth increases; from noon to about four in the afternoon, all is quite still, except some lone woodpecker tapping at some far-off tree.—*Letter of* TORU DUTT *from Garden House, Calcutta, April 25th,* 1875.

He often said to us there was no spot in the world so dear to him as Calcutta.—MRS THOMASON *of* HENRY MARTYN.

As the *Union* slowly made sail up the Hooghly, her sea-worn passengers feasting their eyes on the low tranquil shore, she was met by the *Charlotte* yacht out of Calcutta, sent by the Company to relieve her of her load of Government treasure. Martyn went aboard the yacht, hoping that the smaller boat would make Calcutta faster. That evening they lay in Garden Reach, " very beautiful " in the sunset light. Even to the outward eye there were changes since David Brown had entered Garden Reach some twenty years before. The buildings of the College of Fort William now dominated the stately sweep of the Reach from the north. And beyond them again rose the new Government House, both buildings outward and visible signs of a new dignity that was coming into British life in India. Martyn was to learn on landing of the death of that Governor-General who had first come to India in the same year as David Brown, and also of the great minister who trusted him. For the travellers in the *Union* had yet to hear of the death of Pitt and of Cornwallis.[1]

When in David Brown's first year of service Cornwallis came to Calcutta, he brought her no great originative mind but a calm and dignified common sense. He set out to stabilize life in Bengal and finance in Leadenhall Street by creating a permanent land settlement, a conservative Bengali landed class, and a fixed revenue. A man of such clear-cut and limited ideals went far to reach them; and his industrious and honest fight against corruption meant much for India. But he aimed at a stable and static condition, and in the long run the forces of life are against the man who tries to bind instead of to direct them.

Under Cornwallis, the first peer of the realm whom the merchant city had received, orgies of eating and drinking dear to Jos Sedley and his like grew less, and Calcutta assemblies became more discreet and dignified. Church-going, however, was not yet in fashion, and when the Governor-General said to David Brown that the new Church of St John was " a pretty Church, but it had many critics," that worthy desired with a twinkle that it might have more critics on a Sunday.

Sir John Shore's governorship was a pale and

[1] The Governors-General since David Brown's arrival were Cornwallis, 1786, Sir John Shore, 1793, Mornington (afterwards Wellesley), 1798, Cornwallis again 1805, Sir George Barlow, 1805.

timid sequel to that of Cornwallis. Colour and vigour came with the next administration—colour indeed that appeared on the river in a state barge of green and gold rowed by twenty boatmen in scarlet turbans and rose-coloured livery. When Wellesley on his death-bed asked to be buried at Eton, he was making a fitting request. The outlook that he brought to Calcutta was that of Eton and the Foreign Office. He saw his work in India as part of the Napoleonic struggle. There was in his mind no question of Indian independence, but only of a desperate race between the French and British for dominance there.

One of the most fantastic fruits of the French Revolution had been the planting of a "tree of liberty" in the dominions of Tipu, Sultan of Mysore, while that autocrat conducted correspondence with the French Directory and enrolled himself in a republican club as "Citoyen Tipu."

Wellesley (then Mornington), the friend and favourite of Pitt, came out to India in 1798 conscious that she might be the scene of a death-grapple with France, which had the islands of Mauritius and Bourbon for an assembling place. This consciousness grew and was focussed with the growth of Napoleon's career. If he took Egypt in his stride and came upon India inchoate and unprotected, he might indeed become lord of east and west. But in racing Napoleon, Wellesley set a pace too great for the directors in Leadenhall Street.

One of their letters complains sadly that "neither His Majesty's ministers nor the Marquis Wellesley appear to wish to shrink from responsibility." When in 1805 they recalled him "suspended between

admiration and reproach," he left them responsible
for an empire but looking ruefully at their purses,
and summing up the results of his administration
as " an increased revenue of five millions, and a
debt contracted of twenty millions sterling.   The
great accession of territory made under the same
government has necessarily required an increased
army, at least so long as the power of France
predominates." [1]

They recalled him, but not before he had left
his mark on Calcutta.   On reaching Bengal he
had not disguised his horror at what he found.
" When I arrived there it was in a disgraceful and
a lamentable state."   He put Calcutta into training
as the capital of an empire and introduced a new
magnificence into the life of the dazzled city.   Government House rose, with a stately entrance and cere-
monial stairway.   It was opened with a breakfast
to seven hundred people.   Functions must now be
attended in full dress (white linen had sufficed
before) and no longer were there hookahs in attendance at the Supreme Council.   In the general
tightening up of easy-going ways Wellesley expressed
himself as shocked to find that divine service was
never held at his suburban residence of Barrackpore.
He was no friend to any sort of laxity, and decided
to turn church-going into one of the official functions
of Calcutta life.   He made David Brown senior
chaplain and helped him to choose the lessons for
a most novel function in Calcutta, a thanksgiving
service after the defeat of Citizen Tipu, to which
Wellesley came, and his great soldier brother, in
state through streets lined with troops.   The service

[1] Chatfield's *Hindostan*, 1808, p. 123.

was held in St John's Church with a sentry and his firelock at the door, and servants bearing the gold and silver maces of all the officials. After the fashion of the day when the state wished to pay its compliments to religion, the Governor-General ordered Dr Buchanan's sermon to be printed and circulated. Calcutta had never seen such doings for as Burke said, " The Europeans were commonly unbaptized in their passage to India." " You may easily conceive," wrote the preacher, " the astonishment of men at these religious proceedings. However, all was silence and deep acquiescence. It became fashionable to say that religion was a very proper thing." [1] Society began to come to church. Good David Brown, serene and faithful under patronage as under contempt, would now find the streets around St John's blocked up on Sunday morning with coaches and lacquered palanquins.

The Governor-General, "the marvellous little man " as his subordinates loved to call him, with his unfailing flair for the right man, now saw in David Brown and in Claudius Buchanan who had joined him in 1797, the very leaders needed for a scheme that was to alter the face of Indian administration. Writers who came out at sixteen were not, in Lord Wellesley's opinion, qualified to govern an empire, and in 1800 he sent home his " Notes on the necessity of a special collegiate training of civil servants," marked out a noble site on Garden Reach, put up a worthy building, gathered together upwards of one hundred learned teachers of eastern languages, law and literature, and placed this whole " College of Fort William "

---

[1] See Hough, *Christianity in India*, IX. 1.

under the provostship (the very name breathing his love for Eton) of David Brown.

The Vice-Provost was Claudius Buchanan, a man of restless intellect, who had run away from the home of his boyhood with a fiddle for his sole means of support, and now after strange courses had become the most statesmanlike ecclesiastic of the east, and Wellesley's trusted chaplain. The professor of Bengali was a yet more remarkable man, William Carey, blent of genius and faith, the one-time cobbler and Baptist minister in Midland villages, now translator of the New Testament into Bengali, and the man who established the literary form in workaday prose of that tongue whose poetry has to-day become one of the joys of the whole earth.

Carey was living at Serampore under Danish protection because of the Company's ban on missionaries. But Wellesley foresaw that Bengali must one day replace the foreign Persian as the language of justice, and he determined that Bengali should be taught in the new college. When Brown and Buchanan vouched for Carey as the one man capable of superintending the Bengali studies, Wellesley choked back his suspicions (the local press not knowing what a " Baptist " might be had put about that Carey and his colleagues were Romish priests in the pay of Napoleon) and called forth Carey from his seclusion to be professor of Sanskrit and Bengali.

Wellesley was gone when Martyn came. They sent out Cornwallis to reverse his policy, and Cornwallis was towed up the river in Wellesley's state barge, a dying man. Sir George Barlow now held the reins, but that notable trio at the college

were still working together and turning out men
who would leave their mark on India.

To a Calcutta under Sir George Barlow's rule
and in the inevitable tide of reaction that followed
the withdrawal of Wellesley's imperious hand,
Martyn went ashore at daylight on May 16th, 1806,
and asked for David Brown. He was fifteen miles
away at his suburban home, Aldeen. His colleague
Buchanan had sailed out of the Hooghly as Martyn
entered it, and so it came about that the first man
to welcome Martyn to Bengal was William Carey.
With him, so different in upbringing, so like in
gifts and apostolic spirit, Martyn sat down to his
first breakfast without "the smell of the ship."
Carey bald-headed, unassuming, almost uncouth in
manner, had no small talk, but he never failed
to take fire, like Martyn himself, if the talk turned
to missions.

With him I breakfasted, and joined with him in
worship, which was in Bengalee, for the advantage of a
few servants, who sat however perfectly unmoved. I
could not help contrasting them with the slaves and
Hottentots at Cape Town whose hearts seemed to burn
within them. After breakfast Carey began to translate
with a Pundit from a Sanskrit manuscript.

A chit from Mr Brown during the morning put
his Calcutta house at Martyn's disposal—the
chaplain's rooms adjoining St John's Church. There
in the heart of the city where the moving shadow
of the spire still marks the glaring hours Martyn
retired for solitude and prayer. There too on that
first day he was hunted out by "Mr Brown's
moonshi, a Brahmin" who "came in and disputed
with me two hours about the Gospel." The solitude

of that beginning, broken only by the arguments of the learned visitor, are a strange foreshadowing of what was to come.

Mr Brown soon came to Calcutta and bore Martyn out to his home at Aldeen, buried in foliage of mango, teak and bamboo, with green lawns (since broken up into tanks for the Howrah Water Works) that sloped down to the river and made a playground for his flock of children. Here at the large family table where, whoever might come, motherly Mrs Brown always made room for one guest more, Martyn found his Indian home. Of David Brown he always spoke as a father, and Mr Brown wrote later to a friend that " Martyn lived five months with me, and a more heavenly-minded young man I never saw." It was pure joy to Martyn after work to romp with children. A friend [1] tells us that " when he relaxed from his labours in the presence of friends it was to play and laugh like an innocent, happy child, more especially if children were present to play and laugh with him." Into that grave journal of his there creeps a line that tells much, when he writes of returning to Aldeen with " children jumping and shouting and convoying me in troops to the house. They are a lovely family indeed."

As a " griffin " or new arrival in Calcutta Martyn had calls to pay, and as a new official of the Company he must go to Government House and be presented to Sir George Barlow, who had an unhappy and repellent coldness of manner that often won him personal dislike and does not seem to have been more successful with Martyn than with others.

[1] Mrs Sherwood.

L

" After waiting a considerable time in a crowd
of military men, an aide-de-camp presented me to
Sir G. Barlow, who after one or two trifling questions
passed on." At a later levee Martyn received
" great attention " but was no more able to like
the Governor.

Martyn began at once to preach for David Brown
at the Old Mission Church, and his Calcutta friends
did their best to keep him there, carrying their
appeals " farther than mere civility." Congenial
as his new friends were, the thought of staying in
Calcutta chafed his spirit. He knew that three
of the six chaplains for the Company's fifty-three
stations in Bengal were planted there, together
with the group of Baptist missionaries under
Carey's leadership at Serampore ; and with a true
instinct he felt that Calcutta was dominantly
European, a foreign merchant settlement upon the
mudheaps. He set his heart on a chaplaincy at one
of the great inland centres of population.

Brown and Buchanan wish to keep me here, as I
expected, and the Governor accedes to their wishes. I
have a great many reasons for not liking this ; I almost
think that to be prevented going among the heathen
as a missionary would break my heart. Whether it
be self-will or aught else, I cannot yet rightly ascertain.
. . . I feel pressed in spirit to do something for God.
. . . I have hitherto lived to little purpose more like a
clod than a servant of God ; now let me burn out for God.

Amid the want of activity and decision so remarkable
among the friends of religion here I must begin at last
to act for myself, though I am no more qualified than a
child. At present this is the state of things, I wish to
fix at Benares. . . . If not I must endeavour to be fixed
at Patna as civil chaplain. . . . I shall endeavour to
have an audience of the Governor-General.

His home while he waited for the decision about his station was in a pagoda in David Brown's Aldeen garden, overhanging the broad river. It was a weird place of vaulted cells, its bricks carven with many-armed figures of Hindu gods. Once it had been the shrine of a little black figure wafted there by unseen powers, the idol Radhabullub; but the waters of the sacred river lapped closer and closer to the shrine, until it stood within the sacred limit (300 feet from either bank) where no Brahmin may eat or take a gift. Then Radhabullub left his shrine and retreated, with his conch shells, his cymbals and his offerings, to a grove beyond the sacred limit. The forsaken temple, added by David Brown to Aldeen garden ground, was made by him an oratory. This eerie home of crumbling masonry and creeping vegetation now became Martyn's cell. He revelled in the sense of solitude, the twittering birds, or the moonlight lying placid on the lawns; but to the Cornish saint, as to St Antony in the Egyptian tomb, haunting evil powers were not far from the sometime shrine.

My habitation, assigned me by Mr Brown, is a pagoda in his grounds, on the edge of the river. Thither I retired at night, and really felt something like superstitious dread, at being in a place once inhabited as it were by devils, but yet felt disposed to be triumphantly joyful, that the temple where they were worshipped was become Christ's oratory. I prayed out aloud to my God, and the echoes returned from the vaulted roof. . . . I like my dwelling much, it is so retired and free from noise; it has so many recesses and cells that I can hardly find my way in and out.

Here on a platform built over the placid lapping river, Henry Martyn wrote his sermons for Calcutta

congregations and almost grudged the time they
cost. For the English of Calcutta had David Brown
to their shepherd, and he was constrained to press
on to the unshepherded. Here too he flung himself
greedily on Bengali and Persian and Hindustani,
with a Brahmin and a Moslem teacher with whom
he would sit for hours as they introduced him for
the first time to long winding oriental arguments
upon religion, interminable as the flow of the river
under his pagoda. In Hindustani especially he had
made gigantic strides, and could now point out to
his teacher mistakes in a translation of Genesis.
Sometimes he took boat down to the College of
Fort William for lessons in oriental penmanship,
learning Hindustani roots in the boat as he went,
and returning perhaps in the evening with a crowd
of the Aldeen children in the boat, singing across
the sunset water.

Here in the pagoda, too, he made new friendships.
Five minutes' walk along the river bank brought
him to the apostolic settlement of Carey, Marshman
and Ward, the immortal trio of Serampore missionaries. He found his way there on his first day with
David Brown.

In the cool of the evening we walked to the mission
house, a few hundred yards off, and I at last saw the place
about which I have so long read with pleasure; I was
introduced to all the missionaries. We sat down about
one hundred and fifty to tea, at several long tables in
an immense room. After this there was evening service
in another room adjoining, by Mr Ward. . . . With Mr
Marshman alone I had much conversation.

And John Clark Marshman became more than
them all the friend of Henry Martyn. He was the

son of a Wiltshire weaver, and in boyhood had often walked a dozen miles for the loan of a book. Now in his Serampore house Martyn found "many agreeable sights"; one pundit was translating Scripture into Sanskrit, another into Gujerati, and a table was covered with materials for a Chinese Dictionary. Pacing up and down Mr Brown's garden paths at night, Martyn and Marshman cemented their friendship. Martyn entered keenly into all the joys and sorrows of the Serampore community: the tragic night when they were all agog to welcome Mr Chamberlain and his wife, only to find that Mrs Chamberlain had died on the boat: the Greek Testament lectures to younger missionaries: the preachings to wayside groups under banyan trees, or to immense crowds at fair-time: or the night (when Martyn could not sleep for indignation) of the news that Sir George Barlow, not content with the ban on missionaries in British territory, had forbidden the captain of an American vessel to land two who were bound for Serampore under the protection of the King of Denmark.

In long evenings of talk beside the river the friends would touch on deeper questions. "He is a most lively sanguine missionary," Martyn wrote of Marshman, "and made my heart burn within me." His friend tried to persuade Martyn to stay, for the present at least, in the Bible factory that the dauntless men of Serampore had established in their house for the translation of Holy Scripture into all the main tongues of the east. The work was after Martyn's own heart. He coveted for it the scholarship of Cambridge. Why, he asked Sargent, should it be left to men "who cannot in

ten years supply the want of what we gain by a
classical education?" But he was perfectly convinced that the call to stay in or near Calcutta was
not the call for him.

A yet dearer friend came to the pagoda, a junior
of Cambridge days, Daniel Corrie, afterwards Bishop
of Madras. That plain-faced, genial person,
adoring children and adored by them, fighting
down the claims of rare social popularity, had
recorded his desire to "become the world's
fool for the sake of Christ"; and inspired by
Simeon, but still more by Martyn, now followed
his friend to an Indian chaplaincy. As he lay
in the Hooghly a note came to him to say that
Martyn was awaiting him at the College of Fort
William.

"I set off immediately," says Corrie, "and was
received by him with the most lively demonstrations
of joy." It was pure delight to Martyn to see
that genial expansive countenance again, and to
introduce his friend to David Brown. ("A sensible,
determined pious man" was Corrie's comment in
his journal.) Martyn as guide to Calcutta took
the newcomer for a drive on the dusty "Course"
that evening, "as if I meant to exhibit my re-
inforcement."

Corrie found Martyn eating his heart out at delay
in Calcutta. The sights around him were burning
themselves into his spirit, as not unsimilar sights
had stirred the spirit of St Paul. From his pagoda
he could watch the crowds who climbed the ghat
to worship Radhabullub. Into his prayers or his
translation work there broke the clang of gongs,
with drums or conch shells from the god's new

shrine—" detestable music " to him. He went to visit the temple :

The way up to it was by a flight of steps on each side. The people to the number of about fifty were standing on the outside, and playing the instruments. In the centre of the building was the idol, a little ugly black image, about two feet high, with a few lights burning round him. At intervals they prostrated themselves with their foreheads to the earth. I shivered at being in the neighbourhood of hell.

Again, he went to see the great Juggernaut car in procession near Aldeen. When the car stopped at a neighbouring shrine " the god, with one or two attending deities, was let down by ropes, muffled up in red cloths." Holy water was poured over the image, and Martyn heard the great shout of the one hundred and fifty thousand people who stood with uplifted hands to watch this ceremony.

Before the stumps of images, for they were not better, some of the people prostrated themselves, striking the ground twice with their foreheads. This excited more horror in me than I can well express. . . . I thought that if I had words I would preach to the multitudes all day if I lost my life for it.

Corrie, more than most of Martyn's friends, entered into his haunting sense of the evil " power of the air." He tells of one evening when he was dining at Aldeen, and their eyes were attracted by a flame that rose and quivered on the opposite bank of the river.

We soon perceived that it was a funeral pile, on which the wife was burning with the dead body of her husband . . . by the light of the flames we could discover a great crowd of people, their horrid noise, and senseless music, joined with the testimony of some of the servants, convinced us that our apprehensions were founded on fact. The noise continued until ten o'clock, and the fire was kept burning till that time. My mind was struck with horror and pity. On going out to walk with Martyn to the pagoda, the noise so unnatural, so little calculated to excite joy, raised in my mind an awful sense of the presence and influence of evil spirits.

So Martyn waited in Calcutta, constrained in spirit, reading the life of St Francis Xavier, "exceedingly roused at the astonishing example of that great man," and raising in the city just such a storm as he had excited on the *Union* by his uncompromising sermons. At the Old Mission Church his earnestness was deeply acceptable, but St John's was a scene of trial. It still stands much as Martyn saw it, in the heart of Calcutta with Zoffany's queer altarpiece of the Last Supper, drawn with all the faces taken from old Calcutta characters. Those Sunday morning services at which Martyn sometimes preached before Sir George Barlow and his staff were all but government functions. In side galleries (now pulled down) sat the great ones of Calcutta; the Governor-General on one side, facing the judges of the supreme court on the other. Behind the judges on the north, as being the cooler side, sat the government ladies who had come in palanquins, wearing caps or turbans of sufficient gorgeousness to flaunt under the Governor's very eye. Lesser folk were ranged on chairs on the blue marble floor below. Here, before all the great ones of that little world, the new chaplain stood up to preach.

I knew what I was to be on my guard against—and therefore, that I might not have my mind full of idle thoughts about the opinions of men, I prayed both before and after, that the word might be for the conversion of souls, and that I might feel indifferent except on this score. The sermon excited no small ferment; however, after some looks of surprise and whispering, the congregation became attentive and serious.

Afterwards the storm burst : two other chaplains of the Company felt it their duty to preach counterblasts in which they even appealed by name to their new colleague to turn from doctrines so " inconsistent, extravagant and absurd," and described him (he sitting in the church the while) as " one of those who understand neither what they say nor whereof they affirm." Even to a man of Martyn's humility such orations were not altogether easy to listen to, and it is a very gracious gesture of his spirit that he describes in a rather stilted sentence when he says, " I rejoiced at having the Sacrament of the Lord's Supper afterwards, the solemnities of that blessed ordinance sweetly tended to soothe the asperities and dissipate the contempt which was rising. I think I administered the cup to ―― and ―― [the opposing chaplains] with sincere goodwill." The storm was at its height when Corrie landed and we have the comment of the man who had the art of disarming opposition on his friend who so often aroused it :

A great opposition, I find, is raised against Martyn and the principles he preaches. . . . At three o'clock Martyn preached from Rom. iii. 21–23, the most impressive and best composition I ever heard. The disposition of love and goodwill which appeared in him must have had great effect ; and the calmness and firmness with which he spoke raised in me great wonder.

Perhaps the authorities were not reluctant to send their firebrand chaplain out of Calcutta ; be that as it may his summons came at last to an up-country station, and on September 14, 1806, he wrote to Sargent, "I am this day appointed to Dinapore in the neighbourhood of Patna."

Patna was in those days some six weeks from Calcutta, travelling by a leisurely house-boat towed against the stream. The Browns, and indeed the whole friendly Calcutta group who had hoped to keep Martyn amongst them, quailed at the thought of sending him out alone. He had already shown them his helplessness in sickness, when it was his way to stagger on where a wiser man would have yielded. They dreaded the effect of solitude on his tense nature, and while they told him their kindly fears, the phantom form of Lydia was once more haunting his every thought.

July 12th, 1806. Found Europe letters. . . . My letters were from Lydia, T. H. and Emma, Mr Simeon and Sargent. All their first letters had been taken in the Bell Packet. I longed to see Lydia's. . . . The one I did receive from her was very animating. . . . Mr Simeon's letter contained her praises, and even he seemed to regret that I had gone without her.

Oh, the pity of it ! A letter from Lydia. She had sent him off to the ends of the earth with "the half of a broken hope for pillow at night" and with no leave to correspond with her. In her own eyes she was not free to marry, for Mr John's wedding had never taken place. Had she been wise she would have let ill alone. But Lydia, for all her real goodness, was not of the heroic build. She could not (as she thought) accept Henry's love ; nor could she bear to let it go entirely out of her life, and a few months after Martyn's departure

she began sending letters after him. A series of
six she despatched, of which the first had been lost
at sea. Sisterly or cousinly letters she would have
called them, but they served to rouse in Martyn
all his buried hopes. What lover would not have
found it "animating" to be told that his lady
prayed for him many times every day? Was not
his Lydia giving him now the answer that she was
not ready to give in the moment of hurried parting?
Martyn took the letter to David Brown who
certainly understood from it that the lady was to
be won if she were not won already. His fatherly
heart rejoiced at the prospect of care and sympathy
for his young saint, so determined to strike out a
lonely course. After such a consultation Martyn's
journal says that Mr Brown "strongly recommended the measure of endeavouring to bring her
here, and was clear that my future situation in
the country would be such as to make it necessary
to be married."

A letter from Colonel Sandys, which he opened afterwards, spoke in the highest terms of her. . . . Sat up
late with Mr Brown, considering the same subject . . .
and it dwelt so much on my mind, that I got hardly any
sleep the whole night.

Next day :

Mr Brown's arguments appear so strong that my mind
is almost made up to send for Lydia.

So it came to pass that Martyn sat down in the
pagoda to write his first love letter :

July 29th, 1806. Much of this morning taken up in
writing to Lydia. . . . Staid up till midnight in finishing
the letter to Lydia.

It was very long, as the letter would be of one hitherto pent up in silence and at last able to write his love. There was much to be said too, for this was a letter with a definite proposal that she should break through all her timidities and come to him. His pen flew on after the last boat had splashed homeward on the river and the night was broken only by the wash of water or the sudden cry of a bird. But it was no unrestrained pen, the letter breathes a discipline of spirit remarkable in any lover, but learned only at severest cost by so passionate a soul.

My Dearest Lydia,—

     ... I wish to assure you that I am not acting without much consideration and prayer, while I at last sit down to request you to come out to me in India.

     ... A few weeks ago we received your welcome letter, and others from Mr Simeon and Colonel Sandys, both of whom spoke of you in reference to me. ... Mr Simeon seemed in his letter to me to regret that he had so strongly dissuaded me from thinking about you at the time of my leaving England. ... Mr Brown became very earnest for me to endeavour to prevail upon you. Your letter to me perfectly delighted him and induced him to say that you would be the greatest aid to the mission I could possibly meet with. ... Now with a safe conscience and the enjoyment of the divine presence I calmly and deliberately make the proposal to you. ... If He shall forbid it, I think, that by His grace, I shall even then be contented. ... It can be nothing but a sacrifice on your part.

There follow assurances about the voyage and the climate, so dreadful and so unknown to the Cornish friends; his salary will keep her in comfort, and there will be English ladies at hand. Can she be ready to sail in the February fleet?

(The impatience of the lover made him over-sanguine about dates. Lydia did not receive his letter until March.) She is to come out as "guest to Mr Brown" in any ship where there is a lady of high rank in the service to chaperon her. And will she take Gilchrist's *Indian Strangers' Guide*[1] on the voyage? (a work in which she could learn to read in romanized character such Hindustani sentences as "Hand me the tooth-brush and powder," "I want a palanquin and bearers," "Brush the curtains well that no mosquitoes may remain.")

Then, as it drew on to midnight and the long letter must come to a close, the lover in the ghostly pagoda allowed himself to speak.

You say in your letter that *frequently every day* you remember my worthless name before the throne of grace. This instance of extraordinary and undeserved kindness draws my heart towards you with a tenderness which I cannot describe. Dearest Lydia, in the sweet and fond expectation of your being given to me by God, and of the happiness which I humbly hope you yourself might enjoy here, I find a pleasure in breathing out my assurance of ardent love.

To his vivid imagination his Lydia was almost there. "As soon as she arrives in the river," he wrote to Simeon, "Mrs Brown (a most sensible and zealous woman) will go down fifty or sixty miles to bring her up, so that she will not have the least trouble." "I please myself with the idea of visiting these places the next time in company with Lydia, and of walking with her morning

---

[1] *The Strangers' East Indian Guide to the Hindoostanee or Grand Popular Language of India (improperly called Moors)*, by J. Gilchrist.

and evening on these delightful banks." "Everything I see or do is a source of pleasure."

Her letters meanwhile only buoyed up his hopes. "My dearest Lydia's assurances of her love are grateful to my heart." But she was yet in Cornwall, and the immediate business was to send Henry Martyn off alone to his new station.

The Aldeen family and the Serampore missionaries came to the pagoda for a farewell meeting. They told him that they were "alarmed about the solitariness of his future life." At that moment he could hardly know alarm. The strange interaction of body, mind and spirit were producing in him something more like exultation. Warmth and sunshine had for the moment stayed or seemed to stay the tendency to disease. Hope had flooded the heart of the lover. And the disciple saw before him at last the longed-for task allotted to him by his Master's hand. So, while they sang and prayed under the echoing vault, he was exultant: "My soul never before had such divine enjoyment . . . my joy was too great for my body. I was in actual pain. . . How sweet to walk with Jesus—to love Him and to die for Him."

Next morning he took a house-boat and passed away from the Aldeen garden and the community at Calcutta that would so gladly have kept him in their midst.

CHAPTER IX

DINAPORE

No man (not an Anabaptist) will, we presume, contend that it is our duty to lay before them so fully and emphatically the scheme of the Gospel as to make them rise up in the dead of the night and shoot their instructors through the head.   If conversion be the greatest of all objects, the possession of the country to be converted is the only means, in this instance, by which that conversion can be accomplished.—SYDNEY SMITH's view of Indian Missions, from the *Edinburgh Review, April*, 1808.

Let me be torn to pieces, and my dear Lydia torn from me ; or let me labour for fifty years amidst scorn, and never seeing one soul converted ; . . . Though the heathen rage and the English people imagine a vain thing, the Lord Jesus, who controls all events is my friend, my master, my God, my all.—HENRY MARTYN's view of his life-work on arrival at Dinapore, *December,* 1806.

FOUR of the Calcutta friends brought Martyn on his way up the river, till bad weather turned them back, and he was left for six weeks of leisurely travel alone with his Moslem language teacher and his company of servants and boatmen. All day they towed the boat up-stream and at sunset made her fast and lighted cooking fires on the bank.

Cut off as he was from all but Indian scenes, the river became his teacher as she bore him slowly through the teeming land. She scowled at first and showed him her angry face in such a storm as that of which Tagore wrote [1] that it " droned like a giant snake-charmer's pipe, and to its rhythm

[1] In *Glimpses of Indian Life.*

175

swayed hundreds and thousands of crested waves,
like so many hooded snakes."

I was rather anxious about your little boat the day
you left me, [wrote Martyn to Mr Brown] it blew so
violently. As soon as you were out of sight, the men
laid down the rope and would not track any more for
the day. They were about to put back into a nullah
[a tributary water-course, the refuge of small craft
during river storms] but found that preoccupied by so
many boats, that we were obliged to lie on the naked
shore, exposed to the direct stream and wind. The
budgerow made a good deal of water by beating about
on the ground.

But in general the house-boat passed placidly
on the face of a full and gliding stream between
banks that showed Martyn in an endless picture
the life of Bengal in pleasant October days : muddy
children splashing at the waterside ; sesame or
towering hemp plants standing tall against the
sky ; cotton pods bursting milky-white ; rustling
winds swaying water-rice sown on the river silt ;
coloured groups where women stood in the water
bathing and washing clothes ; bamboo stakes hung
with fishing nets spread out to dry ; " sweet fields
dressed in living green " where the new-sown wheat
was springing ; clusters of thatched roofs among
shivering bamboos or plantains ; each village of
those days guarded by its own absurd mud fort ;
paddy birds standing in line where mud and
water meet ; and over all the wheeling kites
watching the river life with the keen eye of
hunger.

Through the sunny hours when the servants
liked to roll themselves in cotton sheets and sleep
on the roof of the house-boat, Martyn sat at his

books, sometimes with his teacher at Hindustani
and Bengali, sometimes alone at Sanskrit.

Tell Marshman with my affectionate remembrances
that I have seriously begun the Sanscrit grammar, but
I cannot say whereabouts I am in it, being enveloped
at present in a thick cloud with the exceptions, limitations, anomalies, etc.

Sanscrit sleeps a little, though I am daily more
convinced of the need of it in order to know the country
Hindoostanee.

Hindustani he was making more and more his
own as Carey had made Bengali. He brought to
the language already some knowledge of Persian
and Arabic from which on the one side it traced
descent, and he was now adding Sanskrit, its parent
on the other side, and so fitting himself for a critical
mastery of its form and vocabulary. Already, after
six months in the country, he could write to
Marshman at Serampore with a list of mistakes
in one of their Hindustani tracts.

He brought also the delicate ear that was quick
to detect changes of dialect as he passed from
village to village on the Hooghly and the Ganges.
So the river days glided by. "Reading hard all
day." "Employed all the day in translating, in
which work the time passes away pleasantly and
rapidly. The cold mornings and evenings begin to
be very severe."

At sunset when the gaily-painted "budgerow"
was moored, the boatmen in little circles round
their supper fires smoked coco-nut hookahs or told
interminable tales. And Martyn went ashore for
exercise; sometimes with his gun, bringing home
snipe or minas "enough to make a change with

M

the curry " ; sometimes with New Testaments or
some of the leaflets printed at Serampore. He
would plunge into villages where no " sahib " had
been seen before, scaring away graceful companies
of women as they came up from the river with
dripping saris, the household waterpots balanced
against their flanks.

One day he was shown the fresh footprint of a
tiger ; another day the trail of wild buffaloes was
on the path. The *Journal* is full of glimpses of
the myriad life of India.

Went ashore and ascended an eminence to look at the
ruins of a mosque. The grave of a Mussalman [1] warrior
killed in battle, and a room over it, were in perfect
preservation ; and lamps are lighted there every night.
We saw a few more of the hill-people, one of whom had
a bow and arrows ; they were in a hurry to be gone ;
and went off, men, women and children, into their native
woods. As I was entering the boat, I happened to
touch with my stick the brass pot of one of the Hindoos,
in which rice was boiling. So defiled are we in their
sight, that the pollution passed from my hand, through
the stick and the brass to the meat. He rose and threw
it all away.

He talked with all and sundry, testing his
Hindustani wherever he could find a friendly soul
ready to chat with him :

All ran away when they saw me, except one poor old
woman who was ill, and begged. Though she spoke
clearly enough, I could scarcely understand one of her
words, so that I have quite a new language to learn.
When she received half a rupee, she was mute with
astonishment.

People in general were shy of taking his books,

---

[1] Martyn writes Mussalman where we write Moslem or more correctly
Muslim.

but once when he had given away some New Testaments he wrote:

My fame arrived here before me, and some men had travelled on from the spring, having heard that Sahib was giving away copies of the Ramayuna! I told them it was not the Ramayuna, but something better, and parted with as many as I could spare. One poor fellow who was selling gun-rods followed the budgerow along the walls of the fort; and finding an opportunity got on board, and begged and intreated me for one, even with tears. As I hesitated, having given as many as I could spare for one place, he prostrated himself on the earth, and placed his forehead in the dust; at which I felt an indescribable horror, so I could not hold out. When he got it he clasped it with rapture, still thinking it to be the Ramayuna.

So gliding through the teeming land he came at last to Patna and its European suburbs of Dinapore (military) and Bankipore (civil), his new parish, the whole stretching for fourteen miles along the bank of the river which here is two miles wide.

By an early and all-but-forgotten statute of the East India Company it was the duty of their chaplains to teach the natives at their stations, and Henry Martyn, eager as he was for the task, " was almost overwhelmed " at the sight of " the immense multitudes " in this the second city of Bengal—" the multitudes at the waterside prodigious."

He left the house-boat for barrack quarters and surveyed the work before him. " I have now made my calls and delivered my letters, and the result of my observations upon whom and what I have seen is that I stand alone," he wrote to the Aldeen friends. The East India Company's troops, of which two regiments were stationed at Dinapore,

were a reckless fighting force of adventurers from
many European nations, and ne'er-do-weels from
English families. Others besides Martyn found them
"disdainful and abandoned." There was no church,
and he was expected to conduct service at the
drumhead, either in a barrack room with no seats
or in one of the two squares of the cantonments,
with no shade from the Indian sun. "After seeing
the European regiment drawn up I felt as I used
to feel on board ship."

The civilians at Bankipore had never had a
service and were embarrassed when the new chaplain
offered to come and give them one, more especially
as the judge had married a Moslem wife, abandoned
his faith and built a mosque to please her, which
Martyn found on his first call decked out with
flags and lanterns for a Moslem feast. But little
desirous as his countrymen seemed to be of his
services for themselves, they approved still less
of his intercourse with the people of the great
Indian city.

They seem to hate to see me associating at all with
the natives, and one gave me a hint a few days ago about
taking my exercise on foot. But if our Lord had always
travelled about in His palanquin, the poor woman, who
was healed by touching the hem of His garment might
have perished.

Our countrymen, when speaking of the natives, said
as they usually do, that they cannot be converted, and
if they could, they would be worse than they are.
Though I have observed before now, that the English
are not in the way of knowing much about the natives,
yet the number of difficulties they mentioned proved
another source of discouragement to me.

Martyn annoyed the General "by what I said

about the natives." In those days of preposterous superiority the chaplain dared to believe that "these men are not all fools, and that all ingenuity and clearness of reasoning are not confined to England and Europe. I seem to feel that these descendants of Ham are as dear to God as the haughty sons of Japheth."

When he entered Patna itself he speedily found that "haughty son of Japheth" though he were, he was met with equal racial hauteur on the part of a population chafing under the new rule of western aliens, and cherishing memories of the days not so long ago, when Mir Kasim, to avenge commercial injustice, had a hundred and fifty Europeans done to death in their city.[1]

Patna was in India the home of those most formidable Puritans of Islam, the fanatical sect of Wahabis; it was a city full of growling rumour. Martyn was greeted with scowls.

> The thought of interrupting a crowd of busy people like those at Patna, whose every day is a market day, with a message about eternity, without command of language, sufficient to explain and defend myself, and so of becoming the scorn of the rabble without doing them good, was offensive to my pride. The manifest dis-affection of the people, and the contempt with which they eyed me confirmed my dread.
>
> England appears almost a heaven upon earth because there one is not viewed as an unjust intruder.

Altogether his new parish presented no rosy prospect. But Martyn did not ask for roses. He found work to his hand in the hospital and the incessant funerals of a station where one regiment on arriving lost fifteen men in fourteen days. The

[1] The Patna massacre, 1762.

sick men were sometimes ribald, but at other times
Martyn "was much comforted to hear that the
men had great love for him." His barrack quarters,
as the General had warned him, became untenable
in the heat, and he thereupon moved to a bungalow
in the smaller cantonment square, which seemed
to him too sumptuous for a missionary, but which
he for ever filled with a strange assortment of
language teachers, scribes, and poverty-stricken
guests. The house was probably tenantless because
in the rains it was flooded and cut off from the
barracks by a stagnant pond.

Martyn, now master of a house, set aside the
big central room and verandas for a church, retaining only the use of the smaller rooms.[1] He had
forms set out (though superior persons sent their
servants before service with their own chairs and
footstools), and a table behind which he stood.
He begged from the General the help of the band
to lead hymns and chants. The men were paraded,
the station merchants drove up, the ladies were
handed in from their palanquins by officers, the
soldiers' wives in white dresses and mob caps came
across the dusty square under painted umbrellas,
and Martyn at his table, with the light filtering
through the double green lattices behind him, saw
before him, as he told David Brown, a larger
congregation and one in far greater need of
instruction in the Christian faith than would
have been his had he stayed at the Calcutta mission
church.

But he was not content with a flock that came
indeed to his service, but took no further notice

[1] See Harriet Wainwright, *A Sermon Against Calumny.*

of religion. At Dinapore as everywhere his presence was a touchstone; souls here and there accepted his standards and mounted his steep path. Martyn yearned over such and wrestled on their behalf. A Major and his wife who made a marked change of life had to face the music:

The Major was telling me yesterday, almost with tears, of the sneers he met with from nearly all for his religion. . . . He longs to be in England to follow religion unmolested.

I learnt from him that on Sunday evening at the General's he had been bantered on the late change that had taken place in him with regard to religion. I felt such love to him that I could have laid down my life for him.

It was no easier for the men. Martyn put his house at the disposal of the "serious" soldiers twice a week, and never failed to meet the tiny group, for whom sometimes a fair linen cloth was spread and a Communion held in his veranda. They were not more than about half a dozen hardy souls who could gather at any one time. "Six soldiers came last night. To escape as much as possible the taunts of their wicked companions, they go out of their barracks in opposite directions to come to me."

For one part of Martyn's flock in the cantonments no pastoral care had ever yet been shown. With each European regiment of the East India Company there came a half-recognized following of Portuguese and Indian women of the camp. Military regulations forbade Martyn to give Christian marriage to these women and the soldiers. Yet many of the unions with them were lifelong and faithful; and in barracks full of nameless vice made on the whole

for better living among men who were not, like
the King's regiments, looking forward to a return
from foreign service to their English sweethearts.
Since marriage was against the regulations it became
one of the hardest tests for Martyn's "serious"
soldiers to give their women an allowance and cease
to live with them. The camp women, nominally
Roman Catholic or Moslem, but virtually ignorant of
all faiths, had become an institution in cantonment
life. For good or evil they were there and quite
unshepherded and Martyn could not leave them
without care.

I signified to the Colonel that I was ready to minister
in the country language to the native women belonging
to his soldiers of the European regiment, which he
approved, but told me it was my business to find them
an order and not his. So I issued my command to the
sergeant-major to give public notice that there would
be divine service in the native language on the morrow.
The morrow came and . . . 200 women. Instead of
the lessons I began Matthew. I could not keep myself
from attempting to expound a little, and but a little.
The women come, I fear, rather because it is the wish
of their masters. The conversion of any of such
despised people is never likely perhaps to be of any
extensive use in regard to the natives at large; but
they are a people committed to me by God, and as dear
to Him as others; and next in order after the English,
they come within the expanding circle of action.

"The expanding circle of action "—so in a single
phrase he reveals his outlook. His first step beyond
the cantonments was the setting up of four little
primary schools in Patna and its neighbourhood.
The well-greased urchins squatted more or less
contentedly, writing the Persian character in the
sand or on wooden slates and singing out the name

of the letter as they did so. "Thus they learn
both to read and to write at the same time." For
such scholars as mastered the art of reading Martyn
prepared in Hindustani the Sermon on the Mount
and a little book of the Parables of Christ with
explanations, his own first effort at Hindustani composition, corrected again and again with loving
and scrupulous care under the eye of his several
teachers.

I went on to Patna to see how matters stood with
respect to the school. Its situation is highly favourable,
near an old gate now in the midst of the city, and where
three ways meet. . . . The people immediately gathered
round me in great numbers. I told them that what
they understood by making people Christians was not
my intention; I wished the children to be taught to
fear God and to become good men. . . . The General
observed to me one morning, that that school of mine
made a very good appearance from the road; "but,"
said he, "you will make no proselytes." If that be all
the opposition he makes I shall not much mind.

Such little schools, together with the habit of
welcoming Indian friends to their houses, earned
for Martyn and his friend Corrie (now stationed
above him at the rock fortress of Chunar overhanging the Ganges) the title of "the black
chaplains."

Martyn and Corrie wrote to one another once
a week, sending up and down the river accounts
of language difficulties, refractory schoolmasters,
children's progress, or quaint ecclesiastical adventures in neglected communities where all manner
of questions crept in about baptism, marriage and
Christian burial, that had to be solved on the spot
by the isolated young chaplains, in a country where

there was no bishop, and David Brown himself, whom Martyn's letters call "the patriarch," was only in deacon's orders. Those unfettered weekly letters reveal, as more official documents could not, the single-heartedness of the men who wrote.

I trust we shall . . . keep our eyes fixed on the fiery, cloudy pillar [wrote Martyn]. If you see it move when I do not, you will give me the signal, and I will strike my tent and go forward.

Second only to Corrie's letters and occasional visits, as the joy of Martyn's life, was a budget that came periodically from Calcutta. Buchanan with the mind of an ecclesiastical strategist and Brown with the care of a father for his isolated juniors, started together a kind of clerical club for keeping in touch with such chaplains as cared to study the whole Christian position in India. Each man was to send a monthly report of his own task; and other documents of interest were circulated with these, such as Buchanan's researches on the ancient Syrian Churches in the South, or the Latin correspondence which Martyn set up with the Roman Catholic fathers of the Propaganda. The group planned together to supplement the work at Serampore in Bible translation, and collected books on oriental tongues. Martyn heard of the club—"The Associated Clergy" they called it—with enthusiasm.

What a gratification it would be to me to lean my head across your long table to hear what you and your colleagues are planning. But I hope you will send me constant intelligence. Your wish to hear from me can never equal my desire for your letters. The Lord love you and yours.

Among the clerical details of the letters that went down to Aldeen, messages creep in for the children of the house that more than any other was home to him. "Dear little Hannah." "Dear child! Give my love to her." "Tell James and Charles that I expect to find them great scholars when next I see them." "So you intend the new little one for me; I accept the boon with pleasure."

Sorely did he need these Indian friendships, for home letters were few and distressing. His sister Laura died of consumption, and Sally though happily married (so happily that she did not often write to Henry) was also in poor health. And at last the answer came from Lydia. It came to one who dreamed at night of her coming, who after a day "hard at Arabic Grammar" sat at his door looking across the dusty barrack square with his heart at St Hilary and Marazion, and who "hastened on the alterations" in his comfortless house and garden to make it fit for her.

October 24, 1807. An unhappy day; received at last a letter from Lydia, in which she refuses to come because her mother will not consent to it.

He began a letter to her at once:

My DEAR LYDIA,—
Though my heart is bursting with grief and disappointment, I write not to blame you. . . . You condemn yourself for having given me, though unintentionally, encouragement to believe that my attachment was returned. Perhaps you have. I have read your former letters with feelings less sanguine since the receipt of the last, and am still not surprised at the interpretation I put upon them. . . .

You do not assign among your reasons for refusal
want of regard to me. . . . On the contrary you sa
that "*present* circumstances seem to you to forbid m
indulging expectations." . . . Let me say I must b
contented to wait till you feel that the way is clear. . .
If there were no reason for your coming here, and th
contest were only between Mrs Grenfell and me, that i
between her happiness and mine, I would urge nothin
further, but resign you to her. But I have considere
that there are many things that might reconcile her t
a separation from you (if indeed a separation is necessary
for if she would come along with you, I should rejoic
the more). First she does not depend on you alone fo
the comfort of her declining years. She is surrounde
by friends. She has a greater number of sons an
daughters honourably established in the world than fall
to the lot of most parents—all of whom would be happ
in having her amongst them. Again, if a perso
worthy of your hand, and settled in England, wer
to offer himself, Mrs Grenfell would not have in
superable objections though it *did* deprive her of he
daughter. . . .

But the more I write and the more I think of you, th
more my affection warms, and I should feel it difficul
to keep my pen from expressions that might not b
acceptable to you.

Farewell! dearest, most beloved Lydia, remembe
your faithful and ever affectionate

H. MARTYN.

To David Brown :

It is as I feared. She refuses to come because he
mother will not give her consent. Sir, you must no
wonder at my pale looks when I receive so many har
blows on my heart. . . . The queen's ware on its way
out to me can be sold at an outcry or sent to Corrie. I
do not want queen's ware or anything else now.

Was Mrs Grenfell then so obdurate a parent
Or was Lydia only half in love with the man and

alf with the romance of being loved by him?
niece of Lydia tells us that the maternal opposition
was real. "The connexion with the Martyns was
distasteful" to Mrs Grenfell who did not feel the
families equally matched. And she adds, "I should
say that my [great] aunt's ideas of paternal authority,
up to middle life even, were extreme, as I well
remember her expressing them."

An entry in Lydia's diary for May 20, 1806, is
revealing:

"My chief concern now is lest I should have
given too much reason for my dear friend's hoping
I might yet be prevailed on to attend to his request,
and I feel the restraint stronger than ever, that
having before promised, I am not free to marry.
I paint the scene of his return, and whichever way
I take, nothing but misery and guilt seems to
await me. . . . Thou knowest these consequences
of my regard for thy dear saint were not intended
by me, and that when first I regarded him otherwise than as a Christian brother, I believed myself
free to do so, imagining him I first loved *united to
another!*"

Charles Simeon, when he knew that Martyn's
proposal had been sent home, took horse and rode
into Cornwall, the erect precise old bachelor, a
most quaint ambassador of love. But Lydia had
already written her refusal when Simeon came.
"May the Lord comfort me by him" her diary
said as she prepared to meet him. She was edified
by seeing "how a Christian lives." But the hope
of his journey had not been her comfort so much
as Henry Martyn's, and he came away depressed.
Lydia admitted that she had "entered into a

correspondence with Henry Martyn and expressed
too freely her regard," but she once more paraded
her scruple about Mr John. He was not yet married
and she was not free.

Simeon brushed it away and told her no objection
was insuperable except her mother's prohibition
and that he was not disposed to regard as ever
lasting.

But he rode back depressed to Cambridge and
sent out to India a letter which Martyn also found
depressing; while Lydia, with her gift for pro
longing emotional situations, wrote another letter
"to bid him a last farewell."

It was well for Martyn that the greatest task of
his life had just begun to fill his thoughts. The
"Associated Clergy" in their desire for Bible
translation had sent to him to ask if he would
make a New Testament in Hindustani, the existing
one being "unintelligible to the vulgar," and also
a satisfactory version in Persian, since neither
that of Mr Colebrook, the great Sanskrit scholar
nor of the Serampore missionaries, had quite the
idiomatic freedom that was needed. Already
Martyn's uncomfortable church-like house was filled
with strangely assorted guests who hung about him
now a learned Moslem from Patna, now a Roman
Catholic father from the Propaganda, now a Jew
from Babylon, now an Armenian from Jerusalem
("a very agreeable Armenian padre in a black
little cassock exactly such as we wear, or ought
to wear. I feel almost ashamed of my secular
appearance before these very venerable and ap
propriate figures"), now a Prussian sergeant anxious
about his soul. The strangest of them all was now

o be added to the establishment—Sabat, as he
called him, a wild Arab with a wild history whom
Mr Brown was despatching to be his assistant in
translation work. The work was to be his joy and
delight and Sabat an engrossing care, so that the
Martyn of these days, his whole being concentrated
on one end, undistracted by hope of human solace,
moves in a strange calm, finding rest in toil, like
the sleep of a spinning top.

"He wishes, if it please God," wrote Corrie on
a visit in September, 1808, "to be spared on account
of the translations, but with great earnestness he
said, 'I wish to have my whole soul swallowed up
in the will of God.'" [1]

And now at last a "budgerow" was coming up
the Ganges bringing one who saw in vivid colours
and knew how to write down what she saw.

Mrs Sherwood, wife of the paymaster of the
King's 53rd, had been a story-writer from her
childhood and went about the world with a seeing
eye and a warm, compassionate heart. Her *Fairchild Family* was to make her a nursery classic,
but to her gossiping autobiography the Church
owes all its most vivid pictures of Henry Martyn
in India.

The chaplain at their last station, one of the
"Associated Clergy," had given Mr Sherwood a
note for Martyn which he hurried to present on
arrival, leaving his wife in the boat.

Mr Martyn received Mr Sherwood not as a stranger
but as a brother. . . . As the sun was already low, he
must needs walk back with him to see me. I perfectly
remember the figure of that simple-hearted and holy

[1] *Memoirs of Daniel Corrie*, p. 118.

young man, when he entered our budgerow. He was
dressed in white, and looked very pale, which however
was nothing singular in India ; his hair, a light brown,
was raised from his forehead which was a remarkably
fine one. His features were not regular, but the expression was so luminous, so intellectual, so affectionate,
so beaming with Divine charity, that no one could have
looked at his features and thought of their shape or form
—the out-beaming of his soul would absorb the attention
of every observer. There was a very decided air, too,
of the gentleman about Mr Martyn, and a perfection of
manners which, from his extreme attention to all minute
civilities, might seem almost inconsistent with the
general bent of his thoughts to the most serious subjects.
He was as remarkable for ease as for cheerfulness, and
in these particulars his *Journal* does not give a graphic
account of this blessed child of God. . . .

Mr Martyn invited us to visit him at his quarters at
Dinapore, and we agreed to accept his invitation the
next day. Mr Martyn's house was destitute of every
comfort, though he had multitudes of people about him.
I had been troubled with a pain in my face, and there
was not such a thing as a pillow in the house. I could
not find anything to lay my head on at night but a
bolster, stuffed as hard as a pin-cushion. We had not,
as is normal in India, brought our own bedding from the
boats. Our kind friend had given us his own room,
but I could get no rest. After breakfast Mr Martyn
had family prayers, which he commenced by singing a
hymn. He had a rich, deep voice, and a fine taste for
vocal music. After singing he read a chapter, explained
parts of it and prayed extempore. Afterwards he
withdrew to his studies. The conversion of the natives
and the building up of the Kingdom of Christ were the
great objects for which alone that child of God seemed
to exist. It was chiefly while walking with him on the
Plain, on the Saturday and Sunday evenings, that he
opened his heart to us.

This however I can never forget, that Henry Martyn
was one of the very few persons whom I have ever met
who appeared never to be drawn away from one leading
and prevailing object of interest. He did not appear

like one who felt the necessity of contending with the world and denying himself its delights.[1]

She little guessed the struggles that had been the price of serenity for the man whom she described as " walking in this turbulent world with peace in his mind and charity in his heart."

[1] *Life of Mrs Sherwood, chiefly autobiographical*, 1854, p. 340, etc.

CHAPTER X

THE LINGUIST

There is a book printed at the Hirkara Press, called Celtic derivatives—this I want; also grammars and dictionaries of all the languages of the earth. I have one or both in Latin, Greek, French, Italian, Portuguese, Dutch, Hebrew, Rabbinical Hebrew, Chaldee, Syriac, Ethiopic, Samaritan, Arabic, Persian, Sanscrit, Bengalee, Hindoostanee.—HENRY MARTYN *to* DAVID BROWN, *October* 1809.

Christianity has been, as it were, a great searchlight flung across the expanse of the religions; and in its blaze all the coarse, unclean and superstitious elements of the old faiths stood out, quite early, in painful vividness. India shuddered. . . . But the same light which exposed all the grossness gradually enabled men to distinguish the nobler and more spiritual elements in the religions.— J. N. FARQUHAR, *Modern Religious Movements in India.*

DURING Martyn's months in Calcutta he had missed meeting one of her most impressive personalities, Claudius Buchanan, the Vice-Provost of Fort William College.

After penniless wanderings with a violin this sturdy and ambitious person had found his religion and his education among the evangelicals, who sent him to Cambridge. Amongst these men who laid all their stress on the religion of the heart, Buchanan bore a nature fitted for the career of a mediæval prince-bishop. At home he might have been a notable prelate with the ear of statesmen, or, if the reproach of his religious school had debarred him from preferment, a redoubtable party polemic, an honest dealer of shrewd and smashing blows. In India, where he became Wellesley's trusted chaplain, the vast sweep of the problems of a continent delighted him, but the position of the handful of chaplains as an unconsidered appendage of the East India Company caused him grave distress.

His most placid period was during the few years that followed the opening of the College of Fort William, when under Wellesley's approving eye, he bent his great powers to the working out of its ambitious curriculum, and returned in the evening to a little wife for whom his rather condescending courtship had meant entrance into a wider world both of spirit and of intellect.

"It is a new Gospel to me," wrote the bride after listening to his instructions (and Buchanan was a luminous and inspiring teacher), "and I seem to live in a new world, differing far more from my old world than India differs from England." She could not admire him enough, and he approved of her. "Mrs Buchanan is not yet nineteen," he wrote; "she has had a very proper education for my wife. She has docility of disposition, sweetness of temper, and a strong passion for retired life." [1] Under "my Mary's care" Claudius Buchanan spent some contented years, his days busy with college organization, his leisure occupied with schemes for the Church in India. He gave munificently from his salary to provide prizes in home universities and schools for odes or essays on subjects connected with Christianity in the East. To his Mary it was all most wonderful.

[1] Pearson, *Memoirs of Claudius Buchanan*, p. 195.

But she died, and there passed from her rugged husband's life a touch of mellowing softness. He was in danger of hardening into the ecclesiastical strategist. He found, he tells us, "some consolation in writing a few lines to her memory in the Hebrew, Syriac, Greek and Latin languages which I inscribed on a leaf of her own Bible."

That done he turned to survey India and her needs. In 1805 he published his *Memoir of the Expediency of an Ecclesiastical Establishment in British India.* After a clear and succinct statement of existing conditions he suggested (as Grant and Brown had suggested before him) that India stood in dire need of an extension of "our happy establishment." If to-day lovers of India are out of love with the yoking of Church and state, it must at least be acknowledged that Buchanan's proposals were daring in days when there were but three Anglican Church buildings in India, one in each presidency.[1]

"An archbishop is wanted for India," he wrote, "a sacred and exalted character, surrounded by his bishops, of ample revenue and extensive sway."

The sentence gives a picture of his mind, courageous, political, with a curious trust in externals.

As Martyn sailed up the Hooghly Buchanan had passed down it, borne southwards on a survey whose wide sweep delighted his heart. He was on his way to enquire into the state of the Christian Church in South India and describe, in his *Christian Researches in India,* the ancient and then little

---

[1] Three churches served by official chaplains of the Company. The Old Mission Church in Calcutta was an unofficial fourth.

known Syrian Church in Travancore.[1] When he returned his chests were stuffed with manuscripts and his head seething with schemes for Bible translation. He inspired David Brown, and together they started the club known as "The Associated Clergy" and inspired their brethren. Martyn in Dinapore gave his heartfelt admiration to the sweep of Dr Buchanan's intellect and responded gratefully to the vigour of his leadership.

I feel bound to bless our God for the arrival of Dr Buchanan. To him I beg my kindest love, congratulations on his personal preservation and thanks in the name of the whole church for those MSS. he has brought away. My expectation dwells on the lids of those chests; who knows how important the acquisition of them may be?

It is a thought that has lately occurred to me that if Dr Buchanan is disposed to add another to his acts of munificence, he might revive Arabic and Oriental literature in Cambridge by establishing an annual prize there—Arabic and Persian Bibles will soon have to undergo a rapid succession of editions in England, and it is therefore desirable that many persons should be at hand qualified to superintend the printing of them.

Read Dr Buchanan's correspondence with indescribable joy. It will read like a romance in England and the people of God will be in an extasy. But while so many things are calling us to look abroad into the earth, may the people of God mind their own hearts.

Letters now began to come up the river to Dinapore telling Martyn that Brown and Buchanan had comprehensive schemes for "a British Propaganda for uniting all the talents and industry in India." He could not at first get from his leaders

---

[1] So late as 1831 a clergyman in Cornwall could write that "the Syrian Christians and their good Bishop are said to have no existence but in Buchanan's imagination."

all the details of so grand a scheme, but they told
him that his part was to study Hindustani, Persian
and Arabic. He obeyed.

Since your first letter, [he replied to David Brown]
commanding me to change my studies, the dust has
been collecting on Mr Carey's great grammar, [Carey's
Sanskrit grammar was a work of one thousand pages]
and the time formerly devoted to Sanscrit is given to
Persian and Hebrew. I am too shallow in both of
these to touch the Arabic yet. In Hindoostanee translations I begin to feel my ground, and can go on much
faster than one moonshee can follow. I have some
thoughts of engaging another. . . . You have left me
still in the dark respecting the new Propaganda, but I
see enough to rejoice in the zeal that animates you all;
and in time I hope to catch the flame, and with you to
become a living sacrifice.

You can command me in any service which you can
prove to be most favourable to the interests of Zion.

It was in June 1807 that the definite proposal
came to him from David Brown that he should
translate the New Testament into Hindustani (or
Urdu) and supervise translations into Persian and
Arabic, with the help of two men whom they would
send to him as specialists in these languages, Mirza
Muhammad Fitrat of Benares and Nathaniel Sabat,
an Arab educated at Baghdad.

David Brown enclosed a letter of Claudius
Buchanan, which with Martyn's comment on it
throws a curious sidelight on two characters :

In a note of Dr Buchanan's to Mr Brown, which he
sent me is this : " We shall give to Martyn Mirza and
Sabat, and announce to the world three versions of
Scripture in Arabic, Persian and Hindoostanee, and a
threefold cord is not easily broken." This plan of
placing the two with me I accord to, as it seems to be

the will of God ; but annunciations I abhor, except the annunciation of Christ to the Gentiles.

So with diffidence, Martyn accepted the task, hardly realizing at first that it might involve a situation of some little delicacy with his friends the Baptist missionaries at Serampore. Those men of heroic industry had taken for their province the translation and printing of the Scriptures in all the great tongues of India, Burma and China. The vastness of the task undertaken at Serampore can only be seen when it is realized that most of the missionaries there were self-taught in Greek and Hebrew ; some of them only learning those tongues in India for the sake of the translations.

What men so handicapped produced is almost miraculous. In the face of their actual achievements anything seemed possible, and it was hard for them to realize all that was involved in a critical mastery of Greek or Hebrew, or the tentative nature of all first translations made by foreigners.

The friendship between the Baptist missionaries and the Anglican chaplains was real. " I believe you will not find many in England who have less bigotry and more friendship," [1] wrote Carey of David Brown and Claudius Buchanan. None the less there was a little gallantly suppressed sore feeling in Serampore when the chaplains, in starting a Calcutta branch of the new Bible Society, made it clear that not all of the translations of the Society would of necessity be made at Serampore. There was a little tendency to resent the fact that official chaplains had the ear of the government while the

[1] E. Carey, *Memoir of William Carey*, p. 458.

Serampore mission was there on sufferance, and a little natural irritation at the rather lordly tone of Claudius Buchanan's announcements.

But Martyn in his distant station, full of appreciative love for the men of Serampore, and of warm friendship for his "brother" Marshman, was unconscious of the slightly strained feelings for the most part so gallantly controlled. He wrote quite freely and critically, as he would have written of the work of any Cambridge friend, about the quality of their Persian or Hindustani versions; and when his own translations were made, he in his turn showed the scholar's eagerness for all the criticism that his friends could give.

Marshman sent me, you know, some translations. The general style of the Hinduwee is just adapted to the most general use—it will be understood by millions; but it ought to be done with more care. Many important sentences are wholly lost, from faults in the order or other small mistakes. The errors of the press are also very considerable. Remind them that the more haste the less speed.

Had Martyn been in Calcutta there would have been no misunderstanding. As it was he learnt with something of a shock that his Serampore friends were chafed a little by Dr Buchanan's entrusting to so young a "Daniel come to judgment" work which they had expected to see done in Serampore. "Most cordially do I wish to remain in the background to the end of life" he protested, and it was true. But it was too late to draw back from the great enterprise on which he was now launched, and for which his standard was the most exacting.

" Perspicuity is not the only requisite," he wrote ; "a certain portion of grace is desirable and dignity indispensable. The Mahometans are more affected with sound than even the Greeks."

That a man of Martyn's critical power should, after so few years in the country, pass with calm assurance his judgment upon the translations of others, and himself venture upon work for which he had so high a standard is in any case remarkable. It is seen to be still more so when the difficulties of Hindustani study in Martyn's day are taken into account.

He found the language neglected of both eastern and western scholars, and on the whole despised by men of letters. A certain number of small phrase books, not without their modern counterparts, had been published to help civilians to talk to their servants. But Gilchrist and Colebrooke, the chief English representatives among the very few students who had done more serious work on Hindustani, poured candid scorn upon these works : "Hadley's insignificant catch-penny publication, a mere Tom Thumb," wrote Gilchrist, whose Grammar and Dictionary were standard books, and who with some complacency christened works of his own by such names as *The Anti-jargonist* or *The Hindee-Roman Orthoepigraphical Ultimatum.*

Martyn found then a great living language, the tongue of sixty millions, a tongue of hybrid origin, and not yet standardized by any universal work of literature.[1] He was making it more and more

[1] Gilchrist only knew the names of thirty writers in Hindi ; but by 1839 Garcin de Tassy had found the names of 750, including some twelfth century chroniclers in verse and some seventeenth century

his own as Carey had made Bengali, and learning
it always with reference to life, picking out with his
pundit the most used words in the vocabulary, or
fetching in a story-teller from the bazaar to be his
teacher. This language, as yet a tongue of intercourse rather than of books, he by a prophetic
instinct seized on as a great vehicle for religious
truth. Time has proved him right.

De même qu'en Europe les réformateurs Chrétiens
ont adopté les langues vivantes pour tout ce qui a
rapport au culte et à l'instruction religieuse ; ainsi dans
l'Inde, les chefs des sectes modernes hindoues et mussul-
manes se sont servis généralement de l'hindoustani
pour propager leur doctrines. . . . Non seulement ils
ont écrit leurs ouvrages en hindoustani, mais les prières
que récitent leurs sectateurs, les hymnes qu'ils chantent,
sont en cet idiome.[1]

All Martyn's critical skill went into his translation.
He refused to be hurried.

You chide me for not trusting my Hindoostanee to
the press. I congratulate myself. Last week we began
the correction of it : present—a Seid of Delhi, a Poet
of Lucknow, three or four literati of Patna, and Babir
Ali in the chair. Sabat and myself assessors. After
four days' hard labour, five hours each day, we reached
to the end of the second chapter, so when you will have
a gospel I do not know.

When even his scrupulous taste was satisfied
that the work might be sent to the printer, its
publication was delayed by a fire at Serampore.

---

biographies of Hindu saints ; but in pure literature the great mass
of work was translation from Persian, Sanskrit or Arabic rather than
original writing.

[1] Garcin de Tassy, *Préface de L'Histoire de la Littérature Hindoui
et Hindoustani.*

And before the book had come into circulation he had passed from India and the world. But he left it as a legacy of price. His patient consultations with Indian scholars had prepared for it a welcome. It was even set as a text-book in Mohammedan schools in Agra. Martyn himself was too scholarly to hope that his work was final. " I have too little faith in the instruments to believe that the first edition will be excellent," he told David Brown. Yet fifty years later it was written of Martyn's work : " All subsequent translations have, as a matter of course, proceeded upon it as a work of excellent skill and learning and rigid fidelity." [1] So he played his part in introducing the " Great Intruder " whose presence has meant so much of upheaval and stir in the spirit and brain of India.

Hour after hour as the work proceeded Henry Martyn sat in close daily intercourse with Mohammedan scholars, and he learned to know as few men know the Moslem outlook upon life and God. " I read everything I can pick up about the Mohammedans," one of his letters said. But it was in long, eager conversations when dictionaries and reed pens were thrust aside in the interest of the moment, that he gained that astonishing mastery of Moslem ways of thought which won the respect of the doctors of Shiraz.

The conversations, often lasting late into the night, were startling to both parties. Henry Martyn never assumed the superior attitude of the man who cannot be ruffled. It was well seen

[1] Rev. R. C. Mather, LL.D., *Monograph on Hindustani Versions of the Old and New Testaments.*

that he cared with his whole soul for the matters he talked about and the men he talked with. "My tongue is parched," he wrote, "and my hand trembles from the violent onsets I have had this day with moonshee and pundit."

The *Journal* is full of Martyn's notes of conversations. For us they have significance as the first meeting after centuries (Martyn's immediate predecessor as a Christian apologist to Moslem India was a Portuguese Jesuit named Hieronymo Xavier, confessor of Christ at the court of the great Akbar) of two gigantic spiritual forces all unguarded and unaware, coming together with a first rude clash, unsoftened by intercourse and interaction of thought.

On the text "the time cometh, that he that killeth you shall think he doeth God service," he allowed and declared the lawfulness of putting infidels to death, and the certainty of salvation to believers dying in battle with infidels ; and that it was no more strange than for the magistrate to have power to put an offender to death.

He said that prayer was not a duty among the Mahometans, that reading the numaz was merely the praising of God, and that when a servant after doing his master's service well, thought it a favourable opportunity for asking a favour, so the Moslem after doing his duty might ask of God riches or a son, or, if he liked, for patience in affliction. I have never felt so excited as by this dispute. It followed me all night in my dreams.

In the evening had long disputes with moonshee on the enjoyments of heaven, but I felt bitter mortification at not having command of language. However I was enabled to tell the moonshee one thing which rather confused him, namely, that my chief delight even now in the world was the enjoyment of God's presence.

He said with dreadful bitterness and contempt that after the present generation should pass away, a set of fools would perhaps be born, such as the Gospel required.

Mirza said with great earnestness, "Sir, why won't you try to save me?" "Save you?" said I, "I would lay down my life to save your soul: what can I do?" He wished me to go to Phoolwari, the Mussulman college, and there examine the subject with the most learned of their doctors. I told him I had no objection.

So in long intimate talk and in the heat of argument with men who, in spite of themselves, grew to love him and if they sometimes left him in a passion returned again to work with him, Martyn began to learn the religious mind of Islam.

Above all things, [he wrote] *seriousness* in argument with them seems most desirable, for without it they laugh away the clearest proofs. Zeal for making proselytes they are used to and generally attribute to a false motive; but a tender concern manifested for their souls is certainly new to them, and seemingly produces corresponding seriousness in their minds.

But he knew the limitations of argument. "I wish a spirit of enquiry may be excited, but I lay not much stress upon *clear arguments;* the work of God is seldom wrought in this way."

The possibilities of his work in Arabic, the great religious tongue of the Moslem world, fired his imagination. As he began the Arabic New Testament he wrote, "So now, favente Deo, we will begin to preach to Arabia, Syria, Persia, India, Tartary, China, half of Africa, all the south coast of the Mediterranean and Turkey, and one tongue shall suffice for them all."

Brown and Buchanan sent to assist him in this work an extraordinary and tormenting character,

whom they might have chosen expressly for the
discipline of a saint. When Mrs Sherwood first
met him at Henry Martyn's dinner table she poured
out into her diary impressions of " that wild man
of the desert " :

Every feature in the large disk of Sabat's face was
what we should call exaggerated. His eyebrows were
arched, black, and strongly pencilled ; his eyes dark
and round, and from time to time flashing with un-
subdued emotion, and ready to kindle to flame on the
most trifling occasion. His nose was high, his mouth
wide, his teeth large, and looked white in contrast with
his bronzed complexion and fierce black mustachios.
He was a large and powerful man, and generally wore a
skull-cap of rich shawling, or embroidered silk, with
circular flaps of the same hanging over each ear.

She expounded the details of his costume, silk
attire, dagger, ear-rings and golden chain, as though
she could not satisfy her own interest in that striking
figure.

This son of the desert never sat in a chair without
contriving to tuck up his legs under him on the seat,
in attitude very like a tailor on his board. The only
languages which he was able to speak were Persian,
Arabic, and a very little bad Hindustani ; but what
was wanting in the words of this man was more than
made up by the loudness with which he uttered them,
for he had a voice like roaring thunder.

When that mighty voice first resounded through
Martyn's bungalow, Sabat was midway in a wild
career. An Arab of the Arabs, after a life of
wanderings, passions, remorses, protestations, re-
cantations, he was at last sewn up in a sack and
dropped by orders of a Malayan prince to the bottom
of the sea. But his last message, the message
of a lonely prisoner writing in his own blood,

declared that he died in the Christian faith. It had taken the death of one saint and the life of another to win him.

He was first driven to Christianity by remorse. The friend of his youth, with whom he had made the pilgrimage to Mecca, came across an Arabic Bible in Cabul of all unlikely places, and far from any human teacher became a disciple of Christ. The change in him could not be hid, and he had to fly for his life. He came to Bokhara. Sabat his friend was in the city.

"I had no pity," said Sabat afterwards. "I delivered him up to Morad Shah the king." In the market-place they cut off one of the Christian's hands, Sabat the informer standing by in the crowd that watched. Then they pressed him to recant.

He made no answer [Sabat said afterwards], but looked up steadfastly towards heaven, like Stephen, the first martyr, his eyes streaming with tears. He looked at me, but it was with the countenance of forgiveness. His other hand was then cut off. But he never changed, and when he bowed his head to receive the blow of death all Bokhara seemed to say, "What new thing is this?"

Sabat could not ease himself of his friend's last look. In South India he read for himself the book that had made a martyr. Then he all but bullied the chaplain, Dr Kerr, until he gave him baptism. But in sooth, when Martyn first knew him Sabat had gone but a very little way along the Christian path. Martyn welcomed him with eagerness, but soon found that with his coming domestic peace was gone.

Sabat lives and eats with me and goes to his bungalow

at night, so that I hope he has no care on his mind.
On Sunday morning he went to church with me. While
I was in the vestry, a bearer took away his chair from
him, saying it was another gentleman's. The Arab
took fire and left the church, and when I sent the clerk
after him he would not return.

That was the precursor of many storms. At any
moment Martyn looking up from his books would
find flashing black eyes and a livid countenance
glaring at him, while floods of angry Arabic or
Persian poured forth in a voice of thunder de-
manding the instant dismissal of one of the
servants or a fellow translator for some insult;
or threatening eternal wrath because when he
was late for dinner Martyn and his guests sat
down without him. Naturally Sabat looms large
in Martyn's journal.

Poor Sabat fell into one of his furious passions. I
thought of St James's words, "set on fire of hell." He
thirsted for revenge on one of the servants who had
offended him. He went and fetched his sword and
dagger and with lips trembling with rage vowed he
would kill the man.

Sabat has been tolerably quiet this week, but think
of the keeper of a lunatic and you see me. After he
got home at night he sent a letter complaining of a
high crime and misdemeanour in some servant; I sent
him a soothing letter and the wild beast fell asleep.

He said he would never live under the same roof with
Mirza. And why? Because he knew the servants
would at last say, "This belongs to the Hindoostanee
moonshee, and this to the Arabian moonshee," thus
equalizing him with an Indian, and depriving him of
his Arabian honour.

He is angry with me for not hating Mirza too,
according to the Arabian proverb—that a friend is an
enemy of his friend's enemy.

Somehow Martyn managed to love his tormentor. "He is very dear to me. When I think of the circumstances of his life, and look upon him, I cannot help considering it as one of the most singular and interesting events of my life that I was brought acquainted with him. Indeed, everything in the east has been interesting to me." He sat with Sabat night after night when he was ill, and handled his tantrums with a gentleness and humility that few men could have shown.

If in any of our disputes I get the better of him, he is stung to the quick and does not forget it for days. So I avoid as much as possible all questions gendering strifes. If he sees anything wrong in me, any appearance of pride or love of grandeur, he tells me of it without ceremony, and thus he is a friend indeed. He describes so well the character of a missionary that I am ashamed of my great house and mean to sell it at the first opportunity and take the smallest quarters I can find.

Most charming is Martyn's humorous tolerance of Sabat's intellectual bombast.

He loves as a Christian brother [Martyn wrote], but as a logician, he holds us all in supreme contempt. He assumes all the province of reasoning as his own by right, and decides every question magisterially. He allows Europeans to know a little about Arithmetic and Navigation, but nothing more. Dear man! I smile to observe his pedantry. Never have I seen such an instance of dogmatical pride, since I heard Dr Parr preach his Greek sermon at St Mary's, about the τὸ ὄν. He looks on the missionaries at Serampore as so many degrees below him in intellect that he says he could write so deeply on a text that not one of them would be able to follow him. So I have challenged him in their name, and to-day he has brought me the first half of his essay or sermon on a text: with some ingenuity it is the most idle display of schoolboy pedantic logic you ever saw.

When a young officer told Martyn that some friends had fooled him about a supposed text in the Bible which said that men should become bears, Sabat rushed into the conversation. " Oh, if there is such an expression in the word of God it must be true," he said, " *and we will prove it by logic.*" [1]

But as the translation proceeded Martyn found it impossible ever to convince this logician of a flaw in his own work.

Sabat would often contend for a whole morning [Mrs Sherwood says] about the meaning of an unimportant word ; and Mr Martyn has not unseldom ordered his palanquin and come over to us, to get out of the sound of the voice of the fierce Ishmaelite.

" If all the Indian moonshees in Calcutta should unite," said Martyn, " I fear Sabat would not value their opinion a straw. ' He did not come from Persia to India to learn Persian.' "

In Arabic, Sabat's grammar needed watchfulness, but his style was nervous and idiomatic. In Persian his writing was more than usually inter-larded with Arabic phrases ; and Martyn became convinced that it was faulty in style, and that the final New Testament translation in Persian would not be made outside Persia itself.

Before the second edition of the Arabic what say you, [he wrote to David Brown] to my carrying the first with me to Arabia, having under the other arm the Persian to be examined at Shiraz or Teheran ?

So he planned, his mind moving with an almost gay freedom at this beloved task. He speaks with

---

[1] *Memoir of Daniel Corrie*, p. 130.

firm assurance, always the master and never the slave of meticulous grammatical details. He criticizes the setting out of Arabic grammar: " What Erpenius has comprehended in a couple of pages Mr B. has wire-drawn through a folio." He is equally frank over other men's translations. In Arabic—" The New Testament we have, edited by Erpenius, is indescribably bad ; it is not a translation but a paraphrase, and that always wrong." Greatly daring, he will even pass independent judgment on the English Authorized Version. " It appears to me that the two royal authors have suffered more from the plebeian touch of their interpreters, than even the prophets or any others but Job." Nay, the Martyn of these days is audacious. " The books which you mention I shall expect with impatience. Street's version ; Hammond who is a learned man. Horne is all words. Next to oriental translations, my wish and prayer is, that I may live to give a new English version of the Bible from Job to Malachi. Such are some of my modest desires."

A mind like Martyn's could not be incessantly busy with the details of half a dozen languages, without enquiry as to their relation to one another and the nature of all language.

I suppose [he wrote to Corrie] that of all things in the world language is that which submits itself most obsequiously to our examination, and may therefore be understood better than anything else. For we can summon it before us without any trouble, and make it assume any form we please, and turn it upside down and inside out, and yet I must confess the more I look at it the more I am puzzled. I seem to be gazing with stupid wonder at the legerdemain of a conjuror.

In the story of linguistic speculation he stood at a time of change and boundless expectation. The eighteenth century had wondered whether the gift of speech was given to man ready-made or whether it grew. Herder (*Origin of Language,* 1772) supposed that it grew, since nothing direct from the hand of the Almighty could be so illogical and full of caprice as any human speech. Then empire in the east gave a new direction to men's thoughts of language.

Cœurdoux, a French missionary, had sent to the French *Institut* in 1767 a memoir calling attention to the similarity of many Sanskrit words, and some of its flexions, with Latin. And English Sanskrit scholars, Sir Charles Wilkins and Sir William Jones, did their part in creating a tendency to make Sanskrit the mother of tongues. And so with the new century scholars were busy with the genealogy of languages. Men felt that they were on the verge of some great and unifying discovery. Martyn like the rest was on tiptoe with expectation. He rejected Sanskrit speculations and looked on Hebrew, which for Sir William Jones was "rather an object of veneration than delight," as the possible norm and fountain of language.

I have been seized with a philological mania again [he wrote to a friend], and after passing some hours in sleepless cogitation, was obliged to get up to examine all the Greek prepositions, and see if I could not derive them all from the Hebrew.

I am glad you take a liking to Hebrew. It transports me at present. My speculations occupy me night and day. . . . I carry these thoughts to bed with me, and there am I all night long in my dreams tracing etymologies, and measuring the power of some Hebrew letter.

I sit hours alone, contemplating this mysterious language. I sometimes say in my vain heart, I will either make a deep cut in the mine of philology or I will do nothing.

How do you go on in Hebrew? Though my duty calls me to other languages, I am perpetually speculating on that, and the nature of language in general. It goes against the grain with me now to read a little Arabic or Greek, as much as it once did to cram a proposition I did not understand. How or by what magic is it, that we convey our thoughts to one another with such ease and accuracy? Lately I was called on duty to a distant station, the way to which was chiefly on the river. There, far removed from noise, and everything European, I glided along, speculating with as much subtilty as the visionary γυμνοσοφοι who pursue their reveries on the banks. These hermits literally forsake the wo ld; they build a little hut close to the margin of the river and there they sit and muse. . . . It is probable that for some time to come, as long as I am engaged in translation, my thoughts will be rather tinged with philology. . . . But on my own mind I perceive that I must keep a tight rein. I beg your prayers that after having begun in the Spirit I may not leave off in the flesh.

Truly love is better than knowledge. Much as I long to know what I seek after, I would rather have the smallest portion of humility and love than the knowledge of an archangel.

CHAPTER XI

CAWNPORE [1]

This, sir, is a climate which tries the mind like a furnace
Deterioration seems inherent in Indian existence.—LETTER *of*
CLAUDIUS BUCHANAN *from Barrackpore*.

There was a hollow, fearful whistling, like human voices, in the
blast; and Mr Martyn said, "It was often in his mind, that the
prince of the power of the air was permitted to inflict, not only
all storms and tempests, but all diseases and sufferings on man
in the flesh."—MRS SHERWOOD's *Autobiography*.

THE burning winds of the spring in Cawnpore were
blowing, and the Sherwood family stationed there
with the 53rd Regiment were existing as best
they might. Every outer door was shut, and
behind grass screens they sat almost in darkness,
under the punkah in the central hall as the most
endurable place. Captain Sherwood had his table
with account books and journal before him. In
a side room was the family's faithful factotum,
Sergeant Clarke, copying manuscripts. In another
side room a silent ayah chewed and chewed as she
kept guard over the white-faced baby on the floor
with her toys—the motherless Sally rescued by
Mrs Sherwood from starvation and now creeping
back to life.

The Sherwoods had no little child of their own

---

[1] Mrs Sherwood is virtually the writer of this chapter. All the
quotations from her are taken from her autobiography, *Life of Mrs
Sherwood, chiefly autobiographical*, 1854.

in the spring of 1809 ; the two babies born to them in India had died like primroses in an oven : but the motherly woman had hopes of another child in her nursery after the rains. Meanwhile the hot days dragged on wearily. Mrs Sherwood lay on the sofa, a table beside her, with pen and ink and any books she could lay hold of. " Somebody lent me Robinson Crusoe, and Mr Sherwood picked up an old copy of Sir Charles Grandison." On a tiny chair by that sofa, with a tiny table beside it, sat the demurest of little quiet girls, the orphan, Annie Childe, another babe whom Mrs Sherwood had rescued as a little drugged starveling from a heartless nurse. Cared for and daintily clad she looked "a delicate little lady," and passed the long hot days placidly enough at Mrs Sherwood's side.

"I had my orphan, my little Annie, always by me. . . . I had given her a good-sized box, painted green, with a lock and key. She was the neatest of all neat little people, somewhat faddy and par- ticular. She was the child of all others to live with an ancient grandmother. Annie's treasures were few, but they were all contained in her green box. She never wanted occupation : she was either dressing her doll or finding pretty verses in her Bible, marking the places with an infinitude of minute pieces of paper."

They were sitting so on the morning of the 30th of May 1809, the silence only broken by the click of the punkah and the moaning of the hot wind outside, when, the lady tells us, " We suddenly heard the quick steps of many bearers. Mr Sher- wood ran out to the leeward of the house, and ex- claimed, ' Mr Martyn ! '

"The next moment I saw him lead in that excellent man, and saw our visitor, a moment afterwards, fall down in a fainting fit. . . . In his fainting state Mr Martyn could not have retired to the sleeping-room which we caused to be prepared immediately for him, because we had no means of cooling any sleeping-room so thoroughly as we could the hall. We therefore had a couch set for him in the hall. There he was laid, and very ill he was for a day or two. The hot winds left us and we had a close suffocating calm. Mr Martyn could not lift his head from the couch."

Martyn had been transferred by the military authorities from Dinapore to Cawnpore in April 1809, at the hottest moment in the year. He left Sabat and his pretty wife Ameena (a couple who spent their time together in noisy quarrels) to come up by water with all the household goods, and he set out by palanquin, saying good-bye to Dinapore with some regret.

Preparation for departure does not disturb and disorder me as it used to do. The little things of this world come more as matters of course. Still I find it necessary to repeat often in the day, "Thou wilt keep him in perfect peace whose mind is staid on Thee." My men seem to be in a more flourishing state than they have yet been. About thirty attend every night. I have had a delightful party this week of six young men who I hope will prove to be true soldiers of Christ.

That three-hundred-mile palanquin journey in the heat was an absurdity. "I transported myself with such rapidity to this place, that I nearly transported myself out of the world," he told David Brown. At first he travelled by night only. But Mrs Sherwood explains that between

Allahabad and Cawnpore there was no halting-place, and Martyn when he fainted in her hall had been travelling for two days and two nights without a pause, slung in a palanquin that could do nothing to keep out winds that burnt like fire from a furnace.

She took care of him, and he had one of his rare glimpses of domestic life.

"When Mr Martyn got a little better he became very cheerful, and seemed quite happy with us all about him. He commonly lay on his couch in the hall during the morning, with many books near to his hand, and amongst these always a Hebrew Bible and a Greek Testament. Soon, very soon, he began to talk to me of what was passing in his mind, calling to me at my table to tell me his thoughts.

"In a very few days he had discerned the sweet qualities of the orphan Annie, and had so encouraged her to come about him that she drew her chair, and her table, and her green box to the vicinity of his couch. She showed him her verses, and consulted him about the adoption of more passages into the number of her favourites. What could have been more beautiful than to see the Senior Wrangler and the almost infant Annie thus conversing together, while the elder seemed to be in no way conscious of any condescension in bringing his mind down to the level of the child's ?

"When Mr Martyn lost the worst symptoms of his illness he used to sing a great deal. He had an uncommonly fine voice and fine ear ; he could sing many fine chants, and a vast variety of hymns and psalms. He would insist upon it that I should sing with him, and he taught me many tunes, all of which were afterwards brought into requisition; and when fatigued himself, he made me sit by his couch and practise these hymns."

And so the good woman mothered him, knowing that she had found a saint, but a little concerned because he did not seem "very distinct in all his religious views" (there is no indistinctness about the views of the writer of the *Fairchild Family*), and because of a certain vague trustfulness over money. He sent off a coolie to draw for him long arrears of salary, involving the payment to the messenger of some hundreds of pounds counted out in silver into cotton bags. "Mr Martyn said in a quiet voice to us, 'The coolie does not come with my money. I was thinking this morning how rich I should be; and now I should not wonder in the least if he has run off and taken my treasure with him.' 'What!' we exclaimed. 'Surely you have not sent a common coolie for your pay?' 'I have,' he replied."

The money arrived; and Martyn was at a loss to understand his friends' concern about it.

But he was now recovering and must get to the work of his new station. His first impressions, outside the Sherwoods' bungalow, were not cheering.

I do not like this place at all. There is no church, not so much as the fly of a tent; what to do I know not, except to address Lord Minto in a private letter.

I feel fixed at the last place where I shall ever live in India, and sometimes look with interest at the road that leads to Cabul and Candahar. . . . I hear of a Mrs A. as one who is religious, and is even suspected of singing Psalms of a Sunday. Such flagrant violations of established rules seem to mark her for one of our fraternity.

His first service in Cawnpore, himself still a tottering convalescent, was held out of doors on the parade on May 14.

Two officers dropped down, and some of the men. They wondered how I could go through the fatigue. When I looked at the other end of the square which they had formed, I gave up all hopes of making myself heard, but it seems they did hear. There are above a hundred men in the hospital. What time shall I find for doing half what ought to be done?

Already he had made friends, as was his way in every place, with a small group of " serious " soldiers. Mrs Sherwood takes up her pen again :

" As soon as Mr Martyn could in any way exert himself, he made acquaintance with some of the pious men of the regiment (the same poor men whom I have mentioned before, who used to meet in ravines, in huts, in woods and in every wild and secret place they could find, to read and pray and sing) ; and he invited them to come to him in our house, Mr Sherwood making no objection. The time first fixed was an evening after parade, and in consequence they all appeared at the appointed hour, each carrying their mora (a low seat), and their books tied up in pocket-handker-chiefs. In this very unmilitary fashion they were all met in a body by some officers. It was with some difficulty that Mr Sherwood could divert the storm of displeasure. . . . These poor good men were received by Mr Martyn in his own apartment ; and a most joyful meeting he had with them. We did not join the party, but we heard them praying and singing and the sound was very sweet. Mr Martyn then promised them that when he had got a house he would set aside a room for them, where they might come every evening."

Martyn bought a house near the Sepoy lines. "Now, Cawnpore is about one of the most dusty places in the world," said Mrs Sherwood, who disapproved his choice, "and the Sepoy lines are the most dusty part of Cawnpore." His compound was not near enough to his friends, but it had its advantages, for its "funereal avenue" of palm-trees and aloes that rattled in the hot wind, led not to one bungalow but two. This was admirable. Sabat and the goods arrived, and the Arab and his lady were bestowed in the lesser bungalow, while Martyn inhabited the larger, or such part of it as was not filled with "pious soldiers" reading the Bible, scribes copying translations amidst piles of manuscripts and dictionaries, or a medley of guests who gathered from no one knows where. "A vast number and variety of huts and sheds formed one boundary of the compound; these were concealed by the shrubs. But who would venture to give any account of the heterogeneous population which occupied these buildings? For besides the usual complement of servants found in and about the houses of persons of a certain rank in India, we must add to Mr Martyn's household a multitude of pundits, moonshis, schoolmasters and poor nominal Christians, who hung about him because there was no other to give them a handful of rice for their daily maintenance; and most strange was the murmur which proceeded at times from this ill-assorted and discordant multitude." Such was Mrs Sherwood's impression of the *ménage*.

Sabat was as pleased as a child with his new mansion, and work went on apace.

He is gentle and almost as diligent as I could wish [said Martyn]. Everything seems to please him. His bungalow joins mine, and is very neat ; so from morning to night we work together, and the work goes forward. The first two or three days he translated into Arabic and I was his scribe ; but this being too fatiguing to me, we have been since that at the Persian.

The spurt did not last long.

Sabat does not work half hard enough for me. I feel grieved and ashamed that we produce so little, but the fault is not mine. I would never willingly be employed about anything else, but Sabat has no ardour. The smallest difficulty discourages him, the slightest headache is an excuse for shutting up his books, and doing nothing for days.

Sabat creeps on, and smokes his hookah with great complacency if he gets through a chapter a day. I grieve at this hireling spirit, but for peace sake I have long ceased to say anything.

At sunset the translation was dropped, and the frail linguist, whose ardour had exhausted the energies of his various assistants, went out for exercise. Two evenings in the week he spent with his soldiers. On the others he was apt to gravitate towards that friendly household of the Sherwoods. For the soaring linguist was very human. Mrs Sherwood took her airing in an open palanquin, wearing "a lace cap with Europe ribbons," while Captain Sherwood rode, and Martyn would often arrive at their bungalow before his hosts returned. "Two or three times a week he used to come on horseback, with the sais running by his side. He sat his horse as if he were not

quite aware that he was on horseback, and he
generally wore his coat as if it were falling from
his shoulders. When he dismounted, his favourite
place was in the veranda with a book, till we came
in from our airing. And when we returned many
a sweet and long discourse we had whilst waiting
for our dinner. Mr Martyn often looked up to the
starry heavens, and spoke of those glorious worlds
of which we know so little now, but of which we
hope to know so much hereafter. He used often
to show me the pole-star just above the line of the
horizon ; and I have seen the moon when almost
new looking like a ball of ebony in a silver cup."

In August 1809 a little daughter was born to
the Sherwoods, whom they determined to name
after their baby Lucy who had died. When Martyn
came for the christening in the cool of the evening,
the family had not yet returned from the sunset
airing. He told the servants to set in readiness a
table and water in a cool corner of the long veranda,
not knowing that he had chosen for the christening
the very spot where the first little daughter had
been laid dying on a mattress to catch what air
there was.

"Never can I forget the solemn manner with
which Mr Martyn went through the service, or
the beautiful and earnest blessing which he im-
plored for my baby, when he took her in his arms
after the service was concluded. I still fancy that
I see that child of God as he looked down tenderly
on the gentle babe, and then looked upwards."

"This babe in infancy had so peculiar a gentleness of aspect that Mr Martyn called her Serena."
Her parents decided to go down to Calcutta in

October and take the advice of the best doctor in India as to whether they could rear her in Cawnpore. They broke up their household in the full expectation that the mother would be sent home to save her baby's life, and two English ladies, one of them Corrie's sister who had arrived to join her brother, took from Mrs Sherwood the charge of the small orphans she had rescued.

The Sherwoods' last week was spent in Martyn's house. They slept in their house-boats and went to him for breakfast. "In the mornings we all used to set out together, children and servants, to go up from the river to the house, whilst the dew lay yet upon the grass; for it was the beginning of the cold season, and the many aromatic flowers of that southern climate shed their perfume in the air."

The children and ayahs went to rooms set apart for them, and Captain and Mrs Sherwood went into the hall, where Martyn nearly always had some guest for breakfast. "We often sat long over breakfast." Then Martyn turned to his translation, and the Sherwoods went about their business.

"Mr Martyn's house was peaceful, holy and cheerful."

At the sunset airing with the day's work done Martyn enjoyed his friends again, and on their last Sunday he arranged a little chapel with his careful nicety of touch in one of the long verandas, where he gave the Communion to the Sherwoods and to sixteen of his "pious soldiers."

When he had seen them down to their boats for the last time, "blessing our little children," he returned to Cawnpore a lonely man. It is probable that the army society of the place was terrified of Martyn. Otherwise it is hard to explain the gaucherie of their manners to the padre.

It is extraordinary how much I am left to myself here. In the midst of multitudes I am a solitary. . . . The pride of my heart has discovered itself very strongly since I entered this new circle. They sometimes take no more notice of me than a dog, at other times vouchsafe a dignified condescension, so that were it not to become all things to all men in order to save some, I should never trouble them with my company. But how then should I be like Christ? I would rather pass my time with children if I had the choice.

In his loneliness his thoughts would not be kept from Lydia. " I love so true that though it is now the fifth year since I parted from the object of my affections, she is as dear to me as ever," he wrote to Cousin Tom Hitchins in that month when the Sherwoods left. Next month (November 1809) Mr Simeon's letter brought him news that his sister Sally was dying of consumption. He could not hope that a letter would reach her. He began one impulsively ; then turned and wrote instead to her husband : " God make us both from this time live more as pilgrims and strangers upon the earth."

His home letters now let slip the fact that this man with his gigantic plans knew well enough, when he gave it a thought, that the disease which had killed all his near relatives was working in him also. The dusty lines in Cawnpore were trying to him, and he began to confess that every sermon he preached left him in pain. " There is some-

thing in the air at the close of the rains so unfavourable that public speaking at that time is a
violent strain upon the whole body. . . I am sorry to
say that my strength for public speaking is almost
gone. My ministrations among the Europeans at
this station have injured my lungs," he told David
Brown.

They were difficult ministrations even for a
strong man. Soldiers fainted at the out-of-door
parades, and ladies chattered in the General's
drawing-room where he went on for a second
service. He decided to ask for the use of the
billiard-room " which is better than the ball-room,"
but they gave him the riding-school instead. " The
effluvium was such as would please only the knights
of the turf." When the rains came, out-of-door
parades had to be scratched. " The General has
not yet forwarded to Government the proposal for
a church," Martyn wrote after long delay. But
he at length prevailed on the authorities to adapt
an ordinary bungalow near his own for church
services. He watched eagerly over the alterations,
but they went slowly. In December 1809, when
every service was leaving him exhausted, Sabat
challenged him to add to his labours another sermon,
to the strangest congregation that ever gathered
to listen to a saint. Beggars of all sorts found
their way to Martyn's house, among them crowds
of religious mendicants. To save time he gave
out that his alms would be given only once a week.
The news went round the beggar world, and every
Sunday his gates were thrown open to admit a
motley crowd, to whom he gave small coins or
rice.

P

Sabat said to me yesterday, " Your beggars are come, why do not you preach to them ? it is your duty." I made excuses. But the true cause is shame. I am afraid of exposing myself to the contempt of Sabat, my servants, and the mob, by attempting to speak in a language which I do not speak well. This therefore I desire to keep ever before my mind, that I must get to the Kingdom through great contempt.

Next Sunday :

In the afternoon the beggars came, to the number of above four hundred, and by the help of God, I determined to preach to them though I felt as if I were leading to execution.

There was an open space in his garden, green after the rain, with a raised platform of lime at its centre. Here the beggars were seated, and Martyn climbed on to the platform and told them " that he gave with pleasure what alms he could afford, but wished to give them something better— the knowledge of God."

The Sherwoods, encouraged by doctors to remain in India, returned to Cawnpore that December. When Henry Martyn rode to welcome his friends, " he looked, we thought, very ill, and complained of what he called a fire burning in his breast."

But he was full of his new venture with the beggars, though he " looked forward to the next attempt with some dread." Mrs Sherwood went to see what he was doing. She was amazed.

" No dreams," she said, " or visions excited in the delirium of a raging fever could surpass these realities. They were young and old, male and female, tall and short, athletic and feeble, bloated and wizened ; some clothed in abominable rags, some nearly without clothes; some plastered with mud and cow-dung; others with matted, uncombed locks streaming down to their heels; others with heads bald or scabby; every countenance being hard and fixed, as it were, by the continual indulgence of bad passions; the features having become exaggerated, and the lips blackened with tobacco or blood-red with the juice of the henna. . . . One little man used to come in a small cart drawn by a bullock. The body and limbs in general of this poor creature were so shrivelled as to give him, with his black skin and large head, the appearance of a gigantic frog. Another had his arm fixed above his head, the nail of the thumb piercing through the palm of the hand. Another, and a very large man, had all his ribs and the bones of his face externally traced with white chalk, which, striking the eye in relief above the dark skin, made him appear as he approached like a moving skeleton. . . . Such was the view of human nature presented every Sunday evening in Mr Martyn's compound."

Mrs Sherwood stood behind Martyn on the raised platform that evening and on many following Sundays.

"We had to make our way through a dense crowd, with a temperature often rising above 92°, whilst the sun poured its burning rays upon us through a lurid haze of dust. So many monstrous and diseased limbs, and hideous faces, were displayed before us and pushed forward for our inspection, that I have often made my way to the *chabootra* with my eyes shut, whilst Mr Sherwood led me. I still imagine that I hear the calm, distinct, and musical tones of Henry Martyn as he stood raised above the people."

His preaching was as simple as he could make it.

I shuffled and stammered and indeed am persuaded that there were many sentences the poor things did not understand at all. I mentioned Gunga (Ganges), " a good river," but there were others as good. God loves Hindoos, but does He not love others also ? He gave them a good river, but to others as good. All are alike before God. This was received with applause. On the work of the fourth day, " Sun and moon are lamps. Shall I worship a candle in my hand ? As a candle in the house so is the sun in the sky." Applause from the Mohammedans. There were also hisses, but whether these betokened displeasure against me or the worship of the sun, I do not know. I then charged them to worship Gunga and sun and moon no more, but the honour they used to give to them, henceforward to give to God their Maker.

They were no dispassionate audience. Often as he preached bursts of anger would arise, with " shouts and curses and deep and lengthened groans, hissings and gestures till Mr Martyn was compelled to silence. But when the storm passed away again might he be heard going on where he had left off, in the same calm, steadfast tone, as if he were incapable of irritation from the interruption. Mr Martyn himself assisted in giving each person his pice (copper) after the address was concluded ; and when he withdrew to his bungalow I have seen him drop almost fainting on a sofa, for he had, as he often said, a slow inflammation burning in his chest, and one which he knew must eventually terminate his existence."

All that spring they watched him tear himself to pieces ; cheerful enough when he came round

after a day of translation with the sense of something done, and picked up the baby Lucy for a
game before she went to bed ; but plainly enough
a sick man every Sunday when the four services
left him half-fainting with pain and exhaustion.

Accounts of Sally's death reached him in that
spring of 1810, and with them an unexpected joy.
Lydia told herself that he had now no sister of his
own to correspond with and wrote offering to take
a sister's place if he would accept a correspondence
on that basis. He was overjoyed. "My long,
long-lost Lydia has consented to write to me again,"
he told David Brown.

To her he was explicit about his health.

Study never makes me ill—scarcely ever fatigues
me—but my lungs ! death is seated there ; it is speaking
that kills me. Nature intended me for chamber-counsel,
not for a pleader at the bar. But the call of Jesus
Christ bids me cry aloud, and spare not.
You know how apt we are to overstep the bounds
of prudence, when there is no kind monitor at hand to
warn us of the consequence.

When the hot winds blew again in April he had
to confess to David Brown and Corrie that taking
a service always left him with pain in his chest
and hardly able to speak above a whisper. The
references to his health only occurred casually
in letters crowded with details about the translations.

Old Mirza gives me more satisfaction than anyone
in Cawnpore. He seems to take great pleasure in seeing
an intricate sentence in the Epistles unravelled.
I should be more contented to depart if I had finished
the translation of the Epistles.

Or even the translation is forgotten while the scholar moves in another world.

He seems to move in a world by himself [he wrote of St Paul], and sometimes to utter the unspeakable words such as my understanding discerneth not ; and when I turn to commentators, I find that I have passed out of the spiritual to the material world, and have got among men like myself.

But Corrie knew his friend and knew that the health question was serious. " It perhaps would be of importance," he wrote to David Brown, " to get Martyn to resign the service and give himself to the translating and printing of the Scriptures. It is clear that his present labours will bring an early period to his life : I scarce know how to write it, but so it is."

Corrie took boat for Cawnpore to see for himself what could be done. He found Martyn every evening, after ever so little exertion in speaking, reduced to loss of voice, pain in his chest, and such restless fatigue as kept him awake, or troubled his sleep with confused and distressing dreams (" was walking with Lydia, both much affected, and speaking on the things dearest to us both. I awoke, and behold it was a dream ") ; yet buoyed up with hope and plans for his work. " My church is nearly ready for the organ and the bell. . . . My work at present is evidently to translate ; here-after I may itinerate."

" This morning Martyn said he thought a month's silence would entirely restore him." Corrie did what he could. With the General's consent he moved himself and his good sister to Cawnpore to nurse Martyn and take his services for him.

July 31, 1810. On my first arrival [Corrie writes] he recruited greatly for a fortnight, but is now, to say the least, at a stand. He has agreed to go on the river to try the effect of change and solitude. He objects to going to sea at present. . . . The truth is he expects the New Testament will soon be done in Arabic. Your applications for Arabic have set him to work anew with an ardour that nothing but death can repress.

For a few months of bliss Martyn became, far more than he was aware, the central figure of a sort of double household. Corrie, that understanding person, was with him, taking services and setting him free for the beloved translation. Miss Corrie was with the Sherwoods, and in the evening there were the ladies to take for an airing. Of those evenings Mrs Sherwood writes: " I often went out with Mr Martyn in his gig, during that month, when he used to call either for me or Miss Corrie, and whoever went with him went at the peril of their lives. He never looked where he was driving, but went dashing through thick and thin, being always occupied in reading Hindoostanee by word of mouth, or discussing some text of Scripture. I certainly never expected to have survived a lesson he gave me in his gig, in the midst of the plain at Cawnpore, on the pronunciation of one of the Persian letters."

The two households had so many meals together that they found with amusement that the servants were making common cause, and the same cheese appeared on the table at either house. There were hymn-singings in the bungalow, and evening services for which they went together, " not omitting the children," into the unfinished church near Martyn's house.

"We are inexpressibly happy together," said Corrie, and for a time they thought that Martyn was rallying. He himself, engrossed with the great work and delighted with his friends, was generally far too preoccupied to realize that he was ill. When a bout of pain and faintness gave him pause, and he stopped to realize that the family disease had clutched him, he was probably less concerned about it than any of the circle that watched him anxiously. "He spoke of being in a consumption in the tone in which most people would speak of a legacy," said Corrie.

As he flagged more and more they decided to take him on the river. They hired a pinnace in which to go together. Mrs Sherwood describes the mornings in the cabin:

"Mr Martyn sent a quantity of books, and used to take possession of the sofa, with all his books about him. He was often studying Hebrew, and had huge lexicons lying by him. Little Lucy used always to make her way to Mr Martyn when he was by any means approachable. On one occasion I remember seeing the little one, with her grave yet placid countenance, her silken hair and shoeless feet, step out of the inner room of the pinnace with a little mora, which she set by Mr Martyn's couch, then mounting on it, she got upon the sofa which was low, and next seated herself on his huge lexicon. He would not suffer her to be disturbed, though he required his book every instant."

Still he flagged, and they told him he must go to sea. He would not believe them at first; but as the Arabic translation drew to a close and criticisms reached him of Sabat's style, he turned seawards eagerly. If they wanted him to go to sea, why not sail to Arabia and make before he died the perfect version of the Arabic New Testament? On August 22, 1810, he wrote to David Brown :

DEAREST SIR,—

Shall I come down, or shall I not? I have an aversion to Calcutta, with all the talking and preaching to which I shall be tempted there; yet you insist upon it, and sooner or later I must pass through you to the sea, or I shall be buried here. . . . I want silence and diversion, a little dog to play with; or what would be best of all, a dear little child. . . . Perhaps you could learn when the ships usually sail for Mocha. I have set my heart upon going there; I could be there and back in six months. H. MARTYN.

Two days later another letter followed :

Henceforward I have done with India. Arabia shall hide me till I come forth with an approved New Testament in Arabic. I do not ask your advice because I have made up my mind.

. . . So now, dear Sir, take measures for transmitting me with the least possible delay, detain me not, for the King's business requires haste. My health in general is good, but the lungs are not strong. One loud dispute brings on pain.—Yours ever affectionately,

HENRY MARTYN.

The General at Cawnpore granted unlimited leave of absence to one whom he probably looked on as a dying man.

Martyn's last day with his friends was a Sunday. They could not take their eyes off him, believing that they should see his face no more. There was a triumphant glow about him, for it was a great day.

The new bell was rung for the first time to call the people to the opening service in the church that he had made. "There was a considerable congregation," and Sergeant Clarke in his red coat was parish clerk, and Corrie read the prayers. Martyn stood up to preach his first and last sermon in the new church.

"A bright glow prevailed, a brilliant light shone from his eyes. He was filled with hope and joy. Most eloquent, earnest and affectionate was his address."

But when they went to his bungalow after service he sank fainting on a sofa in the hall. There remained one more effort in Cawnpore, the last act of his ministry there, the sermon to the beggars.

"When the sun began to descend we went over to Mr Martyn's bungalow to hear his last address to the *fakeers*. It was one of those sickly, hazy, burning evenings. Mr Martyn nearly fainted again after this effort, and when he got to his house, with his friends about him, he told us that he was afraid he had not been the means of doing the smallest good to any one of the strange people whom he had thus so often addressed."

But Martyn was wrong.

As he preached one of his first sermons to the beggars a group of young men, taking the air in a kiosk on the garden wall, sipping sherbet and smoking, had been struck by the strange proceedings in the English house next door. Down they came from the wall to see what Martyn was about. They pushed through the crowd and stood before him in a row, their arms folded, their turbans

slightly tilted on one side and their lips drawn
up in a superb sneer. But one of them heard
enough to rouse his keenest curiosity. He was a
young Moslem, a sheikh of Delhi, a professor of
Persian and Arabic, but with the heart of a learner.

That gospel preached to the poor seemed to
him something new, and he determined to know
more of Martyn's faith. He did not venture direct
to the Christian preacher, but made interest with
Sabat to be employed as copier of the Persian
gospel. He even sought out Martyn's school-
children and asked them to repeat their lessons.
Then he found a great opportunity when they
gave him charge of a complete copy of the Persian
New Testament on its way to the bookbinder.
He held back the book till he had read it all, and
with the reading came the great decision.

On that last Sunday he was still unknown to
Martyn, but Martyn's plans were known to him,
and Sheikh Salih was making ready to follow the
preacher to Calcutta and ask him there for baptism.[1]

On Monday morning, October 1, 1810, Martyn
must leave Cawnpore. "We were all low, very,
very low," says Mrs Sherwood. Corrie, who had
struggled to save his friend, was white with the
strain of parting. He had found Martyn about
to make a bonfire of all his memoranda, but persuaded him to let him keep them under seal against
his return, and so saved for the Church that journal
by which she knows the mind of Henry Martyn.
"His life is beyond all price to us," Corrie wrote.

[1] He was baptized on Whit Sunday 1811 under the name of Abd
el Masih, and became eventually a clergyman and a notable Christian
leader.

Only Martyn, in a strange serenity, hardly realized their anxiety. He thought that Corrie must have worked too hard, and wrote to him from his boat, " Your pale face as it appeared on Monday morning is still before my eyes, and will not let me be easy till you tell me you are strong and prudent."

So he left them. " I am advised," he told Lydia, " to recruit my strength by rest. So I am come forth with my face towards Calcutta, with an ulterior view to the sea."

CHAPTER XII

TO SHIRAZ

My home
The shimmery-bounded glare,
The gazing fire-hung dome
Of scorching air.

For friend
The dazzling breathing dream,
The strength at last to find
Of Glory Supreme.

From anonymous poem on Saint
John Baptist in ΧΑΡΙΤΕΣΣΙ

Read Ephesians i. It is a chapter I keep in mind every day in prayer. We cannot believe too much or hope too much.

HENRY MARTYN *to* LYDIA GRENFELL
from Muscat, Arabia

MARTYN'S budgerow, paddled from the stern, bore him down stream to the house that was above all others his Indian home.

"Entered the Hooghly," says his journal for November 25, 1810, "with something of those sensations with which I should come in sight of the white cliffs of England." At Aldeen he found the Brown children waiting to convoy him with shouts to the house, and next morning in the city another long-expected meeting took place with friends arrived from England. Thomas Thomason, Simeon's senior curate, that good, serene and diligent person, had been inspired by Martyn's example to break up his home by the riverside at Shelford and to set out in middle life with his calm, methodical wife and their small children, to give the rest of his years to the service of India. Martyn, little if at all conscious how far he had himself inspired both Corrie and Thomason to follow him, hailed the news of his coming with exultation.

Thomason was indeed a notable recruit. His friends had long smiled at his habit in all spare moments of pulling out of his pocket a portion of the Bible. In his own methodical way he had had his Hebrew Old Testament re-bound into sections small enough for pocket use and kept one always at hand. He now brought these years of patient study to the help of the translators in India. On his way out the good scholar was ship-wrecked ; he rescued each child in a sheet and their mother in a counterpane, but every book that he possessed was lost. Martyn found the family living in the heart of Calcutta, patiently collecting house-hold goods once more, and Thomason catechizing the little English children of the settlement with his own babes—" Fair English children, all of them elegantly dressed, standing round the desk and answering the good man's questions."

The Thomasons were shocked at the change in Martyn. " Dear, dear Martyn arrived," wrote the wife, " and we had the unspeakable delight of seeing his face. He is much altered, is thin and sallow, but he has the same loving heart." He sat on the sofa and picked up the old intercourse with them, even to the point when the steady Thomason felt it necessary to prick the bubble of Martyn's airy speculations. "That obstinate lover of antiquity," Martyn wrote of him in a letter, "whose potent touch has dissolved so many of my fabrics heretofore, that I do not like to submit anything to him which is not proof."

After that first long talk Thomason sat down to write to Simeon his impression of the friend so much his junior, who had always been to him both an enigma and an inspiration.

He is on his way to Arabia, where he is going in pursuit of health and knowledge. You know his genius, and what gigantic strides he takes in everything. He has some great plan in his mind of which I am no competent judge; but as far as I do understand it, the object is far too grand for one short life, and much beyond his feeble and exhausted frame. Feeble it is indeed! how fallen and changed! But let us hope that the sea-air may revive him. . . . In all other respects he is exactly the same as he was; he shines in all the dignity of love; and seems to carry about him such a heavenly majesty, as impresses the mind beyond description. But if he talks much, though in a low voice, he sinks, and you are reminded of his being "dust and ashes."

The Martyn of these days seems to have cast a spell over all his friends. They watched him with a kind of awe, as men who dared not interfere. "Can I then bring myself to cut the string and let you go?" wrote David Brown when the Arabian plan was first proposed. "I confess I could not, if your bodily frame were strong, and promised to last for half a century. But as you burn with the intenseness and rapid blaze of heated phosphorus, why should we not make the most of you? Your flame may last as long, and perhaps longer, in Arabia, than in India."

In fulfilment of a five-years'-old promise to

Simeon, Martyn had his portrait painted in Calcutta.[1] It was "thought a striking likeness," but on seeing it David Brown remarked, "That is not the Martyn who arrived in India, it is Martyn the recluse." Martyn acknowledged the truth of the observation. A man could not live alone with Sabat, battling with illness, stripped of every earthly hope save the perfecting of his Gospel, and come out from that seclusion unmarked.

He blamed himself. "It sometimes calls itself deadness to the world," he said, "but I much fear that it is deadness of heart. I am exempt from worldly cares myself and therefore do not feel for others."

The portrait was sent home to the India House, and Charles Simeon went up to London to claim it. His letters from India had left him unprepared for the change in Martyn's face.

It was opened. . . . I could not bear to look upon it, but turned away and went to a distance, covering my face, and in spite of every effort to the contrary, crying aloud with anguish. . . . In seeing how much he is worn I am constrained to call to my relief the thought in *Whose* service he has worn himself so much.[2]

On consultation with the learned in Calcutta Martyn heard little but praise of his own Hindustani New Testament, but Sabat's work, it seemed, and especially his Persian, stood yet in need of polishing. So Martyn determined to take both Persian and Arabic with him, and to go first to Persia. Afterwards he would travel—who knows where? to Damascus perhaps, he said, for there

[1] Now in the University Library, Cambridge.
[2] Carus, *Life of Charles Simeon*, p. 358.

he might enquire as to ancient Arabic versions; or perhaps to Baghdad or the heart of Arabia itself. But Persia must come first.

"All his imaginations of Persia," Mrs Sherwood tells us, "were taken from the beautiful descriptions given by the poets. He often spoke of that land as of a land of roses and nightingales, of fresh flowing streams, of sparkling fountains and of breezes laden with perfumes." A lover of Persian poetry, and especially of Sadi, Martyn had certainly been since Cambridge days; but he was no mere visionary, for he had been also a greedy reader of modern travels, such as Scott Waring's account of his visit to Shiraz, written in 1807.[1] Lord Minto, the statesman who had himself sent Sir John Malcolm[2] to Persia, listened to Martyn's statement of the aims of his journey, and gave him leave to proceed; the Armenians of Calcutta wrote a commendation of him to their brethren in Persia, and "a list of places in Mesopotamia, etc., where there were Christians, and the number of them"; and Martyn was ready to set out.

But to find a ship was not easy. He was told that he had best go to Bombay, and from Bombay to Bosra; but having at length found a coasting trader bound for Bombay, he failed to get a passage. He wrote to Corrie:

The captain of the ship after many excuses has at last refused to take me; on the ground that I might try to convert the Arab sailors, and so cause a mutiny in the ship. So I am half out of heart, and more than half disposed to go to the rightabout, and come back

[1] *A Tour to Sheeraz by the Route of Kazroon and Feerozabad*, by Edward Scott Waring, Esq., of the Bengal Civil Establishment.

[2] See page 247.

Q

to Cawnpore, for there is no ship to be heard of going to Bombay.

He waited on, preaching every Sunday sermons that left him in pain, and kept awake at night by a hacking cough. They gave him the task of preaching for the Bible Society on the first day of 1811. "Mr Brown, foreseeing that I should have to stay over New Year's Day, ordered me to preach for the British and Foreign Bible Society. In consequence I prepared an unwieldy sermon, which has just been delivered. None of the great were present."

The sermon is a revelation of the extent to which Martyn had before him in his prayers and plans the needs of all India, "from Meerut to Cape Comorin," and not India only. "Nay," said that sick man to the godly in Calcutta, "Asia must be our care."

Next week he left them and took ship to carry out his own words, having obtained a passage on the boat that was taking Mountstuart Elphinstone to Bombay as the new British Resident at Poona.

Martyn slipped away from his Calcutta friends. "He suddenly vanished" out of their sight they said. To Lydia he explained that "leaving Calcutta was so much like leaving England that I went on board my boat without giving them notice."

Without taking leave of my too dear friends in Calcutta, I went on board Mr Elphinstone's pinnace, and began to drop down the river.

He reached the ship at the mouth of the Hooghly in two days. She was an Arab coaster, the property of a merchant of Muscat, who ran her with a country-bred captain, Mr Kinsay from Madras, an Arab crew and an Abyssinian slave as overseer. No sooner was Martyn aboard the *Ahmoody* than he " began to try his strength " in Arabic conversation with those sailors. But sickness and fatigue overtook him.

The sea I loath [he wrote to Corrie], I was scarcely well any part of the voyage, and consequently did little but sit the live-long day upon the poop, looking at the flying fish, and surveying the wide waste of waters blue.

" The most agreeable circumstance " in this voyage of six weeks was, he said, the companionship in " the great cabin " of Mountstuart Elphinstone, of whose " agreeable manners and classical acquirements " he wrote enthusiastically. Throughout life Elphinstone shared Martyn's love of the classics. He had gained it as a small boy in the Edinburgh High School, and in spite of the premature breaking off of that schooling, his chief delight wherever he wandered in the East was to turn to the Greek and Latin poets. At Fort William College he added a love for Eastern literature. It was long since Martyn had met with so omnivorous a reader, and he vastly relished the society of one only a few years older than himself who had already seen responsible service in the Moslem border-lands beyond the fringe of British India. They sat long hours on the poop, or went on shore together to walk in the cinnamon gardens of Ceylon (Martyn sent Lydia a piece of fragrant bark) canvassing many questions about books and men.

One of my fellow passengers [he told Lydia] is Mr Elphinstone, who was lately ambassador at the court of the King of Cabul, and is now going to be resident at Poona, the capital of the Mahratta empire. So the group is rather interesting.

When sitting on the poop Mr Elphinstone kindly entertained me with information about India, the politics of which he has had such opportunities of making himself acquainted with.

Mountstuart Elphinstone in his turn enjoyed that voyage, and wrote to a friend :

We have in Mr Martyn an excellent scholar, and one of the mildest, cheerfullest, and pleasantest men I ever saw. He is extremely religious and disputes about the faith with the Nakhoda (the Abyssinian slave), but talks on all subjects, sacred and profane, and makes others laugh as heartily as he could do if he were an infidel. We have people who speak twenty-five languages (not apiece) on the ship.[1]

Or again :

A far better companion than I reckoned on, though my expectations were high . . . a man of good sense and taste, and simple in his manners and character and cheerful in his conversation.

The coaster crawled round Cape Comorin close to the shore, and Martyn, looking up from his Arabic, almost believed himself in Cornwall. He wrote to Lydia describing "the great promontory of India."

At a distance the green waves seemed to wash the foot of the mountain, but on a nearer approach little churches were to be seen, apparently on the beach, with a row of little huts on each side. Was it these maritime situations that recalled to my mind Perran church and town in the way to Gurlyn ; or made my thoughts wander on the beach to the east of Lamorran ? You do not tell me whether you ever walk there, and imagine

[1] See T. E. Colebrooke, *Life of Mountstuart Elphinstone*, I. p. 231.

the billows that break at your feet to have made their way from India.

They called at Goa where the Portuguese held sway, Martyn on the alert for any information about the extent of the Christian faith in those parts. But, he told David Brown,

this place most miserably disappointed me. I did not care about churches or convents, but I did expect to find men, Bishops and Archbishops, learned friars and scowling inquisitors. Certain it is that though we have been shown all the finery of the churches, not a person have we seen that was able to give us the smallest particle of information.

The Inquisition is still existing at Goa. We were not admitted as far as Dr Buchanan was to the Hall of Examination. . . . The priest in waiting acknowledged that they had some prisoners within the walls. . . . We were told that when the officers of the Inquisition touch an individual and beckon him away, he dare not resist.

Here Martyn stood at the tomb of St Francis Xavier whose life had inspired him during his first few weeks in India. It was characteristic of him, as it would have been of that other apostolic man by whose grave he stood, that his attention was drawn away from the tomb with its " paintings and figures of bronze done in Italy " when the friar who guided him let fall a chance word about "the grace of God in the heart." Instantly Martyn forgot his sight-seeing and plunged into conversation with his brother in the faith.

So they drew near to Bombay on Martyn's thirtieth birthday, and his journal shows him turning, as was his wont, from the conversation of the great cabin to a higher communing.

I would that all should adore, but especially that I myself should lie prostrate. As for self, contemptible self, I feel myself saying, let it be forgotten for ever, henceforth let Christ live, let Christ reign, let Him be glorified for ever.

In Bombay he found himself a guest at Government House, and Elphinstone introduced him to good company. For there were in Bombay two men of parts, who would have made their mark in any group of intellectuals.

The older man of the two, Sir James Mackintosh, had been in his young days a friend of revolution and author of *Vindiciæ Gallicæ*. But the Mackintosh of middle life, now looked on as "the lost leader" by the men of drastic political reform, had repudiated his early views in no uncertain tones. "I abhor, abjure and for ever renounce the French Revolution, with its sanguinary history, its abominable principles and for ever execrable leaders," he wrote, and settled down to practise at the Bar. Martyn found him as Recorder of Bombay, consoling himself for exile with a library of the schoolmen and the latest works of foreign philosophy. When he was stirred by congenial society no one could resist his good talk, in which a delicious impertinence just served to remind men of the daring of his early views.

Elphinstone introduced me to a young clergyman [Mackintosh noted in his journal] called Martyn. He seems to be a mild and benevolent enthusiast—a sort of character with which I am always half in love. We had the novelty of grace before and after dinner, all the company standing.

It is a half-pathetic entry from a man who had

once himself been among the enthusiasts and now sat in Bombay reading Dean Swift and recording half-benevolent, half-cynical observations on the men who crossed his path. A week later his comment was a little less genial:

Mr Martyn, the saint from Calcutta, called here. He is a man of acuteness and learning; his meekness is excessive, and gives a disagreeable impression of effort to conceal the passions of human nature.

Later again he wrote in happier tones:

Padre Martyn, the saint, dined here in the evening; it was a very considerably more pleasant evening than usual; he is a mild and ingenious man. We had two or three hours' good discussion on grammar and metaphysics.

So we look at the saint through the eyes of a man of the world who "thought that little was to be apprehended and little hoped for from the exertions of missionaries," an attitude which Martyn had met before.

His introduction to the other man of mark in Bombay society was of greater interest to Martyn, since this was a man whose name was a name to conjure with in Persia. Sir John Malcolm, a soldier turned diplomatist, had twice been sent on embassies to establish British trade and prestige in Persia. He talked Persian fluently, "bribed like a king," scattered presents of "watches and pistols; mirrors and toothpicks; filagree boxes and umbrellas; cloths and muslins; with an unlimited supply of sugar, sugar-candy and chintz." In Persia, later travellers took rank in Persian eyes according as they could or could

not claim acquaintance with Malcolm Sahib.
Martyn found him in Bombay writing his history
of Persia and receiving the censure of Leadenhall
Street for the cost of his missions.

There was a generous gesture about everything
that Malcolm did, since the day when as a twelve-
year-old urchin from the Westerkirk parish school,
standing before the Directors of the East India
Company to demand a cadetship, he had told that
august body that were he to meet Hyder Ali he
would "cut aff his heid." He now gave Martyn
invaluable help, letters of introduction right and
left, much Persian information, and a present of a
Chaldee missal.

The letter that Malcolm wrote to the British
Ambassador in Persia gives one more glimpse of
Martyn as he looked to able men, neither prejudiced against "piety" like the military circle
in Cawnpore, nor yielding him the spiritual sympathy of the circle at Aldeen. It is the last portrait that has come to us from the pen of a fellow
countryman.

His intention is, I believe, to go by Shiraz, Ispahan
and Kermanshah to Baghdad, and to endeavour on
that route to discover some ancient copies of the Gospel,
which he and many other saints are persuaded lie hid
in the mountains of Persia. Mr Martyn also expects
to improve himself as an Oriental scholar; he is already
an excellent one. His knowledge of Arabic is superior
to that of any Englishman in India. He is altogether
a very learned and cheerful man, but a great enthusiast
in his holy calling.

I have not hesitated to tell him that I thought you
would require that he should act with great caution,
and not allow his zeal to run away with him. He declares he will not, and he is a man of that character that

I must believe. I am satisfied that if ever you see him, you will be pleased with him. He will give you grace before and after dinner, and admonish such of your party as take the Lord's name in vain; but his good sense and great learning will delight you, whilst his constant cheerfulness will add to the hilarity of your party.

The man who added to the hilarity of Malcolm's evening parties was pursuing his own course by day, for there is no confining the man of God in the bounds of one social clique.

"My breath is not at all stronger," he wrote to Corrie, "but I have no doubt it would be if I could flee the haunts of men. At this place I am visited from morning to night by the learned natives, who are drawn here by an Arabic tract, which I was drawing up merely for Sabat to help him in his book."

The friends he made while waiting in Bombay for a ship to the Persian Gulf were the usual motley company. Besides the learned of Islam there was "a rope-maker from London who came and opened his heart and we rejoiced together"; a Parsee poet ("he is certainly an ingenious man, and possesses one of the most agreeable qualities a disputant can possess, which is, patience: he never interrupted me; and if I rudely interrupted him, he was silent in a moment"); and a Jew of Bosra, with whom he walked at night by the seaside.

Martyn was given a passage in a ship of the East India Company's navy, sent to cruise in the Persian Gulf against marauding Arab pirates from the coast of Oman. He was to act as chaplain to the European part of the crew of the *Benares*.

In his journal and his letters, especially those to Lydia and to Corrie, " our beloved Daniel in the north," we trace the details of his wanderings. Lydia's proffered letters had never reached him. " When will our correspondence be established ? I have been trying to effect it these six years, and it is only yet in train. But I am not yet without hopes that a letter in the beloved hand will yet overtake me somewhere."

I quitted India on Lady Day. . . . Smooth and light airs left me at liberty to pursue my studies as uninterruptedly as if I were on shore ; and more so, as my companions in the great cabin, being sufficient company for each other, and studious and taciturn withal, seldom break my repose. Every day, all day long, I Hebraize. . . . On the morning of Easter we saw the land of Mekran in Persia.

You will be happy to know that the murderous pirates against whom we were sent, having received notice of our approach, are all got out of the way, so that I am no longer liable to be shot in a battle, or to decapitation after it.

On the Sunday after Easter the *Benares* put into the cove of Muscat for water before pursuing her way up the Gulf to Bushire, and Henry Martyn set foot in Arabia, a land, he said, of " burning, barren rocks. We went through the bazaar, and mounted a hill to look at it, but saw nothing but what was hideous. The town and houses are more mean and filthy than any in India, and in all the environs of the place I counted three trees, date-trees I suppose."

The cove was stifling. Sleep was impossible during the hot nights in shelter of the rocks. But Martyn was about his business.

April 24, 1811. Went with one Englishman, and two Armenians and an Arab who acted as guard and guide, to see a remarkable pass about a mile from the town, and a garden planted by a Hindoo, in a little valley beyond. . . . The little bit of green in this wilderness seemed to the Arab a great curiosity. I conversed a good deal with him, but particularly with his African slave who was very intelligent about religion.

The talk, as so often happened with Martyn, proved more engrossing than the expedition. The slave followed him down to the landing-place and " would not cease from his argument till I left the shore."

So Martyn left Arabian soil. But next day, the ship being still in the cove,

the Arab soldier and his slave came on board to take leave. They asked to see the Gospel. The instant I gave them a copy in Arabic, the poor boy began to read, and carried it off as a great prize.

The *Benares,* having warped out of the stifling cove, was tossed about for days by a north-wester, the more violent of the two prevailing winds that rush up or down the great funnel of the Gulf. On May 21st she came to Bushire, and Henry Martyn landed in Persia at that dilapidated little port surrounded by " a wall with a few bastions which might possibly be a safeguard against the predatory incursions of Horse." [1]

He came into its steamy heat at the hottest season of the year.

" We were hospitably received by the acting Resident. In the evening I walked out by the seaside to recollect myself, to review the past and to look forward to the future."

[1] Scott Waring, *A Tour to Sheeraz*, p. 12.

He at once ordered a Persian costume for travel in the interior, and while it was in making set himself, except when prostrated with headache by the heat of the city, to find out Persian and Arabic opinion on translations of the New Testament.

Learned Mohammedan Arabs enjoyed Sabat's Arabic :

I showed Hosyn, an Arab, the most learned man here, a passage in the New Testament, according to the four versions of Erpenius, English, Polyglot and Sabat. He condemned the three first, but said immediately of Sabat's, " This is good, very good." He read out a chapter in fine style ; in short, he gave it unqualified commendation.

But learned Persians were not equally pleased with Sabat's work in their language. Already his Persian friend in Bombay had criticized it :

He began about the versions of the New Testament, condemning them all. I asked him whether Sabat's Persian was not much superior ? He opened upon a chapter, and pointed out several undeniable errors both in collocation and words, and laughed at some of the Arabic words. When I told him the translator was an Arab who had lived ten years in Persia, he said, an Arab if he live there twenty years, will never speak Persian well.

So the great task remained yet to be done, and Henry Martyn, plunging into Persia, was determined not to come forth again till he brought with him such a version as in all its niceties could satisfy the sensitive Persian ear.

On the night of May 30, 1811, his caravan wound through the sleeping port between blind walls of mud or crumbling stone and set its face towards the distant hills. Martyn had grown a moustache during the voyage ; he now " put off the European " and mounted his riding pony in baggy blue trousers and red boots, a conical cap of Astrakhan and a flowing coat. An Armenian servant followed him on a mule and another mule carried his books. For safety they joined a caravan of about thirty beasts carrying baggage to Sir Gore Ouseley, the British Ambassador, then at Shiraz. In that city of poets and lettered men, Martyn could best pursue his object.

They travelled by night, for the heat of day in early June would be intolerable. As they filed out of Bushire on to the sandy plain that stretched for ninety miles between them and the hills that lift the Persian plateau, Martyn felt all the romance of the first starlight journey with a caravan.

When we began to flag and grow sleepy and the kafila was pretty quiet, one of the muleteers on foot began to sing. He sang with a voice so plaintive, that it was impossible not to have one's attention arrested. At the end of the first tune he paused, and nothing was heard but the tinkling of the bells attached to the necks of the mules ; every voice was hushed. The first line was enough for me. . . . The following is perhaps the true translation :

> *Think not that e'er my heart can dwell*
> *Contented far from thee ;*
> *How can the fresh-caught nightingale*
> *Enjoy tranquillity ?*
>
> *Forsake not then thy friend for aught*
> *That slanderous tongues can say ;*
> *The heart that fixes where it ought,*
> *No power can rend away.*

Thus we went on, and as often as the kafila by their

dulness and sleepiness seemed to require it, or perhaps to keep himself awake, he entertained the company and himself with a song. We met two or three other kafilas taking advantage of the night to get on.

Day caught them still on that sweltering plain. And Martyn, who had almost forgotten it, was forced to remember for once that he was a sick man.

At sunrise we came to our ground at Ahmeda, six parasangs, and pitched our little tent under a tree: it was the only shelter we could get. At first the heat was not greater than we had felt it in India, but it soon became so intense as to be quite alarming. When the thermometer was above 112°, fever heat, I began to lose my strength fast; at last it became quite intolerable. I wrapped myself up in a blanket and all the warm covering I could get to defend myself from the external air; by which means the moisture was kept a little longer upon the body.
But the thermometer still rising, and the moisture of the body being quite exhausted, I grew restless and thought I should have lost my senses. The thermometer at last stood at 126°. . . . At last the fierce sun retired, and I crept out more dead than alive. It was then a difficulty how I could proceed on my journey; for besides the immediate effects of the heat, I had no opportunity of making up for the last night's want of sleep, and had eaten nothing. However, while they were loading the mules, I got an hour's sleep, and set out, the muleteers leading my horse, and Zechariah, my servant, an Armenian, doing all in his power to encourage me.

So they rode on through the coolness of another night, and when daybreak again found them on the unshielded plain they made their preparations.

I got a tattie made of the branches of the date-tree, and a Persian peasant to water it; by this means the thermometer did not rise above 114°. But what completely secured me from the heat was a large wet towel, which I wrapped round my head and body, muffling up the lower part in clothes.

The next day brought them to the bottom of the mountain wall among pits of black naphtha " used by the Persians as we are told it was in (Milton's) hell for lamps, and occasionally given to their camels." [1]

We arrived at the foot of the mountains, at a place where we seemed to have discovered one of Nature's ulcers. A strong suffocating smell of naphtha announced something more than ordinarily foul in the neighbourhood. We saw a river :—what flowed in it, it seemed difficult to say, whether it were water or green oil ; it scarcely moved, and the stones which it laved it left of a greyish colour, as if its foul touch had given them the leprosy.

Little dreamed the man who loved the soft sea-mists of Cornwall of the part that the scarred and burning Persian oil-fields would one day play in political and military history.

Our place of encampment this day was a grove of date-trees, where the atmosphere, at sunrise, was ten times hotter than the ambient air. I threw myself down on the burning ground and slept ; when the tent came up I awoke, as usual, in a burning fever.

And now, after three nights in the saddle, and three sleepless days of fever, they began to climb the mountain ladder to the Persian plateau.

At nine in the evening we decamped. The ground and air were so insufferably hot that I could not travel without a wet towel round my face and neck. This

[1] Scott Waring, *A Tour to Sheeraz*, p. 18.

night, for the first time, we began to ascend the mountains.

There was nothing to mark the road but the rocks being a little more worn in one place than in another. Sometimes my horse, which led the way, stopped as if to consider about the way : for myself I could not guess.

He gave his horse the rein, and rode on drunken with sleep, along paths that hung over dizzy pre-cipices, and up tracks where the travellers behind cower with the sense that the mules must fall back headlong on the hindmost, through desolate places where the moon plays monkey tricks, sometimes riding serene and high, and sometimes as the wild path heaves upward, seeming to sail level with the traveller's bridle. Through such " sublime " scenes Martyn dragged himself on, drugged with overpowering sleep.

My sleepiness and fatigue rendered me insensible to everything around me. At last we emerged *superas ad auras*, not on the top of a mountain to go down again, but to a plain, or upper world.

The first rung of the great ladder was mounted. " We rode briskly over the plain, breathing a purer air, and soon came in sight of a fair edifice, built by the king of the country for the refreshment of pilgrims." Here the thermometer was 110°, tempered for them, however, by a load of ice bought from a mountaineer on his way down to the coastal plain.

Next night they climbed the second rung of that great ladder.

" We ascended another range of mountains and passed over a plain where the cold was so piercing that with all the clothes we could muster we were shivering." They rode on till eight in the morning through country where mountain was heaped on mountain and stone piled on stone as though in some battle of the elder giants. When Martyn arrived at Kaziroon, "there seemed to be a fire within my head, my skin like a cinder and the pulse violent." Here he lay all day in a summer house in a cypress garden still too feverish for sleep, stretching out a burning hand to dip it in water.

So they made two more great ascents, climbing the rugged hills crowned with the greyish green of the wild almond into a cooler air. On the last night of that climb "the cold was very severe; for fear of falling off from sleep and numbness I walked a good part of the way." And now at last they found a place of rest, never forgotten by any traveller who has made that ride.

We pitched our tent in the vale of Dustarjan, near a crystal stream, on the banks of which we observed the clover and golden cup: the whole valley was one green field, in which large herds of cattle were browsing. The temperature was about that of spring in England. Here a few hours' sleep recovered me in some degree from the stupidity in which I had been for some days. I awoke with a light heart and said, " He maketh us to lie down in the green pastures and leadeth us beside the still waters."

There were two more nights of travel before Martyn reached his goal, " gasping for life under the double pressure of an inward fire and an outward burning sun." [1]

---

[1] Sir Robert Ker Porter, *Travels*, I. p. 687.

R

Sleepiness my old companion and enemy again over-took me. I was in perpetual danger of falling off my horse, till at last I pushed on to a considerable distance, planted my back against a wall, and slept I know not how long till the good muleteer came up and gently waked me.

On Sunday, June 9th, they reached Shiraz the many-gated, set white upon her plain. They halted in a garden outside the walls, and next day rode in through the blind narrow streets to the house of a leading citizen, Jaffir Ali Khan, to whom Martyn had letters bearing the magic signature of Malcolm.

The house was thrown open to him.

After the long and tedious ceremony of coffee and pipes, breakfast made its appearance on two large trays: curry, pilaws, various sweets cooled with snow and perfumed with rose-water, were served in great pro-fusion in China plates and basins, a few wooden spoons beautifully carved ; but being in a Persian dress, and on the ground, I thought it high time to throw off the European, and so ate with my hands.

The rich and learned Jaffir placed a room at Martyn's disposal, and here he unpacked such books as he had. His host had been once " a great sayer of prayers, and had regularly passed every afternoon for fourteen years in cursing the followers of Omar according to the prescribed form ; but perceiving that these zealous maledic-tions brought no blessings on himself, he left them off and now just prays for form's sake. His wife [a veiled lady whom Martyn never met while living in her husband's house] says her prayers regu-larly five times a day, and is always up before sunrise for the first prayer." But her husband devoted himself to the pleasures of wealth and literature ; excursions to gardens beside living streams, and the company of poets.

Jaffir Ali Khan heard with the interest of a lettered man of his visitor's anxiety for a true and beautiful translation of the Gospel, and he introduced a brother-in-law who spoke "the purest dialect of the Persian" and offered his assistance in making a new version. "It was an offer I could not refuse," said Martyn, and he at once prepared for months of virtual solitude, "entrenched in one of Persia's valleys" till the great task should be done.

CHAPTER XIII

A YEAR AMONG THE DOCTORS

Yet with the Friend are we, and the Light of the Eye, and the Path of Expectation.—Shamsu-d-Din Muhammad i Hafiz.

The least of His works it is refreshing to look at. A dried leaf or a straw makes me feel myself in good company. . . . If I live to complete the Persian New Testament, my life after that will be of less importance. But whether life or death be mine, may Christ be magnified in me. If He has work for me to do I cannot die.— Martyn's *Journal at Shiraz, January* 1, 1812.

Henry Martyn, "wearing agreeably to custom a pair of red cloth stockings with green high-heeled shoes," went to the palace where a hundred fountains played, and made his bow to the Prince-Governor of Shiraz, in whose city he was now a guest.

On first reaching Shiraz he had found Sir Gore Ouseley, "Ambassador Extraordinary and Minister Plenipotentiary" to the Shah's court, encamped in the plain outside the city walls. When camp was struck and the ambassador and his suite moved on towards Tabriz, Martyn was left alone in that yet mediæval Shiraz where the Prince-Governor was an autocratic tyrant ordering the bastinado, where city gates were closed at sunset, where the Vizier sent a train of mules laden with fruit as a compliment to the stranger, and where men, sipping sherbet cooled with snow, recited the verses of Sadi or of Hafiz, "a poetry which in its endless

260

yet graceful handling of the same overmastering ideas, has all the fantastic wealth of woven traceries and colours burnt in glass, of the purple and gold and crimson shining in the holy place that characterize the art of the thirteenth century." [1]

Martyn, son of another age and world, knew in Shiraz the loneliness of a crowd.

After much deliberation [he wrote to David Brown] I have determined to remain here six months. From all that I can collect there appears no probability of our ever having a good translation made out of Persia. The men of Shiraz propose to translate the New Testament with me. Can I refuse to stay?

Behold me, therefore, in the Athens of Fars, the haunt of the Persian man. Beneath are the ashes of Hafiz and Sadi; above, green gardens and running waters, roses and nightingales. How gladly would I give Shiraz for Aldeen!

Now, good Sir, seeing that I am to remain six months in captivity, comfort me with a letter now and then.

I am often tempted to get away from this prison, . . . but placing myself twenty years on in time, I say why could not I stay at Shiraz long enough to get a New Testament done there, even if I had been detained there on that account three or six years? What work of equal importance can ever come from me?

The story of that sojourn has to be pieced together from Martyn's letters and journal. Letter after letter he sent home by caravan to the coast or by Tartar courier to Constantinople, but none yet reached him from Cornwall, and the Indian packets also were mysteriously delayed.

[1] *Quarterly Review*, January 1892, on Wilberforce Clarke's translation of the *Divan* of Hafiz.

Since ten months [he told Lydia] I have heard nothing of any one person whom I love. I read your letters incessantly, and try to find out something new, as I generally do, but I begin to look with pain at the distant date of the last. . . . I try to live on from day to day happy in His love and care.

He wrote to Lydia, to David Brown and to Corrie long letters that have to be searched before they yield those little details which give the picture of daily life. For the letters are swallowed up with the one supreme interest of his task. When at length an Indian packet reached him, a Persian friend with unquenchable curiosity about the foreigner was anxious to know "in what way he corresponded." "He made me read Mr Brown's letter to me," says Martyn, "and mine to Corrie. He took care to let his friends know that we wrote nothing about our own affairs : it was all about translations and the cause of Christ. With this he was delighted."

The *Journal* too, once full of minute and delicate studies in conscience, becomes now a notebook of the progress of translation and of solitary witness to the faith. There are no longer breathings after Brainerd ; the man stands alone with Christ. The Martyn that moves among the doctors of Shiraz is clothed with an almost magical calm, with the serenity of a man who has forgotten himself in the service of a Greater.

He set up housekeeping in the room allotted to him by his host, with his talkative Armenian servant to do the foraging.

Victuals are cheap enough . . . such a country for fruit I had no conception of. I have a fine horse which I bought for less than a hundred rupees, on which I

ride every morning round the walls. My vain servant
Zechariah, anxious that his master should appear like
an ameer, furnished the horse with a saddle, or rather a
pillion which fairly covers his whole back; it has all
the colours of the rainbow, but yellow is predominant,
and from it hang down four large tassels also yellow.
But all my finery does not defend me from the
boys. Some cry out " Ho! Russ! " others cry out
" Feringhee! " One day a brickbat was flung at me and
hit me in the hip. They continued throwing stones at me
every day until the Governor sent an order to all the
gates that if anyone insulted me he should be bastinadoed,
and the next day came himself in state to pay me a visit.

Most of the day I am about the translation. I am
so incessantly occupied with visitors and my work that
I have hardly a moment for myself. Even from these
Mohammedans I hear remarks that do me good; to-day
for instance my assistant observed, " How He loved
those twelve persons." " Yes," said I, " and not those
twelve only."

Imagine a pale person seated on a Persian carpet,
in a room without table or chair, with a pair of formidable
mustachios, and habited as a Persian, and you see me.
I go on as usual singing hymns at night over my milk
and water, for tea I have none though I much want it.
I am with you in spirit almost every evening.

The long covered bazaar of Shiraz (" like Exeter
Change ") was soon seething with rumour about
the new foreigner who lodged with the wealthy
and respected Jaffir Ali Khan, and who carried
letters from that prince of men, the liberal Malcolm
Sahib. " This is a man of religion, and his coming
here is that he may embrace the true faith and
turn Moslem," said some. " Nay," replied the
politically minded, " but he will pretend to turn
Moslem, and under that pretence he will bring
here more and more English, perhaps five thousand
men from Hindostan, and at last seize the place."

Those who had spoken with Martyn called him a
man of God and a doctor of religion. "A beardless boy," said others, "how should he know anything of the faith?" And to settle the question,
the learned of Shiraz came one by one to sip
coffee and break a lance with the stranger. They
never found him inaccessible. His list of visitors,
as in all places where he dwelt, was very various.[1]

The prince's secretary who is considered to be the
best prose-writer in Shiraz called upon us.

Two young men from the college, full of zeal and
logic, came this morning to try me with hard questions.

Before I had taken my breakfast the younger of the
youths came, and forced me into a conversation. As
soon as he heard the word "Father" in the translation
used for "God," he laughed and went away.

Abdulghanee the Jew Mahometan came to prove that
he had found Mahomet in the Pentateuch. . . He concluded by saying that he must come every day and either
make me a Mussulman or become himself a Christian.

Another day it was a Persian General who came
out of respect to a friend of Malcolm Sahib, or an
Armenian priest who called to see his brother of the
west, or the "chief of a tribe which consists of
twenty thousand families," or an Indian moonshee
who recited his own verses while the Persians
secretly derided his foreign accent.

The interviews were apt to terminate in deadlock, as host and visitor reached one crucial point.

The Moollah Aga Mahommed Hasan, a very sensible,
candid man, asked a good deal about the European
philosophy, particularly what we did in metaphysics.
He has nothing to find fault with in Christianity, except
the Divinity of Christ. It is this doctrine that exposes
me to the contempt of the learned Mahometans.

[1] For the story of one of these visitors which came to light half a
century later, see note on p. 298.

Martyn's serenity, his friends soon learnt, was never the calm of an unfeeling deadness. They could touch him to the quick by anything that concerned the honour of his Lord.

Mirza Seid Ali told me of a distich made by his friend in honour of a victory over the Russians. The sentiment was that Prince Abbas Mirza had killed so many Christians that Christ from the fourth heaven took hold of Mahomet's skirt to entreat him to desist. I was cut to the soul at this blasphemy. Mirza Seid Ali perceived that I was considerably disordered and asked what it was that was so offensive? I told him that " I could not endure existence if Jesus was not glorified ; it would be hell to me, if He were to be always thus dishonoured." He was astonished and again asked " Why ? " " If any one pluck out your eyes," I replied, " there is no saying *why* you feel pain ;—it is feeling. It is because I am one with Christ that I am thus dreadfully wounded."

In spite of the interruptions of garrulous callers, the beloved work went on apace. Sabat's translation, with its fondness for fine words, was found almost useless.

The king has signified that it is his wish that as little Arabic as possible may be employed in the papers presented to him. So that simple Persian is likely to become more and more fashionable. This is a change favourable certainly to our glorious cause. To the poor the Gospel will be preached. We began our work with the Gospel of St John, and five chapters are put out of hand. It is likely to be the simplest thing imaginable ; and I daresay the pedantic Arab will turn up his nose at it ; but what the men of Shiraz approve, who can gainsay ?

During August Martyn's host, " to relieve the tedium of living always in a walled town," pitched a tent for him in a garden in the suburbs, where he found tranquillity, " living amidst clusters of grapes by a clear stream." Here under an orange tree, with greater freedom from interruption, he sat with Mirza Seid Ali hour after hour at the translation, until the cold at night drove him back to the shelter of the city.

The man who thus spent long hours with Martyn had escaped from the Shiah Islam of orthodox Persia to Sufi mysticism. But in nothing had he gone very deep. He was a man of facile intelligence, who told his friends that it was better to gain information about the faith of the Christians than to loiter away the year in the garden.

From him Martyn tried patiently to understand the Sufi beliefs; but he was met by endless meandering discourses about the unity of all being, from one who was himself but a beginner in the Sufi way. "I came to nothing like a clear understanding of the nature of it," Martyn confessed at the end of the explanations.

The facile shallowness of the man came out in his comments on the New Testament :

Mirza Seid Ali read some verses of St Paul which he condescended to praise, but in such a way as to be more offensive to me than if he had treated them with contempt. He observed that Paul had not written ill but something like a good reasoner.

There is another circumstance that gained Paul importance in the eyes of Mirza Seid Ali, which is that he speaks of Mark and Luke as his servants.

Can you give me a proof (said he) of Christianity, that I may either believe or not believe—a proof like that of one of the theorems of Euclid?

Yet Mirza Seid Ali had his deeper moments. "You never heard *me* speak lightly of Jesus," he told Martyn; "no, there is something so awfully pure about Him that nothing is to be said." He grew troubled as his intercourse with the saint grew deeper, and said " he did not know what to do to have his mind made up about religion. Of all the religions Christ's was the best, but whether to prefer this to Soofeism he could not tell."

In such disturbance of mind he decided to take Martyn to meet the greatest religious leader and saint of his acquaintance, the Sufi master at whose feet he sat with reverential awe, and to watch the result of the contact. It was a strange and almost silent interview, when Martyn, no stranger himself to the communion of the Christian mystic, was ushered into the courtyard of Mirza Abul Casim, " one of the most renowned Soofis in all Persia."

We found several persons sitting in an open court, in which a few greens and flowers were placed ; the master was in a corner. He was a very fresh-looking old man with a silver beard. I was surprised to observe the downcast and sorrowful looks of the assembly, and still more at the silence which reigned.

Martyn sat on the ground among the pupils of the sage, Seid Ali whispering in his ear, " It is the custom here to think much and speak little." After a considerable pause he ventured to ask the teacher, " What were his feelings at the prospect of death : hope, or fear, or neither ? "

" Neither," said he, " pleasure and pain are both alike."

I asked, " Whether he had obtained this apathy ? "
He said " No."
" Why do you think it attainable ? "
He could not tell.
" Why do you think that pleasure and pain are not

the same ? " said Seid Ali, taking the part of his silent teacher.

" Because," said I, " I have the evidence of my senses for it. And you also act as if there was a difference. Why do you eat but that you fear pain ? "

With that brief colloquy they relapsed again into silence, and the sages sat unmoved until Martyn came away, his heart yearning over a young disciple whom he had seen preparing the teacher's pipe with great humility, and who had incurred an orthodox father's wrath and left all to find happiness in mystic contemplation.

From the day of that visit followers of the mystic way, among them the young disciple, began to steal into Martyn's rooms under the sympathetic eye of his host.

" I begin now to have some notion of Soofeism," Martyn wrote. " The first principle is this : notwithstanding the good and evil, pleasure and pain that is in the world, God is not affected by it. He is perfectly happy with it all ; if therefore we can become like God we shall also be perfectly happy in every possible condition. This then is salvation."

When they spun interminable theories Martyn was very frank. " There you sit," he told Seid Ali, " and will not take the trouble to ask whether God has said anything or not. No : that is too easy and direct a way of coming at the truth. I compare you to spiders, who weave their house of defence out of their own bowels, or to a set of people who are groping for a light in broad day."

Yet Sufism as he saw it gave him hope for the spiritual future of Persia.

Vast numbers secretly hate and despise the superstition imposed on them [he wrote], and as many of them as have heard the gospel approve it, but they dare not hazard their lives for the name of the Lord Jesus. These Soofis are quite the Methodists of the east. From these you will perceive the first Persian Church will be formed, judging after the manner of men.

During the month of Ramadan, when orthodox Moslems fast by day and feast by night, Martyn was surprised by a visit from the silent sage himself. He conformed outwardly to Islam so far as was necessary to avoid shame and punishment; but at heart he was a rebel, and he came now to ask Martyn for wine, secure that in the Christian's room he would not be betrayed for breaking the regulations he despised.

"I plied him with questions innumerable," wrote Martyn, "but the weary old man had no heart for discussion."

Laying aside his turban, he put on his nightcap and soon fell asleep upon the carpet. Whilst he lay there, his disciples came, but would not believe when I told them who was there, till they came and saw the sage asleep. When he awoke, they came in, and seated themselves at the greatest possible distance, and were all as still as a church.

So the poor old man awoke from his brief comfort of wine and sleep to find himself once more a saintly demi-god. "The real state of this man seems to be despair," wrote Martyn. "Poor soul, he is sadly bewildered."

When winter came and the translators wrapped sheepskins round them as they sat at work, Martyn made his Christmas feast, and bade to it his brethren of the Armenian Church, ignorant and persecuted, sewing patches on to their new coats for fear they should be taken from them by Moslem neighbours. He also bade the Sufi sage and all his following to celebrate the birth of One whom wise men from the east had worshipped. "God will guide whom He will," the poor old man was heard to mutter into his snowy beard; but not another word did he vouchsafe at that strange Christmas feast.

So Martyn reached out towards friendship with these heretics and mystics, for their sakes breaking through the shy, proud reserve of the Britisher, and laying before them all that he had, even his very soul. "I am sometimes led on by the Persians," he said, "to tell them all I know of the very recesses of the sanctuary, and these are the things that interest them."

But long before Christmas time he had awakened hostility amongst the orthodox, and found himself called on to defend the faith before the doctors of Persian Islam. "I am in the midst of enemies," he wrote, "who argue against the truth with uncommon subtlety."

So great was the stir in the city from the presence of the young Frankish teacher that the authorities felt it necessary to assert the true and only faith.

A defence of Islam was prepared, which in the eyes of the learned of Shiraz outweighed all former apologies—"a book which is to silence me for ever," Martyn said. This was the work of Mirza Ibrahim, a majestic and benevolent old man, "Preceptor of all the mullahs," whose manner recalls the traditions of the great mediæval doctors, as he meets an opponent with courteous subtlety.

When this work was put into Martyn's hands

there fell to him, single-handed and almost without books, the task as knight of Christ of meeting the champion of Persian theology. He replied in a tract, the first of a series, in which he shows an astonishing mastery of the whole controversy, and in which he and his opponent throughout preserved high courtesy.[1]

But though Martyn and Mirza Ibrahim might be chivalrous opponents, there were other less courtly antagonists.

As there is nothing at all in this dull place to take the attention of the people, no trade, manufactures or news, every event at all novel is interesting to them. You may conceive therefore what a sensation was produced. Before five people had seen what I wrote, defences of Islam swarmed into being from all the Moulwee maggots of the place, but the more judicious men were ashamed to let me see them.

One of the royal princes was heard to growl that the proper reply to Martyn's writings was the sword. But he remained serene and unmoved among them. "If Christ has work for me to do, I cannot die," he said, and never shirked encounters where he might be called on to confess his faith. Soon all Shiraz was talking of a dinner party at which the great Professor of Canon Law himself had disputed with the stranger.

He invited us to dinner. About eight o'clock at night we went. [October had come and with it the Moslem month of Ramadan, when eating by day is forbidden.] We entered a fine court, where was a pond, and by the side of it a platform eight feet high, covered with carpets. Here sat the Moojtahid in state. The Professor seated Seid Ali on his right hand and me on

[1] The whole controversy was preserved in English, and published by Dr Lee, the Cambridge Professor of Arabic, after Martyn's death.

his left. The swarthy obesity of the little personage
led me to suppose that he had paid more attention to
cooking than to science. But when he began to speak,
I saw reason enough for his being so much admired.
The substance of his speech was flimsy enough; but
he spoke with uncommon fluency and clearness. He
talked for a full hour about the soul. At length after
clearing his way for miles around, he said, that philosophers had proved that a single being could produce
but a single being; that the first thing God had created
was *Wisdom*. . . .

And so on—a winding tissue which Martyn, as he
sat in silence on the many-coloured carpet, had
no desire to call in question, being anxious for
no useless skirmishes among outworks.

The Professor at the close of one of his long speeches
said to me, " You see how much there is to be said on
these subjects; several visits will be necessary; we must
come to the point by degrees." Perceiving how much he
dreaded a close discussion, I did not mean to hurry
him, but let him talk on.

But other listeners were anxious for the clash
of arms, and urged Martyn to bring the Professor
to grips. He did at length respectfully urge the
great lawyer to oblige the company with " something about Islam," and so drew forth a few magisterial statements.

" The Jesus we acknowledge," said he with a
contemptuous smile, " is one who bore testimony
to Muhammad, not your Jesus whom you call
God."

After this the Koran was mentioned, but as the
company began to thin and the great man had not a
sufficient audience, he did not seem to think it worth
while to notice my objections.

It was midnight when dinner was brought in: it was

a sullen meal. The great man was silent; and I was sleepy.

So quite alone he witnessed to the faith. There is a story, perhaps apocryphal, of Martyn when he went to sit under an awning in the Vizier's courtyard and witness the Moslem Passion Play of the death of Hussein. The drama lasted ten days and was played before an audience that sobbed aloud. The story has it that when a scene was reached in which a Frankish ambassador was made to step forward and implore pardon for the victims, the actor knew no Frankish words to say except a few round English curses picked up from travellers. Martyn, stung to the heart at this, leapt on to the primitive stage, and seizing the actor, taught him to say the Lord's Prayer.

The story may be apocryphal; [1] if so, like many legends it has spiritual truth, being faithful to the daring and the impetuosity of Martyn's solitary witness.

On the 24th of February the New Testament was finished. Martyn waited for nothing but the scribing of some gorgeous copies for the hands of Persian royalty, before setting out once more on pilgrimage. They could hardly let him go. They took him out to a garden and seated him on a bed

---

[1] Yet Martyn several times did go to martyr-plays in Shiraz, and we know that he went to the play at the Vizier's in January 1812. Curiously enough, as E. G. Browne was sitting in a Persian house in 1892, his host, speaking of a similar part allotted to a Frankish ambassador in some recent martyr-plays, said, " How I wish you had been here a little earlier, for then we could have borrowed your hats and clothes for the Firangis, and indeed you might even have taught us some words of your language to put in the mouths of the actors who personated them."—E. G. Browne, *A Year among the Persians.*

S

of roses, and made him read them the Bible history
for hours at a time. "Their love seemed to increase," he said, as the time of his departure drew
near. One of them who had seen Martyn's translation of St Matthew, recited to his friends the story
of the Passion of the Lord. "The notes of the
nightingales warbling around," said Martyn, "were
not so sweet to me as this discourse from the
Persian."

Just before he quitted Shiraz, a young man,
bred as a doctor of Islam, came begging for an
interview. He confessed that he had visited
Martyn many times before with the other doctors
to heap scorn on the teacher of a despised sect,
but at every interview he had found his attitude
changing. Martyn's unfailing forbearance to his
violence put him to shame, and his calm reasoning
laid bare sophistries. At last Muhammad Rahim
found himself convinced that the "beardless boy"
was right. Then for shame and fear he had kept
away from his presence for months. But now he
heard that the teacher was going, and he came
at last to make confession of his belief. Martyn
put into his hands that day a copy of the Book,
a Persian New Testament that became his lifelong
companion. Years afterwards Muhammad Rahim
confessed his conversion to a Christian traveller,
and showed the book that was his greatest treasure.
On one of the blank leaves was written, "There is
joy in heaven over one sinner that repenteth.—
HENRY MARTYN."

CHAPTER XIV

THE TRAVELLER

Suddenly I seem to myself to see holy Martin, the bishop, clad in a white robe, with face like a flame, eyes like stars, and glittering hair; and, while his person was what I had known it to be, yet, what can hardly be expressed, I could not look at him, though I could recognize him. . . . He repeats the name of the cross, familiar in his mouth; next, while I gaze upon him, and cannot take my fill of his face and look, suddenly he is caught aloft, till, after completing the immense spaces of the air, I following with my eyes the swift cloud that carried him, he is received into the open heaven, and can be seen no more. . . . A boy enters with a speaking and sorrowful countenance: " Why so sad and eager to speak ? " say I. " Two monks," he answers, " are just come from Tours; they bring the news that Martin is departed."—SULPICIUS SEVERUS, *Life of Martin of Tours* (translated by J. H. Newman).

In that yet mediæval Persia, the aspiring poet or man of letters still laid his book before the Shah on his throne of marble spread with cloth of gold. Fateh Ali Shah,[1] ruler of Persia, over-lord of Georgia and Kurdistan, was not only the statesman who received and balanced the claims of embassies from George III, from Napoleon, from the Tzar Alexander and from the Governor-General Wellesley. He was, as he sat blazing with jewels before a prostrate court, the fountain of taste and the judge of letters for his kingdom. It needed but a pronouncement of praise in his hollow rolling voice, and the fortunes of a volume were made.

[1] 1798–1836.

Henry Martyn, seeing through Persian eyes, determined to gain for the New Testament the respect yielded to a book approved at court.

As his translation work drew to a close he set scribes preparing two volumes of exquisite penmanship for the Shah and for his heir, Prince Abbas Mirza, "the wisest of the princes." The scribes began work in November 1811. They brought him the finished volumes in May 1812, three months after the translator's work was done. Lingering in Shiraz and waiting for their manuscript he "beguiled the tediousness of the day" by an absorbing study of the Psalms in Hebrew, and a translation of the Psalter into Persian. It enthralled him so that he "hardly perceived" the passing of the days. "I have long had it in contemplation," he wrote to Lydia. "I have often attempted the 84th Psalm, endeared to me on many accounts,[1] but have not yet succeeded. The glorious 16th Psalm I hope I have mastered."

When the scribes brought in their fair copies, Martyn wrapped up the costly manuscripts uncorrected. He had none like-minded whom he could put in charge of the precious volumes, and he was determined to lay the books himself in the royal hands, correcting them as he travelled. For he knew that he was a sick man. He must race disease if he desired to see the Book on its way. A long dispute with a Sufi doctor would leave him still with a raw pit of pain where his breath came and went.

He had copies ready for the press. Four were sent by his direction to India that his friends at

[1] See Chapter VI. p. 117.

Serampore might print his translation.[1]   Other
copies he carried with him on his wanderings,
intending, if he lived, to pass them on to some press
in the west, perhaps at his own university of Cambridge. He spent his last hours at Shiraz with his
fellow-translator in giving instructions for the care
and delivery of the Book in case of his own death.

That done, a little before the closing of the gates
at sunset on May 11, 1812, he left Shiraz and
joined a caravan outside the walls, starting that
night to ride across the great Persian plateau
from south to north.

He was riding as servant of the Book to Tabriz
where Sir Gore Ouseley lived ; for he could only
be introduced into the jewelled presence of the
Shah by the ambassador who represented his
nation.

The air of the uplands was cool enough for day
travelling, and the diary is full of notes on the
face of the countryside. Here "no cultivation,
scarcely any plant except the broom and hawthorn " ; then " a vast plain, entirely uninhabited
except where the skirts of it were spotted with
the black tents of the wandering tribes." On
that high plateau it grew cold, even in May :
" hoar-frost, and ice on the pools. The highest

---

[1] The manuscript arrived safely, but not till 1814. It was published
at Calcutta in 1816. Martyn's friend Mirza Seid Ali was actually
sent for from Shiraz that he might see it through the press. When
he came, he told the Calcutta group that he had with him the translation of the Psalms that had been the solace of Martyn's last months
at Shiraz. Martyn no doubt regarded this as an uncompleted task.
He had taken no steps to preserve it for the Church. But it formed
the nucleus of the beautiful Persian Old Testament published in 1846
in Edinburgh and presented to the Shah in 1848.

land between the Persian Gulf and the Caspian
Sea." At night they shuddered in open caravanserais that seemed to let in wind and rain alike.
Martyn after a day's ride drew out of its wrappings
the precious volume prepared for the Prince, and
sat late into the night in some leaky hovel, poring
over the correction of his scribe's exquisite Persian
lettering.

After twelve days of riding they came across
the poppy fields to Isfahan, a city of domes and
minarets and pigeon towers, seen from far across
the plain. Martyn had for companion in the
caravan another Englishman travelling also to
Tabriz to join Sir Gore Ouseley's suite. Consequently they were lodged as foreigners of mark
in one of the palaces of the Shah. Here they
paused a week and there was time for Martyn to
seek out, according to his wont, his fellow Christians
of those parts. He called first on "the Italian
missionary, a native of Aleppo, but educated at
Rome. He spoke Latin very sprightly." Then
to Julfa to visit the Armenians, of whose ancient
and desolate Church he was always a lover, and
with whom he spent many hours.

On the first night of June the caravan left
Isfahan, its plane trees and its fountains, its
niggardly merchants and its dreams of bygone
glory. "Soon after midnight we mounted our
horses. It was a mild moonlight night and a
nightingale filled the whole valley with his notes.
Our way was along lanes, a murmuring rivulet
accompanied us till it was lost in a lake."

At daylight they rode out of these enchanted
scenes on to the great plain of Kashan where fat

melons grow in bare sand, and far away against the blue stands up a snowy mountain wall, the northern barrier of the Persian land.

After eight days they came to Teheran, the half-ambitious, half-squalid city of modern royalty, behind walls of unbaked clay. They reached those walls two hours before sunrise, and all the twelve gates were shut.

"I spread my bed upon the high road, and slept till the gates were open; then entered the city and took up my abode." Here, at the Persian capital, was the favourite palace of the great Shah, with a marble bath where his ladies might play, and a picture gallery for which, when Martyn came, an artist was painting from memory a likeness of Sir John Malcolm, the magnificent ambassador whom Persia could not forget.

Here came the first hitch in Martyn's plans. No muleteers could be found at the moment willing to travel to Tabriz, where lay the British ambassador who would introduce him and his book into the royal presence. It meant delay. And Martyn in 1812 could not brook delay. While life was yet in him he must press on with the Book. He held letters of introduction to the Shah's Vizier. Better than lose the time he could not spare, should he not travel alone to the Shah's summer camping ground, a night's journey outside the city, and ask the Prime Minister himself to bring him to the royal presence?

He ventured. He rode out of Teheran alone with his servant, and found the Vizier lying ill on the veranda of the Shah's tent of audience. Only that many-coloured tent curtain hung between

Martyn and his goal. The Vizier had two royal
secretaries by his couch.

They took very little notice, not rising when I sat
down, as their custom is to all who sit with them ; nor
offering me a water-pipe. The two secretaries on learning my object in coming, began a conversation with
me on religion and metaphysics which lasted two hours.
The premier asked how many languages I understood ;
whether I spoke French ; where I was educated ; whether
I understood astronomy and geography, and then observed to the others that I spoke good Persian. As they
were well-educated gentlemanly men, the discussion
was temperate.

But Martyn had to betake himself to the
caravanserai that night, no nearer to the jewelled
figure in the audience tent, fed with words and
offered no courteous hospitality. He had not
come with the pomp that impresses such diplomats,
and the Vizier had no intention of becoming
sponsor for a lonely stranger.

Martyn spent the evening on the roof of the
inn, sharing the mat of a poor travelling merchant
who supposed that the western powers yet paid
tribute to Mohammedan masters for permission
to live.

Three days later he attended the Vizier's levee
bearing the precious Book. All eyes were turned
on the solitary Frank. In that court where
verbal swordsmanship was the art of arts, a discussion was inevitable, but Martyn knew that
an angry discussion would ruin his chance of
seeing the face of the Shah.

He could not prevent the very clash that he
dreaded. "There was a most intemperate and
clamorous controversy kept up for an hour or

two; eight or ten on one side and myself on the other." He came unfriended; the Vizier encouraged the attack, and the veneer of polish was broken through as they set upon him.

Their vulgarity in interrupting me in the middle of a speech; their utter ignorance of the nature of an argument; their impudent assertions about the law and the gospel, neither of which they had ever seen in their lives, moved my indignation a little.

His indignation, but not his fear. This Martyn seems to have forgotten how to fear. The Vizier who had at first set them by the ears came up at last to the angry group, stilled the hubbub and put to Martyn before them all a crucial question. He challenged the stranger to recite the Moslem creed. " Say God is God and Mohammed is the Prophet of God."

It was an electric moment, the whole court at attention.

I said, " God is God " but added, instead of " Mahomet is the prophet of God," " and Jesus is the Son of God."

They all rose up as if they would have torn me in pieces,

snarling out one of the classic fighting cries of the Moslem world, " He is neither begotten nor begets." " What will you say when your tongue is burnt out for this blasphemy ? "

He heard them in silence.

My book which I had brought expecting to present it to the king lay before Mirza Shufi, the Vizier. As they all rose up after him to go, some to the king and some away, I was afraid they would trample on the book; so I went in among them to take it up, and wrapped it

in a towel before them ; while they looked at it and
me with supreme contempt.

I walked away alone to my tent to pass the rest of
the day in heat and dirt.

A message followed him from the Vizier refusing
to present him to the Shah and referring him to
his own ambassador.

" Disappointed of my object in coming to the
camp," he says, " I lost no time in leaving it."   He
found again his English fellow-traveller who had
secured muleteers and now set off for Tabriz,
travelling for the first nine days along a road
where the Shah himself was soon to pass on his
way to Sultanieh. The north wind from the
Caspian blew over the mountains, and even at
mid-day in June the air was cool. The fresh tang
of the breeze carried Martyn home ; he fancied
himself trudging the roads near Cambridge with
a friend at his side, or following a path by the
Cornish shore with one beloved companion.   " While
passing over the plain, mostly on foot, I had them
all in my mind, and bore them all in my heart in
prayer."

The shadow of the royal progress lay on all the
villages.

All along the road where the king is expected, the
people are patiently waiting, as for some dreadful
disaster : plague, pestilence or famine are nothing to
the misery of being subject to the violence and extortion
of this rabble soldiery.

When they had passed the Shah's camping ground
at Sultanieh they came into a new world, a country
that has been a meeting place of the races of mankind.   The speech around them began to change

from Persian to Turkish, and the caravanserais were the halting place of men whose mules or camels followed the trade routes of the ancient world from east to west.

We found large bales of cotton brought by merchants from Teheran, intended for Turkey. There were also two Tartar merchants, natives of Astrachan, who had brought iron and tea for sale. They wished to know whether we wanted tea of Cathay.

Here in outlandish parts, the two Englishmen fell sick.

June 25, 1812. After a restless night rose so ill with fever, that I could not go on. My companion, Mr Canning, was nearly in the same state. We touched nothing all day.

After another night of fever Martyn was for dragging on, but Mr Canning was not well enough to start. They had before them a stage of eight or ten hours without a house on the way and they had been unable to eat for two days and were suffering from headache and constant giddiness. No doubt it was wiser to delay, but it added anxiety as to whether their supplies could hold out as far as Tabriz. They were becoming desperately short of money.

Next day the servants were down with fever too, and Martyn's head was " tortured with shocking pains." He put it down to exposure to the sun which had great power even though the wind blew cold.

June 29th was a day of acute pain. " I was almost frantic."

" I endeavoured," he says, his Christianity in 1812 anticipating later teachings, " to keep in mind all that was friendly ; a friendly Lord presiding ; and nothing exercising me but what would show itself at last friendly."

The fever passed for that time, leaving him "half dead" but determined to take the road. When they told him at midnight that his horse was ready he "seemed about to sink into a long fainting fit and almost wished it. . . . I set out more dead than alive."

Next day, shivering or burning by turns and almost light-headed, he reached the outer bulwarks of the mountains that guard Persia on the north, "a most natural boundary it is." The face of the land began to be broken up with very rocky foothills where camels graze on scrubby bushes. His horse threaded his way for him through the boulders, for Martyn in high fever could not make his brain obey him, but travelled bewildered through the past, wandering in "happy scenes in India or England." They lost him once ; for riding on ahead he had come to a bridge, and scarce knowing what he did, left his horse and crept under the shadow of the arch, where he sat with two camel-drivers, happy to be still and cool. The caravan passed over the bridge without the sick man's observation, and his fellow-traveller, coming back to search for him, found at first only a grazing horse and feared the worst.

So they passed poor hill villages and came out to the pure clean air, the lovely natural pastures and the churlish shepherds of Azerbaijan. By some miracle Martyn in "fever which nearly deprived me of reason" still sat his horse.

At last, as the dawn of July 7 shone coldly on

the Blue Mosque and the Citadel, he reached the
gate of Tabriz, and " feebly asked for a man to
show me the way to the ambassador's." He
had been two months on the road when Sir Gore
Ouseley and his lady received him at the point
of death.

They did all that they could. The violence
of the fever they could not allay for another fortnight, but they " administered bark " and tended
him as if he were a son. As he lay there under
their kind hands, the sick man knew that he had
no more strength to travel, as he had longed, to
Damascus, to Baghdad, and into the heart of
Arabia to search for ancient versions and perfect
the Arabic New Testament. His task seemed
dropping from his hands. Sir Gore Ouseley told
him that he was too ill to see the Shah or the
Prince, and doubtless dreaded another collision
between Martyn and the mullahs of the court.
But he comforted his guest with the promise that
he would give every possible éclat to the Book
by presenting it himself. The good ambassador
did more. He had extra copies made for high
officials of open mind, who might speak well of the
Book to the potentate. When at length the New
Testament reached the royal hands, the Shah was
graciousness itself.

In truth [said the royal letter of thanks to the am-
bassador] through the learned and unremitted exertions
of the Reverend Henry Martyn it has been translated
in a style most befitting sacred books, that is in an easy
and simple diction. . . . The whole of the New Testament is completed in a most excellent manner, a source
of pleasure to our enlightened and august mind.
If it please the most merciful God we shall command

the Select Servants who are admitted to our presence, to read to us the above-mentioned book from the beginning to the end.

Sir Gore Ouseley did yet more. He carried a copy with him to St Petersburg, and there, at the instigation of a Russian prince, the Bible Society printed the Persian Book, with the British ambassador as volunteer proof-reader. Sir Gore Ouseley's Russian edition came into the world in the year of Waterloo, while the sister edition in Calcutta was still struggling through the press.

So Martyn's task passed into other hands, and he lying sick almost to death in a mansion of Tabriz saw nothing more within his strength in the east. The ambassador had handed him a letter; at last, after more than eighteen months, a letter from Lydia. To her and to Cornwall the sick man turned. Would strength be granted him to reach her? Might he not carry home the New Testament, to be printed perhaps in his own Cambridge? If he could only reach Lydia, surely he would be well enough with her to start for more service in the east.

Made an extraordinary effort and, as a Tartar was going off instantly to Constantinople, wrote letters to Mr Grant for permission to come to England, and to Mr Simeon and Lydia informing them of it.

We have both those letters written by the hand of a man who tells his correspondent that he has not the strength to search his papers for the last home letters.

"I have applied for leave to come to England on furlough; a measure you will disapprove," so he tells Simeon, his feverish brain remembering the relentless standards of work in the Cambridge parish and the brisk upright figure of the leader who never spared himself. "But you would not were you to see the pitiable condition to which I am reduced." A Henry Martyn's plea against some fancied charge of idleness must have been hard reading to his friend. Then the old passion seizes the sick man, and the pen flies in his feverish hand as he turns to the beloved work and warns Simeon about some publication mooted in Cambridge for Moslem readers. Let it not go to press until it has been approved by men who know the east and know eastern ways of seeing, imagining and reasoning. He tells of the last treatise he had written in Shiraz and, with a rare note of satisfaction in any work of his own, records his hope that "there is not a single Europeanism in the whole of it."

But I am exhausted; pray for me, beloved brother, and believe that I am, as long as life and recollection last, yours affectionately,   H. MARTYN.

To Lydia, lest she should dwell on his sickness, he writes of his spiritual solace; "The love of God never appeared more clear, more sweet, more strong." Then, lest she should build on his coming, he adds, "I must faithfully tell you that the probability of my reaching England alive is but small."

The Tartar courier galloped off with the letters and the sick man lay back exhausted. Nothing was left him to do, but to gather strength for the homeward journey.

A month later, "a mere skeleton" after two months of fever, he sat up in a chair and wrote his will "with a strong hand."

August 21–31. Making preparations for my journey to Constantinople, a route recommended to me by Sir Gore as safer, and one in which he could give me letters of recommendation to two Turkish governors.

Sir Gore also procured an order for Martyn to use the Government post-horses as far as Erivan. But Martyn had seen the hardships that the levies of royal underlings brought upon the peasants. "These post-horses I was told were nothing else than the beasts the prince's servants levy on every village. I determined not to use them."

Before setting out he wrote a last letter to Lydia, a letter to be read and re-read on her knees where his portrait hung beneath a print of the Crucifixion in a room that looked out across the shimmer of Mount's Bay.

In three days I intend setting my horse's head towards Constantinople, distant above thirteen hundred miles. . . . Soon we shall have occasion for pen and ink no more ; but I trust I shall shortly see thee face to face.

Believe me to be yours ever, most faithfully and affectionately,   H. MARTYN.

On September 2, 1812, he set out with a little party of guides and servants, while the ambassador and his lady, having done all they could to help him, measured with doubtful eyes the strength of the haggard convalescent against 1500 [1] miles of hardship.

[1] Dr George Smith says that the distance from Tabriz to Constantinople is 1500 miles, though Martyn reckoned it 1300.

At sunset we left the western gate of Tabriz behind us. The plain towards the west and south-west stretches away to an immense distance bounded by mountains so remote as to appear from their soft blue to blend with the skies.

He "ambled on" with the keen sense of the convalescent for the beauty and freedom of the outside world, gazing at "the distant hills with gratitude and joy." His way through Azerbaijan and Armenia always tending westward was the "Royal Road" of ancient Persia along which the service of the Great King passed from Susa to the west. It was marked at each twentieth or twenty-fifth mile by a post-station built of mud bricks, such as went to the building of Babylon the great. Here men and beasts fared much alike as to lodging.

In cities where Martyn had letters of introduction he might hire a room from a citizen. "I was led from street to street till at last I was lodged in a wash-house belonging to a great man, a corner of which was cleared out for me."

A room secured, at the end of the day's hard riding there were the perennial discomforts of such travel : mosquitoes and lice, "the smell of the stable so strong that I was quite unwell," and the incessant crowding and chatter of people who could not or would not understand his desire to rest alone. It was always Martyn too who must be the one to wake at midnight and rouse his party and stand urgent over them as they dawdled round the baggage sleepy and loth to start.

The travelling was hard even for a hale man. He crossed the Araxes ; he left great Ararat upon

T

his left (" so may I, safe in Christ, outride the storm
of life and land at last on one of the everlasting
hills," he prayed, thinking of Noah); he passed
through a rich land of streams where a precious
trunk full of books was dropped and soaked, and
he had a midnight fire built to dry them. He
spent nights in rooms built over or beside the
family stable for the sake of the warmth from
the beasts in winter, but now in September overpowering in heat and stench; and he rode on,
" thinking of a Hebrew letter," and so " perceiving
little of the tediousness of the way. . . All day
on the 15th and 16th Psalms and gained some light
on the difficulties."

So meditating on his songs of degrees, he came
to Erivan, and laid the ambassador's letter before
a provincial governor to whom his distant over-
lord, the Shah, seemed but a shadowy personage.

I was summoned to his presence. He at first took
no notice of me, but continued reading his Koran. After
a compliment or two, he resumed his devotions. The
next ceremony was to exchange a rich shawl dress for a
still richer pelisse on pretence of its being cold. The next
display was to call for his physician, who after respect
fully feeling his pulse stood on one side.

Having sufficiently impressed the thin, sick
traveller with his greatness, he called a secretary
to pick up from the floor the letter of the British
ambassador, and to read it in his august ears.
The letter interested him and he grew languidly
attentive, but his hopes were set on some grapes
and melons cooling before him in a marble fountain,
and he sent the saint away, not knowing that he
had met a man of God.

On September 12 Martyn left his servants waiting for fresh horses, and rode alone to visit his brothers the Armenian monks at Etchmiazin, the mother-city of their church.

The way-worn figure rode into "a large court with monks, cowled and gowned, moving about. On seeing my Armenian letters they brought me at once to the Patriarch's lodge where I found two bishops at breakfast." He struck up at once a friendship with a young monk of his own age named Serope, "bold, authoritative and very able," and full of reforming plans for his Church, "but then he is not spiritual." They talked all day. "When the bell rang for vespers, we went together to the great Church."

Next day Martyn waited on the Patriarch, who received him on a throne, surrounded by standing monks. "I told the Patriarch that I was so happy in being here that I could almost be willing to be a monk with them."

When the young monk who welcomed Martyn had become a silvery-bearded bishop he told a European traveller [1] his impressions of that visit. "He described Martyn to me as being of a very delicate frame, thin, and not quite of the middle stature, a beardless youth, with a countenance beaming with so much benignity as to bespeak an errand of Divine love. Of the affairs of the world he seemed to be so ignorant that Serope was obliged to manage for him respecting his travelling arrangements and money matters. A Tartar was employed to take him to Tokat. He (Serope) was greatly surprised, he said, that Martyn

[1] Mr George Fowler.

was so eminent a Christian; 'since (said he) all the English I have hitherto met with not only make no profession of religion, but live seemingly in contempt of it.'"

Serope took Martyn in hand, changed most of his travelling kit, and bought him a sword against the Kurdish robbers.

So he left them with new baggage and a new train, "a trusty servant from the monastery" carrying his money.

On September 19 they passed from the Persian province of Erivan to the neighbour province of Kars, and so left the domains of the Shah for those of the Sultan of Turkey.[1]

Troubles began.

The headman of the village paid me a visit. He was a young Mussulman and took care of all my Mussulman attendants; but he left my Armenians and me where he found us. I was rather uncomfortably lodged, my room being a thoroughfare for horses, cows, buffaloes and sheep. Almost all the village came to look at me.

Each day there were alarms of Kurdish robbers. Martyn's escort met even poor companies of peasants with suspicion and with pieces cocked, and every travelling party was passed with furtive glances and hands lingering on weapons. Each trifling incident of the way revealed that one of the company, the Tartar guide named Hassan, was a man with the nature of that soldiery which could plait a crown of thorns for a scourged prisoner.

The Tartar began to show his nature by flogging the baggage-horse with his long whip; but one of the poor beasts presently fell with his load.

[1] Both provinces became part of Russian Transcaucasia after the war of 1828, and several shifts of ownership have since taken place on these frontiers.

Or again :

In this room I should have been very much to my satisfaction had not the Tartar taken part of the same bench. It was evident that the Tartar was the great man here : he took the best place for himself ; a dinner of four or five dishes was laid before him. When I asked for eggs they brought me rotten ones.

With a stern vigorous master Hassan might have done good service. With a sick man he showed himself a brute.

September 24. A long and sultry march over many a hill and vale. Two hours from the last stage is a hot spring : the water fills a pool having four porches. The porches instantly reminded me of Bethesda's pool. In them all the party undressed and bathed. The Tartar to enjoy himself more perfectly had his calean to smoke while up to his chin in water.

Kars was left behind, then Erzerum, but fever was winning the race.

September 29. We moved to a village where I was attacked with fever and ague.

October 1. We were out from seven in the morning till eight at night. After sitting a little by the fire I was near fainting from sickness. I learned that the plague was raging at Constantinople and thousands dying every day. The inhabitants of Tocat were flying from their town from the same cause.

October 2. Some hours before day I sent to tell the Tartar I was ready, but Hassan was for once riveted to his bed. However, at eight, having got strong horses, he set off at a great rate. He made us gallop as fast as the horses would go to Chifflik, where we arrived at sunset. I was lodged at my request in the stables of the post-house. As soon as it began to grow a little cold the ague came on, then the fever.

In the night Hassan sent to summon me away, but I was quite unable to move. Finding me still in bed at the

dawn he began to storm furiously at my detaining him so
long; but I quietly let him spend his ire, ate my breakfast
and set out at eight.   He seemed determined to make up
for the delay, for we flew over hill and dale to Sherean,[1]
where we changed horses.   From thence we travelled
all the rest of the day and all night.   It rained.   The
ague came on.   There was a village at hand but Hassan
had no mercy.   At one in the morning we found two
men under a wain with a good fire; I dried my lower
extremities, allayed the fever by drinking a good deal
of water and went on.   The night was pitchy dark so
that I could not see the road under my horse's feet.
We arrived at the munzil [2] at break of day.   Hassan was
in great fear of being arrested here; the governor of
the city had vowed to make an example of him for riding
to death a horse belonging to a man of this place.

He hurried me away without delay; and galloped
furiously towards a village which he said was four hours
distant, which was all I could undertake in my weak
state; but village after village did he pass till, night
coming on, I suspected that he was carrying me on to
the munzil; so I got off my horse, and sat upon the
ground, and told him "I neither could nor would go
any farther."   He stormed, but I was immovable,
till, a light appearing at a distance, I mounted and made
towards it.   He brought in the party, but would not
exert himself to get a place for me.   Sergius told them
I wanted a place in which to be alone.   This seemed
very offensive to them; "And why must he be alone?"
they asked, attributing this desire of mine to pride,
I suppose.   Tempted at last by money they brought me
to a stable room, and Hassan and a number of others
planted themselves there with me.   My fever here
increased to a violent degree; the heat in my eyes and
forehead was so great that the fire almost made me
frantic.   I entreated that it might be put out, or that
I might be carried out of doors.   Neither was attended
to; my servant, who, from my sitting in that strange
way on the ground, believed me delirious, was deaf to

[1] Generally written Sheheran.
[2] The halting place at the end of each stage of about twenty-five
miles.

all I said. At last I pushed my head in among the luggage and lodged it on the damp ground, and slept.

October 5. The merciless Hassan hurried me off. The munzil, however, not being distant I reached it without much difficulty. I was pretty well lodged and felt tolerably well till a little after sunset, when the ague came on with a violence I had never before experienced ; I felt as if in a palsy, my teeth chattering and my whole frame violently shaken.

Two Persians came to visit him as he lay shivering.

These Persians appear quite brotherly after the Turks. While they pitied me, Hassan sat in perfect indifference, ruminating on the further delay this was likely to occasion. The cold fit after continuing two or three hours was followed by a fever, which lasted the whole night and prevented sleep.

October 6. No horses being to be had, I had an unexpected repose. I sat in the orchard, and thought with sweet comfort and peace of my God ; in solitude my Company, my Friend and Comforter. Oh, when shall time give place to eternity ! When shall appear the new heaven and new earth wherein dwelleth righteousness! There shall in no wise enter in anything that defileth : none of that wickedness which has made men worse than wild beasts shall be seen or heard of any more.

There was no later entry in the journal ; but he had not come yet to the end of that impossible ride. Day after day they dragged him on, waking him out of feverish sleep to start before the sun.

Up, O ye lovers and away ! 'Tis time to leave the world
*   for aye ;*
Hark, loud and clear from heaven the drum of parting calls
*   —let none delay ;*
The cameleer hath risen amain, made ready all the camel
*   train,*
And quittance now desires to gain : why sleep ye travellers,
*   I pray ?*

*Behind us and before there swells the din of parting and of
    bells ;*
*To shoreless space each moment sails a disembodied spirit
    away.*
*O heart, towards thy heart's love wend, and O friend, fly
    toward the Friend !* [1]

On October 14, 1812, Martyn bade his Armenian
servant Sergius make a list of his papers and carry
them for him to Constantinople. They had ridden
him to death, but there is no story of that death-
bed. We know that he came at the last " a young
man, wanting still the years of Christ," to Tokat
under its weird pile of castellated hill, a city of
the copper-merchants, but then grim with plague.
We know too that in fever his mind was always
moving among friends in India or in England.

So he came to Tokat, and the mule-bells in
the narrow streets jingled in dying ears. Or
were they sheep-bells ? sheep bells on the moors ?

They probably laid him down to die amid the
babel of an eastern khan. . . That everlasting smell
of the stable ! Why could not the General find
a better place for service than the riding school ?
But then the Lord was born in a stable. A man
could worship there. . . But that raging voice ! If
only the tormenting flood of words might cease !
Was it Sabat or the Tartar ? Sons of thunder,
both of them. Sons of thunder He called them,
yes, and loved them too.

Why that never-ending clatter on the cobbles ?
Little hurrying feet of donkeys. And people too.
Surely so many people were never seen in Truro

[1] Selected Poems from the Divan-i-Shams-i-Tabriz translated by
R. A. Nicholson.

Street before, and all so beautiful. There was Corrie, what a friend he was! and Sally with Cousin Emma, and Sargent and Dr Cardew (but no matter; the lesson was ready to show up)— and Lydia. Of course she would come at last. How her face was shining like a star. How all the faces shone with the light of God. . . Was that an Armenian priest standing at prayer? Simeon had surely come at last with the Bread and Wine. How sweet his voice grew, like the music in King's Chapel! "We praise Thee, we bless Thee, we worship Thee, we glorify Thee, we give thanks to Thee for Thy great glory."

"For Thou only art holy; Thou only art the Lord; Thou only, O Christ . . ."

Some weeks later an Armenian named Sergius, hot from travel, carried a bundle of papers into the house of Mr Isaac Morier at Constantinople, and said that they came from his master who had died on October 16, 1812, at Tokat, where the Armenian clergy gave him Christian burial.

Note for page 264

From " The Memory of Martyn in the Sahara "
Church Missionary Review (December 1912)

In May 1864 the Rev. C. F. Oakley, speaking at Islington, said :

In French Algeria, near El Aghonal, I found some tribes of Arabs who belonged to the oasis of the Beni Nizab. . . . A chief of considerable power invited me to visit him in a place far away in the desert of the South—Beni Salem. I accepted his invitation, and after many days' journey across the sands arrived at my resting-place. I found all the hospitality which an Arab chief could give. . . . He caused a large box to be brought in and opened before my eyes. From this box he took out a very singular collection of Arabic manuscripts and books. At last he came to a book in Persian, the sight of which in the great desert quite surprised me ; it seemed like finding a Russian book in the Scotch Highlands. I said, " How came this book here ? Can you read it ? " " No." " Why then do you keep it with all this care ? " (It was wrapped in folds of silk.) He said in substance what follows :—

" I will tell you, Christian, the history of that book, and you will see why I keep it. My father, like his fathers for many generations, ruled over the tribe of the Beni Salem. When he was young and strong he went as a Hadji on the great pilgrimage to Mecca and Medina. He went on that journey in the year before the Sheikh of the Franks (Napoleon I), uncle of the present Sheikh, went to the land of snow (Moscow). He went to the birthplace and tomb of Mohammed. Thence he went to Persia and visited many towns in that country, among them Shiraz. While he was there, enquiring about many things, he often heard men speak of an Englishman who had come to that city, and at last he went to see him, and was received by him with kindness. During the time they both remained there they often talked together about many things connected with religion, and the Englishman spoke particularly to my father concerning Sidi 'Isa (Jesus Christ), and my father heard him gladly. After a time the Englishman went away, and among the books he used to read was the one I have here, and for the sake of his English friend, my father brought that book home with him when he returned to the Sahara. Many times afterwards my father asked about that Englishman, and heard that he never lived to reach his own land, but died and was buried at Tokat, on his way to Stamboul. But my father never forgot what the Englishman had said to him, and when he was near his death he called me to him and said, ' My son, when I am dead you, like myself, will be head of the Beni Salem. Remember, therefore, that when your father was dying, when the angel of death was near him, he said this to you : If ever there comes to the Sahara an Englishman declaring that he is the servant of Jesus Christ, mark that man, and if he will not travel on one day in seven, nor work on that day, nor do any such things as he does on other days, be kind to that man, be to him as a brother, for the sake of that Englishman who was a brother to me while I was at Shiraz in Persia.' "

Index